HONDURAS
HANDBOOK

HONDURAS HANDBOOK

INCLUDING THE BAY ISLANDS AND COPÁN
FIRST EDITION

CHRIS HUMPHREY

MOON
TRAVEL
HANDBOOKS

HONDURAS HANDBOOK
FIRST EDITION

Published by
Moon Publications, Inc.
P.O. Box 3040
Chico, California 95927-3040, USA

Printed by
Colorcraft Ltd.

© Text and photographs copyright Chris Humphrey, 1997.
All rights reserved.

© Illustrations and maps copyright Moon Publications, Inc., 1997.
All rights reserved.

Some photos and illustrations are used by permission
and are the property of the original copyright owners.

ISBN: 1-56691-099-4
ISSN: 1094-4389

Please send all comments,
corrections, additions,
amendments, and critiques to:

**HONDURAS HANDBOOK
MOON TRAVEL HANDBOOKS
P.O. BOX 3040
CHICO, CA 95927-3040, USA
e-mail: travel@moon.com
www.moon.com**

Printing History
1st edition—November 1997

Editor: Emily Kendrick
Map Editor: Gina Wilson Birtcil
Copy Editors: Don Root, Asha Johnson
Production & Design: Rob Warner
Cartography: Chris Folks, Mike Morgenfeld and Rob Warner
Index: Diane Wurzel

Front cover photo: Military macaws. Photo © Michael Durham/ENP Images

All photos by Chris Humphrey unless otherwise noted.

Distributed in the United States and Canada by Publishers Group West

Printed in China

Although the author and publisher have made every effort to ensure that the information was correct at
the time of going to press, the author and publisher do not assume and hereby disclaim any liability to any
party for any loss or damage caused by errors, omissions, or any potential travel disruption due to labor or
financial difficulty, whether such errors or omissions result from negligence, accident, or any other cause.

*To my parents, Watts and Barbara Humphrey,
for always believing in their prodigal son,
and to Joe Cummings, for a lot of good advice*

CONTENTS

COPÁN AND WESTERN HONDURAS .... **147~181**

ACKNOWLEDGMENTS

The list of those who helped me muddle my way through this first edition is long. My apologies to anyone I've forgotten—take it as faulty memory and bad note-taking rather than lack of appreciation.

Thanks to Peace Corps workers Kevin Postma in El Carbón, all the crew in the Santa Rosa house, Pablo in Raistá (watch where you put your glasses), Christy in Las Marías, Guillermo in Gracias, Stacy and Genevieve in El Corpus, Joceline in Plaplaya, Alison Lyon in La Esperanza, Tamara at Lago de Yojoa, ex-volunteer Glen Peterson on Utila, Dr. Jutta Bayer in the main office, and about two dozen others who gave me excellent advice and recommendations.

To several workers at the Insituto Hondureño de Antropología e Historia, including Rosa Margarita Montenegro, Pastor Gómez Zuñiga, Cármen Julia Fajardo, Kevin Avalos, George Hasseman, and Jenny Garay.

To Guillermo Yuscarán and Don Oscar Martínez López in Catacamas, for great stories; Mosquitia junglemen Jorge Zalavery and Don Beltrán Molina; bush pilot Jorge Goff; Julie Dutcher at Anthony's Key Resort; Jaqueline López in the Santa Bárbara Cohdefor office; Padre Jesús in Choluteca, Padre Marcotulio Izaguirre in La Campa, and Francisco Germán Martínez in Erandique, for a lot of local lore; Mike Brox at Cuban Honduran Cigars in Danlí, for giving me a new addiction (just what I needed); photographer and adventurer Vince Murphy; Dr. James Brady; Derek Parent; Ron Mader; Max Elvir of Lenca Land Trails; Susan and Henrick on Utila; Yair Azubel (thanks for not letting me drown) and the rest of the crew at Utila Water Sports; Bradford O'Neill; and Erasmo Sosa and Davíd Chinchilla at the Instituto Hondureño de Turismo.

For distracting me from my work, thanks to good friend and budding travel writer, or at least fellow vagabond, Grant Raddon; Tom and *las tres demonias* at Shakespeare Books; Álvaro "Julio" Guillén *(pero a la abuelísima, güey")* and Niamh and Anne Lawlor on Utila; Sarah, Ian, and Helen; Dirk and Suyapa in La Ceiba; Sarhan for only getting lost once; and Pritam and Shushila Sandhu.

ABBREVIATIONS AND ACRONYMS

a/c—air conditioning
cm—centimeters
CODEFFAGOLF—Comite para la Preservación de la Fauna y Flora en el Golfo de Fonseca
Cohdefor—Corporación Hondureño de Desarollo Forestal
d—double
Fucagua—Fundación para la Protección de Capiro, Calentura y Guaymoreto
Fucsa—Fundación Cuero y Salado
IHAH—Instituto Hondureño de Antropología e Historia
km—kilometers
Mopawi—Mosquitia Pawisa, or Mosquitia Development
pp—per person
Prolansate—Fundación para la Protección de Lancetilla, Punta Sal, y Texiguat
s—single
tel.—telephone
t—triple
UNAH—Universidad Nacional Autonoma de Honduras
P.N.—Parque Nacional
NO—northwest *(noroeste)*
SO—southwest *(sudoeste)*
NE—northeast *(noreste)*
SE—southeast *(sudeste)*

MAPS

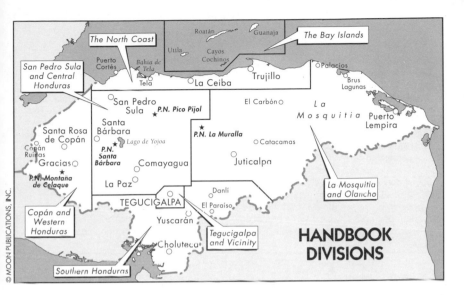

The North Coast

Roatán Guanaja

The Bay Islands

San Pedro Sula and Central Honduras

Puerto Cortés

Bahía de Tela

Utila

Cayos Cochinos

Palacios

Brus Lagunas

Tela

La Ceiba

Trujillo

San Pedro Sula

P.N. Pico Pijol

El Carbón

La Mosquitia

Puerto Lempira

Santa Rosa de Copán

Santa Bárbara

Lago de Yojoa

P.N. La Muralla

Catacamas

Copán Ruinas

P.N. Santa Bárbara

Comayagua

Juticalpa

Gracias

P.N. Montaña de Celaque

La Paz

La Mosquitia and Olancho

Copán and Western Honduras

TEGUCIGALPA

Danlí

El Paraíso

Yuscarán

Tegucigalpa and Vicinity

HANDBOOK DIVISIONS

Choluteca

Southern Honduras

MAP SYMBOLS

Paved Road

Unpaved Road

Railroad Track

Trail

Metropolitan Area

City

Town or Village

Water

Coral Reef

Swamp or Marsh

Mountain or Peak

Point of Interest

Accommodation

Restaurant/Bar

Other Location

International Airport

Airport or Airstrip

© MOON PUBLICATIONS, INC.

LET US HEAR FROM YOU

Writing a guidebook is a lot like taking a snapshot: freezing the image of a place on a giant frame. At the same time, however, it's also like stopping progress: locking the ever-changing details into print. Although we make Herculean efforts to check our facts, the task is an enormous one and sometimes gets away from us. You can help us keep up.

If something we mention no longer exists, if certain suggestions are misleading, if you've uncovered anything new, please write in. Although we try to make our maps as accurate as possible, we are always grateful when readers point out any omissions or inaccuracies. When writing, always be as specific and accurate as possible. Notes made on the spot are better than later recollections. Write your comments in your copy of *Honduras Handbook* as you travel about, then send us a summary when you get home. This book speaks for you, the independent traveler, so please help keep us up to date. Address your letters to:

Honduras Handbook
c/o Moon Travel Handbooks
P.O. Box 3040
Chico, CA 95927-3040
USA
e-mail: travel@moon.com

BOB RACE

INTRODUCTION

Well, it made no difference to him now. He had eaten of the lotus. He was happy and content in this land of perpetual afternoon. Those old days in the States seemed like an irritating dream . . . The climate was as balmy as that of distant Avalon; the fetterless, idyllic round of enchanted days; the life among this indolent, romantic people—a life full of music, flowers, and low laughter; the influence of the imminent sea and mountains, and the many shapes of love and magic and beauty that bloomed in the white tropical nights— with all he was more than content.

—O. Henry, *Cabbages And Kings*

A growing number of foreigners are eating of the same lotus that so entranced U.S. short-story writer and fugitive from the law O. Henry and his fictional consul Willard Geddie at the turn of the century. Long a forgotten Central American country, thought of, when at all, as the ultimate banana republic, Honduras is fast emerging as a favorite travel destination.

It's a surprise it didn't happen sooner. All the ingredients are there: powdery soft beaches lined with palm trees and lapped by turquoise waves, superb coral reef, Mayan ruins, cobblestone colonial villages clinging to green hillsides, the untracked jungles of La Mosquitia, and mountaintop cloud forests teeming with colorful birds and noisy monkeys.

When foreigners return from Honduras, they invariably comment with surprise on the extent of the country's forests, the many possibilities for adventure traveling and visiting remote towns and countryside, the remarkably low costs of food, transport, and accommodations, and how safe one feels traveling there.

But Honduras's greatest asset, and the most important reason travelers find the country a joy to explore, is the relaxed, friendly people. Foreign tourists are still uncommon in many parts of the country, and visitors often feel they're being treated as equals. Hondurans display little of the touchy nationalism or desperation for tourist money that confounds communication in other countries. Anyone who spends any time at all in Honduras with an open mind and friendly disposition will be amazed at how easily Hondurans open themselves up to strangers. They're curious to learn about your country and eager to tell you about theirs.

THE LAND

Shaped like a triangle at the great bend where, after sweeping east into the Caribbean from the base of Mexico, Central America takes a 90-degree turn southward, the main landmass of Honduras is located roughly between latitude 16 degrees N on the north coast and 13 degrees N at the Gulf of Fonseca, and between longitude 83 degrees 15 minutes W at Cabo Gracias a Dios and 89 degrees 20 minutes W near Nueva Ocotepeque. The furthest north-ward Caribbean island possessions of Honduras, the Swan Islands, are located at latitude 17 degrees 30 minutes N.

Approximately two-thirds of Honduras is covered by rugged mountains, or cordilleras. These mountains, the country's principal defining geographic feature, have played an important role in Honduran history, isolating the country from its neighbors and limiting agricultural development.

Flat areas are found mainly along the narrow north and south coast plains, the lowland, jungle-covered plains of La Mosquitia, and a very few inland valleys.

GEOGRAPHY

The second-largest country in Central America, after Nicaragua, Honduras covers 112,491 square kilometers, an area about the size of England. The country's perimeter, not including island possessions, is 2,408 km long, comprised of a 342 km border with El Salvador, a 256 km border with Guatemala, a 922 km border with

Nicaragua, 735 km of north-facing Caribbean coastline, and 153 km of southern, Pacific coastline. At its widest point, between Cerro Montecristo on the border with El Salvador and Guatemala, and Cabo Gracias a Dios, bordering Nicaragua, Honduras extends 675 km.

The only sizable natural lake in the country is Lago de Yojoa, 16 km by 8 km at an elevation of 635 meters. With the construction of El Cajón dam, a larger man-made lake has been created along the Río Humuya.

Mountain Ranges

Although Honduras is blanketed by mountains, they do not fall in neat, parallel chains as in other parts of the Americas. Because of its location at the junction of the Caribbean, North American, and Cocos tectonic plates, the Honduran landmass has been geologically squeezed, resulting in a jumble of small mountain ranges and isolated massifs zigzagging across the country in all different directions and in no apparent order.

In northern Honduras, major mountain ranges include the Sierra Nombre de Dios, which parallels the north coast between Tela and Trujillo, forming a narrow coastal plain and reaching an elevation of 2,480 meters at Montaña Corozal in Parque Nacional Pico Bonito. Further east, the Sierra de Agalta begins in the center of the Olancho department and extends into La Mosquitia, though its name changes to Sierra del Carbón and Sierra del Río Tinto as it heads north. The smaller Montañas del Río Plátano are the only mountains of any size near the coast in La Mosquitia. Also to the east are the Montañas del Patuca and, along the border with Nicaragua, the Cordillera Entre Ríos.

The longest mountain range in western Honduras forms the border with Guatemala, and is called variously the Cordillera del Merendón, Sierra del Espíritu Santo, and Sierra de Omoa during its course from the southwest corner of the country to the Caribbean Sea.

Beginning in far western Honduras near the Salvadoran border, and continuing northeast into the heart of the country in Yoro, a series of short, rugged ranges run roughly northwest-southeast parallel to one another. Closest to El Salvador is the tallest of these ranges, Sierra de Celaque, topped by Cerro de las Minas, the highest peak in the country at 2,849 meters. Further northeast are the Cordillera Opalaca, Cordillera Montecillos, Montaña Meámbar and Montaña de Comayagua, and the Yoro ranges of Pico Pijol, Montaña de Yoro, and Montaña de la Flor.

Isolated ranges include Montaña de Santa Bárbara at the edge of Lago de Yojoa—the country's second highest peak at 2,744 meters—and several mountains in the vicinity of Tegucigalpa.

Except for a few eroded cones in the Gulf of Fonseca, none of the mountains in Honduras are volcanic, in sharp contrast to many peaks in neighboring Guatemala, Nicaragua, and El Salvador.

Valleys

Among this chaotic mountain geography lie numerous intermontane basins of varying sizes, usually between 300 and 900 meters above sea level. The larger valleys, like the Valle de Comayagua, Valle de Catacamas, Valle de Jamastrán, and Valle de Senseti, are intensively worked for crops or cattle, or both.

Major river valleys in Honduras include the broad Valle de Sula, containing the Río Ulúa and the Río Chamelecón; the Valle de Río Aguán; and the Valle de Río Patuca. The Sula and Río Aguán valleys are heavily cultivated by foreign banana companies, while the Río Patuca valley, running through Olancho into the Mosquitia, is mainly covered with rainforest.

The so-called Honduran Depression cuts a lowland gap through the country, following the Río Ulúa, up the Río Humuya into the Valle de Comayagua, over a low pass and down to the Pacific along the Río Goascorán. For many years successive Honduran governments hoped to build a transcontinental railway along this route, which at its highest point on the continental divide is only 870 meters. Another major tributary to the Ulúa, the Río Otoro, also almost meets the Pacific-flowing Río Lempa, separated by a pass of 1,050 meters.

HONDURAS HIGHLIGHTS

SUGGESTED ITINERARY (TWO-WEEK TRIP):

- Two days at the Mayan ruins of Copán
- Three days at the colonial town of Gracias, with side trips to colonial villages and/or a hike up to the cloud forests of Parque Nacional Celaque
- Four days at the beaches of Tela, with visits to nearby Garífuna villages and the nature reserves of Punta Sal, Lancetilla, or Punta Izopo
- Five days scuba diving or snorkeling on the Bay Island of your choice

THE BEST BEACHES, WITH ALL THE AMENITIES:

- West Bay, Roatán
- Trujillo town beach
- Telamar beach in Tela
- Tornabé, near Tela

THE BEST BEACHES, WITH MINIMAL OR NO AMENITIES:

- Water Cay, Utila
- The north-side beaches, Guanaja
- Camp Bay Beach, Roatán
- Triunfo de la Cruz, near Tela
- Miami, near Tela
- Beaches near Palacios, La Mosquitia

BEST BIRDWATCHING SITES:

- Lago de Yojoa
- Jardín Botánico Lancetilla, near Tela
- Parque Nacional La Muralla
- Parque Nacional Cusuco
- Refugio de Vida Silvestre Cuero y Salado

BEST ADVENTURE HIKING REGIONS:

- Reserva de la Biosfera del Río Plátano
- Parque Nacional Sierra de Agalta
- Parque Nacional Pico Bonito
- Parque Nacional Celaque

BEST PLACES TO MEET OTHER TRAVELERS:

- East Harbour, Utila
- West End, Roatán
- Copán Ruinas
- Tela or Trujillo
- Hotel Granada, Tegucigalpa

BEST COLONIAL TOWNS AND VILLAGES:

- Gracias, Lempira
- Belén Gualcho, Lempira
- Ojojona, Francisco Morazán
- Yuscarán, El Paraíso
- El Corpus, Choluteca

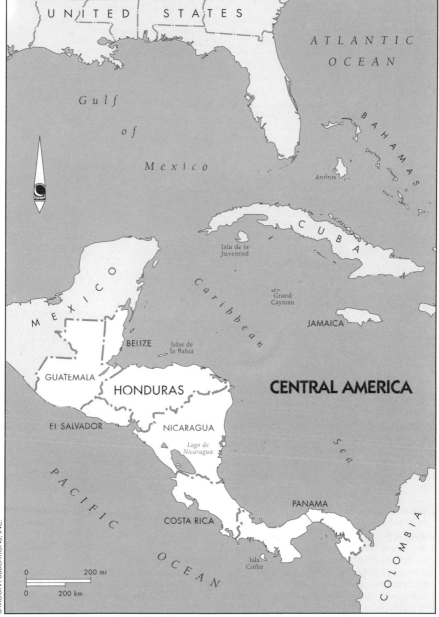

UNITED STATES

ATLANTIC OCEAN

Gulf

of

Mexico

BAHAMAS

Andros

CUBA

Isla de la
Juventud

Caribbean

Grand
Cayman

JAMAICA

MEXICO

BELIZE

Islas de
la Bahía

GUATEMALA

HONDURAS

CENTRAL AMERICA

EL SALVADOR

NICARAGUA

Sea

Lago de
Nicaragua

PACIFIC

PANAMA

COSTA RICA

COLOMBIA

Isla
Coiba

OCEAN

0   200 mi

0   200 km

Coastal Plains

For the past century, Honduras's northern coastal plain has been the country's most intensively exploited region, mainly used to produce bananas and pineapple for foreign fruit companies. For most of its length the plain is quite narrow, in places only a couple of kilometers separate the ocean from the Cordillera Nombre de Dios.

The only places the plain extends inland a significant distance are the valleys of the Ulúa, Chamelecón, and Aguán rivers, and in the broad expanse of La Mosquitia. The Mosquitia plain, in the northeast corner of the country, encompasses more flat land than the rest of the country combined, but because of its thin, acidic soil the region is unsuitable for agriculture.

The Pacific lowlands are on average only 25 km wide, composed mainly of heavily cultivated alluvial soils tapering into mangrove swamps at the edge of the Gulf of Fonseca.

Islands

In the Caribbean, the three main Bay Islands (Islas de la Bahía) of Utila, Roatán, and Guanaja, plus many smaller cays, are considered a continuation of the Sierra de Omoa, a northeast trending mountain range that meets the Caribbean west of Puerto Cortés. Further north are the smaller Swan Islands (Islas del Cisne), also thought to be part of the same geological formation.

Honduras owns several small islands in the Gulf of Fonseca, the largest of which are Isla del Tigre and Isla Zacate Grande, both eroded

The Caribbean and Pacific lowland regions are both known as *tierra caliente* (hot land), where average daytime high temperatures hover between 28° and 32° C throughout the year. Both rain and strong ocean breezes offer some relief, and are often present on the coasts, the Bay Islands, and the islands of the Gulf of Fonseca. Interior lowland regions, such as the Valle de Ulúa, San Pedro Sula, and the Choluteca plains are scorchingly hot for much of the year, particularly during the dry season, with daytime temperatures occasionally hitting 40° C. On the north coast, relief from the heat comes briefly in December and January, when northern cold fronts cool the region down for a few days.

Much of central Honduras, between 500 and 1,800 meters, is *tierra templada* (temperate land). Here temperatures usually stay very comfortable throughout the year, pleasantly warm but not hot during the day and cool in the evening. Tegucigalpa, in a sheltered valley at about 1,000 meters, is a classic example of such a climate zone; daytime highs average 24° C in January and 29° C in April, while lows in those months average 14° C and 18° C, respectively.

The mountain country, above 1,800 meters, is called *tierra fría* (cold land), where temperatures average 16-20° C during the day, and can drop to freezing at night. Strong winds, mist, clouds, and tree cover help keep temperatures down. The highest, cloud-forest covered peaks are the coldest locations in Honduras. Hiking these forests can be pleasantly cool during the day, but be ready for the evening chill.

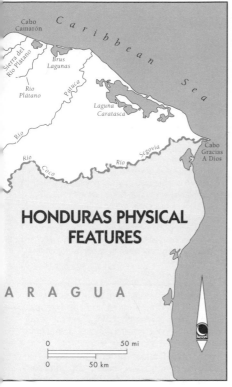

HONDURAS PHYSICAL FEATURES

volcanoes at the southern end of a mountain chain that begins in El Salvador.

CLIMATE

Temperatures
Honduras is situated completely within the tropics—south of the Tropic of Cancer and north of the Tropic of Capricorn—and like most tropical countries, temperature is defined more by altitude than by season. Generally, temperatures change little from month to month in the same location, apart from slight cooling during the rainy season. January and February are the coolest months, while March and April are the hottest, although temperatures rarely vary more than five degrees C on average throughout the year.

Precipitation
Most of Honduras experiences a fairly well defined dry and wet season, though some regional variations exist. The rainy season, called *invierno*, normally begins in May or June and continues to November or December. This wet period is often broken in August and September by a three- to six-week dry spell called *la canícula* or sometimes *el veranillo de San Juan*.

During the first few months of the rainy season, clouds gather in the afternoon, leading to brief rain showers that pass by evening. The later months, particularly October and November, bring much heavier rains, due to hurricanes

BORDER WARS

For over two centuries, Honduras and El Salvador have disputed the border between the two countries, both in a remote mountain region and in the Gulf of Fonseca. This conflict, along with land shortages and immigration pressures, contributed to the outbreak of the so-called "Soccer War" in 1969.

The governments of Honduras and El Salvador signed a peace agreement formally terminating hostilities on 30 October 1980, but, unable to resolve their boundary dispute, submitted the problem to the International Court of Justice at The Hague. The ICJ handed down its ruling in September 1992, awarding Honduras 300.6 square kilometers of the disputed 436.9 square kilometers. Of the six *bolsones,* or "pockets" of land in the mountains, Honduras was given complete control of one and 80% of another, and the remaining four were split nearly evenly with El Salvador.

In the Gulf of Fonseca, Meanguera and Meanguerita Islands were granted to El Salvador, while Honduran ownership of Isla del Tigre was confirmed. The court also ruled Honduras had the right to free passage in the Gulf, an important aspect of the dispute. According to the ruling, the Gulf is not international waters, but is owned in a condominium arrangement between El Salvador, Honduras, and Nicaragua, all of which have gulf coastline.

In spite of the ruling, localized conflicts still occur in the *bolsones.* Honduran and Salvadoran campesinos occasionally attack one another in arguments over land. Both governments appear to be trying to calm tensions rather than fan nationalistic flames.

A parallel dispute also exists over fishing rights. Honduran and Nicaraguan fishermen are regularly taken prisoner for allegedly fishing in the other country's waters, both in the poorly defined Gulf of Fonseca and in the Caribbean. In the Caribbean, Hondurans draw the maritime border at the 15th parallel, while Nicaraguans claim their border extends to the 17th parallel.

---

developing in the Caribbean. These northerlies are often strong enough to cause precipitation all the way across the country to the Pacific coast, while less potent southerlies also bring their own rainfall to the south.

In La Mosquitia and on some parts of the Caribbean coast, rain falls year-round, without a defined dry season. The north coast cities of La Ceiba and Tela, for example, were flooded in March 1996, supposedly the driest time of year. The rest of the country can expect a reliable dry season from December or January to May or June, with steady blue skies and strong sun.

Hurricanes and Tropical Storms

Major tropical storms typically strike Honduras every decade or so, leaving thousands homeless and sometimes dead. Hurricane Fifi in 1974 was a major natural disaster, killing an estimated 10,000 Hondurans, mostly around the town of Choloma. More recently, Tropical Storm Marco struck the north coast in November 1996, destroying 4,000 homes.

Try to avoid the north coast of Honduras during the hurricane season (generally August-November). Even if the hurricanes themselves don't reach the shore, they bring heavy rains; flooding is an annual ritual and can seriously disrupt travel. Cases of cholera and other diseases are also more common during this time.

Other Travel Considerations

During the rainy season, expect road conditions to deteriorate severely. Major highways are well-maintained all year, but often the government will not bother patching other roads during the rains. As a result, many dirt roads become totally impassable, even with four-wheel drive.

MAJOR RIVER SYSTEMS

Río Coco or Segovia—550 km
Río Patuca—500 km
Río Ulúa—400 km
Río Chamelecón—200 km
Río Aguán—225 km
Río Sico or Negro—215 km
Río Choluteca—250 km
Río Guascorán—115 km
Río Nacaome—90 km

Miskitos in a canoe on
the Río Plátano

Also during the rains, water visibility for scuba diving is diminished on the Bay Islands. Divers can take comfort, however, from the fact that those islands are not on the usual hurricane path. Hiking is possible year-round, but it's less muddy during the dry season. If you're planning on rafting or river boating, the best time of year is after the rains, in December or January, when water levels are high.

FLORA AND FAUNA

VEGETATION ZONES

Only a third of the country is suitable for agriculture; 13% is devoted to perennial crops mixed with forest plantations, 11% to intensive annual crops, and nine percent to perennial crops mixed with pastures. The most heavily cultivated areas are the north coast; the Ulúa, Chamelecón, and Aguán valleys; and a few highland basins.

In spite of serious problems with logging and soil erosion, about 65% of Honduras still maintains a forest cover. That's the highest percentage of forestland among Central American nations and is largely due to the country's rugged terrain and relatively low population density.

Humid Tropical Forest
Otherwise known as broadleaf rainforest, this ecosystem once covered much of the Caribbean coast of Honduras. It's now limited to the north-facing slopes of parts of the Cordillera Nombre De Diós, and large expanses of La Mosquitia. The rainforests of La Mosquitia are thought to be the most extensive intact virgin rainforest in Central America.

The rainforest hosts very tall trees, up to 60 meters, with strongly buttressed root systems and dense leaf cover that completely blocks the sun from the forest floor. Tree types include mahogany, cedar, laurel, rosewood, strangler fig, tamarind, oak, ceiba, and many others. Rarely are several trees of the same species grouped together, although to the untrained observer, many trees in the rainforest look strikingly similar.

In virgin rainforest the forest floor is mostly devoid of grasses, shrubs, and herbs, and the soil is thin and nutrient-poor. The annual average temperature in the forest hovers around 25° C, while rainfall averages between 200 and 400 cm a year. At least five cm of rain can be expected every month.

When a rainforest is cleared by humans, and then the land is left alone for a period of time, the resulting growth is an impenetrable mass of thickets, vines, and small trees quite different from the original. Several generations are required for the forest to return to its virgin state.

Arid or Deciduous Tropical Forest

In lowland regions on both the Pacific and Caribbean coasts where rainfall levels are not high enough to support rainforest, deciduous tropical forests are common. A superb example of deciduous tropical forest can be seen in the area around El Corpus, near Choluteca; other patches are found along the valleys of the Ulúa, Humuya, Otoro, Choluteca, and Goascorán Rivers, as well as around Lago de Yojoa and in a few places on the Bay Islands.

Highland Pine Forest

Probably the most extensive type of forest in the country is the pine forest of the central highlands, mainly comprised of ocote *(Pinus montezumae)* but also sometimes including Caribbean pine *(Pinus caribaea)*. Ocotes generally occur between roughly 600 and 1,400 meters, depending on the region. In wetter areas they grow in dense forests laced with epiphytes. In drier areas the ocotes are more widely spaced, often sharing the forest with *encino* or roble oak trees, particularly around water sources.

Cloud Forest

A unique sort of high-altitude jungle thrives on the tops of the highest peaks in Honduras. These jungles are called cloud forests, since they seem perpetually wreathed in damp mists and fog. Although cloud-forested peaks do not receive significantly more rainfall than surrounding regions, temperatures and evaporation levels are markedly lower, so the forest retains a great deal more water.

The result is a dense, towering forest that appears similar to lowland rainforest, but is totally different in composition. The number of tree species is quite low, mainly several types of oak and *aguacate,* but the number of epiphytes is staggering. Bromeliads, orchids, ferns, mosses, and vines hang all over their tree hosts, taking advantage of their position to gather the moisture blowing through the forest.

Two types of cloud forest exist in Honduras. In the southern and western part of the country,

true cloud forest has developed. Here the geographic position of the mountains, in the prevailing wind patterns, has captured a constant cap of clouds, from which the forest sucks its moisture. The true cloud forest is located at elevations of roughly 1,800 to 2,800 meters, and is invariably isolated by a ring of drier pine or liquidambar (sweet gum) forest. Because these forests are biological islands, a variety of endemic plant and animal species are found within them.

In northern Honduras, another type of cloud forest is found at lower elevations. These forests receive more direct rain than those in the south, and rise directly out of the tropical forest below them with only a small intervening band of pine, if any at all. These cloud forests are more accurately characterized as mountain rainforests, and are found as low as 1,000 meters. The forests of Pico Bonito are a prime example.

In a few places at the highest elevations, notably in the Sierra de Agalta, strong winds and high moisture levels have combined to create bizarre dwarf forests. Here gnarled, stunted pine trees only a couple of meters tall grow among a profusion of mosses, ferns, and shrubs.

Although cloud forests do provide a home for species endangered elsewhere in Honduras, they're not as rich in animal—particularly mammal—life as tropical rainforests.

Savanna

Surprising to casual tourists, as well as a few plant biologists, is the presence of grassland savanna in La Mosquitia. The grasslands, dotted with stands of Caribbean pine, receive the same amount of rainfall as the adjacent rainforest and are often submerged during the wettest parts of the year.

A drier type of savanna supporting grasses and occasional stands of acacia and cactus covers parts of Olancho and El Paraíso. Biologists believe these areas were originally forested.

Mangrove Wetland

Much of the Honduran coastline, both Pacific and Caribbean, was once fronted by marshy tidal wetlands supporting red mangroves. Further inland, on drier ground, black and white mangroves replaced the red ones.

Due to expanding fruit cultivation and cattle ranching on the Caribbean coast and shrimp farming on the Pacific, many of Honduras's mangroves have been wiped out. Patches remain in the protected areas of Punta Sal, Punta Izopo, Cuero y Salado, Laguna Guaymoreto, and the Bahía de Chismayo.

FAUNA

Mammals

According to reports surviving from the early colonial era, Honduras once abounded with all variety of game—from jaguars to deer to wild boar. Those days are long gone. In almost all areas with any settlement, most mammals have been hunted out of existence, mainly to provide food or money to poor peasants.

Because of the country's rugged topography, however, a number of isolated regions remain refuges for species extinct elsewhere. The larger national parks, in particular Pico Bonito and Sierra de Agalta, and the rainforest of the Río Plátano Biosphere Reserve are the most likely places to encounter rare mammals.

In the rain and cloud forests, **monkeys** are the easiest mammals to spot. White-faced monkeys, howler monkeys, and capuchins inhabit the forests of Honduras. The noisy howlers are commonly heard in the early morning and late afternoon, when they enjoy unleashing their unearthly roars. Also inhabiting the rain and cloud forests, though rarely seen, are several species of **wild cats,** including jaguars (called *tigres*), mountain lions (called *leones* or *pumas*), ocelots, margays, and jaguarundis. The first two, the largest cats living in Central America, can be dangerous if surprised or cornered, but it's very unlikely you'll run across one. Most cats are nocturnal, so unless you go hiking at night or stumble across their den, chances are you'll never see one.

The largest mammal in the country is the **Baird's tapir,** an odd-looking creature related to the rhinoceros and sometimes measuring over two meters long. The tapir is found in both lowland and highland forests. Other wild forest mammals include opossums; two- and three-toed sloths; pygmy, giant, and tamandua anteaters; white-nosed coatis (called *pizotes*); kinkajous; white-lipped and collared peccaries; agoutis; nine-banded and naked-tailed armadillos, and gray foxes.

Some white-tailed and brocket deer, boars, and coyotes still run wild in eastern Honduras, particularly in parts of El Paraíso and Olancho. More common wild mammals are porcupines, rabbits, squirrels, skunks, raccoons, mice, rats, and several species of bats, including the much-feared **vampire bat**. Contrary to popular myth, vampire bats are uninterested in humans and spend their time prowling among cattle, horses, and other large domestic animals.

Throughout the rest of the country, **cattle** are omnipresent, mainly of the Pardo Suizo (milk cattle) and Brahman (beef cattle) varieties, and sometimes a mix of the two. Other favorite **domestic animals** are pigs, goats, horses, and the ever-present burros.

In the deep waters around the Bay Islands, you might spy several species of **marine mammals,** including seals, spinner and bottlenose dolphins, and sperm, humpback, pilot, and killer whales. The endangered manatee, or sea cow, can still be spotted along the coastline; a small population inhabits the wildlife refuge of Cuero y Salado, west of La Ceiba. River otters, also called nutria, are common in the rivers of La Mosquitia and are sometimes seen elsewhere.

Fish

The greatest variety of fish in Honduras is undoubtedly found in the reefs and surrounding waters of the Bay Islands, which contain an estimated 96% of all the marine life found in the Caribbean. Fish of all sizes, from chro-

ERIN DWYER

mides to barracudas to whale sharks (the world's largest fishes), are found near the islands. Eagle and manta rays are common, as are eels and hammerhead, nurse, and blacktip sharks.

Several species of shellfish are also frequently found in Honduran waters, particularly lobster, shrimp, conch, and a kind of crayfish found in the lagoons and swamps of the north coast. Lobster and shrimp fishing is a major industry on the north coast, and shrimp farming has recently become big business on the Gulf of Fonseca.

Resident freshwater fish include largemouth bass (found particularly in Lago de Yojoa), catfish, mollies, minnows, mojarras, trout, and the endangered cuyamel. This last fish, very meaty and tasty, once abounded in the rivers all along the north coast but has been fished to near extinction everywhere except a few places in La Mosquitia and Olancho.

Reptiles and Amphibians
Honduras holds some 20 species of lizards, including the common iguana and the larger and more intimidating basilisk. The Bay Islands are home to several lizard species found nowhere else in the world.

A great variety of snakes slither through the forests and pastures of rural Honduras. Most of them are harmless. Among the poisonous species are the dreaded fer-de-lance, coral snake, bushmaster, and rattler. Boas are frequently seen.

Crocodiles, caimans, and alligators inhabit many of the lagoons, marshes, and waterways of the north coast, particularly in La Mosquitia, so keep your hands inside the boat when traveling on the water. These reptiles tend to favor places where the current is not strong, so swimming in swift-moving rivers is considered safe.

Turtles, especially hawksbill and green but also loggerhead, Ridley, and leatherback, were once regular guests to the Honduran coasts, but are now endangered.

Birds
For such a small country, Honduras has a wild profusion of bird life. At least 710 species have been identified—more than in the United States and Canada combined. Many are migratory and only visit Honduras during certain times of the year. For a complete listing, the best guide available is the *Field Guide to Mexican Birds,* by Roger Tory Peterson and Edward L. Chalif, which describes over 90% of the birds found in Honduras. Another decent guide, though not as comprehensive, is *A Field Guide to the Birds of Mexico and Central America,* by Irby L. Davis.

Probably the premier **birding location** in the country, in terms of numbers of species, is at Lago de Yojoa, the country's largest inland lake. Reportedly 373 species of birds have been identified in the vicinity of the lake, which lies at the transition zone between the northern lowlands and the central highlands.

Many of the cloud-forest reserves in Honduras are prime birding sites, including La Muralla, Cusuco, Celaque, and others. La Muralla in particular is known for frequent sightings of the beautiful quetzal, a type of trogon with colorful feathering and tail coverts over two feet long.

Surprisingly, the rainforests of La Mosquitia are not the best places to birdwatch, as birds tend to hide their nests well in the thick foliage on the upper stories of the forest. Better birding is possible in farming areas on the edge of the forest, where clearings allow for easier sightings.

The coastal regions of the country host a unique set of bird life, including pelicans, roseate terns, parrots, frigate birds, pelicans, sandpipers, ibises, spoonbills, ducks, storks, fishing eagles, and herons.

HISTORY

Unlike it's violent Central American neighbors, and in spite of its grinding poverty, Honduras has managed to avoid any large-scale social disorder or revolutionary movement in the past 20 years, a fact which can be explained in large part by the country's unique history.

Because of Honduras's broken, rugged landscape and the lack of rich soils, a traditional, land-based elite did not develop during the colonial area as it did in neighboring Guatemala, Nicaragua, and El Salvador. The wealth that was produced from the gold and silver mines was quickly spent or shipped abroad, and did not form the basis for the growth of a powerful upper class.

A land-owning class eventually did arise at the turn of the 20th century. It consisted mainly of North American banana planters, who met no opposition capable of thwarting their takeover of the north coast—the most productive lands in the country.

Thus, in the era following World War II, when social and global conditions led to revolutions across Central America on the part of the lower classes and repressive reactions on the part of elites and the U.S. military, Honduras remained relatively peaceful. Some social disturbances did occur, most notably the Great Banana Strike of 1954 and later land-invasion movements by campesinos, but Honduran politicians and military leaders did not react with the blind opposition characteristic of their more violent neighbors. Labor unions were legalized and limited demands met; the military even undertook a modest agrarian reform program when in power in the 1970s, which helped diffuse a potentially explosive situation in the countryside.

These actions helped engender the belief that Hondurans could advance their causes through organization and political pressure. Apart from an interlude of violence and militarization brought on by the U.S.-led Contra war against Nicaragua, the Honduran system has proved remarkably flexible in accommodating the needs of its people. Though the actual operation of government is almost a caricature of incompetence and corruption, it's somehow sufficient enough to keep Hondurans from resorting to violence.

PRE-COLUMBIAN HISTORY

The First Hondurans

It remains a matter of conjecture whether the earliest settlers in Honduras arrived over land from Asia via the Bering Strait, as many believe, or on rafts from the South Pacific islands. Whatever route they took, the first people to live in what is now Honduras had arrived by about 10,000 B.C.

Next to nothing is known about these early Americans. Archaeologists hypothesize the earliest of them were hunters and gatherers who may have spent only a short time in the region before continuing southward.

Early Honduran Societies

The earliest evidence of settled society in Honduras dates from 2000 to 1500 B.C. It appears localized cultures developed simultaneously in the Valle de Sula, at Yarumela in the Valle de Comayagua, and in Olancho near the village of Talgua in the Valle de Catacamas. The level of interaction between these different societies is a matter of debate, but judging from pottery remains, some intergroup trading took place.

Because of its position in the center of the Americas, Honduras was a crossroads for pre-Columbian indigenous cultures, a border zone of sorts where Mesoamerican and South American indigenous peoples met.

At some point between 3000 and 1000 B.C., three indigenous groups still found in Honduras today migrated to the region. From the northern rainforests of South America came the Pech and Tawahka Sumu. Both groups speak languages related to the Chibchan family and both settled in northeastern Honduras and in Nicaragua. From the north, possibly from as far away as the southwestern United States, came the Tolupan, sometimes also called Jicaque, whose language appears related to Sioux. The Tolupan settled in north-central Honduras.

Around or shortly after the time of Christ, several indigenous groups from Mexico and Guatemala migrated into Honduras. The Toltec-speaking Chorotega are thought to have first settled in western Honduras, and later continued southward to the Choluteca Plain, where they were living at the time of the Spanish conquest. The Nahuatl-speaking Pipil migrated south from Mexico at about the same time.

Not long thereafter, another group moved into western Honduras from Mexico and Guatemala at a time when their culture was beginning an explosion of development. These people—the Maya—went on to build one of the greatest civilizations ever known in the Americas.

The Maya

The Maya crossed the Sierra del Espíritu Santo from Guatemala into the valley of Copán around A.D. 100, conquering the inhabitants of the region. During the next two centuries construction commenced on the city of Copán, and the Maya rulers began to expand their control up the Río Chamelecón to the Valle de Sula and as far east as the shores of Lago de Yojoa.

The first glyph at Copán that can be positively dated was made in A.D. 426 to mark the accession of Yax K'uk'Mo' to the city's throne. Thus began the ruling dynasty of Copán, which spanned four centuries, ending sometime around A.D. 822.

For reasons not entirely clear, Copán was the greatest center for arts, astronomy, and science in the Mayan world. The elaborate stelae erected at Copán are unparalleled anywhere in Mesoamerica, and the city's royal astronomers calculated planetary movements, eclipses, and the yearly calendar with a precision equaled only by modern western science.

Built gradually over the course of 400 years, with old temples buried and new ones built over them, the city of Copán is an impressive testament to the wealth and vision of the Mayan rulers, and their ability to marshal large numbers of laborers. At its height some 24,000 people are thought to have lived in and around Copán.

Mysteriously, classic Mayan civilization abruptly collapsed in the Yucatán, Guatemala, and Honduras around A.D. 900. The collapse is all the odder considering Mayan centers were independent city-states, not part of one great centralized empire. One widely accepted explanation for the demise of Mayan civilization is that the population simply grew too big for the surrounding lands to support. This certainly seems to be the case at Copán, where recent studies confirm massive deforestation and soil erosion just before the city's collapse. Although Maya-speaking people continued to live in the Valle de Copán and still do so today, the city was abandoned entirely.

Honduras in 1502

After the decline of the Maya, Honduras became a complex mosaic of tribes, subtribes, and chiefdoms, with only vague borders be-

altar relief detail, Copán

tween each. This lasted until the arrival of Columbus in 1502 and for a time afterward.

Western and south-central Honduras in 1502 were dominated by the Lenca, a broad grouping composed of several different and often hostile tribes, including the Potón, Guaquí, Cares, Chatos, Dules, Paracas, and Yaras. Although their language does not seem related to any South American group, the Lenca are theorized to have migrated up from Colombia.

The historical account of which languages were spoken by which Lenca tribes is extremely muddled. It's possible the same groups were given two different names by different witnesses, and that others were not Lenca at all. Some tribes were exclusively hunter-gatherers, while others cultivated maize and other crops in the mountain valleys of Comayagua and Sensetí, and around Lago de Yojoa.

In far western Honduras the Chortí Maya held sway over the mountain region along the border with Guatemala as far west and south as El Salvador, and were organized in local chiefdoms.

Throughout western, southern, and northern Honduras at the time of the conquest were trading outposts maintained by the Aztecs. Not far from present-day San Pedro Sula, the city of Naco—the largest urban center in the country when the Spanish conquest began—is thought to have been one such outpost, although others argue it was a Chortí Maya city.

Most of north-central and central Honduras was occupied by the Tolupan in 1502, while further east were the Pech and the Sumu. Each of these tribes survived by hunting, fishing, and practicing limited agriculture. Settlements were small and frequently temporary, and groups moved often to find fresh game and rich soil for planting.

The Choluteca plains, at the time of conquest, were home to the Chorotega and possibly a few settlements of Potón or Lenca.

Unquestionably these various indigenous groups interacted with one another often, either through trade or warfare. In several places, they lived side by side in relative harmony, especially in the valleys of Comayagua, Catacamas, and Agalta, and around Lago de Yojoa. Nonetheless it's clear no group possessed the strength to exercise hegemony over the others, a fact that greatly helped Spanish invaders.

CONQUEST AND COLONIZATION

Columbus' Fourth Voyage

In July 1502, on the fourth and final voyage of Cristóbal Colón (Christopher Columbus), the famed admiral sailed from Hispaniola along the Caribbean coast of Central America, and came upon the island of Guanaja, where he met with the local people and waylaid a trader's canoe laden with axes, copper goods, cacao, and pottery.

Despite the fact that the canoe was seen approaching from the west, Columbus continued east from Guanaja, which he named the Island of Pines. His first stop was at Punta Caxinas, near present-day Trujillo. The first Mass spoken on the mainland of the Americas was held at Punta Caxinas. A simple cross now marks the site.

East of Trujillo Columbus stopped again at the mouth of a large river, which may have been either the Aguán, Sico, or Patuca. Because this was the place chosen to claim the lands for the Spanish crown, Columbus named the river Río de la Posesión.

Continuing further east along the coast of La Mosquitia, Columbus's fleet was buffeted by severe storms until rounding the easternmost point of Honduras and reaching calmer waters off present-day Nicaragua. In honor of the better weather, the point was christened Cabo Gracias a Dios, a name it retains today.

The Conquest Begins

Following this uneventful first visit, Honduras was ignored for the next 20 years, apart from a possible visit by explorers Juan Díaz Solís and Vicente Yáñez Pinzón in 1508. Occupied with consolidating their newfound possessions in the Caribbean, the Spaniards did not return to Honduras until 1522-23, when Gil González Dávila led an exploratory expedition up the Pacific coast from Panama, reaching the Gulf of Fonseca.

In the following couple of years, six Spanish expeditions converged on Honduras, each headed by ambitious soldiers after wealth and glory. Not an auspicious start to colonization, it presaged the trend of placing personal power over group interests—the rule in Honduran government for the next four and a half centuries.

González Dávila, with the approval of the crown, was the first to land on Honduran shores, establishing a small town near the mouth of the Río Dulce, in what is now Guatemala. The explorer marched into the heart of Honduras toward Nicaragua in early 1524. Shortly thereafter, Mexican conqueror Hernán Cortés sent an expedition of his own led by Cristóbal de Olid, who arrived on the north coast in May and quickly set up a small town at Triunfo de la Cruz.

Olid wasn't totally loyal to Cortés, however, and once on his own tried to claim the province for himself. When word of this reached Cortés in Mexico, he promptly dispatched a second expedition, led by Francisco de las Casas, to ensure his authority. Further complications occurred from the incursions of Pedro de Alvarado and Hernando de Soto, who entered Honduras from Guatemala and Nicaragua, respectively. Amid the bickering and fighting, in which Olid literally lost his head, the first permanent settlement was established in the country, at Trujillo.

Impatient with reports of fighting among these various factions, and not trusting anyone, Cortés personally led an expedition to Honduras. Beginning in late 1524, he undertook an incredible multimonth overland trek through the jungles of the Yucatán and the Guatemalan Petén, reaching Honduras in the spring of 1525. Although Cortés briefly took control of the situation in Honduras, by the time of his departure in April 1526, his long absence from Mexico had undermined his position in the royal court, and he never again held positions of power.

Displeased with the turbulent course of conquest, and wanting to ensure direct control over the new colony, the Spanish crown sent Diego López de Salcedo to act as royal governor of Honduras. López de Salcedo anchored off Trujillo on 24 October 1526, and after a few days of negotiations with suspicious colonists loyal to Cortés, he was allowed to land and take office.

Rebellion and Consolidation

The 15 years after López de Salcedo became governor were chaotic for the nascent colony and catastrophic for the indigenous people. Continued infighting, conflicting royal *cédulas* (orders giving authority to conquer and govern a given area), and repeated revolts by native peoples prohibited the Spaniards from sig-

nificantly extending their control across the country.

Several localized attacks against Spanish settlements took place around Trujillo and in the Valle de Sula in the early 1530s, but in 1536 mass rebellion broke out across most of western and central Honduras. Led by the Lenca warrior Lempira, for whom the national currency is named, thousands of Lenca and allied tribes took up arms against the Spaniards. The hostile tribes kept the colony in a precarious position until 1539, when Lempira was assassinated by the Spanish. Localized rebellions continued after Lempira's death, especially in the Valle de Comayagua, but these the Spanish put down easily. For more on Lempira, see the special topic "The Rise and Fall of Lempira."

Victory over the Lenca served the Spanish well, both eliminating further Indian resistance and uniting the conquistadores in the colonial project. Establishing the towns of Gracias a Dios, Comayagua, San Pedro Sula, Choluteca, and Tencoa in the late 1530s laid the foundation for extending Spanish control throughout the region.

As always, gold and silver proved the main impetus for new Spanish settlements. Rich veins were discovered early near Gracias a Dios and Comayagua, and not long after in Olancho and in the hills above the Gulf of Fonseca.

At that time, the province was divided into two sections: Higueras, which comprised present-day western and central Honduras, and Honduras proper, which covered Trujillo, La Mosquitia, Olancho, the region around Tegucigalpa, and the Gulf of Fonseca.

Indian Decline

During this time the indigenous population of Honduras went into a precipitous decline. An estimated 500,000 to 800,000 native people lived in Honduras before 1492, but their numbers began dropping steeply. Diseases for which the Indians had no tolerance preceded the Spaniards, and picked up force when the conquistadores did arrive, ravaging local populations. In addition approximately 100,000 to 200,000 native people were exported from the colony as slaves.

So severe were these depredations, Spanish reports put the number of Indians under Spanish control at just 8,000 in 1541. Although this figure does not include the populations of Tolupan, Pech, and Tawahka outside Spanish influence, it still represents an almost unimaginable decline in population. Though certainly facilitating the conquest, the drastic drop in Indian population also posed serious problems for the Spaniards, who needed labor to work the mines and provide them with food.

The Poorest Colony

Because of labor shortages and the depletion of the richest veins of gold and silver by the end of the 16th century, Honduras quickly became a colonial backwater. Since the possibilities for getting rich were slim, able governors did their utmost to be stationed elsewhere, leaving Honduras with incompetent administrators who were eager to leave at the first opportunity.

Spain's control over Honduras, as with many other regions of Latin America, was through *encomiendas,* a method in which Spaniards received awards of land and the right to use the native people who lived on the land for labor in return for religious instruction.

Farming was difficult; Honduras lacked the rich volcanic soils of its neighbors and the rugged terrain made bringing produce to markets even harder. In the early years of the colony, the only industries of any importance were cattle ranching, often for local consumption, and gathering sarsaparilla, thought at the time to be a cure for venereal disease.

In addition, the developing colony was faced with the presence of pirates on the north and south coast, and later of British settlers in La Mosquitia and the Bay Islands. These raiders, helped by their Miskito allies, made living on the north coast a dangerous undertaking, effectively sealing off the Caribbean coast for the better part of two centuries.

Late in the colonial era, improved technology led to a renewed though short-lived boom in mining, particularly around Tegucigalpa and Choluteca. Farmers in the region of Copán and Gracias also exported large quantities of tobacco to Europe and other colonies. Nonetheless these were mostly small-scale ventures, not enough to attract significant migration to Honduras or lead to notable economic development.

INDEPENDENCE AND 19TH CENTURY HONDURAS

Mexican Empire and Central American Federation

Rather than fighting for their independence from the Spanish empire, Central Americans had it handed to them without a struggle when colonial authority completely collapsed. On 15 September 1821 representatives of the former colonies of Honduras, Costa Rica, Nicaragua, El Salvador, and Guatemala jointly declared independence from Spain in the government palace of Guatemala.

Brief struggles followed within the new countries over how to govern themselves. In Honduras, the two principal cities of Comayagua and Tegucigalpa split on the issue, the former opting to join with Mexico and the latter preferring a union of Central American republics.

By early 1822 the issue had been decided, and the countries declared themselves loyal to Iturbide, the new emperor of Mexico. This would-be empire lasted just over a year, at which point Iturbide was deposed and Central America joined as a federation.

The United Provinces of Central America was a fine idea in theory but in practice foundered on the unpleasant realities of local rivalries, suspicions, and the split between Conservatives and Liberals—a division ongoing in Honduras to the present day. Broadly, Conservatives favored the church, the land-owning elite, and a paternalistic attitude toward indigenous peoples and campesinos, while Liberals supported economic modernization, education, eradicating the power of the church, and a policy of erasing indigenous culture and homogenizing the population. By 1838, after almost nonstop infighting, the union was dead, and each province had become a sovereign nation.

The Birth of Honduras

After a few months of vacillation, Honduras declared itself independent on 15 November 1838, and passed the first of many constitutions in January 1839. Between this time and 1876, Honduras experienced a period of extreme instability and precious little development.

CENTRAL AMERICA'S GEORGE WASHINGTON

Honduras's national hero, Francisco Morazán is one of the most revered characters in Central American history, recognized as a visionary thinker and politician, a humane individual, and one of the finest soldiers ever to fight on American soil. Because of his appreciation for the American Revolution and his tireless efforts to promote Central American unity, Morazán is sometimes referred to as the George Washington of Central America.

Morazán was born 3 October 1789 to an upper-middle-class colonial family in Tegucigalpa. Gifted both physically and intellectually, and imbued with strong self-discipline, he was largely self-taught. He received his only formal education from a priest in the town of Texiguat, at that time the only school near Tegucigalpa. Morazán taught himself French so he could read Rousseau's *Social Contract,* and he continued with Tocqueville, Montesquieu, and the history of Europe.

When Central America declared independence from Spain in 1821, Morazán began working with his friend, Liberal Dionisio de Herrera, who was running Tegucigalpa. Morazán's first command was at the head of a group of soldiers sent to Gracias in 1822 to transport a load of silver and mercury. He was captured by soldiers from Comayagua, but managed to talk his way out of it by claiming he was traveling on business. After the Central American provinces broke away from Mexico and created their own union, Morazán took up arms for the Liberal side. He lost his first battle, defending Comayagua from Conservative troops, and was forced to flee to El Salvador to escape a prison term.

In 1827 Morazán traveled to Nicaragua, where he gathered an army to invade El Salvador, which he did the following year. El Salvador was freed from attacking Guatemalan conservatives. In 1829 he continued by taking Guatemala; in elections the next year Morazán was voted president of the Central American Federation. With one brief interruption, Morazán held this post until 1838. Although the federation experienced constant strain from internal opposition, Morazán managed to institute farsighted reforms in bureaucracy, public education, taxation, freedom of religion, the judicial system, infrastructure, and the development, albeit temporary, of democratic institutions.

Morazán's Liberal policies seriously antagonized the church and elite landowners in all five Central American countries. The forces pulling them apart proved stronger than those holding them together, and in spite of Morazán's best efforts, the union fell apart shortly after he left office. Morazán was forced into exile in Peru in 1840, but he returned two years later. He led a coup in Costa Rica, with the idea of using that country as a base to reestablish the union. His forces were defeated by Conservatives in September of 1842, and on 15 September, ironically the anniversary of Central American independence, Morazán was executed. He was given permission to order his own execution. After correcting the firing squad's aim, he called out, "¡Ahora bien, fuego!" ("Ready, fire!"). According to legend, he was heard to say, "¡Estoy vivo!" ("I'm alive!"), and a second volley killed him.

With his death died any real chance at Central American union, in spite of the obvious advantages of such an alliance. The idea has resurfaced repeatedly over the following century and a half, and may be reappearing even today in the form of the budding Central American Common Market.

BOB RACE

national hero Francisco Morazán

Rivalries between Liberals and Conservatives dominated the political landscape across Central America during this era, and when one side was in power in one country, rulers of the opposite persuasion organized invasions or coups from their territory. Being in the middle of Central America and bordered by Guatemala, Nicaragua, and El Salvador, Honduras was a frequent target of aggression.

As if the squabbles among its Central American neighbors weren't enough, Honduras also had to cope with the machinations of North Americans and British, both private citizens and government officials. American agent E. George Squier and British representative Frederick Chatfield overtly and surreptitiously abused their power to advance the interests of their respective countries, most particularly regarding a trans-continental railroad or canal.

Even more ominous were the activities of private American and British citizens in Honduras. From the U.S. came the messianic, slightly lunatic "grey-eyed man of destiny," William Walker. Convinced he was the savior of Central America, and backed by wealthy U.S. financiers, Walker invaded Nicaragua and declared himself president in 1855. Although his rule was short-lived, Walker performed the heretofore impossible task of uniting all the Central American republics—at least for as long as it took them to defeat and expel the gringo. Unabashed, Walker returned to Honduras in 1860 with the idea of retaking Central America, only to be captured by the British, turned over to Honduran troops, and summarily executed.

Ever more subtle than North Americans, British power brokers contented themselves not with outright invasion, but with contracting a series of debts with the Honduran government. This made a few British bankers and several corrupt Hondurans rich, but crippled the country before it had a chance to get started. In, as one historian puts it, "one of the more dubious transactions in financial history," British bankers lent Honduras a bit less then six million pounds sterling to help construct a national railroad. The government eventually saw merely 75,000 of these pounds, the rest remaining on sticky fingers on both sides of the Atlantic. By 1871 only 92 km of track had been laid, and even that was shoddily built and soon collapsed. Unable to cope with even the interest on the loan, successive governments tried to forget it existed, until by 1916 Honduras owed US$125 million and had to plead for the loans to be renegotiated.

The Liberal Years

One of the first forward-thinking governments in Honduran history began in 1876, with the inauguration of Liberal president Marco Aurelio Soto. A firm believer in modernization, Soto and his successor Luis Bográn did what they could to lay the foundations for development.

During the years between 1876 and 1891, when Bográn was deposed, state finances were regulated, free primary education was promoted, and the legal code was reformed. Convinced of the need for foreign capital to lift Honduras out of poverty, Soto also promoted mining among U.S. investors.

His campaign's most notable success, if it can be termed that, was the founding of the New York and Honduras Rosario Mining Company in 1880, which quickly became the most profitable and productive mine in the western hemisphere during that period. Although the company provided jobs for a thousand Honduran workers and was for a time the most important economic and political player in Honduras, all profits went directly to New York; in the long run Honduras saw little benefit for the concessions it offered.

The Banana Companies

The railroad and mining episodes gave merely a taste of foreign domination compared to the advent of the banana industry on the north coast. U.S.-bound freighters were buying bananas from local producers as early as 1860, but in 1899 the Vaccaro Brothers—later Standard Fruit, and now Castle and Cooke—set up the first foreign-controlled plantations on the mainland near La Ceiba. They were quickly followed by United Fruit and Cuyamel.

Once these foreign companies moved in, small-scale Honduran producers were forced out of business either through land buy-outs or crude threats. Thus, by the beginning of World War I, the three largest companies controlled huge portions of land, the country's only railroads, and over 80% of the Honduran export trade. Much of the land had been given to the companies in return for the construction of railroads, which for the most part were never built.

Along with economic domination, the banana companies showed no compunction about bribing and cajoling government officials and army officers. When quieter tactics proved unsuccessful, financing a revolution was not entirely out of the question, and disputes were often decided in the end by a U.S. invasion.

Reviewing this inglorious period, one historian notes: "North American power had become so encompassing that U.S. military forces and United Fruit could struggle against each other to see who was to control the Honduran government, then have the argument settled by the U.S. Department of State."

THE DEVELOPMENT OF MODERN HONDURAS

The *Cariato*

The perennial instability proved a distraction to the banana companies and the U.S. government, and after the merger of United and Cuyamel in 1929, the political situation in Honduras changed. National Party strongman Tiburcio Carías Andino was able to seize power in 1932 and remain there for 16 years.

Carías, who began his career as a military cook, was a classic example of an uneducated yet extremely shrewd and ruthless *caudillo* (political boss). Social developments were minimal under his rule; the military was professionalized, the opposition and media suppressed, and the fruit companies, particularly United, were given a free hand.

One historian desribed *Cariato* as the kind of time "when members of the opposition were forbidden to travel in automobiles, where the First Lady sold tamales at the Presidential Palace, and the president of Congress justified Carías's long rule by noting that 'God, too, continues in power indefinitely.'"

Following the end of World War II, Central American dictators had become an unnecessary embarrassment to the U.S., and Carías was forced from office in 1948 in favor of protégé Juan Manuel Gálvez. Gálvez ruled for six years, and began the long process of economic moderniza-

tion by developing a central bank, starting a system of income tax, and expanding public works.

The Great Banana Strike

The landmark Banana Strike of 1954 marked the birth of Honduras's powerful and effective organized labor movement. Although sporadic strikes occurred on banana plantations and docks as early as 1916, the 1954 strike was the first large-scale labor action that could not be quickly bought off or put down with force.

Appropriately, the actions leading to the strike began on Labor Day, 1 May 1954. A group of dock workers in Puerto Cortés asked United officials for double pay for work on Sunday, which was mandated by law. Their request was put off several days, and in the meantime their designated spokesman was fired by United.

In response, the dock workers went on strike. They were soon joined by all 25,000 United workers and 15,000 Standard Fruit workers, an expression of pent-up frustration at abysmal working conditions, low pay, and cavalier treatment by banana company officials.

The strike was supported by Hondurans throughout the country, and workers of several other industries struck out of solidarity. Lasting 69 days, the strike was eventually broken by a combination of limited concessions, payoffs to labor leaders, and the establishment of company-friendly unions in competition to the more militant ones. In setting up these "stooge" unions, the American Federation of Labor (AFL) played a prominent role.

Although direct gains from the strike were minimal, it was a watershed for the nascent labor movement. By negotiating with the unions, both the government and the banana companies tacitly accepted their right to exist, and the following year laws were passed on union creation, collective bargaining, and the right to strike.

Growth of Military Power

At the same time, a political watershed was taking place in Honduras. In the face of an incompetent and unpopular government, a group of military officers organized a successful coup d'état on 21 October 1956.

Though elections were held the following year and the military duly turned power back over to civilians, the coup marked the beginning of military influence in the country's politics, a defining

THE SOCCER WAR

In 1969, a brief border war erupted between El Salvador and Honduras, seemingly sparked by a World Cup soccer match between the two countries. The real reasons behind the fighting, of course, were much more serious than a soccer match.

For years land-hungry campesinos from overpopulated El Salvador had been crossing the mountainous border into Honduras, setting up small farms and businesses. By the late 1960s, Salvadoran immigrants comprised roughly 20% of the country's rural population—this at a time when Honduras had begun feeling land pressures of its own. Wealthy Honduran land owners began waging a cynical propaganda campaign that distracted from the country's internal problems and fueled growing hatred against the Salvadorans.

In April 1969, the Honduran government gave Salvadoran settlers 30 days to return to their country; by June some 20,000 had fled. Others were victimized by irate Hondurans and the Mancha Brava, a National Party vigilante squad. Soon after, elimination matches to qualify for the upcoming 1970 World Cup were played between the two countries. In Central America soccer is always a passionate affair, but that year, due to the land disputes, tensions were at fever pitch.

The first match occurred on 8 June in Tegucigalpa. As is common practice, the visiting team spent a sleepless night in their hotel, listening to the screams, horns, and firecrackers of loyal Honduran fans on the streets below. The following day,

the sleepless Salvadoran squad predictably lost, 1-0. A young Salvadoran girl shot herself in grief over the loss. Tens of thousands of Salvadorans, including the president and the soccer team, marched to her funeral.

A week later, Honduras's soccer team traveled to San Salvador for the second match. This time the Salvadoran fans kept the Honduran team awake all night, and at the game, the Honduran national anthem was booed and a rag run up the flagpole instead of the Honduran flag; Honduras lost 3-0 and violence erupted. The Honduran team had to be escorted to the airport by the military, and visiting Honduran fans were beaten. Dozens were hospitalized and two died.

Because of the violence, the third and deciding match was postponed. A month later, on 14 July, the El Salvador military bombed several locations inside Honduras and launched a surprise land attack. The Salvadoran Army made it deep into Honduran territory, but was unable to advance as the Honduran Air Force had destroyed their main fuel-storage station. The war lasted 100 hours. Some 2,000 people, mostly Honduran campesinos, were killed, and 130,000 Salvadorans returned to their country. Apart from releasing nationalistic frustrations on both sides, the war accomplished nothing. A peace treaty was finally signed in 1980, and the International Justice Court in The Hague later settled the border dispute.

The final soccer match was eventually held in Mexico City; El Salvador won 3-2.

---

characteristic of modern Honduran government. A big indicator of this influence were two clauses in the new constitution written by the military: one allowed the head of the military to disregard orders from the president that he considered unconstitutional, and the second gave him control over all military promotions.

Following the 1957 elections, the Constitutional Assembly chose Liberal Ramón Villeda Morales as president. He quickly instituted much-needed social reforms, such as literacy projects, public health care, road building, and agrarian reform. The agrarian reform, in particular, made Honduran land owners and the fruit companies nervous, and when it appeared an even more radical Liberal would win elections after Villeda, the military again took control on 3

October 1963. Colonel Oswaldo López Arellano assumed leadership of the country, and apart from a democratic hiatus in 1971-72, the military stayed in formal power until 1978.

The first half of military rule, until the 1969 war with El Salvador (see the special topic "The Soccer War"), was characterized by a suppression of communist groups and campesino organizations, but at the same time offered limited agrarian and social reform.

Following the war and the failed democratic experiment of 1971-72, López Arellano returned to power, this time convinced of the need for real agrarian reform. Between 1973 and 1976, 31,000 families received 144,000 hectares of land through the National Agrarian Institute (INA). Although it did not eliminate the problems of landless workers, it was a large step in the right direction and a reform that would have been completely unimaginable in the neighboring countries of El Salvador, Nicaragua, and Guatemala.

Following a scandal involving bribes paid by the banana companies to government officials, López Arellano was forced from power in March 1975. His replacement, Col. Juan Alberto Melgar Castro, slowed the pace of reform. Melgar Castro was then ousted in 1978 by a junta led by Gen. Policarpo Paz García, who organized elections in 1981 that nominally returned civilian politicians to power.

Reagan and the Contras

Two external but related developments of extreme importance took place shortly before the 1981 election of Liberal Roberto Suazo Córdova: the 1979 victory of the Sandanista revolution in Nicaragua, and the 1981 inauguration of U.S. President Ronald Reagan. Viewing the world through the paranoid prism of communist-capitalist conflict, President Reagan could not tolerate the presence of the socialist-leaning Sandanistas, and Honduras proved the perfect launching pad for the U.S.-financed and directed counterrevolution.

With the complicity of Suazo Córdova and the fascist armed forces commander Gen. Gustavo Álvarez Martínez, the CIA at first overtly and later covertly directed a stream of training, funds, and weapons to an army of anti-Sandanista Nicaraguans living along the Honduras-Nicaragua border in Olancho and El Paraíso.

Along with the Contras, as the fighters were known, came U.S. military personnel by the hundreds and CIA agents by the dozen, using Honduras as a base not only for the Contra war but also to help the Salvadoran military in its struggle against its leftist rebels. The country had become, in the words of one observer, "a land-based aircraft carrier," the USS Honduras.

Concurrently, the Honduran military tightened its hold over society, although the country was still a formal democracy. Álvarez ruthlessly imprisoned, tortured, killed or "disappeared" labor activists, peasant leaders, priests, and other opponents, often using the infamous hit squad Battalion 3-16. Though the repression never reached the heights it did in El Salvador or Guatemala—

victims here numbered in the hundreds rather than thousands—these strong-arm tactics were unheard of in Honduras, and created widespread discontent even within the military. In 1984 Álvarez was exiled by fellow officers, and his successor, Walter López Reyes, put an end to the blatantly unsavory aspects of repression. Nevertheless, the military remained in firm control behind the scenes.

By 1988 the Contra war began winding down due to U.S. congressional opposition, the Iran-Contra affair, the Central American peace process, and the growing feeling among all Hondurans that they needed to get the Contras out of their country. The Contras were disbanded by early 1990, following the election of Violeta Chomorro in Nicaragua.

The 1990s

Because of the Contra war and subsequent militarization, the 1980s were something of a lost decade for Honduras. In the 1989 elections, National candidate Rafael Leonardo Callejas was swept into office by a large margin, promising a program of economic modernization.

Callejas believed the only way to pull Honduras out of the hole was through a heavy dose of economic adjustment, that is, selling off public industries, laying off public employees, having a floating exchange rate, and encouraging foreign investment. A superbly gifted politician, Callejas managed to push these measures through and generally see them through to the end of his term in 1994, in spite of public and political opposition.

The results were mixed, at best. Unemployment and absolute numbers of people living in poverty rose, but defenders claim it was a necessary price for putting the country's fiscal book in order. Critics retort that many of the privatizations were bought up by Callejas cronies or members of the armed forces, which has since emerged as the strongest economic player in the country. Critics also contend corruption was rife throughout Callejas's term.

The '93 elections brought Liberal Carlos Roberto Reina to power, a long-time politician respected for his personal honesty. He took office in 1994 promising a "moral revolution" to clean the political system of corruption. Reina's success has been debatable. Corruption continues of course, though some say at a lower level than before. Much of Callejas's economic policies have remained intact, and although the country is still a financial basket case, there is room for hope. The *maquiladora* export industry based around San Pedro Sula and Puerto Cortés is booming, and foreign-exchange earnings from tourism are rising steadily.

For the November 1997 elections, the Liberals have nominated party stalwart Carlos Flores as their candidate, while the Nationals picked Nora Gúnera de Melgar, widow of one of the country's military rulers, Melgar Castro. For the first time, the 1997 elections will include a coalition of ex-guerrillas and leftists under the banner of the Unificación Democrático (UDE).

GOVERNMENT

Political System

Since 1982, with the passage of its 16th constitution, Honduras has been formally a democratic country, with a president and 128-member unicameral National Congress elected simultaneously every four years.

The president is by far the most powerful figure in the country. In theory the Congress has wide authority; in practice almost all policy initiatives come from the executive office. The Congress—always ruled by the president's party—generally acts as a rubber stamp.

The system developed partly from the country's long tradition of *caudillo* rulers, and in part from the electoral system. Voters are allowed to choose only one party's slate for national elections, and do not have the option of voting for a president from one party and a congressional deputy from another. Thus, deputies are merely loyal supporters of the president, and do not have a local constituency to answer to.

The judicial system, supposedly independent, is in reality a completely politicized institution. Judges are changed every four years, from the Supreme Court down to local justices of the peace, according to political affiliation.

Honduras is divided into 18 departments: Altántida, Choluteca, Comayagua, Copán, Cortés, El Paraíso, Francisco Morazán, Gracias a Dios, Intibucá, Islas de la Bahía, La Paz, Lempira, Ocotepeque, Olancho, Santa Bárbara, Valle, and Yoro. Each is ruled by a governor, who is appointed and removed at the discretion of the president.

Every four years, the country's 297 municipal governments hold elections for mayor *(alcalde)* and municipal council. Until the 1993 elections, local officials were on the same ballot as national ones, but now voters may split the ticket

between different parties. Rural *municipios* are further divided into *aldeas,* or villages, and *caseríos,* or hamlets.

Political Parties

For the better part of a century, Honduran politics has been formally dominated by two parties: the Liberals and the Nationals. The Liberal Party was created first, in an effort to institutionalize the modernizing liberal reforms of Marco Aurelio Soto and Luis Bográn. The Nationals were born as a splinter group of the Liberals in 1902 at the behest of Manuel Bonilla, who later became the party's first president.

Since their inception, little has distinguished the two parties in terms of policy. For many years the Nationals were linked closely to the military, but that was more an accident of circumstance than a true ideological stance, evidenced by the close cooperation of successive Liberal presidents Suazo Córdova and Azcona with the military in the 1980s.

For the most part, the parties have been vehicles for personal ambition, a fact never much disguised. Campaigns are invariably long on mudslinging and personal accusations and woefully short on political proposals.

In spite of lacking clear ideological differences, each party has certain core areas of support—the Nationals in the rural departments of Copán, Lempira, Intibucá, and Gracias a Dios and in the southern departments of Valle and Choluteca, while the Liberals are more popular in the urban areas and the north coast. Political scientists have suggested that party allegiance is more often merely passed down over generations, much like support for a favorite soccer club, rather than being a real assessment of the options.

Smaller parties have tried to break the grip of the big two, but with little success. Both the Christian Democrats (PDCH) and the reformist Innovation and Unity Party (PINU) have received little more than two percent of the national vote in the past, and are marginalized from any real decision-making. The 1997 elections will witness a new participant, the Democratic Unification Party (UDE), made up of an eclectic collection of ex-guerrillas and leftists, but they are not expected to make a significant dent into the two-party system.

The Military

Some claim the official political system is merely window-dressing for the country's true power broker—the armed forces. The Honduran military is a curious animal. The officer corps is not made up of wealthy elites as is the case in neighboring countries. It's much more egalitarian. In fact, in the absence of a strong homegrown elite, the military has become an elite class itself, with its own interests and agenda often quite different from the country's politicians, business leaders, and landowners. For this reason, the military has never been as rabidly conservative or repressive as other regimes in the region.

Since taking direct power for the first time in 1956, the military has always maintained a watchful eye over civilian politicians, who, knowing the rules of the game, have been careful not to tread on any boots. The exact level of military influence over civilian politicians is a matter of great debate, but it says a lot that current military chief Gen. Mario Hung Pacheco appears in the newspapers on an almost daily basis and is consulted regularly by Pres. Carlos Reina. Nevertheless, recent moves such as the abolition of compulsory military service indicate the balance of power may be equaling out.

Technically the military is under civilian authority, but in practice it manages its own affairs. Changes in leadership have often been presented to surprised politicians as fait accompli, and the Congress duly ratifies the new leader without question. Although it always has a single commander-in-chief, the military is run by a council of officers called the Consejo Superios de las Fuerzas Armadas (CONSUFFAA), which makes decisions collectively.

With the winding down of the Contra war and the curtailing of U.S. military aid to Honduras, along with the fiscal belt-tightening begun by Callejas, the military has started to develop its own financial base. It has been so successful that recently its investment arm, the Instituto de Previsión Militar (IPM), was rated one of the five largest investors in the country. The IPM owns hotels, shrimp farms, a cement factory, and a range of other holdings.

ECONOMY

Honduras is an extremely poor country. For years it has been considered the second-poorest in the hemisphere, after Haiti, though due to the years of civil war Nicaragua is not far behind. Annual per capita income is around US$600, the unemployment rate is a staggering 40%, and some 70% of the population lives below the poverty line.

The Honduran economy grew steadily throughout the 1960s and 1970s, following a policy of import-substitution and promotion of nontraditional exports, but the region's military conflicts during the 1980s sent investment and production into a tailspin. Since the end of the Contra war and the implementation of fiscal reforms by President Callejas, Honduras has become a favorite for foreign investors, particularly Asians. Although growth in 1995 and 1996 was between three-and-a-half and four percent, Honduras still has a long way to go to pull itself out of poverty. At current growth rates, it would take 15 years to achieve the economic level of Guatemala, and 27 years to reach that of Costa Rica.

Agricultural products are still the most important export, particularly bananas, coffee, and shellfish. With that dependency comes the often painful syndrome of having the national economy fluctuate in almost direct relation to the price of these goods in foreign markets, over which Hondurans have no influence.

A fledgling *maquiladora* sector based on the north coast has been posting impressive gains in the past two years, and has powered the rapid growth of San Pedro Sula and Puerto Cortés.

AGRICULTURE

Agriculture, both for export and internal consumption, is the largest segment of the Honduran economy. Over half the population still survives by working the land, though this is changing steadily as the country urbanizes.

In spite of the large percentage of people living and working in the countryside, land ownership is dramatically skewed in Honduras. In 1993, over 60% of the country's arable land was in the hands of the Honduran government and the two largest foreign banana companies, Chiquita and Castle and Cooke.

Agro-exports

In 1996, Honduran agro-exports generated 28% of the GNP, 84% of export earnings, and provided 60% of the nation's jobs.

The original "banana republic," Honduras still depends in large part on bananas, although less so in recent years. Foreign-owned banana companies have been cutting back production in Honduras, and a dispute with the European Community over import taxes has hurt the industry.

Coffee has recently surpassed bananas as the top export earner, bringing in US$237.6 million during the 1995-96 harvest year. Because of rising coffee prices and increased production, coffee earnings are expected to significantly boost the economy during 1996-97. Often produced on less than five hectares of land, coffee provides a living directly to 80,000 families.

Apart from employing many small farmers, coffee cultivation also encourages eco-friendly land use. Of the two strains produced in the country, the finer and more expensive arabica variety requires a shady environment, and thus can be grown in forest areas and serve as an incentive to stop deforestation.

Shrimp farming, particularly along the Gulf of Fonseca, is also a rising industry. From earnings of US$19 million in 1988, the shrimp farms brought in about US$88 million in 1996, providing jobs directly and indirectly to 93,000 Hondurans.

Other nontraditional exports such as melon, black pepper, ornamental flowers, ginger, Chinese peas, and sweet onions have been encouraged by the government, but are still a small part of the agricultural export industry.

Cattle and Lumber

In spite of taking up 30% of the country's arable land, much of it suitable for agriculture, the cattle industry plays a small part in the national economy. In large part this is because ranchers rely on traditional cattle-raising methods dependent on rainfall and pasture feed. These methods result in unreliable, low yields. A few, powerful landowners control most of the ranching.

Considering the great wealth of forests in Honduras, judicious logging holds potential for providing jobs and good income. However, much of the country's forest wealth has been wasted through over-logging, corruption, and mismanagement. Nearly seven million hectares of land were forested in 1964; by 1988 that figure had dropped to only five million. Currently the

ECONOMIC FIGURES

	1990	1991	1992	1993	1994	1995	1996
GDP (% change)	.13.	3	5.6	-3.7	-1.4	3.6	3.5
Exports							
(in millions of US$)	831	792	802	814	1,064	1,092	1,234*
Inflation (%)	23.3	34	8.8	10.7	23.1	29.5	24*
Foreign Debt							
(in millions of US$)	3,773	3,452	3,539	3,904	4,152	4,372	4,300
Deficit (% of GDP)	5.3	.7	2.7	10.6	11	3.6	3.5

*estimates based on first semester figures

forests are disappearing at an estimated rate of 3.6% each year.

The problems of erosion and desertification that go along with logging have hit most of the country, but are particularly severe in the south. In search of valuable mahogany and other hardwoods, pirate loggers have even been cutting dirt roads into the periphery of the Río Plátano Biosphere Reserve.

INDUSTRY AND TRADE

Maquiladoras

Leading the recent boom in foreign investment is the *maquiladora* industry of San Pedro Sula and the north coast. In the early 1990s the government passed legislation allowing foreign export companies to import materials and export finished goods free of tariffs in five specific zones: Puerto Cortés, Choloma, La Ceiba, Omoa, and Amapala.

Taking advantage of these favorable laws, as well as inexpensive labor and a strategic location close to the United States, some 160 factories have since opened, mainly clothing producers. Almost all the factories are in Puerto Cortés and Choloma, with a few in La Ceiba. Expected to generate US$1 billion in exports in 1996 (actual figures were unavailable in late 1997), the *maquilas* directly employ 60,000 Hondurans.

The broader benefits of *maquilas* to Honduras have been widely debated. Although providing much-needed jobs, the jobs are invariably low-skilled and low wage. The *maquilas* do nothing to increase the country's tax base, as they pay no tariffs except for some infrastructure improvements. Also, the factories generally operate on a short-term basis; as soon as better conditions arise elsewhere or Honduran wages increase significantly, they can be expected to relocate.

Trade

The U.S. continues to play a pivotal role in Honduras's foreign trade, providing 43% of the country's imports while buying more than half of its exports. U.S. companies are involved in 73% of all direct foreign investments in Honduras.

Efforts to promote trade among other Central American nations have been generally unsuccessful, in spite of the advancement of the Central American Common Market initiative, which created free trade zone—a nice idea but not particularly useful in practice, as the countries don't engage in much trade with each other.

The Lempira

Honduras's national currency, the lempira, had been dropping steadily in value over the past several years, due to the country's bleak economic outlook. The inflation put a severe strain on Hondurans, and those who could afford it took to buying dollars as a safeguard. But thanks to a recent upsurge in coffee prices and a boom in production, the lempira has stabilized; it actually rose in value against the dollar in early 1997. At last report, the lempira was trading at roughly 12.9 to the dollar.

SOCIETY

THE PEOPLE

Population and Statistics

Honduras has a rapidly expanding population approaching seven million. The annual growth rate averages three percent, and 56% of the population is under 18 years old. Despite this growth, Honduras still has a relatively low population density, averaging around 50 people per square kilometer and as low as two per square kilometer in the wild Mosquitia region.

Although 58% of the population still lives in rural areas, the country is experiencing the fastest urbanization rates in Central America. Most of the urbanization is centered on Tegucigalpa, the north coast cities, and San Pedro Sula, the fastest-growing city in Latin America.

The annual life expectancy in 1993 (latest year for which figures are available) was rated as 67.9, while the mortality rate for babies hovers around 42 per 1,000. The literacy rate is 71%.

Ethnic Diversity

Travelers coming south from Guatemala to Honduras may be surprised at the overwhelming nonindigenous nature of the population. Some 86% of Hondurans are mestizos, also called

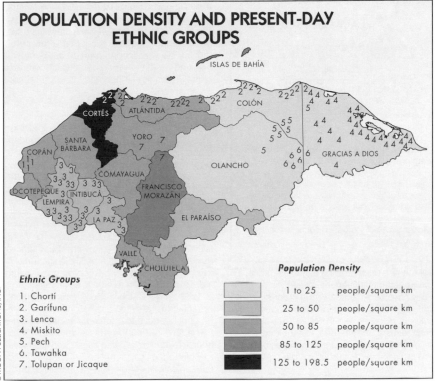

POPULATION DENSITY AND PRESENT-DAY ETHNIC GROUPS

ISLAS DE BAHÍA

CORTÉS
ATLÁNTIDA
COLÓN
SANTA BÁRBARA
YORO
COPÁN
COMAYAGUA
OLANCHO
GRACIAS A DIOS
OCOTEPEQUE
INTIBUCÁ
LEMPIRA
FRANCISCO MORAZÁN
LA PAZ
EL PARAÍSO
VALLE
CHOLUTECA

Ethnic Groups

1. Chortí
2. Garífuna
3. Lenca
4. Miskito
5. Pech
6. Tawahka
7. Tolupan or Jicaque

Population Density

1 to 25	people/square km
25 to 50	people/square km
50 to 85	people/square km
85 to 125	people/square km
125 to 198.5	people/square km

© MOON PUBLICATIONS, INC.

latinos, (persons of mixed European and Central American Indian ancestry). Only 10% are pure blooded Amerindian, while two percent are black and two percent are white.

Because it was only partially controlled by the Spanish, the north coast has a culture markedly different than that of the country's interior. English and North American influences have left their mark on the coast; English is spoken as often as Spanish and the culture is more closely related to the Caribbean islands than the rest of Honduras.

The Bay Islands were settled first by pirates, then, in the early 19th century, by migrants from the Cayman Islands. Today the islands are inhabited by a unique pocket of English-speaking Anglo-Saxons. Due to their history and culture, the islanders have long disdained Honduran authority, preferring to consider the Bay Islands a separate mini-country. Another bastion

of English colonists and pirates for much of the colonial era, La Mosquitia has only recently been brought under effective control by the Honduran government. The region is isolated from the rest of the country by swamps and rainforests, and its residents, like the Bay Islanders, have maintained a sense of separateness.

Amerindian Groups

The extreme decline of the indigenous population in Honduras as compared to Guatemala is not fully understood. For the best analysis on the subject, read Linda Newson's *The Cost of Conquest: Indian Decline Under Spanish Rule in Honduras* (see Booklist).

Small indigenous communities still exist. The Lenca and Chortí Maya can be found in western Honduras, the Tolupan in central Honduras, and the Pech and Tawahka in the northeast. But traditions and language are rapidly being

PEACE CORPS

Hundreds of U.S. Peace Corps volunteers perform their two-year tour of duty in Honduras, one of the highest numbers of any country in the world. Peace Corps participation in the country was boosted during the mid-1980s, as part of a good-relations program connected to the importance of Honduras in U.S. regional policy. Although numbers have been scaled back recently, volunteers still work in most parts of the country, but particularly in western, central, and southern Honduras, as well as La Mosquitia. Volunteers mainly concentrate on agriculture, public health, and the development of tourism potential, with an emphasis on the newly created national park system. The volunteers are usually eager to talk about their sites, and are often excellent sources of information on a particular region.

lost in the face of growing Latino influence. To counteract this influence, indigenous communities have begun organizing in order to defend the destruction of their culture. Although government response to the pressure has been underwhelming, the mere fact of their collective action has encouraged a new consciousness and pride in their Amerindian roots.

Garífuna and Miskitos

Honduras is home to two unique ethnic groups that were created from the mixing of African and indigenous peoples during the colonial era: the Garífuna of the north coast and the Miskitos of the northeast. Rather than fade in the face of modernization, the Garífuna and Miskitos have appeared to grow stronger. For more on these two groups, see the special topics "The Voyage of the Garífuna" and "The Birth of a Race."

RELIGION

Although Honduras is a secular state with guaranteed freedom of religion, it is an overwhelmingly Roman Catholic country. Yet Protestant churches have been on the rise in recent years. Traditional Amerindian religious practices have been all but forgotten, except for a few ceremonies still practiced in rural areas. Superstition and a belief in magic and witchcraft are common among Hondurans in both rural and urban areas.

The Catholic Church

The Catholic church in Honduras has traditionally been one of the poorest and most understaffed in Central America. Approximately 300 ordained priests minister to a population of nearly seven million, and most of the priests are from other countries. In the face of this difficulty, the church began a program called "Delegates of the Word," in which men and women of the laity are trained to be spiritual leaders of a given parish. Now some 10,000 Delegates of the Word live in Honduras, and the movement has spread through much of Central America. A small Jesuit mission continues in the central province of Yoro, run mainly by foreign missionaries.

Unlike other Catholic churches in the region, notably in El Salvador, the Honduran church has not been a major force for social activism. For a time during the 1960s and early '70s, church leadership allowed priests and delegates to pursue the "social option for the poor" and take an activist stance. But the massacre of 10 campesinos, two students, and two priests in Olancho in 1975 at the hands of wealthy landowners put a fast end to the campaign. Since the mid-1980s the church has once again

ETHNIC GROUPS

NAME	ESTIMATED POPULATION	LOCATION
Lenca	100,000	Intibucá, Lempira, La Paz
Garífuna	98,000	Villages and towns on Caribbean Coast
Miskito	29,000	Gracias a Dios
Chortí Maya	4,200	Copán
Pech	2,586	Olancho, Gracias a Dios, and Colón
Tolupan	2,000	Yoro and Francisco Morazán
Tawahka	704	Río Patuca in Gracias a Dios and Olancho

THE VOYAGE OF THE GARÍFUNA

The Garífuna people, who populate the Caribbean coast from Belize to as far south and east as La Mosquitia, are the product of an amazing ethnic and historical odyssey. Most of the 50-odd Garífuna villages are in Honduras, where the group first arrived to Central America in 1797. With their own language, customs, dances, and music, the Garífuna have maintained a distinctive lifestyle in the midst of the Honduran coast society. Colonial-era English and Spanish called the Garífuna "Black Caribs," an accurate description of the two ethnic strains that combined to create a new race.

For the first two centuries following Columbus, the Caribbean island of St. Vincent, in the Lesser Antilles, was left to the Island Carib Indians, who originated from the coast of South America, where Carib speakers still live today. During this time, the island became something of a refuge for black slaves, who were either shipwrecked in the area or escaped from plantations on nearby islands.

Details on the early encounters between the slaves and the Island Caribs are nonexistent, but it must have been a fascinating experience—two completely different cultures, one from Africa and the other from the rainforests of South America, meeting by chance on an island in the middle of the Caribbean. Not only did they get along, but they mixed their blood and their cultures, borrowing from each to develop a new language and new customs. One of many examples of the mixed culture is the *yancunu* Garífuna New Year's dance; it's very sim-

ilar to dances of rainforest Indians in South America, while the music is clearly of West African origin. Possibly in an effort to distance themselves from their past as slaves, the Black Caribs on St. Vincent, and later the Garífuna in Central America, fiercely denied their African blood. In spite of their obviously African physiognomy, both groups insisted they were American Indians.

By the beginning of the 18th century, French settlers from Martinique had begun setting up small-scale plantations of cotton, cacao, and indigo on St. Vincent. They seem to have gotten along peacefully with the Caribs, both Black and "Yellow," as the pure-blooded Indians were called. The French were soon followed by the English, who abortively attempted to colonize the island in 1713. St. Vincent was officially recognized by both countries as neutral territory until 1763, when it was ceded to England in the Treaty of Paris. The British, intent on establishing large-scale sugar plantations, tried to cajole the Garífuna off their valuable island, with little success. When war broke out again between France and England in 1779, the Garífuna and French took the opportunity to seize control of St. Vincent.

The island was formally returned to the English in 1783, at which point the new settlers began pressuring the Garífuna to get off their land. Tensions finally broke out into open war in 1795, pitting the Garífuna and French against English troops. The Garífuna gained a reputation for uncommon feroc-

Garífuna boys

(continues on next page)

THE VOYAGE OF THE GARÍFUNA
(continued)

ity and bravery during the war, which lasted two full years. The Garífuna were led by chief Chatoyer, or Satuyé, who remains a legendary figure among modern Garífuna. The British were finally able to overcome resistance by bringing in massive numbers of troops from Jamaica.

Not underestimating the tenacity of the Garífuna, the British decided to deport them en masse. Among the several sites considered were Africa, the Bahamas, or the island of Hispaniola. Eventually the British decided on Roatán, in the Bay Islands off Honduras, assuming the warlike Garífuna would become a headache for the Spanish.

On 3 March 1797 some 3,000 Garífuna were loaded onto a convoy of 10 boats; the fleet departed St. Vincent, stopping briefly in Jamaica before landing near Port Royal, Roatán on 12 April. For reasons still unclear, the Garífuna did not like the looks of Roatán, which had literally been given to them by the British. A small group crossed to the north side of the island and started the village of Punta Gorda, the oldest continually inhabited Garífuna town, but most continued to the mainland to Trujillo, probably with the help of the Spanish.

The first communities set up by the Garífuna on the mainland of Central America were at Río Negro and Cristales, on either side of Trujillo. The old port had recently been reconquered by the Spanish after 150 years of abandonment, and the Garífuna were welcomed as workers and warriors. Over the next century, groups of Garífuna made their way up and down the Honduran coast, building villages as far north as Belize and as far east and south as the Nicaraguan Mosquito Coast. The Garífuna carved a niche for themselves on the north coast as boatmen, loggers, and mercenary soldiers. They fought defending coastal towns from pirates, and also in the wars of independence.

Although they gave up soldiering long ago and are no longer the first-class canoers of times past, the Garífuna have firmly established themselves as an integral part of the Honduran Caribbean coast. In keeping with their history, the Garífuna are known for their constant travel, either with fishing fleets, the merchant marine, or to Garífuna communities in New York and Los Angeles. Somehow, in spite of this constant movement, the Garífuna have retained a strong sense of ethnic identity. Unlike other minority groups in Honduras, they show no signs of losing their culture. The Garífuna have a built-in resilience immediately apparent on the proud, strong faces and direct gazes that greet visitors to any Garífuna community.

begun to speak up on social issues, but is not considered activist.

Protestants

Protestant churches began to appear in Honduras as early as the turn of the century, particularly in La Mosquitia, on the north coast, and on the Bay Islands. Since the 1980s, evangelical groups, many sponsored by North Americans, have been growing rapidly. Denominations include the more traditional evangelical Baptist and Adventist churches, and Pentacostal churches such as the Assembly of God and the Church of God. An estimated 100,000 people in Honduras belong to Protestant churches.

LANGUAGE

Anyone visiting Honduras after Mexico or Guatemala will be immediately struck by the faster, softer cadences of Honduran Spanish, more similar to the Spanish spoken in Nicaragua and the Caribbean. Words are not as strongly enunciated and are often cut off at the end, with one word running into another. It takes a little getting used to, and you may find yourself saying *"más despacio, por favor"* (slower, please) or *"repita, por favor"* (repeat, please).

Generally, Honduran Spanish is similar to that spoken elsewhere in Latin America, with a few exceptions, particularly the use of *vos* instead of *tú*. Because of British and North American influence, broadly accented Caribbean English is the dominant language on the Bay Islands, although Spanish is increasing with the influx of Latinos from the mainland. English is also spoken along the north coast and in parts of La Mosquitia.

Garífunas and Miskitos mainly use their own languages among themselves, but almost all are bilingual or trilingual, speaking Spanish and/or English as well. Indigenous languages are fading, but some communities still speak Pech, Tolupan, Maya, and Tawahka. Lenca has fallen out of use entirely.

Language Study

After the raging success of language schools in neighboring Guatemala, it's no surprise several Hondurans have set up schools of their own. Language schools can be found in Copán Ruinas, Trujillo, and Tegucigalpa. Generally the schools rate as fairly good to excellent, depending on the teacher. Prices are US$135-150 per week, including five days of one-on-one classes and room and board with a local family. A new school has reportedly been set up in La Ceiba, but its quality has yet to be determined.

VOS

In Honduras as well as several other Central and South American countries, the pronoun "tú" is not frequently heard, and sounds to locals like a sophisticated affectation. More commonly used, and rarely taught to Westerners in their Spanish classes, is "vos."

Essentially vos is used in the same instances as tú, that is, between two people who have a certain degree of familiarity or friendliness, in place of the more formal "usted." The vos form may have originally derived from "vosotros," the second person plural (you all) still used in Spain. However, vosotros is rarely used in Latin America, even in places where vos is common.

For all tenses other than the present indicative, present subjunctive, and command forms, the vos form of the verb is exactly the same as tú. Hence: tú andaste/vos andaste, tú andabas/vos andabas, tú andarás/vos andarás, tú andarías/vos andarías.

In the present indicative, the last syllable is stressed with an accent. The exception is with -ir verbs, in which the final "i" is retained, instead of changing to an "e." Hence: tú andas/vos andás, tú comes/vos comés, tú escribes/vos escribís.

In the present subjunctive, the same construction is followed as with the normal subjunctive, except the vos accent is retained. Hence: tú andes/vos andés, tú comas/vos comás, tú escribas/vos escribás.

However, with normal subjunctive, the tú form includes stem-changes with verbs such as poder, tener, dormir, etc., while the vos form does not include the stem changes. Hence: vos podés, vos tenés, vos dormís.

Vos command forms are derived by simply dropping the final "r" on the infinitive and adding an accent over the last vowel. Hence: vos andá, vos comé, vos escribí. When using object pronouns with vos, "te" is still used. Hence: Yo te lo escribí a vos.

CUSTOMS AND CONDUCT

Typically Latino, Honduran society features customs and traditions similar to those in other countries in the region. Family is of paramount importance, although marriages are often informal due to the expense of weddings and the scarcity of priests. Most Hondurans are Catholic, though not necessarily strict ones.

Perhaps because of the country's history of foreign dominance and seemingly endless poverty, most Hondurans are very fatalistic and not prone to taking initiative. When traveling in Honduras, don't plan on being in a hurry to get anywhere. Things happen at a leisurely pace, and no one rushes. Trying to pressure people to act with haste will get little result other than laying the foundation for an ulcer. Take it easy.

Hondurans are fairly laid-back about clothes in general, but wearing shorts will certainly catch some odd looks in rural villages in the interior. Generally, beachwear should be left to the north coast and the Bay Islands. Public nudity, including swimming naked, is illegal in Honduras.

The litter level in Honduras is disturbingly high. Don't be surprised to see locals toss garbage on the street or out the bus window.

Honduran Women

As in most of Latin America, women are generally not respected by Honduran men, especially in rural society where they are expected to stay indoors and keep quiet when matters of business are being discussed. A budding feminist movement has taken root, but has a long way to go to combat the ingrained machismo. Nonetheless, women are some of the most effective social activists in the country, spearheading initiatives regarding land reform and expansion of public services.

A FEW HONDUREÑISMOS

For a complete Spanish glossary, see the Appendix of this book. Below are a few words and phrases unique to Honduras.

adiós—literally, goodbye, but often used as a casual salutation when passing someone in the street, especially in small towns and villages

catracho—Honduran, used either as a noun or adjective, e.g., *comida catracha* means "Honduran food"

cheque—cool, alright, okay

macanudo—excellent

papa or mama—frequently used to refer to someone you don't know

vaya pués—used after nearly every other sentence, as an all-inclusive "okay" or "understood"

Honduras has a large number of single mothers; it's considered normal for a woman to have one or two children by age 20. Many marriages are informal, and men have few compunctions about leaving their wives for another woman.

Many Honduran women view foreign men with a combination of idealism (the romantic vision of a gringo) and mercenary greed (the possibility of marrying one or getting some of their money). It's relatively common to see an older foreign man escorting around a young Honduran woman; some find this distasteful, others have no problem with it. Mail-order-bride catalogs also commonly list many Honduran women.

For an excellent account of life as a woman in Honduras, read Elvia Alvarado's *Don't Be Afraid, Gringo: A Honduran Woman Speaks From The Heart* (see Booklist).

Women Travelers
Foreign women will likely find themselves the object of a certain amount of unwanted attention while traveling in Honduras. Honduran men tend to view women, to put it crudely, as either virginal mother figures or as sluts. Unfortunately, due in part to representations of women in Western media, most foreigners are viewed as the latter.

One way to cope with the situation is to act conservatively. Tank tops, short skirts, and other skimpy garments do not help in this regard, though certainly on the north coast beach towns and in the Bay Islands these are accepted.

Also, avoid looking men in the eye—this is considered an invitation for the man to introduce himself and try to pick you up. Whether you handle forward men rudely or by trying to ignore them is up to you. Just remember, the more you talk to them, the more encouraged they will be.

campesino family, Montaña de Celaque

BOB RACE

ON THE ROAD

SPORTS AND RECREATION

HIKING AND BACKPACKING

Protected Areas
According to the government, the country's 107 actual or proposed protected areas—national parks *(parques nacionales)*, wildlife refuges *(refugios de vida silvestre)*, biological reserves *(reservas biológicas)*, anthropological reserves *(reservas antropológicas)*, and the one biosphere reserve *(reserva de la biosfera)*,—make up 24% of Honduran territory. Though this may seem an astoundingly large percentage for such a poor, undeveloped country, the reality is that many of the "protected areas" are merely lines on a map in some bureaucrat's office. Faced with a chronic lack of staff and enforcement ability, the government department in charge of most reserves—Corporación Hondureña de Desarrollo Forestal (Cohdefor)—can do little to stop the invasion of land-hungry peasants, cattle herds, and loggers into protected areas. Still, Honduras has more virgin mountain forest and tropical jungle than anywhere else in Central America, and several of the country's parks are truly incredible, not to be missed by the outdoor enthusiast.

The main reserves were established in 1987, and environmental activists have been aggressively pressing politicians to create more. The reserves are composed of a central "core zone" *(zona nucleo)*, meant to be untouchable, and a surrounding "buffer zone" *(zona de amortiguamiento)* where some agriculture and hunting are allowed, depending on the area.

Marked trail systems and camping facilities are rare to nonexistent outside of a few of the most popular parks such as La Tigra, Cusuco, Celaque, and La Muralla. Many of the Peace Corps workers in Honduras—there are hordes of them—are involved with developing certain protected areas as tourist attractions. They have been hard at work drawing up maps, marking trails, building visitor centers, and training guides. The volunteers are often the best sources of information on ways to get into a certain forest and on the flora, fauna, and other sights to look for once there.

Cloud Forests
A sort of high-altitude jungle with towering trees covered with lianas, vines, bromeliads, mosses, and ferns, all wrapped in mist and dripping wet most of the year, the cloud forest is a unique

and magical ecosystem. Although the cloud forests of Costa Rica and Guatemala have had more publicity, Honduras has conserved considerably more virgin cloud forest than either of those countries due to its rugged geography, lack of development, and relatively low population density.

Probably the most visited cloud forest parks in Honduras, because of the ease of access, are La Tigra, just outside of Tegucigalpa, and Cusuco, near San Pedro Sula. Both parks have visitor centers and clearly marked trails, allowing even inexperienced hikers to enjoy the forest and do some birdwatching without fear of getting lost. The forests at La Tigra and Cusuco are not the most pristine, having been logged earli-

er in the century. Nevertheless, patches of virgin forest remain, along with nearly 200 species of birds (including the popular quetzal), a variety of mammals, and countless reptiles and insects.

The two cloud forest parks in the best condition are Montaña de Celaque, near Gracias, and Sierra de Agalta, in Olancho. Sierra de Agalta is Honduras's most extensive cloud forest park and because of its remoteness the forest and its animal inhabitants have been little disturbed by humanity. Unfortunately, the park has virtually no facilities and is not easy to reach. Celaque, though not as large as Sierra de Agalta, has a stunning stretch of primary cloud forest on its high plateau, and can be accessed by casual backpackers along a well-marked trail

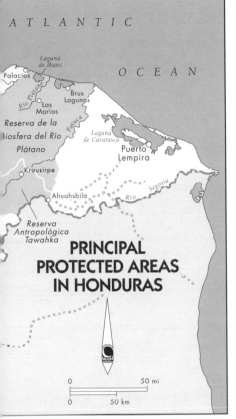

ATLANTIC OCEAN

Laguna de Ibans

Palacios

Brus
Lagunas

Las
Marías

Río Plátano

Patuca

Reserva de la
Biosfera del Río
Plátano

Laguna de Caratasca

Puerto
Lempira

Krausirpe

Ahuahsbila

Río

Segovia

Reserva
Antropológica
Tawahka

**PRINCIPAL
PROTECTED AREAS
IN HONDURAS**

| 0 | | 50 mi |
| 0 | | 50 km |

with two campsites on the way. The highest peak in the country, Cerro de las Minas (2,849 meters) is in Celaque.

La Muralla, in Olancho, is also in relatively good shape. The park is a legendary place for birdwatching; it's an impatient tourist who doesn't catch a glimpse of a quetzal there. Montaña de Santa Bárbara, the second highest peak in the country, looms up above Lago de Yojoa and is also blanketed with pristine cloud forest.

La Mosquitia Reserves

Created in 1980, the **Río Plátano Biosphere Reserve** covers 800,000 hectares of lowland tropical rainforest in the northeast corner of Honduras. This is the legendary jungle of La Mosquitia, the largest remaining broadleaf rainforest in Central America.

The easiest way for visitors to get into the jungle is with one of the guide outfits that leads tours into the reserve. Trips last anywhere from three days to two weeks, and include trips along the Río Plátano in a boat, often combined with short hiking forays into the forest. One company runs rafting and hiking trips from the southern mountains of Olancho down the headwaters of the Río Plátano to the coast, an epic two-week trip.

Freelance trips into the reserve are possible for adventurous travelers who aren't on a tight schedule. The best way to get there is to fly to Palacios from La Ceiba, and contract a boat up the Río Plátano to Las Marías, where guides can be found to take you further upriver or into the jungle. Guides can also be found in Brus Lagunas.

East of the Río Plátano reserve, along a stretch of the Río Patuca populated by Tawahka Indians, the **Reserva Antropológica Tawahka** was recently established. Plans are in the works to connect the Río Plátano and Tawahka reserves to the Bosawas reserve in Nicaragua, preserving a huge stretch of coastal jungle between the two countries.

Other North Coast Reserves

Three reserves on the west half of the north coast protect patches of tropical forest, lagoons and waterways, and the remains of mangrove swamps that once extended almost the entire length of the coast. Outside of Tela are Parque Nacional Punta Sal and Refugio de Vida Silvestre Punta Izopo, the western and eastern arms forming Tela Bay. Between Tela and La Ceiba lies Refugio de Vida Silvestre Cuero y Salado, on land formerly owned by Standard Fruit Company.

Just behind La Ceiba is Parque Nacional Pico Bonito, the largest park in the country after the Río Plátano reserve. Towering Pico Bonito is blanketed with some of the densest tropical jungle in the country. Almost no trails exist in the park, making it serious adventure territory. The jagged terrain and thick jungle hide a wealth of wildlife rarely seen by tourists. A similar but much smaller coastal mountain reserve is Capiro y Calentura behind Trujillo.

PRINCIPAL PROTECTED AREAS

NAME	DEPARTMENT(S)	SIZE (SQUARE KM)	ECOSYSTEM
NATIONAL PARKS (PARQUE NACIONAL):			
Azul Meámbar	Cortés and Comayagua	478	cloud and pine forest
Capiro-Calentura	Colón	49	tropical humid forest
Celaque	Lempira, Ocotepeque, Copán	247	cloud and pine forest
Cerro Azul	Copán	247	cloud and pine forest
Cusuco	Cortés	222	cloud and pine forest
La Tigra	Francisco Morazán	186	cloud and pine forest
La Muralla	Olancho	275	cloud and subtropical forest
Montaña de Comayagua	Comayagua	157	cloud and pine forest
Montaña de Yoro	Yoro and Francisco Morazán	125	cloud and pine forest
Montecristo-Triunfo	Ocotepeque	84	cloud and pine forest
Pico Bonito	Atlántida and Yoro	1,073	tropical and cloud forest
Pico Pijol	Yoro	252	cloud and pine forest
Punta Sal	Atlántida	782	tropical forest, mangrove, lagoons
Santa Bárbara	Santa Bárbara	190	cloud and pine forest
Sierra de Agalta	Olancho	655	cloud and pine forest
WILDLIFE REFUGES (REFUGIO DE VIDA SILVESTRE):			
Bahía de Chismayo	Valle		mangrove
Cuero y Salado	Atlántida	132	mangrove, lagoons
Laguna de Guaymoreto	Colón	50	mangrove, lagoon
Punta Izopo	Atlántida	112	mangrove, lagoons, tropical forest
BIOLOGICAL RESERVES (RESERVA BIOLÓGICA):			
Guajiquiro	La Paz	67	cloud forest
Güisayote	Ocotepeque	128	cloud forest
Lancetilla	Atlántida	41	botanical garden, tropical forest
Yuscarán	El Paraíso	22.4	pine and cloud forest
ANTHROPOLOGICAL RESERVE (RESERVA ANTROPOLÓGICA):			
Tawahka	Olancho, Gracias a Dios		tropical rainforest
BIOSPHERE RESERVE (RESERVA DE LA BIOSFERA):			
Río Plátano	Olancho, Gracias a Dios	5,251	tropical rainforest, savanna

Maps

Topographical maps of scale 1:50,000 covering the entire country are published by the **Instituto Geográfico Nacional.** Generally completely accurate for terrain, the maps are useless when it comes to trails.

The maps cost US$2 each and can be purchased at the Instituto's central office in Comayagüela at the Secretaría de Transporte (SECOPT) on 15 Calle, one block east of 1 Avenida, tel. 25-0752. Some sheets are out of print, but the office staff will usually make a photocopy for you. The office is open Mon.-Fri. 8 a.m.-4 p.m. If your Spanish is up to it, you can write or call for the maps; the staff will send you copies of the sheets you need (have the names handy) if you send them advanced payment for the cost of the maps and shipping.

In the U.S., **Map Link,** 30 S. Patera Ln., Unit 5, Santa Barbara, CA 93117, tel. (805) 692-6777, fax (800) 627-7768, www.maplink.com, sometimes also has the 1:50,000 maps in stock.

Equipment

Generally no special equipment is needed for camping in the cloud forest reserves. Just keep in mind it rains more in cloud forests than in the surrounding lowlands, so come prepared with rain gear, heavy boots, and a change of warm clothes kept in a waterproof bag. Tents are more practical than hammocks for sleeping because of the frequent rain.

Snakebite kits are a good idea, particularly in the coastal, tropical forests. Poisonous snakes are not common in cloud forests. Mosquitoes are common everywhere in Honduras, so come prepared with DEET or another repellent of preference.

Plenty of canned food, pasta, and dried soups are available in local *pulperías,* but carry a few freeze-dried meals if you're planning a long trip away from civilization. Running water in the upper reaches of cloud forests is often drinkable, as long as you're definitely well above any settlements or cattle-grazing areas, but it doesn't hurt to bring a filter or purification tablets. A couple of drops of bleach in each quart of water also works as a purifier.

Exploring La Mosquitia requires special gear suited to the jungle—for more details see the La Mosquitia and Olancho chapter.

HUNTING

Hunting for game in Honduras is more a practice of survival for local campesinos than a sport, but foreigners are permitted to hunt in certain areas. National parks are off limits. The Pacific plains around Choluteca are legendary hunting grounds for white-winged dove, but dwindling populations of the birds have led to restrictions. Hunting is now allowed only for migrant doves and only in certain areas. Deer, quail, wild turkey, and boar are common game in other parts of the country, particularly the Olancho and El Paraíso departments. Hunting season normally runs from the end of November to 15 March.

For more information on hunting seasons, locations, and permits, check with the central Cohdefor office in Tegucigalpa, tel. 23-7703 or 23-8417, or with the Institute of Tourism, tel. 38-3975 or, in the U.S., (800) 410-9680.

Getting permits yourself can be a bit of a nightmare. Most would-be hunters enter the country with an outfitter, who takes care of all the red tape. One frequently used company is Trek International Safaris, P.O. Box 19065, Jacksonville, FL 32245, tel. (800) 654-9915 or (904) 296-3236.

FISHING

Most of the good fishing in Honduras is deep-sea fishing, off either the Bay Islands or the coast of La Mosquitia. Frequent catches include snook, tarpon, kingfish, mackerel, wahoo, blackfin tuna, red snapper, barracuda, and the occasional shark.

On the Bay Islands, fishing charters are easy to obtain and make an excellent change of pace from the islands' main pastime of scuba diving. Flats fishing trips can also be arranged.

The hard-core fisher may want to consider a weeklong trip to La Mosquitia. Guides will take you either out on the open ocean or up mazes of lagoons, rivers, and waterways on the coast. **Trek International Safaris,** P.O. Box 19065, Jacksonville, FL 32245, tel. (800) 654-9915 or (904) 296-3236, runs a lodge in Palacios, while **Pan Angling** in Chicago, Illinois, tel. (312) 263-0328, or in La Ceiba, tel. (504) 43-2487, arranges trips to Cannon Island near Brus Lagunas.

The best inland fishing is at Lago de Yojoa, Honduras's largest natural lake. Largemouth bass were introduced to the lake years ago and a sizable population took hold. Then the lake became a major fishing destination and overfishing depleted stocks. Because of stricter regulations, the population is reportedly on the rebound. Trips on the lake can be arranged with Honduyate, tel. 39-2684 or 57-0774, fax 39-2324; with Motel Agua Azul on the lake shore, tel. 52-7125; or by talking to fishermen at the docks near Peña Blanca.

SCUBA DIVING AND SNORKELING

Probably the most popular form of recreation with foreign visitors to Honduras, in terms of absolute numbers, is scuba diving and snorkeling on the Bay Island reef system. The diving around the three main islands and countless cays is unquestionably world class, rated by some as the finest in the western hemisphere.

Another advantage to diving the Bay Islands is the extremely low cost of certification courses and dive packages. Utila in particular has become a mecca for budget travelers looking for inexpensive explorations of the underwater world. Although divers in Mexico and Belize may hint the low prices are due to inexperienced dive instructors and shoddy gear, the truth is competition among Bay Islands dive shops keeps their standards at a top level, easily as good if not better than elsewhere in the Americas.

BOB RACE

BEACHES

Although it has two coastlines, Honduras's prime beaches are all on the north, Caribbean coast. Truly superb stretches of powdery sand lined by coconut palms can be found all along the coast, from Guatemala to La Mosquitia.

The best "urban" beaches, where tourists can stay at quality hotels, are at Tela and Trujillo. Both have resort hotels and clean beaches right in town. The main beach in Trujillo, in particular, is excellent. La Ceiba and Puerto Cortés have city beaches, but they're dirty and not particularly attractive.

Visitors willing to take day-trips or to rough it a bit in less-than-ideal accommodations will find the country's best beaches at villages between these four main towns. Many Garífuna villages are situated along idyllic beaches, including (from west to east) Bajamar, Miami, Tornabé, Triunfo de la Cruz, Sambo Creek, Río Esteban, Santa Fe, and Santa Rosa de Aguán. Basic hotel rooms are available in all these villages, and it's also usually possible to sling a hammock.

Much of La Mosquitia is lined with miles of wide open, deserted beach, though facilities are minimal. The Bay Islands also boast lovely stretches of beach. Guanaja in particular has great beaches on the north side, with little development so far. One drawback to Bay Island beaches is the omnipresence of sand flies, or *jejenes,* which can make sunbathing an itchy experience.

SPORTS

Fútbol

More of a national religion than merely a sport, *fútbol,* known to North Americans as soccer, is played just about everywhere in the country. Players range from shoeless young men whacking a half-deflated playground ball around a dirt lot to first-division professional teams and the beloved *bi-color,* the white-and-blue clad national team.

Honduras's league, composed of 10 teams, is far from the finest in Central America, but neither players nor fans are lacking in passion. Going to a match is an inexpensive way to catch a glimpse of the fiery spirit lurking inside otherwise tranquil Hondurans. The league has two mini-seasons, from February to June and from August to October, with a championship determined through playoffs. The best teams perennially are Olympia and Motagua, from Tegucigalpa, and España, from San Pedro Sula.

And when discussing the national team, watch out. Don't even think about making jokes concerning their ineptitude—this is no laughing matter. When the team lost to Jamaica in a 1996 World Cup qualifier, held on Independence Day no less, the country was in a tangible funk for days. The next weekend, when the team redeemed national honor by winning a sterling match against hated Mexico 2-1, the euphoria was positively unnerving—strangers hugged each other in the streets, even though the team was already out of World Cup contention.

Béisbol and Basquetbol

Both baseball and basketball are gaining popularity in Honduras. Bay Islanders are particularly fanatical about baseball and can be heard endlessly discussing the latest stats on major-league players in the United States. Surprisingly, a national basketball league was formed recently. So far the quality is a far cry from the NBA.

ARTS AND ENTERTAINMENT

FINE ARTS

Literature

Though Honduras may not be the most prolific country in Latin America's literary world, it has produced two of the most famous early modernist writers in the region: poet and essayist Juan Ramón Molina and historian and journalist Rafael Heliodoro Valle.

Along with Nicaraguan Rubén Darío, Molina (1875-1908) was one of the founders of modernist Latin American poetry and is considered Honduras's national poet. Much of Molina's poetry expresses his existential anguish and a struggle with deep philosophical themes. Although he did not write extensive prose, what he did produce is beautifully lyrical. Shortly after Molina's death from a morphine overdose, his collected works were published in a volume titled, *Tierras, Mares, Y Cielos* (Lands, Seas, and Skies).

One of the most influential Latin American journalists of his era, Rafael Heliodoro Valle (1891-1959) was a prolific writer who published regularly in newspapers across the Americas and wrote extensive histories on the region. In one of his most famous professional coups, Valle in 1945 interviewed reformist Guatemalan president Juan José Arévalo in the Mexican newspaper *Excélsior*. Arévalo candidly discussed the backwardness of his country and the obstacles in the way of development. After Valle's death his most wide-ranging and reflective work, *Historia de las Ideas Contemporáneas en Centro-América* (History of Contemporary Thought in Central America), was published, marking a major landmark in regional historical philosophy.

Modern Honduran literature of note is limited mainly to short stories. Three well-respected authors are Víctor Cáceres Lara, Marcos Carías, and Eduardo Bahr. The latter in particular is known for his politically oriented stories. One exceptional Honduran social novelist is Ramón Amaya Amador, who in 1950 wrote the famed *Prisión Verde* (Green Prison), a story about life as a banana plantation worker.

Visual Arts

Honduras has produced a number of top-quality visual artists, the most famous of which are the so-called "primitivists": Pablo Zelaya Sierra, Carlos Zuñiga Figueroa, and especially José Antonio Velásquez, who painted classic Honduran themes such as tile-roofed villages and rural scenes in a colorful almost childlike style. Velásquez, a self-taught artist, spent much of his time painting the lovely colonial village of San Antonio de Oriente, near Tegucigalpa in the Valle de Zambrano.

More recent artists include Dante Lazzaroni, Arturo López Rodezno, Eziquiel Padilla, Anibel Cruz, and Eduardo "Mito" Galeano. Galeano, who works in the town of Gracias, is known for painting Lenca-oriented themes.

Architecture

Although modern Honduran architecture is unremarkable, a wealth of colonial buildings still stand, particularly in Tegucigalpa, Comayagua, Gracias, and in innumerable other small towns and villages.

Typically, the most visually interesting buildings are the cathedrals and churches. Most are built in a Central American style known as "earthquake baroque," which adapted the dominant styles of Spain to local conditions. Earthquake baroque is known for squat, ground-hugging structures built to resist frequent quakes. Their solidity is relieved by intricate columns, sculptures, and decorations.

Churches built in the 16th and early 17th centuries, most of which have not survived, tended to be much simpler, while those erected in the late colonial period were much more elaborate. One particularly Honduran characteristic in colonial church architecture is the use of folded or pleated patterns on exterior columns.

The interiors of larger churches and cathedrals are invariably decorated with elaborate paintings and sculptures, and are dominated by a carved and often gilded altar piece *(retablo)*. Smaller churches, especially in rural areas, are often painted in a more rustic style, sometimes with mud over plaster.

inside the Catedral de San Miguel, Tegucigalpa

Large, airy wooden houses with porches are common in the north coast banana towns of Puerto Cortés, Tela, and La Ceiba, where North American influences predominated at the turn of the century.

Music

Honduran music consists primarily of Caribbean merengue, salsa, and *cumbia,* with a dash of American pop thrown in. Believe it or not, country music has also achieved some popularity in the discos of the north coast and the Bay Islands.

The only native Honduran music of note is *punta,* the traditional music of the Garífuna. Original *punta* is a stripped-down music form based around a thumping drum accompanied by singing, blowing a conch shell, and dancers performing physics-defying miracles with their hips.

In recent years a modern version of *punta,* called *punta*-rock, has become the rage in Honduras and has gained some recognition abroad. Two of the most popular groups playing *punta*-rock are the Banda Blanca and Garífuna Kids.

The traditional music of the Lenca, Pech, Tolupan, and Maya Indians has, tragically, dwindled in importance over the centuries and is no longer played outside of rare special ceremonies.

CRAFTS

Although not as well known as Guatemala for handicrafts, Honduras does offer several unique *artesanías* for tourists to purchase during their trip. Several villages near Tegucigalpa, especially Valle de Ángeles, are known for their wood carvings and leatherwork, while others like Ojojona are good places to buy simple Lenca-style ceramics.

The region around Santa Bárbara is famed for producing *junco*-palm goods, from simple mats to baskets and hats. When buying *junco,* take a good look at the weave—the tighter the weave, the finer the quality and the higher the price.

On the north coast, you can buy traditional drums of the Garífuna, along with carvings, paintings, and recordings of *punta* music.

ENTERTAINMENT

Discos

It's a sorry town that doesn't have at least one disco where the locals can boogie until the daylight hours on Friday and Saturday. Larger towns and cities invariably have several, often near each other, and many are hopping from Wednesday to Sunday. The north coast towns of Tela and especially La Ceiba are famed for their nightlife, and any visitor with a partying spirit should be sure to go out at least one weekend to check out the scene.

The favored music in discos is salsa, merengue, *punta,* American pop, and the occasional slow country tune. Dancing is generally quite reserved—most couples seem more interested in looking cool rather than really cutting the rug.

Most discos don't get cranking until midnight or later. Fistfights and the occasional knifing are not uncommon, but rarely involve foreigners unless they do something exceptionally stupid like insult someone or try to pick up someone else's date.

Male travelers shouldn't be surprised if they're approached by some surprisingly friendly young women in the discos. Many are prostitutes. Foreign women can expect to get plenty of attention in a disco, even if accompanied by a man. As long as you keep your wits about you and fend off the overzealous men with good humor, all will be well. Going alone is not a great idea.

Pool Halls

Salones de billar, as pool halls are known, are common all over Honduras. They're not always the cleanest of places, and the players are usually a bit rough looking, but if you're desperate to shoot a few racks and tip some beers, it's the place to go.

In the most common game played, simply called "pool," players line up the 15 balls around the side of the table, potting them in numerical order. The shelves on the wall are for each player to keep track of the balls he has sunk. Any number of people can play. Eight-ball is common enough for most pool halls to have a triangle, but is not the game of choice.

Generally it's not recommended women visit pool halls. Even if you're accompanied by a man, expect at the very least to get a lot of looks. Going alone is an invitation to trouble.

ACCOMMODATIONS

Rooms in Honduras range from five-star luxury spreads in Tegucigalpa, San Pedro Sula, and the Bay Islands where you will be waited on hand and foot to a straw pallet in a *campesino's* hut in rural mountain areas. Camping is possible and safe in many rural areas, but designated campsites and RV hookups are nearly nonexistent.

HOTELS AND MOTELS

Rates

Hotel prices are extremely reasonable in Honduras. Budget travelers will have no trouble finding a clean room for US$3-4 per night per person, or less if you're with someone and split the cost of a double room. When getting a double, be sure to specify whether you would like one large bed or two singles. One large bed is less expensive.

Travelers with a bit more money can find well-kept air-conditioned rooms with televisions for anywhere between US$10 and US$30, while luxury resorts charge between US$75 and US$200, depending on location.

Haggling over room price won't get you too far in the lower-end hotels, as prices are fairly rock bottom as it is, but it's worth it to ask if there's anything less expensive *(¿Hay algo más económico?)* from the first price quoted, since owners often assume a foreigner wants the best room. More expensive hotels sometimes charge one rate for foreigners and another for Honduran residents, and it is possible on occasion to negotiate the lower rate, especially if the hotel is not full at the time.

Prices don't vary much throughout the year in most of the country, but during Semana Santa (Holy Week), rooms are more expensive in the north coast beach towns of Trujillo, La Ceiba, Tela, and Puerto Cortés. In La Ceiba prices rise dramatically for the long weekend around the Feria de San Isidro, a famed carnival held each year in mid-May. On the Bay Islands, the high season for tourism is between late December and early April, with a mini-high season in July and August—hotel prices rise during these periods.

A five percent hotel tax is usually, but not always, included in quoted room prices.

Choosing a Room

Although some travelers are loath to do so, checking out a room before taking it is highly recommended. You're paying for it, after all, so take the time to ensure the room is what you want. The location of the room within the hotel is often key—a room facing the street may seem like a good place to watch the bustle of town during the day, but could turn into a noisy nightmare when you're trying to get some sleep.

Especially at less expensive hotels, but at midrange ones also, check the mattress! Nothing worse than having a spring sticking into your back all night long. One time-honored technique if you get stuck with a bad mattress is sleeping on it in reverse; matresses usually give out where the torso falls.

If your room has a bathroom, make sure there is soap and a towel. Also check to see if the water is functioning, and if it's supposed to be hot that it is.

Budget

The vast majority of hotels in Honduras fall into the budget category, charging between US$1 and US$10 per night per person. In cities and large towns, these hotels—called *pensiones, hospedajes,* or simply *hoteles*—are often grouped near each other in the downtown area. In many smaller towns and villages budget rooms are the only choice.

Rooms in budget hotels are invariably extremely basic, often merely cement cubes with a fan, a light bulb dangling from a wire, and a bed of wildly varying quality. Check those mattresses. With heat and mosquitoes common in many parts of Honduras, especially the north coast, a fan can be a key component to a restful night. Overhead fans are preferable as they stir up the air in the entire room and keep the nasty bugs at bay.

Budget hotels frequently offer the choice of *baño privado* (private bathroom) or *sin baño* (without bathroom, that is, shared bathroom). Taking a room *sin baño* is a good way to save a few lempira, but be sure to wear sandals into the communal bathroom to avoid athlete's foot or other fungi.

The better quality budget hotels—usually at least one in every town—send their maids out every day to scour the rooms and place fresh sheets on the beds. Many also have free purified drinking water in the lobby, and provide pitchers for guests to fill up and bring to their rooms.

When hot water is offered, it's invariably in the form of an in-line water heater attached to the shower head, affectionately known among frequent travelers as "suicide showers." These contraptions usually but not always provide a stream of scalding water, but don't get too close to all those dangling wires unless you're looking for an unpleasant zap. The units can be so poorly wired they manage to electrify the entire showerhead. Beware.

Midrange

Formerly limited to cities and major tourist destinations, a growing number of good quality midrange hotels have been springing up in Honduras in recent years, charging between US$10 and US$40 per night. Most large towns have at least one moderately priced spot with air conditioning, TV with cable, clean bathrooms, decent mattresses, and often covered parking.

Hotels in this category range from excellent value for the money to dives who think they can charge extra because they've got an intermittently functioning air conditioner.

Luxury

Full-service, top-class hotels are few and far between in most of Honduras, found only in Tegucigalpa, San Pedro Sula, Copán, the Bay Islands, Tela, La Ceiba, and Trujillo. Quality varies dramatically—some of the newer hotels like the Copantl in San Pedro and several of the resorts on Roatán and Guanaja are very well-managed, while others, like the Christopher Columbus resort in Trujillo, offer service almost laughably poor.

Standard luxury rooms range between US$70 and US$200, or more for suites. The Bay Islands resorts are usually geared toward divers, and offer weekly package rates including three dives daily.

Honduras is a growing destination for wealthier travelers, and many new luxury hotels are planned for construction in the near future, especially on the north coast and Bay Islands. The grandiose Tela Bay Project, just getting underway, may completely change the face of that now-sleepy seaside town, and Holiday Inn plans to build five hotels in Honduras in the next five years.

Camping

Campsites and RV hookups have not yet made it to Honduras, so campers had best come prepared for primitive camping. In most areas in rural Honduras this is no problem. Generally speaking the countryside is the safest part of the country, and the worst hassle you can expect is to get pestered repeatedly by local campesinos to come have a cup of coffee and a chat with them.

When looking for a spot to pitch a tent, it's best to check around and see if you're about to set up on someone's farm. If so, ask permission, "¿Está bien acampar aquí?" Offering a few lempira is also polite, or perhaps inviting the owner over to your camp for a bite to eat.

The few campsites in the country can be found in some of the national parks, such as La Tigra, Cusuco, Celaque, Pico Bonito, La Muralla, and others. Camping is regulated in Cusuco and La Tigra, but fairly laid-back in the other parks. If in doubt, stop in at the local Cohdefor office and ask.

No special gear is needed for camping in Honduras, just come prepared for the conditions. Rain and cold weather are common in the mountains. For information on jungle hiking and camping, see the La Mosquitia and Olancho chapter.

"Dar Posada"

In many villages, especially in the central and western mountains and in some parts of La Mosquitia, no hotels are available for travelers. No worries: just ask around to find a family willing to put you up for the night. The key phrase is *dar posada,* or "offer lodging." Often one family is known to have an extra room and is in the habit of renting it out to passersby for a few lempira ($US50 cents to US$2).

FOOD

Honduras isn't known for its culinary specialties, but the discerning traveler will find plenty of ways to fill the belly and satisfy the taste buds at the same time. From the infinite variations of *plato típico,* the national dish, to the seafood of the north coast and the omnipresent and addictive *baleadas,* Honduran cooks do surprisingly well with limited resources.

When done eating, ask for *la cuenta* ("the bill"), or if the restaurant is a small eatery or food stand, ask *¿Cuánto es?* or *¿Cuánto debo?* ("How much do I owe?"). Tips are not common in most simple eateries, but 10% is expected at any midrange or more expensive restaurant. Some of the better restaurants will add a 10% gratuity to the bill, so check before you leave another tip.

WHERE TO EAT

Those restaurants in Honduras where you can expect table service and a menu are called *restaurantes.* In large towns and cities you'll find high-priced restaurants offering international-style food, or at least creatively prepared Honduran standards. In smaller towns, hotel restaurants are often the best places to get a good meal.

Less pretentious places offering set meals at inexpensive prices are known as *comedores* ("eateries") or, less frequently, *merenderos.* The best way to judge a *comedor* is to check the number of locals eating there. The more, the better. Hamburger joints are very popular in Honduras.

Most town markets have a section inside serving inexpensive and typically good-quality breakfasts and lunches. The quality of street food in Honduras is not as good as in, for example, Mexico. Options are limited to snacks, fruit, and roasted corn.

Ordering and Paying

Most sit-down restaurants will have a menu, called *la carta* or "el menú", but smaller establishments often just serve what they happen to have. To find out the day's pickings, ask *¿Qué hay para comer?* ("what is there to eat?").

WHAT TO EAT

The main meal in any Honduran restaurant is without doubt the *plato típico,* a standard combination of ingredients which can vary dramatically in quality but is always relatively inexpensive.

The centerpiece of the *plato típico* is always a chunk of beef, accompanied by a combination of fried plantain, beans, marinated cabbage, rice, a chunk of salty cheese, and a dollop of sour cream. Possible variations might include saffron rice instead of plain rice, well-prepared beans instead of canned refrieds, or yucca instead of plantain. Tortillas, usually of corn, are served on the side.

A relative of the *plato típico* is the *comida corriente,* also a set meal and usually a bit less expensive than the *plato.* The main course can be fish, chicken, pork, or steak, depending on whatever the cook got a good deal on that day. Fixings are similar to the *plato.*

In a country with a major cattle industry, it's no surprise that beef is a staple of the Honduran diet. Called *bistec* or *carne asada,* the country's grilled beef is not always the finest quality—as with many products the best is reserved for export. Nonetheless, eating beef incurs minimal health risk compared to the second-most popular dish, *chuleta de cerdo,* or pork chops.

AZUCARRÓN PINEAPPLE

Those poor souls who have only tasted the bitter pineapples imported to the United States and Europe are in for a taste sensation after slicing into their first fresh Honduran *azucarrón* pineapple.

The name, which roughly translates as "super-sugary," hints at the mouthwatering pleasures to come. Many foreigners, long convinced they didn't like pineapple at all, have been known to become utterly addicted to the *azucarrón*, buying a fresh one at the market every morning and getting deliciously messy slobbering it down. The *azucarrón's* succulent taste is also the reason it never makes it out of the country. The sugar content is so high the fruit ripens quickly and can't survive the journey to foreign markets without going bad. Fruit companies have long tried to develop varieties with the same taste that won't ripen so fast, but have yet to succeed.

Pollo frito, fried chicken, is also one of the most common dishes in Honduras. It's a rare bus stop or small town that doesn't boast at least one restaurant specializing in fried chicken. One of the more creative and tasty Honduran meat dishes is *pinchos,* a sort of shish kebab typically made with skewered and grilled vegetables and chunks of marinated beef.

A favorite Honduran soup is *tapado,* a vegetable stew often served with beef or sometimes fish. Another, which the squeamish will want to avoid, is *mondongo,* tripe (intestine) stew served in beef broth with cilantro and potatoes or other vegetables.

When on the north coast, the Bay Islands, or near Lago de Yojoa, be sure to take advantage of the often very tasty *pescado frito,* or fried fish. Some of the Garífuna villages on the north coast also whip up a superb grilled red snapper with rice and vegetables. On the Bay Islands locals are fond of skewering a variety of fish and making a stew called *bando* with yucca, other vegetables, and lots of spice.

Langosta (lobster), *camarones* (shrimp), and *caracol* (conch) are all commonly eaten on the north coast, though supply may be limited by the tight restrictions recently adopted to protect the dwindling shellfish population. One superb north coast specialty is *sopa de caracol,* or conch stew, made with coconut milk, potatoes, and sometimes curry. Several restaurants in Tela make mouthwatering *sopa de caracol.*

Main meals are almost always served with a basket of warm tortillas, thin dough pancakes usually made from corn but sometimes from wheat flour. The unaccustomed palate often needs time to adjust to corn tortillas, but once converted the tastebuds will crave the solid, earthy taste. Beans and rice are also frequent accompaniments to a meal.

On the north coast, North American and Garífuna influences have made tortillas less common, and you may find meals accompanied by *pan de coco* (coconut bread), a Garífuna specialty.

Breakfast

The standard Honduran breakfast consists of eggs *(huevos),* tortillas, and a cup of strong, sweet Honduran coffee. Eggs are normally cooked *revueltos* (scrambled) or *estrellados* (fried).

Western innovations like corn flakes and pancakes, frequently served with honey instead of syrup, are on the rise in Honduras but are not common in smaller towns.

Snacks

Travelers searching for the Honduran equivalent of the Mexican taco will be pleased to discover *baleadas,* the snack food of choice. *Baleadas* are flour tortillas filled with beans, crumbly cheese, and a dash of cream, then warmed briefly on a grill. Cheap and filling, *baleadas* make a good light midday meal.

Less frequently seen are *pupusas,* thick tortillas filled with sausage and/or cheese; and *nacatamales,* cornmeal stuffed with pork, olives, or other ingredients, then wrapped in a banana leaf and boiled. North American-style *hamburguesas* are extremely popular, especially on the north coast.

Often sold in street stands are *tajadas,* fried plantain chips served in a small bag with a slice of lime or a dash of salsa. *Tajadas* are also sometimes served in restaurants with a salad of cole slaw and salsa. Sliced fresh fruit such as pineapple and mango is commonly sold in street stands, along with bags of *nance,* a small fruit described by one expatriate journalist in Honduras as "cherry's evil twin."

BUYING GROCERIES

The first word to learn when looking for groceries in most towns and villages in Honduras is *pulpería.* These all-purpose general stores might carry just a few canned goods, drinks, and candy, or might offer a full range of foodstuffs. Almost every population center of any size has a *pulpería*—in fact, if a village has any business establishment at all, it's always a *pulpería.*

Every town of size also has a market *(mercado)* where you can find a wide variety of fruits, vegetables, and meats—vegetarians should brace themselves for the sight of raw flesh covered with flies. Produce is sold in pounds *(libras)* just as often as in kilograms, if not more so; be sure you know the weight before buying. When buying food by the pound, don't just pick up a couple of pieces and ask how much it costs—that's simply an invitation to get ripped off. Check the price per weight and watch it being weighed. It's often worth asking a couple of stalls their prices before buying. Although prices are normally standard, some vendors are not above trying to swindle a few extra lempira out of a naive-looking foreigner.

Western-style supermarkets *(supermercados)* are found only in large towns and cities, and the produce here is often not as good as at the local market.

Tortillas can be bought in bulk at neighborhood *tortillerías,* which make them fresh daily. Good bread is not always easy to come by in Honduras; what there is can be found in *panaderías.* Sweet breads and cookies are more common than sandwich-style loaf breads, as most Hondurans eat tortillas.

DRINKING

Nonalcoholic Drinks
The coffee addict will be pleased to hear that Hondurans brew a mean cup of joe, most often served black with lots of sugar. In contrast to Guatemala, most of the coffee is actually brewed from beans; even in inexpensive *comedores* a fresh cup is more common than Nescafé. If you take milk, be sure to ask for it on the side as it is not normally served.

Blended fruit and milk drinks, called *licuados,* can be found all across the country and make a filling midday snack that could be substituted for lunch. Often they're served with a sprinkle of nutmeg or cinnamon on top, and a healthy dose of sugar. If you don't want either, be sure to advise the proprietor beforehand. Generally the milk is prepackaged and pasteurized, but you may want to check first to be sure.

Fresh fruit juices are also common, and in most establishments are mixed with purified water, but again check first. Two particularly tasty mixes are *jugo de mora* (blackberry juice) and *agua de horchata,* a rice drink with cinnamon. Cartons of good quality orange juice are available all over the country.

Tap water is never safe to drink in Honduras, outside of a few luxury hotels that have their own in-line purifiers. Many hotels buy large bottles of purified water which they keep in the lobby for guests. Agua Azul is a popular brand of purified water sold in containers of various sizes. Be environmentally aware: don't repeatedly buy small plastic bottles and throw them away. Better to buy a gallon or liter jug and fill it up at your hotel. This saves you money and saves Honduras a lot of plastic garbage, which it has plenty of already.

Alcohol
All five brands of beers *(cervezas)* brewed in Honduras are made by the same company, Cervecería Nacional. Of the five, Nacional is the most universally consumed. It's thin and fairly tasteless, though not bad when the weather is hot and the beer is cold. Polar, mainly sold in cans, is similar. Much better are Port Royal, a lager sold in a green bottle with a colorful label, and the heavier Salvavida ("Lifesaver"), sold in a dark brown bottle. Near Tegucigalpa you'll also find Imperial, similar in style to Salvavida.

Several varieties of rum *(ron)* of reasonable quality are distilled in Honduras, but other local spirits such as gin and vodka are nauseatingly bad. The local rot-gut liquor is *aguardiente,* either made in local stills or bought in a bottle. The most popular variety is El Buen Gusto, also called Yuscarán for the town where it's made.

Local wines are not worth mentioning, but several foreign varieties can be found in better supermarkets and liquor stores. Avoid them on the north coast as they don't hold up well stored in the heat.

A word about drinking establishments: waiters in *cantinas* or inexpensive restaurants will often leave the empty beer bottles on the table when you order more. This is not bad service, merely a way to help with accounting at the end of the night.

HEALTH AND SAFETY

As an extremely poor, underdeveloped country, Honduras does not have the best health care for its residents. Nonetheless, the lamentable conditions need not affect travelers who take a few basic precautions.

COMMON AILMENTS

As in just about every country in Latin America, it's essential to watch carefully what you eat and drink. Tap water is absolutely never safe to drink, and be sure to check that any water served at a restaurant or hotel is *agua purificada*. Remember that ice may have been made with tap water. Be particularly aware of salads and uncooked vegetables, and make sure meat, especially pork, is well-cooked. Eating street food is standard practice for many veteran travelers, but someone just arriving in Honduras for a short stay may want to avoid it and save themselves a possible case of **diarrhea.**

If you do develop diarrhea, two courses of action are available: eat as little as possible, drink a lot of water, and let the bug run its course (literally), or take medications such as Pepto-Bismol or Lomatil. Many travelers insist the drugs only prolong the problem, while others swear by them.

Food poisoning is also relatively common. Although it may appear severe at first, with vomiting and uncontrollable bowels, the bug will pass in about a day. Hole up in a hotel room with a good book, a bottle of water, and maybe a few pieces of bread, and expect to feel a bit weak for a couple of days following the illness. If symptoms persist, see a doctor—you may have dysentery. It's extremely important to stay well hydrated if you've got either food poisoning or diarrhea.

DISEASE

Dysentery
Dysentery is a health risk for foreigners traveling in Honduras and other underdeveloped countries. The disease, which results from fecal-oral contamination, comes in two strains: bacillic (bacterial) and amoebic (parasitic). Bacillic dysentery hits like a sledgehammer, with a sudden onset of vomiting, severe diarrhea, and fever. It is easily treated with antibiotics.

Amoebic dysentery, caused by an infestation of amoebas, takes longer to develop and is also more difficult to get rid of. The most effective cure is a weeklong course of Flagyl, a very strong drug which wipes out all intestinal flora. During and after a course of Flagyl, it's important to eat easily digestable food until the body has a chance to re-build the necessary bacterias used for digestion. Yogurt is helpful.

Symptoms for either form of dysentery are not unlike those for malaria or dengue fever, so see a doctor and don't try to diagnose yourself. One of the greatest dangers with dysentery is dehydration, so be sure to drink plenty of water if you even suspect dysentery.

Malaria
The *vixa vivax* strain of malaria is present in most lowland regions of Honduras, and is common on the north and south coasts, the coastal regions of La Mosquitia, and on the Bay Islands. If you're below 1,000 meters, malaria can be present. Thankfully, the Aralen-resistant *P. falciparum* strain has not yet made it north of Colombia.

Symptoms of malaria include high fever, headaches, fatigue, and chills. If these symptoms are present, see a doctor immediately as medical treatment is effective.

Opinions on how to cope with malaria vary wildly. The most frequent recommendation from doctors is to take 500 mg of Aralen (chloroquine phosphate) weekly. Some people react negatively to Aralen, and experience nausea, rashes, fever, or nightmares. Stop taking the drug if you have these side effects.

In high doses, well above 500 mg per week, Aralen has been linked to retina damage and hearing problems. It's not recommended to take the drug longer than six months. If you're on Aralen, continue the course for four weeks after leaving malaria-prone areas. Some travelers, leery of using strong drugs on a regular basis, prefer to carry one high-milligram dose of Aralen with them to use in case malaria strikes, rather than enough for weekly doses. Those who opt for this method should be very careful to avoid mosquito bites by applying repellent, wearing long-sleeved clothes, and using mosquito nets.

Other malaria preventatives include a daily dose of low-level antibiotics such as tetracycline or doxycycline. Antimalarial drugs are available in Honduras.

Other Diseases

Unfortunately, cholera is not uncommon in Honduras, particularly during the rainy season. The best way to avoid it is to be careful with your food and water, don't eat raw fish, and always wash your hands before eating.

The viral disease dengue fever is also a frequent health problem for Hondurans. There is no cure, but it is rarely fatal. The fever is contracted from the bite of an infected mosquito. Symptoms include fever, headache (especially behind the eyes), muscle and joint aches, skin rash, and swollen lymph glands. Usually the fever lasts 5-8 days, followed by about a week of the disease. Tylenol (not aspirin) will help cut the fever and relieve headaches.

A few unconfirmed cases of hemorrhagic dengue, which is fatal, have been reported. Symptoms appear similar to classic dengue at first, which makes it essential to seek medical attention immediately for any of the above symptoms. Hemorrhagic dengue is fully treatable if medical help is found within the first few days of the illness.

AIDS

Although exact numbers are difficult to obtain, it's generally agreed that Honduras has one of the highest AIDS-infection rates in the Americas. San Pedro Sula, in particular, has been hard hit by the disease. The problem persists in part because of the lack of education about health risks and prevention and also as a result of the easygoing Honduran attitude toward sex.

Many HIV-positive prostitutes continue working, either through ignorance or the need for money. Should you choose to sleep with a stranger or newfound friend anywhere in the country, *use a condom!*

Information

For more information on the health situation in Honduras, check the Centers For Disease Control and Prevention (CDC) Health Information for International Travel, tel. (404) 332-4565, or the International Association for Medical Assistance to Travelers, 736 Center St., Lewiston, NY 14092, tel. (716) 754-4883.

PHARMACIES

Most basic pharmaceutical drugs are available in Honduras, many without a prescription. Almost all are generic versions manufactured in Mexico and Guatemala. Nevertheless, it's always best to bring an adequate supply of any prescription medication you require, including blood pressure medicine, insulin, epilepsy drugs, and asthma medication. Keep in mind allergies may be triggered by unfamiliar allergens encountered in a new environment.

Pharmacies in Honduras normally operate on the *turno* system, in which one local shop stays open all night for emergencies on a rotating basis. Often the *turno* pharmacy of the night is posted on a sign in the downtown square. If not, ask at your hotel.

VACCINES

No vaccines are required to enter Honduras, but travelers should be up to date on their rabies, typhoid, measles-mumps-rubella, tetanus, and yellow fever shots. A new Hepatitis vaccine is now on the market, taking the place of the questionable gamma gobulin shot. For Hepatitis A, two shots of Havrix six months apart is now recommended. For Hepatitis B, the recommendation is three shots of Engerix over the course of six months. Each vaccine is good for three years.

BITES AND STINGS

Mosquitoes and Sand Flies

Mosquitoes are found just about everywhere in Honduras, and can be particularly bothersome during the rainy season. Everyone has a favorite method for dealing with the bloodsuckers. It's hard to beat a thick coat of DEET, but many travelers are loath to put on such a strong chemical day after day, especially on a long trip. According to some, eating lots of raw garlic is effective.

Sand flies, or *jejenes,* can be a plague on the Bay Islands, depending on the season and the wind level. Insect repellent will keep them away, and locals swear by Avon's Skin-So-Soft, which is sold on the islands. The bites are annoying but will usually stop itching quickly if not scratched. As their name suggests, sand flies live on the sand, and can be avoided by swimming, sunning yourself on a dock over the water, or just staying away from the beach. A few spots on the islands are known to be free of the pests. Thankfully sand flies are not a severe problem on mainland beaches.

Chagas' Disease

The chronic Chagas' disease, caused by the parasite *Trypanosoma cruzi,* is transmitted by the bite of certain bloodsucking insects (notably the assassin bug and conenose) found from southern Texas through South America. The disease is estimated to affect 12 million people in the Americas. The bugs prefer to bite while victims are asleep, and usually bite on the victim's face. While taking in blood the bugs often deposit feces, which transmits the disease to the victim's bloodstream. Such bug bites are common in Honduras, but before panicking note that only about two percent of those bitten will develop Chagas' disease. Young children are the most susceptible.

After an initial reaction of swollen glands and fever, one to two weeks after the bite, the disease goes into remission for anywhere from five to 30 years, with no symptoms apparent. It may, in fact, never reappear, but if it does, the disease causes severe heart problems sometimes leading to death. There is no cure for Chagas' disease.

To avoid Chagas', avoid being bitten. The bugs are most prevalent in rural areas, often living amid dead palm fronds or piles of wood. If

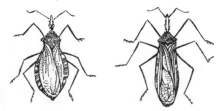

you are sleeping in a thatched-roof hut, try to cover your face with a cloth or put on a bug repellent containing DEET. A spray of pyrethrin insecticide will kill the bugs. If staying in an old hotel, check the room carefully for bugs, including under the mattress.

Chagas' is present in all departments of Honduras except the Bay Islands and Gracias a Dios (La Mosquitia). Infestation is minimal in Atlántida, Colón, and Yoro, while it is a particular problem in Intibucá and parts of Olancho.

Snakes, Bees, and Scorpions

Honduras has its share of scorpions, wasps, bees (including the aggressive Africanized honey bee), and poisonous snakes. Most of the dangerous snakes live in the tropical forests of the Caribbean coast, particularly in the jungles of La Mosquitia, where pit vipers (including the deadly fer-de-lance) and coral snakes are common dangers.

The fer-de-lance is considered one of the most venomous snakes in the world. Bites are fatal unless the victim receives medical help within a few hours after being bitten. The fer-de-lance is easy to spot by the bright patch of yellow under its throat; a marking that earned it the nickname *barba amarilla* (yellow beard).

When hiking in the jungle, wear boots and long pants. Watch where you put your feet, and if possible let a guide precede you. Be particularly careful around piles of dead wood or stones, which offer shade to snakes during the day. Jungle lore holds that fer-de-lance are most frequently found near water holes and light gaps created by fallen trees.

Poisonous snakes are not common in higher altitude pine and cloud forests.

SAFETY

Crime

Street crime is a growing problem in Honduras, although it is still nothing on the level of most U.S. cities. San Pedro Sula is without question the country's most dangerous city, followed by Tegucigalpa and the north coast cities of Puerto Cortés and La Ceiba.

The crime wave has shocked the normally peaceable Hondurans, and to combat it the Armed Forces have begun emergency programs to patrol the streets in San Pedro and Tegucigalpa.

For the most part, the rest of the country is remarkably safe, considering the high poverty. In rural areas foreigners can generally wander around at will with little fear.

Drugs

Though not a drug-producing country itself, apart from some small-scale marijuana growing, Honduras is becoming a favored conduit for South American cocaine on its way north to the United States. The deserted, unpatrolled expanse of the La Mosquitia coast is a choice drop-off point for Colombian drug smugglers. From Mosquitia the cocaine is transported overland through Guatemala and Mexico to the United States. Marijuana cultivation and use is illegal in Honduras.

Police

Since its inception, Honduras's police force, known as Fusep (Fuerzas de Seguridad Pública, or Public Security Forces), had been a division of the armed forces, but in early 1997 it was finally placed under civilian leadership.

Police generally receive little formal training, are relatively incompetent, and often corrupt. Despite this, if you are stopped by Fusep for a traffic infraction or other minor offense, try to go through the proper channels. Do not immediately offer a bribe—this only encourages corruption. As a foreign tourist, you will likely be allowed to go on your way with little fuss unless you've committed a serious crime, since the government is doing its best to develop the tourism industry.

If you are the victim of a crime, the police can be helpful, particularly in smaller towns where it's likely the culprit will be easily found. Policemen are also happy to explain local laws or help tourists with directions.

IMMIGRATION AND CUSTOMS

VISAS

Tourist Requirements

Citizens of western Europe, Canada, Argentina, and Chile are not required to have a visa, and are issued a 30-day tourist card on arrival in Honduras. United States citizens are also sometimes given a tourist card without a visa, though some embassies—for example, in Mexico—say a visa is required. Since the visas don't cost anything, travelers from the U.S. should get one anyway, to be safe.

Citizens of all other countries are required to obtain visas before entering Honduras. Cost usually depends on what that country charges Hondurans for visas. Sometimes it's free, sometimes it can cost up to US$20.

Tourist cards and visas must be renewed every month, up to a six-month maximum stay. Most large towns and cities have a migration office, where your card can be renewed quickly for a couple of dollars. Sometimes you may be asked to get a certain amount of *timbre* stamps, available at a local bank, as payment.

The one office in Honduras where renewing your card is a bit of a nightmare is, ironically, the central migration office in Tegucigalpa. Here you'll be made to wait in a couple of lines and then asked to leave your passport for one to three days. Best to take care of renewal elsewhere when possible.

Foreigners are supposed to carry their passport and tourist card with them at all times, but rarely if ever will it be checked. If you do carry them, be sure to keep photocopies in your hotel room, or better still just carry the photocopies.

CUSTOMS

Travelers entering Honduras are allowed to bring with them anything needed for a vacation, including any sports equipment, plus 200 cigarettes, 100 cigars, half a kilogram of tobacco, and two quarts of spirits. When leaving the country, be sure not to have any pre-Columbian artifacts or coral, particularly black coral, as these could be confiscated either in Honduras or your home country; you could even wind up in jail.

Cars

Foreign cars are allowed into Honduras for a total of six months maximum. Travelers overstaying the limit will be fined. When arriving at the border, be sure to have your title, license, and passport (with visa, if necessary). Insurance is not required.

Thirty-day permits are issued initially, for a US$20 fee. Sometimes you can get a permit for up to three months for an extra US$10. Prices should be clearly posted on signs at border offices, and receipts should be given for every fee. If a border official will not give you a receipt, the fee is probably not required. When in doubt call 36-5594, 36-7538, or 36-6546.

At border posts it is often a good idea to spend a couple of dollars to hire a *tramitador,* a person trained to help with all the paperwork and officials. All *tramitadores* should have identification approved by the government—don't hire someone who is not wearing identification.

If you'd like to renew your permit when the time expires, go to the Dirección General de Aduanas next to the U.S. Embassy in Tegucigalpa. Take two photocopies of your passport, car title, license, and entrance papers, and expect to need at least US$7 in *timbre* stamps (available at most banks), though prices may change.

BORDER CROSSINGS

Official border crossings into Honduras are: El Poy and El Amatillo, from El Salvador; Aguas Calientes and El Florido, from Guatemala; Las Manos, El Espino, and Guasaule, from Nicaragua. Unofficial but regularly used crossings, without migration offices, are Cuyamelito, near Omoa, from Guatemala; Leimus, near Puerto Lempira, from Nicaragua; and several small towns in the mountain region, from El Salvador.

Entering and leaving Honduras by land is generally quick and easy. The best time to arrive is mid-morning, well before lunch break, but most border posts are open until 4 p.m. or 5 p.m. You may be asked to pay a small fee when crossing into Honduras. Technically you shouldn't have to pay anything, but it might be worth the few lempira to avoid an argument with the border guards.

Those leaving Honduras by plane are required to pay an exit fee of US$10.

MONEY, MEASUREMENTS, AND COMMUNICATIONS

CURRENCY

The national unit of currency is the lempira, often shortened to "lemp" by English-speaking Hondurans and expatriates. Bills come in one, two, five, 10, 20, 50, and 100 lempira denominations, while coins come in one, two, five, 10, 20, and 50 centavo pieces. Coins are worth so little they're more of an annoyance than anything with value. Fifty-centavo coins are known as *tostones,* and the slang word for cash is *pisto.* At last report, the exchange rate was roughly US$1:L12.9.

EXCHANGE

Banks or Black Market?
Technically all currency exchange transactions must be done at a bank or in an authorized *casa de cambio* (exchange house), which are rare outside San Pedro Sula or Tegucigalpa. Exchanging money at banks is usually not an arduous affair, especially if you have cash.

Many travelers and Hondurans prefer the convenience of changing money on the black market, which, although illegal, is universally tolerated in the face of the steadily dropping lempira. The exchangers, who usually hang around the central square of most cities and large towns, wave around wads of dollars and lempiras. The rates offered are marginally better than at the banks.

Although the black market may seem a bit shady, the changers are merely businesspeople trying to make a living, and will not rip you off. Nonetheless, it's a good idea to count your money carefully right in front of them to avoid any mistake. As you can tell from how openly the changers operate, there is no risk of getting into legal trouble, unless the government suddenly decides to crack down, which is extremely unlikely.

If you need to change lempiras into dollars, the black market changers are the source.

Banks have strict limits on how many dollars they are allowed to sell.

Traveler's Checks

Any traveler on a long trip without means of accessing money on the road should bring traveler's checks. However, be aware that traveler's checks are not always easy to change in Honduras outside of cities and tourist areas like the Bay Islands or Copán. If you are planning to travel in rural areas, be sure to change enough to cover your time away from the cities.

American Express is by far the most recognized traveler's check—others such as Thomas Cook or Visa are more difficult to exchange. On rare occasions banks may require you to show your original purchase receipt to change checks, so keep it with you.

The American Express agent in Honduras is Mundirama Travel, with offices in Tegucigalpa, al Edificio Ciicsa, corner of Avenida República de Chile and Avenida República de Panamá, tel. 32-3943 or 32-3909, fax 32-0072, and in San Pedro Sula, next to the cathedral on 2 Calle SO, tel. 52-3400 or 53-0490, fax 57-9022.

Credit Cards

Visa and MasterCard are often accepted at the more expensive hotels and restaurants in cities and some large towns, as well as with travel agents, tour groups, and car rental agencies. American Express is much less commonly accepted. In small towns and villages credit cards won't get you much more than blank looks. Visa and MasterCard holders can get cash advances from several banks, for a fee, and from Credomatic offices at no charge. For more information on Credomatic call their Miami, Florida, office at (305) 372-3027 or 372-3015; card application requests tel. (800) 458-2733.

Sending Money

It is possible to receive money wire transfers at both Bancahsa and Banco Atlántida in Honduras. The transfer normally takes three to four days, and charges are not excessive. The money comes in lempiras—often the bank will change some to dollars, but not much. Money can only be received in dollars if a dollar-denomination account is opened at the bank.

Western Union transfers are received at several branches of Banco Sogerin and Banco de Occidente, and at Western Union offices. Money can be sent and received at any Western Union representative—to retrieve the money all you need is the transfer number and a passport. Money is received in lempira, and they charge an exorbitant 10% service fee.

Honduran banks do have ATM cash machines, but they do not yet work with foreign cards. With any luck this will change soon.

WEIGHTS AND MEASURES

Time

Honduras is six hours behind Greenwich mean time, and equal to central standard time in the United States. Daylight saving time is not practiced in Honduras.

Electricity

Almost all outlets in the country operate on 110 volts, and are designed to fit two parallel flat blades. Sometimes a two-pronged round plug is required. A few outlets are 220 volts, but these are extremely rare. If in doubt, ask first.

Power outages and brownouts are frequent in Honduras, especially in the dry season when the El Cajón dam water level is low.

Measurements

Honduras has adopted a confusing mix of metric and nonmetric measurements. US pounds, *libras,* are more frequently used than kilograms as a measure of weight. Twenty-five *libras* equal one *arroba,* and four *arrobas* equal one *quintal.* One quintal equals 46 kilograms. U.S. gallons are used instead of liters for volume, but distance is measured in kilometers and meters rather than miles and feet or yards.

Land sizes are often quoted in *varas,* equal to 838 square meters, or *manzanas,* equal to 0.7 hectares.

COMMUNICATIONS AND MEDIA

Postal Service

Regular mail service *(Correos)* between Honduras and other countries is, at best, a lengthy process. Street addresses are almost nonexistent in Honduras, even in Tegucigalpa and San Pedro Sula. Addresses are usually given as on "X" Calle between "Y" and "Z" Avenidas, or on "X" Calle next to the church, etc. Miraculously, mail does get delivered, though expect to wait anywhere from two to four weeks to receive mail or have it reach its destination. Airmail letters to the U.S. or Europe cost US 50 cents. Packages of up to two kilos can be sent regular mail, and cost US$3 for one kilo and US$6 for two to the U.S. or Europe.

Many post offices now have Express Mail Service (EMS), which reliably sends letters and documents of less than 250 grams to the U.S. in three to four days for US$10-15, depending on the destination, or to Europe in four to five days for US$20-25.

It's possible to receive mail general delivery in any post office in the country. The letters should be addressed to your name, Lista de Correos, town, department, Honduras. A couple of lempira is charged when the mail is collected. Usually offices will hold letters a couple of months, or longer if you advise them ahead of time to await your arrival.

The best places to receive mail general delivery are in large towns—though mail may get lost in the chaos of *Correos* in San Pedro Sula or Tegucigalpa, it may *never* make it out to small towns or villages.

Telephone Service
Hondutel, the national telecommunications company, has offices in every town. You can place international and long-distance domestic

---

USEFUL TELEPHONE NUMBERS

123—AT&T operator
121—MCI operator
191—Long-distance national
192—Information
195—Red Cross ambulance
196—Official time
197—Long-distance international
198—Fire department
199—Police
504—Honduras international area code

---

calls at any of the offices. Prices for three-minute international calls are roughly US$8 to Miami, US$13 to New York, US$23 to France, US$28 to England, and US$23 to Australia.

To place international collect calls from a pay phone, dial the international operator at 197. It is now possible to connect directly with an AT&T operator by dialing 123, or an MCI operator by dialing 121, which makes international calls simple for travelers who subscribe to those companies and carry one of their calling cards.

Media
The five main daily newspapers in Honduras are *La Prensa, La Tribuna, El Periódico, El Heraldo,* and *Tiempo.* All are owned by politicians, and tend to favor one or the other of the two main political parties. *La Prensa* comes the closest to balanced coverage of national news, and has two or three pages of international news including some international sports coverage. Although not as good as *La Prensa* on national news, *La Tribuna* also often features several pages of international wire copy.

Newspapers are usually sold on the street in small stands or merely on a designated street corner. *La Prensa* often sells out by midday. A welcome find for foreign travelers is the English-language weekly newspaper, *Honduras This Week.* Unlike many expatriate-oriented newspapers in the Americas, *Honduras This Week* actually covers issues of importance to the nation, and doesn't shy away from touchy topics like corruption and the military. The paper also has valuable information for travelers and interesting features. It's sold at higher-priced hotels and tourist-oriented stores. Visit *Honduras This Week* on the Internet at http://www.marrder.com/htw/. Their e-mail address is hontweek@hondutel.hn.

Eleven television and 176 radio stations operate in Honduras. Cable television is widely available.

MAPS AND INFORMATION

Maps
Finding totally accurate road maps to Honduras is, unfortunately, an impossible task. Several

*Old and new modes
of transport share
the roads in
Honduras.*

decent maps correctly show the main highways, but invariably mess up the placement of many rural dirt roads, while some incompetent cartographers go so far as to show main highways through areas of virgin jungle and forest.

Formerly Texaco put out an excellent travel map of the country, but its recent edition is difficult to read because of the dark colors used. Nonetheless it's not too bad. Another good one is the International Travel Map of Honduras, available for US$10.95 through **Map Link,** 30 S. Patera Lane, Unit 5, Santa Barbara, CA 93117, tel. (805) 692-6777, fax (800) 627-7768. Map Link also sells the JPK map (US$3.95) of Honduras, a simplified line map of roads with no geographical information.

The **Instituto Geográfico Nacional** publishes a tourist map for US$3, which shows the departments, main roads, and some geographic features. It can be purchased at the Instituto's main office in Comayagüela at the Secretaría de Transporte (SECOPT) on 15 Calle one block east of 1 Avenida, tel. 25-0752.

The Instituto also publishes a complete set of 1:50,000 topographical maps, several sheets of 1:250,000 topographical maps, geological, hydrographic, mineral, and official-boundary maps. The best map of the country available is their large official map, which shows the latest border settlement with El Salvador. It costs US$11, but unfortunately the office was out at last check and awaiting a new printing.

If you need maps of Honduras before going to the country, it is possible to send the institute money and they can send the maps to you, preferably by DHL or UPS. The office staff is friendly, competent, and knowledgable, but you need to speak Spanish and know which maps you're looking for before calling.

Tourist Information

The **Instituto Hondureño de Turismo** (Honduran Tourism Institute) is not the most professional outfit in the world, but it has been improving recently as the government wakes up to the lucrative possibilities of tourism. The Institute's central office in Honduras is in Edificio Europa, 5th floor, on Avenida Ramon Ernesto Cruz, Tegucigalpa (behind the U.S. Embassy), tel. 38-3974 or 22-2124, fax 22-6621.

PUBLIC HOLIDAYS

1 January—New Year's Day
Week leading up to Easter Sunday—Semana Santa
14 April—Día de las Américas
1 May—Labor Day
15 September—Independence Day
3 October—Morazán's Birthday
12 October—Día de la Raza (Columbus Day)
21 October—Armed Forces Day
25 December—Christmas

The Institute recently opened an office in the U.S. that can answer basic questions about traveling in Honduras. Contact them at P.O. Box 140458, Coral Gables, Florida 33114-0458, tel. (800) 410-9608.

A private company in San Pedro Sula, **Servicios Culturales y Turisticos,** can provide tourists with useful information on traveling in the country. Their office is in Edificio Inmosa on 4 Calle between 3 and 4 Avenidas NO, 3rd floor, Room 304, tel.52-3023.

The English-language weekly newspaper *Honduras This Week* is a good source of general news and cultural information on the country, as well as specific travel hints.

The quarterly, free magazine *Honduras Tips* has excellent, up-to-date hotel, restaurant, and travel information on some of the more popular tourist destinations, such as Copán, the north coast, and the Bay Islands. It can be found at many travel agents and better hotels.

GETTING THERE

BY AIR

Several airlines fly direct to Honduras from other countries. From the U.S., **Continental, American, Copa, Taca,** and **Iberia** all fly direct to Honduras from either Houston or Miami. Taca also flies from Belize City, San José, Cancún, and San Salvador, while Copa flies from Mexico City and Panama City, and Iberia flies from Madrid via Miami. La Costeña flies in from Managua, Nicaragua.

Most flights arrive at San Pedro Sula, as the airport at Tegucigalpa is narrow and disliked by pilots. Taca has three flights a week from the U.S. direct to the Bay Island of Roatán.

Standard airfare roundtrip between Houston or Miami and San Pedro Sula is roughly US$550, though better deals can sometimes be found in advance through travel agents.

BY LAND

If you're planning to visit just Honduras and not spend time touring nearby countries, getting there by land isn't the most practical way to go. From the U.S. border, it takes at least three days on buses through Mexico and Guatemala to reach the closest Honduran border post at Aguas Calientes. Those who are on longer trips however, and have some interest in spending time in Mexico or Guatemala, should certainly consider getting there by bus. If you're on your way directly to San Pedro, the north coast, or the Bay Islands, the quickest route from Guatemala is via Esquipulas to Aguas Calientes, near Nuevo Ocotepeque. Many trav-

elers opt for the longer ride through Chiquimula and El Florido, to incorporate a stop-off at the Mayan ruins at Copán on their way through.

If you're coming from or are on your way to Managua, Nicaragua, or further south, the quickest border crossing is through Las Manos, beyond Danlí.

Depending on where your destination is in Honduras, travelers coming from El Salvador will want to cross at El Poy, near Nueva Ocotepeque, or at El Amatillo on the Pacific coast. El Poy is the fastest way to get to the north coast, while El Amatillo is the quickest for Tegucigalpa.

A new route has opened up between Omoa, near Puerto Cortés, and Puerto Barrios, Guatemala. While this crossing once entailed a few hours of hiking through the jungle, it can now be accomplished in either direction in one day, by a combination of buses and river ferries.

A slightly sketchier but still possible crossing is between Puerto Lempira, in the Gracias a Dios department (La Mosquitia) through the border town of Leimus to Puerto Cabezas, Nicaragua. No first-hand information is available on the crossing, but migration officials in Puerto Lempira say it is manageable.

Tica Bus runs international buses to Tegucigalpa from Guatemala City, US$23; San Salvador, US$15; San José, US$35; and Managua, US$20.

BY SEA

U.S. Ferry

Weekly ferry service now runs between Port Isabel, Texas, and Puerto Cortés, Honduras; the ship leaves Port Isabel on Sunday at 6 p.m., arriving in Puerto Cortés Wednesday morning, then leaves Honduras later that day to arrive in Port Isabel Saturday.

Prices depend on how many people are going. The most economical strategy is to go in a group of four, as each cabin has four bunks. One person pays US$228 for a one-way ride with a private cabin, meals and entertainment included. With four people, the same room costs only US$118 per person. Cabins with bathrooms and couches cost more.

The ferry also ships vehicles to Honduras. It's US$599 from the U.S. to Honduras or US$325 back for a passenger vehicle 15 feet long or less. Each additional foot costs US$40. The car may be filled completely—charge is by size, not weight. Passengers traveling with their vehicle must still pay their own fare, although prices are reduced.

It's best to get tickets in the early part of the week in Port Isabel, as the office gets very hectic by the weekend. Reservations are available by phone with a credit card. For more information, call (210) 943-2331 in the United States.

From Belize

Three times a week, launches ply the waters between Dangriga, Belize, and Puerto Cortés, charging US$20 for the two or three hour trip. Sometimes boats can also be found in Mango Creek, Belize, that are going to Puerto Cortés for the same price.

From Guatemala

Twice a week, boats ferry passengers between Livingston, Guatemala, and Omoa, near Puerto Cortés, for US$27.

GETTING AROUND

BY PLANE

Because Honduras is fairly small, flying between destinations in most of the country is not really necessary, with a few exceptions. Should you be in a rush or absolutely hate buses, flights between the two main cities of San Pedro Sula and Tegucigalpa cost US$30 one-way on either Isleña or Taca.

Two areas where it's not a bad idea to arrive by plane are the Bay Islands and La Mosquitia. The islands are serviced by an inexpensive and comfortable ferry, but plane flights from La Ceiba are also inexpensive, and quick. Isleña, Rollins, and Sosa all fly to the Islands daily, charging US$15 to Utila, US$17 to Roatán, and US$22 to Guanaja.

Flying is really the only way to get into La Mosquitia, unless you feel like spending a few days on the deck of a tramp freighter or walking up the coast for a week or so. Isleña flies every day except Sunday from La Ceiba to Palacios for US$43 and to Puerto Lempira for US$45. Rollins flies twice a week from La Ceiba to Brus Lagunas for US$40, and Sosa flies three times a week to Puerto Lempira for US$45.

Between towns and villages in La Mosquitia, travelers may also want to fly, as boat rides are long and often remarkably expensive. The most reliable option is Sami, a rattle-trap little Cessna flying daily between Palacios, Brus Lagunas, Ahuas, and Puerto Lempira. On occasion, it's possible to get a ride with the Alas de Socorro emergency medical service airplane, if it's going in your direction. See the La Mosquitia chapter for more information.

Airfares within Honduras are regulated by the government, so all airlines charge the same amount.

BY BUS

Buses are the most widely used means of transportation by Hondurans. Buses are often essential to visit many of the more out-of-the-way destinations, and budget travelers will be happy to hear that most buses are relatively comfortable and extremely inexpensive For example the four-hour ride between San Pedro Sula and Tegucigalpa costs only US$3.

Direct, first-class bus service is available between main cities like San Pedro Sula, Tegucigalpa, and La Ceiba, but elsewhere don't expect luxury. Many buses are converted U.S. school buses, with bench seating designed for children; so if you're tall, expect a bit of discomfort.

Apart from San Pedro Sula, Tegucigalpa, and Comayagua, the designated bus station in most towns is called simply the *terminal de buses.* In the above-mentioned cities, each company runs its own terminal, and unfortunately they're not centrally located.

Determining bus departure times can be a bit of a guessing game. Some buses leave only when full, which means you should get there early, while others leave at the appointed time, full or not. Generally, long-distance buses leave on a regular schedule.

When you arrive at a station to catch a bus, expect to be accosted by *ayudantes,* or helpers, who will tell you in urgent tones that the bus you want is just out the door and you must buy a ticket immediately. You may then get on the bus and wait another hour before leaving. Another common trick is to tell you the bus is a direct *(directo)* when in reality it stops whenever it sees another potential passenger.

In some buses you are expected to buy a ticket at the station beforehand, while at others the *ayudante* will come around and collect the fare after the trip has begun. If this latter is the case, you will be asked how far you are going, and your fare will change accordingly. Hold on to ticket stubs as the drivers usually collect them at the end of the ride.

In the converted school buses, backpacks and other luggage which does not fit in the overhead racks is stowed in the back, where a couple of seats are normally removed to add space. More expensive buses have compartments below, but if your bag is stashed there by an *ayudante* keep a close eye on the door until the bus pulls out. Bus stations in San Pedro Sula in particular are notorious for having bags ripped off while the unsuspecting victims are on board, awaiting departure.

Apart from the rare express buses, it's customary to flag down a passing bus anywhere along the route—extremely convenient for those traveling in rural areas. Don't bother trying to look for a designated bus stop, just get out on the road and stick out your hand when a bus comes by.

On rare occasions buses will be stopped by police and all men will be forced to get off and line up to be cursorily frisked and have their identifications checked.

The Adventure Shuttle, tel. 57-2380 in San Pedro Sula, operates air-conditioned vans between San Pedro Sula and Copán Ruinas. Private express buses are also available through Transttur, in Tegucigalpa at the Honduras Maya, tel. 39-8400, fax 39-8399; and in San Pedro Sula on 8 Avenida between 5 and 6 Calles SO, tel. 52-4444, fax 52-4441.

HITCHHIKING

Travelers looking to get out into the backcountry of Honduras should be sure to learn the crucial word *jalón.* This literally translates to "a big pull," but in Honduras it means hitching a ride. In many rural areas hitchhiking is the only way to get around, and pickup trucks with room invariably stop to let another passenger pile into the back. When you get dropped off, ask how much you owe for the ride—there's usually a set price.

Not only is hitching safe and convenient in Honduras, but riding in the open air in the back of a pickup beats being crammed into a hot bus for a few hours. Many budget travelers and Peace Corps workers prefer hitching even when buses are available. Women may want to think twice about hitching alone, although many female travelers have done it with no problem.

Hitchhiking is generally only common out on back roads, not on main highways. Some budget travelers insist on hitching everywhere, and it's usually possible, but hitching on main highways is both less common and less safe than in rural areas.

BY TAXI

Taxis are omnipresent in most towns and cities. Meters aren't used, and there's usually a going rate within a certain area. It may be tricky figuring out the going rate. US fifty cents usually gets you around within the downtown area of most towns, while taxis in Tegucigalpa and San Pedro Sula charge closer to US$1.50. For rides further afield, expect to negotiate.

One risky technique is to get in, don't ask the price, and once at your destination hand the driver a 20- or 50-lempira bill, look like you know what the price is, and hope he gives you the

Hitching in pickups is one of the best ways to travel around rural Honduras.

right change. A better plan is to ask a local the prices before hailing a cab.

Taxis are generally collective in Honduras, meaning they stop and pick up passengers along the way and drop them off according to whichever destination is closer. If you're in a hurry and want a nonstop trip, tell the driver and expect to pay extra.

Taxis are invariably found at the downtown square of any town or city, or at the bus station. If you hear someone honking at you as you walk through a town, more than likely it's a taxi—the driver's not being rude, he's just letting you know he's free if you're looking for a ride.

BY BOAT

To The Bay Islands

The ferry MV *Tropical* runs regularly scheduled trips throughout the week to the islands of Roatán and Utila from the Cabotaje dock outside of La Ceiba. If you're really pinching your lempiras or just want the experience, a couple of small freighters leave Cabotaje for the islands every week and will take passengers. The only way to find out about them is to go out to the docks and ask, and the money you spend getting to the docks would probably cover the difference to take the *Tropical*.

Once on the islands, several outfits and resorts offer a variety of cruises and fishing trips. It's also possible to hire local fishermen to take you on freelance trips.

La Mosquitia

Getting to La Mosquitia by tramp freighter has an undeniably romantic appeal, but the reality is somewhat uncomfortable and wet. Should you be after this sort of adventure, get out to the Cabotaje docks in La Ceiba and start asking around. Freighters usually stop in at Brus Lagunas and Puerto Lempira.

In La Mosquitia, *tuk-tuks* (small, motorized canoes) and *pipantes* (dug-out canoes propelled by poles) are often the only transportation available for getting upriver from the coast into the rainforest.

BY CAR

Although it's a long way to drive from the U.S., those who take a car to Honduras can explore large areas of the country accessed only with difficulty by public transportation. Regulations for importing cars are not arduous. Foreign drivers are required to have a license from their country or an International Driver's License, available from AAA. Pickup trucks are the most practical vehicles to bring into Honduras, in terms of both usefulness on the rough roads and finding spare parts.

If you really want to drive around Honduras, but are daunted by the prospect of coming from the U.S. through Mexico and Guatemala, consider shipping your car on the new ferry between Port Isabel, Texas and Puerto Cortés.

For details, see "By Sea" under "Getting There," above. **Hyde Shipping,** with offices in Miami, 3033 N.W. North River Dr., Miami, FL 33142, tel. (305) 638-4262, fax (305) 635-8939, and French Harbour, Roatán, tel. 45-1404, 45-1495, or 45-1512, also ships vehicles for about the same price between Miami, La Ceiba, and Roatán.

Road Conditions

Until quite recently driving in Honduras was a white-knuckle adventure on rutted dirt roads, but the situation has improved dramatically with a road-building binge by successive governments. Honduras now has 14,203 km of roads, including 2,401 km of paved highways, 9,830 km of all-season dirt roads, and 1,972 km of dirt roads passable in the dry season only.

Well-maintained paved highways include: Tegucigalpa-San Pedro Sula, Tegucigalpa-Choluteca, Tegucigalpa-Danlí, Nueva Ocotepeque-San Pedro Sula, San Pedro Sula-Puerto Cortés, San Pedro Sula-Tela, and El Amatillo-Guasaule. The north coast highway from Tela to Trujillo via La Ceiba and Tocoa is paved but in shoddy condition, though it may improve.

Although some older maps don't show them, two all-weather dirt highways cut from Olancho through to the north coast, one via San Esteban and Bonito Oriental, and the other passing La Unión. These are both beautiful drives passing through interesting and rarely visited mountainous regions.

When driving in cities, keep a close eye on signs indicating one-way streets. Most large towns and cities are not difficult to navigate, except Tegucigalpa. The traffic there is horrific and the streets confusing. Better to leave your car at a hotel and get around by taxi during your stay.

Driving at night is not recommended, but if you must for some reason, watch closely for cattle, potholes, and other random obstacles on the road. Keep an eye out for signs warning of upcoming *túmulos* (speed bumps).

Police checkpoints are common throughout Honduras. Signs will tell you to stop, but the best plan is to just slow down as you pass. If the post hasn't been abandoned, the occupants will usually either ignore you or wave you on. Don't expect other drivers to follow the rules of the road. Always drive defensively and expect the unexpected.

Rules of the Road

Traffic rules in Honduras are fairly self-explanatory and similar to rules in the United States. Speed limits are not obeyed, but if you want to be safe, follow them anyway. Right on red is sometimes allowed, sometimes not, so don't risk it. Smoking is not permitted in cars in some cities, such as Tegucigalpa, and seat belts are mandatory.

If you are pulled over for a traffic offense, your license will be taken. You can try to pay a bribe to get it back, but remember the official fines are usually cheaper than a bribe. If you ask for a ticket, you will be given one, and then you have 72 hours to go to traffic court to pay the fine and reclaim the license. In Tegucigalpa, the office is the Dirección General de Tránsito in Colonia Miraflores.

In Case of Accident

If you have an accident with another car, tell someone to go get *tránsito,* the traffic police. Don't leave the scene of an accident before *tránsito* arrives. While waiting, get all information possible about the other driver. When *tránsito* arrives, they will talk to both drivers separately, then write out a description of events for both to sign and date.

An appointment will then be assigned at the *Juzgado de Tránsito* (traffic court), where a monetary arrangement will be made. No one carries insurance, so the judge will arbitrate between the two parties to arrive at an agreement. If no agreement is reached, either party can sue.

In the case of an accident involving a pedestrian, again call the police immediately and do not leave the scene. You may have to spend up to a week in jail, but no more. It's very likely you will be forced to pay a fine to the victim in case of injury, or to the family of the victim in case of death, regardless of who was at fault.

Do not even consider fleeing the scene of an accident. This only creates more serious trouble for you. It's best to follow the process through to its conclusion.

Fuel and Repairs

Gasoline is a bit expensive in Honduras, US$2 per gallon super, and US$1.40 diesel. Regular gas is no longer available in Honduras. Gas stations are common throughout the country, and in places with no gas stations, gas is sometimes sold out of barrels. Be sure to fill up whenever you're planning a trip into rural Honduras, and bring a gas can. Texaco publishes a country map showing the location of their stations.

Mechanical help is relatively inexpensive, but parts can be costly depending on your vehicle. The most common cars in the country are Toyota pickup trucks. Other Japanese makes like Nissan and Isuzu are also common, as are American-made vehicles. Volkswagens are not often seen but do exist.

Be sure to get your vehicle thoroughly checked before leaving for Honduras, and consider bringing a few basic spare parts such as filters (gas, air, and oil), fan belts, spark plugs and spark-plug wires, two spare tires (instead of one), fuses, and radiator hoses. Recommended emergency gear for vehicles includes a tow rope, extra gas cans, water containers, and of course a jack and tire iron. According to Honduran law you are required to have a fire extinguisher and reflective triangles in your car at all times.

Insurance
Apart from policies offered by car rental agencies, auto insurance is virtually nonexistent in Honduras, so you drive at your own risk. This should encourage you to drive defensively, which you should be doing anyway. The English-language newspaper *Honduras This Week* sometimes advertises insurance agents, but policies are generally for a year minimum and thus not practical for most travelers.

Socorro Vial, a service not unlike AAA, is worth contracting should you plan on driving extensively in Honduras. Their coverage provides towing service and mechanical help for US$50 a year, 24 hours a day within 50 km of Tegucigalpa, and 8 a.m.-4 p.m. within 30 km of San Pedro Sula and La Ceiba. For another US$10 they offer medical insurance as well. Their central office is in Tegucigalpa, Avenida República de Chile 202, tel. 31-5551 or 31-4158, fax 32-6133.

Car Rental
Renting a car in Honduras is not cheap. Expect to pay at least US$45 per day with unlimited milage, or more with insurance. Recommended agencies include Toyota, Avis, Hertz, and Molinari.

BY BICYCLE

Remarkably, cyclists rate Honduras as the best Central American country to tour by bicycle. The main highways are in decent condition and highway traffic is low. Because many Hondurans get around by bicycle themselves or walk along the highway, the government has considerately included extra space marked off that bikers can safely cruise on without fear of being run down.

Bicycle touring may seem specialized, but it's actually a wonderful way to really see a country. There's no need to race—determine a comfortable pace for your group and plan your journey accordingly. Drawbacks to biking in Honduras include the extremely mountainous terrain, which will wear you down, and the lack of good quality spare parts. Riding in a group is best.

Mountain biking is a nascent but growing sport among the wealthy in Honduras. Few trails have been developed, but there are plenty of rugged logging roads to explore.

BOB RACE

THE NORTH COAST

INTRODUCTION

More like an entirely different country than a region of Honduras, the steaming hot, banana tree-blanketed plains of the Caribbean coast are worlds away from the rest of the country. The north coast is a polyglot melting pot, closer to the Anglo-African Caribbean islands than the more reserved Hispanic culture of the interior. North coasters are more extroverted: they like to dance, to party, to get out and have a good time.

Settled by the black-Carib Garífuna, North American banana men, Honduran job seekers, and immigrants from across the globe, the north coast is so diverse one never knows whether to address someone in Spanish or English; chances are they know a bit of both. For the traveler, the north coast's most appealing aspect is certainly the perfect trio of sun, sand, and sea. Superb beaches, where you can sling a hammock between two palms and enjoy the gentle offshore breezes in peace, line the entire coast.

The area also contains several of the country's most important natural protected areas, including the mangrove wetlands and lowland jungles of Punta Sal, Punta Izopo, and Cuero y Salado, as well as the mountain jungles, cloud forests, and rivers of Pico Bonito.

Many visitors blow through the north coast on their way between Copán and the Bay Islands, but those who stay a while invariably find themselves entranced by the unique blend of culture and natural beauty. It's no surprise the north coast has the largest contingent of expatriates in the country outside of the Bay Islands.

THE LAND

Most of the north coast is a narrow plain extending roughly 350 km from the Guatemalan border west of Omoa to Cabo Camarón east of Trujillo. Backed by the rugged Sierra de Omoa, Nombre de Diós, and Colón mountain ranges, the plain is only a few kilometers wide for most of its length, extending further inland only along the deltas of the Chamelecón, Ulúa, Lean, and Aguán rivers, which flow north out of the highlands to the sea.

Originally much of the coast was covered by tropical humid forests, but those have long since been converted to fruit and palm plantations. The most intensive cultivation, due to the rich alluvial soils, is along the river deltas. Coastal

NORTH COAST HIGHLIGHTS

- Beach-bumming at Tela and Trujillo
- Visiting the Garífuna villages of Triunfo de la Cruz, Miami, Tornabé, or Santa Fe
- Touring the nature reserves of Cuero y Salado, Punta Sal, Punta Izopo, Lancetilla, or Laguna Guaymoreto
- Rafting on the Río Cangrejal
- Dancing at the discos of La Ceiba
- Partying at the Fiesta de San Isidro, La Ceiba

mangrove swamps were also once extensive but have been hemmed in to a few protected areas (Punta Sal, Punta Izopo, Cuero y Salado) by the steady growth of plantations and cattle ranching.

The coast is usually sweltcringly hot, with mean annual temperatures ranging from 25 to 28° C. The prevailing easterlies of the western Caribbean Sea dump an average 200 centimeters of rain annually, with short dry seasons from February to May and August to September. Both the amount of rain and its timing vary dramatically from year to year, and wet weather can arrive at any time. In 1996 La Ceiba and Tela were flooded in March, supposedly the driest time of year.

Hurricanes are a common annual occurrence, most often coming in October and November and frequently causing flooding, especially in the Valle de Sula. In 1996 Tropical Storm Marco left 60,000 Hondurans homeless on the north coast and destroyed 4,000 houses. As with the entire length of Central America's Caribbean coast, malaria is common, so come prepared.

HISTORY

Pre-Columbian Residents

Archaeological and historical evidence suggests at least three indigenous groups lived on the Honduran north coast in pre-Columbian times, but because of the hot climate and lack of easily cultivated land, habitation was sparse.

The Maya are believed to have extended their influence to western Honduras around A.D. 300, and although settlements were located mostly in the highlands around Copán and near the Guatemalan border, they did farm land in the lower Valle de Sula. On the coast itself, the Maya maintained several important trading posts, the farthest east at Punta Caxinas near Trujillo. Similarly, Nahuatl traders from central Mexico had outposts on the Honduran coast as far east as Trujillo.

Although Jicaque, or Tolupan, Indians inhabited the entire north coast region from the Guatemalan border to Mosquitia, their settlements were almost all in the mountains and they apparently came to the shore only to trade.

1502 to 1860

Following Columbus' first landing on the Honduran coast near Trujillo in 1502, two decades

Fuerte San Fernando de Omoa

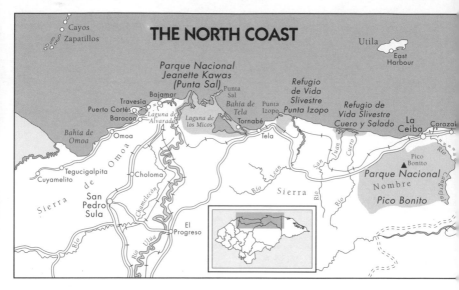

THE NORTH COAST

Cayos Zapatillos · Utila · East Harbour · Parque Nacional Jeanette Kawas (Punta Sal) · Punta Sal · Refugio de Vida Silvestre Punta Izopo · Bajamar · Bahía de Tela · Punta Izopo · Punta Izopo · Refugio de Vida Silvestre Cuero y Salado · La Ceiba · Corazal · Travesía · Puerto Cortés · Baracoa · Laguna de Alvarado · Laguna de los Micos · Tornabé · Tela · Río Lean · Río San Juan · Río Cuero · Bahía de Omoa · Omoa · Omoa · Pico Bonito · Río Congrejal · Tegucigalpita · Cuyamelito · Choloma · Parque Nacional Nombre · Pico Bonito · San Pedro Sula · Chamelecón · Sierra · Río Ulúa · El Progreso · Sierra de · Río Ulúa

passed before Spanish explorers returned. But when they did, they converged on the country in three opposing factions led by Gil González Dávila, Cristóbal de Olid, and Francisco de las Casas. In the midst of their power struggle, the three factions managed to establish settlements by 1525 at Puerto Caballos, now Puerto Cortés, Triunfo de la Cruz, near present-day Tela, and at Trujillo.

Although deposits of alluvial gold were found near Trujillo and at the mouth of the Río Ulúa, these were quickly spent. By the mid-16th century, Spanish attention turned toward more promising mineral deposits inland. Since gold and silver were the conquistadores' main concern, the north coast quickly degenerated into a backwater. The nascent colony was briefly ruled from Trujillo, but by the 1540s the seat of government and most colonists had moved to western Honduras.

If the lack of gold and quality agricultural land, uncomfortable heat, and danger of disease didn't scare away most colonists, the pirates who appeared in the western Caribbean by the mid-16th century certainly did. The pirates sacked the relatively unprotected towns of Trujillo and Puerto Caballos with regularity. So severe was the danger even Spanish traders lived inland and only ventured to the ports when the Spanish

fleets arrived. By 1643 Trujillo had been abandoned and only a small settlement remained at Omoa, near Puerto Caballos.

Having overextended themselves in their conquests, the Spanish essentially wrote off the Honduran north coast until the late 1700s, when expeditions ordered by the reformist Bourbon kings drove English settlers and pirates out of the Bay Islands and Mosquitia.

The Spanish regained control of the coast, but still had no real incentive to populate it on a large scale. The first widespread settlement was undertaken by the Black Caribs, or Garífuna, who were forcibly removed from the Caribbean island of San Vicente by the British in 1797. The Garífuna first established a community in Trujillo, and then migrated up and down the coast, building villages from the edge of Mosquitia as far north and west as Belize.

The violence of the independence wars in the early 19th century, and later fighting among the different Central American countries, increased coastal settlement, driving people from their homes in the central parts of the country to the relatively peaceful coast. Nonetheless, the north coast remained sparsely populated until North Americans and Europeans developed a taste for bananas.

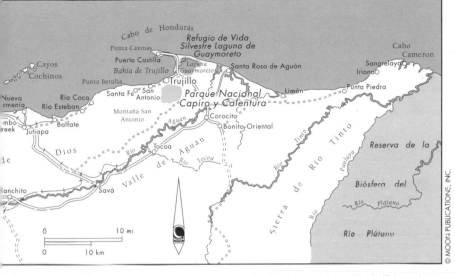

The Banana Industry

The development of the modern north coast—and, some would say, of the entire country—is essentially the story of the growth of the banana industry.

Bananas were introduced to Central America by Spanish missionaries in the first years of colonization, but were cultivated only on a small scale for local consumption. The exportation of bananas began in the 1860s, when small, locally owned plantations on Roatán started to sell their fruit to passing tramp freighters, who in turn sold it to markets in the United States and Europe at an excellent profit. When growers and boat captains realized the moneymaking potential of the trade, more plantations sprang up all along the north coast, particularly around La Ceiba, Tela, and Puerto Cortés.

For the first few decades, Hondurans owned and worked the banana fields, meaning local growers could sell to the highest bidder and make significant profits. By the turn of the century, however, North American exporters realized they could boost their earnings by running plantations themselves, and began gaining control of as much of the Honduran north coast as possible.

This conversion of the north coast into a virtual North American colony was led by three com-panies: United Fruit, based first in Tela and now in La Lima; Cuyamel, which controlled lands west of Puerto Cortés; and Standard Fruit, centered around La Ceiba.

Some land was actually purchased by the companies, but much more was awarded to them by the Honduran government in massive concessions, in return for railroad construction and jobs. Although the government was generally in favor of the concessions, wanting to modernize their backward country, the companies took no chances. To help their cause, they resorted to bribery and arm-twisting, even fomenting the occasional revolution to ensure a friendly administration.

As a result, by the second decade of the century the banana companies held almost one million acres of the country's most fertile land, were making huge profits, and unabashedly manipulated government officials to maintain the status quo. One historian writes: "If Honduras was dependent on the banana companies before 1912, it was virtually indistinguishable from them after 1912."

In the course of building their fiefdoms, the companies completely transformed the north coast. Puerto Cortés changed from a sleepy seaside village into one of the largest ports in

Central America, and Tela and La Ceiba were essentially created out of nothing. Swampland was drained and converted into plantations; railroads were constructed between the plantations and newly built warehouses and docks; and immigrants from across Honduras and the world were drawn by the hope of quick money. Banks, breweries, hospitals, and a myriad of other services were built by the companies to suit their own needs.

Coastal development never strayed far from the direct interests of the banana companies, and fell far short of what many Hondurans had envisioned. For example, railroads were built only between plantations and docks, and the companies preferred to pay annual fines rather than fulfill their contractual promises to extend lines inland, connecting the coast to Tegucigalpa. To this day, the north coast has the country's only railway lines, and now that the companies use trucks, the lines have been allowed to fall into disrepair.

The industry has fallen off steeply from the glory days between 1925 and 1939, when Honduras was the world's top producer and bananas constituted 88% of the country's exports. Still, Standard (now Dole) and United (now Chiquita) remain the top economic force on the north coast, and have diversified into pineapple, African palm oil, and other fruit products. The two companies easily still control the largest amount of land, after the Honduran government, and almost all their holdings are on or near the north coast.

Since the turn of the century the north coast has been the most dynamic economic sector of the country, and with the rise of San Pedro Sula as a major center for light industry and commerce, this trend has accelerated. Although San Pedro is not on the coast, its success is due to the short rail and highway connection to Puerto Cortés, and the city's growth has stimulated the entire north coast. In terms of population and economy, the four coastal departments comprise Honduras's fastest growing region.

PUERTO CORTÉS AND VICINITY

INTRODUCTION

Situated on a deep natural harbor on the northwest corner of Honduras, and only 60 kilometers from the industrial capital of San Pedro Sula, Puerto Cortés is perfectly located to serve as a transfer point for much of the country's imports and exports. It handles the largest amount of boat traffic—though Puerto Castilla near Trujillo moves more total tonnage—and is considered to have one of the best port facilities in Central America. Since a duty-free zone was created in the port area in 1976, a sizable assembly industry has developed, mostly of clothing exported to the United States.

The thriving economy supports a population of roughly 75,700. The city's annual festival day is 15 August.

History
The Spanish first settled west of present-day Puerto Cortés early in the colonial era, recognizing the value of the harbor. The first settlement was named Puerto Caballos (Port Horses), after conquistador Gil González Dávila was

caught in a fierce storm nearby in 1524, and was forced to throw several horses overboard.

Puerto Caballos was repeatedly struck by epidemics and marauding pirates, and by the turn of the 17th century the Spanish relocated to the better-protected harbor of Omoa, to the west. This new port was established in 1870 on the other side of the bay from the colonial one, at the terminus of a new railway line connecting San Pedro Sula to the coast, and the town's name was changed to Puerto Cortés.

Around the turn of the century, Puerto Cortés was a favorite destination for all manner of shady characters, swindlers, and soldiers-of-fortune from the U.S. and Europe. Many were on the run from the law, as Honduras had no extradition treaties until 1912. For a time in the 1890s the Louisiana Lottery, banned in its home state, found refuge in Puerto Cortés and became one of the largest gambling concerns in the world.

Orientation and Getting Around
Although Puerto Cortés is a large city, the downtown area is compact and can easily be explored on foot. Taxis around downtown should cost US 50 cents, or US$1 out to the dock where boats

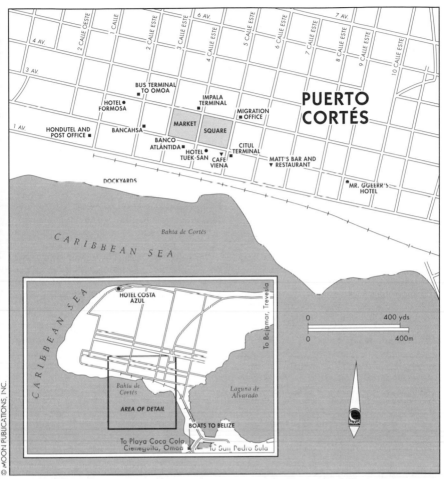

depart for Belize. Buses all leave from within a block of the square. Beware of walking out on 1 Avenida at night as muggings are common.

SIGHTS

A travel writer who condemned Puerto Cortés as "the foulest blot on Central America's coastline" may have been overly unkind—the tropical seediness can be somewhat appealing, if one appreciates that sort of thing—but there's no doubt the port city has little to draw tourists.

The **square** is a reasonably tranquil place to sit, but otherwise there's little to do in town except watching prostitutes and drunks stumble about their business on 1 Avenida. The bustling **dockyards** are off-limits without a special pass, but you can check them out from behind a tall fence.

For a bit of sun and sand near town, **Playa Coca Cola** lies a couple of kilometers west of the city around the bay, a US$1.50 taxi ride or a long hot walk from downtown. Playa Coca Cola is heavily used by locals, and is neither clean nor particularly safe. East of downtown is **Playa El Faro** (Lighthouse Beach), which is not much better.

Quieter and more attractive, but still nothing spectacular, is **Playa Cieneguita,** west of Playa Coca Cola and backed by two hotels. Taxis to Cieneguita cost US$3, or take the Ruta 1 bus from the corner of 2 Calle Este and 3 Avenida to the end of the line; it's a 10-minute walk up the road from there to the beach entrance. The hotels and beach at Cieneguita are usually packed on weekends with wealthy vacationers from San Pedro Sula and completely deserted during the week. All in all, unless one is pressed for time, better beaches can be found at Omoa to the west or Travesía and Bajamar to the east.

ACCOMMODATIONS

In Town
The best inexpensive rooms in town are at **Hotel Formosa,** on 3 Avenida between 1 and 2 Calles Este, tel. 55-0853; US$3 s or US$5 d for a basic room with a fan, US$4 s or US$7 d with private bath, US$12 d with a/c and private bath.

On the square is the dingy **Hotel Tuek-San,** no phone; US$2.50 s with private bath and fan, more for a/c. It has a mediocre cafe downstairs.

Those with a penchant for cockroaches, drunks, and prostitutes can patronize any of several hotels on 1 Avenida, of which the **Hotel Las Vegas** is one of the better-known.

A few blocks east of the square is **Mr. Ggeerr's Hotel,** on 2 Avenida at 9 Calle, tel. 55-0444, offering clean but somewhat claustrophobic rooms with semifunctional a/c and cable TV for US$12 s or US$23 d. The hotel, on the second floor of a large building, has a pool table in the lobby and a bar and restaurant that aren't always open.

On the Beach
Mr. Ggeerr also owns **Hotel Costa Azul,** at Playa El Faro, tel. 55-2260, fax 55-2262. The large oceanfront complex holds a pricey restaurant, swimming pool, and rooms equipped with a/c, cable TV, and telephones; US$30.

At Playa Cieneguita is the **Hotel Playa,** tel. 55-0453 or 55-1105, fax 55-2287, a motel-style arrangement with parking in front of the 12 wood-paneled rooms, each with a small porch. Prices range from US$45 d during the week to US$76 d on weekends. Right next door is the similar **Mar y Más,** tel. 55-1495. Both hotels have outdoor restaurants and pools.

Further up the road toward Omoa is the best accommodation in the area, **Acantilados del Caribe Resort,** tel. 55-1461, fax 55-1403, in U.S. (800) 327-4149. It's built on a private beach and offers two restaurants, a small marina, horseback riding, fishing tours, and other activities. Each cabin has two beds, a porch with hammocks, a/c, TV, and phone, and costs US$48 Mon.-Thurs., US$68 Fri.-Sunday. Less expensive apartments are also available.

FOOD

A surprising and welcome find on the south side of the square in the center of town is **Cafe Viena,** serving inexpensive but well-prepared meals and good coffee from 8 a.m. to 1 a.m. every day in a friendly atmosphere. Check out the great old country tunes on the jukebox.

The new **Matt's Bar and Restaurant,** on 2 Avenida between 6 and 7 Calles Este, tel. 55-0862, is fast becoming a favorite hangout for the local young crowd, with seafood and other dishes for US$4-6 per entree and mellow jazz in the background. Open for dinner only.

The restaurant at **Hotel Tuek-San** has inexpensive, mediocre Chinese food and Honduran standards.

SERVICES

Bancahsa and Banco Atlántida in the center of town exchange dollars and travelers checks Mon.-Fri. 8 a.m.-5 p.m., Saturday 8-11:30 a.m.

Correos and Hondutel are both on 1 Calle next to the main dock entrance. Express Mail Service is available at the post office. The UPS office is on 2 Avenida Este between 11 and 12 Calles, tel. 55-1427.

PUERTO CORTÉS USEFUL TELEPHONE NUMBERS

Police: 55-0420, or dial 199
Fire Department: 55-0223, 55-0500,
   or dial 198
Cruz Roja Ambulance: dial 195
Hospital: 55-0562, 55-0787

The migration office, on the southeast corner of the square, tel. 55-0582, is officially open Mon.-Fri. 8 a.m.-noon and 2-5:30 p.m., Saturday 8 a.m.-noon, but the friendly staff will often open up if a visitor knocks at other hours. Renewing tourist permits and registering after entering from Guatemala is hassle-free here.

Maya Rent A Car has an office on 3 Avenida between 2 and 3 Calles Este, tel. 55-0064, fax 55-1123.

GETTING THERE AND AWAY

Bus
Impala and **Citul,** with terminals on opposite sides of the square, both operate frequent direct buses for the hour-long ride via Choloma to San Pedro Sula; fare is US 80 cents. Local buses take twice as long. A new company, **Expresos del Atlántico,** is about to begin direct service also.

Buses to Omoa (US 20 cents) and Tegucigalpita (US$2), near the Guatemalan border, leave every half hour from the terminal on 3 Avenida and 2 Calle Este. Buses to Bajamar and Travesía leave from next to the Citul terminal, on 2 Avenida and 5 Calle Este.

Car
The road to San Pedro has been under seemingly constant construction since 1995, and is nearing completion. When finished, the four-lane highway should make the 60 km trip a very quick drive.

Train
The only public train in Honduras runs between Puerto Cortés and Tela, a slow ride through an in-

FUERTE SAN FERNANDO DE OMOA

The Caribbean coast of Honduras was sparsely populated throughout the colonial era, making it an easy target for attacks by pirates, marauding Miskito Indians, and later the British Navy. Although pirate assaults began just a couple of decades after the Spanish started to colonize Central America, it was not until the mid-18th century that colonial authorities made serious efforts to combat the marauders and fortify their positions on the coastline.

As early as 1685, the Spanish recognized Omoa as an ideal location for a fort—strategically situated on a deep, protected harbor between English settlements in Belize, the Bay Islands, and Mosquitia. But distractions elsewhere, a lack of funding, and bureaucratic inertia combined to delay actual construction until 1752, when royal engineer Luis Diez de Navarro arrived with a plan for a massive triangular bastion.

Work on the fort was painstakingly slow. For a start, there was no adequate stone in the area; it had to be cut and transported from as far as 150 kilometers away. But more dire was the lack of workers; disease and heat took a brutal toll on the conscripted Indians. Omoa became known as the graveyard of Honduras among the highland Indians, and able-bodied males fled their villages when they heard colonial officials were coming to look for workers. Eventually the Crown brought in black slaves to finish the fort.

Finally completed in 1773, the fort was an intimidating sight. Two of the three sides were 60 meters long, while the ocean-facing base measured 25 meters. The walls were six meters high and two meters thick. The complex overflowed with 150 pieces of artillery, and was surrounded by a moat. Despite its daunting appearance, the fort was never particularly successful. A combined British-Miskito force of almost 1,000 men, led by Commodore John Luttrell, took it in 1779, just six years after the fort's construction. Since that inauspicious first defeat, the fort at Omoa fell variously to Spanish royalists, Francisco Morazán's forces, and later to Guatemalan soldiers. Easier to get into than out of, the fort was finally converted into a prison by the Honduran government in 1853.

In spite of its abysmal record of defense, the visually impressive fort squats ominously in the tropical heat, a kilometer or so from the ocean. The Caribbean has receded in the years since its construction, leaving the fort stranded amid the fields and swamp between the Puerto Cortés highway and the beach.

Admission is US 10 cents for Central Americans and US 20 cents for all others. The fort is open Mon.-Fri. 8 a.m.-4 p.m., Sat.-Sun. 9 a.m.-5 p.m. Next to the fort is a small museum, which at last report was closed to the public due to a renovation project.

SAM THE BANANA MAN

Of the many fascinating and colorful individuals involved in Honduras's banana industry, few if any can top Sam Zemurray, better known as Sam the Banana Man. In an industry run mainly by cold-blooded bankers living in the U.S., Sam was legendary for traveling his plantations on mule back, speaking bad Russian-accented Spanish, and cultivating the loyalty of his workers by personally bringing Christmas presents and throwing parties.

Born Samuel Zmuri, a Bessarabian Jew, Sam immigrated to the U.S. in his youth and got his start in the banana business in Mobile, Alabama in 1895. At the age of 18, Sam offered to buy US$150 worth of ripe bananas that needed to be sold quickly. He fast cornered the market on selling "ripes," and within three years had US$100,000 in the bank.

Heeding the call of the tropics, Sam headed to Puerto Cortés in 1905 as the owner of a formerly bankrupt steamship company, with United Fruit Company and a partner named Hubbard as a temporary financial backer. By 1910, he made the dar-

BOB RACE

Samuel Zemurray

ing move of buying 5,000 acres of land, all with borrowed money, and set up the first foreign-owned plantation in Honduras, along the Cuyamel River west of Puerto Cortés. All the debt scared off his partner, but Sam was happy to get rid of him. Naming his new company the Cuyamel Fruit Company, Sam promptly sank even deeper into debt to acquire more land.

His small plantation could not produce enough bananas to pay off the debts quickly enough for his creditors. Sam needed more land. The usual acquisition method was to grease enough palms to ensure a large concession from the government, but conditions within Honduras made this an unlikely proposition. At the time, the U.S. government was considering taking over the country's customs receipts to cover bad debt, and it was unlikely the U.S. would look favorably on granting Sam a concession. Rather than panic, Sam decided a change of government was in order, so he organized his own revolution to install Manuel Bonilla, a personal friend and the former president of Honduras, who had himself recently been overthrown.

Sam's right-hand man in this adventure was one Lee Christmas, another legendary figure in the early years of the banana industry. A New Orleans railroad man who relocated to Honduras in the late 19th century, Christmas never missed a good fight, and when Sam contacted him in 1910 he was itching for a little "revolutin," as he liked to call it. Christmas, Bonilla, and Sam planned the revolt in New Orleans in December 1910, under the watchful eyes of federal agents who knew full well what they were brewing and were determined to stop it. But Sam managed to dupe the agents with an unusual sleight of hand. The *Hornet,* a 160-foot ship recently bought by Sam and stuffed full of weaponry and eager mercenaries, sailed out to sea on the 20th, but as Christmas and Bonilla stayed in town the U.S. agents had no reason to stop it.

Christmas and Bonilla spent the evening in a famed New Orleans bordello, until the agents outside got tired of watching the fun and went home for the night. Whereupon Christmas declared to Bonilla, "Well, compadre, this is the first time I've ever heard of anybody going from a whorehouse to the White House. Let's be on our way!" Sam met the two on the docks with his own private yacht and ferried them out to the *Hornet,* which was waiting offshore. The drunk warriors sailed off to Honduras, which they took after a month of intermittent skirmishes. With Bonilla safely installed in the presidency, the Banana Man received his coveted concession.

The Cuyamel Company grew in leaps and bounds over the next two decades, making Sam a very wealthy man. Apparently succumbing to pressure from United Fruit, Sam sold Cuyamel to United in 1930 for US$30 million and returned to the United States. It was assumed Sam had tired of the banana business and was looking to enjoy his wealth, but that was not quite the case. Much of United's payment for Cuyamel was in the form of stock, and unbeknownst to the company, Sam had proxies quietly buy up more shares over the years, leaving him with a controlling interest. By 1932, a combination of poor management and the Depression had caused stock prices to fall precipitously. Sam traveled to Boston and attended a board meeting, asking politely for an explanation.

In a condescending reference to Sam's accent, one director said, "Unfortunately, Mr. Zemurray, I can't understand a word you say." Sam reportedly looked at the directors a few seconds, muttered something under his breath, and walked out. He returned a few minutes later with all the papers demonstrating his control of the company, slapped them on the table, and said very deliberately, "You gentlemen have been fucking up this business long enough. I'm going to straighten it out."

Thus began Sam's second coming in the banana industry. He was head of United Fruit for two decades. He quickly reorganized the management strategy of the company, handing responsibility to managers actually on the plantations rather than in U.S. boardrooms, a move fought by the Boston-based managers and cheered loudly by United workers in Central America.

The Banana Man had few compunctions about manipulating local governments to suit his purposes—he is reputed to have uttered the famous quote, "In Honduras, a mule is worth more than a congressman,"—but, unlike most banana men he also actually cared for his adopted country and its people. Under his leadership, United began diversifying away from monocrop agriculture, and developed other products such as pineapple, grapefruit, and African palm. Palm oil in particular has developed into a major industry in Honduras.

To help seek out more nontraditional products for Honduras and all of Central America, and to improve the region's agriculture, Sam funded the Lancetilla Botanical Research Station and the Escuela Agrícola de las Americas at Zamorano, both set up by William Popenoe. Zemurray stepped down as president of United in 1951, but just couldn't stay away from the fray. During the 1954 coup in Guatemala, which was due in large part to the interests of United, Sam directed the company's media efforts. He removed himself from the board of directors shortly thereafter, and died in 1961.

frequently seen stretch of banana country. The four-hour trip in bare, often-crowded cars costs US$1. Some snacks and soft drinks are sold during the trip, and there is a stop at Baracoa, usually long enough to run into the track-side *pulpería*. The train departs Puerto Cortés Friday and Sunday at 7 a.m. Get out to 1 Avenida a few minutes early and look for other passengers waiting. There is no official station; the train seems to stop wherever a large crowd congregates.

Boat

Boats to Dangriga, Belize, and sometimes also to Mango Creek, Belize, leave between 10 and 11 a.m. Monday, Wednesday, and Saturday from a small dock at the mouth of the lagoon. The small launches make the two- to three-hour trip for US$20, but only in good weather, and be

prepared to get wet regardless. Arrive one day before departure to put your name on the list. The office is in a small fish stand on the Puerto Cortés side of the bridge, opposite the dock.

NEAR PUERTO CORTÉS

Omoa

The village of Omoa is built around a small bay 13 km west of Puerto Cortés, where the Sierra de Omoa mountains meet the Caribbean. The town itself was never a major population center, but for strategic purposes the Spanish built the largest colonial-era fort in Central America here.

Omoa is now a sleepy fishing village, its houses and shops scattered along the two-km road between the Puerto Cortés highway and the sea. The main beach, lined with fishing boats and several small restaurants, is unattractive but a quiet and relaxing place to spend a few hours after admiring the fort, located on the main road running between the highway and the beach. About a 45-minute walk south of the highway junction is a small waterfall in the woods—ask someone to point out the trail.

From Omoa a hiking trail winds up into the Sierra de Omoa and arrives at Cusuco National Forest above San Pedro Sula. This multiday trek is normally done in the other direction, but Cusuco officials have reportedly closed the trail recently. The trail may reopen; for more information, call the Fundación Hector Rodrigo Pastor Fasquelle in San Pedro Sula, tel. 52-1014 or 57-6598. Locals celebrate their annual carnival on 30 May in honor of San Fernando.

Accommodations in Omoa until recently were limited to the unsavory **Hospedaje Puerto Grande** between the fort and the beach, with inexpensive but dingy rooms. Fortunately, two expatriate-managed hostels are now open and offer better value.

Roli and Berni's Place, down the road toward the beach from Puerto Grande, on the opposite side of the road, is run by a pair of Swiss travelers who rent a couple of basic but clean rooms for US$3.50 s or US$6 d, with hot showers and a communal bathroom. The porch and yard at the hostel is a great place to relax. The owners also run Yax Pac Tours (P.O. Box 84, Puerto Cortés, tel. 55-1506), offering three-week tours of Honduras and Guatemala with a flexible itinerary for US$1,200, everything included except airfare.

On the beach, **Hotel Bahía de Omoa** is run by a European couple who rent three rooms in their large, modern house with a/c and hot water for US$25-30 d. The owners have a boat and will organize sailing trips and excursions to the nearby Cayos Zapotillos. Reservations can be made by mail at P.O. Box 244, Puerto Cortés.

Of the several beach restaurants, **Champa Virginia** serves some of the better seafood in town; US$2-3 per plate, depending on the size of the fish. The restaurant stays open until 9 or 10 p.m., and the owners are friendly.

At the highway junction are a few *pulperías,* a burger joint, and, opposite the Texaco station, a migration office. Near the fort is a Hondutel. As yet there are no private phone lines in Omoa.

Buses return to Puerto Cortés until 6 p.m. For those returning directly to San Pedro Sula from Omoa, ask the driver to stop at the highway junction outside of Puerto Cortés, where the direct San Pedro buses stop to fill up with passengers.

Getting to and from Guatemala
Formerly a long walk through the jungle, the border crossing to Puerto Barrios in Guatemala can now be accomplished by a combination of buses and canoe rides taking four to six hours, depending on connections. Buses from Omoa or Puerto Cortés go as far as Cuyamelito, a village just past Tegucigalpita, where you can walk or take a US$1 taxi ride to the riverside. From here a canoe escorts travelers to the Río Tinto, where a second canoe continues to the Río Motagua and on to the bus stop on the Guatemalan side. An early departure is recommended to ensure arrival in Puerto Barrios before the migration office closes. Although there is a migration office in Omoa, it's best to take care of exit stamps in Puerto Cortés.

A quicker though less interesting route is to take a boat to Livingston, Guatemala, which leaves Omoa Tuesday and Friday at about noon when the weather is good. The very wet trip costs US$27.

Cayos Zapotillos
Tucked into the Gulf of Amatique are the Cayos Zapotillos, a collection of beautiful little islands whose ownership is unclear. The cays—Hunting Cay, Lime Cay, Nicholas Cay, Raggedy Cay, and French Cay—are claimed by Honduras, Belize, and Guatemala. Until recently not much attention was paid to the dispute, but the three governments have evidently realized the coral reefs and good beaches have excellent tourist potential and have begun bickering about jurisdiction. Boats going to the cays can be hired in Omoa, although it might be necessary to pay for a special trip, which would not be cheap.

Bajamar and Travesía
East of Puerto Cortés on the coast are the two

Garífuna villages of Travesía and Bajamar, which can be reached by frequent local buses. Shortly before Travesía is the inexpensive **Hotel Fronteras del Caribe,** with minimal facilities. There are no hotels in Bajamar, but you can find a room by asking around, or ask any resi-dents you see for permission to sling a hammock on the beach.

Bajamar is the site of the annual National Garífuna Festival, normally held in late July, which draws Garífuna from Belize, Guatemala, and Honduras for a party of dancing and music.

TELA AND VICINITY

INTRODUCTION

Honduran tourism officials, hoping to mimic Mexico's success with planned resorts, have designated Tela Bay as Honduras's Cancún-to-be. Whether their grandiose plans will succeed is anyone's guess, but all the elements appear to be in place: mile upon mile of pristine beaches, sleepy Garífuna villages, two natural reserves chock-full of exotic plant and animal life, and wealthy investors willing to pour millions into developing state-of-the-art tourist complexes. For the time being, however, it's still all hypothetical. Construction has begun on a resort near Triunfo de la Cruz, east of Tela, but Tela residents are still waiting to see what will happen.

Reactions to present-day undeveloped Tela vary wildly. Some visitors are charmed by the town's relaxed seediness, while others take a look at the low-life contingent hanging around the beachfront discos and hastily pack their bags. There's no doubt the downtown beach area is not pristine, but it would be a shame to let this put travelers off from seeing the tranquil beachfront villages and spectacular natural beauty around the bay.

Originally Tela (pop. 77,100) was built as a United Fruit Company town at the turn of the century, but the banana business affects the local economy less since the Tela Railroad Company—United's Honduras division—moved its headquarters to La Lima, near San Pedro Sula, in 1965. Currently the town earns most of its money from African palm plantations, cattle ranching, and tourism.

Street crime has been a problem in Tela, but less so since local merchants recently banded together to pay for several more police officers. Nonetheless, walking around on the downtown beach near the discos or in the south part of town near the railroad tracks after dark is not recommended.

Orientation and Getting Around

A couple of kilometers off the El Progreso-La Ceiba highway, downtown Tela is a compact area bounded by the ocean, the Río Tela, and the railroad tracks. The square is two blocks from the beach. The Río Tela divides the main downtown area from so-called "New Tela," a residential area built by the Tela Railroad Company for its U.S. officials. Apart from a couple of bars and restaurants, the only reason to go to New Tela is to enjoy the beaches in front of Telamar. Taxis anywhere around downtown, to New Tela, or out to the highway should cost US 50 cents pp.

SIGHTS

First stop for most visitors, the town's sweeping **beaches** are wide and fairly clean. The beach in front of the discos and restaurants, however, does not lend itself to peaceful sunbathing—there are just too many people wandering around, and leaving your possessions while taking a dip is an invitation to theft. A better spot is the beach in front of Telamar, in New Tela past the river and the municipal dock. It is very clean and constantly patrolled by the resort's guards.

Dedicated to the fascinating and little-understood Black Carib culture of Honduras's north coast is the **Museo Garífuna,** on the banks of the Río Tela four blocks back from the beach, tel. 48-2904. Open Mon.-Sat. 8 a.m.-6 p.m., the small, two-story museum managed by a friendly and informative staff features displays on aspects of Garífuna life such as fishing techniques, food preparation, household arrangements, and spiritual ceremonies. Downstairs a gift shop sells musical instruments, sculptures, clothes, and other *artesanías.* Admission is US 40 cents pp. In an adjacent building a restaurant serves traditional Garífuna food.

Worth taking a look at on the way to Telamar beach, if only for historical value, is the ruined hulk of the **Tela Railroad Company headquarters,** near the dock in New Tela. It was formerly the command center for the United Fruit empire, which is now based in La Lima, near San Pedro Sula.

Tour Operators

A couple of doors off the square, **Garífuna Tours,** tel./fax 48-2904, offers popular day-trips to Punta Sal for US$16 pp, including a guide and boat transport. Guides are supposedly bilingual, but often speak only minimal English and need to be encouraged to give any information. Still, the trip is an easy way to get to Punta Sal with minimal hassle. Sign up the day before, and be prepared to get wet in the boat. Tours to Punta Izopo, Laguna de los Micos, and the Garífuna village of Miami are also available. The company also rents mountain bikes for US$4 half-day or US$6 full-day.

A lesser-known outfit is **Marymar Tours,** tel. 48-2420, with similar trips to Punta Sal, Punta Izopo, and elsewhere. This family-run operation is located near the entrance to Telamar.

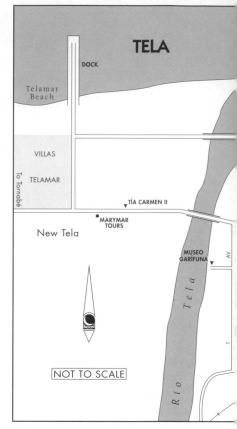

ACCOMMODATIONS

Budget

Many travelers have the unfortunate idea that **Boarding House Sara's** is the only decent budget hotel in town. In truth, despite the hoards of backpackers who patronize it, Sara's is not a particularly good deal. For US$5 you get a fairly grimy double room right next to the discos, which blast music into the wee hours Thurs.-Sunday.

A better value is **Hotel Olas del Mar,** also a dive but with large, breezy rooms and an ocean-facing balcony for US$5 d with private bath and fan. Be sure to request a room on the side of the hotel opposite the discos if you have any desire to sleep.

For a few more lempira, **Hotel Marazul** offers clean, quiet rooms with fans and private bath near the beach for US$3 s or US$6.50 d.

Two cheapies near the bus station are **Hotel Preluna,** charging US$2.50 d in a rickety old wooden house, and **Hotelito Mi Porvenir,** with cell-like but clean rooms for US$3.50 d on the second floor.

Four blocks in from the beach near the post office is **Hotel Posada del Sol,** tel. 48-2111, with clean rooms around a quiet garden and patio for US$4 s or US$7 d with private bath and fan.

Midrange Beach Hotels

Catering mainly to wealthy San Pedro Sula residents who flood in during the weekend are four hotels on the beach west of the discos. Overpriced at

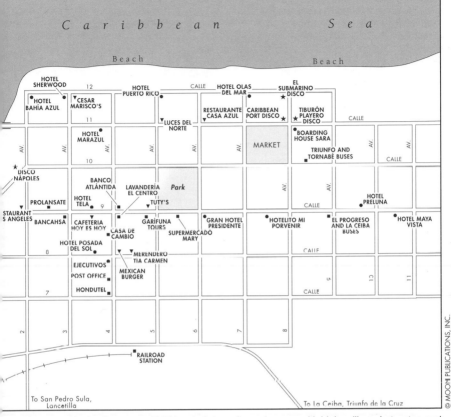

US$23 s or d for basic rooms with TV and a/c is the large **Hotel Puerto Rico,** tel. 48-2413, with an open-air restaurant on the first floor. Some rooms have breezy porches facing the ocean.

Similarly priced but with larger and better-kept rooms are **Hotel Cesar Marisco's,** tel./fax 48-2083, with six modern rooms and superb seafood, and **Hotel Bahía Azul,** tel. 48-2381, at the mouth of the Río Tela.

Hotel Sherwood, tel. 48-2416, fax 48-2294, between Hotel Bahía Azul and Cesar Marisco's, has more elegant rooms, some with private, ocean-facing balconies, for US$38-43 d.

Midrange Hotels in Town

The venerable **Hotel Tela,** tel. 48-2150, two blocks west of the square, offers breezy, tile-floored rooms with high ceilings, hot water, and ceiling fans for US$8 s or US$15 d. The hotel dining room is spacious and elegant.

On the square, the modern **Gran Hotel Presidente,** tel. 48-2821 or 48-2671, fax 48-2992, has comfortable though small rooms with TV, hot water, telephones, and a/c for US$30 d with two beds or US$21 d with one bed. Room service is available from the hotel cafeteria.

Clearly the realization of a personal vision of paradise is **Hotel Maya Vista,** a massive pink structure perched high on a hill just east of the bus station, offering breathtaking views across the bay. Built by French-Canadian owner Pierre Couture, who it seems will keep adding on until there's nowhere else to build, the hotel currently has six double rooms for US$20-50, depending on the size of the room and whether it has kitchen facilities. Pierre and his wife are wonderful hosts and will sometimes whip up a meal for guests if they're in the mood. It's more like staying in a private house than in a hotel. Be sure to make reservations as they often have friends staying with them. Send a fax to Hondutel at 48-2942, and they will respond.

For those looking for self-contained apartments, **Ejecutivos,** tel./fax 48-2047, features eight spacious rooms with kitchens, a/c, and color TVs in a modern, gleaming white building a block from the post office; US$30 d.

Luxury
A sort of tropical suburb, certainly unlike any other resort on the Honduran coast, **Villas Telamar,** tel. 48-2196 or 48-2197, fax 48-2984, in U.S. (800) 742-4276, was built by the Tela Railroad Company in the 1920s to house its U.S. executives. The freestanding wooden houses, each with hardwood floors, wicker and mahogany furniture, a fully equipped kitchen, and immaculately maintained lawn, are located in a well-patrolled complex along a beautiful beach just west of the Río Tela. Facilities include a pool (which can be used by nonguests for US$2), a nine-hole golf course, tennis courts, a sauna, jacuzzi, banquet and conference center, horseback riding, boating, and fishing. Villas go for US$110-350 a night with two to seven double beds, and single rooms and suites are also available for US$60-80. Some houses are in much better condition than others, so it's best to look at what's available before checking in.

FOOD

Inexpensive
Merendero Tía Carmen serves legendary *baleadas* stuffed with various fixings, as well as tacos, simple meals, and fresh juices in a cafeteria a block south of the square. The first batch of *baleadas* usually sells out by 9 a.m. at the latest, but a second batch is made around 4 p.m. A second Tía Carmen's across the bridge in New Tela has *baleadas* all day until 10 or 11 p.m., and the owners are much friendlier, too.

Opposite Garífuna Tours next to the square, **Tuty's** serves excellent *licuados* and juices, and decent breakfasts as well, Mon.-Sat. 6 a.m.-2 p.m. Be prepared to wait; service is terrible.

A popular spot for inexpensive meals and beers downtown is **Cafeteria Hoy es Hoy,** on 9 Calle between 3 and 4 Avenidas, open daily 8 a.m.-10 p.m. For inexpensive burgers, *tortas,* and tacos for lunch, try **Mexican Burger** near the post office.

Restaurant Los Angeles, 9 Calle between 1 and 2 Avenidas, serves up a decent chop suey and other Chinese dishes daily for lunch and dinner.

Midrange
A favorite among foreign visitors is **Luces del Norte,** on the corner of 11 Calle and 5 Avenida between the square and the beach. Service can be painstakingly slow but it's worth the wait for the divine curried conch soup, lobster, grilled snapper, and very good breakfasts. The restaurant has a large secondhand-book exchange. Open daily 7 a.m.-10 p.m.

Also serving a sublime conch soup and other seafood dishes is **Cesar Marisco's,** 3 Avenida, tel. 48-2083, with open-air seating facing the beach; open daily 7 a.m.-10 p.m.

If you've overdosed on seafood and are looking for a change of pace, try the expatriate-run **Restaurante Casa Azul,** 11 Calle and 6 Avenida, for well-prepared Italian food. The small menu includes lasagna, fettuccine, addictive garlic bread, and a wine selection (though the wines don't hold up well in the tropical heat) for US$3-5 per plate. The restaurant at the **Hotel Bahía Azul** serves excellent breakfasts at a reasonable price, but their other meals are not as good a value.

BOB RACE

The **Museo Garífuna restaurant** prepares hearty traditional Garífuna dishes, including cassava, *tapado* (a fish, cassava, and coconut dish), and *machuca* (fish with banana and coconut milk). The service is attentive and the setting, an open-air porch on the river's edge, is peaceful. Open for three meals a day Mon.-Sat. until 9 p.m., with live music and dancing on Saturday evenings.

ENTERTAINMENT

Tela is second only to La Ceiba for nightlife on the north coast. A cluster of discos on the beach on the east side of town, including **El Submarino, Caribbean Port,** and **Tiburón Playero** are the center of the action, with large crowds meandering back and forth between them until daybreak on weekends. The crowds can get violent, with shootings and knifings not uncommon, although mostly the violence stems from drunken brawls over girlfriends and is not aimed at foreign visitors. Expect to be propositioned by prostitutes and persistent drug dealers. In town, **Disco Nápoles** is also a hopping spot, considered to have the best dancing in Tela.

Telamar has a more upscale bar/disco on the beach, with occasional live bands. Across from the bus station is a decent nameless **pool hall** with reasonably well-kept tables, beer for sale, and a relatively clean atmosphere.

INFORMATION AND SERVICES

Bancahsa and Banco Atlántida, both downtown, change traveler's checks and cash Mon.-Fri. and Saturday mornings. For quicker, hassle-free exchange, Casa de Cambio Teleña is open Mon.-Fri. 8-11:45 a.m. and 1-4:30 p.m., Saturday 8 a.m.-noon.

Hondutel, open daily 7 a.m.-9 p.m., fax 48-2942, and Correos, open Mon.-Fri. 8 a.m.-4 p.m., Saturday 8 a.m.-noon, are on the same block two blocks southwest of the square.

One block west of the square is **Lavandería El Centro,** open Mon.-Sat.; US$2 for one load wash and dry. **Supermercado Mary** on the square has a good selection of groceries and is open Mon.-Sat. 8 a.m.-8 p.m., Sunday 8 a.m.-noon.

TELA
USEFUL TELEPHONE NUMBERS

Police: 48-2079, or dial 199
Fire Department: 48-2350, or dial 198
Cruz Roja Ambulance: 48-2121, or dial 195
Hospital Rotario: 48-2073, 48-2051

Prolansate, tel./fax 48-2042, is a local environmental organization that helps manage nearby natural protected areas—a mission that does not always endear its staff to ranchers, developers, and land-hungry campesinos. The Prolansate office is downtown next to the cinema; open Mon.-Fri. 7 a.m.-noon and 2-5 p.m. Simple maps and some tourist information are available.

GETTING THERE AND AWAY

Bus

Surprisingly, there are no direct buses from Tela to San Pedro Sula. Travelers must either take a bus to El Progreso from the downtown terminal, and transfer to a San Pedro bus, or take a taxi out to the highway at Tío Jaime's Restaurant and flag down one of the La Ceiba or Trujillo buses going to San Pedro (US$2) which pass every half hour or so. The restaurant sells tickets for direct buses to Tegucigalpa (US$5, three runs daily, last bus leaves at 1 p.m.).

Those going via El Progreso would do well to wait for the twice-daily direct bus, which takes an hour to make the trip (US$1, Mon.-Fri. 7:30 a.m. and 8:45 a.m.; Saturday and Sunday 3 p.m. and 4:15 p.m.). The local bus on that route (US 50 cents, every hour or so) takes at least twice as long. Buses to La Ceiba, none direct, take two to three hours, but should take less time if the highway ever gets repaired (US$1, every half-hour or so until 6 p.m.).

Car

The 68-km, two-lane road to El Progreso through African palm and banana plantations is in good shape, and the additional 28 km to San Pedro Sula is an excellent four-lane highway. To the east, on the other hand, the 101 km of "pavement" to La Ceiba is abysmal and takes at least an hour and a half even in a private car. Don't go very fast unless you want to break an axle slamming into a lurking pothole.

Train

The train to Puerto Cortés (4-5 hours, US$1), which travels through coastal banana plantations, leaves from the decrepit train station several blocks south of the square Friday and Sunday at 1:45 p.m.

WEST OF TELA

Tornabé

Seven km west of Tela via a rough dirt road is the quiet Garífuna village of Tornabé. Lined along a dirt road just back from the beach, it's a perfect place to relax and be mesmerized by the sun and waves. Further west, between Tornabé and Miami, work has begun on the Tela Bay Project, a massive planned tourist complex located in the buffer zone of the Punta Sal National Park. Local fishermen are often happy to take visitors out to Punta Sal for a negotiable fee, either dropping them off for the day or acting as guides.

Near the center of town the Garífuna couple **Chola and Tritio** manage basic candlelit cabins, US$3 s or d, with home-cooked seafood and beers for sale.

One of the finest accommodations in Tela Bay, in terms of peace and quiet per dollar, is **The Last Resort**, tel./fax 48-2545, or in Tegucigalpa tel./fax 36-9287. Air conditioned cabins with private bath go for US$55 a night—a bit expensive, but it's the perfect place to go if you're looking to get away from it all but still have all the creature comforts. The restaurant serves mouthwatering seafood and is worth patronizing even if you're not staying at the resort. A motorized catamaran is also available for excursions.

Buses between Tornabé and Tela (US 25 cents) depart several times a day at irregular hours, the last in either direction usually at 5 p.m. Buses leave Tela from near the market. Trucks leave Tornabé heading west to Miami Mon.-Sat. three times daily, charging US 30 cents for the 20-minute ride.

Miami

The idyllic Garífuna village of Miami rests on a narrow sand spit, backed by the broad Laguna de los Micos and fronted by the Caribbean. Unlike Tornabé or Triunfo, Miami is almost totally undeveloped, with most families still living in the traditional Garífuna thatched huts. Facilities are minimal—if you want to spend more than the day here ask around for food and a room or

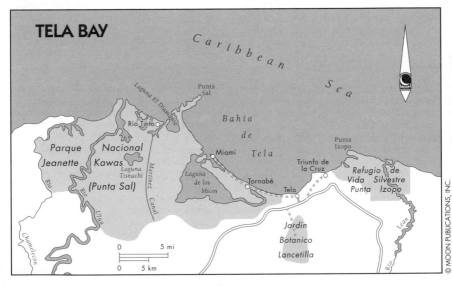

TELA BAY

Caribbean Sea

Punta Sal

Laguna El Diamante

Río Tinto

Bahía de Tela

Punta Izopo

Parque Nacional Jeanette Kawas

Laguna Tisnachí

(Punta Sal)

Miami

Triunfo de la Cruz

Refugio de Vida Silvestre Punta Izopo

Martínez Canal

Laguna de los Micos

Tornabé

Tela

Río Ulúa

Río

Chamelecón

0   5 mi

0   5 km

Jardín Botánico Lancetilla

Río Lean

© MOON PUBLICATIONS, INC.

JEANETTE KAWAS, ENVIRONMENTAL ACTIVIST

The national park at Punta Sal is named for Jeanette Kawas, the former president of Prolansate, an environmental organization dedicated to protecting Punta Sal, Punta Izopo, Lancetilla, and Texiguat. In Honduras, as Kawas discovered, defending the environment is more than signing petitions and sending out leaflets, as it is in the U.S. or western Europe. It's a matter of life and death.

Several different groups and individuals have claimed ownership of Punta Sal land, including Honduran colonel Mario "El Tigre" Amaya and an African palm cooperative run by the National Campesino Union, among others.

Kawas forcefully advocated the creation of a national park at Punta Sal. Although the effort was ultimately successful—national-park status was granted in November 1994—she paid the price for her activism. Kawas was killed in April 1995, and her murder remains unsolved.

BOB RACE

Jeanette Kawas

a place to sling a hammock. One room with space for a hammock is usually available next to the only store in Miami.

Motorized and paddle canoes can be rented to explore the lagoon. More territory can be covered with the motor, but it also scares wildlife away. Locals say camping on the inland side of the lagoon is possible, and would be excellent for early morning birdwatching.

Small boats are also available to take visitors to Punta Sal. For the budget camper, the absolute cheapest way to get out to Punta Sal from Tela is to get to Miami by bus and truck, then walk eight km on the beach out to the point.

Parque Nacional Jeanette Kawas (Punta Sal)

One of the most biologically diverse natural reserves in Honduras, the 782 square km of protected territory around Punta Sal includes humid tropical forest, mangrove swamp, coastal lagoons, rivers and canals, rocky and sandy coastline, coral reef, and ocean. Almost 500 types of plants have been identified within the park, as well as 232 animal species, including endangered marine turtles, manatees, jaguars, ocelots *(tigrillos)*, caimans, white-faced and howler monkeys, wild pigs, pelicans, and toucans.

Most tours arrive by boat at the base of the point on the east side, offering visitors a chance to enjoy a beautiful beach before taking a half-

hour hike over the point to the lovely cove on the far side. This steep trail is a good opportunity to see the abundant and colorful bird life, as well as noisy troops of howler and white-faced monkeys.

Apart from the rugged and beautiful 176-meter-high Punta Sal, most of the reserve's territory is flat, and encompasses the Los Micos, Diamante, Río Tinto, and Tisnachí lagoons, the Martinez and Chambers canals, and the Río Ulúa. The Río Chamelecón forms the western boundary of the park. Traveling up these waterways by boat provides excellent opportunities for viewing wildlife—binoculars and mosquito repellent at the ready.

No facilities are available in the park apart from one small *champa* on the point which sells meals to tour groups. Camping on the beach is accepted and would be a superb way to spend a few days; come prepared with food, fresh water, and a tent or hammock. Although tour operators like to tout the great snorkeling, there's little in the way of interesting reef, possibly because the water is usually too choppy to enjoy. Certainly don't expect anything on the level of the Bay Islands.

Although most visitors arrive by boat, road access exists to villages in the southern part of the park, leaving from a sign-posted turnoff on the west side of the Tela-El Progreso highway, past Lancetilla.

There is currently no entrance fee to the park.

EAST AND SOUTH OF TELA

Triunfo de la Cruz

Another Garífuna town similar to Tornabé, Triunfo is eight km east of Tela. The beach in town, though lined by fishing boats and not kept conspicuously clean, is an excellent quiet place to sunbathe and swim in the warm waters. Locals are not bothered by visitors, and though they may not seem very friendly at first, neither do they hassle the few backpackers who come in search of a little peace and sun. Still, beware of sleeping on the beach in Triunfo, as tourists have reported being robbed at gunpoint. The beaches are safe during the day, but at night it's best to stick to one of the hotels.

Tourism officials are reportedly helping organize a group of locals to perform a traditional *dugu* dance for visitors. Triunfo's annual festival is held on 3 May, the Day of the Cross.

Roughly in the center of town, on the beach, are a cluster of simple thatched cabañas run by **Panchi** for US$3.50 d, and next door are concrete ones managed by **Margarito Colón** for US$6 d. A friendly watchman keeps an eye on things so visitors can relax without fear of theft. Others in town rent out rooms for similar prices.

Jorge's Restaurant, just east of the hotels, serves up some of the meatiest and most succulent fried snapper this author has ever tasted, as well as a hearty, veggie-filled conch stew. Locals will come around the hotels to see if anyone wants breakfast cooked for them.

Several buses daily run to and from Tela (US 30 cents). The buses leave Tela from near the market, the last returning to Tela in mid-afternoon. A taxi to Triunfo costs about US$3, and sometimes one that has just dropped off passengers in Triunfo will give a ride back to Tela for US 50 cents. Formerly the two- to three-hour walk to Tela via the small village of **La Ensenada** was a pleasant way to return from Triunfo, but recently several muggings have been reported, so don't go alone. Nearby is the site of Cristóbal de Olid's first landfall on Honduras, marking the beginning of Spanish colonization. Triunfo was originally established as a settlement by Olid, but the colonists soon moved elsewhere and the area was not permanently occupied until the Garífuna moved there from Trujillo in the early 1800s.

Jardín Botánico Lancetilla

A small miracle of botanical science five km south of Tela, Lancetilla was first set up in 1925 by the legendary William Popenoe of United Fruit Company, who is also responsible for starting the Escuela de Sciencias Agrícolas in the Valle de Zamorano, near Tegucigalpa. Initially Lancetilla was designed as a research station for testing different varieties of bananas, but Popenoe's endless inquisitiveness soon led to experiments with fruits and plants from all over the world. One of Honduras's most profitable agricultural products, the African oil palm, *Elaeis guineensis,* was first introduced by Popenoe in Lancetilla, and further work was done with coffee, cinchona (the source of quinine, for years the only treatment for malaria), cacao, rubber, mango, and a myriad of other plants.

Although Popenoe left Lancetilla in 1941 to go to Zamorano, United Fruit continued the work he began until 1974, when Lancetilla was turned over to the Honduran government. The garden has since become part of the Escuela de Sciencias Forestales and is still a fully functioning research station.

Lancetilla boasts one of the most preeminent collections of fruit trees, flowering trees, hardwoods, palm trees, bamboo, and other assorted medicinal and poisonous plants in Latin America. Named after the indigenous lancetilla palm, *Astrocaryum standleyanum,* Lancetilla contains 764 varieties of plants in 636 species, 392 genera, and 105 families on a mere 78 hectares in the William Popenoe Arboretum, and a further 60 species of fruit and hardwood trees in the experimental research station.

The Lancetilla Biological Reserve, in the surrounding hillsides, contains both primary and secondary tropical humid and subtropical humid forest. Getting into the reserve requires some effort as there are no trails designed for tourists. For the US$5 entrance fee, visitors are given an hour-long guided tour of a section of the arboretum, and are then free to wander the paths for the rest of the day. Many plants are labeled to help identification. Labels are color-coded as follows: green indicates hardwood, red indicates fruit, yellow indicates ornamental, and most important, black indicates poisonous. Feel free to sample fallen fruit, but be sure not to try anything from a black-labeled tree! Keep an eye out for the mangosteen trees, *Garcinia mangostana,* a

Malaysian native considered by some connoisseurs to produce the finest fruit on the planet. Mosquitoes are often fierce in the arboretum, so be sure to come prepared.

Just under two km from the visitor's center, past groves of palms and bamboo, are two swimming holes along the Río Lancetilla. Though unspectacular, they're a good way to cool off after a hot walk.

You can arrange guides and purchase maps of the arboretum and a self-guided tour of one of the trails at the large, wooden visitor's center. There's also a cafeteria here, a pleasant place to write a letter or wait for a guide while sipping a cold drink.

Lancetilla is open Mon.-Fri. 7:30 a.m.-3 p.m., Sat.-Sun. 8 a.m.-3 p.m. Bunk beds are available in a hostel for US$4 a bed, but these are often taken by the many research and student groups who visit the gardens. Check with Prolansate in Tela, tel. 48-2042, to make reservations.

The highway turn-off to Lancetilla is just south of the power station outside of Tela. You could take an El Progreso bus, get off at the junction, and walk the 45 minutes into the gardens, or take a taxi from town for US$3.50. Another good option is to rent a bike at Garífuna Tours and pedal out at your own pace. The entrance fee is collected at a *caseta* at the highway junction, where there is also a small nursery selling fruit and palm-tree seedlings for US$1-2.

Refugio de Vida Silvestre Punta Izopo

Visible around the bay to the east of Triunfo is Punta Izopo, Tela Bay's second largest protected area, covering 112 square km, of which about half is a buffer zone and half is a supposedly untouchable nuclear zone. Much less frequently visited than Punta Sal but with similar ecosystems and wildlife, the swamps and waterways stretching into the jungle south of the point are superb for bird and animal watching.

Inside the reserve's boundaries are the small Río Plátano (not to be confused with the river of same name in Mosquitia) and Río Hicaque, the larger Río Lean on the point's eastern side, as well as kilometers of swamps, lagoons, and estuaries. Several small settlements are also located inside the boundaries of the reserve, including Hicaque, Las Palmas, Coloradito, and the intimidatingly named Salsipuedes (Get Out If You Can). Near the base of Punta Izopo a massive, US$60 million tourist development named Marbella is being built with the backing of the World Bank and the Central American Bank for Economic Integration. The project is opposed by environmentalists, who say the hotel will harm the ecosystems in the reserve, and by some Triunfo residents, who are unsure they want a huge tourist resort right next door to their quiet community.

The easiest access to the reserve is with a tour operator such as Garífuna Tours or Marymar Tours in Tela. Both normally take a dirt road east from Triunfo to the Río Plátano, where the river trips begin. A low-budget option is to hunt around Triunfo for a local willing to rent a dory (US$5 a day would be a reasonable amount for a two-person wooden boat with oars) and paddle out to the point with a companion. Don't try it alone as it's a lot of work to fight the waves. Once at the point you can muck around on the beach or walk around the point (beware the hordes of sand flies), or cross the low sandbar into the Río Plátano or Hicaque and paddle up the waterways.

LA CEIBA AND VICINITY

INTRODUCTION

The largest city on the north coast, with a population of just over 100,000 and growing, La Ceiba is not particularly attractive on first glance, but those who give it a chance may find themselves charmed. The beaches are dirty, there is no architecture of interest, and it's almost always steaming hot, but La Ceiba has a certain carefree Caribbean joie de vivre that has earned it the nickname "Honduras's girlfriend."

The most overt expression of this spirit is the unsurpassed nightlife and dancing scene centered on a strip of discos right along the beach, where you can boogie until all hours practically every night of the week. There's no doubt about it—*ceibeños* know how to party. As the saying goes, "Tegucigalpa piensa, San Pedro trabaja, y La Ceiba divierta" ("Tegucigalpa thinks, San Pedro works, and La Ceiba has fun"). The town's good times culminate in the annual Feria de San Isidro, or Carnaval, a weeklong bash of dancing and music held in May.

La Ceiba is a convenient base to explore nearby nature refuges such as Pico Bonito, the Cuero y Salado wetlands, and the rapid-filled Río Cangrejal, as well as the nearby beach towns of Corozal and Sambo Creek. It's also an inevitable stop-off point for travelers on their way to the Bay Islands, Trujillo, or Mosquitia, and is a good place to stop and take care of any business that needs attending while on the road.

History

For most of its existence, La Ceiba has been a Standard Fruit Company town, and essentially this is still the case. The area's first settlers were a few Garífuna families from Trujillo who built a village on the west side of the estuary in 1810. They were followed by Olancho immigrants fleeing violence in their homeland in the 1820s. One of these *olanchanos,* Manuel Hernández, built his house near a massive ceiba tree, which became the town's informal gathering place. The tree was cut down in 1917 to make way for the customs building, but the name stuck.

In the late 19th century, La Ceiba was in the midst of the booming banana industry. The first banana plantations on the mainland were planted near the mouth of the Río Cangrejal, and others soon followed in the vicinity. But the population of La Ceiba was still only about 2,000 when the Vaccaro brothers of New Orleans arrived in 1899, scouting for banana lands. They were awarded a concession at Porvenir, just west of La Ceiba, and quickly built a railroad track to transport their fruit to La Ceiba, where it could be shipped north. By 1905 the Vaccaros had moved their company headquarters to La Ceiba, and began transforming the town.

The company offices and housing for American employees were built in what came to be known as the Mazapan district, unsubtly surrounded by high cyclone fencing. The Vaccaros—who by 1926 had named their operation the Standard Fruit and Steamship Company—built the city dock, managed the town port, supplied the city's electric power, set up the first bank, built the D'Antoni Hospital, and even brewed the first version of Salvavida, one of Honduras's most popular beers.

Standard's business quickly expanded to the Trujillo region and into the rich Aguán Valley, and in the process attracted workers from across the globe, turning La Ceiba into one of the north coast's great cultural melting pots, along with Puerto Cortés. Garífuna, Honduran campesinos, Jamaicans, Cayman Islanders, North Americans, Arabs, Italians, Spanish, French, and Cubans, to name only the most prominent, all lived side by side in La Ceiba—their mark can still be seen on the city today.

Standard Fruit—now Dole—is still La Ceiba's largest employer, although it has long since diversified into pineapple, African palm oil, and a myriad of other agricultural products. Most of its produce is now shipped out of Puerto Castilla, near Trujillo; the dock in La Ceiba is no longer used.

Orientation and Getting Around

Although La Ceiba is the largest city on the north coast, visitors usually spend most of their time in

LA FERIA DE SAN ISIDRO

In a town notorious for partying, the Feria de San Isidro is *the* party in La Ceiba—a several-day bash culminating in a blowout Saturday night that attracts some 200,000 revelers from across Honduras and the Caribbean. The country may have other national celebrations, but the Feria—held in mid-May—is Honduras's time to cut loose.

According to La Ceiba legend, three Spanish immigrants started the Feria. The Spaniards—supposedly named Norquer, Artuche, and Pallares—arrived in the village in 1846, bringing with them the tradition of honoring San Isidro Labrador, a patron saint of campesinos. According to custom they held a party in honor of the saint. The annual fiesta became a popular event with the Garífuna, who although hardly campesinos themselves, are always ready for a reason to get out and dance. It quickly became a local institution. The Feria was declared La Ceiba's official annual fiesta in 1886, and in 1929 the tradition of parades and floats was added.

On the final Saturday of the Feria, floats bearing scantily clad women proceed down Avenida San Isidro beginning in the late afternoon, headed by the Queen of the Carnaval. After the parade has passed, well-known Honduran and Central American bands on stages lined up and down the length of the avenue crank up, and the music keeps going until morning.

Many visitors, expecting to see crazed dancing in the streets, come away from Carnaval a bit disappointed. The only ones dancing, usually, are the fans at the rock stage who have a grand time headbanging and slam dancing, and the occasional group of gringos in front of one of the salsa or *punta* stages.

The secret, for those who really want to dance, is to enjoy the stage music on the avenue until midnight or 1 a.m., and then head out to the discos on 1 Calle. Normally packed anyway on weekends, the discos are bursting at the seams during the Feria, and should not be missed by the serious partyer. When out on the streets during the Feria, beware of pickpockets in the crowds.

Saturday may be the official biggest party, but many locals insist the "real" bash is on Friday night in Barrio La Isla, with bands on 4 Calle on the east side of the estuary from downtown. Other mini-ferias take place the previous Sunday in Sitramacsa and Miramar colonias, Monday in Barrio Bellavista, Tuesday in Barrio Alvarado, Wednesday in Colonia Alhambra, and Thursday in Colonia El Sauce. La Ceiba on the Sunday following Carnaval is usually utterly and completely dead, with most people rousing themselves only if there's a decent soccer match on TV.

---

a relatively small area bounded by the square, the sea, and the strip of discos and beach to the east of the estuary, which divides the downtown area from the La Isla and La Barra neighborhoods. Taxis within this area should only cost US 50 cents pp, but expect drivers to stop and pick up other passengers. The main drag in town is Avenida San Isidro, running from the ocean south past the square all the way to the Burger King on 22 Calle.

SIGHTS AND RECREATION

La Ceiba is not bursting with tourist attractions. The town's beaches are downright filthy and not very safe, which is unfortunate since they could be cleaned up without much effort. The only halfway decent bit of sand and sea is **La Barra Beach,** east of downtown, between the

Partenon Beach Hotel and the mouth of the Río Cangrejal (hence the beach's name: "barra" is used in Honduras to designate a river mouth).

The downtown **square** is nothing special, but take a look at the crocodile pen on the south side, where a dozen or so reptiles sit immobile for hours sunning themselves on their concrete pedestals, looking like statues. The nearby main commercial district, centered on Avenida Atlántida and Avenida 14 de Julio, between 4 and 6 Calles, is a lively and colorful scene. The central market is a 1931-vintage, weather-beaten wooden building at 6 Calle and Avenida Atlántida.

Anyone with an entomological inclination should be sure not to miss the **Museo de Mariposas,** tel. 42-2874, e-mail: rlehman@gbm.hn, displaying over 5,000 Honduran butterflies and 400 from other countries. Also included are examples of the two largest butterflies in the world, as well as over 1,000 other insects. Apart from

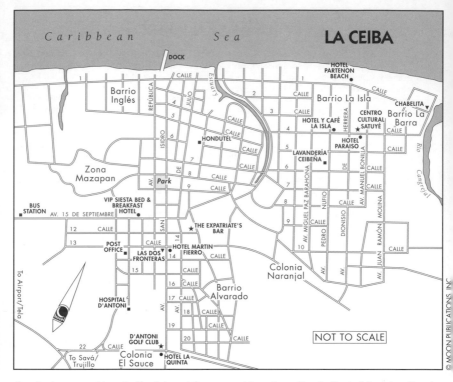

the displays are videos in English and Spanish, posters, maps, and all the gear needed to become an amateur butterfly collector, including traps and ultraviolet lights. The museum is in Colonia El Sauce just south of the golf course, Segunda Etapa, Casa G-12, US$1.50 entrance for adults, US$1 for students. Open Mon.-Sat. 8 a.m.-noon and 2-5 p.m.; closed Wednesday afternoons.

At the southern end of Avenida San Isidro is the **D'Antoni Golf Club** for the links addict. Two rounds on the nine-hole, relatively flat course cost US$20 for nonmembers; club rental is an additional US$3. The tennis courts, pool, restaurant, and bar are for members and their guests only.

Tour Operators

Several outfits run rafting trips on the Río Cangrejal. Less than an hour south of La Ceiba, the river is considered to have some of the best whitewater rafting in Central America. Two La Ceiba companies specializing in rafting are **Ríos Honduras,** tel./fax 43-0780, and **Tropical River Rafting,** tel./fax 43-2055.

For hiking and boat trips to Pico Bonito, Cuero y Salado, and other nearby natural areas, two recommended tour operators are **Euro Honduras Tours,** 1 Calle at Avenida Atlántida, tel. 43-3893, tel./fax 43-0933, a very well-managed outfit with guides who speak English, French, and German; and **La Moskitia Eco Aventuras,** on Parque Bonilla, tel. 42-0104, tel./fax 37-9398. La Moskitia specializes in trips to Mosquitia, including the famed Olancho-to-coast 10-12 day expedition (for more information see the Olancho and Mosquitia chapter), but also runs customized local trips.

Ecotours, on San Isidro between 4 and 5 Calles, tel. 43-4026, leads decent inexpensive tours of sites in the vicinity of La Ceiba, but has received poor reviews on its longer trips to Mosquitia.

ACCOMMODATIONS

Fittingly for a city of its size and strategic location—the center of the north coast—La Ceiba has dozens of hotels in all price ranges. With a little effort, visitors should have no trouble finding a room that suits exactly their taste and budget. During Carnaval week hotel owners raise prices considerably, sometimes as much as double, and rooms fill up fast. Generally it's possible to get a room as late as Wednesday during Carnaval week, but after that don't count on it.

Budget

Most inexpensive hotels are found between the square and the ocean, on or between Avenidas San Isidro, Atlántida, and 14 de Julio. For the real lempira-pincher, there are a string of not-recommended dives on Avenida República, parallel to the railroad tracks.

Unquestionably the best inexpensive deal, and often full of backpackers and Hondurans

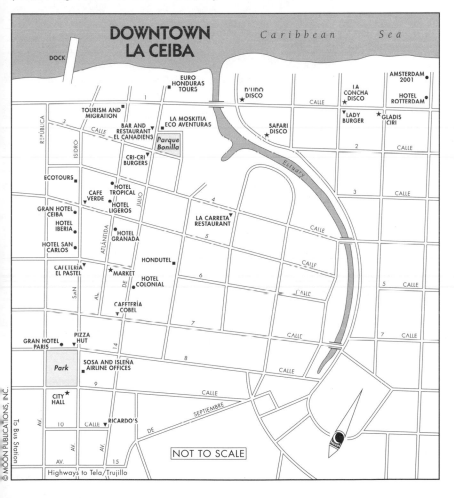

DOWNTOWN LA CEIBA

Caribbean Sea

DOCK

EURO HONDURAS TOURS

D'LIDO DISCO

LA CONCHA DISCO

AMSTERDAM 2001

HOTEL ROTTERDAM

TOURISM AND MIGRATION

LA MOSKITIA ECO AVENTURAS

SAFARI DISCO

LADY BURGER

GLADIS CIRI

BAR AND RESTAURANT EL CANADIENS

Parque Bonilla

Estuary

CRI-CRI BURGERS

ECOTOURS

CAFE VERDE

HOTEL TROPICAL

HOTEL LIGEROS

LA CARRETA RESTAURANT

GRAN HOTEL CEIBA

HOTEL IBERIA

HOTEL GRANADA

HOTEL SAN CARLOS

HONDUTEL

CAFETERIA EL PASTEL

MARKET

HOTEL COLONIAL

CAFETERIA COBEL

PIZZA HUT

GRAN HOTEL PARIS

Park

SOSA AND ISLEÑA AIRLINE OFFICES

CITY HALL

RICARDO'S

SEPTIEMBRE

NOT TO SCALE

To Bus Station

Highways to Tela/Trujillo

© MOON PUBLICATIONS, INC.

*Avenida San Isidro
during La Feria*

as a result, is **Hotel San Carlos,** in the middle of town on Avenida San Isidro between 5 and 6 Calles, above a busy *comedor.* Lots of interesting characters populate the funky rooms, which go for US$3 s and US$4 d with private bath and fan. Some rooms are much better than others but there usually aren't many choices available.

For a few more lempira, the popular **Hotel Tropical,** on Avenida Atlántida between 4 and 5 Calles, tel. 42-2565, offers cleaner and airier rooms, some with TV and a/c, for US$4 s and US$6 d with private bath and fans. The two-story cement-and-plaster building is often filled with Bay Islanders and people in from Mosquitia, but there are usually a couple of rooms open each day. Beers, soft drinks, and bottled water are sold in the lobby—a major bonus on those sweltering afternoons when you're recuperating from a hangover. A reader reported finding an assassin bug in his room.

Next store to the Tropical is **Hotel Ligeros,** tel. 43-0181, with similar rooms for slightly more money, and down a block toward the market on the opposite side of the street is **Hotel Granada,** tel. 43-2451, with relatively clean rooms around a dingy interior courtyard for US$6 s or US$7 d with private bath. Check the mattresses as some are terrible.

A favorite among backpackers, possibly for its location on the beach near the discos, is **Amsterdam 2001,** a ramshackle little dive run by a foul-tempered old Dutch sailor who is no fan of Americans and doesn't appear overly fond of anyone else, either. Beds in the communal room

go for US$3—no great value, considering the San Carlos offers a private room with bath for the same price downtown.

Behind the Amsterdam is the new, two-story **Hotel Rotterdam,** tel. 43-2859, run by the same family but with much friendlier management. Clean rooms with private bath and fans cost US$9 d—no singles available.

Rooms in Barrio La Isla

If you want to stay in the mainly Garífuna neighborhood of La Isla, east of downtown on the other side of the estuary, a decent option is **Hotel y Café La Isla,** on 4 Calle, tel. 43-2835, charging US$6 s and US$7 d with fan and private bath.

A more upscale option—in fact a bit out of place on the dirt roads of La Isla—is **Hotel Paraiso,** a couple of blocks further east on 4 Calle, tel. 43-3535, with clean rooms equipped with cable, a/c, and phones in a modern building with a parking lot and cafeteria. Rooms cost US$12 s or US$18 d.

Midrange

An excellent value located in a quiet neighborhood a few blocks south of the square is **Hotel Martin Fierro,** on Avenida San Isidro at 13 Calle, tel./fax 42-2812. The 10 rooms feature a/c, cable TV, and private baths (as well as some slightly tacky artwork—framed pictures of 18-wheelers in dreamy lighting!) for US$10 s or US$14 d. The attentive and friendly owners offer coffee in the sitting room, and the second-floor porch is a fine spot to smoke a cigarette and watch the day go by.

Two decent hotels downtown, next to each other on Avenida San Isidro between 5 and 6 Calles, are **Hotel Iberia,** tel. 43-0401, and **Gran Hotel Ceiba,** tel./fax 43-2737 or 43-0876. Each offers rooms with a/c, cable TV, hot water, and phones for US$14 s or d, US$20 d with two beds. Both have parking lots.

The only midrange beachside accommodations in La Ceiba are at **Hotel Partenon Beach,** tel. 43-0404, a large complex with three buildings and 110 rooms stretched across a large part of La Barra beach east of downtown. Prices range from US$14-35 d, depending on the room's location and whether it has a fan or a/c. Facilities include a pool, outdoor bar, and screened-in patio restaurant; the Greek owners also plan to open a casino soon.

Useful for those arriving late or departing early by bus is **Gran Hotel Libano,** tel. 43-1102, behind the bus station. It's not a bad deal at US$9 s or US$12 d with TV and a/c.

Luxury

First opened in 1912, the **Hotel Gran Paris** on the square is a Ceiba landmark, and although it may have seen better days it is still a social center for the city, patronized by wealthy Hondurans and foreigners alike. It has 65 rooms, equipped with a/c, TV and phones, and set around an interior courtyard with a pool and bar. Rates run US$28 s, US$31 d, or US$50 suite. Downstairs is a cafeteria and tranquil patio with bar and swimming pool, which nonguests may use for a fee.

Probably a better value for the price downtown is **El Hotel Colonial,** on Avenida 14 de Julio between 6 and 7 Calles, tel. 43-3977, fax 43-1955. Classy but understated, the Colonial has 50 rooms with all the amenities for US$24 s or US$27 d, with a cafeteria, patio bar, parking lot, and sauna (as if it's not hot enough outside).

The small and efficiently managed **VIP Siesta Bed and Breakfast Hotel,** south of downtown on Blvd. 15 de Septiembre, tel. 43-0968 or 43-6970, fax 43-0974, is a favorite with business travelers, offering modern, spacious, and tastefully decorated rooms for US$22 s, US$27 d, or US$50-60 suite. The restaurant is open for breakfast only. The management will arrange a car and English-speaking driver if requested.

Hotel La Quinta, at the south end of Avenida San Isidro, tel. 43-0223, 43-0224, 43-0225, or 43-3194 to -3196, fax 43-0226, is the plushest spot in town, with 110 rooms spread out over a large area interspersed with grassy patios, two pools, and a casino. Rooms range US$23-80, depending on size and location. Inside is Maxim's Restaurant, serving excellent seafood and steaks for US$7-10 per plate and sporting an extensive wine selection.

FOOD

Eateries in La Ceiba consist of beer and burger joints or cafeterias, with little midrange quality food. Apart from the places listed below, innumerable restaurants line 1 Calle and the beach, usually with heavy emphasis on burgers and seafood.

Inexpensive

For excellent breakfasts, *baleadas, pastelitos, platos del día* (daily specials), fresh juices, and other assorted goodies, **Cafeteria El Pastel** is hard to beat. On the corner of Avenida San Isidro and 6 Calle, with doors open to both streets, this is a great place to relax with a coffee and ease into the day. With similar food and prices, though much more crowded (possibly because of the air-conditioning), is **Cafeteria Cobel** on 7 Calle between Avenida Atlántida and Avenida 14 de Julio.

Cri-Cri Burgers on Parque Bonilla cooks up a mean pepper steak sandwich as well as decent burgers, french fries, and other munchies, and is a good place to people-watch if you can stand the full-volume music.

On Avenida Atlántida near the market is **Comida Rápida Maldonado,** with inexpensive burgers and beers. For well-prepared Mexican snacks like *carnitas* and tacos, as well as excellent burgers and fries, try **Las Dos Fronteras** on the corner of 13 Calle and Avenida San Isidro, open Mon.-Sat. 8 a.m.-10 p.m., Sunday 5-10 p.m.

Pollitos La Cumbre near the highway turnoff toward Savá and Trujillo is open 24 hours, great for that late-night craving.

Midrange

Chabelita, in a small wooden house east of the Partenon Beach Hotel, right before 1 Calle runs into the Río Cangrejal, is considered universally to have the best seafood in town. Superb conch soup, fried snapper, and monster shrimp are served at reasonable prices for lunch and dinner daily, although sometimes not on Sunday.

The Expatriate's Bar, as the name suggests, is a favorite haunt of many foreign residents living in La Ceiba, particularly those from the United States. The large thatched-roof bar and patio is on the second story of a building on 12 Calle, two blocks east of Avenida San Isidro. Doors open at 4 p.m., earlier during the U.S. football season. Apart from American-style chicken wings, burgers, nachos, and burritos, a large selection of Honduran cigars are sold at the bar. The food is not cheap, but portions are sizable.

One of the better downtown restaurants is **La Carreta,** 4 Calle two blocks east of 14 de Julio, specializing in steaks but also serving decent seafood for US$5-10 per meal. Open for lunch and dinner every day. A favorite among foreigners for reliable pizza, lasagna, salad bar, and air-conditioning is **Pizza Hut** on the square, open daily until 10 p.m.

Expensive

The classiest restaurant in town, apart from Maxim's at the La Quinta Hotel perhaps, is **Ricardo's,** on Avenida 14 de Julio at 10 Calle, tel. 43-0468. The atmosphere is upscale but not overly stuffy, with casual but neat attire recommended. The seafood and steaks are both excellent, and the conch soup is particularly good. Pastas and vegetarian dishes are available. Entrees cost US$7-20, and reservations are accepted.

ENTERTAINMENT

Discos

As the party capital of Honduras, La Ceiba boasts a roaring nightlife, mainly centered around the discos on 1 Calle east of the estuary, the so-called *zona viva,* or live zone. Foreigners, mainly men, have been known to get addicted to the scene, spending days or weeks on end drinking, dancing, chasing local women, and consuming the odd illicit substance until all hours night after night.

The only slow nights are Monday and Tuesday, and even then the discos are open until at least midnight. On weekends the strip is quite an adventure, with large crowds in all the discos and milling around on the street until daybreak.

The odd shooting or stabbing is not unheard of, and fistfights are considered just good fun. Generally, unless you do something stupid like try to pick up someone's date, none of the violence is directed at foreigners. The crowd is totally mixed—Latinos, Garífuna, Bay Islanders, Miskito Indians, and gringos all enjoy themselves shoulder to shoulder.

A few warnings: While it may be obvious in the sober light of day, in a drunken haze distinguishing a friendly young woman from a prostitute is not an easy task. In fact it's a fine line at La Ceiba discos. Use common sense, don't carry much money, and if sex is what you're after, don't forget protection! Foreign women may be more relaxed if they go with a male companion or a couple of female friends. It's not the wisest plan for a female traveler to hit the discos alone, although if you did you'd certainly get a lot of attention (possibly unwanted or inappropriate attention, however). Finally, the area between the discos and many downtown hotels is not the safest at night, especially near Parque Bonilla. Walk in groups and stick to the main avenues on the way home.

One musical twist sure to amuse some foreigners, expecting to hear only the hot rhythms of salsa, merengue, and *punta,* is the popularity of country music on the north coast. Don't be surprised to walk into a disco and see couples doing a slow two-step to the latest Garth Brooks hit.

Casual dressers beware: Walking into a disco wearing cut-offs, a T-shirt, and sandals won't get you much respect and certainly not many offers to dance. Break out that dress shirt, pair of slacks (or at least jeans), or sundress buried in the bottom of the pack for those special occasions.

D'Lido is the king of the discos, open 24-7 and always raging on the weekends, with two bars, tables, a patio, and in the center a large dance floor with a crowd shimmying to reggae, disco, rap, *punta-*rock, and the occasional country tune. Cover charged on weekends only.

Just east of D'Lido is **La Concha,** a somewhat lower-key spot, and further on is **La Kosta.** Another popular disco, **Safari,** favors country music; it's on 2 Calle right on the estuary. **Gladis Ciri,** on the south side of 1 Calle a couple of blocks east of D'Lido, is a Garífuna dance hall with almost no Latinos in sight, although no one seems to mind the occasional gringo patron.

A mild-mannered snack stand by day, **Lady Burger** turns into a traditional *punta* dance venue most evenings, with a Garífuna group dancing and singing, accompanied by drums and conch-shell horns. This is not a place to go dance, but rather to watch the performance and sip inexpensive beers.

On 4 Calle in La Isla is **Centro Cultural Satuyé,** a mainly Garífuna dance hall.

Bars

If the disco scene sounds a bit too energetic, but you'd still like to go out for a few drinks, try the **Bar and Restaurant El Canadiense** on Parque Bonilla, run by a friendly French-Canadian and his Honduran wife. Younger travelers and expats, especially Europeans, enjoy coming here for a mellow chat or to watch the latest sports on TV while sipping a beer or munching on a sandwich. Normally open Mon.-Sat. 8 a.m.-11:30 p.m., with good breakfasts.

On San Isidro is the **Cafe Verde** *champa* bar, with expensive mixed drinks. It's favored by wealthier expats and the prostitutes after their cash.

INFORMATION AND SERVICES

Several banks downtown will change dollars and traveler's checks, including Bancahsa, Banco Atlántida, and Banco de Occidente. The latter also receives Western Union wires. Credomatic, Avenida San Isidro between 5 and 6 Calles, tel. 43-0684, offers free cash advances on Visa cards.

Correos is on Avenida Morazán between 13 and 14 Calles, several blocks southwest of the square, open Mon.-Fri. 8 a.m.-4:45 p.m., Saturday 8 a.m.-noon. Express Mail Service is available. UPS is in the same building as the Hotel Iberia on Avenida San Isidro, tel. 43-0115 or 43-0116.

Hondutel, one block east of Avenida 14 de Julio between 5 and 6 Calles (look for the orange tower), is open 24 hours a day. Faxes are sent and received 8 a.m.-4 p.m. only.

The migration office is on 1 Calle between Avenida San Isidro and Avenida Atlántida, open Mon.-Fri. 8 a.m.-noon and 2-5 p.m. Renewing tourist cards is quick and painless, and costs US$2 with no *timbre* stamps required.

For airline tickets and other travel information, try **Paso Travel Service,** a block south of the square on Avenida San Isidro, tel./fax 43-1990, tel. 43-3186. Some English is spoken.

Run by an English-speaking owner who spent some time in the U.S., **Lavamatic Ceibeña,** on Avenida Pedro Nufio between 5 and 6 Calles in Barrio La Isla, not far from downtown, has American-style self-service washers and dryers. Open daily 7 a.m.-10 p.m, US$1.50 wash and dry.

Information

The **Consejo Municipal de Turismo,** 1 Calle between Avenida San Isidro and Avenida Atlántida, in the same building as the migration office, tel. 43-2863, offers a limited amount of information and some maps; Mon.-Fri. 7:30-11:30 a.m. and 1-5 p.m., Saturday 7:30 a.m.-noon. A tourist information booth in the square has been closed down and appears likely to remain so.

Mopawi, an organization working in Mosquitia, has an office on Avenida República half a block south of the docks on the west side of the railroad tracks, tel. 43-0553. Little general information is available here, but sometimes workers know of boats leaving for Mosquitia.

Car Rental

Agencies include **Toyota,** at the airport, tel. 43-1976; **Maya,** at La Quinta Hotel, tel. 43-3071, fax 43-0226; and **Molinari,** at Gran Hotel Paris, tel. 43-0055, fax 43-2371.

GETTING THERE AND AWAY

Because of its strategic location in the center of the north coast, La Ceiba is a major transportation hub for the Bay Islands, La Mosquitia, and other towns and villages on Honduras's Caribbean coast.

LA CEIBA USEFUL TELEPHONE NUMBERS

Police: 48-0241, or dial 199
Fire Department: 42-2695, or dial 198
Cruz Roja Ambulance: 43-0707, or dial 195
Hospital D'Antoni: 43-2234, 43-2264

Air

As elsewhere in Honduras, all domestic airlines offer the same government-mandated ticket prices. Most planes are of the twin-propeller, dozen-seat, unpressurized variety. Arrive one hour before flight departure. At the airport are a small restaurant and a couple of snack stand/gift shops, one of which usually sells day-old copies of the *Miami Herald* and some international magazines.

Golosón International Airport is 12 km from downtown La Ceiba on the highway toward Tela. Taxis from town to the airport normally cost US$3. Airport taxis parked at the terminal charge US$5 to town, but you can walk out to the highway and flag down a passing cab for US$2 to the square or a downtown hotel. Be sure to call or go to the airline offices to double-check prices and flight days, as they are likely to change, particularly to Mosquitia.

Isleña Airlines has offices downtown on San Isidro opposite the square, tel. 43-0179 or 43-2344, and at the airport. Isleña flies several times daily to Roatán, Tegucigalpa, and San Pedro Sula, and flies daily except Sunday to Utila and Guanaja. To Mosquitia, Isleña flies daily except Sunday to Palacios via Trujillo, and to Puerto Lempira on Monday, Tuesday, Thursday, and Saturday.

Aerolineas Sosa also has offices right next to Isleña downtown on Avenida San Isidro, tel. 43-2519 or 43-1399, and at the airport, tel. 43-0884. Sosa flies to Utila three times a day Mon.-Sat., to Roatán four times daily, and to Guanaja once a day Mon.-Saturday. To Mosquitia, Sosa flies to Brus Lagunas on Monday and Friday, and to Puerto Lempira on Tuesday, Thursday, and Saturday.

Rollins, at the airport, tel. 43-4181, has daily flights to Utila, Roatán, Tegucigalpa, and Palacios, and also flies to Brus Lagunas Wednesday and Saturday. **Caribbean Air,** at the airport, tel. 45-1933 or 43-4045, flies to San Pedro Sula twice daily, Roatán four times daily, Guanaja every day, Utila Mon.-Sat., and Belize City Wednesday and Sunday (US$78). **Taca,** tel. 43-1912, in the U.S. (800) 535-8780, has flights once a week direct to Miami, New Orleans, and Houston, and every day to Miami via San Pedro Sula.

Bus

All buses leave from the central terminal on Blvd. 15 de Septiembre west of downtown, just across the railroad tracks. Taxis to or from the terminal cost US 50 cents, though taxis parked in the terminal itself will charge more going into town. Walk out to the road for a less expensive one. Small meals and snacks can be bought at stands and eateries at the terminal. Destinations, times, and prices are as follows:

- **San Pedro Sula:** direct, three hours, US$2.20, 12 departures daily between 5:30 a.m. and 6:30 p.m. with Catisa.
- **Tegucigalpa:** direct, six and a half hours with a stop for food at Santa Rita, Yoro, US$6, six departures daily with Traliasa or Etrucsa, normally the first bus leaves at 3 a.m. and the last bus leaves at 11:30 a.m.
- **Tela:** local, two hours (less if they ever fix the road), US$1, every hour between 4:30 a.m. and 6 p.m.
- **Trujillo:** local, four hours, US$2.50, eight buses between 4 a.m. and 4 p.m.
- **Tocoa:** local, two and a half hours, many daily between 4:30 a.m. and 5:15 p.m.
- **Olanchito:** local, three hours, US$1.40, eight daily between 6:30 a.m. and 5:30 p.m.
- **Nueva Armenia** and **Jutiapa:** 90 minutes, US 80 cents, usually twice daily at irregular hours.
- **Balfate, Río Esteban,** and **Río Coco:** US$1.30 to Río Esteban, US$1.50, three hours to Río Coco, three buses daily at 7:30 a.m., noon, and 1:30 p.m. (or whenever the bus is full).
- **Corozal** and **Sambo Creek:** usually four daily with the last at 6 p.m. (times very vague), US 20 cents to Corozal, US 40 cents to Sambo Creek. To get to these villages you can also hop on any westbound bus to Tocoa, Trujillo, Jutiapa, or Olanchito, get off at the highway turnoff, and walk the short distance into town.

SAMPLE ONE-WAY AIRFARES FROM LA CEIBA

Utila: US$15
Roatán: US$17
Guanaja: US$22
Trujillo: US$18
Palacios: US$30
Brus Lagunas: US$43
Puerto Lempira: US$45
San Pedro Sula: US$23
Tegucigalpa: US$30

• **La Unión:** (for Cuero y Salado) several daily, US 40 cents.

Car

The 103-km, two-lane highway to Tela is currently in a sad state of disrepair, and takes at least 90 minutes in a private vehicle. Government officials claim the road will be repaired in the near future, but they've been saying that for a long time.

East of La Ceiba the highway continues along the coastal plain to Jutiapa, where it cuts through a low point in the Cordillera Nombre de Dios into the Valle de Aguán at Savá. This 80-km stretch is in relatively good shape. At the highway junction at Savá, you can drive west to Trujillo on a progressively deteriorating road, a total of 166 km from La Ceiba. Traveling east to Olanchito on a well-paved highway, it's a total of 123 km from La Ceiba.

Boat

Until 1995 the municipal dock at the end of Avenida República handled the town's boat traffic, and was a great place to search out rides to Mosquitia or the Bay Islands, as well as watch the hustle and bustle of dockside activity. Unfortunately the dock was sold to, of all companies, Standard Fruit, as part of the government's privatization drive. The new municipal dock is at Cabotaje, several kilometers east of town, a US$3 taxi ride from the square.

The **MV** *Tropical* departs Cabotaje to Roatán (US$7, two hours) and Utila (US$5.50, two hours) on the following schedule: Monday to Roatán 5 a.m. and 3:30 p.m., to Utila 10:30 a.m.; Tues.-Fri. to Utila at 10 a.m., to Roatán 3:30 p.m.; Saturday to Roatán 11 a.m.; Sunday to Roatán 7 a.m. For reservations or more information, the *Tropical* office can be reached at tel. 42-0780.

Boats frequently pull in and out of Cabotaje on the way to Mosquitia. If you want to catch a ride, get out to the docks and start asking around. Some boat captains welcome a few extra lempira, while others refuse to take passengers. The *Captain Rinel,* which makes regular trips to Brus Lagunas and Puerto Lempira, has an office in the Cosmo building on San Isidro between 4 and 5 Calles, and often takes passengers. If you take this route into Mosquitia, which certainly has romantic value, be ready to sleep on deck no matter what the weather for two to four days,

---

DISTANCES FROM LA CEIBA

Tela: 103 km
San Pedro Sula: 202 km
Tegucigalpa: 445 km
Tocoa: 108 km
Trujillo: 166 km
Jutiapa: 33 km
Savá: 80 km
Olanchito: 123 km

---

and bring all the food and water you will need. These are not passenger boats, but small, rusty cargo freighters, and amenities are minimal or nonexistent.

WEST AND SOUTH OF LA CEIBA

Refugio de Vida Silvestre Cuero y Salado

Formed by the estuaries of the Cuero, Salado, and San Juan rivers, which flow off the flanks of the Cordillera Nombre de Dios to the south, the Cuero y Salado Wildlife Refuge comprises 13,225 hectares of wetlands and coastline filled with plant and animal life endangered elsewhere in Honduras. Jaguars, howler and white-faced monkeys, manatees (the reserve's mascot), turtles, crocodiles, caimans, fishing eagles, hawks, and several species of parrots are among the 196 bird and 35 mammal species identified within the reserve's boundaries.

The swampy mangrove-covered wetlands perform several important ecological functions. The dense walls of mangrove roots in the water act as a nursery for marine animals such as shrimp and several fish species, who make their way out to the open ocean after they've had a chance to grow. The vegetation serves as a way station for many migratory birds, and as a buffer zone protecting the surrounding area during ocean storms and floods coming down from the mountains.

Much of the north coast formerly was covered with similar wetlands, but a lot has since been converted to pasture or plantations—a process all too evident as Cuero y Salado is surrounded by encroaching cattle-grazing land. An estimated 40% of the reserve's wetlands have been drained since 1987, when the land was donated by Standard Fruit to become a re-

LA CIEBA AREA

Caribbean Sea

Refugio de Vida Silvestre
Cuero y Salado

VISITOR'S
CENTER

El Porvenir

La
Ceiba

Corozal

Sambo
Creek

GOLOSÓN
INT'L
AIRPORT

Armenia
Bonito

VISITOR'S
CENTER

La
Unión

Río San Juan

Río Cuero

Río

La
Masica

Parque

Río Maria

Las Mangas

To Tocoa

Río Corozal

Pico Bonito
(2,435 m)

Río Bonito

Nacional

Yaruca

MOON

To Tela

San
Marcos

Río Perla

Montaña de Corozal
(2,480 m)

Pico

Sierra Nombre de Dios

Río San Lorenzo

Bonito

Olanchito

San
Lorenzo

Río

Río Aguan

0   10 mi

0   10 km

© MOON PUBLICATIONS, INC.

serve. The situation is so grim environmentalists are considering asking the army to help patrol to keep ranchers out. The reserve is also threatened by chemicals leaking in from nearby pineapple and African palm plantations.

It's recommended visitors make reservations, though it's not required. Reservations ensure a bed in the bunkhouse (US$7 a night) and a guide for a two-hour trip up the reserve's waterways. The tours cost US$13 for the entire boat, which can fit several passengers. For reservations contact Fundación Cuero y Salado (FUCSA), Edificio Ferrocarril Nacional, Zona Mazapan, Apt. 674, La Ceiba, Atlántida, tel./fax 43-0329. The

FUCSA office is in an old railroad building behind the Standard Fruit building in La Ceiba, just a couple of blocks west of the square.

Morning is the best time for viewing animal life, but late afternoon can be good as well. The guides are usually volunteers at the reserve, and are very knowledgeable about the ecosystems and wildlife in the area. They can usually help visitors get a good look at a troop of howler monkeys or some of the more colorful bird species in the reserve. Be sure to bring some repellent or long sleeves—the mosquitoes aren't too bad on the beach or the encampment, but can be fierce in the swamp.

For tourists, the interior section of the reserve is accessible by boat only, but don't be surprised to see a couple of locals fishing further in the swamps. They know all the paths to get into the reserve and don't mind getting munched by mosquitoes to catch a free meal for their families.

A US$10 (for foreigners) or US$1 (for Hondurans) entrance fee is charged above the price of the boat ride and bunk. You can camp free on the 12-km-long beach, but you'll still have to pay the entrance fee. Locals will cook up a meal for unprepared visitors, but it's usually best to come with food. The beach is a great spot for a bonfire cookout.

Cuero y Salado is 30 km from La Ceiba. To get there without a car, take a bus from La Ceiba to La Unión, and get off at the railroad tracks. From here, unless arrangements were made with FUCSA to be picked up for a ride in the reserve's bone-rattling car (US$5), a local will offer to take you in by *burra*, a few boards with train wheels underneath propelled by a pole (US$7). The sweaty operation is worth every penny. Alternatively, it's a two-hour walk along the rails to reach the headquarters. When returning, keep in mind the last bus leaves for La Ceiba at 3 p.m. The Bar El Bambú at the end of the train line makes a fine place to sip a cold beer or soft drink while awaiting the bus.

If coming by car, take the highway toward Tela. Past the airport, shortly after crossing the Río Bonito bridge, a dirt road heads off to the right through endless pineapple fields. Follow this to La Unión and the railroad tracks. A right turn on the way leads to Porvenir, which has decent beaches. As there is no road in to the headquarters, arrange to leave the car at Bar El Bambú while in the reserve.

Parque Nacional Pico Bonito

Chances are the first thing you noticed when you arrived in La Ceiba, especially if you came in by plane, was that massive emerald green spike of a mountain looming beyond the airport. This is the 2,435-meter-high Pico Bonito, centerpiece of the national park of the same name. Covering 107,300 hectares

BOB RACE

in the departments of Atlántida and Yoro, of which 49,000 hectares is a buffer zone, Pico Bonito is the largest protected area in Honduras apart from the Río Plátano Biosphere Reserve. It is also one of the least explored, mainly because most of it is dense, trackless jungle, ranging from humid tropical broadleaf forest in the lower regions to cloud forest on the peaks.

Some 20 river systems pour off the park's mountains; the rivers display their fullest splendor during the fall rainy season. Because of its rugged, natural isolation, Pico Bonito is a refuge for animal life seen only rarely in other regions of the country. Still, getting in to a place where one might run across a jaguar or ocelot requires some serious effort.

The park's main access is just south of the village of Armenia Bonito, which is reached by turning down a dirt road south off the La Ceiba-Tela highway just west of the airport, before reaching the Río Bonito. Past Armenia Bonito, a rough dirt road continues south, deteriorating as it goes, which gives an idea of how many visitors make it out to the park. After crossing a small, usually dry creek, the road passes through a dilapidated iron gate and continues to the edge of the Río Bonito, where there is a sizable rancho.

The proprietor of the ranch is Germán Martínez, the park *vigilante*. Germán collects a US$3 entrance fee per day and can supply mattresses and a key to the visitor's center. The 1 de Mayo buses leaving from Parque Bonilla in La Ceiba drive out to Armenia Bonito frequently; fare is US 10 cents. The visitor's center is about a 90-minute walk from Armenia Bonito.

Situated just off the edge of the Río Bonito, surrounded by jungle and usually deserted, the visitor's center is a lovely, tranquil place to spend a couple of days. Be sure to bring plenty of food; none is available. A trail has been developed past the visitor's center up to a look-out point with great views out over the Caribbean. The circular trail takes 3-5 hours and is a good route to look for monkeys, birds, and other animals. Another trail continues up the river valley.

For the adventurer, it would be hard to find more of a challenge in Honduras than a trip to the top of Pico Bonito. It may look like a relatively short jaunt, but in fact it takes a solid 9-10 days of hacking through the jungle while clinging to a steep, muddy hillside, hoping there are no snakes nearby. Germán has taken a few expeditions to the top, and will gladly take other fearless climbers for a mere US$10 a day. If he's not available, other men in nearby ranchos also know the route.

For an even tougher challenge, the truly obsessed adventurer can contemplate getting to the top of Montaña Corozal (2,480 meters), the park's highest peak. It's in the heart of the park, hidden from view by Pico Bonito. There have been no known expeditions to the top of Montaña Corozal.

It is also possible to enter the park on the south side, in the Yoro department near Olanchito, where the lower elevations are blanketed with pine forest instead of tropical jungle. The villages of San Marcos and San Lorenzo are good jump-off points on this side. A group of Zapotal Indians, a subgroup of the Jicaque, control 3,500 hectares of parkland on this side.

For more information on the park, contact the administration office, in La Ceiba's Colonia El Sauce (across from the golf course), tel./fax 43-3844. From the main entrance to El Sauce, the unmarked office is in the fourth house on the right side.

Río Cangrejal

Forming part of the eastern boundary of Parque Nacional Pico Bonito, the Río Cangrejal tumbles off the flanks of the jungle-covered mountains through a narrow boulder-strewn valley before reaching the Caribbean at La Ceiba. Anyone spending a couple of days in La Ceiba should be sure to visit the middle or upper reaches of the river, at least on a day-trip, to enjoy the spectacular scenery, take a dip in one of the innumerable swimming holes, or raft some of the finest whitewater in Central America. Unfortunately, the Honduran government is considering building a dam on the river, a singularly shortsighted plan as it would destroy the river's excellent tourism potential. The project is still in the planning stages, so with luck officials will come to their senses before construction begins.

To visit the river valley by private transportation, drive out the highway from La Ceiba toward Tocoa. Just outside of town a bridge crosses the river, which at this point is wide and not particularly impressive. On the far side of the bridge a dirt road turns off to the south, and follows the valley through the villages of Las Mangas, Yaruca, and Toncontín, ending in Urraco. The road beyond Urraco over the mountains to Olanchito has deteriorated to a path, which would make an adventurous hike or mountain-bike ride.

Usually a couple of buses daily make the bouncy and uncomfortable run between La Ceiba and Urraco. Instead of trying to figure out when the bus leaves, you could take a taxi or city bus out to where the dirt road turns off the highway and hitch upriver.

Balneario Los Lobos, signposted, charges US 20 cents for a swim. There's no real reason to swim there—many other free spots can be found upriver—but take the trail from the *balneario* to the **Cascade El Bejuco,** a waterfall visible on the opposite mountainside.

Las Mangas, where the road crosses a bridge, is a particularly lovely spot to admire the emerald green mountainsides and go for a swim. David González rents cabins at Las Mangas for US$15-20, with food available. He can be contacted at the Hotel Caribe in La Ceiba, tel. 43-1857, which is owned by the same family. David can also arrange hiking or rafting trips.

For those interested in rafting or kayaking with a tour outfit, see "Tour Operators" under "Sights and Recreation" above. The class II-IV rapids can be enjoyed year-round, but are best run during or just after the fall rains when the river is deep.

EAST OF LA CEIBA

Playa de Perú

One of the better beaches near La Ceiba, Playa de Perú is reached by a 1.5-km dirt road turning off the Tocoa highway between kilometer markers 205 and 206, about 10 km east of downtown La Ceiba. It's not possible to walk to this beach from town since the mouth of the Río Cangrejal is in the way.

Río María

One the finest freshwater swimming holes in Honduras is on the Río María, which passes underneath the highway between kilometer markers 207 and 208, east of Playa de Perú. On the east side of the highway bridge a path follows the river up a short distance until the path forks, one branch crossing the river and another leading up a hill to the left. Head up the hill, away from the river, for 15 minutes or so until the path comes back toward the river, audible below. Keep an eye out for a small trail cutting down a steep hillside; after a short but treacherous stretch this path arrives at the river's edge at a lovely waterfall with a pool at its base. If you're in doubt about the route, ask a local kid to guide you to the falls for a few lempira.

This is just the first of a series of waterfalls and pools created by huge boulders along the river, all surrounded by jungle—a wonderful place to spend a relaxing afternoon picnicking, reading, or just lazing around. The area is supposedly an ecological reserve, but apparently in name only.

It's best to go during the week as a crowd often shows up on weekends, but should there be too many people for your tastes, just head downriver a bit and find a quieter pool. There have been some reports of thievery here, so leave valuables at home.

Corozal

Not one of the more attractive Garífuna settlements on the Honduran coast, Corozal is a fairly dirty fishing village on the beach a couple of kilometers west of Río María. In town are a couple of basic *comedores* and the inexpensive **Hotel Hermanos Avila.** Nearby is **Playa de Zambrano,** a decent though unspectacular stretch of beach.

On the highway near the entrance to Corozal is **Villa Rhina,** tel. 43-2517 or 43-1222, fax 43-3558, a new resort-hotel set into the hillside with views out over the Caribbean. On the 10-acre grounds are three freshwater pools, a small waterfall, and a trail up into the forest above, where you can catch views of the Cayos Cochinos. Each of the attractive wood-paneled, air-conditioned rooms costs US$30 d. The hotel is well-run, but the location—above the highway and away from the beach—is not the best.

Sambo Creek

A few kilometers east of Corozal and somewhat more appealing is Sambo Creek, another Garífuna village at the mouth of a small river. Just west of town, near the mouth of the Río Cuyamel, lies a stretch of clean and deserted beach that would make for good camping, if the local family living nearby doesn't mind. A bit further west is **Playa Las Sirenas,** which, although clean, charges a ridiculous US$10 a night to camp.

In Sambo, **Hotel Avila** has basic rooms for US$4-6 per night, and the **Restaurante Mi Rancho** serves excellent seafood in traditional Garífuna style. Ceibeños often make the trip out to Sambo just to eat there.

On the south side of the highway on Río Cuyamel is a reputedly excellent swimming hole.

Jutiapa, Nueva Armenia, and Further East

Just before the highway turns inland through the hills toward Savá and the Valle de Aguán, 33 km from La Ceiba, is the small town of Jutiapa, where a road turns off down to Nueva Armenia at the sea's edge. From here you can find rides on a fishing boat out to the Cayos Cochinos for US$4-5 pp. Most boats leave in the early morning, so the best plan is to arrive in the afternoon and arrange a ride for the following day. A simple hotel in Nueva Armenia offers inexpensive rooms.

A couple of kilometers west of Jutiapa, on the south side of the highway at kilometer marker 225, is the **Usha Natural Curing Center,** run for over 20 years by the legendary Dr. Sebi, world-famous for his natural detoxification and curing techniques. Usha offers both day treatments and multiday stays in cottages; either way you'll enjoy the natural saunas and hot springs, curing sessions, and vegetarian food. The center is open Mon.-Sat. 8 a.m.-4 p.m., Sunday 10 a.m.-4 p.m. Reservations can be made in the U.S. at the Fig Tree in Miami, Florida, tel. (305) 252-1800 or 252-9536.

East along the coast beyond Jutiapa are the small, tranquil villages of Balfate, Río Esteban, and Río Coco. From Río Coco adventurers could make their way by foot or boat around the point to Trujillo in a day or two.

VALLE DE AGUÁN

From Jutiapa, the highway turns south into the hills, crossing into the broad Río Aguán valley. The Río Aguán winds out of the mountains of Yoro, to the west and south, and is also fed by tributaries flowing north out of Olancho. It meets the Caribbean east of Trujillo, at the Garífuna town of Santa Rosa de Aguán. One of the most fertile regions in the country, the Valle de Aguán is owned in large part by the Standard Fruit Company (now Dole), and is covered by a sea of banana, pineapple, and African palm plantations.

SAVÁ

A hot agricultural town on the south side of the Río Aguán where the La Ceiba highway meets the Olanchito-Tocoa-Trujillo road, Savá is a common transfer point for bus travelers. The town holds a couple of nondescript *comedores* and a gas station, but no hotels nor reasons for wanting one.

At Savá, the La Ceiba road meets another highway continuing west to Olanchito or east to Tocoa and Trujillo. On the way to Olanchito, on the west side of the Río Mame 28 kilometers from Savá, a dirt road turns off south. This road leads to La Unión in Olancho—86 km away and the closest town to **La Muralla National Park**—and eventually on to Juticalpa and Tegucigalpa. For travelers on their way directly to Tegucigalpa and not interested in stopping at La Muralla, the road from Corocito (east of Tocoa) through San Esteban is a quicker route.

OLANCHITO

The second-largest community in the Valle de Aguán after Tocoa, Olanchito sits in the heart of Standard Fruit lands. The town was founded in the 17th century by migrants from San Jorge de Olancho, a colonial town near Catacamas that was destroyed by a natural disaster. The town church, set on a palm-lined square, holds a small statue of San Jorge, the town's patron saint. The statue was reputedly carried here from San Jorge de Olancho by the original migrants. The 23 April festival in the saint's honor is quite a bash, with some 20,000 people dancing in the streets.

Most of the year, though, Olanchito is hot, dusty, and altogether uninteresting to the casual traveler. For anyone curious to see what a classic company town looks like, take a taxi or bus to nearby **Coyoles,** where practically all the buildings were built and are still owned by Standard Fruit. Almost all Olanchito residents, apart from a few small-scale ranchers and farmers, derive their income either directly or indirectly from Standard.

Accommodations

Should you have some business in Olanchito, or an odd desire to overnight in this out-of-the-way but friendly agricultural town, several decent hotels lie within two blocks of the square. The best inexpensive accommodations are at **Hotel Colonial,** tel. 44-6972, offering clean, sparsely furnished rooms, each with fan and private bath, for US$2.50 s or US$4 d. The rooms are set around a courtyard, and there's even room for parking.

A step up in quality is **Hotel Valle Aguán,** tel. 44-6618, where the modern, fan- and TV-equipped rooms surround a quiet courtyard; US$7 s or US$10 d. On the courtyard is **Restaurante La Iguana,** one of the better eateries in town. The **Hotel Olimpic,** tel. 44-6324, is a somewhat better deal at US$8 s or d with a refrigerator or US$10 with a/c.

Food

Most restaurants in town are cheap and basic. One of the better ones is **Burger Cheese,** serving burgers and beers until midnight or later. The only upscale restaurant in town apart from La Iguana at the Hotel Valle Aguán is **La Ronda,** on the western edge of town. Favored by a contingent of gringo missionaries working near Olanchito and locals with a few extra lempira to blow, La Ronda has a large menu including steak, chop suey, chicken, shrimp, and soups for US$4-6 an entree.

Services

Bancahorro and Bancahsa in the center of town change dollars and traveler's checks. Hondutel and Correos share a building five blocks south of the main street. Gas is available in town.

Getting Away

It's possible, but not easy, to continue west from Olanchito to Yoro. The road deteriorates beyond Olanchito; swollen rivers can flood the route, cutting it off entirely. Buses do make the trip, however. One goes from Olanchito to San Lorenzo (two hours), where you change to another to Yoro (90 minutes).

The last bus from Olanchito to La Ceiba leaves at 3:30 p.m., but it's usually possible to catch a later bus to Savá and there change to another bus continuing to La Ceiba or Trujillo.

TOCOA

A bustling agricultural town 29 kilometers east of Savá, Tocoa has nothing whatsoever to attract a tourist. Even the downtown square is ugly, although the bizarrely designed church, reportedly the work of a Peace Corps volunteer, is interesting enough.

Though lacking in tourist attractions, Tocoa is a magnet for land-hungry migrants who use the rapidly growing city as a base to invade the Río Sico and Río Paulaya valleys on the western edge of the Río Plátano Biosphere Reserve. Many of these homesteaders are moving in on protected land, but little can be done to stop them, even if the government wanted to, which it doesn't always—it's easier to sacrifice a remote stretch of jungle than deal with the thorny problem of land redistribution in the rest of the country.

Accommodations

Because of all the agricultural and business activity in Tocoa, several hotels offer rooms of varying quality. The super-basic **Hospedaje Rosa** on the main drag charges US$2.50 for a room with private bath and fan. **Hotel Victoria,** a block away, costs US$7 with a/c—a good deal. And adjacent to Bancahorro, the upscale **Hotel San Patricio,** tel. 44-3401, boasts a/c, TV, and a parking lot; US$11.

Food

The classiest restaurant in town is **La Gran Villa,** on the northwest end of the square on the road to the bus station, tel. 44-3943. The restaurant offers shrimp, conch, and steak dishes at US$4-7 per entree, as well as sandwiches, breakfasts, and a full bar. It's open Mon.-Sat. 8 a.m.-9 p.m.

Next to Hotel San Patricio is the **Dragon de Oro,** featuring chop suey *estilo hondureño* (Honduran-style). Find cheap eats at **El Cazador** on the south side of the square.

Services

Bancahsa, Banco Atlántida, and Bancahorro in the center of town all change dollars and usually traveler's checks. The **bus station** is four blocks north of the square, next to the market. Last

GETTING TO MOSQUITIA THE HARD WAY

Flying into Palacios, Brus Lagunas, or Puerto Lempira is by far the easiest way to get into Mosquitia, but for those with a sense of adventure (or a fear of light aircraft) it is possible to get to Palacios by a combination of truck and boat.

Two six-wheel trucks leave Tocoa daily at 7 a.m. and 11 a.m. (times subject to change) for a grueling but fascinating seven-hour, US$9 trip to the Garífuna village of Sangrelaya. It's best to get there early to ensure a good seat—inside the cab is best, but if that's been taken try to get a bonch seat with your back against the cab, which offers some support on the long and bumpy ride. The truck leaves the Trujillo highway at Corocito, and passes Bonito Oriental, Limón, and Iriona before arriving at Punta Piedra, where the road ends. From there the truck follows the beach, often half in the water and half on sand, sometimes at heart-stopping steep angles, to Sangrelaya, passing several small villages along the way.

From Sangrelaya, *lanchas* can be hired to Plaplaya or Batalla for roughly US$35 per boat, and from here onward to Palacios or Raísta. The boat trip from Sangrelaya can be very wet, so be prepared. All told, the trip is more expensive than the plane, but incomparably more adventuresome.

bus to Trujillo leaves at 6 p.m., last to La Ceiba leaves at 4 p.m. The 24-hour **Texaco station** on the highway can give you a fill-up.

Getting Away
From Tocoa it's 59 kilometers to Trujillo via a poorly maintained paved road passing Corocito, which is the turn-off to Bonito Oriental, San Esteban and Olancho, and Sangrelaya at the edge of Mosquitia. Between Tocoa and Trujillo, slow down when approaching bridges as the bumps can be bone-rattling. Gas is available at Corocito.

TRUJILLO AND VICINITY

INTRODUCTION

Coralio reclined, in the mid-day heat, like some vacuous beauty lounging in a guarded harem. The town lay at the sea's edge on a strip of alluvial coast. It was set like a little pearl in an emerald band. Behind it, and seeming almost to topple, imminent, above it, rose the sea-following range of the Cordilleras. In front the sea was spread, a smiling jailer, but even more incorruptible than the frowning mountains. The waves swished along the smooth beach; the parrots screamed in the orange and ceiba-trees; the palms waved their limber fronds foolishly like an awkward chorus at the prima donna's cue to enter.

—O. Henry, *Cabbages And Kings*

One of many foreigners who have been waylaid by Trujillo's lotus-land vibes, American writer O. Henry renamed the town Coralio for his short story, but the description is as good as one could ask for. Although it is the country's oldest settlement, Trujillo still feels like a forgotten, sleepy corner of Honduras, where it seems no one is in a hurry to do anything.

Even the local tourist industry has failed to take off, despite the obvious attractions of a broad bay lined by a beach and palm trees, a national park close to town comprising jungle-covered mountains and mangrove lagoons, and several quiet Garífuna villages not far away. The main drawback has been its location: Trujillo is four hours by crowded, bumpy bus from La Ceiba, and about twice that from Tegucigalpa. However, in late 1996 Isleña began regular daily plane service from La Ceiba, which may boost the number of visitors.

The capital of the Colón Department, Trujillo has about 30,000 residents. Its annual patron festival is held on 24 June in honor of San Juan Bautista.

History
Though Trujillo was officially founded on 18 May 1525 by Juan de Medina, acting under orders from Hernán Cortés, the natural bay had long before drawn other settlers. According to colonial testimony and archaeological evidence, Trujillo Bay had been occupied for many hundreds of years before the Spanish arrived. Trujillo was apparently something of a pre-Columbian cross-roads, site of Pech and Tolupan villages as well as settlements of Mayan and Nahuatl traders from Mexico and Guatemala.

The early Spanish colonists established their new town on the site of an Indian village named Guaimura, amid approximately a dozen other villages totaling several thousand inhabitants. Trujillo was named for the Spanish hometown of Medina's superior officer Fernando de las Casas.

In the first years after conquest, Trujillo was the administrative center of the new colony, housing both the governor of Honduras and the only bishopric, established in 1545. But the lure of gold in the mountains soon drew colonists to the interior towns of Gracias a Dios and Comayagua, which by the middle of the century had superseded Trujillo.

Trujillo faded into a backwater colonial port. The constant threat of pirate assault on the poorly guarded harbor was all the more reason for colonists to relocate. French corsairs first attacked in 1558, and others followed repeatedly from their bases on the Bay Islands and in Mosquitia. Since colonial authorities were unable to mount an effective defense, even the Spanish merchants who depended on the port took to living inland and only came to the coast when the Spanish fleet arrived.

In 1642 English pirate William Jackson led an assault on Trujillo with 1,500 men, almost en-

bust of San Juan de Medina

economy relies on the port, the departmental government, and the fledgling tourist industry.

Orientation

The center of Trujillo is on a rise above the beach, and consists of a small square surrounded by government buildings, the church, and a few stores. The town continues several streets back up the hill, where the bulk of hotels and restaurants are located. To the west of downtown is Barrio Cristales, the first Garífuna settlement on mainland Honduras.

Robberies have been reported in the vicinity of Trujillo, but generally the downtown area, the main town beach, and the airport beach are safe. Less safe are the more deserted stretches of beach between Trujillo and Santa Fe and east of the airport beach toward Puerto Castilla.

SIGHTS

First and foremost among Trujillo's attractions is the **beach** right below town—a wide, clean swath of sand lined with *champa* restaurants and lapped by the protected waters of the bay. Swimming and sunbathing here is safe, but don't tempt fate by leaving possessions lying around unguarded. The bay is not as clear as waters off the Bay Islands (and might get worse if a planned oil refinery is built at Puerto Castilla), but still it's warm, fairly clean, and calm. The **airport beach,** east of town in front of the airport and dominated by the Christopher Columbus Hotel, is an equally fine spot for relaxing, usually a bit quieter as it's further from town.

East of the airport, beaches continue all the way around the bay to Puerto Castilla, but robberies have been reported on these deserted stretches; stay at the two beaches mentioned above unless you go with a group.

For all its storied history, Trujillo retains little in the way of colonial monuments. The most interesting is the **Fortaleza de Santa Bárbara,** which was built piecemeal beginning in 1575. Along with the fort at Omoa, Trujillo's fort was notably unsuccessful, falling continually to attackers over the course of the colonial era. Invaders were repelled with success only after the arrival of the Garífuna in 1799. The Garífuna were superb soldiers, who gained experience

tirely destroying the town. While Trujillo residents were still recovering from the blow, the next year Dutchman Jan Van Horn arrived and finished the work entirely. Those who hadn't been killed gave up the port as a lost cause, and Trujillo was deserted by the Spanish for almost 150 years. It was intermittently used by the British.

In the late 18th century the Spanish began a major counteroffensive to turn back British settlements along Central America's Caribbean coast. As part of this effort, Trujillo was reoccupied by a contingent of soldiers in 1780. Although the Spanish colony was on its last legs, the new settlement took hold. It received a boost in 1799 after several hundred Garífuna, deported by the British from the island of San Vicente, built a village just west of Trujillo in what is now Barrio Cristales.

As with the rest of the north coast, Trujillo participated in the banana boom of the early 20th century. Both Standard and United Fruit acquired lands in the area. Standard still controls much land in the nearby Aguán Valley, and ships most of its produce out of nearby Puerto Castilla. Trujillo's

TRUJILLO

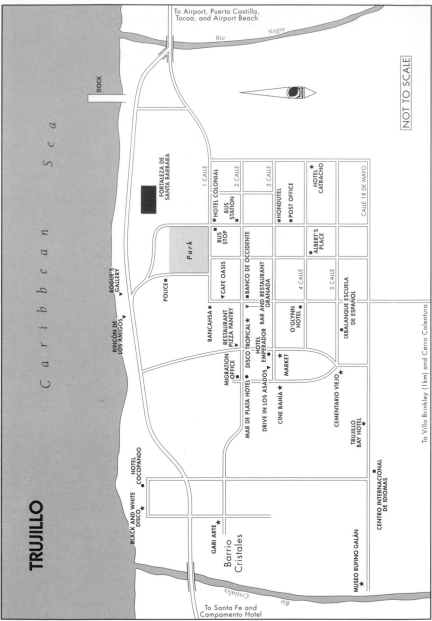

To Airport, Puerto Castilla,
Tocoa, and Airport Beach

Rio Negro

DOCK

NOT TO SCALE

C a r i b b e a n   S e a

FORTALEZA DE
SANTA BARBARA

ROGUE'S
GALLERY

RINCÓN DE
LOS AMIGOS

Park

POLICE

1 CALLE

2 CALLE

3 CALLE

HOTEL COLONIAL

BUS
STATION

BUS
STOP

CAFE OASIS

BANCO DE OCCIDENTE

HONDUTEL

POST OFFICE

HOTEL
CATRACHO

CALLE 18 DE MAYO

ALBERT'S
PLACE

4 CALLE

5 CALLE

BANCAHSA

RESTAURANT
PIZZA PANTRY

DISCO TROPICAL

HOTEL
EMPERADOR

MIGRATION
OFFICE

BAR AND RESTAURANT
GRANADA

O'GLYNN
HOTEL

IXBALANQUE ESCUELA
DE ESPAÑOL

MAR DE PLATA HOTEL

DRIVE IN LOS ASADOS

CINE BAHIA

MARKET

CEMENTARIO VIEJO

TRUJILLO
BAY HOTEL

HOTEL
COCOPANDO

BLACK AND WHITE
DISCO

GARI ARTE

Barrio
Cristales

MUSEO RUFINO GALÁN

CENTRO INTERNACIONAL
DE IDIOMAS

Rio Cristales

To Santa Fe and
Campamento Hotel

To Villa Brinkley (1km) and Cerro Calentura

© MOON PUBLICATIONS, INC.

WILLIAM WALKER'S LAST ADVENTURE

Legendary filibuster William Walker, "the gray-eyed man of destiny" as he was called in his years of fame, was possessed by a burning desire to govern parts or all of Central America. His stated reasons were varied, among them the desire to expand slavery and to establish U.S. control over the fractious republics before England did. But the more important driving force behind his actions seems to have been a slightly crazed messianic fervor.

Walker invaded and briefly ruled Nicaragua from 1855-57. His presence prompted the heretofore impossible task of unifying El Salvador, Guatemala, Honduras, and Costa Rica in a common goal—namely getting rid of the pesky gringo. After a series of bloody battles, Walker surrendered in Nicaragua on 1 May 1857, and returned to New Orleans. His hero's welcome there took the sting out of his defeat, and as convinced as ever of his destiny to rule Central America, he soon organized another expedition to reconquer Nicaragua.

Walker departed New Orleans in June 1860, planning to first take control of the island of Roatán, then join forces with Honduran Liberal Party leader Trinidad Cabañas to overthrow the Honduran government. However, the British, who at that time occupied Roatán but were about to turn the island over to Honduras, got wind of the plan and put off their departure. When Walker arrived off Roatán and saw the Union Jack still flying, he changed plans and decided to take Trujillo. Landing on the bay a few kilometers from town at night, Walker and his 200 men marched on the fort at dawn and took it in a 15-minute battle.

Walker quickly hoisted the flag of the Central American Republic over the fort, and reassured the townspeople of his good intentions. However, he made the fatal mistake of taking over Trujillo's customs house, which unbeknownst to him was technically managed by the British. This gave British forces in Roatán the pretext they needed to help Honduras attack Walker. The British warship *Icarus,* commanded by Capt. Norvell Salmon, soon appeared in the harbor, and word came of a force of 700 Honduran soldiers just outside of town. Rather than give in to the inevitable, Walker chose to lead his men out of town during the night. They made their way east into Mosquitia in hopes of joining forces with Cabañas.

Walker eventually found a deserted encampment on the banks of the Río Negro and stopped to regroup. But there he and his men came under attack from Honduran soldiers. They fought off the attack for five days, but with many of his "Immortal" soldiers dead or wounded, and himself ill with a fever and shot in the cheek, Walker knew he was defeated. When the *Icarus* appeared near the scene of the battle, Walker surrendered to Salmon, figuring he and his men would at worst return in shame to the United States.

Walker's men were placed under the protection of the British flag, but Salmon had no sympathy for Walker; he turned him over to the Hondurans in Trujillo. At first Walker protested, but soon became resigned to his fate. On 12 September 1860, Walker was led to the outskirts of town—now the site of the town hospital—flanked by two priests and a crowd of heckling Hondurans, clearly relishing the sight of the famed invading gringo's execution. Walker remained calm, received his last sacraments from the priests, and stood straight in the face of the firing squad.

from a half-century of guerrilla warfare against the British on San Vicente. The last real battle for the fort took place in 1910, when a Honduran general landed here in an unsuccessful attempt to launch a coup. The fort was closed in 1969 when its guard troops were called into action against El Salvador in the "Soccer War." Shortly thereafter it was converted into a tourist attraction. Several colonial-era cannons are still set up on the fort's ramparts. Known locally as El Castillo, the fort is open daily 9 a.m.-noon and 1-4 p.m. Admission is US 10 cents for adults, 5 cents for children, free for Hondurans.

Although Trujillo was the site of the first cathedral in Honduras, the original church was destroyed long ago. The unexceptional **Catedral de San Juan Bautista** was built in 1832 and remodeled 1930-39.

The **Museo Rufino Galán,** on the edge of the Río Cristales on a hillside above town, houses an eclectic collection of Trujillo bric-a-brac from across the centuries, given, bought, found, or fallen out of the sky—literally. Probably the most impressive display is the remains of a U.S. transport plane that crashed nearby in 1985. Don't expect any displays, signs, or other niceties: this is the life's work of a born pack rat. Some pre-Columbian pieces are hidden amid the junk. The museum costs US$1, and an additional 60 cents to swim in some murky pools. Don't bother swimming here, the ocean is much better.

The **cementerio viejo (old cemetery),** south of downtown, is worth a visit to see the grave of the "gray-eyed man of destiny," William Walker, whose filibustering days came to a violent end in Trujillo on 12 September 1860. Apart from Walker's grave, the cemetery also offers an interesting if decrepit assortment of grave monuments from across 300 years of Trujillo history.

ACCOMMODATIONS

Budget

A favorite hotel among backpackers is the **Mar de Plata,** which although cheap at US$4 s and US$6 d is extremely dingy, especially on the first floor. Rooms are concrete cells with bad fans, and the shared bathrooms are not too clean. **Hotel Catracho** has more character, with wooden rooms and porches round a courtyard for the same price, but with private bathrooms.

A far better deal are the low-priced rooms at the **O'Glynn Hotel,** tel. 44-4592. Although the owners push the overpriced US$30 a/c- and TV-equipped modern rooms, the annex has comfortable, wooden rooms with high ceilings and porches for US$5 s or US$6 d, with clean shared bathrooms. In the lobby of the hotel is a complete set of framed topographical maps of the region, an interesting collection of pre-Columbian jade figurines, and a copy of the testimony of the founding of Trujillo on 18 May 1525 in the name of Cortés, written by Capt. Francisco de las Casas.

Also not a bad deal is **Hotel Emperador,** tel. 44-4446, opposite the market, where a small courtyard is surrounded by a few clean rooms with private bathroom and fan; US$6 s or US$7.50 d. Rooms equipped with TV are available for a bit more.

Run by an American expatriate in an incongruous but attractive red-brick house a couple of blocks behind the square is **Albert's Place,** tel. 44-4431. It looks like a little piece of England plopped down on the Honduran coast, and with good reason. It was built by an evidently homesick Brit almost a century ago. Albert charges a mere US$8 s or d for homey and colorful rooms with high ceilings, and can arrange meals for a bit more.

In Barrio Cristales is **Hotel Cocopando,** a three-story concrete structure on the beach charging US$5 s or US$6 d with fans. The restaurant serves decent fish and a mean *chuleta de cerdo,* and the disco next door rages on weekends.

Midrange

Apparently in perpetual construction, at least until the American owner runs out of room or gets bored, the **Villa Brinkley,** tel./fax 44-4444 or 44-4545, is an architectural oddity perched on a hillside above town. Currently 20 wood-and-plaster rooms of differing sizes, all tastefully decorated, are available for US$18-30—an excellent value. Some come with kitchenettes and sunken bathtubs. The food varies between good and excellent, depending on the current cook. Outside is a pool and expansive patio, with great views out over town and the bay. Apartments in a separate building rent for US$12-35 per night. The Turtle Tours office is in the hotel.

Campamento Hotel and Restaurant, tel. 44-4244, fax 44-4200, a couple of kilometers west of Trujillo on the road to Santa Fe, rents 10 beach bungalows for US$30 d or t. The atmosphere is peaceful, the beach is clean, and the restaurant serves good seafood. On the south side of the airstrip, opposite the Christopher Columbus Hotel, is the modern, two-story **Trujillo Bay Hotel,** tel./fax 44-4732. Rooms with a/c, TV, hot water, and porches cost US$25 s, US$35 d, which is not a bad value, although the location is not the best.

Conveniently located on the corner of the square, but gloomy and unfriendly, is **Hotel Colonial,** tel. 44-4011, with a/c- and TV-equipped rooms for US$23 d.

Luxury

A sprawling, lime green complex spread across the beach in front of the airport, the **Christopher Columbus Hotel,** tel. 44-4966 or 44-4249, fax 44-4971, may not be aesthetically elegant but it has all the amenities for a pampered vacation. The 70 air-conditioned rooms range from US$55 s to US$120 for a suite with views of the ocean and the mountains behind. Up to two children under 12 stay free. Service at the hotel was initially extremely poor, but has reportedly improved recently. The private, patrolled beach is very safe, and the hotel supplies all manner of beach and water toys for guests. Other amenities include a swimming pool and tennis courts.

Built around a set of natural hot springs on the eastern slopes of Parque Nacional Capiro y Calentura, just outside of Trujillo on the road to Tocoa, is **Silin Hotel Resort and Spa,** tel. 44-4249 or 44-4247, fax 44-4248, in the U.S. (708) 766-7509, fax (708) 766-8061. Rooms with a/c and TV go for US$43 d, which includes a massage and use of the hot springs. Nonguests may use the baths for US$3, or get a massage for US$6. At the hotel is the Restaurant Praga, open daily 7 a.m.-9 p.m.

FOOD

In Town

Apart from a couple of *merenderos* on the square, there is little in the way of inexpensive food in Trujillo. Almost all restaurants are midrange, usually US$3-6 for a full meal and a bit less for breakfast. If you're on a budget you may have to resign yourself to eating a lot of *baleadas* or hitting the market and cooking meals yourself. One decent low-priced spot is **Drive-in Los Asados,** a block west of the market, up the hill, which serves enchiladas, *pastelitos, tajadas,* burgers, and other snacks. The patio restaurant is a friendly place to have a few beers and chat with locals.

Cafe Oasis, opposite Bancahsa downtown, serves healthy breakfasts and good vegetarian meals on a small patio. It also has a small book exchange. Open Mon.-Sat. 9 a.m.-6 p.m.

One of the oldest restaurants in Trujillo is **Bar and Restaurant Granada,** a block south of the square. The Garífuna owners serve a large selection of meals, with heavy emphasis on seafood; US$4-10 per entree. Open daily 8 a.m.-11 p.m.

Similar is the **Restaurant Pizza Pantry,** which despite its name has a large menu including hearty breakfasts, shrimp, lobster, steak, salads, and a full bar; US$4-10 per entree. The pizza is not bad. Open daily 7 a.m.-10 p.m.; service can be slow.

On the Beach

Among the many restaurants lining the beach in front of town, **Rincón de los Amigos** is the current favorite. Run by a trio of friendly expats (though owners seem to change with regularity), the large thatched-roof restaurant has tables on the beach, hammocks to relax in, and a bar. The seafood is usually good, although the selection is limited to the day's catch. Expect to enjoy a full meal; there is little in the way of snacks or light meals. Many travelers find themselves spending entire days at the Rincón, lounging in the hammocks, chatting, drinking, and taking an occasional dip in the ocean. Open daily 8 a.m. 11 p.m.

Nearby is the **Rogue's Gallery,** otherwise known as Jerry's, with similar food to Rincón and also a frequent haunt of travelers and expatriates. On the airport beach, just east of Christopher Columbus, is the **Bahía Bar,** a restaurant and bar with tables and hammocks under champas out on the beach. Service can be painfully slow, but with the waves and sun to lull you into a daze, what's the rush? The fish sandwiches are excellent, as are the fresh juices. The seafood, pizzas, and other dishes are also good. A long-time Trujillo expatriate institution, the Bahía has recently changed ownership and it remains to be seen if quality is maintained. The new owners don't plan on making any changes. Even if you're not hungry, this is a fine place to get a cold drink and relax on the beach.

Right next door is **Gringo's Bar and Restaurant,** similar in price and style to the Bahía. **Chino's Bar and Grill,** further east at the far end of the airport, has a full bar with a good music selection and lots of seafood. The Honduran owners also rent out cabins behind the bar for US$25 35.

ENTERTAINMENT

Rincón de los Amigos is a late-night hangout popular with travelers and a few locals. If you're after something a bit more energetic, the **Disco Tropical** next to the Restaurant Granada downtown is the weekend party spot in Trujillo.

The **Black and White Disco** next to the Hotel Cocopando on the beach in Barrio Cristales is also popular on weekends, favoring *punta* music for the mainly Garífuna crowd. **Cine Bahía** is a block south of the Mar de Plata Hotel.

INFORMATION AND SERVICES

Shopping
In Barrio Cristales, **Gari Arte,** tel. 44-4207, sells a variety of Garífuna *artesanías,* including drums, carvings, jewelry, paintings, *punta* cassettes, and T-shirts.

The **Supermercado Popular** on the square has a large selection of groceries, and is open Mon.-Sat. until 7 p.m. The public market, a couple of blocks south of the square, does not offer much variety, but has a basic selection of staple fruits and vegetables at inexpensive prices.

Services
Just off the square, Bancahsa is the easiest place to exchange dollars and traveler's checks, and get cash advances on a Visa or Master-Card. Western Union wires are received at Banco de Occidente.

The migration office is opposite the Mar de Plata Hotel, and renews tourist cards quickly and painlessly. Hondutel, a couple of blocks south of the square, is open Mon.-Fri. 7 a.m.-9 p.m., Sat.-Sun. 8 a.m.-4 p.m. Faxes are received at 44-4200. Correos is right next to Hondutel.

The only tourist agent in Trujillo is **Turtle Tours,** in the Villa Brinkley Hotel above town, tel./fax 44-4431. Apart from arranging tours of Mounts Capiro and Calentura and the crocodile farm on the Guaymoreto lagoon, the agency also rents 350cc and 650cc enduro motorcycles for US$35 a day or US$22 half day. The *merendero* on the west side of the square acts as an agent and will drive you up to the hotel if you want to rent a bike. Bicycles were once

rented as well, and may be again in the near future. The owners speak German, English, and Spanish.

Isleña Airlines sells plane tickets at the Christopher Columbus Hotel, which is owned by the airline.

Information
Fundación para la Protección de Capiro, Calentura y Guaymoreto, a.k.a. **Fucagua,** tel./fax 44-4294, staffs an office on the second floor of the kiosk in the middle of the square, in the same room as the town library. The office can provide you with a simple map and descriptive pamphlet of the surrounding natural areas.

Language Schools
A new reason for a longer stay in Trujillo is the two Spanish schools which have recently set up shop in town. Reports on the quality of the teachers vary, but the prices are comparable to or better than schools in Guatemala, and it's hard to beat the location.

Run by the same company that manages a school in Copán Ruinas, the **Ixbalanque Escuela de Español,** tel. 44-4461, offers four hours of daily one-on-one lessons for five days, plus seven days room and board with a local family, for US$135. No one in the Trujillo office speaks English, so you may want to make reservations via the Copán Ruinas office at tel. 61-4432 or fax 57-6215.

Centro Internacional de Idiomas, tel./fax 44-4777, charges US$150 for the same services. Reservations can be made in the U.S. by mail to TGU 00068, P.O. Box 025387, Miami, FL 33102-5387 or on the Internet at www.world-wide.edu/honduras/cici/.

GETTING THERE AND AWAY

Air
Isleña Airlines began daily flights to Trujillo in 1996. The flight is a stop-off on the La Ceiba-Palacios route, and costs US$18 to La Ceiba and US$20 to Palacios. With connections through La Ceiba, flights to Tegucigalpa cost US$48, San Pedro Sula US$40, and Roatán US$25. The La Ceiba flight departs at 12:45 p.m. and the Palacios flight leaves at 10:45 a.m.

TRUJILLO USEFUL TELEPHONE NUMBERS

Police: 44-4038, 44-4039, or dial 199
Hospital Salvador Paredes: 44-4093

*There is no Red Cross or fire department in Trujillo. Call the police in an emergency.

BOB RACE

Car
The 166-km, two-lane highway to La Ceiba is in fairly bad shape until Tocoa, where it improves somewhat. The drive can be done in two-and-a-half to three hours.

If you're driving to Tegucigalpa from Trujillo, the dirt road turning off from Corocito and heading through the mountains of Olancho is faster and much more scenic than the route via La Ceiba and San Pedro Sula. The dirt road runs through a relatively isolated area, so certainly only drive in the daytime, and be prepared for a dusty, bumpy four or five hours before reaching the pavement near Juticalpa.

A dirt road also leaves Corocito east to Limón and continues on as far as Punta Piedra, near the edge of La Mosquitia. There is no way to drive into La Mosquitia.

NEAR TRUJILLO

Santa Fe and San Antonio
A large Garífuna town 10 km west of Trujillo, Santa Fe is strung along a sandy road parallel to the unattractive beach. Cleaner patches of beach can be found nearby to the east and west of Santa Fe. A two-story concrete building one block south of the main street has rooms for rent for around US$5 d, and others may rent out rooms for visitors.

Comedor Caballero, better known as Pete's Place, is worth making a trip to Santa Fe. The one-room restaurant, with the kitchen right next to the tables, serves up superb conch stew, lobster tail, shrimp in wine sauce, snapper, pork chops, and other dishes daily for lunch and dinner. Meals cost US$4-10, but it's well worth the splurge. Pete presides over the cooking with an eagle eye, and is a wealth of information on the area.

Reportedly a small patch of reef known as **Cayo Blanco** lies offshore in front of Santa Fe; it could be reached with the help of a local fisherman.

Beyond Santa Fe the dirt road continues to the smaller villages of San Antonio and Guadalupe. Rooms can be found in San Antonio by asking around, and there is a small hotel in Guadalupe.

Thrice-daily buses ply the dirt road between San Antonio, Santa Fe, and Trujillo, leaving at irregular hours. The last bus normally returns to

Bus
Cotraipbal, tel. 44-4932, runs direct buses to San Pedro Sula (US$5.50, 5-6 hours) at 3 a.m., 5 a.m., and 8 a.m.; to Tegucigalpa via Olancho (US$6, 8-10 hours) at 3 a.m., 4:30 a.m., and 9 a.m. The buses leave from the terminal one block south of the square.

Regular buses to La Ceiba (US$2.50, four hours) leave from the square every two hours between 2 a.m. and 2 p.m. Tocoa buses (US 90 cents, two hours) leave every hour from the square until 4:30 p.m. Two buses daily go to Santa Rosa de Aguán (US$1, 90 minutes) usually around 10 a.m. and 2 p.m., though times frequently change.

To Limón, take a Tocoa bus to Corocito, then hitch from there. Buses to Santa Fe and San Antonio leave from opposite the Tiendo O'Glynn, Mon.-Sat. at irregular hours. Usually three buses daily run to Santa Fe for US 70 cents. A private taxi to Santa Fe would cost US$6.

Frequent buses run Mon.-Sat. between Trujillo and Puerto Castilla for US 50 cents.

Trujillo midafternoon. From Guadalupe, in the dry season, you can follow trails around the point west past the settlements of Plan Grande and Manatí Creek to Río Coco, and from there get a bus onward to Jutiapa and La Ceiba. It would also be easy to arrange a boat ride out this way for a nominal fee with the fishermen who pull up daily near the dock in Trujillo.

Parque Nacional Capiro y Calentura

Comprising 4,537 hectares between 667 and 1,235 meters above sea level, Capiro y Calentura National Park is centered on the two jungle-clad peaks right behind Trujillo. The park has few trails or tourist facilities as tourism was a secondary reason for establishing the reserve, after protecting Trujillo's water supply. The easiest and most common access is via the dirt road past Villa Brinkley, which winds up the mountain to the radio towers just below the peak of Cerro Calentura. Formerly the U.S. Drug Enforcement Agency maintained a radar station here, but now the caretakers of a Hondutel tower and the Catholic radio station antenna are the only occupants.

The 2-3 hour walk up to the towers from town is best done in the early morning, when it's cool and the birds are most active. Muggings have been reported on the road, so it might be wise to go in a group. Although a visitor's center has been built at the bottom of the road, it is currently empty. From the radio towers, a trail goes east a short distance to a lookout point with great views out over the bay and Laguna Guaymoreto. The peak of Cerro Calentura is a bit further east, but no apparent trails exist. To get out there would require a machete. From the radio towers you can see out over the Valle de Aguán.

Another frequent hike in the park is up the Río Negro, in a valley between Cerro Capiro and Cerro Calentura. The trail follows a water pipe along the river to a dam, above which are two small waterfalls.

Just outside the western edge of the park, a colonial-era **stone road** cuts over the mountains to the village of Higuerito on the south side of the mountains. The trail begins east of the village of Campamento, on the road to Santa Fe. Somewhere in the side of the mountains—good luck finding them—are the **Cuyamel Caves,** which archaeologists say have been used as a ritual site since pre-Columbian times.

Puerto Castilla

The largest container port in Honduras in terms of total tonnage transferred (Puerto Cortés handles more ships), Puerto Castilla is 28 km from Trujillo, just inside Punta Caxinas. Most of the freight shipped out of Puerto Castilla is agricultural products and raw materials, much of it produced by Standard Fruit. Unless shipping is a personal fetish, there is little reason to go out to Puerto Castilla. Beaches both on the bay side and the ocean side of the point are dirty and not particularly safe.

Fishing in Puerto Castilla's deep harbor is reputedly excellent. Waters drop straight down to 20 meters, allowing deep-water fish to be caught right off the docks. Boats can sometimes be found at Puerto Castilla going to Mosquitia or the Bay Islands. Ask around the docks or talk to the port captain for more information.

Rumors abound in Honduras about a massive oil refinery to be built in Puerto Castilla, and tensions are running high on both sides of the debate. Although it wouldn't do much for Trujillo's fledgling tourism industry, many powerful and well-connected people are backing the project, so it may well come to pass.

To visit the site of the first Mass celebrated on the mainland of the Americas, when Columbus landed here in 1502, ask the driver of the Puerto Castilla bus to let you off at the **Monumento a Colón,** a concrete cross on the beach reached by a short walk from the road. Spain reportedly donated funds for a more grandiose monument, but the money mysteriously vanished.

Refugio de Vida Silvestre Laguna de Guaymoreto

The Guaymoreto Wildlife Refuge, covering over 7,000 hectares, surrounds a broad lagoon formed by the Cabo de Honduras, east of Trujillo. The lagoon, canals, mangrove swamps, and a small island are excellent bird and monkey viewing areas. Getting into the reserve without guides is not easy—better to take an inexpensive day-trip with Turtle Tours, tel./fax 44-4431. The highlight of this trip is a visit to the Hacienda Tumbador crocodile farm. For those who want to freelance it, get out to the Guaymoreto bridge, which is shortly after the turnoff to Puerto Castilla just outside of Trujillo, and ask around for a boat to take you into the lagoon.

Santa Rosa de Aguán and Further East

Situated on a sand spit at the mouth of the Río Aguán, about an hour east from Trujillo by car, Santa Rosa de Aguán is a lovely, unspoiled Garífuna town infrequently visited by foreigners. Perhaps because the town is accessible by boat only, as it's on the far side of the river from the end of the road, it has a singularly isolated feel. Most buildings are thatched huts, although a few concrete houses have been built. There is one bar, not far from the dock.

Locals are very friendly and inquisitive about visitors. They'll be glad to help find someone willing to cook a meal or rent a room. One "hotel" in town has rooms for US$5 d. Camping on the endless, windswept beach is also possible. The water currents are treacherous, so don't go in above where you can stand. Mosquitoes can be fierce, but the perpetual breeze usually keeps them at bay.

To get to Santa Rosa, take the twice-daily Trujillo bus to the edge of the Río Aguán, where there are a couple of stores and a restaurant/bar, then pay US 20 cents for a *cayuco* (canoe) to take you over to the far side. If you're in a private vehicle, the turnoff to Dos Bocas and on to Santa Rosa de Aguán is exactly 22 km from the junction to Puerto Castilla, outside of Trujillo.

According to locals, you can walk to **Limón,** another Garífuna town to the east, in a day along the beach. Time estimates vary, so be ready for a long walk, but the beach looks beautiful the entire way, so camping out would be no hardship. Limón can also be reached by road from the turnoff at Corocito.

BOB RACE

THE BAY ISLANDS

INTRODUCTION

Many travelers coming to Honduras for a vacation have a visit to the Bay Islands on the top of the agenda. The three islands of Roatán, Utila, and Guanaja, plus some 60 smaller cays, are the country's prime tourist attraction—Caribbean jewels of sand, coconut palms swaying in the steady trade winds, green and blue waters, and one of the most spectacular coral-reef systems in the Americas, which attracts scuba divers from the world over.

For novice divers, finding a more convenient place to get a beginner's scuba certification or advanced training would be difficult. Eager instructors by the dozen are just waiting around for their next client, ready to take potential divers through the paces for rock-bottom prices in calm, clear, 28° C waters.

Diving and snorkeling may be the activities of choice among Bay Island visitors, but life above the waves has its own appeal. Centuries of pirate raids, immigration, deportation, and conquest have left a fascinating cultural and racial gumbo of British, Spanish, African, and native American influences that have combined to create the unique society of the Bay Islands.

High season for Bay Islands tourism is from Christmas to Easter, with a mini-high season July-September.

THE LAND

The Bay Islands, arrayed in an arc between 29 and 56 km off the Caribbean coast of Honduras, are the above-water expression of the Bonacca Ridge, an extension of the mainland Sierra de Omoa mountain range which disappears into the ocean near Puerto Cortés. The Bonacca Ridge forms the edge of the Honduran continental shelf in the Caribbean. Thus, on the northern, ocean-facing side of the three main islands shallow waters extend only just beyond the shore before disappearing over sheer underwater cliffs to the deep waters, while on the south side the waters fronting the Honduran

BAY ISLANDS HIGHLIGHTS

- Scuba diving
- Snorkeling on West Bay Beach, Roatán
- Slinging a hammock on Water Cay, Utila
- Partying Saturday night on Utila
- Visiting the north-coast beaches on Guanaja
- Seeing the dolphins at Anthony's Key, Roatán

mainland are much shallower. The height of the islands generally increases west to east, from the lowland swamps of Utila to the modest mid-island ridges of Roatán to two noteworthy peaks on Guanaja, the highest being 412 meters.

Flora and Fauna

Ecological zones in the Bay Islands include pine and oak savanna, arid tropical forest, beach vegetation, mangrove swamp, and iron shore, or fossilized, uplifted coral. Much of the once-dense native pine and oak forests have not survived centuries of sailors seeking masts, immigrants looking for building material, and hunters setting fires to scare game. The only forests left are on the privately owned island of Barbareta, in the hills above Port Royal, Roatán, and in a couple of remote corners of Guanaja.

Bay Island coconut palms, normally a reliable source of liquid refreshment and shade, have been struck in the last couple of years by Lethal Yellowing (LY), a mysterious plant disease responsible for the death of millions of palms in Florida, Jamaica, and Mexico. The plague is confined to various stands in Flowers Bay and West Bay, Roatán, and efforts are being made to cure trees with antibiotic injections and to replace dead stands with LY-resistant Jamaica and Creole coconut breeds.

Once abundant, many of the animal species endemic to the Bay Islands have been hunted to extinction or to the brink of it: manatees, seals, fresh- and saltwater turtles, white-tailed deer, green iguanas, basilisk lizards, boa constrictors, yellow-crowned and red-lored Amazon parrots, frigate birds, brown pelicans, and roseate terns have all vanished or are now seen only rarely. As recently as 30 years ago crocodiles were frequently seen crossing streets in Utila; when one was spotted (and promptly killed) in December 1995 the event was a major local news item.

In spite of the depredations of hunters, 15 species of lizard still survive on the island, along with 13 species of snake (including the poisonous but rarely seen coral), over 120 bird species (most of which are migratory), wild pigs, the small ratlike agouti, two species of opossum, and 13 species of bat.

BOB RACE

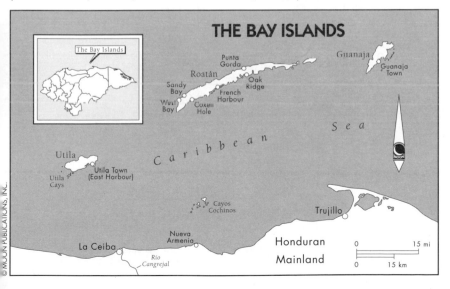

THE BAY ISLANDS

© MOON PUBLICATIONS, INC.

COPING WITH THE BLOODSUCKERS

Sand flies and mosquitoes can be voracious on the Bay Islands, so come prepared. Sand flies (also called *jejenes* and "no-see-ums") can be a true nightmare on the beach, turning the arms and legs of an unsuspecting sunbather into pincushions of little red welts. DEET, Skin-So-Soft, and coconut oil are all good repellents, as of course are long, loose-fitting clothes. A good strategy for enjoying a sunbathing session without getting gobbled is to sit out on a dock over the water; sand flies don't stray far from the beach. A good stiff breeze will get rid of them entirely, so with luck the trade winds will be blowing during your trip.

The Bay Island Conservation Association (BICA), with offices on all three islands, coordinates efforts to protect different endangered species as well as the islands' remaining forests by overseeing reserves at Port Royal and Carambola in Roatán, Turtle Harbor in Utila, and, supposedly, the entire island of Guanaja. More funds are to be made available for tighter environmental protection as part of a major new Inter-American Development Bank program for the Bay Islands.

Climate

The Bay Islands have a superbly comfortable climate, with year-round air temperatures ranging between 25 and 29° C and east-southeast trade winds blowing steadily most of the year. Daytime temperatures average 27° C, 21° C at night—hot but not stifling during the day and pleasant for sleeping at night.

Annual rainfall averages 220 cm, more than half of this coming in October and November, the height of the hurricane season. The best water visibility is when there is the least rain, usually March to September. Water temperature ranges from 26° C midwinter to 30° C in summer.

HISTORY

Pre-Columbian Residents

In spite of almost 50 identified archaeological sites, little is known of the early inhabitants of the Bay Islands. Most archaeologists now agree, after years of dispute, that pre-Columbian islanders were related to the mainland Pech, who prior to conquest lived close to the coast near Trujillo.

The first full-time residents are thought to have arrived no earlier than A.D. 600. After A.D. 1000 several major residential areas sprang up, such as Plan Grande in eastern Guanaja and the "80-Acre" site in eastern Utila. Because all the sites are located inland between 10-20 meters above sea level, it is believed the first islanders hated sand flies more than the current residents, and fled the shoreline to escape the pests.

The islander Pech grew manioc (cassava) and corn, hunted for deer and other game, fished from dugout canoes for reef fish and shark, and carried on a lively trade with the mainland Maya and Pech, as evidenced by discoveries of obsidian, flint, and ceramics with mainland designs.

Most pre-Columbian sites have long since been thoroughly sacked by fortune hunters both foreign and local. The best place to see examples of pottery and jade is in the museum at Anthony's Key Resort in Sandy Bay, Roatán. Locals may still try to sell visitors "yaba-ding-dings," as they call the artifacts, but after years of looting there aren't many pieces left to sell.

Conquest and Colonization

Believed to be the first European to visit the Bay Islands, Columbus landed near Soldado Beach on Guanaja in late July 1502 on his fourth voyage. After anchoring and sending his brother Bartholomew ashore for a look around, the Admiral named the island "Isla de los Pinos" (Island of the Pines) in honor of the impressive forests. He then commandeered a passing merchant canoe laden with goods from the mainland and forced its owner to accompany him to the Mosquitia Coast to serve as an interpreter. He remarked in his journal on a "very robust people who adore idols and live mostly from a certain white grain with which they make fine bread and the most perfect beer."

When the Spaniards returned on a slaving expedition in 1516, they made off with 300 Indians after a brief skirmish, only to have the would-be slaves take over the ship near Cuba and promptly set sail back to their home. But other ships looking for slaves soon followed, and not

THE BAY ISLANDS REEF SYSTEM

Coral reefs represent one of the most complex ecosystems on the planet, comparable in diversity to tropical rainforests. The Bay Islands reef is particularly varied because of its location on the edge of the continental shelf, at the transition between shallow-water and deep-water habitats. Some 96% of all species of marine life known to inhabit the Caribbean—from tiny specks of glowing bioluminescence to the whale shark, the largest fish in the world—have been identified in the waters surrounding the Bay Islands. Divers and snorkelers flock here in droves to experience a dizzying assortment of fishes, sponges, anemones, worms, shellfish, rays, sea turtles, sharks, dolphins, and hard and soft corals.

What is Coral?

Contrary to what many people understandably assume, coral is a nonswimming animal, not a plant. Each "branch" of coral is made up of hundreds or thousands of tiny flowerlike polyps. Each polyp is a thin-membraned invertebrate that compensates for its flimsy body by extracting calcium carbonate from the sea water and converting it into a brittle limestone skeleton. Through this continual, tireless construction process, the bizarre and beautiful undersea forests seen by divers and snorkelers are created, at a rate of about a centimeter per year.

Tiny, extended tentacles bring in some food drifting by in the water, but the anchored coral polyps must supplement their intake by housing miniscule algae cells; these cells in turn produce nutrients for the polyps through photosynthesis. Because of this symbiotic relationship, coral always grows in relatively shallow waters, where the sun can penetrate. It also means drops in water clarity due to pollution or erosion from construction, agriculture, or deforestation can be fatal for coral, robbing the algae of the light needed to photosynthesize.

The main reef-building coral in shallow areas is leafy lettuce coral *(Agaricia tenuifolia)*. This species virtually excludes other corals from many spur tops, growing in some areas to within 10 cm of the surface. In areas with greater wave energy, such as along the north sides of the islands, forests of treelike elkhorn coral *(Acropora palmata)* are common. Star coral *(Montastrea annularis)*, brain coral *(Diploria spp.)*, boulder brain coral *(Colpophylia natans)*, and elegant columns of pillar coral *(Dendrogyra cylindrus)* are often seen on the fore reef,

at a depth of 10-15 meters. Black coral does live around the Bay Islands, usually in deeper waters on reef walls. Many shallower patches have been destroyed by jewelry makers. In the water, black coral appears silver, only turning black when exposed to the air.

Fire coral, or hydrocoral, is not a true coral but a "battery of stinging nematocysts on tentacles of coral polyps," as Paul Humann, author of three good resources on reef systems, describes it. Learn what fire coral looks like right away, and keep well clear of it, as even a light brush can be painful. Should you accidentally bump into it, remember never to rub the affected area or wash it with fresh water or soap, as this can cause untriggered nematocysts to release their barbs. Two recommended treatments are vinegar or meat tenderizer, both of which immobilize the nematocysts.

The Reef

It's often claimed that the Bay Islands reef, together with the Belize reef system to the north, is the second-longest reef in the world after the Australian Great Barrier Reef. In truth, the Bay Islands reef is completely distinct from the Belize reef—not only does a 3,000-meter-deep undersea valley separate the two, but they are different kinds of reef. The Belize system is a barrier reef, with the coral wall separated from shore by a lagoon at least a mile wide, while the Bay Islands system is a fringing reef, essentially beginning right from the shore. Sections of the north side reef on the Bay Islands show characteristics of developing into a barrier reef in time, but are still considered fringing reef.

Reef geography is generally the same on all three of the main islands: the north side forms almost a complete wall, with only a few narrow passages allowing access to the small lagoon between the reef and the shore. The Guanaja north-side reef is much farther offshore (about a mile in places) than on Utila and Roatán. Much of the north-side reef is formed by precipitous cliffs dropping off to water depths of 50-2,000 feet, while the south-side reef frequently starts literally at the water's edge and slopes down at a more gentle grade. The southern reef is generally more broken up than the north, with channels, headlands, and cays. Sea mounts—hills of coral rising up off the ocean floor—

(continues on next page)

THE BAY ISLANDS REEF SYSTEM
(continued)

and spur-and-groove coral ridges are common, and are often the best places to see diverse sealife.

The Cayos Cochinos reef system shares similar characteristics as the other islands, except it lacks steep dropoffs and lagoons on the north side.

The Health of the Reef
Generally speaking, the Bay Islands reef is in pretty good shape. According to a recent study, the Roatán reef has 30% live coral cover (the rest covered by sand, seagrass, sponges, rubble, algae, dead coral, fire coral, etc.), a healthy percentage compared to other Caribbean reefs.

Tourism poses the most direct threat to the reef, since coastal development generates runoff and other forms of water pollution. Degraded water quality leads to algae blooms, which steal sunlight, oxy-gen, and other nutrients from the coral, literally choking the reef to death. The proliferation of divers is also beginning to take a toll on the reef; some oversaturated dive sites have been closed off to allow for recovery. These days dive boats more regularly tie off on buoys instead of anchoring on the reef, but divers continue to bump and grab coral in spite of frequent warnings. Each brush with a piece of coral wipes off a defensive film covering the polyps, allowing bacteria to penetrate. Just one small gap can compromise the defenses of an entire coral colony.

Black coral, formerly common around the Bay Islands, has been depleted in recent years by jewelry makers, whose work can be seen in several local gift shops. For those tempted to buy a piece, remember it is illegal to take black coral into the United States.

---

long after that, in 1530, the first *encomienda* was awarded on the Bay Islands. *Encomiendas* granted a conquistador rights to demand labor and tribute from the local inhabitants, supposedly in return for good governance and religious education.

This new economy had barely been established when European freebooters began appearing on the horizon, drooling at the thought of all the gold mined in the interior of Honduras passing through relatively isolated and unprotected Trujillo. French raiding boats appeared in 1536, followed by the English, who used the Bay Islands as a hideout for the first confirmed time in 1564 after capturing four Spanish frigates.

By the early 17th century, the persistent use of the Bay Islands as a base for pirate assaults and, briefly, as a settlement area for the British Providence Company had become a serious threat to the Spanish, so colonial authorities decided to depopulate the islands. By 1650 all the native islanders had been removed, most ending up in the malarial lowlands on Guatemala's Caribbean coast. This only made the islands more appealing to the pirates, who pursued their ventures unabated.

The many pirates who sheltered on the islands before the British military occupation in 1742—including Morgan, Coxen, Morris, Van Horn, and a host of others—spent most of their time hunting, fishing, or fixing up their boats, and never bothered to set up any buildings beyond temporary camps. Smaller groups preferred to anchor in the bay on the south side of Guanaja, with at least seven escape routes through the cays and reef, while larger fleets stayed at Port Royal, Roatán, with just one narrow, easily defensible entrance.

Following the declaration of war between England and Spain in 1739, British troops occupied Port Royal for several years, building two small forts and granting homesteads in Port Royal and Sandy Bay. The Spanish were awarded the islands as part of the Treaty of Aix-la-Chapelle in 1748, and the last settlers were finally removed in 1751. The British returned in 1779 following another outbreak of war. In 1782 Spaniards attacked Port Royal with 12 ships and took the forts after two days of fierce fighting. The forts and surrounding town were destroyed and Roatán was left uninhabited.

Development of the Modern Bay Islands
The first immigrant settlement in the Bay Islands that has survived to the present day is the Garífuna village at Punta Gorda, Roatán.

Some 4,000 Garífuna were unceremoniously dumped on the deserted island on 12 April 1797 by the British.

The Garífuna were followed in the 1830s by a wave of immigrants, both white and black, leaving the Cayman Islands in the wake of the abolition of slavery there. Although some isolated settlers lived on the islands when the Cayman Islanders arrived, the newcomers laid the foundations for the present-day towns. They moved first to Suc-Suc Cay off Utila in 1831, and shortly thereafter to Coxen Hole, Flowers Bay, and West End in Roatán and finally to Sheen and Hog Cays off Guanaja, which would eventually become Bonacca Town.

As the Bay Islands continued to be a useful geopolitical tool for the British, now wrangling for control over Central America with the United States, they were initially claimed by the British. In 1859, the British were forced to recognize Honduran sovereignty over the Bay Islands, but many islanders continued to think they were part of the British Empire until the early 20th century, when the Honduran government first began asserting its authority over the islands.

Current Society

The economy of the Bay Islands has long relied almost entirely on the ocean, despite brief forays in the banana and pineapple exportation business in the late 19th century. Fishing has always been a mainstay of the economy, supplemented by a modest boat-building industry (which has declined in recent years) and by money islander men earned working on cruise or cargo ships for several months of the year.

This low-key existence began to change, starting in the late 1960s, when tourists discovered the islands' reefs, beaches, and funky culture. Since the late 1980s, as Central American conflicts wound down, the pace has picked up dramatically. In 1990 an estimated 15,000 tourists came to the islands, by 1993 that number had doubled to 30,000, and it is thought to have doubled again in 1996.

In the last couple of years in particular the Bay Islands seem to have hit a sort of tourism critical mass and been deemed "in." New buildings—especially in Roatán—are no longer small homey hotels and quirky expatriate houses but multimillion dollar resorts, luxury mansions, and

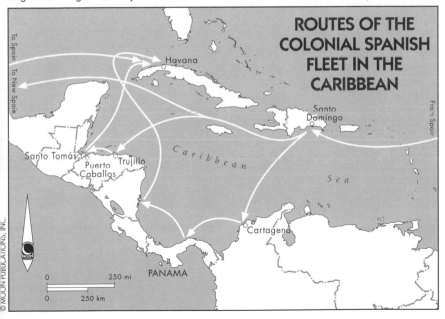

ROUTES OF THE COLONIAL SPANISH FLEET IN THE CARIBBEAN

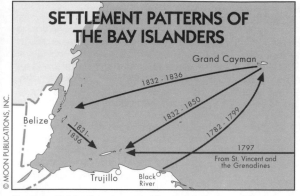

SETTLEMENT PATTERNS OF
THE BAY ISLANDERS

Grand Cayman

1832 - 1836

1832 - 1850

1782 - 1799

1831-
1836

1797
From St. Vincent and
the Grenadines

Belize

Trujillo   Black
            River

© MOON PUBLICATIONS, INC.

mates put the population at about 24,000 for all three islands, with an annual growth rate of nine percent, compared to just under three percent for the entire country. Considering rising prices from tourism, an increase in crime, and the growing intrusion of the Honduran government—most recently a rude awakening from the tax man, also looking for a slice of the foreign-exchange pie—it's no surprise some islanders have mixed feelings about their tourism boom.

fenced-off housing compounds. A total of US$100 million in tourist-related developments is slated for the next three years. The changes have benefitted many islanders immensely, and most now live off the tourist trade in one way or another. But some now wonder if they have completely lost control of their islands' future.

Even before the tourist boom, islanders had always maintained a better standard of living than their mainland countrymen (still called Spaniards by the islanders). Consequently a steadily growing stream of Latino immigrants have come over to get a piece of the good life, a trend that is changing the face of the islands and that many islanders are not too happy about. Recent esti-

The Inter-American Development Bank and the Honduran government are beginning to implement a US$24 million program of infrastructure and environmental projects on the Bay Islands—projects that aim to alleviate some of the harsh effects of tourism-related development on the marine and terrestrial ecosystems and on islander society. Strict regulations will be placed on construction and road building to safeguard against erosion, which, apart from being an unfortunate loss of scarce topsoil, also hurts the reef. Sewage and water projects will also be undertaken. Guanaja, Utila, and Roatán are supposed to benefit equally from the loan, but because of the heavy concentration of development on Roatán that island is expected to receive the most attention.

ROATÁN

Rattan-Island is about 30 miles long and 13 broad, about eight leagues distant from the coast of Honduras . . . The south side is very convenient for shipping, having many fine harbours. The north side is defended by a reef of rocks that extend from one end of the island to the other, having but few passages through, and those of but small note, being mostly made use of by the turtlers . . . It is likewise very healthy, the inhabitants hereabouts generally living to a great age.

—Thomas Jefferys,
Geographer to the King of England, 1762.

Jefferys may have been a bit off on the measurements—Roatán is actually about 40 miles long and only a little over two miles wide—but he did accurately describe the natural features that have long made Roatán the choice of Bay Island immigrants, from the first pirates 400 years ago to the resort builders and dive fanatics of today.

Theories on the source of the island's name vary wildly. The most popular explanation, supported by Jefferys and many other colonial-era chroniclers, is that Roatán is a derivation of rattan, a common vine found in the Caribbean. Another possibility is that it's a severe corruption of the Nahuatl expression *coatl-tlan,* "place of women." A third, far-fetched hypothesis is that the name comes from the English expression "Rat-land," referring to the island's pirate inhabitants.

Tourists and retirees began arriving on Roatán in the 1960s, and in recent years the influx has increased dramatically. Roatán has been deemed respectable—enjoying fawning write-ups in travel publications and the limelight of frequent celeb sightings—and is now home to a large expatriate community consisting mainly of Americans but also including many Europeans.

After some 15 years of raging real-estate speculation and building fever, few nooks and crannies have escaped the scrutiny of developers. Remote sections of coastline on all sides of the island have been divided up in lots for development as private homes or resorts. Nevertheless, towns like West End and Sandy Bay remain relatively slow-paced and not outrageously expensive when compared to other Caribbean islands.

Some 16,000 people, roughly two-thirds of the Bay Islands' population, live on Roatán. Coxen Hole, the island's largest town, is the department capital. Sand flies can be a plague here, so come prepared (see the special topic "Coping with the Bloodsuckers").

GETTING THERE

Air

As the most frequently visited of the three Bay Islands, Roatán has plenty of air service. **Sosa,** tel. 45-1154, **Caribbean,** tel. 45-1466 or 45-1933, **Isleña,** tel. 45-1088, and **Rollins,** tel. 45-1967, offer several flights daily to and from La Ceiba (US$23). Connections are available to San Pedro Sula, Tegucigalpa, and the Mosquitia. Caribbean also flies to Belize City twice a week. **Taca,** tel. 45-1387, offers three flights a week to and from the U.S. (once a week each to and from Houston, New Orleans, and Miami) as well as connections to other Central America cities. Travelers leaving Roatán for foreign destinations are required to pay a US$25 departure tax.

The airport is three km from downtown Coxen Hole, on the highway toward French Harbour. Taxis from town cost US$1.50, *to* town sometimes more, depending on how wealthy you look. Taxis to and from West Bay run about US$5. You can walk from the airport to Coxen Hole in about 20 minutes, or just walk the short distance out to the highway and await a bus heading into town. The buses run every half hour or so until midafternoon.

Boat

The **MV *Tropical*** runs daily between La Ceiba and the municipal dock in Coxen Hole; the two-hour ride costs US$7. Some snacks are available on the boat, and a movie is shown in the

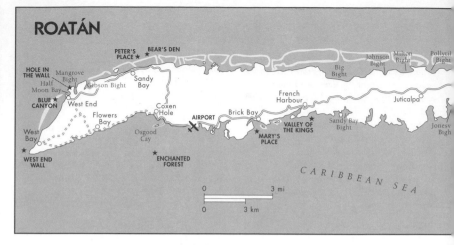

ROATÁN

cabin. Tuesday through Friday the *Tropical* leaves La Ceiba at 7 a.m. and Roatán at 10 a.m. On Saturday it leaves Roatán at 7 a.m., La Ceiba at 11 a.m., and Roatán again at 2 p.m. Sunday it leaves La Ceiba at 7 a.m. and Roatán at 3:30 p.m. Monday it leaves La Ceiba at 5 a.m., Roatán at 7:30 a.m., and La Ceiba again at 3:30 p.m. Offices are on the docks in Coxen Hole, tel. 45-1795, and at the Cabotaje dock in La Ceiba, tel. 42-0780.

Coxen Hole's **port captain,** tel. 45-1262, can be helpful (if you speak Spanish) in arranging rides to the other islands, Mosquitia, Belize, or elsewhere. Better yet, prowl from dock to dock asking boat crews where they are going and when. Some boats refuse to take passengers, while others are happy for the extra cash.

GETTING AROUND

Roatán has the Bay Islands' only major highway; it runs east-west connecting various island settlements. While the majority of visitors are likely to stay put in West End, Sandy Bay, or the confines of their resort, the more adventurous may wish to explore Roatán's less accessible corners. Buses operate along the highway, and hitchhiking is a viable option for reaching places with regular traffic but off the main highway, such as Flowers Bay, Camp Bay Beach, or Port Royal.

Buses and Tours
Most of the island can be covered on Tica minibuses, which leave Coxen Hole frequently from 7 a.m. until late afternoon. The buses run to Sandy Bay (US 40 cents), West End (US 60 cents), French Harbour (US 40 cents), Punta Gorda (US 90 cents) and Oak Ridge (US 90 cents). All buses leave from the main street in Coxen Hole—the smaller minibuses to West End leave from the park next to the H.B. Warren Supermarket, while the larger (less frequent) east-side buses depart from a little further east up the street.

Tica also operates comfortable new vans and a 30-seater bus for island tours or excursions. Day rates or a set price for a trip can be negotiated. Those who have limited Spanish should request Matilde Zuñiga, the only English-speaking driver. It's about US$80 for an eight-seat van on a full-day island tour. Call 45-1764, 45-2206, 45-1809 or 45-1290 for more information.

Car Rental
Several companies rent compact cars and small four-wheel-drives at rates ranging US$45-55 per day. **Toyota,** tel. 45-1166, and **Avis,** tel. 45-1568, both have offices opposite the highway from the airport. Other agencies include **Roatán Rent-A-Car,** closer to Coxen Hole, tel. 45-1944; **Sandy Bay Rent-A-Car,** with offices in Sandy Bay, tel. 45-1710, fax 45-1711, and West End, tel. 45-1925; and **Bay Island Rent-A-Car,** on the highway in Sandy Bay, tel. 45-1815.

Bay Island Rent-A-Car also rents scooters, when they're working, for US$25 a day. These would be a great way to get around if it weren't for the seemingly psychotic taxi and minibus drivers and the narrow, pot-holed, occasionally cow-filled roads.

Bringing Your Car
For those who just can't do without their own set of wheels, it is possible to ship a car from either Miami or La Ceiba. One frequently used operator is **Hyde Shipping,** with offices in Miami, at 3033 N.W. North River Dr., Miami, FL 33142, tel. (305) 638-4262, fax (305) 635-8939, and in French Harbour, Roatán, tel. 45-1404, 45-1495, or 45-1512. Shipping a standard-size car to Roatán from La Ceiba costs US$60, from Miami US$600.

Cruises, Fishing Trips, Charters
The clear, clean waters surrounding Roatán, stroked by steady trade winds most of the year and stocked with most of the known fish species in the Caribbean, are superb for sailing and fishing trips. Many boat owners offer half- and full-day cruises, snorkel trips, cocktail cruises, deep-sea and flats fishing, or combinations of the above.

Several companies offer cruises to the Cayos Cochinos, Barbareta, Morat, Guanaja, and elsewhere in the vicinity. **Far Tortuga Charters,** information at Librería Casi Todo, tel. 45-1255, fax 45-1659, offers cruises aboard its trimaran *Genesis.* **Casablanca Charters,** information at

Rick's American Cafe in Sandy Bay, sails the 38 foot ketch *Defiance III* out of West End for US$50 full day, US$30 half day. Captain Harold Ebright, a PADI Divemaster, takes the **SV Honky Tonk** out for overnight or half-day charters. For information call 45-1222 (or hail Ebright on VHF channel 16).

Roatán Sail and Dive Charters, tel. 45-1620, operates two boats: a 54-foot catamaran sleeping eight, and a 60-foot ketch monohull sleeping six.

RECOMMENDED ROATÁN DIVE SITES

WEST END:
- West End
- Blue Channel
- Hole In The Wall

SANDY BAY:
- Peter's Place
- Bear's Den

FRENCH HARBOUR/SOUTH SIDE:
- Mary's Place
- Valley of the Kings
- Enchanted Forest

EAST END:
- Pigeon Cays
- Morat Wall

DIVING RULES AND ETIQUETTE

- Don't dive alone.
- Know your limitations and only dive if in good physical condition.
- Always follow the dive tables.
- No spear fishing.
- Don't remove any marine organisms, alive or dead.
- Don't anchor anywhere in or near coral—use the buoys.
- Don't litter or discharge foreign substances into the water.
- When diving, always fly a diver-down flag and lower the flag when all divers are back on board. When passing moored boats, or boats flying a diving flag, always pass on seaward side at least 150 feet away, even in a small boat.
- Avoid contact with any living part of the reef.
- Always observe proper buoyancy techniques and secure dangling equipment.
- Never sit or stand on coral formations, or grab coral to steady youself.
- Don't grab, poke, ride, or chase reef inhabitants.
- Don't feed the fish.
- Discourage reef degradation by refusing to buy black-coral jewelry, sea turtle products, shell ornaments, etc.
- If you find garbage on the reef, gently remove it and bring it back to shore.
- Take only photographs, leave only bubbles.

The charter offers eight-day, seven-night dive and fish trips for US$3,700 a couple and US$7,100 for six people, everything included. Destinations are worked out between guests and captain. This recommended charter is a favorite among honeymooners, with many annual repeat customers.

Two deep-sea fishing outfits are **Hot Rod Charters,** tel. 45-1862 or 45-1522, which charges US$300 half day, US$500 full day for a trip aboard a fully equipped 35-foot *Trojan,* and the **Coco View Resort,** tel. 45-1011, fax 45-1013, which takes out *The Huntress,* a 39-foot sportfishing boat. Oak Ridge residents **Carmen and Sandy Byrd,** tel. 45-2163, fax 45-2230, will take one or two people out on their 16-foot skiff for a full day of flats fishing; US$165, plus US$10 more to rent gear.

The **French Harbour Yacht Club** in French Harbour, tel. 45-1478 or 45-1460, fax 45-1459, is a likely place to look for **crew jobs** or rides on yachts.

WEST END

Although it is the main tourist town of Roatán and lined with cabañas, restaurants, and dive shops, West End remains a slow-paced seaside village and an undeniably superb location to lose yourself in the relaxing rhythms of Caribbean life. Even during the high season (Dec.-April) people and events move at a languid pace up and down the sandy, ocean-side road that constitutes "town." It's a telling sign that the road has been left rutted and unpaved—cars and bicycles must slow to a snail's pace, bouncing along, while pedestrians are free to wander at leisure, stopping to browse for T-shirts or to admire yet another spectacular sunset right off shore.

Construction of new houses and cabañas continues, but in an unobtrusive way—new developments are tucked away among the palms and don't dominate the visual landscape. You're not overwhelmed by wealthy tourists in West End, as it has no luxury resorts. The roughly 400 local residents have not lost their easy friendliness, and fortunately seem to be influencing the newcomers more than the newcomers are influencing them.

Sights
West End's main attractions are natural and in plain view: beaches, 28° C bright blue water, and, a couple hundred yards offshore, the coral reef, marked by a chain of buoys. The waters around West End are kept very clean, and visitors can jump in pretty much wherever it's convenient. The best beach in town is **Half Moon**

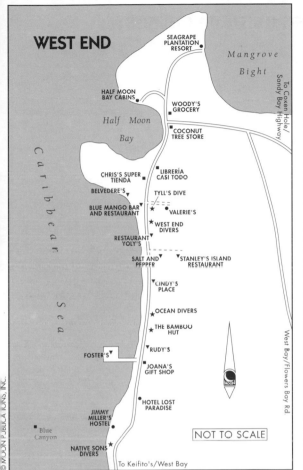

WEST END

SEAGRAPE PLANTATION RESORT

Mangrove Bight

To Coxen Hole/ Sandy Bay Highway

HALF MOON BAY CABINS

Half Moon Bay

WOODY'S GROCERY

COCONUT TREE STORE

C a r i b b e a n   S e a

CHRIS'S SUPER TIENDA

LIBRERÍA CASI TODO

BELVEDERE'S

TYLL'S DIVE

BLUE MANGO BAR AND RESTAURANT

VALERIE'S

WEST END DIVERS

RESTAURANT YOLY'S

SALT AND PEPPER

STANLEY'S ISLAND RESTAURANT

CINDY'S PLACE

OCEAN DIVERS

THE BAMBOO HUT

FOSTER'S

RUDY'S

JOANA'S GIFT SHOP

West Bay/Flowers Bay Rd

HOTEL LOST PARADISE

JIMMY MILLER'S HOSTEL

Blue Canyon

NATIVE SONS DIVERS

NOT TO SCALE

To Keifito's/West Bay

© MOON PUBLICATIONS, INC.

Bay, a swath of palm-lined sand right at the entrance to West End, bordered by points of iron shore (fossilized, raised coral) on either side forming the namesake shape. Another good place to swim and sunbathe is the dock in front of Jimmy Miller's hostel at the south end of town. Both of these spots also happen to be near two of the best snorkeling sites off West End. The reef passes right across the mouth of Half Moon Bay, an easy swim from shore, with particularly fine reef near the southern two points. Sea turtles and rays are often seen in the sand flats and shallower sections of reef here.

One of the buoys in front of Jimmy's hostel marks the entrance to **Blue Canyon,** a spectacular channel cutting through the reef. It's a bit of a swim for snorkelers, so take your time heading out to conserve energy for the reef and the trip back.

There are several other sites on the reef off West End, but in looking for them beware of boat traffic. Snorkel gear can be rented from any of the dive shops for US$5 or from Cindy's Restaurant for US$3. A passport or US$10 deposit is usually required.

Dive Shops

Although not as numerous as on Utila, West End's half-dozen fully equipped dive shops offer dives and courses for all levels and in several languages. Minimum standard prices have been set by the local government to avoid the sort of cutthroat competition rampant on Utila, so courses and dive packages generally cost about the same everywhere: US$200 for a standard open-water certification, US$160 for the advanced open-water, US$60-75 for a resort course, US$30 per dive, US$25 each with five or more dives. Generally all shops have two dives daily, one morning and one afternoon, and start new certification courses every couple of days.

Tyll's Dive, fax 45-1245, is one of the oldest shops in West End and has a full range of courses and a friendly staff. Tyll's also organizes sailing trips on a 42-foot yacht.

Ocean Divers, tel. 45-1005, in Canada (514) 934-2255, in the U.S. (800) 458-3281, in Europe 31-7114-1557, runs a hotel with their dive shop and offers package rates for diving and courses. An open-water certification package including five days accommodations, breakfast, and transport to and from the airport costs US$342-399. Weeklong dive packages, with

DIVING IN THE BAY ISLANDS

Upon arrival in the Bay Islands, prospective divers can be overwhelmed with the number of dive shops and courses. How to know what's best for you? First, try to realistically decide if you are ready to go diving. Bay Islands dive instructors have many stories of would-be students who, believe it or not, could barely swim or were actually scared of the water. Although it's relatively cheap and it's fun, if you just can't get rid of that lurking panic after a couple of shallow dives, accept the fact that diving is not for you. One of the best ways to find out how you will react to scuba diving is to try snorkeling a few times first to see how you feel in the underwater world. Snorkelers can often hitch rides on dive boats and enjoy the same sites without all the gear.

Novices ready to take the plunge have a choice of either a **resort course** or **open-water certification.** A resort course, normally costing US$50-80, is an introductory dive for those who aren't sure if they'll like diving or not. It involves a half-day of instruction followed by a shallow, controlled dive.

The open-water certification, as taught in the Bay Islands, normally includes two days of classroom instruction and shallow-water training, followed by two more days of open-water dives, gradually descending to a maximum depth of 15 meters. A 50-question multiple-choice test on material that has been drilled into your head is the last step to becoming a certified open-water diver. You are then allowed to dive without an instructor—but never without another diver. Never dive alone.

Dive shops will sometimes take **referrals,** wherein a person completes the academic and shallow-water training at home and finishes the open-water dives with the shop. Considering that the shallow-water training could be accomplished for less money in balmy, clear Caribbean waters instead of the local YMCA pool, there's not much attraction in this option unless your time on the islands is extremely limited.

Many newly certified divers come out of their course feeling slightly uneasy about the idea of diving without that reassuring veteran instructor at their shoulder, and may want to immediately continue their controlled training with the **advanced open-water course.** The advanced course provides specific instruction in undersea navigation and multilevel diving—essential for planning your own dives—and includes two diving highlights: the night dive and the deep dive (to 40 meters). Although dive shops and PADI may imply otherwise (one of PADI's nicknames is Put Another Dollar

room, breakfast, and 13 dives, tanks and weights included, cost US$510-573.

West End Divers, tel./fax 45-1531, one of the more popular shops in town, has two dive boats and lots of new equipment. **Seagrape Divers,** tel. 45-1717, at the north end of town, has three boats and usually offers the minimum prices for courses.

Native Sons Divers, tel. 45-1335, next to Jimmy's at the south end of town, was opened in 1994 by an islander with divemaster experience at the Reef Resort in Oak Ridge and Cross Creek Divers in Utila. He offers certification through PDIC, a relatively new U.S.-based organization, and has new gear and two small boats.

Other Recreation
Sea kayaks can be rented at the Bamboo Hut Restaurant, next to Ocean Divers, for US$4 per hour or US$18 per day, or from Sea Blades Kayaks, run by Librería Casi Todo for US$12 half-day, US$20 full day. Sea Blades offers guided tours for US$45 full day with lunch included.

Belvedere's, tel. 45-1171 (or VHF channel 16), operates **glass-bottom-boat tours** for US$8 pp with three persons minimum, as does the Coral Reef Explorer, tel. 45-1402 or ask at the Coconut Tree Store.

For fun and convenient transportation, Chris' Super Tienda rents **mountain bikes** for US$10 a day.

WEST END ACCOMMODATIONS

Hotels in West End mostly fall into the moderate range, from US$20-60 for a double, generally in a cabin with ceiling fan, screened windows, and private bathroom. The budget traveler will be glad to hear, however, that inexpensive digs are still available. There are no luxury resorts in West End.

Budget
Jimmy Miller's Hostel has the cheapest beds in town—mattresses laid out on a wooden floor in a large communal room upstairs with mos-

In), divers are not required to have an advanced certification to do either deep or night dives.

So you've decided you're ready for the open-water course—how to choose between all the different dive shops? Price is not much of a factor, as everyone pretty much charges the same amount. At last report, open-water courses in Utila cost about US$150, on Roatán and Guanaja more like US$200-250. The Roatán municipal government has actually set minimum prices to avoid price wars like those that occasionally hit Utila.

Another variable to consider is the **certifying organization** used by the dive shops. In the Bay Islands, almost everybody uses PADI (Professional Association of Dive Instructors), the most widely recognized certification in the world. A couple of shops are PDIC, a newer, U.S.-based organization that has less of an established reputation.

Perhaps the most important criteria for choosing a shop is the quality of the instructors and equipment and the shop's reputation for safety. A good instructor can mean the difference between a fun, safe, and informative course and one that just follows the book, or worse. Ask how many dives an instructor has—100 is very few, 500 is a decent amount, 1,000 or more is a lot. Also, an instructor with 100 or so dives is likely to have gone through all or most of his or her courses on the Bay Islands,

where conditions are excellent almost all the time. Consequently, that instructor will have less experience dealing with emergency situations than a diver trained in, for instance, the North Sea or the northern Pacific off California. Instructors with training in commercial diving, mixed-gas diving, cave diving, or military diving tend to be more safety-conscious and cautious.

Finally, look at the gear you would be using. The newer, the better. Especially crucial is having an air compressor in good condition, to ensure clean air in your tank. A large dive boat makes for easier water entry/exit and a less choppy and wet ride to and from the dive sites than a small one. Those prone to seasickness should bring motion sickness pills, which are sold by many dive shops.

At least two well-known companies offer packages allowing divers to spend an entire week aboard a fully equipped live-aboard dive boat. If this interests you, contact the **Bay Aggressor,** in the U.S. at P.O. Drawer K, Morgan City, LA 70381, tel. (800) 348-2628 or (504) 385-2628, fax (504) 384-0817; or **Peter Hughes Diving,** in the U.S. at 6851 Yamuri St., Ste. 10, Coral Gables, FL 33146, tel. (800) 932-6237 or (305) 669-9391, fax (305) 669-9475. Both charge about US$1,200 for one week, everything included except transport to Honduras.

---

quito nets overhead. He also has two private rooms and a rudimentary kitchen downstairs. A couple of hammocks can be slung on the porch, pleasant sleeping when there's a breeze. Jimmy's is not for those in need of creature comforts (hose shower, nowhere to store valuables), but the price is certainly right at US$2.20 for a dorm bed. The hostel is at the south end of town right on the beach.

Valerie's is a quiet, comfortable, and inexpensive hotel/hostel behind Tyll's Dive Shop, with dorm beds for US$5 with use of kitchen and comfortable patio, safe lock-up, mosquito nets, and bunk beds. Private rooms are US$10-20 d, some with porches and hammocks. Travelers are often found playing cards and socializing on the patio.

Many local residents rent rooms out of their house for US$8-15 d—ask around.

Midrange
Located 15 minutes from West End on the way to West Bay, **Keifito's Beach Plantation,** fax 45-1648, has quiet, clean cabins for US$22 d that

make for a great reasonably-priced getaway. It's located on a tree-covered hillside sloping down to the water. The coastline here is rocky, but there is a large dock to sunbathe on and swim off, and West Bay Beach is only a few minutes' walk away. Excellent, inexpensive food is served at the restaurant, situated on a breezy deck overlooking the sea. The staff is very friendly.

West End icon **Foster Diaz,** tel./fax 45-1008, the owner of Foster's Bar and Restaurant, has several cabins for rent in West End and West Bay for US$20-50, some with kitchens and private porches. Foster also organizes snorkel tours, fishing trips, and other excursions.

Half Moon Bay Cabins, tel. 45-1015, in the U.S. (800) 989-9970, fax (813) 933-1977, on the northern point of Half Moon Bay, offers frequently recommended waterfront cabins for US$48 d with fan, US$65 with a/c, free snorkel gear for guests , a reef right out front, and great seafood at the restaurant. More information is available from Rick McLaughlin, 1305 Ellicott St., Tampa, FL 33603.

*Foster's restaurant
and bar is a popular
gathering spot in
West End.*

At the far north end of town is **Seagrape Plantation Resort,** with a dive shop and 10 unspectacular but clean duplex bungalows set amid palm trees for US$42 d. Dive and meal packages are available.

A long-time resident of West End, **Hotel Lost Paradise,** tel. 45-1306, fax 45-1388, rents rooms in a main building and in cabins on stilts in the sand for US$50 s or d with fan, US$68 with a/c. Meal plans are available, as are better rates for multiday stays.

WEST END FOOD AND ENTERTAINMENT

Inexpensive
Finding low-priced food in West End isn't easy. One of the few inexpensive restaurants in town, **Cindy's Place** serves up homestyle chicken, fish, and steak, with mashed potatoes, salad, fries, or other fixings for US$3-5. Run by friendly islanders, it's a relaxed place to hang out and talk, inside or at one of the picnic benches on the lawn. They don't sell beer but you can buy some next door.

Stanley's Island Restaurant, on the porch of a house a hundred paces up the hill from the main road (look for the sign), serves inexpensive, unpretentious food like tacos, *pastelitos* (deep-fried pastries stuffed with meat and potatoes), enchiladas, grilled fish, and a nightly vegetarian dish. Closed Sunday.

The restaurant at **Keifito's Beach Plantation,** a 15-minute walk south of West End along the beach, has very tasty grilled sandwiches for US$2 and filling, reasonably priced breakfasts. Closes at 5 p.m. on Tuesday and Thursday, open until 8 p.m. other days.

Midrange
The choice breakfast spot in town is unquestionably **Rudy's,** where the owner will serve you up a steaming cup of coffee and invariably reply heartily "Still alive!" when you ask how he's doing. The response is so famous it appears on a specially made T-shirt. Rudy whips up superlative, filling banana pancakes, excellent omelettes (you pick the fixings), and fresh juices (the mango is nectar of the gods) for US$2-4. He also receives and sends faxes for a fee (fax 45-1205) and has cabins for rent.

Restaurant Yoly's next to West End Divers has an authentic pizza oven and makes a very respectable pie for US$3-5. This popular post-dive dinner spot is open in the high season Mon.-Sat. 5-9 p.m., in low season Monday, Wednesday, and Friday only.

An American couple operates **Belvedere's,** a tiny Italian restaurant on the dock behind Chris' Super Tienda, with a rotating menu including eggplant parmesan, spaghetti, lobster, lasagna, and chicken for US$4-7. Open Sun.-Thurs. for dinner only.

For the culinary world tour, check out **Salt and Pepper,** featuring revolving international specials Mon.-Sat., a different cuisine nightly from Thai to Italian to Greek. The small, highly recommended restaurant is open for breakfast, lunch, and dinner, US$4-12 per entree.

Entertainment

Along with all his cabins, Foster Diaz is the owner of **Foster's,** one of the social centers of West End. The restaurant/bar is a two-story wooden contraption built on a dock over the water, with a couple of hammocks swinging between the wood beams and always a few people hanging about drinking beers. Occasionally bands or DJs play on weekends. Foster also operates a water taxi to West Bay.

The **Blue Mango Bar and Restaurant** offers happy hour nightly 5:30-6:30 p.m., and organizes parties and dances regularly. Light meals and snacks are served until midnight normally, later on weekends. It's closed Monday.

The **Bamboo Hut** shows movies nightly at 7:30 p.m.

MORE WEST END PRACTICALITIES

Shopping

For handicrafts, jewelry, batik, swimsuits and other assorted odds and ends, check out **Joana's Gift Shop,** tel. 45-1392, across from Foster's. **Librería Casi Todo,** tel. 45-1255, across from the church, has a small selection of new and used books and some English-language publications, and also acts as the local Isleña agent.

Chris' Super Tienda sells T-shirts, sunscreen, Skin-So-Soft, postcards and a few groceries, and will place local calls for a fee.

The best, and really only, grocery store in West End is **Woody's,** with a decent selection of packaged goods and the occasional slightly limp-looking vegetable. H.B. Warren in Coxen Hole is far superior. The **Coconut Tree Store** at the entrance to town usually has *The Miami Herald* for sale at US$2.20 daily, US$4 on Sunday.

Exchange

Several stores and dive shops will change dollars, and sometimes travelers' checks, but never at a good rate. Take care of exchange in Coxen Hole whenever possible.

Getting There and Away

Minibuses to and from Coxen Hole leave frequently between 7 a.m. and 5 p.m., US 60 cents each way. Collective taxis cost US$1.30.

WEST BAY

Until recently people raved about West Bay being one of the last great untouched beaches on the island, a place where islanders and visitors alike often went to sling a hammock, build a bonfire, and pass the night drinking rum with friends. Little did those happy campers know the land along the bay was being subdivided and sold, both to islanders and foreigners. Once the real-estate feeding frenzy subsided, in 1994, the construction boom began. Now the beach is lined with cabañas, private homes, a new housing development, and a few hotels.

Despite the development, West Bay Beach—sometimes called Tabiyana Beach—is still a stunning spot: 1.5 km of powdery, palm-lined sand lapped by exquisite turquoise-blue water. At the south end of the beach, where a wall of iron shore juts out into the water, the coral reef meets the shore. For anyone who wants a low-key encounter with an exceptionally fine reef without a long swim or any scuba gear, this is *the* place. It's almost too beautiful—more like an aquarium than a section of live reef, with brilliantly colored fish dodging about, the odd barracuda lurking, gently waving sponges and sea fans, just a few feet from the beach.

The reef comes closest to shore at the beach's south end, but for anyone willing to swim out a bit the entire bay is lined by excellent reef. Keep an eye out for boats when in the water. Several resorts take guests out to West Bay for daytrips, which means the beach can get crowded during the middle of the day, but in the early morning and late afternoon it's generally quiet.

Near West Bay

West Bay was formerly connected by trail to Flower's Bay, a small and little-visited village on the south side of the island toward Coxen Hole. This trail still exists, but the new housing construction in the hills around West Bay makes it difficult to find. It's also possible to walk to Flowers Bay by dirt road in about an hour—

red-lored Amazon parrot

Cabañas Roatana, tel./fax 45-1271, U.S. address c/o Johan and Liz Mathias, Jackson Shipping, 5353 W. Tyson Ave., Tampa, FL 33611, about midway up the beach set back slightly from the shore, has well-equipped rooms for US$60-90 (depending on the season and whether the room has a/c or not) in a large two-story house. Meal packages are available and scuba or fishing trips can be arranged by the American owners.

At the south end of the beach is the somewhat overpriced Tabiyana Beach Resort, tel. 45-1038, fax 45-1033, with 10 rooms in four buildings, some with kitchenettes, for about US$85 pp. Both guests and nonguests can rent kayaks and snorkel gear.

Food
Formerly in West End, Bite on the Beach is the favorite spot in West Bay to grab a snack or a meal. Enjoy seating on a breezy seaside deck, and filling but reasonably priced (US$3-7 per entree) dishes such as shrimp, fried fish, chicken, soups, and burritos. Open for lunch and dinner Wed-Sat., lunch only on Sunday, closed Monday and Tuesday.

West Point Restaurant, near Bite on the Beach, serves slightly pricey but good quality seafood including king crab, lobster, grouper, and shrimp, prepared by a European chef with creative recipes. Open daily 8 a.m.-10 p.m., US$5-11 per entree, with quiet patio seating. The owners also rent snorkel gear and can arrange rooms in Foster's West Bay cabins.

JB's, a bar/restaurant toward the south end of the beach, offers a revolving menu of seafood and American-style meat and potatoes daily for US$5-10 per entree.

Getting There and Away
From West End you can walk to West Bay (45 minutes along the beach, past the new development on the point), or take a water taxi (US$1 from Foster's and elsewhere) or car (a four-km dirt road turning off the Coxen Hole highway near the entrance to West End). West Bay residents are considering instituting a toll for cars as they collectively paid for the road to be built and are receiving no help from the municipality in maintaining it.

start out on the dirt road back toward West End and take the only turn-off to the right. A dirt road also runs between Flowers Bay and Coxen Hole, along the island's south shore.

In the hills between West Bay and West End are the remains of several pre-Columbian Indian burial sites and settlements. Jimmy Miller in West End knows the whereabouts of a couple of them and will take visitors there on horseback for a fee, as will several others in town. There's not much to see beyond a few mounds and potsherds, but it's an interesting excursion and a break from the water.

Accommodations
Foster Diaz runs several cabins and duplexes near the north end of West Bay beach (inquire either at his restaurant in West End or at the West Point Restaurant, see below) from US$15-40 d, including a small room built into the branches of a mango tree, complete with electricity and running water.

SANDY BAY

With a full-time population of about 1,200, Sandy Bay is considerably larger than West Bay, but somehow it doesn't feel larger. Development has arrived, but it's mostly limited to private houses rather than hotels and resorts. Anthony's Key Resort (AKR), which literally splits Sandy Bay in two, is a massive tourist complex, but most guests don't venture off the grounds into town, resulting in little impact on the life of locals.

The waters around Sandy Bay and Anthony's Key Resort were the first-established section of the Roatán Marine Reserve, created in 1989, and the snorkeling and diving are superb. The sizable beach in Sandy Bay is somewhat muddy, not well-kept, and generally not the best for sunbathing.

Sights and Recreation

The only dive shop in Sandy Bay not run by a hotel is **Tino's Diving and Eco Adventures,** tel. 45-1920 or 45-1712. It's owned and operated by the amiable Tino Monterroso, who has worked at many of the local resorts as a divemaster. He operates two small boats and charges US$30 per dive, less for a package of dives, and US$265 for PADI open-water certifications with at least two people. Apart from being an experienced diver, Tino is a legendary explorer and has lots of stories to tell.

The Institute for Marine Sciences (IMS) at AKR, with its famous bottle-nosed dolphin shows and encounter program, is one of the main attractions at Sandy Bay. Shows are held daily except Wednesday at 10 a.m. and 4 p.m., Saturday and Sunday also at 1 p.m., US$4 admission. Dolphin dives, 35-40 minutes of controlled but unstructured swimming with dolphins over open-water sand flats, cost a certified diver US$100, US$15 extra to rent equipment. You can snorkel for 30 minutes with the dolphins for US$75. Divers and snorkelers are always accompanied by an Institute trainer. The IMS has several exhibits on invertebrates, reptiles, birds, fish, coral-reef life, and the geology of the Bay Islands, as well as a small but worthwhile bilingual museum on local archaeology and history. Admission to the IMS and museum only, excluding the dolphin show, is US$2; the facility is open daily except Wednesday 8 a.m.-5 p.m.

Carambola Botanical Reserve, located off the highway opposite the entrance to AKR, is the only developed inland reserve on the Bay Islands. Well-built trails wind through forests of ferns, spices, orchids, flowering plants, fruit trees, and even a few mahogany on the way to the top of Carambola Mountain. Along the way is a turnoff to the fascinating Iguana Wall, a section of sheer cliff that serves as a protected breeding ground for iguanas and parrots. There are vestiges of pre-Columbian ruins in the reserve, and great views from the peak over the surrounding reef and, in the distance, Utila. If manager Irma Brady is at the visitor's center, she can provide a great deal of information on the reserve's flora and fauna, but the other staffers in general are not very knowledgeable. For more information call Bill or Irma Brady at 45-1117. Entrance costs US$3; open daily 8 a.m.-5 p.m.

Accommodations

Sandy Bay's hotel selection is limited, but rooms can be found in all price ranges except rock-bottom. The only reasonably priced rooms in town are at **Beth's Place,** tel. 45-1266, a rambling wooden house set in the trees on a hill between the beach and the highway. The friendly American owner of the same name lives upstairs and rents out clean rooms with a kitchen downstairs for US$8 per night or US$50 per week. Only nonsmokers are allowed as Beth is allergic to tobacco. She has a large collection of books and magazines and a porch to read them on, and snorkeling equipment for US$4 per day. Coming from Coxen Hole, Beth's driveway turns off the highway to the right just before Rick's American Cafe.

The Oceanside Inn, tel. 45-1552, in the U.S. (407) 850-9795, just west of AKR, offers eight large, wood-paneled rooms at US$30 s, US$44 d, US$54 t, with a restaurant/bar and a gift shop with a decent cigar selection. Dives can be arranged with Tino Monterosso's dive shop.

The slightly worn **Sunrise Roatán Resort ,** tel. 45-1265, fax 45-1318, has clean wooden rooms around a porch for US$39 s or US$48 d, but the location away from the beach near the highway is not the greatest. The hotel runs a dive shop on the shore in Sandy Bay with three boats.

Dive Resorts

For those looking to really get away from it all for a week, **The Inn of the Last Resort,** tel. 45-1838, fax 45-1848, in the U.S. c/o C.O.J. Travel, tel. (800) 374-8181 or (305) 893-2436, might be the place for you. Set on a tree-covered, isolated peninsula, the Inn has no phones or TVs to disturb complete relaxation, only a huge selection of books, a breezy bar/restaurant, and the nearby reef. Rooms come with a/c and ceiling fans. Weeklong dive vacations cost US$695 pp for a couple, US$595 pp for five days, with three meals daily and frequent fishing trips.

Closer to a full-size tourist town than a hotel, **Anthony's Key Resort,** tel. 45-1327, fax 45-1329, U.S. reservations (800) 227-3483 or (305) 666-1997, fax (305) 666-2292, is one of the premier vacation resorts on Roatán and, for that matter, in all of Honduras. AKR manages 56 cabins both on the small and serene Anthony's Key and on a tree-covered hillside on the mainland. Full-week diving and meal packages are available for US$600-675 pp for a couple. Prices include tanks, weights, transport to and from the airport, an excursion to West Bay beach, and a room with overhead fan and potable tap water. There's fantastic swimming and snorkeling on all sides and a fine sunbathing beach on the cay. Dive-shop facilities are excellent, with several large boats and new equipment, and an underwater photo/video shop, tel. 45-1003, fax 45-1140, offering one-day slide processing and camera rentals (sometimes for nonguests as well) for about US$60 a day for the Nikonos V system with strobe.

Food

The best place to get a decent, inexpensive meal in Sandy Bay is **The Ceiba Tree Restaurant,** just opposite the entrance to the Sunrise Resort on the highway. Simple meals, *pastelitos,* and other snacks, soft drinks, and beer are served daily at lunch and dinner (US$3-5 a meal) in a screened porch.

Rick's American Cafe, set up on a hillside above the highway, is one of the more popular expat bar/restaurants on the island. After climbing up the precipitous staircase patrons can relax with a beer on the large wooden deck and watch the latest ball game on cable TV, while awaiting an order of steak, nachos, an Ameri-

can-style burrito, or a burger (US$5-10 a plate). Rick's is open daily for dinner and also for brunch on Sunday.

On the beach in Sandy Bay is a nameless eatery in a small shack with very basic meals and snacks.

Services

On the grounds of AKR is the **Episcopal Medical Center,** tel. 45-1515, at night 45-1500, also VHF channel 26, home to the only recompression tank on the Bay Islands, where divers who don't follow the tables end up spending uncomfortable hours wondering if they will avoid permanent damage. (For more information, see the special topic "Decompression Sickness.") There are no X-ray facilities, but the doctors can treat any ailments resulting from diving and other illnesses as well. Open Mon.-Sat. 9 a.m.-noon and 1:30 p.m.-5 p.m., Sunday 9 a.m.-noon.

Sandy Bay is just off the West End-Coxen Hole highway; minibuses and taxis pass frequently in both directions.

COXEN HOLE

A dusty, unremarkable town of weather-beaten wooden houses and shops, Coxen Hole is visited most frequently to change money, buy groceries, or take care of other business. All buses across the island are based out of Coxen Hole, and the airport is three km outside of town.

Named for pirate captain John Coxen, who lived on Roatán 1687-1697, the town was founded in 1835, when several families arrived from the Cayman Islands and settled on the harbor.

Osgood Key, just across the harbor from town, is really the only sight worth visiting in Coxen Hole, with a seafood restaurant and bar and cabins for rent at about US$20 d. To get there take a free water taxi from McLaughlin Lumber, and don't forget to bring your snorkel gear.

Accommodations

Though most sun- and sand-seekers proceed directly from the docks and airport to West End, Sandy Bay, or elsewhere, there are a few decent options for spending a night in Coxen Hole.

The inexpensive **Hotel Noemi Allen,** tel. 45-1234, just over the bridge at the western end of Main Street, has rooms for US$6 s or d with fan in a large wooden house. It's in a slightly seedy neighborhood, but the owner is friendly and overall the hotel is a good budget value.

Hotel Coral, on the second story of a large Victorian in the center of town, is a bit pricey at US$6 for a dingy single with shared bathroom or US$11 for a double. If no one is around in the hotel ask for assistance at the pharmacy across the street. A better value is the **Hotel El Paso** on the eastern side of town, with clean rooms for US$9, fans, and shared bath.

The only relatively upscale rooms in town are at **Hotel Cay View,** tel. 45-1202, fax 45-1179, in the U.S. (800) 222-8383, with private bath and a/c as well as a restaurant/bar for US$28 s or US$31 d.

Food and Entertainment
Good-quality snacks, breakfasts, and espresso drinks are sold at the **Que Pasa Cafe,** inside the Librería Casi Todo II, on the road out toward West End, but that's about it for tourist-quality food in Coxen Hole.

Comedor La Roca features some of the cheapest eats on the island, and it's not bad either, served out of a stand on the dirt road leading to the public market. It offers enchiladas, *baleadas,* and *comida corrientes.* Locals frequent **Comedor Gloria,** on the western edge of town, for its inexpensive set meals, soups, *pastelitos,* and other snacks.

For a night of thumping *punta* music, gyrating hips, and the occasional violent altercation, the **Harbour View Disco** is the spot of choice.

Shopping
Imapro, near the airport, tel. 45-1945, sells woodwork made in their own factory, as well as cards, books, and other gifts. The company also has shops in El Progreso and San Pedro Sula. **Yaba Ding Ding**—the islanders' nickname for pre-Columbian artifacts—sells batiks, tie-dyes, paintings, and furniture, all made by the owners. Closed Sunday.

Librería Casi Todo II on the road out toward West End has a larger selection of books than the West End store, as they haven't been picked over as much. Still, the selection weighs over-whelmingly toward romance and espionage. Inside is the Que Tal Cafe, serving coffee, breakfasts, and snacks.

In the center of town is **H.B. Warren,** the best supermarket on the island.

Services and Information
Banffaa, tel. 45-1030 or 45-1091, and Bancahsa, tel. 45-1767, both cash traveler's checks and advance cash on Visa cards, and are open Mon.-Fri. and Saturday in the morning only. Credomatic, tel. 45-1196, will also advance cash on a Visa, for no fee.

On the small square in the center of town are the Correos, migration office, and port captain. Up the hill behind Bancahsa is Hondutel, fax 45-1206, open daily 7 a.m.-noon and 12:30-9 p.m.

The Bay Islands Conservation Association (BICA) office is in the Cooper Building in downtown Coxen Hole, tel. 45-1424. Some pamphlets and maps are available, as well as *The Bay Islands: Nature and People,* an informative bilingual paperback by Susan Jacobson.

Columbia Tours, in the second story of a converted house across from the Cooper Building downtown, tel./fax 45-1747, can arrange plane tickets.

The *Coconut Telegraph,* in the Cooper Building, Ste. 301, tel. 45-1660, fax 45-1659, is a monthly magazine on the Bay Islands with heavy emphasis on Roatán; it's sold in various stores in West End and Coxen Hole for US$1.40.

In case of emergency call the **police** at 45-1099, 45-1138, 45-1190, or 45-1199; or the **fire department** at 45-1198.

The Coxen Hole **Municipal Hospital,** tel. 45-1499, is not the finest operation in existence—better to go to the medical center at AKR for most problems—but does have the only X-ray machine on the island.

FRENCH HARBOUR AND VICINITY

A large south-coast town set about one km off the highway on a wide peninsula 10 km east of Coxen Hole, French Harbour is home to one of the island's two major fishing fleets (the other is based in Oak Ridge). This is a working town, a world apart from the nearby resorts of Fantasy Island and Coco View. Apart from watching the activity on the docks, French Harbour is not particularly visually attractive. Nevertheless, the town has a cheerful character that Coxen Hole lacks. Plenty of snorkel and dive sites can be found on the nearby reef, but there isn't much of a beach.

French Harbour is thought to be named for a Frenchman who had one of the first homesteads in the area during the British military occupation in the 1740s.

Accommodations

The basic **Hotel Brooks** occupies the second floor of a rickety wooden house between the bus stop and the docks. It's not a bad deal at US$3 s or d with shared bath. Better still is **Hotel Gabriela,** a bit further up the same road, with double bed, a/c, and bathroom for US$8. Nearby **Hotel Joe** and **Harbor View Hotel** are pricier and no better in quality.

For the best rooms in town, try **Casa Romeo,** tel. 45-1518, fax 45-1645, a large stylish wooden house built on the dock, with a cool and quiet restaurant downstairs serving excellent seafood (the prices reflect the quality). Seven bright, whitewashed and breezy rooms with a/c, fans, and harbor views cost US$35 s, US$45 d, or US$75 pp with three meals and transport to the airport included.

On the other side of the point from the docks, **The Buccaneer,** tel. 45-1032, fax 45-1845, built in 1967, has comfortable rooms that face the ocean and are equipped with a/c, TVs, and telephones; US$50 s, US$66 d. Next door is Rita's Uruguayan Steak House, run by the hotel; open daily 7 a.m.-10 p.m.

The **French Harbour Yacht Club, Hotel and Marina,** tel. 45-1478 or 45-1460, fax 45-1459, is a local social center for expats, with a large bar and restaurant (good pizza) overlooking the marina and a message board to look for crew jobs. Outside on the breezy deck is a small pool. The hotel has 18 rooms with TV, telephone, and ceiling fan for US$38-55 s or d. Rooms 1-9 have ocean-facing porches. Massage, laundry, car rental, boat rental, taxi service, and island tours are all available. Marina dockage rates are US$8-16 per night, depending on boat size. Water is included, but cable TV hookup is US$2 more and electricity is metered.

Food and Entertainment

The one quality restaurant in town is **Gio's,** tel. 45-1536, across from the Banffaa Bank, with excellent seafood (the crab is a specialty) and steaks at tourist prices.

Apart from Gio's and the hotel restaurants, French Harbour has little in the way of decent food. Several small, rather dirty *comedores* line the main street, of which **Johnny's Restaurant** serves some of the tastier food.

Two discos get the locals hopping in town on weekends: **Al's** and **Bolongo's.** The former has a better DJ favoring merengue and salsa while the latter has a slightly more upscale (read: safer) atmosphere.

Getting There and Away

The Coxen Hole-Oak Ridge buses, which run until late afternoon, pull all the way into town so there's no need to slog out to the highway. A collective taxi to Coxen Hole costs US$3-4.

Brick Bay

Formerly called Brig Bay, Brick Bay is a secluded cove on the south side of the island just off the Coxen Hole highway not far west of French Harbour. Keep an eye out for a sign pointing to **Romeo's Resort,** tel. 45-5525, in the U.S. (800) 903-4525 or (305) 559-0511. This long-time Roatán resort, which recently changed hands, has 30 rooms for US$75-109 per night for a couple, some with a/c, others with fans. Weeklong diving and meal packages go for US$769, or US$719 for nondivers. Romeo's also rents a house with five rooms on the hillside and operates a small marina.

East of French Harbour

The narrow, two-lane highway (bicyclists beware) running east of French Harbour to Oak Ridge winds for most of its length along the ridge in the center of the island, affording superb views of both coasts and the surrounding reef. Between French Harbour and the Punta Gorda turnoff the highway passes Juticalpa, a small Latino community and the only sizable inland settlement anywhere on the Bay Islands. Once heavily forested, these central island mountain slopes have been almost entirely denuded of their original cover and now support either secondary scrub growth, pasture, or farmland.

BOB RACE

33576, tel. (800) 282-8932, fax (904) 588-4158, is not quite as luxurious as Fantasy Island or Anthony's Key, and many guests swear by it for that very reason. Sixteen rustic, wooden rooms with fans are built over the water on a small cay; the main building holds more rooms. No TVs or telephones can be found anywhere in the hotel, which is accessible by boat only. Diving is excellent right offshore—the reef wall starts 100 feet from the hotel and the wreck of the 140-foot *Prince Albert* is entombed in 65 feet of water nearby. One week with lodging, meals, and dives costs US$775 pp, or slightly less during the Sept.-Jan. off-season.

PUNTA GORDA

The oldest permanent settlement in Roatán, Punta Gorda ("wide point") was founded shortly after 12 April 1797, when some 3,000 Garífuna deportees from the Caribbean island of St. Vincent were stranded on Roatán by the British. After settling in Punta Gorda, many Garífuna continued on, migrating to Trujillo and from there up and down the Caribbean coast of Honduras, Nicaragua, Guatemala, and Belize. The anniversary marking their arrival is cause for great celebration in Punta Gorda. Garífuna from all over the coast attend the event. For most of the year, though, Punta Gorda is simply a sleepy seaside town—dozens of *cayucos* pulled up on the beach, a steady breeze blowing in the palms, and Garífuna residents moving at a very deliberate pace, happy to spend a few minutes or hours chatting with a visitor.

The beaches in town are not the best, but not far up the coast you'll find fine patches of open sand, like Camp Bay Beach to the east. Local boat owners will be happy to take you for a negotiable fee. There's great snorkeling and diving on the reef near Punta Gorda, but watch out for boat traffic if you swim out from town, and remember the north side of Roatán is choppier then the south and west.

Practicalities

On the main road looping through town (both ends connect to the highway) are a couple of *pulperías* and *comedores,* a pool hall, and one hotel, **Los Cinco Hermanos,** with six rooms at US$5 s or d upstairs in a worn wooden house. Mediocre lunch and dinner are served in the hotel's *comedor.*

Not far east of French Harbour are two of the best-known luxury resorts on Roatán: Fantasy Island and Coco View.

Situated on its own isolated 15-acre island complete with two shimmering man-made beaches, nearby reef, full dive shop, four dive boats, jet skis, tennis courts, sailboards, and myriad other services and recreation equipment, **Fantasy Island Resort,** tel. 45-1191 or 45-1222, fax 45-1268, in the U.S. at Fantasy Island Travel Services, 5353 W. Tyson Ave., Tampa, FL 33611-3225, tel. (800) 676-2826 or (813) 835-4449, fax (813) 835-4569, offers the complete get-away-from-it-all vacation. One-week packages including diving, lodging, and meals cost US$869-1050 pp for a couple, depending on the room. Four-night packages go for US$600-640. Each of the 83 rooms is decorated in tropical style with a/c, fan, TV, refrigerator, and balcony with ocean view. Inside the spacious main building are three bars, a 120-person conference center, and plenty of helpful staffpeople always milling about.

The Coco View Resort, tel. 45-1011, fax 45-1013, in the U.S. at P.O. Box 877, San Antonio, FL

Ben's Dive Resort, tel. 45-1916, in the U.S. (800) 484-1177, ext. 0224, opened in 1996 by a local resident with many years experience as a divemaster at different resorts and dive shops in Roatán, is a unique sort of dive-hotel. The four well-built wooden cabins, small dive shop, and restaurant are all run and managed by Ben and his wife, a hospitable couple who seem to be friends with everyone in town. Ben knows plenty of north-side dive sites infrequently visited by other dive shops and is a patient instructor/divemaster. Guests will enjoy gorging on the excellent seafood (conch fritters, calamari, lobster) as well as on sandwiches, steaks, and breakfasts. A local *punta* band plays in the restaurant every Saturday night. One week lodging-meal-and-dive packages cost US$550 pp alone, US$500 pp with two, US$450 pp with three, including three boat dives a day and one night dive. Packages cost US$100 less Oct.-Dec., and PADI certifications are available.

OAK RIDGE

From the highway coming downhill to the water's edge, it seems Oak Ridge (capital of the José Santos Guardiola municipality, which covers eastern Roatán) is scattered all over the place, clinging to hillsides, cays, and peninsulas all around a large harbor, which is literally the center of town. The harbor has always been the town's entire reason for existence. It first served as a refuge for pirates fleeing Spanish warships, then as the center of a major boat-building industry, and now as home to a fishing fleet and processing plant.

Perhaps because of its relative remoteness, more of Oak Ridge's 4,655 residents are obviously of English descent than elsewhere in Roatán.

Practicalities
Buses stop at the mainland dock next to a Bancahsa (which changes cash and traveler's checks and advances money on Visa cards) and the fish-processing plant. From there a visitor can walk along the shore, past the fish plant all the way around the western end of the harbor, over a small bridge, and out to a narrow point facing the ocean.

Just past the fish plant on this road, on the left hand side, a sign marks a room for rent—a small cabin next to a private house, on the water, for US$8 d with bathroom and a clean, large bed. Not far past the hotel are two *comedores* on each side of the street, both with inexpensive and relatively tasty meals.

Apart from a couple of stores and a weather-beaten wooden church, there's not much on the point, though it's interesting to check out the town and docks. The ocean-facing side of the point has no beach, only exposed, rocky coral which makes it difficult to get out to snorkel on the reef.

From the dock by the bus stop water taxis will take a visitor over to the cay ("cayside") for US 40 cents or so, though some drivers may try to charge you more. Cayside is much the same as the point; several houses sit amid the trees behind the rocky, coral-covered shore-line. Most cayside visitors are coming to the **Reef House Resort,** tel. 45-2142 or 45-2297, in the U.S. at P.O. Box 40331, San Antonio, TX 78229, tel. (800) 328-8897 or (210) 681-2888, fax (210) 341-7942, the only major tourist setup in Oak Ridge and one of the oldest dive resorts on the island. The owners dive many little-known sites nearby, including an excellent wall right in front of the hotel. One week with lodging, meals, and dives goes for US$725 pp for a couple; five days costs US$550 pp for a couple.

Near Oak Ridge
Not far from town in both directions, but especially east, are several beaches. Dory captains on the main dock near the bus stop will transport you there for US$5 or US$10 return. Longer trips to Barbareta (US$40), Pigeon Cay (off Barbareta), Helene (US$20), Port Royal, or through the mangrove canals are also possible. Bargain hard, and remember it's the least expensive to go with a group of people and split the cost of the boat.

EASTERN ROATÁN

Paya Beach
Between Oak Ridge and Punta Gorda a dirt road turns off the highway to the east, marked by a sign for the **Paya Beach Resort,** tel. 435-2139; in the U.S., (888) 662-2466, fax (409) 628-3554, e-mail: info@payabay.com, www.payabay.com. This small hotel occupies an isolated private beach on the north coast. Its seven rooms, each

with a fan and ocean-facing balcony, run US$75 pp with three meals a day or US$48 pp without meals (though there's nowhere else to eat out there). Dives can be arranged through Ben's Dive Resort in Punta Gorda, and the owners also organize tours to Helene and Barbareta.

Camp Bay Beach

Just east of Paya Beach along the same road, past the village of Diamond Rock, is Camp Bay Beach. The largest undeveloped beach left on Roatán, it's a veritable tropical daydream lined with nothing but coconut palms swaying in the steady breeze. This idyllic state will soon change, though, as property lots on the beach are frequently seen advertised for sale in local magazines and real-estate listings; enjoy it while you can. For the time being, this is still the sort of place you could find a secluded spot to pitch a tent or sling a hammock, if you've got a car or can manage to get out there on your own. No buses go out to Camp Bay, but rides from the highway can often be found in the morning and early afternoon. Also, a pickup drives every day from Oak Ridge to Diamond Rock in the early morning (6-7 a.m.). The beach is 13 km from the Oak Ridge highway turn-off.

Port Royal

The dirt road continues past Camp Bay over the hills to Port Royal, once the site of English pirate camps, now the site of luxury homes for retired expatriates. Named for the famous port in Jamaica, Port Royal was long the favorite anchorage for marauding pirates because of its protected, defensible harbor. It was chosen by the British military as their base in the 1740s for the same reasons. The British built two small forts to guard the harbor: Fort Frederick on the mainland, with one rampart and six cannons, and Fort George on the cay, with one rampart and 17 cannons. In spite of their heavy armaments, the forts didn't see much service before their destruction in 1782 by a Spanish expedition. The remains of Fort George can still be seen, while the foundations for Fort Frederick now hold a private home.

Currently no lodging or restaurants exist in Port Royal, but it's rumored Julio Iglesias and Oscar de la Renta will be opening a US$12 million resort here in the near future.

Old Port Royal, further east, is thought to be the site of the ill-fated Providence Company settlement, dating from the 1630s and 1640s. This is the deepest harbor on the island, though it's no longer used for commerce.

The hills above Port Royal were declared the **Port Royal Park and Wildlife Refuge** in 1978 in an effort to protect the principal watershed for eastern Roatán and several species of endangered wildlife. The refuge has no developed trails for hikers.

East End Islands

East of Port Royal, Roatán peters out into a lowland mangrove swamp, impassable by foot or car, which connects to the island of **Helene,** sometimes called Santa Helena. Just east of Helene is the smaller island of **Morat,** and further east is **Barbareta,** a two-by-five kilometer island home to pristine virgin island forest and several lovely beaches. All three islands are surrounded by spectacular reef.

On Barbareta is the **Barbareta Beach Club,** P.O. Box 63, La Ceiba, Honduras, fax 42-2629, VHF channel 88a, in the U.S. tel. (205) 990-8948, fax (205) 928-1659, a fully equipped resort set on 1,200 acres of thick forest and palm-lined beach. Rooms run US$220-280 pp with meals for three nights. Rooms in the lodge are less expensive than in the beach bungalows. Each of the available activities for guests—diving, windsurfing, hiking, mountain biking, fishing—costs extra, but prices are not outrageous. Reservations are required.

Southeast of Barbareta are the **Pigeon Cays,** a perfect spot for a relaxed day of picnicking and snorkeling with no one around. Boats to Barbareta, Morat, Helene, and the Pigeon Cays can be hired at the main dock in Oak Ridge.

UTILA

Perhaps because of its small size and relatively recent popularity as a tourist destination, Utila has the feeling of being lost in a tropical time warp. Listening to the broad, almost incomprehensible islander English coming out of islanders with names like Morgan and Bodden, it seems pirates ran amok here just a few years instead of two centuries ago. Life on Utila still moves at a sedate pace; local conversation is dominated by the weather, the state of the fishing industry, and spicy gossip about the affairs of the 2,000-odd inhabitants.

In the past few years, though, Utila has come face to face abruptly with the late 20th century. A steadily growing stream of budget travelers flow in from across the globe, all eager to get scuba certification for as little money as possible (about US$150 at last check). With its semiofficial designation as the low-budget Bay Island, Utila has become one of those great backpacker hot spots like Kathmandu, Marrakech, or Lake Atitlán—packed with young Europeans and Americans out for a good time in the sun.

While a boon to business owners (dive shops have been popping up like mushrooms after a spring rain), many of the locals are not so sure about their new economy and their backpacker visitors. Prices have been rising steadily, as has the crime rate, which some blame on the influx of Latino immigrants chasing the tourist dollars. Some islanders are vocal in their belief that the backpacker crowd is a negative influence on their community. Still, keeping in mind how rapidly island society is changing, don't let this stop you from trying to get to know islanders, many of whom are eager to talk to foreigners who are likewise open to interaction.

Utila's name reputedly derives from a contraction of *ocotillo,* which in Nahuatl refers to a place with a lot of black smoke. The smoke came from burning the resinous ocote pine, supposedly used by pre-Columbian islanders in a type of distilling process. The smallest of the three main islands, Utila is 11 kilometers long and five kilometers wide, with two-thirds of its area covered by swamp. Two small hills on the eastern part of the island, Pumpkin Hill and

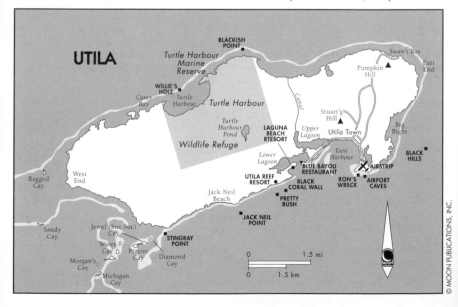

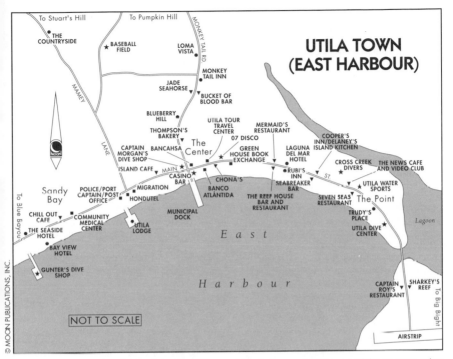

Stuart's Hill, are volcanic in origin. Sand flies can be voracious on Utila, so come prepared.

As of August 1996, the Bay Islands Conservation Association (BICA) in Utila began collecting a US$5 tourist tax from all visitors. The primary goals for the money are helping to fund more patrols of the Turtle Harbour Marine Reserve on the north side of the island, paying for environmental education in schools, and setting up more mooring buoys for dive boats. Visitors are given a pass when they pay the US$5, which must be shown to the plane or boat company before a ticket will be sold off the island.

UTILA TOWN (EAST HARBOUR)

Almost all Utilans live in East Harbour, on the south side of the island. Universally called Utila, the town wraps around a large harbor that's protected from the open ocean by an arm of reef. The town is divided into four parts: the point, between the airport and downtown; Sandy Bay, between downtown and the western edge of town; the Center, near the main intersection by Captain Morgan's Dive Shop, Bancahsa, and the municipal dock; and Monkey Tail Road, which cuts inland perpendicular to the shore.

Although not a large town in total population, Utila's collection of wooden houses, dive shops, hotels, and restaurants is spread across a large area. To cover the ground between your hotel, dive shop, and favorite restaurants and bars, a fleet of rusty and grievously mistreated **mountain bikes** are available to rent for US$1.25 a day from a stand near the main intersection. Make sure to check your steed thoroughly before riding off into the sunset—many have flat tires or a chain rusted solid—and be sure to use a flashlight when riding at night.

Pedestrians should keep an eye or ear peeled for maniac cyclists and three-wheeled motorcycle drivers. Locals appear to derive a secret thrill from whipping along the roads passing unsuspecting gringos as close as possible to scare them. Visitors may also notice that, unlike everywhere else in Honduras, baseball, not soccer, is the sport of choice on Utila. If you want one of those bonding sports conversations, a pertinent comment on the major leagues will always kick things off.

The town's generator runs 6 a.m.-midnight.

RECREATION

Dive Shops

If there's any complaint to be leveled against Utila, it's that all anyone ever talks about is diving. All things considered, that's no surprise. Word has gotten out that Utila offers possibly the least expensive open-water scuba certifications in the world, and business has been booming ever since. Competition between shops is fierce, with hail-fellow-well-met European and American divemasters trying to sign up new customers as the unsuspecting travelers walk in from the airport, backpacks still on their backs. Sixteen shops are now in business in Utila, though with the price wars it's unclear how many will survive. This is wonderful news to the discerning would-be diver, who will wisely spend a day or two asking around among other travelers and investigating several dive shops before deciding where to go and what courses to take.

Note: Whispered comments may be heard about Utila shops cutting corners on safety, but most of the whispers come from Roatán shops and competing Utila shops. Diving accidents do occur regularly in Utila, but invariably they are the result of a diver disregarding the diving tables, diving alone, or breaking some other rule. There have been no cases of a diver drowning or getting decompression sickness while in an open-water course.

Prices now stand at US$125-150 for an open-water or advanced open-water course and US$25-30 for two-tank dives. Most shops have open-water courses starting every other day, available in English, Spanish, German, French, Italian, Swedish, Hebrew, and probably a couple

of other languages as well. Listed below are five of the more popular and responsible dive shops.

Utila Water Sports, tel./fax 45-3239, has safety-conscious instructors and a large dive boat, when it's not in use by the Laguna Beach Resort (same owners).

Utila Dive Center, tel. 45-3326, fax 45-3327, was the first dive shop opened on the island, in 1991, and has 30 new tanks, a new compressor, and a room in the shop to rest in.

Captain Morgan's, tel. 45-3161, located on the corner downtown, has a reputation as a fun-loving dive shop with a friendly staff.

Cross Creek Divers, tel./fax 45-3234, offers US$2 rooms with its courses and has fax and Internet services at the office.

Gunter's, tel. 45-3113, is run by a local artist/character who has been diving in Utila for years and has a good group of instructors. The shop, on a dock in Sandy Bay at the western edge of town, also runs boats out to Water Cay.

Kayaking and Boating

Gunter's, tel. 45-3113, rents sea kayaks for snorkeling or taking forays into the canal or to the north side. Yacht skippers should call VHF channel 16 to request check-in and clearance-procedure information with Utila Harbour Authority (in Spanish), or go visit the port captain's office next to the police station. Anchoring is permitted in East Harbour and in the Utila Cays Channel for a US$10 monthly fee; always use anchor lights, and do not empty bilges in the harbor or near land. Larger boats may dock at the municipal wharf for a daily docking fee.

steer clear of stinging fire coral

BOB RACE

ACCOMMODATIONS

In keeping with its status as the least expensive Bay Island, the majority of Utila rooms fall into the budget category, about US$4-5 double. A couple of hotels aim for travelers with a few more lem-

RECOMMENDED UTILA DIVE SITES

SOUTH SIDE:

- Stingray Point
- Jack Neil Point
- Pretty Bush
- Black Coral Wall

NEAR THE AIRPORT:

- Ron's Wreck
- Airport Caves
- Black Hills

NORTH SIDE:

- Blackish Point
- Willie's Hole
- Ragged Cay

pira to spend on cleanliness and privacy, and a few low-key resorts are competing to corner the high-end market. Except for the resorts, all hotels are in small, wooden buildings, often converted houses, so their proliferation is not overwhelming. Architecturally at least, Utila has not been greatly changed by the tourist influx.

Budget

The Countryside, as the name suggests, is about a 15-minute walk outside of town, set amid trees and fields. The US$2.50 rooms are very basic but guests have kitchen rights and there's usually a festive crowd of backpackers hanging out.

One of the best deals in town (and often full as a result) is **Blueberry Hill,** an eclectic assortment of small wooden buildings on stilts built around the owner's house on Monkey Tail Road. Airy rooms each with kerosene stove, bathroom, and lots of character go for US$4 d.

A bit further up the road, past the Bucket of Blood Bar, is the **Monkey Tail Inn,** a fairly grimy small wooden house with six rooms, a small porch, and an intermittently cleaned bathroom, US$4 d, US$2.50 s. Colorful graffiti from generations of backpackers covers the walls, particularly in the room to the right of the front door. The owners live in the house next door and own the small store across the street. For just a little more, **Loma Vista** has clean, sunny rooms with communal kitchen facilities and a porch for US$5 d.

Located a few houses up from the Monkey Tail, Loma Vista is often full.

Cooper's Inn on the point has clean rooms with fans and mosquito nets for US$4.50 d. The owners organize glass-bottom-boat trips, and excellent dinners are served downstairs at Delaney's Island Kitchen. The inn is conveniently close to several of the dive shops, for those out-of-bed-into-the-dive-boat mornings. **The Seaside Hotel,** tel. 45-3150, near Gunter's Dive Shop on the west edge of town in Sandy Bay, has 11 basic rooms for US$5 d with bathroom and fan, and some newer rooms for US$10 d.

Rubi's Inn, next to the Reef House, offers clean, breezy rooms with fans for US$4 s or US$6 d. The inn sits right over the water on the point, and has kitchen facilities and a front porch.

Midrange

Formerly one of the best deals in town, **Trudy's Place,** tel. 45-3195, fax 45-3103, on the point, has gone up to US$8 pp for rooms in a clean wooden house. Note, though, that guests taking a course with the affiliated Underwater Visions dive shop stay for free. **Laguna del Mar Hotel,** across the street from Trudy's, is owned by the same family and has slightly more expensive rooms.

In Sandy Bay, opposite the hulking, half-constructed building on a hillside known locally as Darren's Folly (a favorite spot for unauthorized parties), is the **Bay View Hotel,** tel. 45-3114, with 11 neat, whitewashed rooms around a grassy lawn at the water's edge for US$10 s, US$15 d.

Dive Resorts

Far and away the best hotel in East Harbour itself is **The Utila Lodge,** tel. 45-3143, fax 45-3209, in the U.S. contact Roatán Charters, P.O. Box 877, San Antonio FL 33576-0877, tel. (800) 282-8932 or (352) 588-4132, fax (352) 588-4158. The lodge, run by Americans Jim and Kristy Engle, occupies the dark wood building behind Hondutel. It has its own dock for fishing boats and dive boats, as well as eight rooms with a/c and private balconies. Rates of US$725 a week include three all-you-can-eat meals and three boat dives daily. Nondivers pay US$625 a week. Daily rates are available. Jim is an avid fisherman and will arrange flats or deep-sea fishing trips for guests.

DECOMPRESSION SICKNESS

The thought of getting decompression sickness, better known as "the bends," certainly sends a chill through every novice diver's spine. It's important to remember, however, that if a diver follows the tables, it won't be a problem. Those who end up in trouble are invariably the ones who consider themselves exempt from the laws of physics and the averages used to create the diving tables.

Decompression sickness occurs when a diver returns to sea-level pressure too rapidly. While under increased pressure in the water, the nitrogen in a diver's breathing mixture is absorbed by blood tissues, where it can remain in solution with no ill effects. If a diver does not stay down too long (and hence did not absorb too much nitrogen) and goes up at a rate that allows for outgassing, all will be well. When the pressure is reduced too rapidly, the nitrogen returns to a gaseous form, producing bubbles in tissue and blood cells, causing severe pain and serious problems in the central nervous, peripheral nervous, or cardiopulmonary systems. One dive instructor compared it to shaking a bottled carbonated beverage and then opening it: the bubbles just want to explode out. When a diver ascends too fast, the same process is happening inside his or her tissues.

Due to this need to decompress, dive tables were developed to analyze how much gas the body has absorbed over different lengths of time. All recreational diving is nondecompression diving, intended to allow a diver to make a controlled ascent straight to the surface in the event of an emergency. When near the limits of the tables, a short 3-5 minute decompression stop in five meters of water is recommended.

If a diver is suspected of having decompression sickness, lay the person on his or her left side (in the hope that a bubble will not lodge in the heart) and administer 100% oxygen if possible. If the diver is not breathing, administer CPR. Keep the diver warm and get medical attention as soon as possible. Decompression symptoms sometimes may appear anywhere from three to 24 hours after diving. Symptoms include pain in the extremities, severe headache, impairment of speech or vision, seizure, shortness of breath or respiratory arrest, paralysis, or complete collapse.

All divers should wait a full day after their last dive before flying above 1,000 feet.

The Episcopal Medical Center in Roatán, which operates the only recompression chamber in the Bay Islands, offers **diving insurance** through all dive shops for US$2 a day. Although shops don't push it (so as not to seem more expensive), it is worth buying; emergency treatment, in the unlikely event of an accident, can be very pricey.

On the south side of the island, and the west side of the canal, is **Laguna Beach Resort,** tel./fax 45-3239 (Utila Water Sports), in the U.S. at 1004 Jacquelyn St., Abbeville, LA 70510, tel. (800) 66UTILA or (318) 839-0013, fax (318) 839-5024. The resort opened in January 1996 and offers six bungalows (ceiling fans standard, a/c optional) set on a private sandy peninsula, accessible by boat only, with great swimming and snorkeling right out front. One week with meals and dives on a large (thus, stable) dive boat goes for US$750 pp. Flats and deep-sea fishing, windsurfing, and sea-kayaking trips are available.

The **Utila Reef Resort,** tel. 45-3254 (the Reef Dive Shop in town), in the U.S. tel. (800) 263-9876, is a two-story thatched-roof building west of Laguna Beach, also built on the island's south coast on a small private beach. Each of the five rooms has a fan, a/c, hot water, 24-hour power and water, and ocean-facing balconies. Rates run US$865 for one week with full meals and three boat dives daily. A black-coral wall is just one of many beautiful scuba and snorkel sites right nearby. The Louisiana Cajun owners like their meals zippy, so be prepared for a spicy kick unless you request severe blandness.

FOOD

Inexpensive

Supremely addictive *baleadas* are sold by the **"baleada ladies,"** as they are affectionately known, for US 30 cents each at the intersection near Captain Morgan's dive shop. These very astute mainland immigrants saw a need for cheap eats and have filled the niche with raging success. Placidly whipping out a steady stream of fresh tortillas filled with beans, cheese, and soaked onions (a tasty twist on the traditional version), the ladies invariably attract a crowd to their outdoor stands during the lunch and dinner shifts.

Thompson's Bakery, on Monkey Tail Road not far from the main intersection, sells wildly popular and inexpensive breakfasts daily 6 a.m.-noon. It's always packed with divers stuffing themselves with pancakes, omelettes, coffee, and the famous johnnycake (biscuits served plain or like a McDonald's Egg McMuffin) and washing it all down with a mug of coffee before running out to their 7:30 a.m. dive. Delectable chocolate chip cookies and other cakes are sold to go.

One of the low-budget culinary secrets in town is **The Chill Out Cafe,** past the church in Sandy Bay, serving healthy and inexpensive sandwiches, small meals, sodas, and beer daily from 7 a.m. until there are no more customers.

The Island Cafe serves sandwiches, light meals, and salads for US$2-4 on the porch of an old wooden house in the center of town; open for dinner only Mon.-Sat., no beer sold. Also set in a large converted house is **Chona's,** opposite the 07 Disco, featuring burgers, steak, and fish for US$2-4. Meals here are cooked at a snail's pace, but there's plenty of cold beer and conversation to keep you occupied while you wait. This favored hangout for locals and travelers alike is open for lunch and dinner daily except Tuesday.

For the best fried chicken in town, as well as inexpensive *baleadas,* fried fish, burgers, and *comida corrientes,* try the **Seven Seas Restaurant** on the point, open for breakfast, lunch, and dinner every day.

Midrange

Certainly one of the more unusual finds in Utila is **Delany's Island Kitchen,** managed by a Danish chef cooking nightly dinner specials like Swedish meatballs, lasagna, and veggie burgers for a ravenous crowd of divers. It's best to arrive before 8 p.m. as they frequently run out of food due to high demand. Closed Sunday; US$3-5 per meal.

Also with a creative, rotating menu is **Sharkey's Reef,** considered by some to have the best food

in town. Located just before the airport, Sharkey's usually has four dinners to choose from for US$3-5 each. It's open Wed.-Sun., and is a popular spot for late-night conversation and beers.

The Jade Seahorse, opposite the Bucket of Blood Bar on Monkey Tail Road, serves healthy US$3-5 meals, *burrito-baleadas* (a unique concoction), large fruit shakes, and US$2-3 breakfasts in a creatively decorated dining room filled with wooden furniture, backgammon and chess boards, and soft music in the background. The quality food and low-key ambience are fast making this new restaurant a favorite gathering spot for travelers staying in hotels on Monkey Tail Road.

Always full of travelers hankering for the solid (though unspectacular) lasagna, pizza, salads, burgers, and daily specials is **Mermaid's Restaurant,** on the point. Service can be fatally slow, but the tables, on a dimly lighted patio, make a pleasant place to chat. Open lunch and dinner except Friday night and Saturday afternoon; US$3-6 per meal.

Across from Sharkey's near the airport, **Captain Roy's Restaurant,** tel. 45-3190, has an extensive menu of juicy barbecued ribs and burgers, steaks, pizza, shrimp, and fish, served in an air-conditioned dining room for US$3-6 a meal. A bar and cocktail lounge are attached.

ENTERTAINMENT

Two discos in the center of town, **07** and **Casino,** turn into scenes of extreme debauchery late Saturday night into the wee hours of Sunday morning. The 07 tends to have a more mixed crowd of travelers and locals bopping to techno, funk, and Euro-disco sounds, while the Casino favors thumping *punta* and Caribbean sounds for the mainly local crowd. Usually groups of people stand around in the street in between the two discos, looking for entertainment and frequently finding it in the form of drunken brawls. Cheap beer and rum and cokes are the only drinks available; there's no cover charge at either disco.

One of more *tranquilo* bars is the venerable **Sea Breaker,** basically a wooden porch on the water with a thatched roof over part of it. It's a great place to sit and talk for hours under the

the relaxing Sea
Breaker

stars, with mellow music and inexpensive drinks.

The Bucket of Blood Bar up Monkey Tail Road is an island institution. Although not as lively as it once was, it's still a good place for a late-night beer session. The colorful name has spawned a popular T-shirt, on sale at the bar.

A slightly more upscale crowd tends to patronize **The Reef House Bar and Restaurant,** offering tasty Mexican-style *bocas,* good music, and sports on the TV. The breezy top-floor patio is a choice spot to hang out but beware the steep stairway if you've had a few. Closed Wednesday.

The billiard aficionado need not fear: there is one small **pool hall** tucked away in a house behind the Bucket of Blood where you can get your fix until about 11 p.m. nightly, beers served. Although temporarily closed at last report, **The News Cafe and Video Club** next to Utila Water Sports normally shows movies nightly.

After a late night at the bars, and especially on Saturday night/Sunday morning after the discos, it's a good idea to walk home in a group. Muggings are not common but not unheard of either.

MORE UTILA TOWN PRACTICALITIES

Shopping and Information
The Green House Book Exchange on the point rents books at US$1 a day or exchanges them two-for-one, or one-for-one with a US$1 charge. The owners are very knowledgeable about Utila, the Cayos Cochinos, and other parts of Honduras as well. Open Mon.-Fri. 9-11 a.m. and 4-6 p.m. and occasionally other random hours as well.

Several groceries in town sell fresh produce, cheese, milk, and other perishables, but they often run out on Sunday and Monday, before the next boat arrives. The **BICA** office, tel. 45-3260, where travelers need to buy their US$5 visitor's card, is a small wooden building in front of Mermaid's Restaurant, open Mon.-Fri. 7 a.m.-7 p.m., Sat.-Sun. 6-8 p.m. Pamphlets, maps, books, and T-shirts are also for sale.

The Utila Times, tel. 45-3101, fax 45-3234, is the island's news and gossip sheet, an entertaining source of local information printed (usually) monthly and sold for US$1 at various locations.

Exchange
Both Bancahsa and Banco Atlántida change traveler's checks and will give a cash advance on a Visa card; open Mon.-Fri. 8-11:30 a.m. and 1:30-4 p.m., Saturday 8-11:30 a.m. Henderson's will also exchange traveler's checks and cash.

Services
Migration, Hondutel, and Correos are all located near each other on Sandy Bay Road, next to the police station. Hondutel and Correos are both open Saturday morning.

Utila Tour Travel Center, next to the 07, tel. 45-3368, tel./fax 45-3386, is an Isleña agent, and can arrange tickets with any airline.

In an emergency contact the **police,** tel. 45-3145, or dial 199. For medical attention, the **Community Medical Center** opposite the church on Sandy Bay Road, charges US$4 per visit, Mon.-Fri. 8 a.m.-noon. In emergencies contact Dr. Dan, the American expat who runs the center, at his home in the harbor on the yacht *Tabitha,* VHF channel 6.

Getting There and Away

Monday through Saturday, several flights a day ferry passengers between Utila and La Ceiba. All flights on all three airlines cost US$23 one-way. Buy **Isleña** tickets at Utila Tour Travel Center, tel. 45-3368, tel./fax 45-3386; **Rollins** tickets at Captain Roy's Restaurant, tel. 45-3190; and **Sosa** tickets at Hunter and Morgan's Store, tel. 45-3161.

The **MV** *Tropical* departs La Ceiba for Utila on Monday at 10:30 a.m. and Tues.-Fri. at 10 a.m., returning to the mainland Monday at noon and Tues.-Fri. at 11:30 a.m.; US$5.50 each way. Travelers can spend the two-hour ride inside watching a video or outside on deck enjoying the breeze.

The much less luxurious and slower **MV** *Starfish* leaves Utila for La Ceiba Monday at 5:30 a.m.; US$4.50. The advantage of taking the *Starfish* is arriving in La Ceiba early enough (8:30 a.m.) to make bus connections elsewhere. The trip also has undeniable atmospheric value—watching a hazy sunrise over the Caribbean from a rusty tramp freighter, admiring the views of Pico Bonito looming up on the mainland. No reservations are needed, just show up on the main dock at about 5 a.m. For those really counting their lempira, the owners of the *Starfish* are happy to let passengers sleep on deck the night before, saving one night at a hotel and ensuring you don't oversleep.

ELSEWHERE ON THE ISLAND

The Blue Bayou Restaurant, a couple of kilometers west of downtown, is a good spot to spend a relaxed half-day lazing in the hammocks strung among the palms, reading a good book, or snorkeling off the dock. The food is not the best, but it only costs US$1 to use the hammocks all day. The owners also rent a couple of unappealing rooms and an unwieldy wooden canoe for paddling up the nearby canal (Gunter's sea kayaks are much better).

The point at Blue Bayou marks the southern entrance to the cross-island canal. About halfway up the canal is a small dock where a trail heads west to **Turtle Harbour Pond,** site of a small pre-Columbian ruin. On the north side of the island west of where the canal lets out are a couple of small, deserted beaches accessible by boat only.

One of the best stretches of sand on the island is **Jack Neil Beach,** on the southwest side of Utila, just before the Utila Cays. The owners of the Green House Bookstore plan to build a hotel here soon.

From the end of Monkey Tail Road a five-km dirt road continues across the island to **Pumpkin Hill Beach** on the north side. Much of the coast here is covered with fossilized coral and rocks, but a few patches of sand provide good spots to put down a towel and relax in splendid isolation. Negotiating a safe passage into the water to swim and snorkel is no easy task, but in calm weather the determined will make it. Near the beach is **Pumpkin Hill** (270 feet high), riddled with caves, one of which is the sizable **Brandon Hill Cave,** reputedly the site of pirate's treasure. The smooth dirt road out to the beach makes a great 15-minute mountain-bike ride or hour's walk.

Closer to town is **Stuart's Hill,** like Pumpkin Hill a former volcano. From the top are good views over town and the south side of the island, and nearby are the barely visible remnants of a pre-Columbian ceremonial site.

The "Airport Beach," at the far end of the airstrip, is not exactly a sandy paradise, but there are a couple of good snorkeling sites just offshore. A path continues north past the airport to a small secluded cove, and further on to a larger one called **Big Bight,** which has a small patch of decent sand—a good locale for a lazy day of snorkeling, sunbathing, and trying to figure out how to split open a coconut without a machete. The coral reef ridges in the bay are not in the best health, but there are plenty of interesting formations and marine life to admire with snorkel and fins. Big Bight is about two km north of the airport.

UTILA CAYS

The Utila Cays are a collection of 12 tiny islets located off the southwest corner of the island. Some 400 people live on **Jewel (or Suc-Suc) Cay** and **Pigeon Cay,** which are connected by a narrow causeway and generally referred to jointly as Pigeon Cay. These islanders are descended from the first residents who came to Utila from the Cayman Islands in the 1830s. Originally the migrants settled on the main island, but soon moved out to the cays, reputedly to avoid the sand flies. If you found Utila residents to be an odd Caribbean subculture, the Pigeon Cay population is odder still—a small, isolated group who tend to keep to themselves, but nevertheless welcome the occasional visitor with friendly smiles.

At the end of the causeway on Jewel Cay is a small hotel with simple rooms for US$5 d. Decent food can be found at three restaurants. Try the great fish cakes at the Pigeon Cay Restaurant, run by Dutchman Jan Olsman, who also manages Sea Fan Divers and takes visitors to Water Cay. On Pigeon Cay is a small seafood market, a great place to stock up with fresh fish for a Water Cay cookout. Surprisingly for such a tiny town, Pigeon Cay sports a disco that's hopping on Saturday night. There are no beaches on the cay, but snorkeling is great and the waters are sparkling clear.

If you'd like to rent a private island, Morgan and Sandy Cays are managed by George Jackson on Pigeon Cay, tel. 45-3161. A cabin is available on **Diamond Cay** (sometimes called Dimond Cay), a tiny islet right in front of Jewel Cay.

If you were to conjure up the ideal tropical beach paradise, your picture might be something very close to **Water Cay.** Almost within shouting distance of Pigeon Cay, Water Cay is a patch of sand several hundred meters long, wide at one end and tapering to a point on the other; the only occupants are coconut palms and one small caretaker's shack. Piercingly blue, warm water and a coral reef just a few yards out ring the cay. There is no permanent resident on the island, and visitors are welcome to camp out with tents or hammocks as long as they like, within reason, for US$1.30 a night. The caretaker (who shows up most days but doesn't live on the island) rents hammocks for another US$1.30 a night, though they're not the finest quality—better to bring your own. The best snorkeling is off the south side, though it can be a bit tricky finding an opening in the wall. Water Cay is a popular impromptu party locale for locals and travelers, especially on weekends and on the full moon.

WATER CAY COOKOUT

With driftwood everywhere for bonfires and no one around to bother campers, Water Cay makes the perfect spot for a fish cookout. Come prepared with all the fixings—foil, lemons, garlic, onions, and maybe a few sweet potatoes for good measure. When arriving from Utila, stop off at Pigeon Cay for 10 minutes and go to the local fish market and pick up a fish or three, depending on how many feasters are expected. Once you've chosen an appropriate spot, build a roaring fire, wrap everything up in foil, and toss them into the coals for a few minutes.

If you're lucky, a group of islanders might be holding their own cookout, and can show you how to whip up some *bando,* a spicy seafood and vegetable stew. Be sure not to forget liquid refreshments—one drink with an appealing tropical style is made by chopping open a coconut and spiking the milk with rum. As the milk dwindles the mix becomes progressively more lethal, and may quickly lead to an early collapse in a hammock.

GUANAJA

Guanaja has somehow ended up as the forgotten Bay Island, overlooked in the rush of travelers and migrants to Utila and Roatán. This oversight is surprising considering Guanaja's fantastic reef, wide-open north-side beaches, and quirky fishing towns.

But the days of Caribbean backwater status are fast coming to an end. In the last two years Guanaja's real estate market has boomed as more and more expatriates seek their own little chunk of paradise. While Roatán is a bastion of American immigrants, more Europeans seem to be buying up lots on the deserted beaches on Guanaja's north side. The construction boom is expected to begin in the coming years.

Contrary to conventional belief, it is possible to survive on the island on a budget, though not as easily as on Utila. But the few extra lempiras are worth it to catch a glimpse of what Utila and Roatán looked and felt like 30 years ago. And for those with a bit more to spend, dive resorts range from funky, homey little hotels to fully equipped luxury spreads.

The waters surrounding Guanaja constitute the only complete marine reserve in the Bay Islands, but until recently active conservation efforts have been minimal. Currently Texas A & M University is conducting a study on Guanaja's reef in conjunction with the Posada del Sol Resort.

GUANAJA TOWN

Past travel writers have insisted on calling Guanaja Town the Venice of the Bay Islands, an unfortunate misnomer as visitors inevitably come away disappointed with this architectural oddity of a town. Built on rickety wooden causeways over a maze of canals, Guanaja Town was founded in the 1830s by immigrants from the Cayman Islands. They constructed their homes on what was then Hog and Sheen Cays. These two tiny little islets, with a total of one km of land space connected by a shoal, have since been built to cover 18 square km by generations tossing their garbage out the window, and eventually covering it over with sand, shells, and coral.

Guanaja Town may look hopelessly defenseless in the face of a hurricane, but the fringing reef, sandbars, and islets ringing the town to the south protect it from all but the fiercest storms. It is sometimes referred to as Bonacca by the locals, which derives from "Bonacre" ("good acre"), one of the early names for Guanaja.

With no beaches or other obvious attractions, Guanaja Town is worth a visit only to meet the islander townsfolk and take care of any business you might have. Anyone who spends a couple of days wandering the maze of causeways that comprise the island will soon make a few acquaintances and start to hear the endlessly entertaining local gossip and tall tales.

Dive Shops
Diving Freedom is a small outfit with only one launch and not a lot of equipment, located in the same building as the Coral Cafe. Owner Hugo Cisneros offers PDIC (a relatively new U.S.-based certification organization) open-water courses for US$200, but will go cheaper because business is tough. Individual dives cost US$25, or less in packages. Hugo will go to all sides of the island, and will also take snorkelers out for a small fee when he goes diving.

RECOMMENDED GUANAJA DIVE SITES

SOUTH SIDE:
- Pond Cay Wrecks
- Wreck of the Jado Trader
- Jim's Silver Lode
- Vertigo

WEST, EAST, AND NORTH SIDES:
- Final Wall
- Pinnacle
- Dianna's Reef
- Volcano Caves
- Black Rock Caves
- Siberia Eel Garden

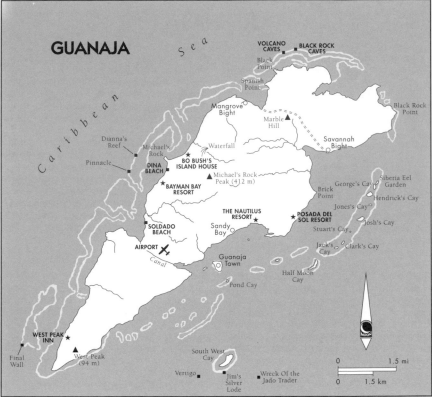

GUANAJA

Caribbean Sea

VOLCANO CAVES
BLACK ROCK CAVES
Black Point
Spanish Point
Mangrove Bight
Black Rock Point
Marble Hill
Savannah Bight
Dianna's Reef
Michael's Rock
Waterfall
Pinnacle
DINA BEACH
BO BUSH'S ISLAND HOUSE
Michael's Rock Peak (412 m)
George's Cay
Siberia Eel Garden
Brick Point
Hendrick's Cay
BAYMAN BAY RESORT
Jones's Cay
THE NAUTILUS RESORT
POSADA DEL SOL RESORT
Josh's Cay
SOLDADO BEACH
Sandy Bay
Stuart's Cay
AIRPORT
Jack's Cay
Clark's Cay
Canal
Guanaja Town
Half Moon Cay
Pond Cay
WEST PEAK INN
Final Wall
West Peak (94 m)
South West Cay
Vertigo
Jim's Silver Lode
Wreck Of the Jado Trader

0   1.5 mi
0   1.5 km

© MOON PUBLICATIONS, INC.

Harder to contact is **Jado Divers,** run by Mateo Curloin, with an office just past Hondutel on the same side. Look for the red-and-white "diver down" sign. During the day he can be contacted on VHF channel 65.

Local boat owners will gladly take out snorkelers, for a fee, to any of dozens of nearby sites. The reef surrounding Southwest Cay is particularly good for snorkeling.

Accommodations

Although not as grim as many travelers assume, the budget hotel selection is limited to the top end of the "budget" category, and even then only if there's two of you. Solo travelers can expect to pay for two beds regardless. The midrange options are scarce as well, and there are no resorts in Guanaja Town.

On the northern end of the main street is the **Hotel Miller,** tel. 45-4327, on the second floor of a large building. A double room costs US$10-15 with hot water, fan, and homey decorations, more for a/c and TV. Similar is the **Carter Hotel,** tel. 45-4203, US$9 s, US$10 d with bath—though water is not always reliable.

In a concrete building set back off the main street in the middle of town, the **Hotel Rosario,** tel. 45-4240, has rooms with a/c and TV for US$22 d. At the south end of the main street is the **Hotel Alexander,** tel. 45-4326, a large house on the water. Each of the 12 rooms has a sea-facing balcony and private bath; US$35 s or

US$45 d, more for a/c. A penthouse with three double beds, kitchenette, and TV is also available for US$150 a night. Less expensive rooms (US$7-10) are for rent in a private house on the left just before Hotel Alexander.

Next to the airstrip is the **Airport Hillton,** where unexceptional rooms with private bath rent for US$28 d. There's no reason to stay here except misguided paranoia about missing a flight.

Food and Entertainment

Tasty and inexpensive meals, including great beef soup, are served at **Wilma's,** on a side street just past the Nest Restaurant (not as good). Open for three meals a day.

Two Italians run **The Up and Down Restaurant,** a couple of blocks off the main street, serving pizza, spaghetti, lasagna, and other Italian dishes for US$3-7 in a friendly international atmosphere. Open for lunch and dinner daily, with bar service until midnight, or later on weekends.

Across the street from Up and Down is **Joe's,** which has no sign, but serves legendary inexpensive chicken *guisado* (stewed) or *a la plancha* (fried). One local described the perfect meal to a pair of eager visitors who followed his detailed instructions and were greatly rewarded. First, find Joe's and place your order; the *guisado* is preferred. Go outside, turn right, then turn right immediately into an alley next to the pool hall. A

couple of doors up on the left Miss Mina makes great fresh *pan de coco* (coconut bread) in her one room place. Once you purchase a dozen or so hot rolls—this must be accomplished between 6 and 7 p.m. when the bread comes out of the oven—return to Joe's trying not to wolf down too many pieces of warm bread en route. Finally, when your food arrives gorge thoroughly on bread, beer and chicken, and thank your guidebook author for recommending the *guisado,* as you will have lots of tasty juice to mop up with your bread.

Two doors away from Banco Atlántida on the same side of the main street is **Emma's** (no sign), serving decent and inexpensive breakfasts, burgers, *pastelitos,* and coffee.

The Coral Cafe in the center of town doesn't have much in the way of good food (microwaved burgers are the main course) but it serves as an informal town square, with everyone stopping in to chat and have a soft drink or beer. Cafe owner Hugo Cisneros helps locate boats heading over to the big island, sells Sosa airline tickets, and manages the Diving Freedom shop. Across the street is a good bakery.

The **Mountain View Disco,** a rickety old wooden dance hall built over the water, is the local weekend hot spot.

Services

Banco Atlántida, tel 45-4262, and Bancahsa, tel. 45-4178 or 45-4335, change both dollars and

boarding the MV Tropical

traveler's checks. **Guanaja Properties,** tel./fax 45-4299, tel. 45-4276, is the largest real estate office on the island. Some **tourist information** is available from Kenia Lima in the mayor's office, tel. 45-4119.

Police can be reached at tel. 45-4310. There is no fire department on Guanaja.

Getting There and Away

Both Sosa, tel. 45-4359, and Isleña, tel. 45-4208, fly once a day from La Ceiba to Guanaja via Roatán for US$30. The airstrip is on the main island, with no terminal except a simple shelter, though a terminal was under construction at last report. Boats invariably come out to meet the flights, and charge US$1-2 for the 15-minute ride to town. Both airlines have agents in Guanaja where tickets can be purchased.

Although there is no regular ferry service between Guanaja and the mainland, ships frequently depart to various destinations up and down the Honduras coast and throughout the Caribbean. The port captain, tel. 45-4321, may be of some help in locating rides.

ELSEWHERE ON THE ISLAND

The favored locales for high-end vacationers on Guanaja have always been the several dive hotels scattered around the island—self-contained operations ranging from the luxurious Posada del Sol resort to the homey four-room Island House. Resorts normally book weeklong meal-and-dive packages, including transport to and from the airport.

Budget travelers can seek out less expensive rooms in Mangrove Bight, stay at the tent camp on West End Bay, or freelance camp on one of many immaculate north-side beaches.

Private boats arrive and depart frequently each day, heading between Guanaja Town and various parts of the island. Usually islanders arrive in town in the morning, shop or sell goods, and leave again about midday. Ask around, especially at the Coral Cafe, where Hugo can often help arrange rides. A ride to Mangrove Bight, an hour or so away depending on the size of the outboard, normally costs US$1.50. Boats heading to Mangrove Bight can easily drop visitors off at Dina Beach or Michael's Rock, both superb beaches. Regular boats to Savannah Bight leave

Guanaja Town daily at 7 a.m., returning immediately, for US 60 cents. An express boat trip to Michael's Rock or vicinity costs about US$25.

Dive Resorts and Hotels

One of the premier dive resorts in the Bay Islands, **Posada del Sol,** tel. 45-4186 or 45-4311, tel./fax 45-4186, in the U.S. at 1201 U.S. Hwy. 1, Ste. 210, N. Palm Beach, FL 33408, tel. (800) 642-3483 or (407) 624-3483, fax (407) 624-3225, has 23 Spanish-style rooms with ceiling fans set on 70 acres of mountainside and beachfront property on the main island's south side. Among the many amenities are: freshwater pool, tennis court, two beaches, restaurant and bar, in-house massage therapist, Nautilus equipment, kayaks and snorkel gear, staff-organized trips to Barbareta, town tours, and archaeological hikes. Weeklong dive-and-meal packages cost US$756 pp for two people, US$917 for one; three night packages are US$339 pp. Prices include three dives daily on one of three 42-foot dive boats, one night dive per week, and unlimited shore diving.

On the north side of the island is the **Bayman Bay Resort,** tel. 45-4179, in the U.S. at 7481 W. Oakland Blvd., Ste. 307A, Ft. Lauderdale, FL 33319, tel. (800) 524-1823 or (954) 572-1902, fax (954) 572-1907, featuring 18 wooden cottages distributed across 100 acres of wooded hillside fronted by a white-sand beach. Each cottage is decorated with local art and equipped with ceiling fans and louvered windows to let the trade winds blow through. Weeklong packages, include diving and three buffet-style meals daily, cost US$700-750.

Casa Sobre El Mar, on Pond Cay, south of Guanaja Town, tel. 45-4269, VHF channel 78, in the U.S. (800) 869-7296 or (615) 443-1254, may not be the biggest resort on the island, but it's certainly the most colorful—a bright green-and-orange wooden house built by American owners Ivey and Betty Garrett. It's filled with books, pictures, ornaments, fishing and diving gear, fish in tanks, monkeys, a parrot, and even a pet boa constrictor. This "ma and pa dive resort" has three rooms with hot water and serves up three healthy meals daily. A constant breeze keeps all bugs away. Rooms are upstairs, with a porch, and cost US$75-85 a day for divers, US$20 less if you're not diving. Diving is excellent on all sides of the cay, including a reef wall and the wreck of a small freighter in 85 feet of water right in front of the hotel's dock.

One of the more relaxed, friendly, and less expensive dive hotels in the Bay Islands is **Bo Bush's Island House,** fax (via Hondutel) 45-4146, built and managed by Bo and his wife. Bo is a bilingual, experienced island diver with over 5,000 dives under his belt and a fast boat, and he knows a whole world of north side dive sites including caverns, walls, reef gardens, wrecks, and more. The comfortable stone-and-wood house set into the hillside can sleep eight, but Bo's boat can only handle six divers. Meal-and-dive packages cost US$590 a week or US$80 a day. Meals and room only costs US$40 a day. The isolated hotel has a positively tranquilizing atmosphere, with wide stretches of deserted beach all around. Bo, a very friendly and laid-back host, will happily take guests on hiking trips and island tours.

In Sandy Bay, **The Nautilus Resort,** tel. 45-4389, in the U.S. c/o Action Travel, 151 S. Division St., Carterville, Il 62918, tel. (800) 224-3866 or (618) 985-2818, fax (618) 985-2841, has only six rooms on 25 acres of land, with a 1,000-foot sand beach and a nearby waterfall. Weeklong dive-and-meal packages cost US$700 pp double occupancy.

Mangrove Bight

On the northeast side of Guanaja is Mangrove Bight, a small town with a mixed population of Latino and islander families, all dependent on the modest local fishing fleet. Like most island towns, Mangrove Bight is built right on the water, with many houses actually set on posts in the small bay. Electricity in town currently shuts off at 10 p.m., but the town generators may soon be replaced by 24-hour power lines. Mangrove Bight is usually stroked by a steady breeze, which keeps the sand flies and mosquitoes to a minimum.

Shandra Miller rents out a clean, breezy cabin over the water with a bathroom and two double beds for US$10 pp. Book it through Hugo at the Coral Cafe in Guanaja. Others in town likely will rent a room out for less if you're willing to hunt around a bit. A couple of *comedores* in town serve up inexpensive eggs, burgers, and other dishes.

A few points of rock sticking up out in the bay in front of Mangrove Bight indicate the location of the **reef.** It's a fair swim out but doable for strong snorkelers who keep their eyes peeled for boat traffic. Once to the reef, poke around to find a sufficiently deep opening to pass through, and get ready for a heart-stopping drop-off into the blue depths below on the far side. Visibility is not fantastic and the water is a bit choppy, but it's worth the effort to snorkel around the drop-off. Snorkelers may want to get in and out of the water from the western edge of town as the local "sewer system" consists of outhouses over the harbor. Shandra has fins and a mask for her guests to use.

Near Mangrove Bight

From Mangrove Bight a dirt road heads southeast past an unused airstrip and across a low point in the interior of the island to **Savannah Bight,** about an hour and a half away through mosquito-filled pastureland. About halfway there you'll pass **Marble Hill,** an anomalous, tree-covered outcrop on the west side of the road. On the far side of the hill is the largest known pre-Columbian ceremonial site on the Bay Islands, **Plan Grande.** Thankfully the site was mapped in the 1930s before being completely pillaged of its pottery and jade artifacts and destroyed. Little remains of either the ceremonial site or a large residential complex nearby, but locals will take a visitor to poke around for a fee. The road between Mangrove Bight and Savannah Bight offers good views of the mountains in the center of the island.

For the industrious, a trail leads from the western end of Mangrove Bight up a small valley, over a peak, and down the other side to Sandy Bay. The summit of the 412-meter peak is flat and reportedly a good spot for camping. Needless to say, the views from the top are stunning. Fresh water can sometimes be found but it's best to bring enough for the whole trip, which could be done in a long day.

About a 45-minute walk west of Mangrove Bight by trail begins a stretch of beautiful beach winding around to **Michael's Rock,** a rocky headland jutting into the ocean. The entire beach is lovely, but the best sections—two stretches of powdery sand and brilliant pale blue water separated by a grove of coconut palms—are right on either side of the headland. In its current state, this is a superb beach on which to sling a hammock or pitch a tent and enjoy a couple of days in isolation, but this may change soon. Rumor has it the Camino Real hotel chain is planning to build a resort here. Small patches of reef around Michael's Rock offer snorkeling possibilities, but the main reef is about a mile off-shore.

On the way to Michael's Rock is Bo Bush's Island House, a friendly, low-priced dive hotel that also makes a great place for nondivers to relax and enjoy the beach. Not far from Bo's place a small creek comes out of the hills, and a trail follows it a half hour uphill to a small **waterfall** surrounded by lush vegetation.

Don't forget to come prepared for sand flies; they can be fierce on the north side beaches.

Elsewhere on the North Side
From Michael's Rock, **Dina Beach** is visible further southwest, but walking is difficult as the trail passes through thick underbrush in order to by-pass rocky coastline. It's better to get dropped off by boat and picked up later instead of trying to walk it from Mangrove Bight. This is a great beach for camping, but there's no fresh water anywhere nearby so be sure to bring enough.

Southwest of Dina Beach is Bayman Bay Resort, separated by more rock headlands. Further southwest still, near the mouth of the canal, is **Soldado Beach,** the reputed site of Columbus' landing in 1502. Nearby is a half-built monument marking the event—Spain donated money for a small museum, but somehow the money didn't go as far as originally expected.

Even larger unoccupied beaches are to be found on **West End Bay,** west past the canal on the north side of the island. So far the only facility in West End is the **West Peak Inn,** a small restaurant and lodging run by a British expatriate. Sleeping accommodations in tents cost US$28 per day, including three healthy meals. Kayaks and some diving equipment are available, and a nearby trail ascends to the top of West Peak (94 meters) for views across Guanaja and over to Barbareta and Roatán. More development is expected soon on West End Bay.

THE OTHER BAY ISLANDS

CAYOS COCHINOS (HOG ISLANDS)

The Hog Islands, called the Masaqueras by the early colonists, consist of two main islands and 13 small cays surrounded by pristine reef, 19 kilometers off the Honduran coast. The two larger islands are covered with thick tropical forest and ringed by excellent white-sand beaches.

The Cayos were declared a marine reserve in 1994. All marine and terrestrial flora and fauna within a 460-square-km area is protected, from fishing, development or any other harmful activity. From any point of land in the islands, the reserve extends eight kilometers in all directions. The cays are managed by the Smithsonian Tropical Research Institute, which has an office on Cayo Pequeño.

The marine reserve has caused some anxiety among a community of Garífuna, who have lived on one of the cays for generations and who survive by subsistence fishing. There has been some talk of kicking the Garífuna out, but government officials say this will never happen.

Practicalities
The only "official" accommodations in the Cayos are at **Plantation Beach Resort,** Apto. Postal 114, La Ceiba, Atlántida, Honduras, tel. 42-0974, in the U.S. c/o A-1 Scuba and Travel, tel. (800) 628-3723. The resort was included in the original management plan for the reserve. The hotel's mahogany and stone cottages with decks and hammocks are tucked into a small valley on the site of a former pineapple plantation on Cayo Grande. One week with meals and diving costs US$795; two PADI instructors provide certification courses. Traveler's checks and cash are accepted, credit cards and personal checks are not. Those looking for some hiking to complement their diving will find numerous trails over the 140-meter peak or around the shore to the north side, where there is a lighthouse and a small village. The resort boat, a twin 300hp 42-footer, comes to La Ceiba every Saturday and charges US$75 for the roundtrip.

Those who wish to appreciate a different side of the Cayos for considerably less money can take a boat from Nueva Armenia, near Jutiapa on the mainland coast, to the Garífuna village of **Chachauate,** on Lower Monitor Cay.

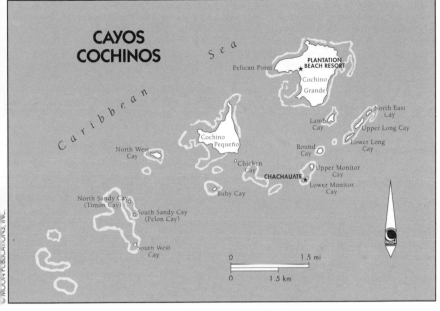

This is the sort of place, as one visitor commented, where you should go with an open mind and heart. Because of its isolation, Chachauate is one of the more traditional and friendly Garífuna villages in Honduras, so keep that in mind and try to be a relaxed and amiable guest. A couple of *pulperías* can supply minimal food, but there are no hotels or restaurants, so visitors will have to ask locals to cook food and help find a room to stay in (or at least permission to sling a hammock). There's great snorkeling all around, but visitors should bring their own gear, as well as fresh water and a few other supplies like fruit or crackers. Boats to the Cayos leave from Nueva Armenia most days in the early morning and will take passengers for US$5-7 each way.

SWAN ISLANDS

Three days by boat from Guanaja or Puerto Lempira are the tiny Swan Islands, the northernmost possession of Honduras in the Caribbean and an extension of the same geological formation that forms the Bay Islands. The Swan Islands lie some 160 km from the Honduran coast. Columbus landed on the islands in 1502, four days before arriving at Guanaja, and named them the Santa Anas in honor of the saint on whose day the islands were discovered. Because the islands are a good source of fresh water, they were frequently used as a way station by Caribbean voyagers over the centuries, and as a result their ownership has long been disputed. As late as 1893 an U.S. captain believed he had discovered them (not realizing he was 391 years late) and so claimed them for the United States. The U.S. finally ceded ownership of the Swan Islands to Honduras in 1974, but the CIA continued to maintain a radio station there until recently.

Currently the islands are populated by Jamaican fishermen who have permission from the Honduran government to reside there on a temporary basis. The 14-mile reef surrounding the islands is reportedly in superb condition, and several Spanish galleons supposedly lurk in the waters below.

The Swan Islands—two small cays and many smaller islets, all owned by the state and declared a marine sanctuary—can be reached by private boat, helicopter, or plane (there is a small landing strip), or with one of the supply boats from Jamaica that bring in provisions for the fishermen.

BCB RACE

COPÁN AND WESTERN HONDURAS

INTRODUCTION

Along with the Bay Islands, the famed ruins of Copán are probably one of the most often visited sites in Honduras. But invariably travelers continue right on to the Caribbean coast from Copán without taking the time to explore other areas of the country's western highlands. It's their loss—this is one of the most naturally beautiful and least-explored areas in all of Central America. Here the adventurous can lose themselves for weeks, traveling the mountain roads and footpaths between isolated colonial villages like Erandique, La Campa, and Belén Gualcho, or climbing to the unsurpassed cloud forests of Montaña de Celaque, Honduras's highest peak.

Outside of Copán Ruinas, the colonial town of Gracias, and the region's unofficial capital of Santa Rosa de Copán, few tourist services exist in the western highlands. Yet the lack of creature comforts is more than compensated by the thrill of visiting lovely villages seemingly lost in the mists of history, where locals may not know quite what to think of a passing foreigner but will invariably invite them in for a cup of strong black coffee and a chat.

Western Honduras is also one area where the country's indigenous highland culture remains. This is Lenca territory, the land of Lempira, a famed Indian chief who battled the conquistadores to a standstill before being tricked and killed, and for whom the national currency is named. In the hills around Copán near the Guatemalan border are villages of Chortí Maya, a people related to their highland cousins to the northwest.

THE LAND

Western Honduras is an extremely mountainous region with little flat land apart from small, intermontane valleys. The mountain ranges, which include the Celaque, Opalaca, de las Neblinas, and Merendón, are the highest in the country, topping out at 2,849 meters at Cerro de las Minas on Montaña de Celaque. Unlike nearby El Salvador and Guatemala, the mountains of western Honduras are not volcanoes, but are formed of metamorphic rock overlain mostly with limestone. Soils in the region are generally thin and unpro-

COPÁN AND WESTERN HONDURAS

GUATEMALA

Sierra del Espíritu Santo

Quimistán

Chamelecón

Ulúa

El Puente

La Entrada

Río Jicatuyo

Valle

Santa Bárbara

Río

Río Copán
Santa Rita

El Florido

Copán Ruinas

Valle de Copán

San Agustín

Dulce Nombre

San Juan de Opoa

Montaña de Puca

San Rafael

Santa Rosa de Copán

Higuito

Río

Montaña Verde

Monte Verde

Cucuyagua

Valle de Cucuyagua

Río

P.N. Montaña

Gracias

Sierra

Reserva Biológica Montaña de Güisayote

Corquín

Cerro de las Minas (2,849 m)

de Celaque

de

Opalaca

Esquipulas

Belén Gualcho

La Campa

Mejocote

To Siguatepeque

Agua Caliente

Valle de Ocotepeque

La Labor

San Manuel Colohete

San Juan

Valle de Sensenti

Caiquín

Nueva Ocotepeque

Sierra Celaque

San Sebastián

Sierra

La Esperanza

El Poy

Yamaranguila

P.N. Trifinio-Montecristo

de las

Río

Tomalá

Río Mocal

Neblinas

Erandique

Tambla

Valladolid

Gualince

San Francisco de Opalaca

EL

Río Sampul

La Virtud

Candelaria

SALVADOR

Mapulaca

Río Guarajambala

San Antonio

Río Lempa

Santa Lucía

0   10 mi
0   10 km

© MOON PUBLICATIONS, INC.

COPÁN AND WESTERN HONDURAS HIGHLIGHTS

- Seeing the ruins of Copán
- Visiting the colonial town of Gracias and hiking in the nearby cloud forest of Parque Nacional Celaque
- Touring the highland colonial villages of Belén Gualcho, La Campa, San Manuel Colohete, or Erandique

ductive, apart from some of the intermontane valleys, which are covered with a fertile loam.

The two major valleys in western Honduras are the Valle de Copán, along the Río Copán, and the Valle de Sensetí between Nueva Ocotepeque and Santa Rosa de Copán. Much of the region is still covered with *ocote* pine forest, mixed in with oak and liquidambar (sweet gum) at higher elevations, although deforestation is a serious problem in many areas as campesinos cut wood for fuel or to clear more farm or grazing land.

At elevations above 2,200 meters, dense cloud forest covers mountain peaks. A sort of high-altitude jungle, cloud forests contain towering trees blanketed with moss, vines, and ferns, and dripping wet all year round. Again, deforestation has taken a serious toll on the cloud forests. A classic example can be seen at Güisayote, near Nueva Ocotepeque, where a narrow strip of cloud forest covers the ridgeline but is surrounded by denuded slopes.

The rainy season in western Honduras is normally May through September, but wet weather can hit at any time in the mountains. If you're planning on camping, come prepared. Generally the area receives between 75 and 200 cm of precipitation a year, more in the mountains and less in the valleys. During the rains, the temperature ranges from cool to downright cold, while during the dry season it's normally quite comfortable—warm in the daytime and pleasantly cool at night.

HISTORY

Pre-Columbian Era
By all accounts western Honduras was heavily populated by different indigenous groups, but archaeologists disagree on exactly which ones.

Evidence from the Spanish suggests the Indians currently known as Lenca were at least a half-dozen distinct tribes during colonial times. Tribes included the Potón, Guaquí, Cares, Chatos, Dules, Paracas, and Yaras, who lived in an area stretching from Olancho to El Salvador.

At the time of conquest the Lenca were a relatively small group centered around the mountains near present-day Erandique. They had established villages, but were essentially hunters and engaged in little agriculture. Loyalties existed only among those who spoke the same language, and tribes were constantly at war with their immediate neighbors.

Farther west, toward the Guatemalan border in the Copán and Chamelecón Valleys and in the department of Ocotepeque, the Chortí Maya dominated. The Chortí were the immediate descendents of the Classic Maya who had built Copán several centuries earlier. Although they were a relatively sedentary agricultural society, their political organization did not extend much beyond a group of neighboring villages.

Nahuatl-based place names which have survived to the present day suggest Mexican traders or immigrants also lived in western Honduras, though their numbers were not large.

Conquest and Colonization
Spanish conquistadores began their conquest of present-day Honduras in 1524, 22 years after Columbus first landed near Trujillo. The first forays into western Honduras came from Guatemala, when an expedition led by Juan Pérez Dardón took control of the Río Copán region under orders from Pedro de Alvarado.

By 1530 other expeditions from both the Honduran coast and from Guatemala converged on the mountainous region around Celaque. Captain Juan de Chávez was sent by Alvarado to establish a town, but was forced to return to Guatemala when he found himself facing thousands of hostile Lenca warriors led by Lempira.

In addition to Chávez's report, other stories of fierce Indian resistance driven by Lenca leaders Tapica and Etempica along with Chortí Maya leaders Mota and Copán Galel flooded into Alvarado's office, convincing the notoriously cruel conquistador to personally lead an expedition

*17th century church,
San Manuel Colohete*

into the region. In 1536 Alvarado cut a bloody swath through western Honduras, massacring Indians and burning houses in Laepera and Opoa.

Alvarado's actions only further enraged the Lenca, Maya, and other tribes, and his apparent victory over the region proved ephemeral. The town of Gracias a Dios was founded in late 1536 as a Spanish base, but early the following year the entire province was in open revolt, led by Lempira from his fortress at Peñol de Cerquin. Not until 1539, after two years of fierce warfare, was the revolt extinguished and Spanish control over the region consolidated.

Part of the Higueras province, western Honduras was extremely poor throughout the colonial period. The small mines of gold and silver found near Gracias a Dios were quickly spent, and treasure-seeking conquistadores headed for richer prospects in Peru and Mexico. After a few short years as the administrative center of Central America in the 1540s, western Honduras faded into a badly governed and sparsely populated region, surviving on the meager income from cattle production and the tobacco industry.

Independence to Present
Located between El Salvador, Guatemala, and the two main cities of Comayagua and Tegucigalpa, western Honduras was a major crossroads during the wars of independence and the resulting struggles between the Central American republics. Although many battles were fought in the region, there were no major prizes to be captured apart from Santa Rosa de Copán, which was at the time a major center for tobacco production.

Since the mid-19th century, western Honduras has steadily declined in importance to the national economy. The mining boom around Tegucigalpa and the burgeoning banana industry on the north coast at the turn of the century only drew workers eager to escape the region's poverty away from western Honduras.

To this day western Honduras is one of the poorest parts of the country, inhabited mainly by peasants, many of whom survive by subsistence farming supplemented by meager corn or coffee production. Much of the U.S. Peace Corps' work in Honduras has focused on encouraging nontraditional agricultural products and soil-conservation measures in the region.

COPÁN RUINAS TOWN

For many visitors, Copán Ruinas is the first Honduran town they see after crossing over from Guatemala, and it's hard not to be charmed by the relaxed friendliness of the place. In contrast to many Guatemalan mountain towns, Copán Ruinas evinces an overwhelming sense of safeness, due in large part to the lack of resentful, tense vibes between locals and foreign visitors. Any afternoon and evening in the square one can watch schoolchildren playing, elders leisurely passing the time of day, some young man plucking a tune on his guitar under the admiring gaze of his girl.

In addition, Copán Ruinas is a physically beautiful town, with a shady square, cobblestone streets, and an attractive locale amid the green hills of the Río Copán Valley. Copán Ruinas was originally a small village, an outlying settlement of the larger Santa Rita, before archaeology and tourism improved its fortunes.

Much of the agricultural land in the Copán Valley is dedicated to tobacco, as it has been since colonial times. For many years Copán tobacco was famed through the Americas and well-known in Europe. In the 1960s other strains were introduced to the valley, and pests brought in by the foreign varieties quickly wiped out the Copán plant. Much of the tobacco is now used to make the national cigarettes, and some goes to the Flor de Copán cigar factory in Santa Rosa de Copán.

The biggest event of the year in Copán Ruinas is the annual festival in honor of the town's patron saint, San José. The festival takes place on 19 March.

SIGHTS

Although nothing on the level of the new Sculpture Museum at the ruins (see "The Ruins of Copán," below), the small **Museo Regional de Arqueología** on the square is worth a visit to admire its extensive collection of statuettes, jade sculptures, and the complete tomb of a shaman, laid out in a case just as it was found at the Las Sepulturas site. The museum is open Mon.-Sat. 8 a.m-noon and 1-4 p.m.; US$2.50 entrance fee.

The old **cuartel,** an old barracks building atop a hill five blocks north of the square, is a fine spot to admire views over the town and the Río Copán Valley.

ACCOMMODATIONS

Because Copán Ruinas is accustomed to tourists of all incomes from backpackers to luxury travelers, hotels are available in all price and quality ranges. Almost all are located right in the center of town.

When arriving in town by bus, expect to be surrounded by a horde of young men offering to find you a room. They may tell you certain hotels are full, and they may be lying. Nevertheless they will find a room for a couple of lempira tip.

Budget

Hotel Los Gemelos is the favored backpacker spot in town, with good reason. This friendly, family-run small hotel, down the hill northeast of the square, has a dozen neat plaster-and-tile rooms around a small courtyard for US$3 s or US$4 d, communal bathrooms, a sink for washing clothes, and an attached souvenir shop.

Across the street from Los Gemelos is the American-owned **Hotel California and Tres Locos Bar,** with small rooms in a grass courtyard behind the bar, nicely decorated with handicrafts and art, for US$5 s or d. The bar closes at 9 p.m. so no worries about late-night noise.

Probably the cheapest room in town is at **Hotel Posada,** just north of the square, with basic but reasonably clean double rooms for US$3.50. Near the highway bridge leaving town toward the ruins is the two-story, motel-style **Hotel Paty,** tel. 61-4021, with a large parking lot out front. Fairly clean, sparse rooms go for US$5 d with no fan and communal bath, or US$12 d with fan and private bath. National newspapers are sold here around 9 or 10 a.m. every day.

The owner of the Casa de Café (see "Midrange," below) is building a dormitory-style hostel, which should be open by the time of publication.

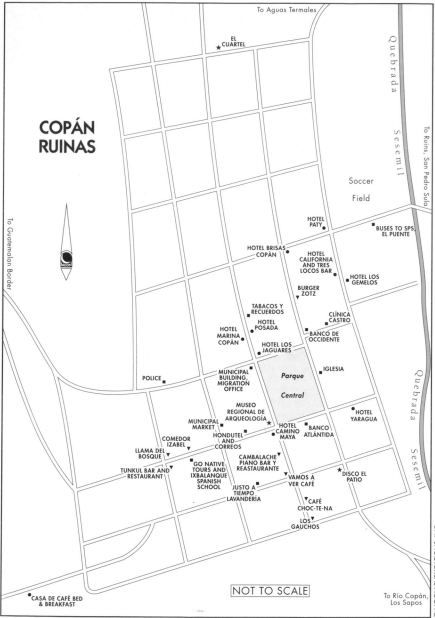

COPÁN RUINAS

To Aguas Termales

★ EL CUARTEL

Quebrada Sesemil

To Ruins, San Pedro Sula

Soccer Field

To Guatemalan Border

HOTEL PATY ●

● BUSES TO SPS, EL PUENTE

HOTEL BRISAS COPÁN ●

HOTEL CALIFORNIA AND TRES LOCOS BAR ●

● HOTEL LOS GEMELOS

BURGER ZOTZ ▼

TABACOS Y RECUERDOS ■

HOTEL POSADA ●

CLÍNICA CASTRO ●

HOTEL MARINA COPÁN ■

● BANCO DE OCCIDENTE

HOTEL LOS JAGUARES ●

Parque Central

● IGLESIA

MUNICIPAL BUILDING, MIGRATION OFFICE ■

POLICE ■

MUSEO REGIONAL DE ARQUEOLOGÍA ★

● HOTEL YARAGUA

MUNICIPAL MARKET ■

COMEDOR IZABEL ▼

HONDUTEL AND CORREOS ■

HOTEL CAMINO MAYA ■

■ BANCO ATLÁNTIDA

LLAMA DEL BOSQUE ▼

TUNKUL BAR AND RESTAURANT ▼

GO NATIVE TOURS AND IXBALANQUE SPANISH SCHOOL ■

CAMBALACHE PIANO BAR Y REASTAURANTE ■

VAMOS Á VER CAFÉ ▼

★ DISCO EL PATIO

JUSTO A TIEMPO LAVANDERÍA ■

▼ CAFÉ CHOC-TE-NA

LOS GAUCHOS ●

NOT TO SCALE

● CASA DE CAFÉ BED & BREAKFAST

To Río Copán, Los Sapos

Quebrada Sesemil

© MOON PUBLICATIONS, INC.

Midrange

Formerly a bit of a dive, **Hotel Yaragua,** tel. 61-4464, fax 61-4050, on the southeast corner of the square was at last report completely rebuilding its rooms. The hotel plans to offer double rooms for US$15 with hot water and TV.

A block north of the square is **Hotel Brisas Copán,** tel. 61-4018, with quiet, clean rooms with hot water, fans, and TV for US$18 d or US$27 t. The owners live in the adjacent building, which is separated from the hotel by a pleasant patio open to guests.

Two similarly priced options on the square are **Hotel Camino Maya,** tel. 61-4446 or 61-4518, fax 61-4517, offering modern rooms in a two-story building, and **Hotel Los Jaguares,** tel. 61-4075 or 61-4451, with slightly more inviting tile-floored rooms and an outdoor patio. Both hotels charge US$35 s or US$44 d, and have private parking. The Cafe Elisa is downstairs in the Camino Maya.

A unique setup several blocks southwest of downtown is **Casa de Café Bed and Breakfast,** tel. 52-7274, fax 52-0523, run by an American-Honduran couple. Behind their very lovely house are several wood-paneled guest rooms, tastefully decorated and featuring elegant wooden writing desks. From the hammocks on the patio, you'll enjoy unmatched views over the Río Copán Valley below. Though a bit isolated, this place is perfect for relaxing and soaking in the area's vibes. Rooms cost US$38 d with breakfast.

Luxury

The only top-notch hotel in downtown Copán Ruinas, at least at the moment, is **Hotel Marina Copan,** tel. 61-4070, 61-4071, or 61-4072, fax 61-4477. Rooms in the one-level colonial-style building feature dark wood furniture and paneling. Some of the 40 rooms have terraces and gardens—well worth requesting. Among the hotel amenities are a small pool on the main patio, a sauna and gym, a bar, and a recommended restaurant. Hotel service is very good. Prices range from US$70 s to US$105 suite.

Set on a hillside above the San Pedro Sula highway at Km 164 is **Posada Real de Copán,** tel. 61-4480 through -4497, or in San Pedro tel. 56-8740, fax 56-8748. A Best Western hotel, it's equipped with a sizable patio swimming pool, two bars, a restaurant, and conference room. The 80 rooms each have a/c, cable TV, and purified tap water. Many offer views of the valley and ruins below.

Farther up the highway, past Santa Rita, is the venerable **Hacienda El Jaral,** tel. 52-4457, tel./fax 52-4891 or 52-5067, founded as a working ranch in 1870. Now run as a stylish hotel by the great-grandson of the original owner, it's set on a private lagoon with a large heron population. The US$50 d rooms are in 19th-century cabins, each with hot water, ceiling fan, TV, and refrigerator. Activities include horseback riding, hiking, mountain biking, and tubing on the nearby Río Copán.

The **Gran Hotel Gobernantes** in Santa Rita, tel. 61-4528, was completing construction at last report and should be open by the time of this book's publication.

FOOD

Inexpensive

Despite its slightly odd name, **Café Choc-Te-Na** offers unexotic but clean, tasty, and low-priced meals and snacks including vegetarian dishes, spaghetti, *baleadas, licuados,* and breakfasts. It's open daily 7 a.m.-9 p.m. in a simple cafeteria two blocks south of the square.

Two blocks west of the square is **Comedor Izabel,** a local favorite for well-prepared standards including beef and chicken dishes, vegetarian soup, *baleadas,* tacos, and breakfasts. Open daily 7 a.m.-9 p.m. More of a snack stand, and also popular with locals, is **Burger Zotz,** featuring burgers, *baleadas, licuados,* and other munchies served daily 8 a.m.-10 p.m. Half a block north of the square, Burger Zotz is often full of schoolchildren in the afternoon.

Midrange

Vamos a Ver Café, run by European owners who know what travelers like, has a creative menu with vegetarian options, excellent sandwiches with imported cheese on homemade bread, a large selection of coffees, and pleasant indoor and outdoor dining areas. Movies are shown nightly for US$1, and the restaurant is open daily 7 a.m.-10 p.m.

Something of a Copán Ruinas institution, **Tunkul Bar and Restaurant** is a favorite gathering spot for expatriates and moneyed travelers; it often hosts tourist-oriented social events. Meal prices are reasonable, and the *baleadas* and burritos are notoriously huge. The garlic chicken is a specialty. The patio-bar is two blocks west of the square and has a billboard with tourist information. Open daily 7 a.m.-midnight. Across the street from the Tunkul is **Llama del Bosque**, with a large menu and full bar service at slightly upscale prices.

A more relaxed, unpretentious place to have a meal or a few drinks is **Cambalache Piano Bar y Restaurante,** just off the southwest corner of the square. It's popular with locals and travelers who come to enjoy the sociable ambience and good music. Meals from the extensive menu are served either in the bar or in a quieter interior courtyard. Open 7 a.m.-11 p.m.

Those looking for a more traditional restaurant could try **Los Gauchos,** an Argentine-style steak house with heavy emphasis on beef, but also serving fettuccine and other pastas, paella, and shrimp (though this might not be a wise choice for seafood, so far from the coast). Open for lunch and dinner daily.

INFORMATION AND SERVICES

Shopping
As a major tourist destination, Copán Ruinas has its share of souvenir shops, many with Guatemalan and Salvadoran as well as Honduran crafts, including *junco* palm goods, leather, ceramics, jade and wood sculptures, and the ever-present T-shirts. Shops include **Mahchi, Yax Pac, Honduras Es Amor (near the ruins), Sac Nic Te,** and **Copán Galel,** all located within a couple of blocks of the square. **Tabacos y Recuerdos** opposite the Marina Copán Hotel has a decent selection of Honduran cigars.

Services
Banco de Occidente on the northeast corner of the square changes dollars, quetzales, and traveler's checks, as well as advancing cash on Visa cards Mon.-Fri. 8 a.m.-noon and 2-5 p.m., Saturday 8 a.m.-noon. The local migration office is inside the municipal government building on the square, open Mon.-Fri. 8 a.m.-4:30 p.m.

Hondutel, open daily 8 a.m.-9 p.m., and Correos are next to each other half a block west of the square.

Justo a Tiempo Lavandería, a block southwest of the square, will wash your grubby duds for US$1 per pound, Mon.-Sat. 7:30 a.m.-5:30 p.m. The American owner also runs a book exchange.

Emergency
Apart from dealing with crimes, the local **police,** tel. 61-4060, can also arrange ambulance service.

Clínica Castro, tel. 61-4504, is run by a competent doctor who speaks some English. His office, a half a block north of Banco de Occidente, is open Mon.-Sat. 8 a.m.-noon and 2-4:30 p.m.

Tours
Go Native Tours, tel. 61-4432, fax 61-4004, runs day-trips to nearby hot springs, caves, villages, El Rubí waterfall, and other sites for US$25-45 pp, depending on the length of trip.

Spanish School
For those who become hypnotized by the easy lifestyle of Copán Ruinas and want a reason to extend their stay, **Ixbalanque Spanish School,** tel. 61-4432, fax 57-6215, offers five days of one-on-one classes and a week of housing with a local family for US$145. The classes and family stays are generally very good—the families tend to be more interested in interacting with foreigners than similar setups in Guatemala.

GETTING THERE AND AWAY

To La Entrada, San Pedro Sula, and Santa Rosa de Copán
Etumi buses to La Entrada (2-3 hours) and on to San Pedro (another two hours) leave every hour or so between 4 a.m. and 5 p.m. from the bridge at the north end of town. "Direct" buses to San Pedro (which often stop along the way anyhow) leave Copán at 4 a.m. and 5 a.m. Buses straight through to Santa Rosa de Copán leave daily at 8 a.m., but you can also take a bus to La Entrada and wait for a San Pedro-

Santa Rosa bus there. Supposedly there are normally two Santa Rosa buses daily, but at last report one was out of commission. Best to double-check all bus departure times as they frequently change.

The 72-km road between Copán Ruinas and La Entrada is paved, but often in bad shape, especially during the rainy season.

To the Guatemalan Border

The Copán Ruinas-El Florido border crossing between Honduras and Guatemala is the crossing most frequently used by Central American travelers, although the route through Santa Rosa de Copán-Nueva Ocotepeque-Esquipulas is considerably easier. The main advantage to the El Florido-Copán Ruinas crossing is that it allows the traveler to see the ruins, right on the way in or out of the country.

Buses to El Florido, at the border, leave Copán Ruinas frequently and charge US 80 cents for the half-hour potholed 12-km trip. Pickup trucks ply the same route and are often easier to find as they drive through town picking up passengers before leaving. The price should be the same, but be sure to ask before getting on as drivers might try to get more out of unsuspecting travelers. The last bus/pickups leave to the border around 3 p.m. and return around 4 p.m.

The border itself is in the middle of a field, with no services except a *pulpería* on the Honduran side and moneychangers offering bad rates. There have been some reports of Honduran officials requesting extra crossing fees—insist on receipts for all fees charged, and if they won't give one don't pay. The border is supposedly open daily 6 a.m.-6 p.m., but this seems to fluctuate. The best time to arrive is midmorning, well before lunchtime.

From El Florido, buses continue on to Chiquimula, Guatemala for US$1.50; it's two-and-a-half bumpy, dusty hours away.

NEAR COPÁN RUINAS

In addition to viewing the Mayan ruins, many hikes and excursions can be made in the hills and valleys around Copán Ruinas. The countryside is generally very safe for wandering, and local campesinos are invariably friendly and helpful to visitors who lose their way.

Eight kilometers northeast of Copán Ruinas on the highway to La Entrada is the lovely cobblestone village of **Santa Rita,** which was originally the main Spanish town in the area. Formerly the village was named Cashapa, which means "sweet torilla" in Chortí Maya. The last buses back to Copán Ruinas pass at around 5:30 p.m.

About a half-hour walk from Santa Rita, across the Río Copán, is **El Rubí,** an attractive set of twin waterfalls pouring through a series of boulders. Because of the profusion of trails, it's best to get a local to show you the way up. Trails from Santa Rita also continue up over the mountains to the south, ending up in **San Agustín,** where rides can be found to Dulce Nombre de Copán and on to Santa Rosa de Copán. The hike can be done in one day, and passes along sections of the old Camino Real and near the virgin cloud forests of Monte Quetzal.

Spelunkers shouldn't miss the **cave** 30 km northeast of Copán Ruinas (ask locals for more specific directions). Almost two km long, it's filled with stalactites, stalagmites, and bats, and it has a river running through it.

One can also stroll along the Río Copán in any direction, and enjoy the rural beauty of the valley. Most of the fields in the area are dedicated to tobacco; those odd-looking buildings all over the place are drying ovens for the leaves. If all this hiking has stiffened up the muscles, consider a trip to the **aguas termales** (hot springs) about 20 km north of Copán Ruinas by dirt road. Pickup trucks often travel this road and will give you a ride for US$1-2.

THE RUINS OF COPÁN

HISTORY OF THE MAYAN CITY OF COPÁN

Although not the largest Mayan city—at its height a population of 24,000 lived in the surrounding region, as compared to over 100,000 at Tikal—Copán was, as one noted archaeologist put it, "the Athens of the New World." It was the premier Maya center for arts and astronomy during the 400 years when the city was at the peak of its development.

The Early Years

The rich bottomland in the Río Copán Valley attracted farmers of unknown origin as early as 1000 B.C., but archaeological evidence indicates the Maya did not settle the area until about the time of Christ. Construction on the city is thought to have begun around A.D. 100, and the recorded history of the city does not begin until 426, when Copán's royal dynasty began. Some archaeologists believe the dynasty began when outsiders conquered the city and took over administration of the valley.

Detailed information on Copán's earliest rulers is difficult to obtain, in part due to the ancient Mayan tradition of destroying monuments built by past rulers or building over temples erected in their honor. Not until 1993 were references to Copán's first ruler discovered, buried deep under the Hieroglyphic Stairway beneath a subtemple referred to as Papagayo.

The Papagayo temple was built by the second ruler, nicknamed Mat Head for the odd headdress he is always depicted wearing. In the temple, Mat Head erected a stela in his own honor that also refers to his father, **Yax K'uk'Mo'**. According to the stela, Yax K'uk'Mo', the city's first ruler, took the throne in A.D. 426 and governed until A.D. 435. The 1993 excavation under the Papagayo temple uncovered the tomb of Yax K'uk'Mo'. Evidence indicates he was a powerful shaman who was revered by later rulers as semi-divine.

Little solid information is available on the next seven members of the dynasty, apart from a few names and dates. Apparently ruling only a small, provincial settlement at that time, these leaders created few lasting monuments or hieroglyphics telling of their deeds.

The Height of the Royal Dynasty

The period of greatest architectural construction, considered to be the height of Copán's dynasty, began on 26 May 553, with the accession of **Moon Jaguar** to the throne. Moon Jaguar, Copán's 10th leader, built the Rosalila Temple, which was discovered in 1989 buried under Structure 10L-16. A replica of the temple can now be seen in its full glory in the Copán Museum.

After Moon Jaguar, a series of rulers of unusual longevity governed Copán, providing the stability and continuity necessary for the city to flourish. **Smoke Imix,** the city's 12th ruler, took the throne 8 February 628 and ruled for 68 years, leaving more inscribed monuments and temples than any other ruler. Frequently depicted in full battle regalia and with representations of the jaguar god Tlaloc, Smoke Imix is thought to have been a great warrior. His successor, **18 Rabbit,** was also a prolific builder, who gave final form to the Great Plaza and the Ball Court and encouraged the development of sculpture, from low-relief to the nearly full-round style of later years. Despite these achievements, 18 Rabbit's reign ended in tragedy; he was captured in battle by the nearby city of Quirigua, formerly a vassal state of Copán, and beheaded on 3 May 738.

The Decline

Possibly because of the devastating blow of 18 Rabbit's death, the 14th ruler, **Smoke Monkey,** erected no stelae in his own honor, and built only one temple during his 11-year rule. He apparently conducted the city's affairs in a council with nobles, demonstrating the weakness of the regime. In what archaeologists consider an attempt to regain the dynasty's former glory, Smoke Monkey's successor, **Smoke Shell,** dedicated the impressive Hieroglyphic Stairway, the longest hieroglyphic inscription known in the Americas. The 2,500 glyphs narrate the glorious past of Copán, but the poor construction of

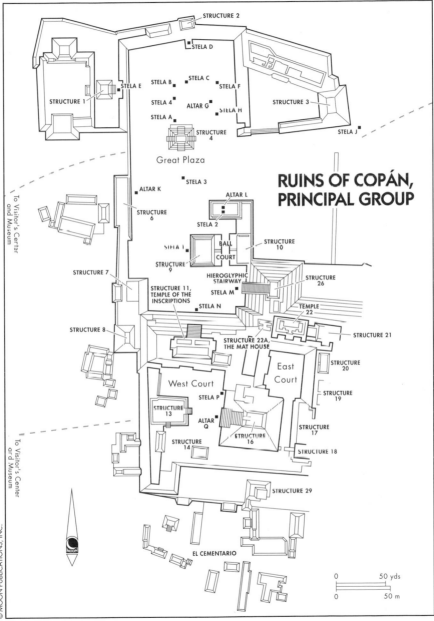

STRUCTURE 2

STELA D

STELA E

STRUCTURE 1

STELA B   STELA C

STELA 4   STELA F

STRUCTURE 3

STELA 4

ALTAR G   STELA H

STELA A

STRUCTURE 4

STELA J

Great Plaza

STELA 3

RUINS OF COPÁN, PRINCIPAL GROUP

ALTAR K

ALTAR L

STRUCTURE 6

STELA 2

To Visitor's Center and Museum

STELA I   BALL COURT   STRUCTURE 10

STRUCTURE 9

HIEROGLYPHIC STAIRWAY   STRUCTURE 26

STRUCTURE 7

STRUCTURE 11, TEMPLE OF THE INSCRIPTIONS

STELA M

STELA N   TEMPLE 22

STRUCTURE 8

STRUCTURE 22A, THE MAT HOUSE   STRUCTURE 21

STRUCTURE 20

East Court   STRUCTURE 19

West Court

STELA P

STRUCTURE 13

ALTAR Q   STRUCTURE 17

STRUCTURE 16   STRUCTURE 18

STRUCTURE 14

STRUCTURE 29

To Visitor's Center and Museum

EL CEMENTARIO

0   50 yds

0   50 m

© MOON PUBLICATIONS, INC.

REDISCOVERING COPÁN

. . . working our way through the thick woods, we came upon a square stone column, about fourteen feet high and three feet on each side, sculptured in very bold relief, and on all four of the sides, from the base to the top. The front was the figure of a man curiously and richly dressed, and the face, evidently a portrait, solemn, stern, and well fitted to excite terror. The back was of a different design, unlike anything we had ever seen before, and the sides were covered with hieroglyphics . . . The sight of this unexpected monument put at rest at once and forever, in our minds, all uncertainty in regard to the character of American antiquities, and gave us the assurance . . . that the people who once occupied the Continent of America were not savages.

—John Lloyd Stephens,
Incidents of Travel In Central America, Chiapas, and Yucatán, 1841

Likely because of its supremely beautiful artwork, unsurpassed by any other Mayan city, Copán has long attracted explorers and archaeologists and occupies a special place in the study of the ancient Maya. As a result of this long and close attention, the history of Copán is one of the best-understood in the Mayan world.

The Colonial Years
After the great Mayan city collapsed and was overtaken by jungle in the 9th century, the outside world knew nothing of Copán until 1576, when Don Diego Garcia de Palacio wrote an official report on the ruined city to King Philip II. Garcia's report was descriptive and quite accurate, obviously the product of first-hand observation: "They [the ruins] are found on the banks of a beautiful river in an extensive and well-chosen plain, which is temperate in climate, fertile, and abounding in fish and game. Among the ruins are mounds which appear to have been made by the hand of man as well as many other remarkable things."

Garcia's portrait of Copán would stand as the most informative for the next three centuries. In 1689 historian Francisco Antonio Fuentes y Guzmán unearthed Garcia's report. Fuentes related the city to an incident that took place in the Chiquimula region in 1530, an Indian revolt led by one "Copán Galel, who had an army of 30,000 warriors" and fought the Spanish from a heavily fortified town surrounded by a moat. Fuentes concluded that this town and the ruins were one and the same, but modern historians and archaeologists reject the idea, placing Copán Galel's fortress farther south in current-day Ocotepeque. Nevertheless Copán Galel may have been the source for the ruin's name.

19th-Century Adventurers
Other historians after Fuentes rehashed Garcia's initial description, but apparently did not actually go to Copán. The next recorded visit came in April 1834, when the Guatemalan government commissioned Col. Juan Galindo, a naturalized Irishman whose real name was John Gallagher, to investigate the ruins. Galindo spent a couple of months at the site, but added little useful information to what Garcia wrote. He did, however, make the valuable observation that Copán bore striking similarities to Palenque, the Mexican ruins he had also visited. Galindo noted that the two sites seemed to be related.

Copán became known to the wider world by the work of John Lloyd Stephens and Frederich Catherwood, two uniquely talented men who visited, and then bought, the ruins in 1839. An American diplomat, adventurer, and author, Stephens had already published the famous travelogue *Incidents of Travel in Arabia Petrea* before he convinced U.S. president Martin Van Buren to send him on a diplomatic mission to Central America. Stephens was accompanied on the expedition by his friend, the English architect-artist Catherwood.

The pair spent several weeks at the ruins, clearing underbrush, taking measurements, and sketching buildings and artwork. After many more adventures and explorations in Guatemala and the Yucatán, Stephens and Catherwood returned to the U.S. and published *Incidents of Travel in Central America, Chiapas, and Yucatán*, which was an immediate success and went on to become one of the most widely read books of the time, going through 10 editions in three months. It was just the sort of report needed to awaken a fascination with Mesoamerican civilization. While Westerners from the U.S., Great Britain, and other developed nations had until then held a vague knowledge that ruined cities existed somewhere in Central America, Stephens's detailed measurements and lively descriptions, accompanied by Catherwood's accurate and elegant drawings, captured the public's imagination.

The First Archaeologists

Largely because of *Incidents of Travel,* legendary British archaeologist Alfred P. Maudsley made his way to Copán in 1881. Although he stayed for only three days, the enigmatic and beautiful artwork entranced Maudsley. He returned four years later to begin a full-scale project of mapping, drawing, photography, excavation, and reconstruction that would continue off and on until 1902. Maudsley's voluminous work on Copán and several other Mayan sites was compiled in the five-volume *Biología Centrali-Americana,* which was enhanced considerably by the superb drawings of Annie Hunter. Hunter's representations of glyphs are extraordinarily accurate and still used in research today.

Maudsley was followed by a long line of Mayanist scholars, who continued the work of excavation and reconstruction, gradually building a more accurate picture of what Copán originally looked like, and building what has become known as the "traditional" model of Mayan civilization. Foremost among these scholars were Sylvanus Morley and J. Eric Thompson. Completely enamored with Mayan art and astronomical science, Morley and Thompson contributed more than any others to the prevailing view of the Classic Maya as peace-loving philosophers living in something akin to a New World Athens, minus the warfare.

Modern Theories of Copán

Beginning in the mid-1950s, this traditional, elite-oriented view, which saw the Classic Maya as a miraculous, almost flawless society, began to break down. As archaeologists began investigating smaller pre-Classic sites and the residences of ordinary ancient Maya, a more complex, richer picture of Mayan society began to emerge. The new theories held that

Mayan society developed like many other ancient civilizations—amid warfare, trading, agricultural innovation, and exploitation of the lower classes.

Probably the most stunning breakthrough in understanding the Maya came in 1959 and 1960, when archaeologists Heinrich Berlin and Tatiana Proskouriakoff began deciphering Mayan hieroglyphics—a process that continues to this day. Archaeologists had long understood that hieroglyphics were a form of writing, but they could do little more than guess at the meanings.

The work of Berlin and Proskouriakoff has been taken up by noted linguists and archaeologists such as Yurii Knorosov, Linda Schele, David Kelley, Floyd Lounsbury, and others, with considerable success. It is now recognized that the glyphs are nothing more or less than a history of the cities where they have been found, recording in stone events such as battles and dynastic successions. Using clues provided by *Relaciones de las Cosas de Yucatán,* written by Bishop Diego de Landa, epigraphers can now translate some glyphs into the ancient Mayan language.

Because of the abundance of stelae and carvings at the site, Copán has been a major focus of the deciphering efforts, and the history of the city is perhaps better understood than that of any other ancient Maya center. In 1975 the Peabody Museum of Harvard, which sponsored Maudsley's initial investigations, began a second major project at Copán. This project is undertaking important investigations overlooked by earlier efforts, including studying outlying, residential areas such as Las Sepulturas for clues into everyday life among the ancient Maya, and making excavations under many of the buildings in the Principal Group to learn about the city's growth over time.

---

the staircase itself reveals Smoke Shell could not mimic the impressive work of his predecessors.

The final leader in Copán to complete his reign, **Yax Pac** governed the city 58 years, and apparently attempted to legitimate his rule through the veneration of the Jaguar Tlaloc warrior-sacrificial cult. Depictions of the cult cover monuments built during his reign. One of the most important monuments left by Yax Pac is the famous Altar Q, a square bench illustrating all 15 prior rulers of the dynasty around its sides, with the first, Yax K'uk'Mo', passing the baton of leadership to Yax Pac. Although he may not

have known it when he commissioned it, Yax Pac left on the small stone altar a brief résumé of the city's entire history.

A 17th leader, **U Cit Tok',** assumed the throne on 10 February 822. But for reasons which remain a mystery, his rule was never completed. Evidence for this is the pathetic Altar L, which he ordered built to commemorate his rule; it was only half completed before being abandoned.

The debate over the reason for the collapse of the Classic Maya kingdom has raged since serious archaeological work began at the turn of the century. The most accepted current expla-

the Ball Court

nation for Copán's collapse pits the blame on environmental factors. By the final decades of the 8th century, the city had grown to cover some of the best alluvial bottom land in the river valley, and consequently farmers were pushed farther up the hillsides, where land was not as productive. Recent investigations indicate that during this time the Río Copán Valley experienced droughts, deforestation, massive soil erosion, and sudden floods during the rainy season. It's likely Copán simply outgrew its environment.

Although the city center was abandoned, evidence suggests the population in the region did not drop drastically until about 1200, when the region reverted to the small village groups found by the Spanish when they entered the valley in 1524.

THE RUINS

The ruins of Copán are about a kilometer east of Copán Ruinas on the road toward San Pedro Sula, set off the road in a 15-acre archaeological park along the edge of the Río Copán. After buying your US$10 entrance ticket, walk up the path from the visitor's center (where there is a small cafeteria and gift shop) into the woods to the entrance gate, where a guard will take your ticket.

The Great Plaza

Past the gate, where colorful macaws hang out eyeing the visitors, the path continues through the woods briefly before opening out onto the Great Plaza. In this expansive grassy area, which was graded and paved during the heyday of the city, are many of Copán's most famous stelae—free-standing sculptures carved on all four sides with pictures of past rulers, gods, and hieroglyphics. Red paint, traces of which can be seen on **Stela C,** built in 730, is thought to have once covered all the stelae. It is a mix of mercury sulfate and resins from certain trees. Most of the stelae in the Great Plaza were erected during the reign of Smoke Imix (628-695) and 18 Rabbit (695-738), at the zenith of the city's power and wealth.

All of the stelae are fascinating works of art, but one of particular interest is **Stela H** (730), which appears to depict a woman wearing jewelry and a leopard skin under her dress. She may have been 18 Rabbit's wife.

At the south end of the Great Plaza is the **Ball Court,** probably the best-recognized and most-often-photographed piece of architecture at Copán. It is the third and final ball court erected on the site, and was completed in 738. No exact information is available on how the game was played, but it is thought players bounced a hard rubber ball off the slanted walls of the court, keeping it in the air without using their hands. Atop the slanted walls are three intricate macaw heads on each side, as well as small compartments which may have been used as dressing rooms by the players. Macaws were considered sacred by the Maya.

The Acropolis

South of the Ball Court is the Acropolis, a massive architectural complex built over the course of the city's history. Some of the most fascinating archaeological finds in recent years have come from digging under buildings in the Acropolis and finding earlier temples which were buried and built over. At its highest, the Acropolis is 30 meters above the Great Plaza, and is estimated to weigh over three million tons.

Rising from the southeast corner of the Plaza, and now unfortunately covered with a roof to protect it, is the equally famous **Hieroglyphic Stairway,** the longest hieroglyphic inscription found anywhere in the Americas. The 72 steps contain more than 2,500 glyphs. It was built in 753 by Smoke Shell to recount the history of Copán's previous rulers. Since the city was declining in prestige at that point, the stairway was shoddily made compared to other structures, and collapsed after an earthquake. Tragically, early archaeologists reassembled the steps in random order, rendering the story Smoke Shell told indecipherable. The National Geographic Society recently located a photograph of the stairway taken by a Mexican visitor before the earthquake, and, using this as a template, archaeologists hope to rebuild the stairway and read the story again.

Underneath the stairway a tomb was discovered in 1989. Laden with painted pottery and jade sculptures, it is thought to have held a scribe, possibly one of the sons of Smoke Imix. In 1993, farther down below the stairway, archaeologists found a subtemple they dubbed **Papagayo,** erected by the second ruler of Copán, Mat Head. Deeper still, under Papagayo, the tomb of the founder of Copán's ruling dynasty, Yax K'uk'Mo', was unearthed. Thus scientists consider this site, called the **Founder's Room,** to be the original center of Copán, around and over which the city grew. The earliest known glyph at Copán was found here.

The broad, broken staircase bordering the south side of the Great Plaza rises to the **Temple of the Inscriptions,** so-called for the hieroglyphic blocks comprising it.

A small, not visually arresting building called the **Mat House** occupies a corner of the Acropolis between the Temple of the Inscriptions and the Hieroglyphic Stairway. Archaeologists have been particularly interested in this building. It was erected in 746 by Smoke Monkey, not long after the shocking capture and decapitation of his predecessor, 18 Rabbit. Decorated with carvings of mats all around its walls, the Mat House was evidently some sort of communal government house; the mat has always symbolized a community council in Mayan tradition. Following 18 Rabbit's death, the Copán dynasty weakened so much that Smoke Monkey was forced to govern with a council of lords, who were commemorated on the building according to their neighborhood. The original facade of the Mat House is in the Sculpture Museum.

Next to the Mat House is **Temple 22,** thought to be a "Sacred Mountain," the site of important rituals and sacrifices in which the ruler participated. South of Temple 22 is the **East Court,** the site of much current excavation. Evidence suggests this was the original plaza for Copán— archaeologists have uncovered a smaller version of the court built by Yax K'uk'Mo', the first ruler of the dynasty, and traces of older construction dating to A.D. 100.

On the eastern side of the East Court, the Acropolis drops off in an abrupt cliff down to where the Río Copán ran for a time, before it was diverted to its current course in 1935. Since the river ran alongside the Acropolis, it ate away at the structure, leaving a cross-section termed by Sylvanus Morley, "the world's greatest archaeological cut."

Between the East Court and the nearby West Court is **Structure 16,** the site of one of the most important recent discoveries at Copán. Underneath the pyramid, in 1989 Honduran archaeologist Ricardo Agurcia found the most complete temple ever uncovered at Copán. It's called **Rosalila** (Rose-lilac) for its original paint, which can still be seen. The temple was erected by Copán's 10th ruler, Moon Jaguar, in 571. Tunnels accessing Rosalila are closed to the public, but a full-scale replica of the temple is the centerpiece of the Sculpture Museum. Structure 16 was a temple dedicated to war, death, and the veneration of past rulers.

At the base of Structure 16 is a square sculpture known as **Altar Q,** possibly the single most fascinating piece of art at Copán. For many years, following the theory of archaeologist Herbert Joseph Spinden, it was believed the altar illustrated a gathering of Mayan astronomers in the 6th century. However, recent breakthroughs in deciphering Mayan hieroglyphics have revised that view. The altar, as it turns out, is a brief history of the entire Copán dynasty, depicting in stunning relief each of the 16 rulers seated around the edge of the altar, with the first ruler, Yax K'uk'Mo', passing the ruling baton on to the last, Yax Pac, who ordered the altar built in 776. Near the altar the bones of 15 jaguars were uncovered, presumed to have been sacrificed in honor of the warrior god Tlaloc when the altar was dedicated.

South of the West Court is an area known as **El Cementerio,** where archaeologists have found the remains of many graves in recent years. Lately much of the original sculpture work at Copán has been removed from the grounds and replaced by exact duplicates. Although this is a bit disappointing for visitors, it is essential if the city's artistic legacy is not to be lost forever, worn away by the elements and thousands of curious hands. Most of the finest stelae and carvings can now be seen in the Sculpture Museum.

Adjacent to the Principal Group in the park is a kilometer-long **nature trail,** with examples of ceiba, strangler fig, and other plants characteristic of the jungle originally covering the Copán Valley. Beware the *chichicaste* thorn shrub, which will give you a nasty sting if you touch it.

Las Sepulturas

Two km up the highway toward San Pedro Sula from the main ruins is the residential area of Las Sepulturas. Ignored by early archaeologists, in recent years Las Sepulturas has provided valuable information about the day-to-day lives of Copán's ruling elite. The area received its macabre name ("The Tombs") from local campesinos, who farmed in the area and in the course of their work uncovered many tombs of nobles who were buried next to their houses, as was Maya custom.

Although the ruins have been rebuilt extensively, they are still not as visually interesting to the casual tourist as the Principal Group, and most of the sculpture has been removed. One piece that remains is the **Hieroglyphic Wall** on Structure 82, a group of 16 glyphs cut in 786, relating events from the reign of Yax Pac, Copán's last ruler. On the same structure is a portrait of **Puah Tun,** the patron of scribes, seated with a sea-shell ink holder in one hand and a writing tool in the other.

VISITING THE RUINS OF COPÁN

The ruins are open 8 a.m.-4 p.m. every day, and it's highly recommended to get in right when the gates open. In the early morning hours you'll be able to enjoy the ruins in relative solitude, and you'll have good low-angle light for your photographs. This is also the favorite time for a group of white-tailed deer who live in the woods to come out and wander around the ruins. Whenever you go, be sure to keep an eye out for Pancho the monkey, who strolls around waiting for tourists to give him a hug.

When walking around the ruins, refrain from walking on stairways that have been roped off, and try not to lean on sculptures, stelae, or buildings, as salts on the skin can corrode the stone, especially when multiplied by the 60,000 or so visitors who come to Copán each year. It should go without saying, but let it be said: it is illegal to remove any stones from the park.

Two pamphlet-guides to the ruins are sold at the ticket office: *History Carved in Stone,* by William Fash and Ricardo Agurcia Fasquelle, and *Copán, Legendario y Monumental,* by J. Adan Cueva. The former, written in English, has an excellent interpretation of the growth of the city and advances in archaeology, but does not discuss each monument individually. The latter, in English and Spanish, is weak on recent advances in archaeology, and although it does give a description of many major sites, they are often incomplete and not entirely useful.

Guides can be hired at the site for about US$10 for a two-hour tour. In addition to providing information on the ruins themselves, guides often relate interesting local legends and tall tales about the area.

In **Plaza A** of Las Sepulturas the tomb of a powerful shaman who lived around 450 was discovered; it can be seen in its entirety in the Museo Regional in Copán Ruinas. In this same area traces of inhabitation dating from 1000 B.C. were found.

Las Sepulturas is connected to the Principal Group by an elevated road, called a *sacbé,* which runs through the woods. Archaeologists expect to open the road to the public by 1998, but currently visitors must go around by the highway. Be sure to bring your ticket as you must show it to get in to Las Sepulturas.

Other Sites

South of Copán Ruinas, in the hills on the far side of the Río Copán just opposite the ruins, is the small site of **Los Sapos** (The Frogs). Formerly this rock outcrop carved in the form of a frog was quite impressive, but it has since been worn almost completely away. Nonetheless it's a good destination for a two- or three-hour roundtrip walk, and the site itself provides great views out over the valley. The location was thought to be a birthing spot, where Mayan women would come to deliver children. To get there, leave town heading south, and follow the main road over the Río Copán bridge. On the far side turn left and follow the dirt road along the river's edge. The road will begin to head up into the hills, and after a few minutes a ranch comes into view on the left. Pay a nominal fee here (US 50 cents or so) and follow a trail another five minutes to the site.

Higher up in the mountains beyond Los Sapos is another site known as **La Pintada**, a single glyph-covered stela perched on the top of a mountain peak, with fantastic views. By foot or horseback La Pintada is about 3-4 hours from Copán Ruinas.

THE SCULPTURE MUSEUM

As of the summer of 1996, Copán has had a museum befitting the ruins' importance in the world of the ancient Maya. Designed by Honduran architect Angela Stassano, the museum is built into a hillside and illuminated by a massive, open air skylight. Apart from the full-scale reconstruction of a buried temple, which is the centerpiece of the building, the museum contains some of the finest examples of Mayan sculptures ever found.

The museum's architecture was designed to depict different aspects of Mayan cosmology. Visitors enter through a tunnel, representing the mouth of the underworld in Mayan mythology, as well as the tunnels used by archaeologists in uncovering the buried temples, tombs, and buildings at Copán. The four sides of the building are aligned with the cardinal points of the compass, which were fundamental to the Maya, and also represent the four sides of a cornfield. The two-story design symbolizes the Mayan concept of a lower underworld and the aboveground reality. The first floor contains sculptures of skulls, bats, and other images of death and violence, while the upper floor displays facades from buildings and many of the original stelae commemorating Copán's leaders.

Dominating the center of the museum is a full-scale replica of the Rosalila Temple found under Structure 16 in 1989; the temple was built in 571. The bright colors may be a bit of a shock at first, but all Mayan buildings were once covered with plaster and brightly painted. It will certainly change your attitude toward the Mayan aesthetic—not one of somber elegance but a more exuberant, technicolor style. With time, exposed to the elements from above, the temple's colors are expected to fade somewhat, replicating the process that must have taken place at the original temple.

Although not cheap—an extra US$10 on top of the ruins' entrance fee—a visit to the Sculpture Museum is a must for anyone really interested in the ancient Maya who lived at Copán. Apart from displaying the originals of some of the best-known stelae and sculpture in the Mayan world, the museum contains many pieces never before seen by the public. These pieces give a full view of the prodigious ability of the Mayan craftsmen. The informative signs are in English and Spanish. Take the time to read them all—it's a short course in Mayan history and archaeology.

the "Old Man" of Copán

LA ENTRADA
AND THE RUINS OF EL PUENTE

LA ENTRADA

Nothing more than a highway junction with a town built around it, La Entrada is a good base from which to visit the nearby ruins of El Puente, the second-most developed Mayan site in Honduras after Copán.

Should it be necessary to spend the night in La Entrada, the **Hotel San Carlos,** tel. 98-5228 or 98-5187, is the only decent option in town. A three-story modern building right at the highway junction, the San Carlos charges US$10 s with fan and TV, or US$23 d with a/c. The hotel also has the best restaurant in town.

While waiting for a bus to Copán (72 km), Santa Rosa de Copán (44 km), or San Pedro Sula (126 km), fill up on *baleadas* and other cheap eats at El Triangulo store and lunch counter, next to the Texaco station. Buses to all these destinations frequently pass, the last usually around 5-6 p.m.

EL PUENTE

Located north of the Florida Valley on the banks of the Río Chinamito, two km north of the Río Chamelecón junction, the Mayan ruins at El Puente were first visited by an archaeologist in 1935, when Danish explorer Jens Yde drew a detailed map of the structures. El Puente then received little attention until 1984, when the Japanese Overseas International Cooperation Agency began work on the site in an effort to create a second archaeological attraction in Honduras.

Because it does not have the name recognition or the incredible artwork of Copán, El Puente is not as saturated with tourists as its more famous neighbor. As a result, it makes for a very pleasant and relaxing side trip on a journey between Copán and the north coast.

The 210 known structures at El Puente cover two square km, but only the main group has been restored. Generally oriented east to west, the main group has five well-defined plazas, and is dominated by **Structure 1,** an 11-meter pyramid with six platforms; it is thought to have been a funerary temple.

Other buildings of note include **Structure 10,** a long pyramid on the south side of Structure 1 that holds an ornate burial chamber, and **Structure 3,** a pyramid complex whose south staircase holds an example of an *alfarda,* an inclined plane of decorative stonework. Tunnels allows visitors access into both of these buildings.

At the entrance to the site is a small museum with displays on the site itself and on Mayan culture in general. The ruins entrance ticket, US$2 for Central Americans and US$5 for everyone else, includes admission to the museum, which is soon to have a cafeteria.

From the museum it's about a one-km walk down a shady dirt road to the ruins, which are set admist grassy fields at the edge of a small river. Although the main buildings don't take long to admire, the location is a pleasant place to relax or picnic for a couple of hours. A nature trail is being developed by a Peace Corps volunteer at the site, and you can also take a dip in the river to cool off.

El Puente is in the municipality of La Jigua, five km from the La Entrada-Copán Ruinas highway. The turnoff is at La Laguna, where you can possibly catch a ride with a passing pickup truck up the road to the ruins. This road continues past El Puente to a lonesome stretch of the Guatemalan border. Traffic is fairly regular but not entirely dependable—better in the morning. A return ride can often be found with trucks carrying workers from the site back to La Entrada. A taxi from La Entrada costs US$15-20 roundtrip with a couple of hours at the ruins.

SANTA ROSA DE COPÁN

INTRODUCTION

Situated on a hilltop with a commanding view of the surrounding mountainous countryside—including the country's highest peak, Montaña de Celaque, to the east—Santa Rosa de Copán is a perfect base for exploring the fascinating and beautiful western highlands. Apart from a local cigar factory, Santa Rosa doesn't boast any specific tourist sites in itself, but visitors frequently find themselves staying longer than they planned in this overgrown village of 32,400 people. The climate is pleasantly cool, accommodations and food are inexpensive, and the residents are happy to see outsiders enjoying their town, of which they are justifiably proud.

Although technically only the capital of the Copán department, Santa Rosa functions as the capital for all of the western highlands. Almost all commerce in the region passes through Santa Rosa, and campesinos from rural areas wander the city's streets looking for merchandise or carting produce.

History

Little is known about the area surrounding Santa Rosa de Copán during pre-Hispanic times. Archaeologists generally agree the region was a transition zone between the Lenca tribes, centered further east and south, and the Chortí Maya, who inhabited the hill country along the Guatemalan border. The remnants of indigenous villages have been discovered at several sites near Santa Rosa, such as El Pinal, Yarushin, and Zorosca, but none within the town limits.

Early in the colonial period the Spaniards established a major settlement nearby at Gracias a Dios, but Santa Rosa itself was not settled until 1705. Juan García de la Candelaria, a cap-

tain of the Gracias town militia, applied for and was granted an *encomienda* in the name of Santa Rosa de los Llanos, also known as La Sábana. The site was strategically chosen on a hill above a fertile valley, along the royal road between Guatemala City and Gracias; the town quickly prospered as a transport way station and a cattle-ranching area.

A major boost in the nascent town's fortunes came in 1793, when the crown chose to move the Royal Tobacco Factory from Gracias to Santa Rosa, as it was nearer to the producing regions of the Copán Valley than Gracias. Santa Rosa grew steadily after this, with migrants coming from Guatemala and directly from Spain to establish their own small farms and businesses. In the late colonial period and well into the present century, the tobacco industry based in Santa Rosa was by far the most important economic activity in western Honduras, and as a result the city quickly eclipsed Gracias as the most important urban center in the region.

Santa Rosa, along with Comayagua and Tegucigalpa, was deeply involved in the independence wars and the resulting strife between the different Central American republics. Honduran president José Trinidad Cabañas briefly made Santa Rosa the country's seat of government in 1853, when Honduras was under constant threat from Guatemala. The importance of Santa Rosa was officially ratified in 1869, when the department of Copán was established and Santa Rosa designated its capital.

Orientation and Getting Around

Santa Rosa's downtown is a compact area of several blocks, but the town extends in all directions. The central market is east of the square, near the Ocotepeque highway, which continues down around the edge of town before looping

northwest on its way to San Pedro Sula. The bus station is on the highway down the hill about one km north of downtown. Taxis anywhere in Santa Rosa should cost US 50 cents.

SIGHTS

Probably the most interesting attraction in Santa Rosa, apart from just the relaxed ambience, is the **Flor de Copán cigar factory,** tel. 62-0185, two blocks west of the square on Ave. Centenario. It's not hard to find the factory—just follow the strong smell wafting out of the block-long building where 180 workers hand-roll some 20,000 cigars a day, almost all for export to the U.S. and Europe.

Free tours of the factory range 15 minutes to an hour in length, depending on the guide. Afterwards visitors are allowed into the bodega to buy a few cigars. Prices are generally about a third of U.S. prices, but surprisingly the Hotel Elvir just up the road sells them for even less than the factory. The Santa Rosa mark is considered the lightest, while the Don Melo is considerably stronger. Zino is the factory's top-of-the-line brand.

The simple, whitewashed *catedral* on the square was first built in 1798, then rebuilt in 1880. In the middle of the square is a two-story kiosk built in 1900, which now houses a small snack stand.

A block south of the square is the **Casa de la Cultura,** which sells some books and artwork but offers little information on the region. For great views over the town and surrounding mountains, take a walk up the hill on the south side of town.

ACCOMMODATIONS

Almost all hotels in Santa Rosa fall into the budget range, with only two midrange options. Most hotels are within three blocks of the square.

Budget
At the absolute bottom of the price and quality range are **Hospedaje San Pedro** and **Hospedaje Suyapa,** both renting cell-like rooms for US$1.20 s. One of the best inexpensive places to stay, if only for the company, is the **Peace Corps house,** a private house rented by volunteers so

they'll have a place to stay when they come into town from their villages. If the house isn't full (and it usually isn't), visitors can stay in one of the bunks for US$2.20 a night, and enjoy playing a stereo or swapping a book with one of the several hundred paperbacks left by generations of volunteers. If no one answers the door, ask at Pulpería Paty across the street if anyone is around. The volunteers are often excellent sources of information on nearby places worth visiting.

Two blocks east of the church is **Hotel Copán,** tel. 62-0265, with reasonably clean rooms for US$3 s, US$5 d, more for private bathroom. Two blocks west of the square is the similarly priced **Hotel Santa Eduviges.** The family-run **Hotel Castillo,** tel. 62-0368, has some of better inexpensive rooms in town, for US$2.20 s, US$4 d, or a little more with private bathroom.

Midrange
Unquestionably the best hotel in town is **Hotel Elvir,** tel./fax 62-0103, with spotless, modern rooms equipped with TV, bathroom, and lots of hot water for US$15 s, US$21 d, or US$24 t, credit cards accepted. The staff is very helpful and the cafeteria serves tasty and reasonably priced food. Room service is available. Max Elvir, a tireless promoter of tourism in the area, runs **Lenca Land Trails** out of the hotel, offering tours of surrounding villages and natural areas, including Celaque, Monte Quetzal, Belén Gualcho, San Manuel Colohete, and any other place you might want to visit. Rates depend on how many people want to go, but are quite inexpensive, and Max is an excellent and affable guide.

For travelers getting in late or leaving early, **Hotel Grand Mayaland,** tel. 62-0233, across from the bus station on the highway below town has modern rooms for US$9 s, US$15 d with TV, telephone, bathroom, and intermittent hot water.

FOOD AND ENTERTAINMENT

Inexpensive
Ever popular with travelers, Peace Corps volunteers, and locals is **Chiky's Mexican Restaurant,** on the corner of 1 Calle SO and 1 Ave. SO, an unpretentious and inexpensive eatery serving burgers, *tortas, plato típico,* and other assorted munchies in a ramshackle wooden building with benches and picnic tables. It's a great spot to drink a few beers and chat or watch TV—the owner is always willing to flip the channel, especially if a sporting event is on.

Pollos Copanecos, a block south of the square on 1 Ave. SE, serves up a mean fried chicken and french fries, Mon.-Sat. until 8 p.m. Almost worth a trip down the hill is the *comedor* at the bus terminal, which serves an excellent vegetable soup with everything in it but the kitchen sink.

Midrange
For a good selection of well-cooked Honduran standards for US$2-4 per entree, try **Rincón Colonial,** a block from the square on 1 Ave. SE, normally open daily until 10 p.m. A block farther away from the square on the opposite side of 1 Ave. SE is the similar **La Hacienda;** it also features a full-service bar.

The American-owned **Pizza Pizza,** on Calle Centenario at 5 Ave. NE, serves up a decent pie as well as grinders, spaghetti, and garlic bread, all at reasonable prices. It's open daily until 9 p.m., and also sells some books and the *Honduras This Week* English newspaper.

Across the street from Pollos Copanecos is the slightly pretentious **Flamingo's,** with an extensive and relatively overpriced menu ranging US$4-6 per plate.

A Garífuna family from Santa Rosa de Aguán on the north coast manages **La Gran Villa,** a restaurant specializing in seafood located on the highway toward San Pedro Sula, west of the bus station. Open daily until 9 p.m., La Gran Villa serves conch soup, snapper, shrimp, and other dishes—all excellent if a fresh shipment recently came in. Entrees run US$3-4.

Entertainment
Apart from going to **Chicky's** or **La Hacienda** for a few drinks, Santa Rosa offers little in the way of late-night party entertainment. The **Cine Hispano** next to the *catedral* shows a nightly double feature.

INFORMATION AND SERVICES

Hondutel, open daily 7 a.m.-9 p.m., and Correos are next to each other on the west side of the square. The migration office is one block northwest of the square.

SANTA ROSA DE COPÁN
USEFUL TELEPHONE NUMBERS

Police: 62-0918, 62-0840, or dial 199
Fire Department: 62-0823, or dial 198
Cruz Roja Ambulance: 62-0045, or dial 195
Hospital: 62-0128, 62-0093

Bancahsa, one block west of the square on Calle Centenario, changes traveler's checks and can advance cash on Visa cards. Banco de Occidente and Banco Atlántida exchange dollars and, sometimes, traveler's checks.

Super Lavandería Florencia, on Calle Centenario between 4 and 5 Calle SO, washes clothes Mon.-Sat. for about US$2 per load. Hotels might charge less.

GETTING THERE AND AWAY

Bus
Unless otherwise noted, all buses depart from the main bus terminal on the San Pedro Sula highway north of town. Depatures, times, and prices are as follows:

• To **Gracias,** eight buses daily between 7:15 a.m. and 5:30 p.m., US$1, about 90 minutes.
• To **Nueva Ocotepeque** and on to the **Guatemalan border,** six buses daily between 6 a.m. and 4:30 p.m., US$1.20-1.50, 2-2.5 hours.
• To **Copán Ruinas,** normally two buses daily in the late morning and early afternoon, US$1.50, three hours.
• To **San Pedro Sula,** four direct buses daily which take only two and a half hours instead of four (worth planning on) at 8 a.m., 9:30 a.m., 1:30 p.m., and 3 p.m., US$2.
• To **Tegucigalpa,** two buses daily, 4 a.m. leaving from the downtown square, 9:45 a.m. leaving from the Sultana office on the highway east of the Texaco station, US$4, six hours. On Sunday, departures are 9:45 a.m and 10:45 a.m., both from the highway office. To inquire about tickets, either go to the office or call 62-0940 or 62-0151.
• To **Belén Gualcho,** two buses daily at 7 a.m. and 10:30 a.m., US$1, two hours.

• To **San Agustín,** one bus daily at 3 p.m. Note that from San Agustín, you can pick up a trail heading over the mountains to Santa Rita, near Copán Ruinas.

Car
The highways to La Entrada (44 km), San Pedro Sula (170 km), Gracias (47 km), and Nueva Ocotepeque (92 km) are all paved and generally well-maintained, except at the height of the rainy season.

NEAR SANTA ROSA DE COPÁN

A portion of the old **Camino Real** passes near Santa Rosa, beginning in the village of San Agustín, beyond Dulce Nombre de Culmí. An old colonial road system once maintained by the crown, the Camino Real has been paved over in many places to form present-day main highways. From here you can walk over the crest of the mountains down to Santa Rita, near Copán Ruinas, in a day. Near the trail, on the left (south) side close to the crest, is the privately owned **Monte Quetzal,** a pristine, undeveloped mountain with dense cedar forest and plenty of its namesake birds. Reportedly the mountain is soon to be incorporated into Honduras's system of national protected areas. Max Elvir of Lenca Land Trails knows the owner and can arrange trips there.

Between Santa Rosa and San Juan de Opoa, on the road to Gracias, is **Parque La Montañanita.** Although not much more than a weekend picnic area for Santa Rosa residents, it's a good place to camp out.

Sixteen kilometers from Santa Rosa on the San Pedro highway is a dirt road turnoff to the east leading to **Quezailica,** a small town centered around the beautiful **Santuario del Milagroso Cristo Negro,** built in 1660 and declared a national monument in 1987. In the church is a carved wooden Black Christ, made by an unknown artist who was apparently a student of famed sculptor Quirio Cataño, who made the Black Christ of Esquipulas. A major Chortí Maya community in pre-Hispanic times, this area contains many relics of the Chortí Maya, including a carved rock monolith in the shape of a face found hidden in the church's atrium, now sitting outside the church.

NUEVA OCOTEPEQUE AND VICINITY

NUEVA OCOTEPEQUE

A classic dirty border town, Nueva Ocotepeque does have one major advantage—its setting amid the beautiful mountains at the junction of Honduras, Guatemala, and El Salvador. The town's name derives from the words "ocote," a local pine tree, and "tepec," meaning hill. Most travelers who enter here understandably get on the first bus heading in whatever direction they're going, but the hiking aficionado may want to dawdle a couple of days to see the nearby **Reserva Biológica Montaña de Güisayote,** on the crest of the mountains rising right behind town, or **Parque Nacional Triunfo-Montecristo,** which forms the border of the three countries.

Practicalities

Of the several budget hotels in town, **Hotel Turista,** on the main street next to the square, is a good value, with clean rooms for US$2 s, US$3 d, or a bit more with private bathroom. **Hotel San Juanito** two blocks off the avenue behind the main bus stop, also has inexpensive, large rooms.

The only moderately upscale accommodation in town is **Hotel Sandoval,** tel. 63-3098, fax 63-3408, a modern three-story building one block off the main drag with rooms ranging from US$10-25, depending on the number of people and whether or not it's air-conditioned. The hotel restaurant, open daily 7 a.m.-9 p.m., has the best food in town. Credit cards are accepted.

Other than the Hotel Sandoval restaurant, eating options are limited to a number of unremarkable *comedores* serving standard *plato típico,* eggs, or chicken and rice. The restaurant at the Congolón bus stop is not bad.

Hondutel, across from the Hotel Sandoval, is open daily 7 a.m.-9 p.m. Banco de Occidente exchanges dollars and traveler's checks, but changing Salvadoran colones or Guatemalan quetzales is best done with moneychangers at the border.

Getting There and Away

Buses run frequently between Nueva Ocotepeque and the Guatemalan border at Aguas Calientes (22 km) and to El Poy at the Salvadoran border (7 km) until midafternoon. It's always best to get to the border early to ensure rides onward.

When arriving from Guatemala, it's possible to get a bus from Aguas Calientes going directly to San Pedro Sula, five and a half hours, US$3, five departures between 8 a.m. and 3 p.m., with a stop at Santa Rosa de Copán. From Nueva Ocotepeque, you can catch any of the buses coming from Aguas Calientes onward to San Pedro Sula for US$2.70, or take a direct midnight bus for US$4.

Several buses daily travel between Ocotepeque and Santa Rosa, charging US$1.20 for the two-hour ride.

NEAR NUEVA OCOTEPEQUE

Reserva Biológica Montaña de Güisayote

The Güisayote reserve is what you would call a last-ditch effort to save a patch of disappearing cloud forest. The reserve covers a ridge above Nueva Ocotepeque, and the remaining strip of forest looks for the world like a mohawk haircut, surrounded by denuded hillsides.

It may not be anything like Celaque or some of Honduras's other mountain reserves, but Güisayote has a number of endangered birds and mammals hanging on in the reserve, including quetzals, blue foxes, wild hogs, monkeys, and maybe even a couple of pumas. It's possible to visit the reserve easily in a day from Nueva Ocotepeque with or without a vehicle.

One of the reasons the forest has been so severely decimated is that the Honduran Army built a road along the ridge at the time of the 1969 war with El Salvador in order to patrol the frontier, which gave farmers and ranchers easy access into hills. That same road is now being allowed by environmental authorities to deteriorate into a trail, which can be used by hikers in the reserve.

To get to Güisayote, take any Santa Rosa-bound bus from Nueva Ocotepeque and get off at El Portillo ("The Pass")—at 2,000 meters this is the highest point of any paved road in Honduras. El Portillo is a collection of huts at the pass, from which a dirt road turns south up into the hills, following the ridge to a Hondutel tower a few kilometers inside the reserve. A half-hour walk past the Hondutel tower, the road comes to a three-way junction. The left road turns into a path descending the hillside, while the middle and right-hand roads continue into the forest. According to locals, the middle road continues around the mountain to the villages of Ocotlán and Plan de Rancho, from where one can catch a truck ride back to Nueva Ocotepeque. The right-hand branch leads to Cerro El Sillón ("Big Chair Mountain"), the massive wall behind Nueva Ocotepeque. At 2,310 meters, it's the highest peak in the vicinity.

Those visiting the park by car can drive as far as the junction, and from there must walk. It might be best to leave the vehicle at the rancho near the Hondutel tower, and pay a few lempira to have the owners watch over it while you hike.

In the southern section of the reserve is a large mountain lake called Laguna Verde; ask a local *campesino* to guide you there. North of El Portillo another dirt road follows the ridge through another, smaller patch of forest.

The topographical map covering Güisayote is Nueva Ocotepeque 2359 II. The government office on the north side of the square in Nueva Ocotepeque will give tourists free photocopies of a section of the topo map with the reserve boundaries marked.

Parque Nacional Triunfo-Montecristo

This national park, jointly administered by Honduras, Guatemala, and El Salvador, comprises a cloud-forested mountain peak forming the boundary between the three countries. The park is accessible from the Honduran side, but only with difficulty. One local forestry officer's advice for accessing it was, "Take a bus into El Salvador, where buses go up to within a few minutes walk of the peak." Clearly the concept of actually walking up is not big in Montecristo. If you are interested in hiking it from the Honduran side, go to the village of Santa Fe, and then on to El Mojonal, where trails continue up to the peak. Guides are essential as trails are nothing more than vague footpaths. From the top, you can see the Pacific on a clear day.

The topographical map covering the Honduran portion of the park is Montecristo 2359 III.

GRACIAS AND THE LENCA HIGHLANDS

One of the undiscovered treasures of Honduras, the mountain country between Gracias, La Esperanza, and the Salvadoran border is a beautiful region comprising pine forest and infrequently visited colonial villages. Foreign tourists are making their way to Gracias, at one time the administrative center for Spain's Central American empire, and to the nearby Montaña de Celaque, the country's highest peak, blanketed with spectacular, lush cloud forest; but travelers rarely go beyond these spots.

However, the area offers much more; the dirt roads and trails connecting the highland villages of Belén Gualcho, La Campa, San Manuel Colohete, Erandique, and beyond are adventures waiting to happen. Here you can lose yourself for weeks at a time admiring the seemingly long-lost colonial architecture and the rugged countryside. The Lenca campesinos populating the region are extremely friendly, and although they might wonder what you're doing out there, the worst that will happen is you'll be invited in for so many cups of coffee you'll never get anywhere.

Note: Few amenities are available anywhere in the region, apart from a couple of decent hotels and restaurants in Gracias. Travel is mainly on foot or by hitching rides on pickup trucks bouncing over bad dirt roads, and food is almost exclusively rice, beans, tortillas, and coffee. But if you're not in a hurry (and you'd better not be), a ride, a meal, and a bed always seem to be found for very little money.

GRACIAS

History

Founded in the earliest phase of the conquest of Honduras, Gracias a Dios was relocated twice before being established at its current location on 14 January 1539 by Bishop Cristóbal de Pedraza and Juan de Montejo under orders of Francisco de Montejo, then ruler of Honduras. In those early years, the would-be colonists were engaged in a fierce struggle against the Lenca leader Lempira, and the settlement was apparently moved for strategic reasons. The second location reportedly served as the main Spanish base for quelling the revolt, after which the town was moved farther south to its present location.

According to tradition, the town received its name because one of the conquistadores had a heck of a time finding any land flat enough for a town in the mountainous region. When a suitable spot was located, the Spaniards reportedly said "Thank God we've finally found flat land!" Hence, Gracias a Dios.

With the establishment of the *Audiencia de los Confines* at Gracias on 16 May 1544, the town became the administrative center of Central America. The *Audiencia* was a royal court of sorts with power to impart civil and criminal justice, and a jurisdiction ranging from the Yucatán to Panama. Larger towns in Guatemala and El Salvador quickly became jealous of the prestige accorded Gracias, and forced the *Audiencia* to be moved to Antigua, Guatemala in late 1548.

Following the removal of the *Audiencia*, Gracias fell into a long, slow slide that has continued to the present day. When the little gold and silver in the area was quickly worked within a couple of decades after the conquest, local colonists had little to fall back on beyond cattle ranching and tobacco production. Gracias remained an important administrative center for Honduras throughout the colonial period, but by the early 19th century nearby Santa Rosa de Copán had taken over the tobacco industry, and not long after also became the de facto regional capital.

Currently Gracias survives on providing services for surrounding villages, cattle ranching, and the nascent tourist industry.

Sights

Of the four churches in Gracias, **La Merced,** a block north of the square, is by far the most attractive. Its ornate sculpted facade was built between 1610 and 1654. The main church on the square, **La Iglesia de San Marcos,** was built in the late 19th century. Next door, currently being used as the *casa cural,* is the building which once housed the *Audiencia de los Confines.*

In the center of a shady square a few blocks southwest of the main square is **La Iglesia de San Sebastián,** known locally as La Ermita. On the west side of La Ermita is the **Galeano House** (Casa Galeano), residence of a prominent long-time Gracias family. The elderly Señor Galeano is extremely knowledgable on local history and is usually happy to speak to a polite visitor who speaks Spanish. Don't be put off by his throat speaker, just listen closely. His son Eduardo "Mito" Galeano is a respected Honduran painter who will sometimes show visitors examples of his work.

Last of the four local churches is **La Iglesia de Santa Lucía,** two km down the road toward the Celaque visitor's center.

Perched on a hill just west of downtown, **El Castillo de San Cristóbal** was built in the mid-19th century to help defend Honduras against the turbulence raging across Central America at the time. In spite of its impressive construction, the fort never saw any action, and now doubles as a local lovers' lane. The remains of Honduran and Salvadoran president Juan Lindo (served 1847-52), who ordered the fort's construction, are entombed inside. In addition to admiring the two cannons, a good reason to visit the fort is to check out the views across Gracias, the surrounding countryside, and Montaña de Celaque looming up to the southwest. The fort's gates are open daily 7 a.m.-noon and 1-5 p.m.

Accommodations

All hotels in Gracias are in the budget range, though quality varies. The best rooms in town are at **Hotel Erick,** tel. 98-4066, one block north of the square, where rates range US$5-10 s or d, depending on whether the bathroom is shared or private. Hot water is available, which makes all the difference after a trip up the mountain. Some complain the owners are less than friendly, but at least they know how to keep clean rooms. The attached store is a good place to stock up on camping food for trips to Celaque.

Posada del Rosario, tel. 98-4516, run by the owners of Restaurante Guancascos, has three rooms for rent in a small house four blocks west of the square; US$6 s, US$7 d, with hot water. **Hospedaje Corazón de Jesús,** and the nearby **Anexo,** are for those really guarding their lempira. Extremely basic rooms with communal bath go for US$1.30 s, US$2 d.

Food and Entertainment

Restaurante Guancascos, tel. 98-4516, also known as Los Lencas, has cornered the market on travelers. Run by a friendly and knowledgeable Dutch woman, the restaurant offers the only creative cooking in Gracias, including vegetarian dishes. The only drawback is that it may take a while for your order to get to the table. Books, artwork, and some topographical maps are for sale, and camping gear

rental and rides up to the Celaque visitor's center are also available (US$8 per carload). The restaurant, on the southwest corner of the square, is open Mon.-Sat. 7 a.m.-10 p.m., Sunday 7 a.m.-8 p.m.

For standard Honduran meals prepared with a bit more care than usual, and at slightly higher prices then your average *comedor,* **La Fonda** is worth checking out. The owners also arrange rides to the Celaque visitor's center.

Several other *comedores* within a couple of blocks of the square serve *plato típico* and chicken for around US$1 a plate. For *pastelitos, baleadas,* and other snacks, try **Helados Tatiyana,** two blocks north of the square.

Restaurante Iris, in the less than ideal hotel of the same name next to La Ermita church,

serves three basic meals daily, and turns into a **disco** every Saturday night.

Information and Services

Hondutel and Correos are a block south of the square. The town's telephone lines seem to go on the blink with regularity, so don't plan on having to call anyone.

Banco de Occidente, a block west of the square, is currently the only place to change dollars and traveler's checks. The migration office is just north of the square, near the police station.

Some information and a useful photocopy of a topographic map of Celaque, with the trail marked, is available at the Cohdefor forestry office, near the entrance to town from Santa Rosa de Copán.

Getting There and Away

Buses to **Santa Rosa de Copán** leave from near the market roughly every hour or so until midafternoon. Not far up the Santa Rosa highway is a dirt-road turnoff up the mountains to **San Rafael,** reached by hitchhiking only. From here you can catch a once-daily bus onward to Santa Bárbara through a little-seen and very beautiful region of central-western Honduras. The bus to Santa Bárbara from San Rafael leaves at 4:30 a.m.

Looking at a map it may appear the quickest route from Santa Rosa de Copán to Tegucigalpa is via Gracias, but the 80 km dirt road from Gracias via San Juan to La Esperanza is in severely rough shape and takes at least four hours in the dry season. The road is sometimes impassible during heavy rains. Nonetheless the pine-forested countryside is exceptionally beautiful, and for those not in a hurry this is a great trip.

One *busito* (minibus) to La Esperanza leaves daily from the southeast corner of Gracias, near the river, at 6 a.m., but hitchhiking might be quicker and more comfortable. Another *busito* leaves from the same spot daily at around 11 a.m. and goes to San Juan, where the road turns off to Erandique.

A bus leaves Gracias daily at 2 p.m. for the nearby villages of La Campa and San Manuel Colohete, on the southeast side of Montaña de Celaque. Again, hitchhiking would be quicker and more comfortable.

Hot Springs

The perfect remedy for those aching limbs after slogging up to the top of Celaque is a visit to the **aguas termales,** about five km east of Gracias on the road to La Esperanza. Three pools— one at 40° C, the other two at 37° C—have been built around the springs, which are surrounded by forest. One of the pools is long enough to take a few swimming strokes across, a very pleasurable experience in the warm water. A small restaurant at the pools serves up soft drinks, beers, and very tasty snacks and meals, and a barbecue pit is available for rent. Entrance is US 80 cents pp; open daily 8 a.m.-6 p.m., bathing suit required. To get there without a car, either hitch a ride up the La Esperanza road to the turnoff, or start walking up the road and keep an eye out for a path heading off to the right—a shortcut to the pools.

PARQUE NACIONAL MONTAÑA DE CELAQUE

One of the premier parks in Honduras, Celaque boasts the country's highest mountain at 2,849 meters, as well as a truly magnificent cloud forest on the high plateau, more impressive than anything this author has seen elsewhere in Guatemala, Honduras, or Costa Rica. This is the real forest primeval—towering trees covered with vines, ferns, and moss forming a dense canopy completely blocking out the sun, very little undergrowth between the trees, and everything dripping wet even when it's not raining. Celaque means "box of water" in Lenca; 11 major rivers begin on Celaque's flanks, which gives you an idea of how wet it is.

The park covers 266 square km total, with 159 square km in the core zone above 1,800 meters. Although treacherously steep on the flanks, Celaque levels off in a plateau at about 2,500 meters, which is where the true cloud forest begins. Up on the plateau you can spend hours or days admiring the astounding flora and quietly keeping an eye out for quetzals, trogons, toucans, hawks, or any of the other 150 bird species identified in the park, as well as for the rarer mountain mammals such as jaguars, armadillos, or tapir. An ever-popular goal for foreign visitors, quetzal sightings are commonplace on Celaque, particularly on the hillside leading up to the highest peak.

An added bonus to this natural wonderland is the well-developed trail leading to the peak, which passes a visitor's center and two encampments on the way. This makes Celaque accessible for the casual backpacker who wants a serious hike but doesn't want to hire a guide or try to navigate by compass and topographical map.

The Visitor's Center

The Celaque visitor's center, staffed by the affable guard Miguel, is a very comfortable setup some nine km from Gracias at the base of the mountain. Several bunks are available for US$1 a night (in addition to the US$1 park entrance fee), and Miguel's wife will cook up meals upon request. Miguel will also act as a guide for US$15 a day, though it's not necessary for hiking up the trail to the peak since it's well marked.

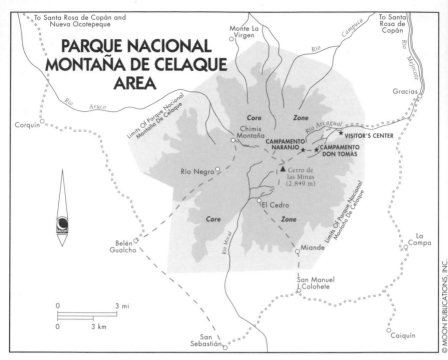

PARQUE NACIONAL MONTAÑA DE CELAQUE AREA

The center, at the edge of the forest next to the Río Arcágual, is a very peaceful spot to relax, and plenty of easy day hiking is possible nearby, along the river.

To get to the visitor's center from Gracias, either arrange a ride at Guancascos or La Fonda restaurants, or start walking and hope a pickup truck comes by. It's about a two-hour walk from Gracias to the center.

On the Trail

The trail up the mountain follows the river for a short while, ascends a steep hillside, then parallels the mountain, going upward at a less steep grade for about two hours to **Campamento Don Tomás** at 2,050 meters. Here there is a tin shack with three bunks inside and an outhouse. The shack is sometimes locked, so it's best to check with Miguel beforehand.

Beyond the camp, the trail heads straight up a steep hillside. This is the hardest stretch of trail by far, and climbing it often entails clinging to roots and tree trunks to pull yourself up the invariably muddy path. After two to three hours, the trail reaches **Campamento Naranjo,** nothing more than a couple of flat tent sites and a fire pit on the plateau's edge, at 2,560 meters. Wipe off the sweat and mud, and soak in your surroundings: the cloud forest.

From Campamento Naranjo it's another two hours or so to the peak, but it goes up and down over gentle hills instead of straight up. Keep a close eye out for the plastic tags tied to tree branches—the lack of undergrowth makes it easy to lose track of the trail. The final ascent to the top of **Cerro de las Minas** is a half-hour of fairly steep uphill, but go slow and listen for the quetzals and trogons that live there. The peak is marked by a wooden cross, and if the clouds haven't moved in you'll have superb views over the valleys to the east. Near the peak is a sizable waterfall, which may soon have a trail leading to it. From the visitor's center to the peak is six km and about 1,500 meters in elevation gain.

You could, theoretically, hike all the way from the visitor's center to the peak and back in a day, but it would be a brutal day and would leave no time for enjoying the cloud forest. A better plan for a short trip would be to spend the night in the shack at Campamento Don Tomás (bring sleeping bags), hike up to the plateau in the early morning, and either come back down to the camp or make it all the way out to the visitor's center that night. To get all the way out, be sure to leave the plateau not long after midday. If you leave the trail take good care to keep clear bearings (with a compass), as it's very easy to get lost on the plateau.

If you want to spend a bit more time in the cloud forest, bring a tent and camp a couple of nights at Naranjo. You could spend more than one night at the shack, but that would mean hiking up and down the steepest stretch of trail each day to get up to the cloud forest. Whatever your plans for Celaque, remember it's often cold and always wet, so come prepared with proper clothing, including stiff boots, waterproof jacket, and a warm change of clothes kept in a plastic bag. Both campsites are next to running water. Many visitors drink the water untreated, as there is no human habitation above, but the cautious will want to treat the water first.

The Cohdefor office in Gracias sells photocopies of the relevant section of the Gracias topographical map, with the trail and camps marked, for US 30 cents. This is much more useful than the actual topo itself. A map is not really necessary if you're just planning to hike up the main trail, but it does give an idea of the lay of the land and is not bad to have just in case. The topographical maps covering the entire park are: Gracias 2459 I, La Campa 2459 II, San Marcos de Ocotepeque 2459 III, and Corquín 2459 IV.

VILLAGES AROUND CELAQUE

La Campa

Sixteen kilometers from Gracias by a fairly well maintained dirt road is the Lenca village of La

CLIMBING CELAQUE THE HARD WAY

For some people, the idea of hiking up a well-marked trail to a cloud forest in Honduras is altogether too easy to really get the adrenaline flowing. Never fear—there are more adventurous routes to the peak. But before venturing off into the woods, beware. The terrain on Celaque is incredibly rugged, confusing, and often blanketed with fog. Locals who live within the boundaries of the park have been known to get lost themselves. In 1996 one El Cedro resident wandered around the plateau for three days, hungry and half-frozen, before he eventually struck the Gracias trail and was helped out by a passing group of foreign hikers.

Apart from the easy trail up the Gracias side (which locals call the gringo trail, *el sendero gringo*), the most common route begins in Belén Gualcho, reached via bus or truck from Santa Rosa de Copán. From Belén Gualcho it's a several-hour hike up to the lovely village of Chimis Montaña, set on a hilltop at about 2,000 meters on the west side of the plateau. At Chimis you can usually find someone willing to guide you by footpaths up to the Gracias trail, from where you can descend without further help and the guide can return home.

Another option is to go from Gracias to San Manuel Colohete, and from there hike up about five or six hours to the village of El Cedro, where Julian Vazquez is one local who definitely knows the route to **El Castillo,** as Cerro de las Minas is known. From El Cedro it's a brutal three- or four-hour (at Julian's pace) hike straight up through thick forest to the Gracias trail, which is reached shortly before the final ascent to the peak.

Before leading one wayward guidebook author from El Cedro to the peak, Julian's last guiding venture was taking up a group of U.S. marines, who must have seemed like aliens from outer space when they landed their chopper on the local soccer field. Evidently they were looking for a thrill after all those slow days at the airbase outside of Comayagua. According to Julian, they kept up with him a lot better than the woefully out-of-shape author.

A reasonably fee for a day's guiding is about US$8-10 or so. These villages are desperately poor, so any small gifts of food, pens, flashlights, or other useful items (please, not candy!) are greatly appreciated. Although visitors are extremely rare on this side of the mountain, locals are friendly and hospitable.

Campa, known locally for its earthenware pottery. Those who only have a short time to spend in this region should consider a day-trip from Gracias to La Campa to get an idea of what village life is like in the rural mountains of western Honduras. With only about 400 residents tucked into a small valley, La Campa represents that supremely calm, quiet, uncomplicated life where it seems nothing, not even visits from outlandish foreigners, disturbs the rhythm of everyday life.

The **Iglesia de San Matías** in the center of town was begun in 1690, and reconstructed in 1938. It's a fine example of the churches found in many nearby villages. The local priest is very knowledgeable on the region and happy to talk with visitors. The smaller **La Ermita** church on a hill above town was built in 1890.

Apart from the churches, the town holds just a couple of *pulperías* and several houses selling pottery. A small *hospedaje* may soon be built across from the entrance to the church, but as yet there are no accommodations in La Campa.

During the week leading up to 22 February, La Campa transforms from a sleepy village into the bustling site of one of the best-known annual festivals in the region. Pilgrims from all over western Honduras and Guatemala flood the town to pay homage to the town's patron saint, San Matías, and participate in the celebrations, which include the traditional *guancascos* exchange of saints, music, and ritual dancing.

The canyon behind town can be reached by trail, and reputedly several caves line the river bank. On the hill behind the church a trail winds upward, leading to **Cruz Alta,** four km away, a good day-hike through the forest. This hill has long been venerated by people throughout the region. According to local legend, long ago the valley was struck by a series of earthquakes, which terrified the populace. So strong were the quakes that a new mountain was created. In hopes peace would return, the local priest advised the people to carry crosses and sacred images to the top of the new mountain. When this was accomplished, the quakes ceased, and since then the hill has been considered sacred.

Caiquín

West of La Campa, the road to San Manuel Colohete deteriorates severely. Three kilometers from La Campa a dirt road turns off, leading another five km to Caiquín. A colonial chapel stands in the center of the village. Reportedly the Caiquín church holds some well-preserved paintings on the plaster walls and a fine wooden altar.

San Manuel Colohete

Arriving on the back of a pickup truck from Gracias and La Campa, cresting the hill, and viewing San Manuel below is a heart-stopping experience. The village sits on a rise above the junction of three rivers pouring off the side of Celaque, which soars skyward in a sheer wall that dwarfs the whitewashed village. It feels as though San Manuel has been lost in the mists of time, utterly remote and disconnected from anything save the stunning landscape surrounding it.

Similar in design to La Merced church in Gracias, the plaster, tile-roofed *Iglesia de San Manuel* features an ornately sculptured facade, and remnants of centuries-old mud paintings are still visible around the wooden altar. Only the most insensitive won't be entranced by the church's primitive elegance. Locals don't know when it was built, but the best guess is at the end of the 17th century.

One local *comedor,* near the entrance to town, supplies basic, inexpensive meals, while a superbasic *hospedaje* just off the square offers a US$1, grim bed. If the *hospedaje* is full, you could certainly rough it under the porch of the government building on the square, if you ask nicely.

Don't be surprised if San Manuel residents don't know quite what to make of a foreign visitor, especially if not accompanied by a Honduran. But the worst that will happen is everyone will stare wordlessly at you, and the children will pester you relentlessly. Keep a friendly smile on your face and all will be well.

San Manuel is 14 km by very rough dirt road west of La Campa.

Beyond San Manuel

If the dirt road to San Manuel seemed bad, check out the stretch continuing on to San Sebastián, a similar village farther west around Celaque, also with a simple *hospedaje*. If no ride is available the

cowboy guitarist near El Cedro

road can be walked in three to four hours, and from there you can continue several more hours on a remnant of the old Camino Real to Belén Gualcho, where you'll find a basic hotel and a ride to Santa Rosa de Copán.

Straight up the mountain from San Manuel by trail are the tiny villages of Miande and El Cedro—basically collections of huts clinging to the hillside. From El Cedro you can find guides to go up to the peak of Celaque and from there down to Gracias, or conversely, find trails continuing to Chimís Montaña or down to Belén Gualcho. The main trails in this vicinity are accurately marked on the topographical maps, and if in doubt just ask passing campesinos, who are usually all too happy to stop and find out what a stranger is doing passing through these parts.

Belén Gualcho

On the western flanks of Celaque, accessible by dirt road from Santa Rosa de Copán or trail from San Sebastián, is the village of Belén Gualcho, dominated by two colonial-era churches considered to be among the most beautiful in the country. The town holds a couple of *comedores* and a simple hotel, and its Sunday market, which attracts campesinos from all over the surrounding region, is quite a sight.

Belén's annual festival is held 24 June in honor of San Juan. The story goes that in years past, a spirit was so impressed by Belén's festival that every year he arrived on a black mule and took part in the revelry himself, afterwards disappearing into the hills. But one year a group of young men thought it would be amusing to attach a bunch of firecrackers to the mule's tail. Offended by this evident lack of respect for his otherworldliness, the spirit rode off in a huff and has never returned.

Buses drive twice a day between Belén and Santa Rosa de Copán, via Corquín.

ERANDIQUE

About halfway between Gracias and La Esperanza is San Juan, where a rough dirt road turns south 24 km to Erandique, an exceptionally beautiful rural colonial town set amid the Sierra de las Neblinas. The mountains around Erandique were used by Lenca warrior Lempira as his base to fight the Spanish conquistadores.

Erandique has three squares, each fronted by a small but very fine colonial-era church. Formerly each of the squares had a massive tree in front, planted over a century ago, but now only two survive. One of these remaining two was nearly split in half when struck by lightning. The one intact tree is impressively huge, dwarfing the square and the church behind it. A large statue to Lempira now rests in the center of the main square.

Visitors to Erandique will be asked immediately if they would like to buy opals—the surrounding countryside is one of the most famous areas in the Americas for the precious stone. Several different grades of opals are mined nearby, including black, white, river, garden, rainbow, milk, and the valuable aurora opals. Honduran opals are considered particularly valuable because of the frequent presence of scarlet coloring. Local campesinos are also always turning up obsidian arrowheads and other objects from pre-Columbian and conquest times, often trying to sell them to visitors for very little money.

Apart from the occasional opal-buyer, Erandique doesn't receive many foreign visitors, so you may be the recipient of a few curious but friendly stares from town residents. As one Honduran visitor put it, "visiting Erandique is like seeing the rural Honduras of half a century ago." The town's annual festival is held on 20 January in honor of San Sebastián.

Practicalities

Erandique has only one *hospedaje,* behind the store on the first square in town, where the bus stops. The small rooms are suprisingly clean and cost only US 80 cents per night—can't beat that. There are no restaurants in town, but ask around for someone who will cook a meal, and expect something very basic.

One minibus runs between Gracias and Erandique daily, leaving Erandique at 5 a.m. and Gracias at 11 a.m. for the two-and-a-half-hour, US$1.50 trip.

Hiking Near Erandique

The pine-forested mountains around Erandique are excellent for hiking, with footpaths leading in all directions. For a short afternoon trip, ask the way to **Las Cuatro Chorreras,** a wide waterfall about a half hour's walk south of town down the valley.

Those with an interest in history may want to make a pilgrimage to **Peñol de Cerquín,** Lempira's unconquered fortress in his war against the Spanish. Ask a local for the path leaving Erandique and winding its way up the southeast flank of Montaña Azacualpa to **San Antonio Montaña.** San Antonio is perched on the side of the mountain and is more a scattering of huts than anything else. The trail rounds the side of the mountain near San Antonio's schoolhouse, and from that spot the Peñol can be seen in the valley below. From the schoolhouse a trail continues downward, or you can continue up the trail on the far side of Azacualpa, which eventually connects to the Erandique-Mapulaca road. This roundtrip can be done easily in a day, with plenty of time to admire the views, but a trip to the Peñol would require one night of camping.

Other nearby mountains such as **Coyucatena, Congolón,** and **Piedra Parada** (according to local lore, the site of Lempira's assassination) can also be hiked up—generally trails lead everywhere. Reportedly a monument to Lempira sits atop Cerro Congolón. From Erandique, you could walk to the towns on the Salvadoran border or northwest towards Celaque and Gracias in a couple of days, if equipped with good maps and a compass or a local guide. Camping is safe, but it's always best to check with a local *campesino* before pitching a tent.

Lenca mother and child

THE RISE AND FALL OF LEMPIRA

Ever wondered why Honduras has such an odd name for its currency? Unbeknownst to many outside the country, western Honduras was the site of one of the fiercest rebellions against the Spanish invaders, led by a Lenca warrior whose name means "Man of the Mountain."

Spaniards first penetrated the mountainous region of present-day western Honduras in the early 1530s. From the start the native Lenca, led initially by a chief named Etempica, fiercely resisted the newcomers. By 1536 the situation in the province had grown so precarious, the Spanish leaders called on Pedro de Alvarado to lead an expedition from Guatemala to pacify the region. The legendarily bloodthirsty conqueror of Guatemala waylaid a few indigenous villages in the Río Mejocote Valley, and sent Juan de Chávez further south to found Gracias a Dios. Instead, Chávez ran into thousands of Lenca warriors enraged by Alvarado's actions and spoiling for a fight.

Chávez wisely left the region without founding a town. Later in the same year, three colonists were on their way from the Spanish base at Siguatepeque when they were waylaid and killed by unknown Indians. On hearing of the event, Honduran governor Francisco de Montejo led a strong contingent of soldiers into the region and called a meeting of native chiefs. All but one of the chiefs showed up and were promptly hanged by the Spaniards.

The only chief who did not come to the meeting was one Lempira, described by the Spaniards as about 35-40 years old, "of medium stature, with strong arms, brave, and intelligent." Rather than being cowed by the Spanish violence, Lempira gathered a large force of warriors at Peñol de Cerquín, a natural fortress, and several other mountain redoubts near what is now Erandique. Through either intimidation or negotiation, Lempira convinced the Cares tribe, traditional enemies of the Lenca, to join the fight against the Spaniards. Legend has it Lempira swayed wavering Indians by saying, "How is it so many brave men in their own land can be subjugated miserably by so few foreigners?"

At that time the Spaniards did indeed have very few men in Honduras, as it was not a rich province when compared to the treasure-laden regions of Peru and Mexico. Just as Montejo thought he had subdued the region with his show of force, Lempira coordinated surprise attacks on several Spanish settlements in Honduras from his fortress at Peñol de Cerquín. When the conquistadores learned of his role they assembled a force led by Capt. Alonso de Cáceres to take the fortress.

Lempira had chosen his spot well. The steep, rugged Peñol did not allow the Spaniards to employ their horses, and unable to take the fortress by force they resolved to lay siege. But after six months the Peñol had not been taken, and other Indian groups, seeing Lempira's success, began their own uprisings across the province.

At this point, several different versions of the story are told. In the classic version, Cáceres was ordered to retreat to Siguatepeque by Montejo, but before leaving he resolved to trick Lempira. Calling on the Lenca chief to discuss peace, Cáceres hid a soldier among the Spanish horses, and just as Lempira was disdainfully rejecting any terms short of Spanish withdrawl, the soldier shot and killed him with an arquebus.

Much of this history is derived from *Historia de America,* written by Spanish historian Antonio de Herrera almost 100 years after the events in question. More recently, Honduran and Canadian historians uncovered a document in Seville, Spain from the Audiencia de México. In the report, made in 1558, Spanish soldier Rodrigo Ruiz states he killed the Lenca leader, who he called "Elempira," in single combat, and took his head back to Siguatepeque as proof of his actions.

Yet another version comes from the Lenca town of Gualcinse, not far from the Peñol, and at the time of the revolt one of Lempira's allies. Local tradition has long held that Lempira was indeed shot while listening to a peace proposal by the Spaniards, but that he was only wounded, and his warriors carried him off to hiding. According to the Gualcinse account, a contingent of Spaniards heard of Lempira's whereabouts, came to the town, and killed him on his sickbed. They then cut off his head and brought it back to Siguatepeque. This sequence of events would explain why according to Honduran tradition Lempira was killed at Piedra Parada, which although nearby is clearly not the same location as Peñol de Cerquín.

(continues on next page)

THE RISE AND FALL OF LEMPIRA
(continued)

So pick your favorite story—we'll never know the whole truth. From all the supporting witnesses reported in the Ruiz document, it's clear the soldier played some essential role in killing Lempira, but whether through treachery or single combat remains a mystery. In some manner Lempira's uprising and death must have been a last gasp for the Lenca; the formerly fierce warriors never again threatened Spanish rule in the region.

Beyond Erandique

The road out of town heads up over the mountain behind town and continues on to Mapulaca near the Salvadoran border. Little traffic passes on this road even in the dry season, but hitchhiking is possible. It might be quicker to find a guide and walk by trails through the lovely countryside. From Mapulaca, another rough dirt road winds its way north via Valladolid and Tomalá to La Labor, where it meets the Nueva Ocotepeque-Santa Rosa de Copán highway. This is serious adventure-travel country—pickup trucks are the only means of transport all the way. Don't plan on getting anywhere quickly.

LA ESPERANZA

The capital of the Intibucá department, La Esperanza lies in the heart of the most traditional Lenca region in the country. Although the town itself only has a population of about 5,000, the market area often swarms with residents from surrounding villages coming in to trade their produce or buy goods. The market is especially lively on weekend mornings, when you can watch Lenca women wearing colorful dresses and headscarves doing business. The 8 December festival in honor of the Virgin de la Concepción is one of the most interesting of Honduras's annual celebrations, involving a ritual exchange of saints with the nearby village of Yamaranguila.

Set in a mountain valley surrounded by pine forest in the heart of the Sierra de Opalaca at 1,980 meters, La Esperanza has a cool climate with daytime temperatures normally hovering between 10 and 20° C. Originally the Lenca village of Eramaní, which means "Land of Pottery" in Lenca, La Villa de La Esperanza was officially founded on 23 September 1848. The Spanish name derives, according to local legend, from a priest who came to the area with his younger cousin during colonial times, to convert the Lenca. The young cousin became enamored with a local girl, and fathered a child with her. The priest promptly sent his cousin away in anger, but the girl and her child never gave up hope *(esperanza)* that the young Spaniard would return.

The cave visible on a hill just above town has a small chapel inside known as **La Ermita,** which is the site of religious services during Semana Santa and other special occasions. The main street running past the square turns into a stairway leading up to the cave.

Practicalities

Two of the better hotels in town are **Hotel Solis,** tel. 98-2080, and **Hotel La Esperanza,** tel. 98-2068, each with clean rooms and hot water for US$7 d, or more with private bathroom. Less expensive is **Hotel El Rey,** tel. 98-2266, charging US$1.70 s, or US$3 s and US$6 d with private bath.

Cafeteria Manuel has one of the best lunch deals in town, US$2 for a huge plate of food, and vegetarian dishes available also. Just off the square is **Lucky's Burger,** a good spot for burgers, chicken, and beers, although you might starve before the food arrives. **Pizza Veniccia** has surprisingly decent pizza for this remote corner of Honduras.

Hondutel and Correos are next to each other on the square. Banco de Occidente near the square can change dollars, but usually won't take traveler's checks.

Getting There and Away

La Esperanza is connected by a well-maintained, 67-km paved road to Siguatepeque. The road heads down out of the mountains, across the Río Otoro Valley, past the town of Jesús de Otoro, and back up into the mountains to the junction with the San Pedro Sula-Tegucigalpa highway.

Buses to **Siguatepeque** leave roughly every two hours from the terminal near the market, charging US$1 for the 90-minute ride.

Buses to **Tegucigalpa** (four hours, US$2.20) leave the terminal five times daily between 5 a.m. and 1 p.m., while buses to **San Pedro Sula** (four hours, US$2.20) leave three times daily between 6:30 a.m. and 11 a.m.

Dirt roads leave La Esperanza onward to **Marcala** (35 km), where you can continue on paved roads to La Paz, near Comayagua, and also to **Gracias** (80 km). No buses ply these routes, but hitchhiking is easy and safe. Get out to the junction early, and expect to pay a few lempira for the ride. The standard rate to Gracias, four hours away through beautiful mountain scenery, is about US$1.50.

South of La Esperanza dirt roads continue to the villages of **Santa Lucía** (87 km) and **San Antonio** (93 km), in the hotter canyon country near the border with El Salvador. There has been some conflict in this region recently between the two countries over the so-called *bolsones,* pockets of land disputed since the end of the 1969 Soccer War. What little violence that has taken place, however, has been in extremely remote settlements and would not affect passing travelers.

Near La Esperanza

Seven km from La Esperanza is one of the most traditional Lenca communities in the country, **Yamaranguila.** Although not fully accustomed to tourists, residents are friendly to visiting outsiders, and on certain holidays traditional dances like the *guancascos* can be seen. Inquire with the local *alcalde* (mayor). Near Yamaranguila is a very impressive waterfall—just ask directions to **La Chorrera.**

On the dirt road heading to San Francisco de Opalaca, just outside of La Esperanza, is **Laguna Chiligatoro,** a good place for a swim on a hot day.

There are four supposedly protected natural areas in Intibucá: Montaña Opalaca, Mixcure, Montecillos, and Montaña Verde. Unfortunately much of the forests have already been severely logged, leaving little of the original flora and fauna intact. Because of its isolated location, only **Refugio de Vida Silvestre Montaña Verde** (Montaña Verde Wildlife Refuge) is still worth visiting, but getting into the forest is no easy task. Located near the border of the Lempira department, in the San Francisco de Opalaca municipality, Montaña Verde can be reached by first getting to the village of Monte Verde, where a guide can be hired to explore the mountain. As yet no trails exist, and there are no facilities in Monte Verde. Topographical maps covering the reserve are 1:50,000 La Iguala 2559 IV and La Unión 2560 III.

GUANCASCOS: A LENCA TRADITION

The language and many of the traditions of the Lenca have been lost over the past four and a half centuries, for reasons not entirely clear to anthropologists. One communal ritual that has been preserved, and can still be seen on certain days in a few towns in the Lenca highlands, is the *guancascos.* A bilateral ceremony between two towns, usually neighboring, the *guancascos* commemorates an agreement reached in the past over the division of land. Formerly a strictly indigenous ritual, the *guancascos* since colonial times has incorporated elements of Catholicism.

On the designated day, processions from each town, carrying images of their patron saints, meet at a location between the two and exchange the images. After dancing, praying, and the lighting of fireworks to scare off bad spirits, the processions walk together to the church of one town, which has been decorated with pine branches and filled with copal incense smoke. Special speeches are given in the church by representatives of both towns, and this is followed by a party of dancing and drinking.

Formerly the dance of the *guancascos,* called *La Danza del Gorrobo,* was performed with specific instruments and elaborate masks and costumes. This custom is no longer widespread, and can be seen only in a few of the most traditional Lenca towns, such as La Campa, Lempira on 24 February and La Esperanza, Intibucá on 8 December.

BOB RACE

SAN PEDRO SULA AND CENTRAL HONDURAS

A far-flung region comprising the country's industrial and financial capital (San Pedro Sula), its largest lake (Lago de Yojoa), and the mountainous landscapes of Santa Bárbara and Yoro, central Honduras has much to offer. Travelers can take care of business and enjoy city life in San Pedro Sula, fish and boat on Lago de Yojoa, admire the gushing waterfall at Pulhapanzak, buy handicrafts and visit colonial villages near Santa Bárbara, or hike and birdwatch in the cloud forests of Cusuco, Santa Bárbara, and Pico Pijol.

SAN PEDRO SULA

INTRODUCTION

Situated on the southwestern edge of the broad, fertile Valle de Sula, up against the flanks of the Sierra Merendón, San Pedro Sula (often shortened to San Pedro) is a bustling, hot, modern city. If Honduras's governmental capital is Tegucigalpa, its business and financial capital is San Pedro Sula.

Unless they come to San Pedro on business, most foreign visitors stop in the city only briefly. In spite of its nearly five centuries of existence, San Pedro has virtually no remaining colonial architecture, and apart from one good museum, not much to attract tourists. If you need to take care of some business while on the road,

though, San Pedro is a good place to do it. The city is easy to get around in and has just about every sort of store or business you could hope to find in Honduras. The hotel and restaurant se-

---

**SAN PEDRO SULA
AND CENTRAL HONDURAS
HIGHLIGHTS**

- Birdwatching and boating on Lago de Yojoa
- Visiting Santa Bárbara, one of the friendliest towns in the country
- Seeing the colonial churches of Comayagua
- Hiking in the national parks of Cusuco, Santa Bárbara, or Pico Pijol

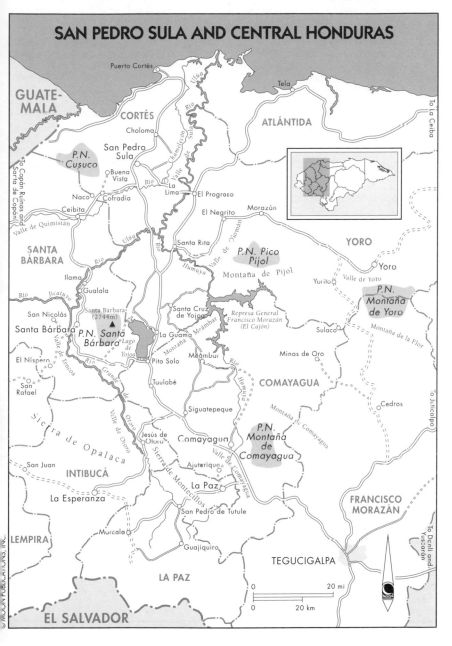

SAN PEDRO SULA AND CENTRAL HONDURAS

lection is excellent, covering all price ranges and tastes, and *sampedranos,* as local residents are known, are friendly and relaxed.

A word of warning: San Pedro is well-known for its prostitutes, but also carries the dubious distinction of being the AIDS capital of Central America, so take the necessary precautions. Further, the city has the highest crime rate in the country. Muggings are not unheard of, so pay attention to who's around you and where you are, especially after dark.

San Pedro is at about 40 meters elevation, and the climate is steaming hot all year round, with daytime temperatures varying between 30 and 40° C. Rains in the Valle de Sula, which normally hit between July and November, can be torrential.

History

The Valle de Sula is one of the longest-inhabited regions of Honduras. A village site recently excavated along the Río Ulúa was dated to 1100-900 B.C. Little is known about the site's builders other than some apparent contact with the Olmecs of central Mexico, implying a fairly high degree of development.

The Maya are believed to have maintained settlements along the Valle de Sula, but the center of their society was farther west and south in the mountains along the present Guatemalan border. The largest Indian settlement in the region, found when the Spanish first penetrated the interior of Honduras, was at Naco, in a small valley on the far side of the Sierra Merendón from San Pedro.

La Villa de San Pedro was founded on 27 June 1536 by Pedro de Alvarado, conqueror of Guatemala, on the flat area of the Valle de Sula, far enough from the edges of the Chamelecón and Ulúa rivers to protect it from flooding. An early base of operations for the Spanish in their

MAQUILAS: POST~MODERN SLAVERY OR GOLDEN OPPORTUNITY?

The driving force behind San Pedro's annual economic growth of five to six percent unquestionably comes from the 160-odd export-oriented *maquila* factories in the region. Owned by Koreans, Taiwanese, Americans, and some Hondurans, the *maquilas* mainly assemble clothes for export to the United States. They were first set up in the early 1990s after the Honduran government passed laws allowing factory owners to import equipment and material and export assembled products duty-free. The only taxes paid by *maquilas* are on the employees and to the municipal government to help improve local infrastructure.

Because of its strategic location in the middle of Central America, only an hour from Puerto Cortés, which is itself but a two day boat trip to Miami, and because of the extremely low local wages, San Pedro has become a favored *maquila* center for foreign factory owners. To many labor organizers outside Honduras, especially in the United States, the low wages and less-than-ideal conditions translate into a sort of modern slavery. In July 1996 the New York-based National Labor Committee accused television celebrity Kathie Lee Gifford of exploiting Honduran workers, mainly women, in a factory producing clothes bearing her name. The case was publicized widely after the news program "Hard Copy" aired a story on the factory, and the U.S. Congress heard testimony from one 15-year-old factory worker, Wendy Diaz.

Honduran labor organizers agree the conditions in many *maquilas* are less than ideal. Verbal abuse, compulsory overtime, unreachable production quotas, and dismissal for pregnancy are all common. Nonetheless, local union leaders say many *maquilas* treat their workers with respect, subsidize lunch, and offer free medical care. They also note that although child labor is frequent, in Honduras it's unrealistic to expect families to care for their children until age 18, and that if young people don't work in the relatively high-paying *maquilas,* they will find other work elsewhere.

The clamor in the U.S. passed right over like Honduras's annual tropical storms, and the *maquilas* continue expanding and attracting workers from all over the country. Forty cents an hour may seem like slave wages to a foreigner, but for many Hondurans it represents a chance to provide their families with good food and even savings for their future.

SAN PEDRO SULA

To Choloma,
Puerto Cortés

Río Bermejo

Río Piedras

CERVECERÍA
HONDUREÑA

14 CALLE
13 CALLE
12 CALLE
11 CALLE
10 CALLE
9 CALLE
8 CALLE
7 CALLE
6 CALLE
5 CALLE

MERCADO
GUAMILITO

4 CALLE
3 CALLE

ESTADIO
GENERAL
FRANCISCO
MORAZÁN

RESTAURANTE
EL MORRO

RESTAURANTE
DON UDO'S ▼

CAFÉ DES
ARTES ▼

2 CALLE
1 CALLE
2 CALLE

12 AV
11 AV
10 AV
9 AV
8 AV
7 AV
6 AV
5 AV
4 AV
3 AV
2 AV
1 AV

25 AV
24 AV
23 AV
22 AV
21 AV
20 AV A
20 AV B
8 AV
16 AV
15 AV
14 AV
13 AV

CINE
GÉMENIS

PAT'S
STEAKHOUSE

ANTOJITOS
MEXICANOS

RESTAURANTE
▼ LAS TEJAS
EL MEXIQUENSE

CLÍNICA
BENDAÑA

PARQUE
CENTRAL

3 CALLE
4 CALLE
5 CALLE
6 CALLE

1 AV
2 AV
3 AV
4 AV
5 AV
6 AV
7 AV
8 AV
9 AV

Av. CIRCUNVALACIÓN

To El Progreso,
Airport

7 CALLE
8 CALLE
9 CALLE
10 CALLE
11 CALLE
12 CALLE
13 CALLE
14 CALLE
15 CALLE
16 CALLE

LA HUERTA
DE ESPAÑA

APART–HOTEL
EL ALMENDRAL

HOTEL COPANTL

Av. CIRCUNVALACIÓN

18 CALLE
19 CALLE
20 CALLE

NOT TO SCALE

To Tegucigalpa, Santa
Rosa de Copán

conquest of Honduras, San Pedro quickly faded in importance during the colonial period. After 1600 San Pedro was virtually abandoned, in part because of pirate and Indian attacks and also because colonists had moved on in their search for gold and silver in the highlands. Until approximately 1660 the town was a center for contraband activity.

During the later part of the colonial era, *sampedranos* survived on business generated by cattle ranchers and sarsaparilla, which grew wild in the region and at the time was considered a miracle drug by Europeans, who believed it cured venereal diseases.

In the mid-19th century San Pedro's fortunes took a turn for the better, when commerce picked up at the port of Omoa, and San Pedro became a frequent stop-off point for goods on their way in or out of the country. But it was the growth of the banana industry and the reopening of Puerto Cortés in the late 19th century that jump started San Pedro's economy, and it has continued growing steadily. Currently San Pedro is the fastest growing city in all of Central America, with a population of roughly 465,000.

Orientation and Getting Around

San Pedro Sula is laid out in a straightforward grid pattern, divided into northern and southern sections by 1 Calle and into eastern and western sections by 1 Avenida. Avenues *(avenidas)* run north-south, streets *(calles)* east-west. The central part of the city is ringed by Avenida Circunvalación.

The casual visitor should not have much need to venture beyond Avenida Circunvalación. Most hotels, restaurants, businesses, and bus stations are within eight blocks of the downtown square. The western and southwestern section of Circunvalación is the nicer part of town, with many upscale restaurants, hotels, and nightclubs. Most taxis charge US$1.30 for a ride anywhere within Circunvalación, more beyond. The local bus system is cheap, but routes are circuitous and it's often more convenient to hop a cab for those infrequent trips away from downtown.

SIGHTS

Parque Central

San Pedro's downtown square is always crowded and is a pleasant place to people-watch. The square often hosts impromptu music performances or the occasional evangelical preacher delivering a sermon. The adjacent **catedral** was built in 1949, and is not particularly interesting from an artistic standpoint. Running south from the center of the square is the *peatonal,* or pedestrian walkway, filled with moneychangers and vendors.

Museo de Antropología e Historia

One of the finer museums in the country, the Museo De Antropología E Historia, 3 Avenida between 3 and 4 Calles NO, tel. 57-1496 or 57-1798, is the most interesting cultural site in San Pedro. Its two floors of exhibits outline the development of the Valle de Sula from 1500 B.C. to the present. The displays, labeled in Spanish only, track Sula civilization from its earliest traces at the Playa de los Muertos site through the classic Mayan-era settlements at Los Naranjos, to the colonial and modern eras. It's interesting to note that the banana industry, an important part

San Pedro Sula's cathedral

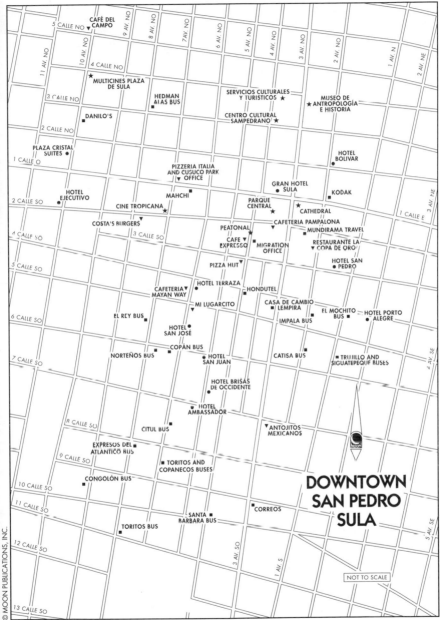

DOWNTOWN SAN PEDRO SULA

NOT TO SCALE

© MOON PUBLICATIONS, INC.

of the valley's economy, is barely mentioned, perhaps in concession to nationalist sentiment.

Noteworthy exhibits include the many different phases of Ulúa ceramics, sculptures from the Naranjo site reminiscent of the giant Olmec heads of La Venta, Mexico, examples of Spanish weaponry, details of the construction of the fortress at Omoa, and, oddly enough, a comprehensive history of beer production in Honduras.

Apart from the permanent historical exhibit, the museum has one gallery for rotating exhibits, and a gift shop well-stocked with T-shirts, calendars, books, cards, and artwork. Outside is a small patio cafeteria. The museum is open Tues.-Sun. 10 a.m.-4:15 p.m. Admission is US 50 cents.

Centro Cultural Sampedrano
Around the corner from the museum, on 3 Calle between 3 and 4 Avenidas NO, is the Centro Cultural Sampredrano, which frequently holds concerts and dramatic performances, usually for US$3-4 per show. San Pedro's main drama group is **El Círculo Teatral Sampredrano.** For information on upcoming performances call 53-3094. The Centro also has a small library open to the public and stocked with books written in Spanish.

Cervecería Hondureña
On the north end of San Pedro, on the road to Puerto Cortés, is the country's largest brewery, where Salvavida, Port Royal, and Nacional are all made. Tours of the brewery are available by prior appointment—call 53-3310, 53-1201, 53-3308, or 53-3314, all extension 3876.

RECREATION

Golf
Two golf clubs near San Pedro are open to the public: Las Lomas Golf Course in Choloma, on the road to Puerto Cortés, tel. 53-3106; and La Lima Golf Course on the highway to El Progreso, just past La Lima. Both courses rent golf clubs.

Fútbol
For a taste of Honduras's national sporting passion, consider watching a soccer match at **Estadio General Francisco Morazán,** on 1 Calle O between 13 and 14 Avenidas. Tickets for reg-

ular season matches cost US$2-4, depending on seats; national team matches cost a bit more. Tickets can be bought in advance at the stadium, but usually it's no problem to get a ticket right before the match. If it's a sellout, scalpers will be offering tickets for not much more than face-value. Crowds tend to be impassioned, but it's generally very safe, certainly not like watching a match in many European countries. Watch out for pickpockets.

ACCOMMODATIONS

San Pedro has a wide selection of hotels of all varieties and price ranges. Many of the less expensive hotels are in the southwest quadrant of the city, within 10 blocks of the square.

Budget
The large, well-managed **Hotel San Pedro,** on 3 Calle between 2 and 1 Avenida SO, tel. 53-1513 or 53-4014, fax 53-2655, is a favorite among foreigners and locals alike, with good reason. Options range from US$4 s for a basic partitioned room with fan to US$12 for a large room with TV and a/c, all cleaned daily. Free purified water is available, and there's a TV in the lobby. Check-out time is a relaxed 2 p.m. The hotel is close to the Tela, La Ceiba, and Puerto Cortés bus stations.

Another low-priced good deal is **Hotel San José,** on 6 Avenida between 5 and 6 Calles SO, popular with Peace Corps volunteers. It's clean, and offers tile-floor double rooms with fans and bathrooms for US$5. Similar to the San José but not quite as nice is **Hotel San Juan,** just around the corner on 5 Avenida and 6 Calle SO, tel. 53-1488.

A five-story building, **Hotel Brisas de Occidente,** on 5 Avenida between 6 and 7 Calles SO, tel. 52-2309, has huge, empty tile rooms looking like something out of a Paul Auster novel. Rooms are always available, and not a bad deal either if you like the ambience—US$3.50 for a double bed with fan, shared bath only.

Hotel Porto Alegre, east of 1 Avenida on 5 Calle SE, tel. 57-2188, features quiet, clean, airy rooms for US$6 s or d with bathroom and fan, or US$8 with TV. Nearby are buses to Lago de Yojoa, Trujillo, and Siguatepeque.

Midrange
Hotel Ambassador, on the second floor above some of the shops on 7 Calle between 5 and 6 Avenidas SO, tel. 57-6824 or 57-6825, has 32 quiet rooms with a/c, TV, telephone, and hot water for US$16 s or US$23 d, less with fan instead of a/c. Some rooms have balconies, and the hotel cafeteria offers room service. Less expensive, though a bit gloomier, is **Hotel Terraza,** on 6 Avenida between 4 and 5 Calles, tel. 53-3108, fax 57-4798, charging US$12 for two beds with fan and TV, or US$15 with a/c.

Hotel Ejecutivo, on 2 Calle and 10 Avenida SO, tel. 52-4289, fax 52-5868, is patronized by expatriates who appreciate the quiet neighborhood, good service, and modern rooms with a/c, TV, telephone, and hot water; US$27 d.

In Colonia Trejo, southwest of Avenida Circunvalación, is **Apart-Hotel El Almendral,** on 16 Avenida B and 12 Calle B SO, tel. 52-1989 or 52-1992, fax 52-4476, a well-managed two-story hotel in a quiet, safe neighborhood. Each room has a/c, TV, telephone, hot water, a small stove, and a refrigerator stocked with drinks. Rooms cost US$38-50. Reservations are recommended as the hotel is often full. Nearby is **El Almendral II,** which does not have stoves, but does have bathtubs and balconies. Both buildings have washers and driers for guest use only and interior parking lots.

Right in the center of town, **Hotel Bolivar,** at 2 Calle and 2 Avenida NO, tel. 53-3224 or 53-3218, fax 53-4823, is slightly overpriced at US$30 s or d, considering the rooms are slightly dark and basic. But it does have a/c and TV, and is quiet and certainly centrally located.

Luxury
For years *the* hotel in San Pedro, the **Gran Hotel Sula,** facing the downtown square, tel. 52-9992 to -9999, fax 52-7000, in the U.S. (800) 223-6767, has been surpassed in quality by the Copantl but is still favored by many business travelers and tourists for its central location. The double rooms all have private balconies, telephone, TV, a/c, and throw rugs over tile floors, and cost US$95 or US$130 for a suite. Corporate rates are available. Typewriters and NordicTrack exercise machines are available in rooms for a small fee. The upscale **Granada Restaurant** serves lunch buffets and dinner à la

carte, and the diner-style **Café Skandia** is open 24 hours, with a patio overlooking the small pool. The tobacco shop sells day-old *Miami Herald* newspapers and many English magazines and books.

An eight-story modern pink tower on the road heading out of town toward Tegucigalpa, **Hotel Copantl,** tel. 56-8900 or 56-7108, fax 56-7890, has 200 modern, quietly tasteful rooms with TV, a/c, and direct telephone lines; US$170 d up to US$350 for a suite. Helpful employees always mill about the cavernous lobby, extensive terraces, and swimming pool, ready to run errands or answer questions. Among the many facilities at the Copantl are a beauty parlor, a tobacco and gift shop selling many English-language publications, a travel center/information desk, a convention center, a casino, two bars, three restaurants, a health spa, and six tennis courts.

A new addition to the high-end market in San Pedro is **Plaza Cristal Suites,** in Barrio Guamilito on 10 Avenida between 1 and 2 Calles NO, tel. 52-2302, fax 52-3227. It's run by a U.S.-Honduran partnership with hotel experience in the U.S. and strong ideas about service and quality. The converted apartment building features 19 suites, each with a living room, bedroom, kitchen, a/c, color TV, and direct telephone line. Rates range from US$60 for a studio suite up to US$160 for a three-bedroom suite. The owners live at the hotel and are quick to respond to any requests or complaints.

FOOD

Inexpensive
Ever popular with budget travelers and locals, **Cafeteria Mayan Way,** in a run-down building on 6 Avenida between 4 and 5 Calles SO, has a distinctly funky yet somehow appealing atmosphere. The inexpensive meals are surprisingly tasty, considering the look of the place. Open Mon.-Sat. 6 a.m.-midnight, it's a good place for breakfasts and *comida corrientes.*

Run by a Garífuna family, **Mi Lugarcito,** on the corner of 5 Calle and 6 Avenida SO, is a good spot for very inexpensive *comida corrientes, baleadas,* burgers, tacos, and breakfasts. Open Mon.-Sat. 7:30 a.m.-6:30 p.m.

Five blocks west of the square on 2 Avenida O, **Costa's Burgers** is a popular lunch and snack spot serving burgers, sandwiches, and light meals. Open daily until 10 p.m. Several clean *comedores* in the **Mercado Guamilito,** between 8 and 9 Avenidas and 6 and 7 Calles NO, serve inexpensive *comida corrientes.*

Cafes

Cafeteria Pampalona on the square always has a large crowd of cigarette-smoking, coffee-guzzling locals chatting or reading the newspaper at the formica tables, and soft elevator music playing overhead. The espresso is very good, and the extensive menu is not overly expensive at US$2.50-4 a full entree or US$1.70 for breakfast. Trying to get some service can be a chore—the squadron of sharp-dressed waiters will studiously avoid your inquiring gaze as they languidly polish silverware. At the height of the lunch and dinner rush they may refuse to serve just coffee. Open daily 8 a.m.-8 p.m.

Cafe Expresso on the *peatonal,* just off the square, serves up a decent espresso in a modern, coffee-bar atmosphere. Wealthier *sampedranos* enjoy sipping a cappuccino or latte and savoring a fine quiche or crepe at **Café del Campo,** in a converted house on 10 Avenida at 5 Calle NO. The food is a bit pricey, but the sandwiches, steaks, fish, and shrimp are very good quality, and breakfasts are not unreasonable at US$2-3 for an omelette or pancakes with coffee. Open Mon.-Sat. 7 a.m.-10 p.m.; seating inside or on the patio.

Café Skandia in the Gran Hotel Sula is a diner-style cafe conveniently open daily 24 hours, great for that late-night craving. The service is good and the food reasonably priced; breakfasts are a good deal.

Italian

For an excellent pizza, don't miss **Pizzeria Italia,** on 1 Calle at 7 Avenida, west of the square, tel. 53-0094. Large pizzas, big enough for one person with a monster appetite or two looking for a midsize meal, cost US$3-4 depending on ingredients. The lasagna, cannelloni, ravioli, and spaghetti are also good. The two small dining rooms are often full on weekends. Wine and beer are available. Open Tues.-Sun. 11 a.m.-10 p.m.

Nearby is **Restaurante Vicente,** on 7 Avenida between 1 and 2 Calles, tel. 52-1335, owned by the same people as Pizzeria Italia. This is more of a sit-down restaurant, with many standard Italian dishes at very reasonable prices.

The always-reliable **Pizza Hut** has two restaurants in town, one on the *peatonal,* tel. 57-8383, and the other on Blvd. Morazán, tel. 58-0358.

Honduran

Restaurante Las Tejas, on Avenida Circunvalación at 9 Calle SO, tel. 52-2705, is popular for its well-prepared steaks, shrimp, seafood, *pinchos,* and chicken at midrange prices. Open Mon.-Fri. 10:30 a.m.-2:30 p.m. and 5-11 p.m., Sat.-Sun. 10 a.m.-10 p.m.

Chinese

The air-conditioned **Restaurante La Copa de Oro,** near the square on 2 Avenida between 2 and 3 Calles SO, offers decent Chinese food daily 10 a.m.-7:30 p.m.; US$2.50-4 an entree.

Mexican

With restaurants downtown at 3 Avenida between 7 and 8 Calles SO and on Avenida Circunvalación at 7 Calle SO, **Antojitos Mexicanos** is an excellent inexpensive spot to munch a couple of Mexican-style *tortas, chilaquiles,* enchiladas, or tacos and wash them down with a beer or soft drink. The downtown branch is open daily 8 a.m.-9 p.m., while the one on Circunvalación is open daily 10 a.m.-midnight, sometimes later on weekends.

El Mexiquense, in a residential neighborhood at 10 Calle and 14 Avenida SO, tel. 57-3131, offers traditional Mexican dishes such as *mole, pierna adobada, carnitas, queso fundido, alambres,* and tacos *al pastor,* whipped up by a Mexican cook for US$2-4 per meal—very reasonable considering the quality of the food. Open daily 11 a.m.-11 p.m., later on Friday and Saturday.

Cuban

Run by Cuban owners, **Restaurante El Morro,** a block west of Avenida Circunvalación on 1 Calle, tel. 53-3935, features excellent dishes and service in a quietly elegant dining room. The *ropa vieja,* shredded meat in an onion-tomato sauce, is particularly good, and prices are reasonable at US$5-9 an entree. Two small private dining rooms are available at no extra cost with reservations. Open Tues.-Sat. 11:30 a.m.-3 p.m. and 6:30-11 p.m., Sunday 11 a.m.-5 p.m.

Spanish

La Huerta de España, on 2 Calle and 21 Avenida SO, tel. 52-3775, is two eateries in one—a formal restaurant and a cafeteria-deli, both with Spanish meats, cheeses, wines, and other dishes. Restaurant specialties include paella, *tortilla de patatas, conejo* (rabbit), *callos a la madrileña* (beef in a tomato sauce), and lots of seafood. Open daily from 11 a.m. until midnight or later.

Steak and Seafood

Considered one of the classier spots in town, although you might not believe it looking at the fake windmill out front, **Restaurante Don Udo's,** in a residential neighborhood west of Avenida Circunvalación on 1 Calle at 20 Avenida O, tel. 53-3106, offers a variety of international dishes and a decent wine list. The restaurant has indoor and patio seating, and is open Mon.-Thurs. 5 p.m.-midnight, Fri.-Sat. 6 p.m.-1 a.m., and for brunch on Sunday 11:30 a.m.-2:30 p.m.

A favorite with the local jet set and businesspeople with expense accounts, **Pat's Steakhouse,** on Avenida Circunvalación at 5 Calle SO, tel. 53-0939, is generally thought to have the best cuts of beef in town. Good seafood is available also, and the wine list is extensive. The atmosphere is cool and casual yet elegant—proper attire and reservations recommended. Open daily noon-3 p.m. and 6 p.m.-midnight.

ENTERTAINMENT

Café des Artes, on 1 Calle between 14 and 15 Avenidas O, near the stadium, tel. 53-2380, is one of the nicer bars in San Pedro. It's got an upscale, young, hip atmosphere and good music on the stereo, not so loud that you can't have a good talk. The Spanish-style tapas make great munchies to go with your drinks. Open 6 p.m.-2 a.m.

Among the many discos in town, **Confetti's** is the current favorite, followed by **Henry's,** both in the southwest section of Avenida Circunvalación, an area known as the *zona viva.*

For a more interesting experience, check out **Terraza's,** colorfully referred to by some locals as a "disco de la mala muerte" ("disco of the bad death"), and known for its eclectic mix of artsy types, homosexuals, junkies, and hookers. Near Terraza's is the **Flamingo Night Club,** considered one of the less sleazy topless dance clubs in town. Clients pay for table dances, and pay a bit more to take the dancers home. If prostitutes are on your agenda, be sure to bring condoms, as San Pedro is the AIDS capital of Central America.

Cinemas showing first-run movies in San Pedro include **Cine Aquarius,** 10 Avenida and 2 Calle NO, tel. 53-1188; **Cine Gémenis,** 12 Avenida and 1 Calle O, tel. 52-6060; **Multicines Plaza de Sula,** 10 Avenida and 4 Calle NO; and **Cine Tropicana,** 7 Avenida and 2 Calle SO, tel. 53-0391.

INFORMATION AND SERVICES

Shopping

San Pedro has one of Honduras's best handicraft markets at **Mercado Guamilito,** between 8 and 9 Avenidas and 6 and 7 Calles NO. The several dozen *artesanía* stalls sell a wide variety of handicrafts from across the country, including woodwork, paintings, sculptures, weavings, and more. Also here you'll find a regular food market, many flower stalls, and several *comedores* serving light meals. It's a very pleasant place to shop—the salesfolk are all friendly, and the market is spacious.

T-shirts and some artwork are also often sold from stalls on the square and along the *peatonal.* Two high-quality handicraft stores in San Pedro are **Mahchi,** on 1 Calle between 6 and 7 Avenidas O, tel. 52-9208, open Mon.-Fri. 8 a.m.-

---

SAN PEDRO SULA USEFUL TELEPHONE NUMBERS

Cruz Roja Ambulance: 53-1283, or dial 195
Fire Department: 56-8790, 56-6180, or dial 198
Police: 52-3128, 52-3171, or dial 199
Clínica Bendaña: 53-1618, 53-1614, 53-4437, 53-4429

5 p.m., Saturday 8 a.m.-noon, and **Imapro,** on 1 Calle between 4 and 5 Avenidas E, tel. 57-3355, open Mon.-Fri. 8 a.m.-noon and 1-5 p.m., Saturday 8 a.m.-noon. Imapro sells mainly woodwork made in their El Progreso factory, along with T-shirts, postcards, maps, and books, while Mahchi features paintings, rugs, sculptures, and other artwork.

Danilo's is the premier store for leather goods in San Pedro, with a factory/store in Colonia Trejo at 18 Avenida between 8 and 9 Calles SO, tel. 52-0656, open Mon.-Fri. 8 a.m.-6 p.m., and a store at 10 Avenida between 2 and 3 Calles NO, open Mon.-Sat. 8 a.m.-6 p.m.

The main market in San Pedro is between 5 and 7 Calles and 4 and 5 Avenidas SE. A smaller one is nearby on 9 Avenida between 7 and 9 Calles SE. One good supermarket near downtown is **Supermercado El Centro** on the corner of 2 Calle and 13 Avenida SO, open daily 8 a.m.-8 p.m.

For those who like to roll their own cigarettes, the only store in the entire country to buy rolling papers is **Nicholas Larach** on 3 Avenida between 4 and 5 Calles SO. Large sheets of rice paper *(papel de arroz)* are sold for US 25 cents each, and are good for many rolls.

Almacen El Estudiante has an eccentric collection of secondhand romance novels, childrens' classics like the Great Brain, Encyclopedia Brown, and Narnia series, and a few literary classics, all stacked in several large piles and sold at inexpensive prices. The store is on 3 Avenida between 7 and 8 Calles SO.

Photography Supplies
Film, including some for slides, and other photography supplies are sold at **Foto Indio** on 7 Avenida between 2 and 3 Calles SO; open Mon.-Sat. 7:30 a.m.-6 p.m. The **Kodak** shop on 1 Calle and 2 Avenida O also sells some slide film, and can develop slides, but reports on the quality have varied. If you're desperate, **Foto Flash** on 2 Calle between 2 and 3 Avenidas NO can do basic camera repairs.

Medical Attention
Clínica Bendaña, on Avenida Circunvalación SO between 9 and 10 Calles, tel. 53-1618, 53-1614, 53-4437, or 53-4429, is a high-quality, full-service private clinic capable of handling medical emergencies and treating illnesses. Most of the doctors speak at least a bit of English. Open 24 hours.

Money Exchange
Many banks in town can change dollars or traveler's checks, but the hordes of moneychangers on the square and along the *peatonal* are certainly a lot quicker and usually offer a slightly better rate. It may seem shady to a foreigner, but there have been no reports of anyone getting ripped off.

If the black market makes you nervous, try **Casa de Cambio Lempira** on 3 Avenida between 4 and 5 Calles SO; open Mon.-Fri. 9 a.m.-5 p.m., Saturday 9 a.m.-noon. **Credomatic,** at Edificio Crefisa, 5 Avenida and 2 Calle NO, tel. 57-4350 or 53-2404, advances cash on Visa cards for no charge.

The American Express agent in San Pedro Sula is **Mundirama Travel Service,** tel. 52-3400 or 53-0490, fax 57-9022, right next to the cathedral downtown. It's open Mon.-Fri. 8 a.m.-5 p.m., Saturday 8 a.m.-noon.

Communications
The central Hondutel office, on the corner of 4 Avenida and 4 Calle SO, tel. 57-2222, fax 52-4923, is open 24 hours a day, but after 9 p.m. a guard lets you in. However, this is not the best neighborhood to be in that late.

Correos, 9 Calle and 3 Avenida SO, tel. 57-0707, is open Mon.-Fri. 8 a.m.-5 p.m., Saturday 8 a.m.-noon, and has Express Mail Service. More reliable though significantly more expensive are **DHL,** in Edificio Aida one block north of the Banco Sogerin building on 1 Calle, tel. 57-9250 or 57-9251, and **UPS,** in Edificio Panamericana, 3 Calle and 2 Avenida NO, Barrio Guamilito, tel. 57-8805, tel./fax 57-8921.

Migration
The migration office is half a block south of the square on the *peatonal,* on the east side of the street on the second floor, tel. 53-3728. Open Mon.-Fri. 8 a.m.-4 p.m., it offers hassle-free permit renewal.

Information
Information on San Pedro Sula and many other destinations in Honduras is available at **Servi-**

CONSULATES IN SAN PEDRO SULA

Belize: Km 5 on highway to Puerto Cortés, tel. 51-1740, 51-0717
Belgium: Edificio Banco de Ahorro, tel. 53-3059, fax 52-7257
Chile: Colonia Bella Vista, 3 Avenida #407, fax 56-1634
Costa Rica: 11 Calle A, 22 Avenida A #126 SO, tel./fax 52-8564
El Salvador: 3 Avenida and 1 Calle NO, Edificio Bancatlan, Room 1204, tel. 57-5851, fax 52-9706
Finland: Almacén Lady Lee, exit to La Lima, tel. 53-2706, 53-1642
France: 21 Avenida between 9 and 10 Calle NO, tel. 57-4187
Germany: at Berkline Industrial, exit to Puerto Cortés, tel. 53-1244, fax 53-1868
Great Britain: 2 Calle between 2 and 3 Avenida SO, Edificio Martínez Valenzuela #604, tel. 57-2063, fax 57-4066
Guatemala: 8 Calle between 5 and 6 Avenida NO, #38, tel. 53-3560
Haiti: Edificio Los Alpes, 8 Calle between 14 and 15 Calles NO, tel. 53-3944
Holland: Plaza Venecia, 14 Avenida between 7 and 8 Calles SO, tel. 52-9724, 57-1815, fax 52-9724
Italy: Edificio La Constancia, 3rd floor, 5 Avenida between 1 and 2 Calles NO, tel. 52-3672
Mexico: 2 Calle and 20 Avenida SO, #205, Río Piedras, tel. 52-3293, 53-2604, 53-2605
Nicaragua: 6 Calle and 16 Avenida NO #36, tel. 52-9069
Norway: Km 1 on the highway to El Cármen, tel. 57-0153, 52-2458, fax 59-0856
Spain: 2 Avenida between 3 and 4 Calles NO, #318, Edificio Agencias Panamericanas, tel. 58-0708, fax 57-1680
Uruguay: 2 Calle between 16 and 17 Calles NO, #16, tel. 53-3094, 53-4178, fax 57-8365

cios **Culturales y Turísticos,** a private company that works with the Honduran government. Their office is in Edificio Inmosa on 4 Calle between 3 and 4 Avenidas NO, 3rd floor, Room 304, tel. 52-3023.

Tour Operators

Cambio Central America/Honduras Expeditions, Edificio Copal, second floor, 1 Calle between 5 and 6 Avenidas O, tel. 52-0496 or 52-7274, fax 52-0523, runs tours across Honduras, including expeditions to the La Mosquitia jungle, Copán, Lago de Yojoa, Tela, Omoa, and many other destinations. Their mailing address is P.O. Box 2666, San Pedro Sula.

Explore Honduras Tours, Edificio Posada del Sol, 1 Calle and 2 Avenida O, tel. 52-6242, fax 52-6093, also offers local tours and trips to Copán, the Bay Islands, and Lago de Yojoa. A day tour of a La Lima banana plantation costs US$35 pp.

The train aficionado might want to look up **Banana Life Tours,** tel. 52-6036. Their customized railroad cars travel through banana plantations between San Pedro Sula, Puerto Cortés, and Tela; US$25 pp for a three-and-a-half-hour trip with breakfast included. Trips to

the wetlands at Refugio de Vida Silvestre Cuero y Salado by a combination of car, train, and boat cost US$90 pp.

Travel Agents

Two companies that can arrange airline tickets are **Mundirama Travel Service,** next to the cathedral at 2 Calle SO, tel. 52-3400 or 53-0490, fax 57-9022, which is also the American Express agent; and **Discovery Travel,** Edificio Gold Brand, Apto. 786, on 1 Calle between 7 and 8 Calles O, tel. 52-1873 or 52-1804, fax 57-6845.

Car Rental

Several car rental agencies operate in San Pedro. A few have multiple locations. **Dollar Rent A Car** has offices downtown at 3 Avenida between 3 and 4 Calles NO, tel./fax 52-7627 or 57-0820; at the airport, tel. 68-2337; and at Hotel Copantl, tel. 57-3542. **Maya Rent A Car,** tel. 52-2670 or 52-2671, fax 52-8890, staffs an office at the airport and at 3 Avenida between 7 and 8 Calles NO. At the airport and the Gran Hotel Sula is **Monilari Rent A Car,** tel. 53-2639, 52-2704, or 68-2580. **Toyota Rent A Car** is at 4 Avenida between 2 and 3 Calles NO, tel. 57-2644 or 57-2666.

GETTING THERE AND AWAY

San Pedro is the central transportation hub for northern and western Honduras, and is frequently the gateway to the country for foreign visitors on their way to the north coast or Bay Islands. Most bus travelers in Honduras will eventually find themselves passing through San Pedro at one time or another.

Air

Aeropuerto Internacional Ramón Villeda Morales, 13 km from downtown San Pedro, opened a terminal for international flights in late 1996; the old terminal now services domestic flights. At the terminal are Bancahorro and Banco Atlántida for exchanging money, Hondutel, Correos, a bookstore, duty-free shops, and a Danilo's leather store. Snacks only are sold at the airport, but across the parking lot is the inexpensive **Cafetería Chalet La Mesa,** handy for those waiting for a flight. Taxis from town to the airport cost about US$5. You could take an El Progreso bus and get off at the airport turnoff, but that still leaves a two-km walk, so it's best just to spring for the taxi. If you're leaving the country on an international flight, expect to pay a US$10 departure tax.

Isleña Airlines, tel. 52-8335, tel./fax 52-8322, flies direct to La Ceiba twice daily (US$30 one-way) and Tegucigalpa once daily (US$30 one-way), with connections to the Bay Islands and La Mosquitia.

Sosa Airlines, tel. 68-1742, flies daily to La Ceiba, with connections to Roatán and Utila.

Taca Airlines flies daily to Belize City, Miami, San Salvador, and Tegucigalpa. Taca has an office downtown at Centro Comercial Prisa, 1 Calle and 9 Avenida O, tel. 53-2646 or 53-2649, fax 53-2641. At the airport call 68-2398 or 68-2399.

American Airlines offers one flight daily to Miami. Their office is at Centro Commercial Firenze, 16 Avenida between 1 and 2 Calles NO, tel. 58-0518, 58-0519, or 58-0520.

Continental flies daily to Houston. Their downtown office is at the Gran Hotel Sula, tel. 57-4141; at the airport call 68-1917 or 68-1918.

Copa flies to Mexico City and Panama on Tuesday, Thursday, and Saturday. The downtown office is in Edificio Salame Gattas, 10 Avenida and 2 Calle, tel. 53-2709 or 53-2624; at the airport call 68-1170 or 68-2399.

Iberia flies Friday and Monday to Madrid by way of Miami. Their downtown office is at Edificio Quiroz, 2nd floor, 2 Calle between 1 and 2 Avenida SO, tel. 57-5311 or 53-4609; at the airport call 68-2165.

Bus

As in Tegucigalpa, bus stations in San Pedro are unfortunately scattered across town. Each company maintains its own station. Almost all terminals are in the southwest (SO) quadrant.

• To **Puerto Cortés:** Three companies offer direct buses leaving between 6 a.m. and 5 p.m.; US 70 cents, one hour. Expresos del Atlántico is on 8 Calle and 7 Avenida SO; Impala is on 2 Avenida between 4 and 5 Calles SO, tel. 53-3111; and Citul is on 6 Avenida between 7 and 8 Calles.

• To **La Ceiba:** Catisa, on 2 Avenida between 5 and 6 Calles, runs 12 direct buses daily between 5:30 a.m. and 6 p.m.; US$2, three hours. Buses stop at the turnoff to Tela. Buses to **El Progreso** leave from the same station frequently all day.

• To **Trujillo:** Direct buses leave twice daily at 11 a.m. and 2 p.m. from the gas station on 1 Avenida S between 5 and 6 Calles; US$4, six hours. Travelers can get off at Tela and La Ceiba.

• To **Tegucigalpa:** Companies running frequent buses include El Rey, on 7 Avenida between 5 and 6 Calles SO, tel. 57-8355; Transportes Norteños, on 6 Calle between 6 and 7 Avenidas; Hedman Alas, at 3 Calle and 8 Avenida NO, tel. 53-1316; and Saenz, on 8 Avenida between 4 and 5 Calles SO, tel. 53-4969. Each offers departures usually every hour between 6 a.m. and 6 p.m.; US$3, four hours. El Rey offers earlier departures at 2:30 a.m. and 4:30 a.m. Hedman Alas also runs three **direct luxury buses** with a/c, TV, and bathrooms daily at 5:45 a.m., 11:30 a.m., and 4:45 p.m.; US$6. Saenz operates six similar luxury direct buses leaving every two hours daily between 6 a.m. and 6 p.m.

• To **Siguatepeque:** Local buses leave from the gas station on 1 Avenida S between 5 and 6 Calles every hour between 4:30 a.m. and 4:30 p.m.; US$1, two hours.

• To **Santa Rosa de Copán:** Toritos and Copanecos, on 6 Avenida between 8 and 9 Calles SO, tel. 53-1954 or 53-4930, run four direct buses daily departing at 8 a.m., 9:30 a.m.,

2 p.m., and 3:30 p.m.; US$2, two and a half hours. Local buses take considerably longer—best to plan on getting a direct bus. The local last bus to Santa Rosa leaves at 5 p.m.

• To **Nueva Ocotepeque and the Guatemalan border:** Toritos at 11 Calle between 6 and 7 Avenidas SO, tel. 57-3691, and Congolón at 8 Avenida between 9 and 10 Calles SO, tel. 52-2268, alternate days, offering six departures daily to the border with stops at Santa Rosa de Copán and Nueva Ocotepeque. Buses leave at midnight, 12:30 a.m., 6:30 a.m., 10:30 a.m., 1 p.m., and 3 p.m. The first two departures cost US$5, the last four US$3; all take five and a half hours to reach the border.

• To **Copán Ruinas:** Direct buses leave from the corner of 6 Calle and 6 Avenida SO twice daily at 11 a.m. and 2 p.m.; US$3.50, four hours.

• To **Santa Bárbara:** Cotisba on 4 Avenida between 9 and 10 Calles SO, tel. 52-8889, runs regular buses roughly every hour between 5:20 a.m. and 6 p.m., 2.5 hour ride, US$1, and two direct buses at 8 a.m. and 4 p.m., 1.5 hour ride, US$1.30.

• To **El Mochito and Lago de Yojoa:** Several buses leave between 6 a.m. and 5:30 p.m. daily from 4 Avenida between 1 and 2 Calles SE; US$1, three hours. It costs less to Pulhapanzak Falls and Peña Blanca.

Car
As the country's major industrial center, San Pedro Sula is well-connected by paved road to the north coast and western and central Honduras. Highways to Santa Rosa de Copán,

---

DISTANCES FROM SAN PEDRO SULA

Tegucigalpa: 246 km
El Progreso: 20 km
Puerto Cortés: 57 km
Tela: 90 km
La Ceiba: 202 km
Trujillo: 440 km
Santa Bárbara: 108 km
Santa Rosa de Copán: 170 km
Copán Ruinas: 198 km
Nueva Ocotepeque: 262 km
Yoro: 136 km

Nueva Ocotepeque, Copán Ruinas, Tela, La Ceiba, Trujillo, Yoro, and Tegucigalpa are all fairly well-maintained and can be driven on safely year-round. During the height of the rainy season, however, road conditions tend to deteriorate.

Train
At last report, train service between San Pedro Sula and Puerto Cortés had been suspended, and officials don't think it will resume any time soon. For the latest information, check at the train station on 1 Avenida and 1 Calle, or call 53-4080.

NEAR SAN PEDRO SULA

Parque Nacional Cusuco
Situated on one of the highest sections of the Sierra Merendón, a north-south-trending mountain range dropping into the Caribbean Sea near Omoa, Cusuco covers roughly 10,000 hectares, of which 1,000 hectares fall in the core zone above 1,800 meters. The park forms part of the watershed for the Río Motagua, on the north and west side, and for the Río Chamelecón, on the south and east. The highest point in the park is Cerro Jilinco at 2,242 meters. In the 1950s, the forest around Cusuco was heavily logged by the Río Cusuco Company. Logging ended in 1959 when the region was declared a reserve on the recommendation of Venezuelan ecologist Geraldo Bukowski. The national park was established in 1987.

Cusuco is a popular park for foreign visitors, both because of its proximity to San Pedro Sula and because of the great wealth of bird life in the cloud, pine, and subtropical forests. Over 100 species have been identified in the park, and it's estimated that up to 300 species may actually be here. It's also inhabited by many endangered mammals, including the park's namesake, the armadillo *(cusuco)*.

A visitor's center, with maps and displays on local flora and fauna, and four trails have been built in the park. Ask the *vigilante* here to tell you where the three well-known birdwatching spots are. The trails—El Danto (two km), El Quetzal (one km), La Mina (2.5 km), and El Pizote (two km)—are well marked and not too steep or strenuous, but they can be muddy so bring boots and watch your footing. Another trail, continuing along the ridge of the Merendón down to Omoa, makes an excellent two- to three-day hike, but it has recently been closed by the foundation managing the park. With luck it will reopen soon. Although guides are not necessary to navigate the main trails, they can be of use in helping spot animals and birds. You can find guides in the village of Buenos Aires, on the way to the visitor's center.

No camping is allowed in the park itself, but you can pitch a tent at a site along the road between Buenos Aires and the visitor's center for free. As at La Tigra near Tegucigalpa, entrance prices for Cusuco went up to US$10 for foreigners in 1996, a steep price to pay considering the facilities and the fact that the forest is not in as pristine shape as several other parks in the country. However, the location near San Pedro is certainly convenient, and the price is worth it for those who don't have the time or inclination to venture further afield. Hondurans pay US$1.

The main access to the Cusuco visitor's center is by car to Cofradía, a small town on the Santa Rosa highway 16 km from the turnoff outside of San Pedro Sula. From the signposted turn at Cofradía continue 26 km up a dirt road to Buenos Aires and on to the visitor's center. If you don't have a car, get off any Santa Rosa or La Entrada bus at Cofradía, then hitch a ride in a pickup to Buenos Aires or the nearby village of Tomala. From Buenos Aires, if no ride is available, it's a two-hour, five-km walk to the visitor's center.

It's possible to drive to the visitor's center straight up into the hills behind San Pedro Sula, via a dirt road passing through Las Peñitas, El Gallito, Naranjito, and Bañaderas before reaching Buenos Aires. This road is not in the best of shape, but offers great views over the city and across the Sierra Merendón.

For more information on the park, call or visit **Fundación Hector Rodrigo Pastor Fasquelle,** above Pizzeria Italia on the corner of 1 Calle and 7 Avenida O, tel. 52-1014 or 57-6598; open Mon.-Fri. 8 a.m.-noon and 1-5 p.m. Apart from a basic pamphlet and map, little practical hiking details are available, but the foundation library is an excellent source for ecological information on the park and Honduras in general. The topographical maps covering the park are the 1:50,000 Cuyamel-San Pedro Sula 2562 I, Valle de Naco 2562 II, Quimistán 2562 III, and Cuyamelito 2562 IV.

BOB RACE

La Lima

Sixteen kilometers from San Pedro Sula, just off the highway to El Progreso, is the center of United Fruit's (now Chiquita Brands) banana operations in Honduras—La Lima. For those interested in touring a banana plantation, the best option is to take a day tour with **Explore Honduras Tours,** tel. 52-6242, fax 52-6093; US$35 pp.

DEPARTMENT OF YORO

EL PROGRESO

A dusty, hot agricultural city of 124,000 in the center of the Valle de Sula, El Progreso offers little of interest to tourists. Most travelers who stop in El Progreso are changing buses.

Practicalities
Near the exit to Tela, next to the market, is **Hotelito Max,** tel. 66-0221, offering basic, concrete rooms with bathrooms for US$6 d for one bed, US$10 d two beds. The hotel has an interior parking lot. Two blocks east of the main bus terminal is the four story **Hotel Las Vegas,** tel. 66-4667 or 66-4588, with a range of rooms, from US$7.50 d with one bed and fan to US$13 d for two beds, a/c, and TV. Downstairs is the **Restaurante Copa Dorada,** open 7 a.m.-midnight with room service available.

Find cheap eats at **Mitchel's Cafeteria** on the main street, 1 Avenida. On the Tela-San Pedro bypass road is one of the better restaurants in town, **Los Tarros,** tel. 66-1290. Specializing in steaks *a la parrilla,* Los Tarros also serves seafood, chicken, soups, sandwiches, and, unusually, pitchers of Port Royal, Salvavida, and Nacional beer on tap. Open daily 11 a.m.-10 p.m., air-conditioned dining room, US$3-6 per full meal. **El Pichón,** across from the main bus terminal, is a good place to grab snacks and fresh juices while awaiting your bus.

Dollars and traveler's checks can be changed at Bancahorro and Banco Atlántida, both on 1 Avenida.

Buses to San Pedro Sula and Yoro depart from the main bus terminal, just off the square. San Pedro buses leave frequently all day long, US 40 cents, 20 minutes; to Yoro every hour or so between 5 a.m. and 5 p.m., US$1.30, three and a half hours; to Morazán (for Pico Pijol), every hour between 6 a.m. and 6 p.m., US 70 cents, two hours.

Buses to Tela leave from a different stop, four blocks west of the main terminal. Direct buses leave Mon.-Fri. at 3 p.m. and 4:15 p.m., Sat.-Sun. 8 a.m. and 8:45 a.m.; US$1, 45 minutes. Try to plan on the direct as the local buses take about two hours, stopping at seemingly every kilometer.

El Progreso is connected to San Pedro by a new, 28-km, four-lane highway passing La Lima and the airport. Continuing north to Tela, the highway narrows to two lanes but is still in fairly good condition. East and south, a road cuts from El Progreso back to the San Pedro-Tegucigalpa highway at La Barca, passing Santa Rita. From Santa Rita another two-lane paved road winds up into the mountains to Morazán and Yoro.

MORAZÁN TO YORO

Morazán
Morazán, a dusty town of 8,500 set two km off the Yoro highway, is 45 km from Santa Rita in the middle of the Valle de Cataguana, below the Sierra de Pijol. Morazán makes a good base for visiting Parque Nacional Pico Pijol, as it's the closest town with lodging and supplies.

The town has a couple of inexpensive *hospedajes* and *comedores,* a gas station, and several stores selling camping supplies.

YORO'S MYSTERIOUS LLUVIA DE PESCES

A swampy field called El Llano del Pántano one and a half kilometers southeast of the town of Yoro is the site of a most unusual annual rainstorm, according to local legend. During the height of the rainy season, usually sometime in mid-June, a fierce storm will hit in the middle of the night, and in the morning residents find the field full of flopping fish! Thus the annual event has become known as the "Lluvia de Pesces," or "The Rain of Fish."

More skeptical minds have theorized that the fish come upriver from a tributary of the Río Aguán, and use the inundations from the heavy rain to reach the marsh, where they are accustomed to laying their eggs. Reportedly some Japanese scientists came to Yoro not long ago to solve the mystery, and came away mystified.

Parque Nacional Pico Pijol

One of the less-explored natural reserves in the country, the mountains of Pico Pijol are a major water source for the El Cajón reservoir and San Pedro Sula. The land has been set aside as a protected area more in the interests of resource conservation than tourism. No trails have been developed in the 11,206-hectare park apart from those used by locals, but it is possible to explore the upper reaches of the forest with the help of guides. The highest peak in the reserve is Pico Pijol, at 2,282 meters. On the western edge rises Cerro El Sargento, 1,852 meters, from where you can see San Pedro Sula on a clear day. Four major rivers flow off the mountains: Río Pijol, Río Pataste, Río Chilistagua, and Río Jacagua.

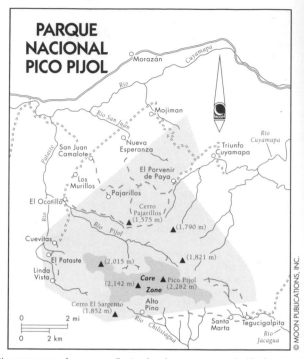

Much of the mountains' lower-elevation forest cover has been cut down to make room for coffee plantations, *milpas* (cornfields), or grazing land, but the core zone of the park, above 1,800 meters, is still in good shape. The south side of the Río Pijol Valley, rising up to the high ridge, is particularly pristine, due to the steepness of the hillside. The forest above El Pataste is also in good condition.

To get into the park, look for *desvio* La Regina, a turnoff from the Yoro highway between El Negrito and Morazán, between Km 37 and 38 near a Fusep police post. This dirt road leads to a junction; to the left lies the village of San Juan Camalote and to the right the road continues to Los Murillos and El Ocotillo, ending at Cuevitas. From there you can walk by trail to El Pataste and Linda Vista, where you can find guides to lead you up Cerro El Sargento, Pico Pijol, and other peaks. The few names marked in the register atop Pico Pijol attest to the difficulty of scaling the peak. A visitor's center and lodge is planned for Los Murillos.

Along the Río Pijol, reached from the village of El Ocotillo, is a triple waterfall called **Las Pirates**, an excellent swimming spot surrounded by forest. On the southeast side of the park, near the village of Tegucigalpita, is a major cave system of unknown depth, with wide chambers and an underground waterfall near the cave mouth. Take the dirt road near El Negrito to reach Tegucigalpita.

Buses drive between Morazán and some of the villages around the park—ask in Morazán for the latest information, as it changes regularly. For more information on Pico Pijol, contact the office of **Ecopijol** in Morazán. Ecopijol dispenses pamphlets and maps of the park, but the local Peace Corps volunteer is usually the best source of information on the park. The **Cohdefor** office in Morazán also has a large topographical wall map that can give you an idea of the park's geography. Topographical maps covering the park are 1:50,000 El Negrito 2661 I and Las Flores 2661 II.

Yoro

Beyond Morazán, the highway heads over a low hill and enters the Valle de Yoro, ending at

THE TOLUPANS OF MONTAÑA DE LA FLOR

Formerly one of the most widespread indigenous groups in Honduras, the Tolupans—or Jicaques, as they are called by Latinos—now number less than a 1,000. Almost all of them live in one community, in the mountains forming the border between the Yoro and Francisco Morazán department ments.

In pre-conquest times, the Tolupans lived across a broad swath of present-day Honduras between northern Olancho and the Sierra de Omoa, near Guatemala. Unlike their neighbors the Pech, who came originally from the jungles of South America, the Tolupans seem to have migrated to the region from the southwestern United States, as their language is closely related to that of the Sioux.

Because the Tolupans generally refused to convert to Catholicism and opted to fight or retreat into the mountains rather than accept Spanish colonization, they were a constant target of colonists needing laborers. Many thousands are thought to have died in the construction of the fortress at Omoa, and countless others were enslaved or perished working in dye factories or transporting sarsaparilla.

By the mid-19th century, only about 8,000 Tolupans still clung to their traditional ways in the mountains of Yoro, living in villages surrounded by wooden palisades deep in the forests, and avoiding contact with outsiders whenever possible. Unfortunately for these remaining communities, they happened to live in an area rich in sarsaparilla; in the 1860s, the world market for this root boomed when it became all the rage to add to beverages. The governor of Yoro, Jesús Queróz, ordered his soldiers to force the Tolupans to gather the root year-round, even in the tor-

rential rainy season, and march it to the coast at Trujillo or Tela.

This bleak period of slavery, which continued into the 20th century, was burned deep into the minds of the surviving Tolupans. They still speak of how when an Indian died from exhaustion or disease while carrying sarsaparilla, the soldiers only stopped the column long enough to redistribute the dead man's load, but not long enough to bury him.

A group of three Tolupan families, desperately trying to flee the Yoro soldiers and be left in peace, learned of an unpopulated forest on the far side of the Montaña de Yoro, out of the jurisdiction of the Yoro governor. They fled there in 1864, just ahead of pursuing soldiers. The small group, led by men who had taken the names Juan Martínez, Francisco Martínez, Pedro Soto, and León Soto, settled in a region called Montaña de la Flor, at that time raw forest.

The village of Montaña de la Flor now has about 600 inhabitants, all descendents of those first three families, and is the only Tolupan community retaining some of its original traditions. Most villagers still speak Tolupan, although all also speak Spanish. They do not drink alcohol, do not practice Catholicism, and for the most part disdain surrounding Latino villagers and their money-oriented ways.

How long their traditional ways will continue is uncertain, as Montaña de la Flor can now be reached by road from nearby Latino villages and towns, and some Tolupans have married with Latinos. One can hope they will fare better than their former compatriots in Yoro, who only vaguely remember their Tolupan past.

---

the town of Yoro. The church in Yoro holds the remains of Padre Manuel de Jesús Subirana. Known as La Santa Misión, he was a tireless missionary and protector of the native Tolupan in Yoro; he died 27 November 1864. Subirana is still revered among the campesinos of the region, many of whom consider him a saint. In the dry season, you can continue by bus from Yoro along the Río Aguán Valley to Olanchito.

South of Yoro, not far from the village of Yorito, is the colonial mission **Luquigüe,** considered one of the best preserved missions in the country. Luquigüe was established in 1751 by

Franciscan missionaries in an effort to convert the Tolupan Indians who lived in the region at that time. The friars were generally unsuccessful; the Indians were kept there only by force. They fled whenever possible, and the mission was abandoned shortly after Independence in 1821.

This region, especially on the south side of Montaña de la Flor, is the last bastion of the Tolupan, who once lived from the Guatemalan border to Olancho. The best way to get to their main settlement at Montaña de la Flor is via Cedros, north of Tegucigalpa.

Between Yoro and Montaña de la Flor is the 154-square-km **Parque Nacional Montaña de Yoro,** a mountain mesa covered in cloud forest and reaching a height of 2,282 meters. Little information is available on the ecological status of the park, or on the best ways to get into the forest.

LAGO DE YOJOA AND VICINITY

Honduras's largest natural lake, Lago de Yojoa is roughly 16 km long by eight km wide, at an altitude of 635 meters, right along the San Pedro Sula-Tegucigalpa highway. The setting, backed by the majestic mountains of Santa Bárbara and Cerro Azul/Meámbar, is spectacular.

The lake is drained naturally on the south side by Río Tepemechín, which leads eventually into the Río Ulúa, and on the north by the Río Blanco Canal, a channel that powers a hydroelectric plant at Cañaveral. Because of its location in the transition zone between the Valle de Sula and the central highlands, and its extensive marshes, the Lago de Yojoa region boasts the country's largest variety of bird species. One count put the number of species at 373. Whatever the exact number, the lake and surrounding forests are a birder's paradise. One particularly good spot is at Hotel Agua Azul and the nearby Isla del Venado.

The shores of the lake are dotted with innumerable ruins, mostly believed to be of Mayan origin, including Los Naranjos. Along with the Valle de Sula, Lago de Yojoa is thought to have been one of the most heavily populated areas in Honduras in pre-Hispanic times, used as a home by the Lenca, Maya, and perhaps other groups.

Largemouth bass fishing in the lake was once legendary, attracting anglers from across the globe, but the bass population has declined due to overfishing. Because of recent protection efforts, the lake's fish stock is reportedly on the rebound. Yacht and fishing trips can be arranged on the lake by contacting Richard Joint of **Honduyate,** tel. 39-2684 or 57-0774, fax 39-2324. Honduyate also rents a house on the edge of the lake at Gualquieme. You can arrange less expensive fishing trips by talking to local fishermen, especially at Las Marías near Peña Blanca. If you go this route, it's best to come equipped with your own gear. Fishermen will also gladly take you on a lake tour for a negotiable fee.

Getting detailed information on the status of the lake's ecology is no easy task. **Ecolago,** a new organization run out of Hotel Agua Azul, is more of a good idea than an actual environmental monitoring station, although with luck, the situation will improve. The lake's water level was seven and a half meters below normal in 1996, but that seems to change constantly rather than express a long-term trend.

Regular buses ply the roads around the lake, between Peña Blanca and El Mochito, La Guama, and Pulhapanzak Falls. If no buses are immediately apparent, just stick out your thumb—hitchhiking is fairly reliable.

LAGO DE YOJOA

Peña Blanca
Not much of a town itself, Peña Blanca lies at a major crossroads near the northwest corner of the lake. From here roads continue to El Mochito around the west side of the lake, to Agua Azul and La Guama along the north side, and along the Río Lindo past Pulhapanzak Falls to the San Pedro-Tegucigalpa highway to the north.

Two km from Peña Blanca are the docks at **Las Marías,** used by many fishermen. You can hire boats to go out on the lake from here. Nearby is the mouth of the canal that feeds the power plant, a good place for a swim.

In Peña Blanca you'll find the inexpensive **Hotel Maranata,** the only real budget-class hotel on the lake, and several low-priced *comedores.*

Buses leave Peña Blanca daily in late morning to San Luis Planes, a village set high on the northern flanks of Montaña de Santa Bárbara, where you can find guides to take you into the cloud forest.

Los Naranjos
Roughly four km from Peña Blanca on the road to El Mochito is the village of Los Naranjos; nearby lies a ruins site of the same name. The Mayan site is extensive, but almost entirely unexcavated, meaning there's not much for the casual visitor to see beyond a lot of mounds.

El Mochito

On the south side of the lake, at the foot of Montaña de Santa Bárbara, is the mining town of El Mochito. There's not much to interest tourists, but a couple of dirt roads lead from there up into the mountains (for details see "Parque Nacional Santa Bárbara" in the "Near Santa Bárbara" section under "Santa Bárbara and Vicinity," below).

North Side

Following the road east of Peña Blanca, through coffee plantations with good views over the lake and the mountains of Santa Bárbara, are the hotels of **Las Glorias,** tel. 56-0736, and **Brisas del Lago,** tel. 52-7030. The former, cabins with a/c and TV in a forested area, has a good deal more character than the latter, an imposing concrete structure that looks more like a government building than a resort. Rooms at either cost US$30 d.

The most popular accommodations on the lake are four km east toward La Guama from Brisas del Lago at **Hotel Agua Azul,** tel. 52-7125. The rustic, slightly weather-beaten wooden cabins on a small rise above the lake cost only US$20, with fans and bathroom. The hotel has a great wooden porch restaurant offering unbeatable views out over the lake. The reasonably priced food is good, though service is slow. Pedal boats and motor launches are available for rent. The nearby **Isla del Venado** and the rocks at **La Venta** are good places to birdwatch.

Near the entrance to the hotel is the office of **Ecolago,** supposedly an environmental organization monitoring the lake. No information is dispensed here, and the office is usually deserted. The best person to talk to about the lake is the local Peace Corps volunteer, who can be found by asking at the Hotel Agua Azul.

Parque Nacional Cerro Azul/Meámbar

The road from Peña Blanca hits the San Pedro-Tegucigalpa highway at **La Guama,** an unattractive highway town at km marker 166. From La Guama a dirt road heads east to the village of San Isidro, which stands at the base of Parque Nacional Cerro Azul/Meámbar.

The park covers 312 square km ranging between 415 and 2,080 meters, and contains patches of lowland humid, pine, and cloud forest. About 15 km of trails lead into the park, mostly through patches of cloud forest. None of the developed trails lead to the highest peaks, which are covered with a dwarf forest similar to that found in Sierra de Agalta. Experienced guides can be found in San Isidro, through the Proyecto Aldea Global (Global Village) office, and also in the village of Las Delicias.

An environmental education center has been built in Los Pinos town, where six cabins are available for rent. For more information on the cabins and the park, contact Aldea Global, tel. 73-2741, or visit their office in San Isidro or Siguatepeque.

Topographical maps covering the park are 1:50,000 Taulabé 2660 III and Santa Cruz de Yojoa 2660 IV.

Pito Solo

At the southeast corner of the lake, where the Santa Bárbara road meets the San Pedro-Tegucigalpa highway, is the village of Pito Solo. The only rooms there are at **Los Remos,** tel. 57-8054, an unattractive one-level ranch-style place reminiscent of, in the words of one guest, the Bates Motel. Rooms are none too clean and cost US$13 d, although negotiations are possible. The food is bad and the pool is foul.

From Pito Solo it's 157 km to Tegucigalpa, 97 km to San Pedro Sula, and 53 km to Santa Bárbara.

Cavernas de Taulabé

Approximately 17 km south of Pito Solo, at km marker 140, are the Cavernas de Taulabé, which have been explored to a depth of 12 km without hitting the bottom. The first few hundred yards of the cave have been lit and have steps, but beyond that bring a flashlight and watch your footing. It might be best to hire a guide for exploring, as it's easy to get lost. Entrance costs US 40 cents, guides go for about US$3-4 for a couple of hours. Ask about the legendary *bandito* who hid out in the caves for months. Locally made honey is frequently sold along the highway near Taulabé.

NORTH OF THE LAKE

Of the several *balnearios* along the Río Lindo, in its course flowing out of Lago de Yojoa to the Río Ulúa, by far the most popular is the 43-

the impressive Pulhapanzak Falls

meter-high **Pulhapanzak Falls.** To get to the falls, take a bus from Peña Blanca to the San Pedro Sula-Tegucigalpa highway and get off at San Buenaventura. From San Buenaventura, walk 1.5 km to the signposted turnoff to the falls.

If in doubt, ask any local to point the way. If coming from Tegucigalpa, get off at La Guama and catch a bus to Peña Blanca and on to San Buenaventura.

Above the Río Lindo is a restaurant and large open field. In the center of the field are a few mounds covering what are thought to be Mayan-era ruins. Past the restaurant is a swimming hole above the falls—don't swim too close to the drop-off!

To properly admire the falls, follow the trail down along the edge of the river to a viewpoint below. The land around this part of the river is private property and is still covered with dense forest, a visually pleasing background for the falls.

Entrance to the falls costs US 40 cents, and the owners are happy to have people camp out for another 40 cents, either with a tent on the lawn or in a hammock. Sunrise here can be very beautiful. The area is usually packed on weekends and deserted during the week.

Between San Buenaventura and Peña Blanca is a power-plant station at **Cañaveral.** In front of the office are two sculptures from Los Naranjos, one a headless statue and the other a large dish, which were unearthed during the construction of the canal in 1962. Next to them is an example of one of the turbines used in the power plant.

Just beyond the power plant is **Balneario Cabo Cañaveral,** a well laid-out series of pools along the river that unfortunately aren't kept too clean. Entrance is US 40 cents.

SANTA BÁRBARA AND VICINITY

SANTA BÁRBARA

Cupped in the lush, hot lowlands not far from the Río Ulúa, at the base of the Montaña de Santa Bárbara towering above, Santa Bárbara enjoys a sublimely beautiful setting. It's also an exceptionally friendly town, where locals seem pleasantly surprised to see foreign visitors and take pleasure in getting to know them. It's the sort of place where you want to find things to do, just so you can continue soaking in the relaxed atmosphere. Fortunately, there are several worthwhile side trips from Santa Bárbara—to outlying villages, an abandoned castle, and of course, up into the forests of the national park.

The mountain countryside surrounding Santa Bárbara is well-known as one of the country's top coffee-producing regions, and also as the center for the *junco* palm industry. Baskets, hats, and other handicrafts are made from *junco* palm.

History
Santa Bárbara was founded in 1761 by several families who moved to the region from Gracias, reportedly escaping usurious priests. Santa Bárbara remained relatively small until April 1815, when the nearby town of Tencoa, one

of the first Spanish settlements in Honduras, was flooded by the Río Ulúa. Tencoa's surviving inhabitants moved to Santa Bárbara, and the combined population became the biggest town in the region.

Sights
The 110-year-old **Catedral de Santa Bárbara** facing the town square (Parque Central) features an intricately carved wooden altar with painted statues of saints. Just outside of town are two *balnearios* in rivers coming off the mountain—**La Torre** and **Santa Lucía.**

A visit to the long-abandoned **Castillo Bográn** in the hills above Santa Bárbara makes a great day-trip. From the square, get someone to point out the castle, visible on a ridge southeast of town. The castle is four km from Santa Bárbara on a dirt road leading to the village of Las Crucitas. Pickups occasionally drive the road and will give you a lift for a few lempira,

or you can walk it in one or two sweaty hours, depending on your pace. Actually getting in to the castle requires some serious bushwacking and scrambling, but it is possible for the determined.

Accommodations
Not accustomed to accommodating many foreign visitors, most hotels in Santa Bárbara are on the lower end of the price scale, but comfortable rooms can be found without difficulty.

Gran Hotel Colonial, tel. 64-2665, one and a half blocks from the square going toward the hills, features two floors of clean, tile-floored rooms around a small courtyard. Rates range from US$4 s or d with a communal bathroom to US$6 s or d with private bathroom. All rooms have fans; TV and a/c are available for a slightly higher price.

One block southeast of the square is **Boarding House Moderno,** tel. 64-2203, a large, quiet

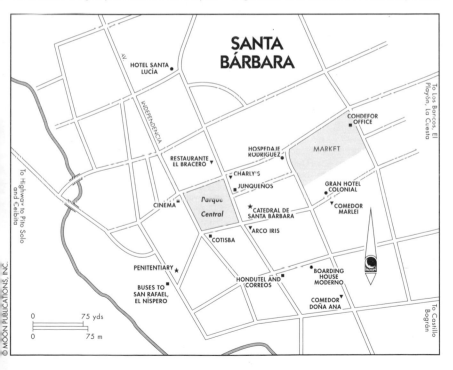

building charging US$4 s with bathroom, US$6 s or US$8 d with fan and hot water, more for a/c. The front desk sells sodas and fruit juices. For less money, **Hotel Santa Lucía,** two blocks north of the square, tel. 64-2531, is a very good value at US$1.80 s with shared bath, US$2.50 s with private bath, US$5 d private bath. The tile rooms are clean and have fans.

A block east of the square is the ultracheap **Hospedaje Rodriguez,** for the real lempira-pincher at US$1.20 s, US$2 with private bath. The tiny rooms are often full.

Food and Entertainment

The best meals in town are unquestionably offered at **Comedor Doña Ana,** an unusual setup. Meals are served in the house of a middle-class Santa Bárbara family, two blocks southeast of the square; it's decorated with paintings, old photographs, and sculptures. It feels a bit like eating in your grandmother's house. Three reasonably priced set meals are served Mon.-Sat. during standard meal times (7-9 a.m., noon-2 p.m., and 6-8 p.m.).

Restaurante El Bracero, half a block north of the square, probably has the most extensive menu in town, although the food is unexceptional. It's one of the few places in town to get mixed drinks. Open daily 9 a.m.-11 p.m. Decent chicken, as well as burgers and *comida corriente,* can be had at **Cafetería Pollo a la Costa,** half a block from the square on Avenida Independencia; open daily until 9 p.m.

Charly's, on the northeast corner of the square, is a good spot for *baleadas,* tacos, pastries, juices, yogurt, and other snacks; open daily 9 a.m.-10 p.m. **Arco Iris,** on the southeast corner of the square, adjacent to the cathedral, also has very good fresh juices and ice cream. Right across from Hotel Colonial is **Comedor Marlei,** with reasonable, inexpensive *comida corriente.*

Occasional weekend dance parties are held at **Disco Chalet El Tejado,** next to Hondutel. The town **cinema** is on the northwest corner of the square.

Information and Services

Hondutel, open Mon.-Fri. 7 a.m.-5 p.m., receives faxes at tel. 64-2550. Correos is right next door, a block south of the square. Banco de Occidente and Bancahsa will usually change dollars, but not always traveler's checks.

Hammocks of fair quality are sold by inmates of the local penitentiary, who are always amused to get visitors. The penitentiary is a block down the hill west of the square.

Estela de Zamora, on Avenida Independencia, is one of the finer stores in town selling *junco*-palm goods. The owners have been in business for 30 years and are happy to explain the differences in quality of various products.

Getting There and Away

Junqueños, tel. 64-2113, runs buses twice daily to **Tegucigalpa,** leaving Mon.-Fri. at 7 a.m. and 2 p.m., Sat.-Sun. 9 a.m. and 2 p.m.; US$2.20, four and a half hours. The office, right next to the church on the square, also sells some *junco* handicrafts.

Cotisba, tel. 62-8889, runs buses roughly every hour between 4 a.m. and 5 p.m. to **San Pedro Sula,** 2.5 hour ride, US$1, with one direct bus leaving at 8 a.m., 1.5 hour ride, US$1.30. Their office is on the southwest corner of the square, nearly opposite Junqueños.

Buses to **San Rafael,** a village in the mountains south of Santa Bárbara, leave from next to the penitentiary, a block below the square, at noon; three hours. From San Rafael, you can continue by hitching to Gracias. The bus returns from San Rafael at 4:30 a.m.

Buses to **El Níspero** leave at 11 a.m. from next to the penitentiary, and return at 6 a.m.

From San Pedro Sula or Santa Rosa de Copán, the road to Santa Bárbara turns off at **Ceibita,** between Km 32 and 33. From Ceibita (where there is often a lot of fruit for sale), it's another 61 km to Santa Bárbara.

East out of Santa Bárbara, the highway leads to Pito Solo, where it meets the San Pedro-

BOB RACE

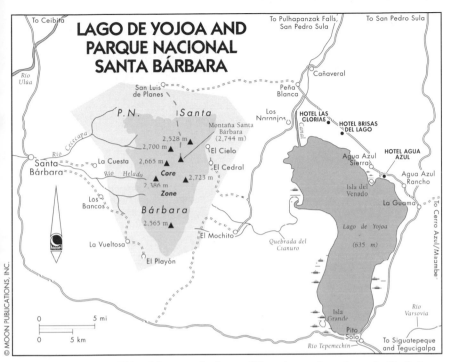

LAGO DE YOJOA AND PARQUE NACIONAL SANTA BÁRBARA

Tegucigalpa highway. This 53-km stretch of road is not as frequently traveled as the one toward Ceibita, and is in worse condition, but passes through beautiful countryside.

NEAR SANTA BÁRBARA

Parque Nacional Santa Bárbara

Surrounding the peak of Santa Bárbara, the second-highest in the country at 2,744 meters, Parque Nacional Santa Bárbara covers about 13,000 hectares of cloud, pine, and semihumid tropical forest. Montaña de Santa Bárbara is not part of any major mountain range, but an anomalous, solitary massif rising up between Santa Bárbara town and Lago de Yojoa. The highest point in this massif is called Pico Moroncho. The forest on top of the mountain is dense, wild, and in fairly pristine condition due to its isolation.

Although as yet no signposted trails have been developed in the park, it's possible to get into the forest from several of the villages around the edge of the mountain. From Santa Bárbara, you can catch a ride on a truck or drive 20 minutes by dirt road to **La Cuesta** or **Los Bancos** and **El Playón,** and look for guides. In El Playón, Mario or Reino Orellano are usually willing to take visitors into the forest for a negotiable fee.

Probably the best access is via **San Luis Planes,** a village set in a high valley on the north side of the park; you can get there by bus from Peña Blanca on Lago de Yojoa. From San Luis a clear trail leads to a rough cabin in the forest at **Los Chávez.** The cabin may become the park's visitor's center. Ask Profesor Mauro in San Luis for the keys to the cabin. From Los Chávez a trail continues to the peak, but you may need a guide to find it. Cohdefor is planning to mark this trail for visitors.

From El Mochito, on the south shore of Lago de Yojoa, you can get a truck to **El Cedral** and continue on foot or horseback to **El Cielo,** where guides can be found to lead you to the peak.

For more information on the park and access to it, stop in at the Santa Bárbara Cohdefor office and speak to Jaqueline López, an extremely knowledgeable and helpful official who manages the park. The topographical map covering the park is 1:50,000 Santa Bárbara 2560 I.

Villages Near Santa Bárbara

The department of Santa Bárbara is dotted with colorful colonial villages infrequently visited by foreigners. Many, such as **Gualjoto, El Níspero, Los Bancos, and San Vicente,** are known for producing *artesanías.* **llama,** on the road toward Ceibita and San Pedro Sula, is famous for its *junco* goods as well as its traditional colonial church.

Not far from Santa Bárbara are the ruins of **Tencoa,** one of the first Spanish towns in Honduras. This was the original site of Santa Bárbara until the town moved to its current site because of a flood in Tencoa.

Set high on a mountain divide separating Santa Bárbara from the Gracias region is **San Rafael,** with a lovely colonial-era church. A daily bus from Santa Bárbara travels to San Rafael, and the adventurous can continue onward to Gracias by hitchhiking down the dirt road. No hotels exist in San Rafael, but locals will rent rooms for a night. This little-visited mountain region is exceptionally beautiful.

SIGUATEPEQUE

Set in a broad valley amid highland pine forest in the center of Honduras, Siguatepeque (pop. 45,700) enjoys a cool and comfortable climate—a pleasant change for those coming from steamy San Pedro Sula or the north coast. In spite of its long history—the town was one of the first bases for the Spanish in their conquest of Honduras—little colonial-era architecture remains in Siguatepeque. And there are few other attractions per se to interest foreign visitors. The main reason to visit Siguatepeque, besides any business you may have with the Escuela de Ciencias Forestales (the Honduran national forestry school), is to enjoy a walk in the surrounding pine forests. With inexpensive hotels and good restaurants, Siguatepeque is a pleasant place to break up a trip from the north coast to the capital or beyond. Perhaps because of the school, Siguatepeque has a distinctly upscale feel to it for a town in the middle of the country.

ORIENTATION AND SIGHTS

Unusual for a Honduran town, Siguatepeque has two main squares. The one with the church on it is known as the *"parque"* while the other, two blocks west, is called the "plaza." The town is about 1.5 km off the San Pedro-Tegucigalpa highway.

At the highway intersection is the **Escuela de Ciencias Forestales,** the national forestry school. For those who read Spanish, the school library has some useful books on the country and its natural resources; some of the books are for sale.

About an hour's walk or a US$1.30 taxi ride outside of town is a small park at **Calanterique,** which means "mountain of water" in Lenca. The park has places to camp as well as picnic benches. About four km down the highway west to La Esperanza is the village of **El Porvenir,** a local center for Lenca pottery, sold out of several houses on the road.

PRACTICALITIES

Accommodations

A very good value on the southeast corner of the *parque* is **Boarding House Central,** tel. 73-2108, charging US$2.50 s, US$4 d, or US$4 s, US$6 d for private bath, hot water, and TV—worth a bit of a splurge. The *comedor* in the Boarding House is not so great, but it's convenient for beers or soft drinks.

On the same side of the *parque,* next to the cinema, is the two-story **Hotel Versalles,** tel. 73-2157, also a good value at US$2 s or US$3.50 d, US$2.50 s or US$5 d with private bath. The clean rooms surround a courtyard. A step up in price and quality is **Hotel Gomez**, tel. 73-2860, a two-story motel-style place around an interior parking lot. The clean rooms go for US$6 s or US$8 d with TV and hot water, a bit less without TV. A half a block from the plaza, the hotel has a decent cafeteria.

Opposite Banco de Occidente, just north of the plaza, **Hotel Panamericano**, tel. 73-2202, has similar rooms and prices to the Gomez, and also offers a/c.

Food and Entertainment

An extremely pleasant find out here in the middle of Honduras is **Pizzeria Venezia**, run by an Italian expatriate who came to Siguatepeque for its cool climate. The unpretentious, popular restaurant between the two squares serves up a superb, inexpensive pizza as well as pasta and sandwiches, daily 10 a.m.-10:30 p.m.

La Villa, a Mexican-style restaurant next to the *parque*, has excellent fajitas, quesadillas, nachos, *tortas*, burritos, burgers, and breakfasts for US$1.50-3 per meal. The owner spent some time in the U.S. and came back with a firm belief in the importance of good service. Open daily 7 a.m.-9 p.m.

Comedor Central between the two squares is a popular spot for inexpensive *comida corriente, pastelitos,* and other standard Honduran food. On the southeast corner of the plaza is **Fruti Licuados,** a good place to grab a fruit drink or *pupusas.* **Caffe Goldivar** just south of the *parque* serves inexpensive breakfasts, *comida corriente,* and decent coffee in a cafeteria-style atmosphere.

On the highway to San Pedro, at Km 118, is possibly the best deli-supermarket in Honduras, **Granja d'Elia,** tel. 73-2414. All sorts of quality vegetables, meats, cheeses, and other goodies are available daily until 8 p.m.

Cine Aeropuerto on the *parque* shows movies nightly.

Services

Hondutel on the *parque* is open daily 5:30 a.m.-9 p.m., and receives faxes at tel. 73-2008. Right next door is Correos, with Express Mail Service available. Tourist cards can be renewed hassle-free at the migration office, just off the *parque.*

Banco de Occidente and Banco Atlántida will change dollars and traveler's checks.

Getting There and Away

Siguatepeque is 125 km from San Pedro and 117 km from Tegucigalpa, with well-maintained highway in both directions. Toward Tegucigalpa the winding stretch of highway down into the Comayagua Valley is called "Cuesta La Virgen." The easiest way to get to San Pedro or Tegucigalpa is to take a US 40-cent taxi ride out to the highway and catch the next bus that comes by in your direction. If you don't feel like waiting on the highway however, **Empresas Unidas,** tel. 73-2149, runs buses to Tegucigalpa from the plaza every two hours between 4 a.m. and 4 p.m.; US$1, a little over two hours.

To La Esperanza, take a US 80-cent taxi ride to the highway turnoff, a couple of kilometers from Siguatepeque toward San Pedro, where buses leave roughly every two hours, charging US$1 for the 90-minute ride. If there are no buses around just stick out your thumb. The paved road to La Esperanza is 67 km, dropping down into the Otoro (upper Ulúa) Valley, past the town of Jesús de Otoro, and climbing back up into the mountains of Opalaca to La Esperanza.

COMAYAGUA

INTRODUCTION

Comayagua, Honduras's original capital city, is on the northwestern edge of the broad Valle de Comayagua, the largest flat region in central-western Honduras. The 390-square-kilometer valley lies roughly equidistant between the Caribbean and Pacific coasts. Comayagua (pop. 70,600) lies at the junction of the Río Chiquito and the Río Humuya.

Because it was long the country's political and administrative center, Comayagua has a wealth of colonial monuments. Just outside of town, in the middle of the valley, is the Enrique Soto Cano Air Force Base, better known as Palmerola, used by the U.S. military.

History

The fertile Valle de Comayagua attracted settlers long before the Spanish arrived in the region in 1537. For centuries, the valley had been a bastion of the Lenca, but during the years before Columbus, Nahuatl-speaking migrants from central Mexico moved into the region, apparently coexisting peacefully with the original inhabitants. The attractions of the area were obvious, and are further illustrated through the name Comayagua, which is thought to mean "abundance of food" in Maya.

It's unclear when the first conquistadores passed through the valley, but Alonso de Cáceres founded Santa María de Comayagua on 7 December 1537, under orders from Francisco Montejo. The first city was destroyed shortly thereafter by Indians in the region, who rose with Lempira in revolt against the Spaniards. In fact, the valley was the last bastion of Indian rebellion to be put down, holding out until the first months of 1539.

Comayagua was reestablished the same year, and by 1557 the crown recognized it as a city. Not long after, veins of silver were found nearby, further encouraging Spaniards to settle there. By 1573 Comayagua was the most important city in the province, surpassing Gracias a Dios. It was made the administrative capital, which it remained through the rest of the colonial period.

Comayagua was a center for intrigue and a target for attack during the wars of independence and Central American union. It was pillaged and burned several times in the mid-19th century, most notably in 1837 by Guatemalan general José Justo Milla. When Honduras was established as an independent country, Comayagua was declared the capital. The rise of Tegucigalpa in the late 19th century as a center for gold and silver production led to a bitter rivalry between the two cities, which was finally settled in 1880 when President Marco Aurelio Soto changed the seat of government to Tegucigalpa.

Since then—a black day for every Comayagua resident—the city slid into a sort of genteel poverty, trying to retain the pretensions of a capital but without the economic or political power base. These days Comayagua mostly survives on the valley's agriculture and cattle industries, as well as on money derived from the nearby Palmerola Air Force Base. The U.S. military presence in town is quite noticeable to anyone who sticks around for a couple of days, although the future of the Palmerola base is uncertain. Several ex-military personnel operate businesses in town.

Orientation

Downtown Comayagua is set a couple of kilometers off the San Pedro-Tegucigalpa highway, with the "Boulevard" running between. Watch out for your axle—at last report the Boulevard was one of the most potholed stretches of road in Honduras.

Comayagua is centered around the broad downtown square (Parque Central), with a kiosk in the middle and many benches. One block north is the shady **Plaza San Francisco,** with concrete benches, and two blocks south is the smaller **Plaza La Merced.** Walking to the main sights in town is no problem, but a taxi might be desired to get out to the highway or to the bus stations. Palmerola Air Force Base is a couple of kilometers south of Comayagua on the south side of the highway toward Tegucigalpa.

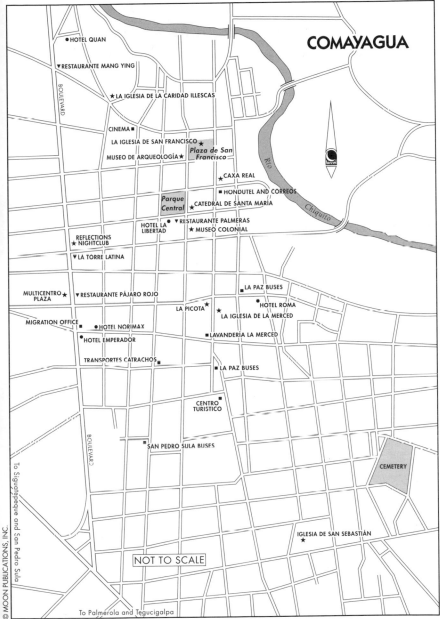

COMAYAGUA

- HOTEL QUAN
- ▼ RESTAURANTE MANG YING
- ★ LA IGLESIA DE LA CARIDAD ILLESCAS

BOULEVARD

- CINEMA ■
- LA IGLESIA DE SAN FRANCISCO ★
- MUSEO DE ARQUEOLOGÍA ★

Plaza de San Francisco

Río

- ★ CAXA REAL
- ■ HONDUTEL AND CORREOS

Parque Central

- ★ CATEDRAL DE SANTA MARÍA
- HOTEL LA ● ▼ RESTAURANTE PALMERAS
- LIBERTAD ★ MUSEO COLONIAL

Chiquito

- REFLECTIONS
- ★ NIGHTCLUB
- ▼ LA TORRE LATINA

- MULTICENTRO ★
- PLAZA
- ▼ RESTAURANTE PÁJARO ROJO
- ★ LA PAZ BUSES

- LA PICOTA ★
- ★ HOTEL ROMA
- LA IGLESIA DE LA MERCED

- MIGRATION OFFICE
- ● HOTEL NORIMAX
- ● HOTEL EMPERADOR
- ■ LAVANDERÍA LA MERCED

- TRANSPORTES CATRACHOS ■
- ■ LA PAZ BUSES

- CENTRO
- TURISTICO ■

BOULEVARD

- ■ SAN PEDRO SULA BUSES

CEMETERY

NOT TO SCALE

- IGLESIA DE SAN SEBASTIÁN
- ★

To Siguatepeque and San Pedro Sula

© MOON PUBLICATIONS, INC.

To Palmerola and Tegucigalpa

SIGHTS

As the capital of Honduras for over 300 years, and the religious seat of the colony under Spanish rule, many colonial buildings still stand in Comayagua, though many are in sorry states of disrepair. All are located within walking distance of the square.

Catedral de Santa María

The imposing Catedral de Santa María, also known as La Iglesia de la Inmaculada Concepción, was built on the site of the original Comayagua plaza over the course of more than a century, between 1580 and 1708. The prolonged construction stemmed from problems obtaining funds and the need to rebuild the foundation in the late 17th century.

The church's facade is particularly elaborate, decorated with sculpted columns and eight statues set in niches. The one tower, built in 1650, holds one of the oldest known clocks in the world. The Reloj Arabe, as it is known, was made around 1100 and graced the side of La Alhambra in Granada, Spain, before it was donated to Comayagua by King Felipe II.

Inside the cathedral are three *retablos* in baroque style, with sculptures by Andrés y Francisco de Ocampo dating from the 1630s. The cathedral is normally closed from 11:30 a.m. to 2 p.m., and shuts its doors for the day at 4 p.m.

Museo Colonial

A block south of the Catedral is the **Museo Colonial,** with an eclectic collection of religious art from Comayagua's five churches, including paintings, chalices, statues, vestments, old documents, and an impressive wooden confessional. Many of the pieces were brought to the museum out of fear they would be stolen from the churches, a growing problem in recent years. Open Mon.-Sat. 9:30-11:30 a.m. and 2-5 p.m., Sunday 10 a.m.-noon and 2-5 p.m.; entrance US 25 cents.

Museo de Arqueología; La Iglesia de San Francisco

One block north of the square is the Museo de Arqueología, on one side of the Plaza San Francisco, in a building that was Honduras's seat of

government for a short time in the 19th century. Many of the displays relate to digs made in the area of El Cajón dam, before the region was submerged by water. The museum is not extensive, but the collection of jade art, jewelry, pottery, and copies of petroglyph art are well worth a look. Labels are in Spanish only. US$1 entrance for foreigners, US 15 cents for Hondurans; open Wed.-Fri. 8 a.m.-noon and 1-4 p.m., Sat.-Sun. 9 a.m.-noon and 1-4 p.m.

Next to the museum is the shady Plaza San Francisco, with the Iglesia de San Francisco on the north side. The church, originally called La Iglesia de San Antonio, was built in 1574 in a simple style, and rebuilt completely between 1610 and 1620. An earthquake in 1784 badly damaged the structure, and the roof collapsed in 1806. Three years later another quake knocked down the bell tower. A second reconstruction was completed in 1819.

The church has an ornate carved *retablo* and a gory statue of Christ. Hours are variable— ask around for the caretaker to let you in if it's closed. He may let you go up into the three-story bell tower, but watch out for the rotten wood planks if you go up!

Caxa Real

Around the corner from the Plaza de San Francisco are the crumbling remnants of the colonial Caxa Real, or tax-collection house, built between 1739 and 1741. Destroyed by the earthquake in 1809, only part of the front of the building remains standing. The inscription above the door states the building was constructed under direction of Lt. Col. Don Francisco de Parga, under orders of Royal Field Marshal Don Pedro de Rivera

---

IF YOU ONLY HAVE ONE DAY IN COMAYAGUA, DON'T MISS:

- Catedral de Santa María, to see the ornate carved facade, ornate altar, and 800-year-old clock
- Museo Colonial, for the display of religious art from several Comayagua churches
- Museo Regional de Arqueología, for a short tour of prehistoric art in central Honduras
- Iglesia de La Merced, built in 1550

the remnants of the Caxa Real

Villalón, to serve as the Royal Treasury for King Felipe and Queen Isabel.

Iglesia de La Merced
Comayagua's first cathedral, La Merced was built in 1550 on the reputed site of the first Mass spoken in the valley. Its baroque facade possibly dates from the early years of the 18th century. Many of the paintings and sculptures in the church date back to the 16th century.

Across the street there's a small square with a pillar in the center, known locally as **La Picota.** It was erected in 1820 in honor of the liberal Spanish Constitution of 1812.

Iglesia de San Sebastián
Some 10 blocks south of the square stands Iglesia de San Sebastián, built in 1581 as a site for blacks and Indians in the city to pray. The towers were added in later years, and rebuilt in 1957 in a rather unattractive style. Guatemalan troops used the church as a barracks when the city was invaded in 1837. The church's architecture is generally fairly elemental, but the *retablo* inside, crafted by Blas de Mesa, is worth admiring. The remains of Honduran president and general José Trinidad Cabañas are buried under the church floor, marked by a engraved stone.

Iglesia de La Caridad Illescas
Several blocks northeast of the square, La Caridad was also intended during the colonial era for the *mestizo,* black, and Indian population who lived in the neighborhood. Construction on the church began in 1629. Of the several religious artworks within, of particular note is the gold- and silver-lined *retablo* dedicated to Santa Lucía.

RECREATION

If you're sweaty after walking around to the churches and museums, you could take a dip in the pool at **Centro Turistico Comayagua,** six blocks southeast of the square. Open Tues.-Sun. 10 a.m.-10 p.m., the pool is not huge but big enough for a few strokes. The pool and adjoining bar/restaurant are usually crowded on weekends.

ACCOMMODATIONS

Budget
Centrally located right on the square, **Hotel La Libertad** is popular with backpackers looking for a cheap bed. Unfortunately, the rooms are not too clean, many of the mattresses are in terrible shape, and the water supply is irregular.

Behind La Merced church, **Hotel Roma,** tel. 72-1702, has simple, clean rooms for US$3 s or US$4 d with communal bathroom, US$6 d with private bath. **Hotel Emperador,** across from the Norimax, tel. 72-0331, has unexceptional rooms for US$5 s or d with one large bed and bathroom, US$7 d with two beds. TV and a/c are available for a few dollars more.

Midrange

Hotel Quan, tel. 72-0070, could be classified either as budget or midrange, as it has rooms ranging from US$3.50 s or US$6 d with shared bath to US$13 s or US$16 d for a/c, refrigerator, TV, and hot water. The hotel, popular with visiting Americans, is kept spotlessly clean, the management is very helpful, and the neighborhood northwest of downtown near La Iglesia de La Caridad is quiet.

Just off the Boulevard, across from Hotel Emperador, is **Hotel Norimax,** tel. 72-1210, a three-story building with clean rooms for US$12 d with TV and fan, US$14 d with a/c. No singles available. The front-facing rooms have balconies, but the noise from the buses pulling past makes it worth requesting a room in the back.

FOOD AND ENTERTAINMENT

Inexpensive

Finding decent, inexpensive food in Comayagua can be a bit of a chore. One of the better places downtown is **Restaurante Palmeras,** a couple of doors down from Hotel La Libertad on the square, with low-priced breakfasts, *comida corriente, baleadas,* and other munchies.

Midrange

Restaurante Pájaro Rojo, on the Boulevard, tel. 72-0690, has a good selection of well-cooked Honduran standards such as *pinchos,* steaks, and several seafood dishes for US$3-6 per meal, with patio seating. Open Tues.-Sat. 11 a.m.-10 p.m., Sunday 11 a.m.-9:30 p.m.

For a taste of Americana, check out **Dave's Burgers,** on the highway toward Tegucigalpa not far past the gas stations. The fishburgers are excellent, though not huge so you may want two, and the burgers, club sandwiches, and BLTs aren't bad either; US$2-3 per sandwich. The place, run by an American ex-serviceman, is open Tues.-Thurs. noon-10 p.m., Fri.-Sat. noon-11 p.m., and Sunday noon-8 p.m.

Restaurante Mang Ying, on the Boulevard near Hotel Quan, tel. 72-0567, serves up a heaping plate of chop suey, chow mein, and other dishes at reasonable prices. Open daily 9:30 a.m.-10 p.m., the restaurant is popular with American military personnel serving at Palmerola.

Another expatriate-owned eatery is **Betsy's Sweet Shop,** in the MultiCentro Plaza on the Boulevard, which sells brownies, cheesecake, cinnamon rolls, and deli sandwiches, as well as a selection of handicrafts. Open Mon.-Sat. 10 a.m.-7 p.m.

Expensive

Generally regarded as the classiest place in town, **La Torre Latina,** on the Boulevard next to Reflections Nightclub, tel. 72-1193, is a quiet, small restaurant serving shrimp, lobster, steaks, chicken cordon bleu, and much else for US$5-10 per plate. Open Mon.-Sat. 11 a.m.-3 p.m. and 5-11 p.m.; neat dress recommended.

Entertainment

Reflections Nightclub on the Boulevard, owned by an American ex-serviceman, attracts a mixed crowd of locals and military personnel dancing to the DJ music. Unlike some of the other clubs in town, Reflections is considered safe and relatively violence-free. Open Wed.-Sat. 10 p.m.-4 a.m.

INFORMATION AND SERVICES

Three and a half blocks south of the square is **New Souvenirs,** tel. 72-1071, with *artesanías* from Honduras, Guatemala, and Nicaragua, including carvings, carpets, pottery, stone sculpture, and some paintings. Open daily 7:30 a.m.-5 p.m. The market district is along the two main streets leaving the square to the south, extending for several blocks.

Hondutel is behind the Cathedral, open daily 7 a.m.-9 p.m. Next door is Correos, with EMS fast-mail service available. The migration office is opposite Hotel Emperador, just off the Boulevard.

COMAYAGUA USEFUL TELEPHONE NUMBERS

Police: 72-0080, 72-0307, 72-0053, or dial 199
Fire Department: 72-0091, or dial 198
Cruz Roja Ambulance: 72-0091, or dial 195

Bancahsa, Banco de Occidente, Banco Atlántida, and others will exchange dollars or traveler's checks.

Lavandería La Merced, a block south of La Merced church on the opposite side of the street, is open Mon.-Sat. 8 a.m.-5:30 p.m., and charges US$1.20 per load wash and dry.

For general medical problems, **Centro Médico San Rafael,** tel. 72-0068, has a competent doctor and won't charge too much. Open 24 hours.

GETTING THERE AND AWAY

Bus
Buses to **Tegucigalpa** are offered by Transportes Catrachos, five blocks south of the square, tel. 72-0260. The buses run every half hour between 5 a.m. and 5:30 p.m.; US$1, 90 minutes. Buses to **San Pedro** leave from two blocks farther south, three times daily at 4:45 a.m., 6:45 a.m., and 12:45 p.m.; US$1.00, three hours. For more informatiion call 72-1208. Alternatively, you can take a taxi out to the gas stations at the highway and flag down a bus headed in either direction with minimum hassle.

Buses to **La Paz** leave frequently between 7 a.m. and 6 p.m. from two stops near La Merced church; US 30 cents, 30 minutes.

Car
From Comayagua, the highway west to Siguatepeque (32 km) and San Pedro Sula (160 km) and east to Tegucigalpa (85 km) is kept in good condition all year. In either direction, the road ascends steeply into the mountains ringing the Comayagua Valley.

NEAR COMAYAGUA

Parque Nacional Montaña de Comayagua
Only seven km from Comayagua is the edge of Parque Nacional Montaña de Comayagua, covering 18,000 hectares, of which 6,380 hectares are core zone. The highest point in the park is **El Portillo,** 2,407 meters. The forest is not one of the country's finest, certainly noth-

ing compared to Celaque or Sierra de Agalta, but sizable patches of cloud forest remain, populated by quetzals, toucans, eagles, deer, monkeys, and a few pumas.

You can hike into the park from the villages of **Río Blanco** and **Río Negro,** both reached via dirt road from **San Jeronimo,** 12 km from Comayagua by dirt road. Off the road to La Libertad, you can also enter through **Tres Pinos** or **Zona Helada.**

The **Cohdefor office** in Comayagua has little information on the park, but there is a useful full-size topographical map on the wall. Cohdefor workers may be able to help you get into the park or suggest guides. To get to the office, take the highway toward San Pedro Sula, and keep an eye out for a dirt road turning southwest, marked by a Cohdefor sign. Best to take a taxi from town.

Topographical maps covering the park are 1:50,000 Comayagua 2659 II and Agalteca 2759 III.

Enrique Cano Soto Air Force Base (Palmerola)
For much of the 1980s, Palmerola was essentially a U.S. military enclave, from where the Contra war against the Sandinista government in Nicaragua was directed. More recently, the base has been used in the war against drugs.

Growing pressure from Honduran citizens and politicians against U.S. presence has led to a reduction in the number of personnel at the base. In 1995 over 2,000 U.S. military were housed here; that number dropped to 450 by 1996. The base is now officially under the Honduran flag. Negotiations are underway to lease Palmerola to the U.S. on a long-term basis.

Tenempua
In the hills above Comayagua on the road to Tegucigalpa are the ruins of Tenempua, thought to have been built originally before the time of Christ, and used by the Lenca in their war against the Spanish. The site is on an imposing promontory on the north side of the highway, reached by trail. Remnants of walls and a ball court are visible, and petroglyphs can be found in the area.

LA PAZ AND VICINITY

The capital of the department of the same name, La Paz has little to interest the casual traveler. However, located on the southern edge of the Comayagua Valley, it's a good stop-off point for those interested in visiting the mountain country south toward the Salvadoran border. Near La Paz are the ruins of **Yarula,** believed to be one of the oldest ruins sites in Honduras. Only a few mounds are visible.

Practicalities
One block from the market is **Hotel y Restaurante Alis,** tel. 74-2125, with decent accommodations and food. Rooms cost US$3.50 d, US$6 d with bathroom. **Merendero Criollos,** just off the square, has inexpensive *comida corriente* and snacks.

Bancahsa and Banco Atlántida will both change dollars but not traveler's checks.

Six buses daily leave to **Marcala** between 6:30 a.m. and 3:45 p.m.; US 80 cents, two hours, paved road. To **Guajiquiro,** one bus leaves daily at noon, takes the Marcala road for a half hour, then turns into the hills for another bumpy two and a half hours. Buses to **Comayagua** leave all day until late afternoon; US 30 cents, 30 minutes. All buses leave several blocks north of the square, between the market and the soldier statue.

San Pedro de Tutule and Guajiquiro
Roughly 20 km from La Paz, set two km off the highway, is the town of San Pedro de Tutule, a market town for the villages in the surrounding mountains. San Pedro de Tutule is one of the last bastions of pure Lenca Indians in the country, along with the region around La Esperanza.

High in the mountains above Tutule, about two hours by rough dirt road, is the Lenca village of Guajiquiro. From here you can hike up into the **Reserva Biológica Guajiquiro,** covering 67 square kilometers of pine and cloud forest, interspersed with patches of farmland. The highest part of the reserve rests on a high mesa, with several small peaks of about 2,200 meters.

Topographical maps covering the reserve are 1:50,000 Opatoro 2658 III and San Pedro de Tutule 2658 IV.

Toward El Salvador
Not far from the El Salvador border is an impressive set of petroglyphs. To visit them, take a bus to Santa Elena, then continue by truck to the village of Azacualpa. From here it's two and a half hours by trail to the site, with a guide. Ask for the *"piedras pintadas."*

BOB RACE

BOB RACE

TEGUCIGALPA AND VICINITY

TEGUCIGALPA

INTRODUCTION

Honduras's capital, a city of somewhere between 700,000 and one million people, depending on who you ask, occupies a high mountain valley around 1,000 meters above sea level. The Río Choluteca runs right down the middle of it. The valley is ringed by mountains, with only a narrow valley to the north allowing the Río Choluteca to continue on its course to the Pacific.

Opinions of Tegucigalpa—called "Teguc" (Tegoose) by locals—vary wildly. Some visitors are uninspired and can't wait to catch the next bus out of town, while others are charmed by the mix of colonial and modern buildings, the mountain setting, and relaxed atmosphere. Certainly visitors have no problem finding places and sites to see, including several colonial churches, three museums, a large market area, and plenty of handicraft stores, all in the downtown area. In the surrounding hills are the colonial mining villages of Santa Lucía, Valle de Ángeles, and Ojojona, which make for great day-trips. And Parque Nacional La Tigra, just a dozen kilometers from the city, has a well-developed network of trails through its cloud forest.

Because of its altitude, Tegucigalpa has a pleasant climate year-round, ranging from pleasantly warm during the day to cool at night. The mean annual temperature is 28° C, although it can get considerably cooler during the rainy season.

History
Both archaeological work and historical records suggest the Tegucigalpa Valley was not a major population center, at least in the years shortly before the Spanish conquest. It's postulated that the mainly Lenca population was dependent on the larger settlements in the nearby Comayagua Valley. Many believe the city's name derives from the Lenca words meaning "land of silver," but, as the Lenca had no interest in silver and are not likely to have named a place because of it, others have suggested "place of the painted rocks" and "place where the men meet." The ending "galpa," common in the region, means "place" or "land."

Exactly when the Spanish first came into the area is unclear. In the early 1540s at the latest, Alonso de Cáceres is likely to have passed through the region on his way to Olancho, under orders from Francisco Montejo, but he made no report on the valley. According to one Hon-

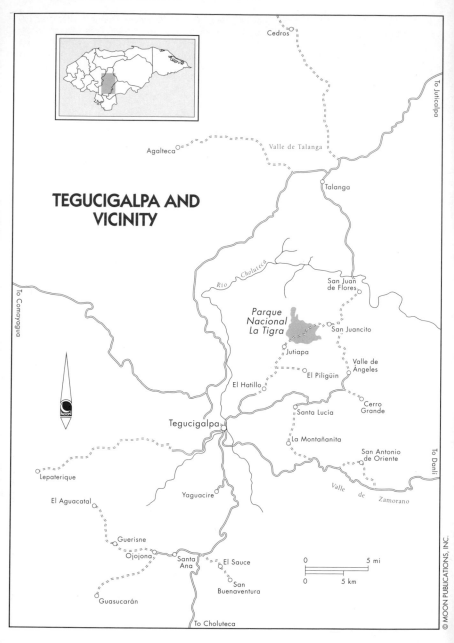

TEGUCIGALPA AND VICINITY

Cedros

To Juticalpa

Agalteca

Valle de Talanga

Talanga

To Comayagua

Río Choluteca

San Juan de Flores

Parque Nacional La Tigra

San Juancito

Jutiapa

Valle de Ángeles

El Piligüin

El Hatillo

Cerro Grande

Santa Lucía

Tegucigalpa

La Montañanita

San Antonio de Oriente

To Danlí

Lepaterique

Yaguacire

Valle de Zamorano

El Aguacatal

Guerisne

Ojojona

Santa Ana

El Sauce

San Buenaventura

Guasucarán

To Choluteca

0   5 mi

0   5 km

duran historian, it's probable that residents of Comayagua, who were combing the new colony for precious metals, found the first veins of silver near Santa Lucía by 1560. An official report to the Spanish authorities dated 1589 states silver was found in Tegucigalpa 12 to 15 years prior. According to local legend, the first strike was made on 29 September, Saint Michael's day; hence, San Miguel is the city's patron saint.

Whatever the exact date, by the late 16th century miners were building houses and small mine operations along the Río Choluteca and in the hills above. Tegucigalpa had no formal founding, like Comayagua, Gracias, or Trujillo, but grew haphazardly, by chance, and remained a relatively small settlement of dispersed houses connnected by trails for the first years of its existence. The original name for the settlement was Real de Minas de San Miguel de Tegucigalpa, but by 1768 the mines were producing enough wealth to merit the title "Villa."

By the end of the colonial period the city's mineral wealth allowed it to eclipse Comayagua in economic importance. Because of the rivalry between the two cities, the legislature of the short-lived Central American Republic alternated between the two, and in 1880 Pres. Marcos Aurelio Soto moved the capital definitively to Tegucigalpa. The story goes Soto made the move out of anger toward the Comayagua aristocracy for snubbing his Indian wife, but more likely he was following his Liberal principles by locating the government where the economy was strongest.

In the early 20th century Honduras's economic expansion was centered on the north coast, and the lack of a cross-country railroad left Tegucigalpa behind in development. The mines at La Rosario provided some stimulus, but most of the profits went to New York rather than Tegucigalpa. To this day Tegucigalpa has no major industry to speak of, and survives mainly on the government and a small financial community. In 1932 the Distrito Central was created, bringing neighboring Comayagüela and Tegucigalpa under a unified government.

Orientation

Downtown Tegucigalpa is centered around the *parque central,* with the Parroquia de San Miguel Arcángel (also known simply as the Catedral) on

PATRONATOS: GETTING BY IN THE SLUMS

Like almost all cities in Latin America, Tegucigalpa has grown at an alarming rate over the past several decades, from about 200,000 people in 1950 to somewhere close to a million today. As any visitor to Tegucigalpa quickly notices, most of these newcomers have settled in the mountains ringing the city, in shanty villages crawling up the hillsides from the valley floor. Immigrants simply go to the edge of the existing city and build a home out of cardboard or tin, later improving with wood or cement blocks when they've got the money. Basic social services have followed this explosive, unplanned growth at a much slower pace. As the Library of Congress's Area Handbook states matter-of-factly, "For the vast majority of Tegucigalpa's urban population, living conditions are dismal." Water, sewage systems, electricity, telephone lines, bus routes, and paved roads, not to mention health care and schools—all have been long in coming to the barrios. Most residents would say these services wouldn't have come at all were it not for the pressure put on the government by the *patronatos.*

An example of Hondurans' propensity and ability to organize themselves collectively, the *patronatos* have their origin in religious festivals. Each barrio has traditionally had its own patron saint, and committees, called *patronatos,* were formed among residents to help organize and pay for the fiesta on their saint's day. When people realized they would have to fight to get any services from the government, the *patronatos* took on the task, collecting donations, organizing demonstrations, and meeting with officials. The *patronatos* are invariably dominated by women, and this has added to their effectiveness. Often the groups shame government bureaucrats into fulfilling their demands. One *patronato* member tells the story of how a group of 75 women tore down a fence around land they wanted to use to build a health center, and then went downtown to confront the official responsible for putting up the fence. After much yelling, he finally agreed to let them use the land, saying, "What can you do with these women who talk like battleships?"

one side and many of the city's main business-es and government buildings in the surrounding blocks. Most of the sites of interest to tourists are in walking distance of downtown. Because of the city's broken geography and haphazard construction over the centuries, Tegucigalpa does not have an ordered street plan and can be a bit confusing to navigate at first, but this only adds to the city's charm.

Colonia Palmira, just east of downtown, is one of the more upscale neighborhoods in Tegucigalpa. Here you'll find many of the city's high-priced hotels and nicer restaurants. Further east continue Avenida La Paz and Boulevard Morazán, two major parallel avenues. Partway up Avenida La Paz is the U.S. Embassy. A massive building, it's frequently used as a reference point in giving directions. Southeast of downtown extends Avenida Juan Pablo II, where many discos are found, and Boulevard Suyapa, which leads to the Basilica de Suyapa and the National University.

Across the Río Choluteca from downtown is Comayagüela, a noisier and poorer sister city to Tegucigalpa. The main city market and all of the long-distance bus stations are in Comayagüela. Some travelers may find it convenient and inexpensive to stay in Comayagüela, but take care walking around at night.

Getting Around

The main sights downtown can easily be covered on foot, but buses or taxis are needed to get to many of the bus stations and far-flung parts of the city. Taxis in Tegucigalpa are more expensive than in smaller towns, usually charging US$1.50-3 around town, depending on where

A STATUE OF MORAZÁN?

In the center of the square in Tegucigalpa is a statue that may not be what it seems. Apparently sometime around the turn of the century, a delegation of Honduran congressmen were sent to Paris to commission a statue of national hero Francisco Morazán. Unfortunately, when they arrived in Paris, they wound up spending most of the commission money enjoying the pleasures of that great European capital. At the last minute, realizing their bind, they found in an art store a used statue of Ney, one of Napolean's famous generals. Deciding no one in Honduras would be the wiser, they had a new plaque inscribed for Ney's statue, and presto! It's Morazán. Or, at least, so goes a favorite though possibly apocryphal story. More recently a Honduran historian claims to have unearthed a receipt in the French National Archives from a Parisian sculptor contracting him to make a statue of Morazán. Who's right? We'll probably never know.

you're going, or US$4 out to the airport. One call-ahead taxi service is **Cotatyh,** tel. 33-7318, which can take you out to the airport, on city tours, or up to Valle de Ángeles or Santa Lucía.

Colectivo **taxis,** which run set routes, are inexpensive, but figuring out which taxis go where can be a nightmare. One useful *colectivo* drives between Puente La Isla near the stadium out to Colonia Kennedy for US 25 cents.

Most buses cross the city from one end of Comayagüela to the far end of Tegucigalpa, passing

TEGUCIGALPA HIGHLIGHTS

If you only have one day to tour Tegucigalpa, don't miss:
• The Parque Central and the Cathedral, to people-watch and admire colonial religious art
• The Galería Nacional de Arte, to see one of the finest art collections in Central America
• La Villa Roy, for a brief tour of the nation's archaeology and anthropology
• Parque La Leona, for views over the city and a visit to the colonial Buenos Aires neighborhood

If you have time for day-trips, consider:
• Hiking in La Tigra cloud forest and to the Rosario mines
• Shopping for handicrafts at Valle de Ángeles
• Visiting the colonial village of Ojojona and the nearby petroglyphs at El Sauce

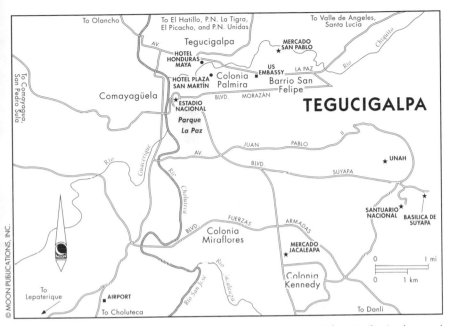

right by the *parque central*, and charge US 10 cents. Two useful buses are the 21 Tiloarque-La Sosa, which runs from Mercado Mayoreo up 6 Avenida in Comayagüela, through downtown, and out Avenida La Paz to where the Valle de Ángeles and Santa Lucía buses leave, and the 32, which goes from Comayagüela out Boulevard Suyapa to the National University.

If at all possible, avoid driving in Tegucigalpa, as the traffic is hideous. Armed with a decent map the city is not all that difficult to navigate, but the endless wait, especially during rush hour, can be enough to give you an ulcer.

SIGHTS

Parque Central

Tegucigalpa's downtown square is a great place to hang out, relax, and people-watch. It's invariably full of people walking around, buying newspapers, selling odds and ends, or just hanging out. Beware of sitting under the trees as you may find yourself the object of target practice from the pigeons above.

A *peatonal* (pedestrian street) extends several blocks west of the square and is lined with shops, restaurants, street vendors, and moneychangers.

Parroquia de San Miguel Arcángel

Otherwise known as the Catedral, the Parroquia was built between 1765 and 1782 on the site of a simpler wooden church, and is a fine example of late colonial architecture. Although the design is relatively simple, the vaulted ceiling and domed altar are impressive. The gold-and-silver altarpiece sculpted by Guatemalan artist Vicente Gálvez is incredibly intricate. Presiding over the altar is a statue of San Miguel, the patron saint of Tegucigalpa. Several sculptures and paintings decorate the interior, including ones by famed colonial artist José Miguel Gómez.

The Catedral was damaged so badly in the earthquake of 1808 it was practically abandoned for almost 30 years before being reinforced. It was damaged again during the 1975 earthquake that struck Guatemala.

La Merced and Galeria Nacional de Arte

A block south of the square is La Iglesia de La

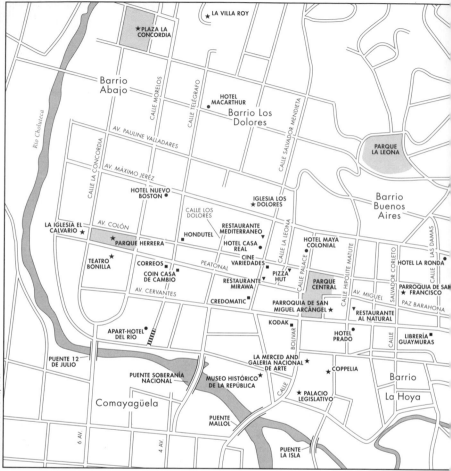

Merced, built in the mid-18th century and featuring a beautiful gilded altarpiece flanked by two smaller *retablos*. The building next door to the church, built in 1654, was originally a convent, then in 1847 became the National University. In 1996 the building changed again, this time into the Galería Nacional de Arte, tel. 37-9884, arguably the finest art gallery in Central America.

The gallery traces the evolution of Honduran art, beginning downstairs with rooms dedicated to prehistoric pictographs and petroglyphs, stone and ceramic art from the Mayan era, and a stunning collection of colonial paintings, sculptures, and gold and silver religious art. The pieces were all chosen for their visual beauty rather than historical importance. Upstairs, several rooms contain paintings from classic Honduran artists Pablo Zelaya Sierra, Carlos Zuñiga Figueroa, and José Antonio Velásquez, as well as lesser-known painters and sculptors such as Eziquiel Padilla, Dante Lazzaroni, Arturo López Rodezno, and Anibel Cruz.

DOWNTOWN TEGUCIGALPA

CALLE DIONISIO GUTIÉRREZ

TAURO/ARIES ■

HOTEL
GRANADA III ●   HOTEL
                    GRANADA II
GRATION   LA GRAN
                       MURALLA
CALLE FINLAY
        HOTEL ●
        GRANADA I   ■ MERCADO   AV. JUAN GUTEMBERG
                       SAN MIGUEL ▼ RESTAURANTE
AKESPEARE   NANKING
BOOKS   ▼ PANCHO'S

        CAFÉ ▼
        PARADISO

AV. PLAZUELA

        ● ALONDRA

        Barrio
        San
        Rafael

0   250 yds

0   250m

For such a small, economically deprived country, Honduras has produced an unusual number of fine visual artists, and the museum is an excellent tour of the country's artistic history. The artwork is laid out tastefully, with good lighting, and in logical progression. Don't miss this museum. It's open Tues.-Sat. 10 a.m.-4:30 p.m., Sunday 10 a.m.-2 p.m.; US$1 entrance fee.

Next to the church and art gallery is the Palacio Legislativo, or National Congress. It's known laconically by locals as El Sapo ("the frog") be-

cause the bizarre architecture makes it seem as though the building is about to hop away.

Museo Histórico de la República

A block west of the Congress building is the Museo Histórico de la República, housed in the old Presidential Palace. The building, designed by Italian architect Augusto Bressani, took 10 years to build due to the political instability in Honduras at the turn of the 20th century. It served as the office and home of the president from 1916 to 1992, when Rafael Callejas declared it a museum and moved his offices to Colonia Miraflores.

The museum is great for those interested in Honduran history, but is otherwise not particularly gripping. Many of the displays consist of photos or drawings of famous personages accompanied by long descriptions in Spanish of their importance to Honduran history. Rooms are dedicated to, in order, Independence, Central American Federation, the Conservative Reaction (1838-76), Liberal Reform (1876-1910), Consolidation of the Nation (1932-1949), and modern history. Unsurprisingly, there is little information on the importance of Honduras's military or the U.S. government in the recent Honduran history display.

On the first floor is a computer database on Honduran history, in Spanish; upstairs you'll find the presidential dining room and a display of Honduran artwork.

The museum is open Wed.-Sun. 8:30 a.m.-noon and 1-4 p.m., and costs US$2 for foreigners, US$1 for Hondurans, children under seven admitted free. As of mid-1997 the museum was closed for remodeling, and expected to reopen by early 1998.

Parroquia de San Francisco

Facing a small, shady park three blocks east of the square is the oldest extant church in the city, first built in 1592 and reconstructed in 1740. Inside the church are a gilded altarpiece and several colonial-era religious paintings. The building next door, formerly the Franciscan monastery, is now used by the Army.

Parque Herrera and Teatro Bonilla

Six blocks west of the square is the shady, attractive Parque Herrera, in front of which stands the Teatro Nacional Manuel Bonilla, built in 1915.

La Villa Roy

THE INSTITUTO HONDUREÑO DE ANTROPOLOGÍA E HISTORIA

The facade is nothing spectacular, but the interior is exquisite, designed in the style of the famed Athenée of Paris. The theater seats 600 in rows on the ground floor and in the compartments above. For information about upcoming performances, ask at the box office or call 22-4366.

On the west side of the park is **La Iglesia El Calvario,** dating from the mid-18th century and housing several *retablos* and an image of the Virgen de la Soledad.

Iglesia Los Dolores

Dominating a large square filled with vendors, Los Dolores is a large, bright white church with a fairly plain facade but featuring several attractive pieces of religious art inside, including relief paintings of the stations of the cross, an ornate altar, and a painted dome. The church, built in 1732, is several blocks northwest of the downtown square.

La Villa Roy

La Villa Roy was donated to the public by the wife of ex-president Julio Lozano Diaz in 1974, and now houses the **Museo Nacional de Honduras,** one of the most interesting and comprehensive historical museums in the country.

The main rooms cover Honduran anthropology, ethnology, prehistoric archaeology, the era of contact with the Spanish, and the colonial era. The ethnology display is particularly interesting, offering descriptions of the lifestyle and traditions of Honduras's ethnic groups.

Normal hours are Wed.-Sun. 8:30 a.m.-3:30 p.m.; admission US$1 for Central Americans, US$2 for others. For more information call 22-0079, ext. 722.

Just below the museum, on the way back into downtown, is the small **Plaza La Concordia,** featuring several replicas of Mayan sculptures.

Parque La Leona

Set among the winding cobblestone streets and colonial houses of the picturesque Buenos Aires neighborhood, Parque La Leona makes a pleasant spot to take a rest and admire the views over downtown and the valley. The park is a 15-minute walk from the square up a steep hill.

Parque La Paz

Atop Juana Laínez hill in the center of Tegucigalpa, near the National Stadium, is Parque La Paz, commemorating the peace treaty ending the so-called "Soccer War" between El Salvador and Honduras in 1969. The road winding up to the top starts next to the fire station behind the stadium. On top is a stone monument with a huge flag perpetually fluttering in the breeze, surrounded by trees which limit the views somewhat. The only way up if you don't have a car is on foot or in a taxi.

Basilica de Suyapa and Santuario Nacional

Honduras's patron saint, La Virgen de Suyapa, is venerated in a simple white plaster chapel set on a small square on the eastern outskirts of

Tegucigalpa, near the National University (Universidad Nacional Autonoma de Honduras, UNAH). The Basilica de Suyapa, built in 1749, houses the tiny, six-centimeter-tall statue of the virgin in a wooden case behind the altar. According to legend, the statue was discovered in a cornfield in 1743. The church is often packed with worshippers from across the country praying to the virgin.

Near the chapel, set on a hillside and dominating the skyline in that part of the city, is the **Santuario Nacional,** a massive, cavernous church built in 1958. It's painted in bright colors and covered with pictographic stained-glass windows. Shortly after the church was built, the statue of La Virgen de Suyapa was placed here. Local legend has it that she didn't much care for her new sanctuary—when she was moved into it, she vanished and reappeared in the chapel. Evidently she understands the problems of crowd control, however, and allows herself to be brought to the new church during the annual fiesta in her honor, 25 Jan.-4 Feb., when many thousands of worshippers come from across the country to see her.

Parque Naciones Unidas
On the top of Montaña El Picacho off the road to El Hatillo, Parque Naciones Unidas commands views over the entire Tegucigalpa Valley. Built in the 1940s, the pine-forested park is a fine place to escape the noise of the city for a while and breathe clean air. The park also features a frequently used soccer field and a small zoo. Buses to El Picacho leave from behind Los Dolores church on Sunday only—during the week take an El Hatillo bus, get off at the intersection, and walk one and a half km into the park, or take a cab. Entrance is US 40 cents.

Fútbol
Soccer matches are frequently held on weekends in the Estadio Nacional (National Stadium), within walking distance from downtown. Ticket prices are US$2 for national team matches and US$1.25 for normal league games. It's often possible to buy tickets at the box office right before the game, but for big matches it might be better to buy a day in advance.

Sights in Comayagüela
The **San Isidro Market** just over the bridge in Comayagüela, between 5 and 7 Avenidas and 1 and 2 Calles, is worth a visit to check out the hustle and bustle—it's the city's largest market. The old market building partially burned down recently and a new one has yet to be built, but business continues unabated in the empty lot and surrounding streets. Beware of pickpockets in the market crowds.

At the Banco Central de Honduras building on the corner of 12 Calle and 6 Avenida in Comayagüela is the **Museo Numismático,** reportedly boasting the largest collection of antique

the Santuario Nacional in Tegucigalpa

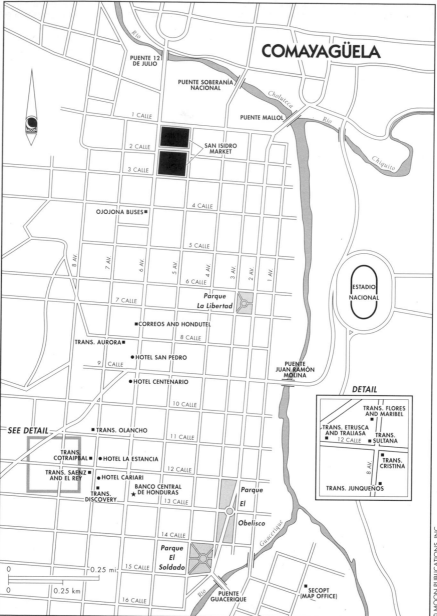

COMAYAGÜELA

PUENTE 12
DE JULIO

PUENTE SOBERANÍA
NACIONAL

PUENTE MALLOL

1 CALLE

2 CALLE

SAN ISIDRO
MARKET

3 CALLE

4 CALLE

OJOJONA BUSES ■

5 CALLE

8 AV.
7 AV.
6 AV.
5 AV.
4 AV.
3 AV.
2 AV.
1 AV.

6 CALLE

7 CALLE

Parque
La Libertad

ESTADIO
NACIONAL

■ CORREOS AND HONDUTEL

8 CALLE

TRANS. AURORA ■

9 CALLE

● HOTEL SAN PEDRO

● HOTEL CENTENARIO

PUENTE
JUAN RAMÓN
MOLINA

10 CALLE

DETAIL

TRANS. FLORES
AND MARIBEL
■

SEE DETAIL

■ TRANS. OLANCHO

11 CALLE

TRANS.
ETRUSCA
AND TRALIASA
■

12 CALLE

TRANS.
SULTANA
■

TRANS.
COTRAIPBAL ■

● HOTEL LA ESTANCIA

8 AV.

TRANS.
CRISTINA
■

TRANS. SAENZ ■
AND EL REY

12 CALLE

● HOTEL CARIARI

TRANS.
DISCOVERY ■

BANCO CENTRAL
DE HONDURAS
★

TRANS. JUNQUEÑOS

13 CALLE

Parque
El
Obelisco

14 CALLE

Parque
El
Soldado

15 CALLE

0   0.25 mi

0   0.25 km

16 CALLE

PUENTE
GUACERIQUE

■ SECOPT
(MAP OFFICE)

Río Choluteca

Río Chiquito

Guacerique

© MOON PUBLICATIONS, INC.

coins and money in Central America. Unfortunately the museum was closed to the public at last report. For the current status call 37-7979, ext. 108, Mon.-Fri. 9 a.m.-4 p.m.

ACCOMMODATIONS

As you would expect for a capital city, Tegucigalpa offers a wealth of hotel rooms in all price ranges. Most visitors will want to stay in the downtown area, which is where many hotels are located. Comayagüela, across the Río Choluteca, also has many hotels in the budget and midrange catagories—useful for travelers arriving late or departing early by bus, since most buses pull into Comayagüela.

HOLY WEEK IN TEGUCIGALPA

Although many of the capital's residents flee the city to vacation spots during Holy Week (Semana Santa) leading up to Easter Sunday, others stay behind to watch and participate in Tegucigalpa's traditional processions, which tell different parts of the biblical Easter story during the course of the week.

The series of parades begins with the Procession of the Triumphant Arrival, representing Christ coming into Jerusalem on a donkey, and is followed by the Lord of Humility Procession on Tuesday, the ominous male-only Procession of Chains on Thursday, the Holy Cross Procession on Good Friday, the late night Virgin of Solitude Procession, the Holy Burial Procession, and the festive Procession of the Empty Tomb on Easter Sunday, celebrating Christ's resurrection.

Each procession begins at the Catedral on the main square in Tegucigalpa and continues along Calle Real and Avenida Centenario (6 Avenida) in Comayagüela, ending at the Iglesia de la Inmaculada Concepción.

In former years, families along the procession path would set up *descansos,* or resting stops, for participants to stop and pray at small, homebuilt altars. Many city residents would also decorate elaborate carpets, or *alfombras,* to lay out along the road. *Descansos* and *alfombras* are still often seen, but not as frequently as in the past.

Budget
Hotel Granada I, on Avenida Juan Gutemberg in Barrio Guanacaste, tel. 37-2381, is something of a Tegucigalpa institution, attracting travelers, Peace Corps workers, and Hondurans with its three floors of clean, inexpensive tile-floored rooms; US$4 s, US$5 d with shared bath, or US$7 s, US$8 d with private bath. The communal bathroom on the second floor has an endless supply of hot water, and the hotel also has a TV lounge and a very good, inexpensive *comedor* on the second floor. Drinking water is free, and the reception sells soft drinks. Around the corner from the Granada I are the Granada II, tel. 37-4004, and Granada III, tel. 22-0597, each charging US$7 s, US$9 d with private bath.

Half a block north of the square on Calle Palace, **Hotel Maya Colonial,** tel. 37-2643, offers high-ceiling plaster-walled rooms around a courtyard in a colonial-era building for US$6 s or d, US$9 d with two beds. Some rooms have great old bathtubs, but unfortunately there's no hot water! Drinking water is free.

The inexpensive **Hotel Casa Real,** on Calle Salvador Mendieta, tel. 37-5914, rents timeworn but appealing rooms for US$3 s or d with one bed, shared bath, US$5 s or d with private bath, more with two beds. The rooms facing the street are noisy in the morning and during the day, but they quiet down at night.

In an alley next to Iglesia Los Dolores are several very cheap but also filthy *hospedajes,* only fit for the extremely poor willing to fight off the drunks who hang around the alley. Around the corner from Los Dolores is **Hotel Goascorán #2** (not to be confused with #1, one of the dives in the alley), a good value at US$2.50 s with shared bath or US$4 with private bath.

For a bit of a splurge in the budget category, the American-owned **Hotel Nuevo Boston,** at Maximio Jeréz 321, just west of Los Dolores church, tel. 37-9411, offers very quiet rooms set around two small courtyards. The rooms have fans and hot water, and rent for US$9 s or US$15 d; more for the larger rooms facing the street.

Midrange
Unique **Apart-Hotel Del Río,** tel./fax 22-1889 or 37-6678, rents 10 apartments of varying sizes in a converted mansion above the Río Choluteca. Each apartment has a kitchenette, and some have

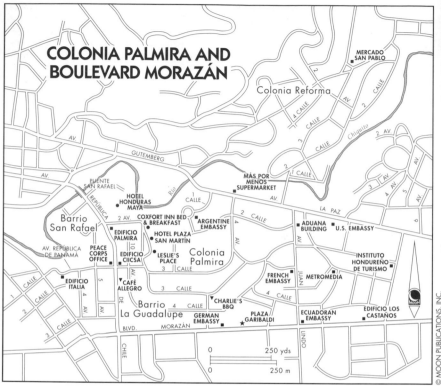

COLONIA PALMIRA AND
BOULEVARD MORAZÁN

Colonia Reforma

MERCADO
SAN PABLO

GUTEMBERG

MÁS POR
MENOS
SUPERMARKET

HOTEL
HONDURAS
MAYA

Barrio
San Rafael

COXFORT INN BED
& BREAKFAST

EDIFICIO
PALMIRA

HOTEL PLAZA
SAN MARTÍN

ARGENTINE
EMBASSY

ADUANA
BUILDING

U.S. EMBASSY

AV. REPÚBLICA
DE PANAMÁ

PEACE
CORPS
OFFICE

EDIFICIO
CIICSA

LESLIE'S
PLACE

Colonia
Palmira

INSTITUTO
HONDUREÑO
DE TURISMO

EDIFICIO
ITALIA

CAFÉ
ALLEGRO

FRENCH
EMBASSY

METROMEDIA

Barrio
La Guadalupe

CHARLIE'S
BBQ

GERMAN
EMBASSY

MORAZÁN

PLAZA
GARIBALDI

ECUADORAN
EMBASSY

EDIFICIO LOS
CASTAÑOS

BLVD.

CHILE

LINDO

0   250 yds

0   250 m

© MOON PUBLICATIONS, INC.

balconies and telephones; US$25-40 per room, weekly and monthly rates available. The house has a large reading room, as well as a porch and garden overlooking the river. It's conveniently located just a couple of blocks from downtown, yet in a quiet neighborhood. Reservations are suggested as the bilingual owners often host groups.

On either side of Hotel San Martín, just above the Honduras Maya, are two bed and breakfasts. **Coxfort Inn Bed and Breakfast,** tel./fax 31-5692 or 31-5849, run by English-speaking owners who live on the premises, has very cozy, tastefully decorated rooms with TV and telephone for US$40 a night, or US$35 when staying a week. Guests have use of a small pool and gym. **Leslie's Place,** tel. 39-0641, fax 31-2957, in a converted house with a pleasant patio, offers eight rooms decorated with new furniture and equipped with TV and telephone for US$59 s, US$74 d.

Hotel MacArthur, tel. 37-5906 or 38-0414, fax 38-0294, in Colonia Dolores, a residential neighborhood close to downtown, features well-lit, airy modern rooms with hot water and telephone for US$21 s, US$25 d, or US$29 s and US$34 d with a/c and TV also. The well-managed hotel also has a reasonably priced cafeteria.

Luxury

On a hill overlooking downtown from the east, the **Honduras Maya,** tel. 32-3191 or 32-3195, fax 32-7629, has long been the hotel of choice for wealthy guests both foreign and local. The Maya has 189 rooms with all the amenities for US$140 s, US$155 d, or a special executive suite for US$230 with fax and direct phone lines. The downstairs cafeteria is overpriced and the service is poor, but the Restaurante La Veranda is good. Other services include an outdoor pool and ample patio; a souvenir shop selling English-language newspapers, magazines, and books; a travel agent; a hair stylist; and a large convention center. Next door, under different ownership, is the **Casino Royale,** the only casino in Tegucigalpa.

A block up the hill from the Maya is **Hotel Plaza San Martín,** tel. 37-2928 or 37-2930, fax 31-1366, the second major luxury hotel in town. You can see the fortresslike structure, painted gleaming white with pastel accents, from all over the city. Quieter than the Maya, the San Martín is favored by wealthier Hondurans, and has 110 rooms with balconies for US$102 s, US$122 d, or US$147 suite. The hotel has a restaurant, bar, and cafeteria.

Hotel La Ronda, tel. 37-8151 to -8154, in the U.S. (800) 446-2747, is considered the finest hotel in the heart of downtown, with 72 modern, air-conditioned rooms going for US$50 s or d and US$80 suite, breakfast included. The elegant dining room at Restaurante La Rondalla serves highly recommended food. Upstairs is a solarium dining room, and the bar often has a live combo playing.

Adjacent to the cathedral, **Hotel Prado,** tel. 37-0121 to -0127, fax 37-2221, offers 70 rooms, each with a/c and refrigerator, some overlooking the square, for US$60 s, US$70 d, US$80 suite. Price includes breakfast at Restaurante La Posada. The hotel's Bar El Cabildo often features live music.

If you want to stay outside of the center of town, the modern, motel-style **Hotel Alameda,** on Boulevard Suyapa, tel. 32-6902 or 32-6920, fax 32-6932, offers 75 rooms with a/c, TV, telephone, and hot water for US$65 s, US$75 d, and US$85 t. The hotel boasts two pools, a bar, restaurant, interior parking, and a professional, helpful staff.

Comayagüela Accommodations

The four-story **Hotel San Pedro,** on 6 Avenida between 8 and 9 Calles, tel. 22-8987, is popular for its ultracheap, clean rooms at US$2 s or US$3 d with communal bath, or a bit more with private bath. **Hotel La Estancia,** near several bus terminals on 7 Avenida between 11 and 12 Calles, tel. 37-3564, is a good value at US$4 s or d with communal bath, hot water, and overhead fans. The quiet rooms surround a small interior courtyard.

Hotel Cariari, next to the Discovery terminal on 7 Avenida between 12 and 13 Calles, tel. 38-6285, features 12 clean, quiet rooms for US$3.50 s, US$5 d communal bath, or US$4 s, US$6 d private bath, all with overhead fans.

For a nicer room, check out **Hotel Centenario,** on 6 Avenida between 9 and 10 Calles, tel. 37-7729 or 22-1050, charging US$13 s or d with one bed or US$21 with two beds. All rooms have TV and telephone.

Camping

Camping is allowed at Parque Naciones Unidas, atop El Picacho overlooking Tegucigalpa. Reach the park via the road leading to El Hatillo.

FOOD

Tegucigalpa could hardly be considered a culinary mecca, but with a little poking around you'll find a variety of different cuisines and price ranges to suit all tastes.

Inexpensive

Half a block from the square next to Hotel Maya Colonial is **El Ranchito,** open daily 8 a.m.-7 p.m., serving low-priced *baleadas,* tacos, and other snacks.

For *pupusas* and beer 24 hours a day, check out **Pupusas Sacaclavo** ("Nailpuller"), on Avenida Máximo Jeréz near the square. It's pretty much a dive, but one of the few places for late-night munchies downtown.

Pancho's, on Avenida Miguel Barahona, east of Iglesia San Francisco in the Barrio Guanacaste, is a popular spot for their excellent and low-priced *alambres, tortas, tacos al pastor, queso fundido,* and other Mexican-style meals. The music and relaxed atmosphere make it a good spot to hang out, drink some beers, and chat with friends. Open Mon.-Sat. 9 a.m.-9 p.m.

Cafes

The quiet **Café Paradiso,** on Avenida Miguel Barahona in Barrio Guanacaste, tel. 22-3066, is a bookstore/cafe serving good coffees and pastries and offering a small but interesting collection of Spanish-language books and *artesanías.* Open Mon.-Fri. 9 a.m.-8 p.m., Saturday 9 a.m.-6 p.m.

Vegetarian

Behind the cathedral, **Restaurante al Natural,** tel. 38-3422, is a shady enclave of quietness and healthy food serving inexpensive, creative dishes such as stuffed potatoes or avocados, spanish tortillas, omelettes, salads, juices, and breakfasts. Open Mon.-Fri. 8 a.m.-7 p.m., Saturday 8 a.m.-3 p.m.

Coppelia, on Calle La Isla a block behind La Merced church, is a good spot for *licuados* and fruit salads. Open Mon.-Sat. 7 a.m.-7 p.m.

Seafood

The Hungry Fisherman, at República de Chile 420, tel. 32-6493, is the best seafood restaurant in town, offering a selection of oysters, shrimp, lobster, conch, or red snapper for US$8-10 per entree, soup and salad included. Open daily 11 a.m.-2 p.m. and 5-10 p.m.

Steaks

El Arriero, at Avenida República de Chile 516, just up from the Honduras Maya, tel. 32-5431, serves pricey but excellent South American-style cuts of beef. Open Mon.-Sat. 11:30 a.m.-3 p.m. and 6-11 p.m., Sunday 11:30 a.m.-10 p.m.

Barbecue

Near the village of El Hatillo, in a converted tannery in the forests above Tegucigalpa, is **Café USA,** tel. 21-8354, with Texas-style ribs, chicken, sausage, and brisket for US$7-10 per meal. The restaurant is 1.5 km beyond the Hatillo church—look for the signs.

Chinese

Opposite Hotel Granada, **La Gran Muralla** serves huge portions of chop suey and other dishes, big enough to feed two if you're not ravenous. Try the good daily specials. Open 10 a.m.-9 p.m.

A couple of blocks further east on the other side of the street is **Restaurante Nanking,** on the ground floor of the hotel of the same name, offering a monster chop suey for US$2 and

other dishes in a spacious dining room. Open daily 11 a.m.-10 p.m.

Restaurante Mirawa, with dining rooms on Avenida Morazán and on the *peatonal* just off the square, has great wonton soup and inexpensive meals. It's open daily 10 a.m.-9 p.m.

Mediterranean

They call themselves **Restaurante Mediterraneo,** but their selection of Mediterranean food is limited to a Greek salad and "suflaky." No matter—the menu is extensive, prices are reasonable, and service is excellent. The diner-style restaurant is a favorite place for people to have drinks and talk, and the waitresses will bring you an endless supply of *bocitas* (snacks) while you drink. Open Mon.-Sat. 9:30 a.m.-10 p.m., on Calle Salvador Mendieta.

Italian

Café Allegro, on República de Chile above the Honduras Maya, tel. 32-8122, serves well-prepared but not overly large portions of pasta, pizza, and other Italian dishes—including an interesting assortment of soups (peanut, broccoli, cauliflower, and others)—in a quiet patio dining area; US$3-6 per entree. This restaurant is favored by Peace Corps volunteers and European travelers. Open daily 10 a.m.-10 p.m. Above the restaurant are communal rooms for rent at US$6 pp, and downstairs is a gift shop with carvings, furniture, paintings, and books.

Closed temporarily at last check, Restaurante Roma just off Avenida República de Panamá near the corner of República de Chile, is reported to have very good pizzas and other Italian dishes.

The ever-popular **Pizza Hut** has three restaurants in town: right off the square, tel. 37-5717; on Avenida Juan Pablo II, tel. 32-1500; and in Comayagüela, tel. 38-2320. All are open daily until 10 p.m.

Brazilian

Between Boulevard Morazán and Avenida La Paz, at the eastern edge of town, is **Restaurante Jacare D'Amazonia,** tel. 36-6734, serving a variety of traditional Brazilian dishes such as *chimol,* chicken heart, meat kebabs, lamb, and *farfola de yucca* in an all-you-can-eat format for US$14 pp. Special parties and live music can be arranged with advance notice. Open Tues.-Sun. 10 a.m.-midnight.

European

Restaurante Kloster, on Boulevard Morazán, tel. 36-6198, serves a variety of European dishes such as steak with béarnaise or bordelaise sauce, chateaubriand, duck in Cointreau and orange sauce, German sausage, pâté, and much else for US$7-12 per plate. The restaurant has a deli and wine shop attached. Open Mon.-Sat. 11 a.m.-2:30 p.m. and 5:30-11 p.m.

Honduran-European

One of the more creative restaurants in Tegucigalpa is **Alondra,** in a converted house opposite the Honduras Maya on República de Chile, tel. 31-5909. Among their specialties are shrimp and mushrooms soaked in whiskey, chicken in wine sauce, and steak *al jalapeño.* Neat attire and reservations are recommended. Open Mon.-Sat. noon-2 p.m. and 7-10 p.m.

ENTERTAINMENT

Dancing

Plaza Garibaldi on Boulevard Morazán is a sort of combination bar-restaurant-disco with a lively ambience that attracts locals and foreigners alike. The small dance floor gets packed on weekends with couples dancing until the wee hours.

Of the several discos in town, **Back Streets, Alejandro's,** and **Tropical Port,** on Avenida Juan Pablo II, and **Confetti's,** on Boulevard Morazán, are all good and fairly safe.

Bars

Tobacco Road Tavern on Avenida Miguel Baharona, also a bookstore, is a good place for a quiet beer. American owner Tom Taylor sells a selection of Danlí cigars, and the place is an informal traveler's gathering spot. It's normally open Mon.-Sat. until 11 p.m., but hours can vary. **El Barrilón** at the end of Boulevard Morazán serves pitchers of Imperial beer on tap.

Casino

Next to the Honduras Maya is **Casino Royale,** tel. 32-2217, fax 31-5815, open daily 1 p.m.-6 a.m. The casino offers gamblers a choice of slot machines, blackjack, poker, baccarat, or roulette.

Billiards

Mr. Pool, a block north of the square on Avenida Máximo Jeréz, is well lit and has many tables. Open daily 9 a.m.-11 p.m., the pool hall has a heavy male atmosphere although women are allowed.

Cinemas

Movie theaters in Tegucigalpa showing first-run movies include **Cine Variedades,** two blocks from the square, tel. 22-0003; **Tauro/Aries** in Barrio Guanacaste near the Hotel Granada; and **Multicines Plaza,** in Miraflores, tel. 32-2227 or 32-2233.

SHOPPING

Gifts and Handicrafts

Mundo Maya Gift Shop, tel. 22-2946, two blocks east of the square on Calle Adolfo Zuñiga, sells wood carvings, paintings, postcards, T-shirts, books, and some *artesanías* from La Mosquitia.

Carmen, on Avenida República de Chile 338, tel. 32-2807, has a good selection of wood, ceramic, and porcelain sculptures, paintings, and painted masks from across the country. On Avenida Cervantes east of the square are several souvenir shops, including **Tikamaya, Regalo Maya, Don Quijote, Tesoros Maya,** and **Caoba.**

Books

Metromedia, near the American Embassy in Edificio Casa Real, Avenida San Carlos, tel. 32-7108, offers a good selection of English-language magazines, newspapers, and new and used novels. Open Mon.-Sat. 10 a.m.-8 p.m., Sunday noon-5 p.m.

Downtown on Avenida Miguel Barahona, **Shakespeare and Co. Books** has a small room filled to the ceiling with shelves of used English-

pottery at Ojojona

language books at inexpensive prices, with heavy emphasis on romance and adventure novels. Open Mon.-Sat. 9 a.m.-11 p.m., although they close early if there are no customers.

Possibly the best Spanish-language bookstore in Honduras is **Librería Guaymuras,** on Avenida Cervantes, tel. 22-4140, which stocks an excellent collection of novels, poetry, and books on Honduran and Central American history, society, and politics. Open Mon.-Fri. 8:30 a.m.-12:30 p.m.and 1-6 p.m., Saturday 8:30 a.m.-12:30 p.m.

Groceries

Más Por Menos, on Avenida La Paz below the American Embassy, is a full-service grocery open daily. **Mercado San Miguel,** next to the Hotel Granada in Barrio Guanacaste, has a decent selection of fruits and vegetables.

Maps

Topographical, road, mineral, resource, and other maps published by the Honduran government can be purchased at the **Instituto Geográfico Nacional,** at the Secretaría de Transporte (SEC-OPT) in Comayagüela, 15 Calle one block east of 1 Avenida, tel. 25-0752. The office stocks a large but not complete selection of 1:50,000 and 1:250,000 topographical maps, but the staff will often make a photocopy of ones not available for sale. Maps are inexpensive, the bureaucratic hassles are nonexistent, and the staff is knowledgeable and friendly. Open Mon.-Fri. 8 a.m.-4 p.m.

INFORMATION AND SERVICES

Communications

The main Hondutel office is on Avenida Colón west of the square, open 24 hours a day. The office receives faxes at tel. 37-9715, Mon.-Fri. 8 a.m.-4 p.m. and Saturday 8 a.m.-noon. Other offices are in Comayagüela on 6 Avenida between 7 and 8 Calles, open daily 7 a.m.-8:30 p.m., and in Colonia Kennedy.

The downtown Correos occupies an attractive old building at the end of the *peatonal.* It's open Mon.-Fri. 8 a.m.-7 p.m., Saturday 8 a.m.-1 p.m. In Comayagüela, the Correos is next to Hondutel on 6 Avenida; open the same hours. Express Mail Service is available at both offices.

DHL is on Avenida República de Chile near the Honduras Maya, tel. 35-8012 to - 8020. **UPS** is in Edificio Palmira right across from the entrance of the Honduras Maya, tel. 39-4287 to - 4289 or 31-1244.

Exchange

Any of the dozen or so banks downtown will change your dollars or traveler's checks, but it's easier to go to either a *casa de cambio* (try **Coin Casa de Cambio** at the end of the *peatonal,* open Mon.-Fri. 9 a.m.-5 p.m. and Saturday 9 a.m.-noon) or one of the many men waving thick wads of lempiras and dollars along the *peatonal.* Though it may appear shady, the independent moneychangers are honest businesspeople and will not rip you off. Still, it's always recommended you count your money right then and there.

If you need to change some money at the last minute before getting on a bus in Comayagüela, try Banco Atlántida, on the corner of 6 Avenida and 11 Calle. Credomatic, a block west of the square on Calle Salvador Mendieta, tel. 31-1058, advances any amount up to the limit of your Visa or MasterCard in lempiras for no fee. Open Mon.-Fri. 8 a.m.-5:30 p.m. and Saturday 8 a.m.-2 p.m.

The American Express agent in Tegucigalpa is **Mundirama Travel,** Edificio Cliisca on the corner of Avenida República de Chile and Avenida República de Panamá, tel. 32-3943 or 32-3909, fax 32-0072. They will sell checks to cardholders only—no cash. The office holds mail up to six months and is open Mon.-Fri. 8 a.m.-noon and 1-5 p.m., Saturday 8 a.m.-noon.

Migration and Customs

The central migration office is on Avenida Máximo Jeréz, tel. 38-1957, ext. 24. In general, try to renew tourist cards elsewhere, as doing it here requires waiting in line and leaving your passport at least one day. Offices in other cities and towns are usually much quicker, hassle-free, and less expensive. Open Mon.-Fri. 8:30 a.m.-4:30 p.m.

The Aduana (Customs) office for dealing with car permits is on Juan Lindo just off Avenida La Paz, next to the U.S. Embassy, tel. 36-6650, 36-8754, or 36-8566, ext. 108. Open Mon.-Fri. 8:30 a.m.-4:30 p.m.

EMBASSIES AND CONSULATES IN TEGUCIGALPA

Argentina: Colonia Rubén Darío, Avenida José María Medina 417, tel. 32-3376 or 32-3274
Brazil: Colonia La Reforma, Calle La Salle 1309, tel. 36-5223 or 36-5867
Canada: Edificio Los Castaños, Boulevard Morazán, tel. 31-4538 or 31-4548
Colombia: Edificio Palmira, 4th floor, across from Honduras Maya, tel. 32-9707 or 32-5131
Costa Rica: Residencia El Triángulo, 1 Calle 3451, tel. 32-1768 or 39-0787
Chile: Edificio Compañía de Seguros Internacionales, Boulevard Morazán, tel. 31-3703 or 32-2114
China: Avenida República de Panamá 2024, Colonia Palmira, tel. 32-4490 or 31-1484
Denmark: Boulevard Los Próceres, Edificio La Paz, tel. 36-6407 or 36-6645
Dominican Republic: Colonia Miramonte, in front of Banco Continental, tel. 39-0129
Ecuador: Avenida Juan Lindo 122, Colonia Palmira, tel. 36-5980, fax 36-6929
El Salvador: Colonia San Carlos 2A, #219, tel. 36-7311 or 36-0045
France: Colonia Palmira, Avenida Juan Lindo 3A, tel. 36-6800 or 36-6432
Germany: Edificio Paysen, 3rd floor, Boulevard Morazán, tel. 32-3161 or 32-3162
Great Britain: Edificio Palmira, 3rd floor, across from Honduras Maya, tel. 32-0621 or 32-0618
Guatemala: Colonia Las Minitas, 4 Calle, Arturo López Rodezno 2421, tel. 32-9704 or 32-5018
Holland: Colonia Alameda, Avenida Principal, Edificio Festival, tel. 31-5007
Israel: Edificio Palmira, 5th floor, across from Honduras Maya, tel. 32-4232 or 32-5176
Italy: Colonia Reforma, Calle Principal 2602, tel. 36-6810 or 36-8027
Japan: Colonia San Carlos between 4 and 5 Calles, tel. 36-6828 or 36-6829
Mexico: Colonia Palmira, Avenida República de Brasil 2028, tel. 32-6471 or 32-4039
Nicaragua: Colonia Lomas del Tepeyac B-M-1, tel. 32-4290 or 32-9025
Panama: Edificio Palmira, 2nd floor, across from Honduras Maya, tel. 31-5441
Peru: Colonia Alameda, Calle Rubén Darío 1902, tel. 31-5261 or 31-5272
Poland: Colonia Palmira 5A, tel. 31-5628
Portugal: Colonia Alameda, Avenida Principal, Edificio Festival, tel. 31-5007
Spain: Colonia Matamoros, #80, tel. 36-6875 or 36-6589
Sweden: Colonia Miramontes, Avenida Altiplano 2758, tel. 32-4935
Switzerland: Edificio Galerías, Boulevard Morazán, tel. 32-6239 or 32-9692
United States: Avenida La Paz, tel. 36-9320 to -9329
Venezuela: Colonia Rubén Darío, Calle Arturo López, tel. 32-1886 or 32-1879

Health
The private **Clínica Viera,** across from City Hall (the Alcaldia) on Avenida Colón, tel. 37-3160, stays open 24 hours and can take care of most health problems.

Legal Help
For immigration or criminal problems, or help in dealing with official paperwork, lawyer **Carlos de la Rocha,** tel. 36-3853 or 36-1847, has been recommended. Long-time Honduran resident **Bradford Bell,** tel. 36-7782 or 36-5455, is a specialist in business and property law.

Peace Corps
The central Peace Corps office is in a large brick building on the corner of Avenida República de Chile and Avenida República de Panamá, tel. 32-1753 or 32-2451. Casual visitors are not allowed in, but if you're trying to get a message to a volunteer, this is the place to leave it.

Spanish Classes
Reportedly the best Spanish classes in the city are at **Centro Cultural Alemán,** in Barrio Los Dolores on Calle La Fuente, tel. 37-1555, open Mon.-Wed. and Friday 1-4:30 p.m. and Thursday 10 a.m.-noon and 3-4:30 p.m. It's best to call ahead and make reservations for the popular one-on-one classes.

Laundry
Superc Jet Lavandería, on Avenida Juan Gutemberg just west of where it crosses a bridge and becomes Avenida La Paz, charges US$1.50 per load; open Mon.-Sat. 8 a.m.-6:30 p.m.

Information
The **Instituto Hondureño de Turismo,** on the fifth floor of Edificio Europa, Avenida Ramon Ernesto Cruz behind the U.S. Embassy, tel. 38-3974 or 22-2124, fax 22-6621, can be of some use if you have a specific query, but is generally unaccustomed to dealing with individual travelers.

Travel Agents
Three travel agents in Tegucigalpa who can arrange plane tickets and take care of other

---

TEGUCIGALPA USEFUL TELEPHONE NUMBERS

Cruz Roja Ambulance: 37-8654, or dial 195
Fire Department: 32-1183, 32-5474, or dial 198
Police: 37-1400, or dial 199
Clínica Viera across from Alcaldia, 24 hours: 37-3160

---

basic services are: **Honduras Copán Tours,** across from the Honduras Maya, tel. 32-9736 or 32-9964, fax 32-6795; **Fiesta Americana,** on Boulevard Morazán next to Burger King, tel. 32-4666 or 32-3766; and **Mundirama,** in the Cliisca building on the corner of Avenida República de Chile and Avenida República de Panamá, tel. 32-3943 or 32-3909, fax 32-0072.

Tour Operators
Explore Honduras, tel. 36-9003 or 36-7694, fax 36-9800, in Edificio Medicast, Ste. 206, Boulevard Morazán, runs recommended tours of Tegucigalpa, La Tigra, Valle de Ángeles and Santa Lucía, as well as further afield to Copán, Lago de Yojoa, the north coast, and La Mosquitia.

Near the Más Por Menos supermarket, just off Avenida La Paz, is the office of **Honduras Traveling,** tel. 36-8511 or 36-8512, fax 36-8513, which runs tours of the city and vicinity, Comayagua, and Amapala.

For top-notch adventure and rafting tours in La Mosquitia, contact **La Moskitia Eco Aventuras,** tel. 21-0404, fax 21-0408, e-mail: moskitia@david.intertel.hn.

Photography
The **Kodak** shop on the southwest corner of the square sells and develops slide and print film, although there have been some complaints about the quality of the slide developing.

If your camera's giving you problems, **Jorge Calderón** can handle basic repairs and will tell you if the problem is beyond his capabilities, rather than trying to take it apart anyhow. His office, cluttered with the corpses of cameras from times past, is on the first floor of Edificio Colonial, on the north side of the square, and is open Mon.-Fri. 8 a.m.-5 p.m.

GETTING THERE AND AWAY

Air
Toncontín International Airport is six km from downtown on the highway leading out of town to the south. At the airport are several car rental agencies, Hondutel, two banks and a lot of moneychangers, a snack bar, and a souvenir shop.

Airport taxis cost US$5 to downtown, or more with three people. If you don't have much luggage, it's cheaper to walk right out front to the main road and catch a bus there. All the buses passing in front of the airport to the north go to downtown.

If you're leaving the country on an international flight, expect to pay a US$10 departure tax.

Isleña, tel. 33-1130 or 33-1894, flies to San Pedro Sula (US$30 one-way) once daily and La Ceiba (US$40 one-way) four times daily, with connections to the Bay Islands and La Mosquitia. **La Costeña,** tel. 34-6628 or 34-6632, flies Mon.-Sat. to Managua for US$65 one-way. **Taca/Lahcsa,** tel. 31-2472 or 33-5756, flies daily to San Salvador (US$100 one-way), San Pedro Sula (US$30 one-way), and Miami; and four times a week to San José (US$80 one-way), Cancún (US$210 one-way), and New Orleans.

Continental, tel. 33-7676 or 33-4697, flies to Houston daily. **American Airlines,** tel. 32-1414, flies daily to Miami.

Bus
Unfortunately for travelers, Tegucigalpa has no central bus station. Terminals are all operated by individual bus lines, and are mostly located in Comayagüela. As times change often, its best to double-check the schedules listed below either by phone or in person. Don't bother trying to make reservations by phone—they are rarely respected.

• To **San Pedro Sula:** Offering hourly service between 6 a.m. and 6 p.m. are Hedman Alas, on 11 Avenida between 13 and 14 Calles, tel. 37-7143; Transportes Saenz and Transportes El Rey, both at 12 Calle and 7 Avenida, tel. 37-6521 or 37-8561; and Transportes Norteños, tel. 37-0707. The Norteños and El Rey buses are US$2, while the Hedman Alas and Saenz

TEGUCIGALPA CAR RENTAL AGENCIES

Budget: airport office, tel. 33-5161, fax 33-5170
Hertz: downtown, across from Honduras Maya, tel. 39-0772 or 39-0774, and at the airport, tel. 34-3784
Maya: Avenida República de Chile 202, tel. 32-0682 or 32-0992
Molinari: at Honduras Maya, tel. 32-8691, and at the airport, tel. 33-1307
Avis: at the Honduras Maya, tel. 39-5711 or 32-0088, fax 39-5710, and at the airport, tel. 33-9548
Toyota: in Colonia El Prado, tel. 33-5790, and at the airport, tel. 34-3183

direct service is US$3. Saenz has one early departure at 2 a.m. Both Hedman Alas and Saenz also operate luxury buses for US$6.
• To **Siguatepeque:** Transportes Maribel, at 8 Avenida between 11 and 12 Calles, tel. 37-3032, has seven departures between 6 a.m. and 4:45 p.m.; US$1, two hours.
• To **La Paz:** Under the same roof as Transportes Maribel, at 8 Avenida between 11 and 12 Calles, is Transportes Flores, offering nine buses between 7:30 a.m. and 5 p.m.; US$1, 90 minutes.
• To **Santa Bárbara:** Transportes Junqueños, at 8 Avenida between 12 and 13 Calles, tel. 37-2921, leaves Mon.-Thurs. and Saturday at 7 a.m. and 2 p.m., Friday at 7 a.m. and 4 p.m., Sunday at 9 a.m. and 2 p.m.; US$2.30, four hours.
• To **Santa Rosa de Copán:** Sultana, at the corner of 12 Calle and 8 Avenida, tel. 37-8101, runs two buses daily at 6 a.m. and 10 a.m; US$3.60, six hours (not direct).
• To **La Ceiba:** Operating three buses a day at varying hours, usually two in the morning and one in the afternoon, are Etrusca, on 12 Calle between 8 and 9 Avenida, tel. 20-0137; Traliasa, also on 12 Calle between 8 and 9 Avenida, tel. 37-7538; and Cristina, on the corner of 12 Calle and 8 Avenida, tel. 20-0117. All charge US$5 for the five- to six-hour ride.

• To **Juticalpa** and **Catacamas:** Transportes Discovery, on 7 Avenida between 12 and 13 Calles, tel. 22-4256, offers three direct and nine local buses daily between 6 a.m. and 2:30 p.m.; US$2.40 to Juticalpa direct (two hours), US$1.50 local (three hours), and US$2.70 to Catacamas direct (three hours), US$1.90 local (four hours). Empresa Aurora, on 8 Calle between 6 and 7 Avenidas, tel. 37-3647, also runs local buses to Juticalpa and Catacamas between 4:30 a.m. and 5:30 p.m.

• To **San Francisco de la Paz, Gualaco,** and **San Esteban:** Transportes Olancho, on the corner of 7 Avenida and 11 Calle, tel. 37-7355, runs two buses daily via Juticalpa at 6 a.m. and 6:30 a.m. The six-hour ride to the end of the run at San Esteban costs US$3.

• To **Tocoa** and **Trujillo** via **La Muralla:** Cotraipbal, on 7 Avenida between 11 and 12 Calles, tel. 37-1666, runs three buses at 5 a.m., 9 a.m., and noon. The nine hour ride to Trujillo costs US$5.

• To **Yuscarán, Danlí,** and **El Paraíso:** Discua, tel. 32-7939, operates buses to Danlí every 45 minutes between 6 a.m. and 6:30 p.m. from Mercado Jacaleapa in Colonia Kennedy. (*Colectivo* taxis run out past Mercado Jacaleapa from Puente La Isla, between downtown and the stadium, for US 25 cents.) The two-hour ride to Danlí costs US$1; it's a bit more to El Paraíso. Some buses only go to Danlí, but from there frequent buses continue to El Paraíso. Buses to Yuscarán also leave from Mercado Jacaleapa daily at 8:45 a.m. and 4 p.m.

• To the **South Coast:** Royery, tel. 38-2863, runs buses to Guasaule daily at 6 a.m., 8 a.m., and 3:30 p.m. (US$1.80); to San Marcos de Colón five times daily between 4 a.m. and 4 p.m. (US$1.70); and to Choluteca seven times daily between 6 a.m. and 6 p.m. (US$1.40). The buses leave from 6 Avenida and 23 Calle in Comayagüela.

Buses to Cedeño leave Mercado Mayoreo four times daily between 6 a.m. and 2:30 p.m. (US$1.80); to El Amatillo a couple every hour between 4:30 a.m. and 5 p.m. (US$1.30). Buses also leave from Mercado Mayoreo to Choluteca and Cedros frequently, and to Minas de Oro at 1 p.m. and 2 p.m. To get to Mercado Mayoreo, take any Carrizal or Cerro Grande-bound city bus from right in front of the *parque central.*

• To **Ojojona:** Buses leave as soon as they fill up from the corner of 6 Avenida and 4 Calle near the market in Comayagüela; US 25 cents, 45 minutes.

• To **Santa Lucía** and **San Juancito,** for La Tigra: Buses leave from Mercado San Pablo, off Avenida La Paz. Santa Lucía buses leave every 45 minutes between 6 a.m. and 6 p.m. (US 20 cents), while a couple of buses leave to San Juancito at irregular hours (US 40 cents).

• To **Valle de Ángeles:** Buses leave every hour from the Medalla Milagrosa church, near Hospital San Felipe on Avenida La Paz; US 30 cents. Any of the Santa Lucía, San Juancito, or Valle de Ángeles buses can be caught at the Dippsa gas station at the end of Avenida La Paz.

• To **El Hatillo** and points west of La Tigra: Buses leave from Parque Herrera in downtown Tegucigalpa four times a day to Limones (US 25 cents), once a day to Jutiapa (US 35 cents).

International Buses

Air-conditioned Cruzeros del Golfo buses to **San Salvador, El Salvador** and **Guatemala City, Guatemala** leave from Barrio La Granja in Comayagüela at 6 a.m. and 1 p.m., charging US$17 to San Salvador. Tica, tel. 38-7040, offers 9 a.m. departures to **Managua, Nicaragua** (US$20), **San José, Costa Rica** (US$35), San Salvador (US$15), and Guatemala City (US$23).

DISTANCES FROM TEGUCIGALPA

Yuscarán: 77 km
Danlí: 93 km
Choluteca: 142 km
San Pedro Sula: 246 km
Comayagua: 85 km
Siguatepeque: 117 km
Juticalpa: 192 km
Catacamas: 232 km

NEAR TEGUCIGALPA

SANTA LUCÍA

A picturesque colonial village of tile roofs and cobblestone streets perched on a hillside 13 km above Tegucigalpa, Santa Lucía has been the Peace Corps training center for 15 years, and is a growing destination for wealthy Hondurans looking to escape the city. For much of the colonial period Santa Lucía was home to some of the richest mines in Honduras. The town produced so much wealth for the crown, King Felipe II sent a wooden statue of Christ in appreciation, which can still be seen in the local church.

Apart from enjoying the views and admiring the colonial church, there's not much to do in Santa Lucía, but it's a pleasant place to spend an afternoon wandering around. A dirt road continuing past the church up into the forest makes for an easy hike with great views over the town, Tegucigalpa below, and La Tigra forest. The road continues across the mountaintop to the Danlí highway, reached in two or three hours walking, where you could hail a passing bus down to Tegucigalpa.

A trail descends from Santa Lucía to Tegucigalpa, but it lets out in some tough shanty villages on the outskirts of the city, and robberies have been reported, so that walk is not recommended.

Practicalities

There are no hotels in Santa Lucía, so plan on making your visit a day-trip.

Restaurante Dónde El Francés, run by, you guessed it, a Frenchman, is one kilometer from Santa Lucía on the road to the highway. Crepes, rabbit in wine sauce, kidney in liquor, snapper, and other creative dishes are served in a funky little dining room or out in the garden. Open daily 7 a.m.-8 p.m.; US$2-6 per entree.

Restaurante Miluska, in the center of town, tel. 37-0472, offers Czech- and Hungarian-style food Tues.-Sun. 10 a.m.-8 p.m.; US$3-6 per entree.

The last bus to Tegucigalpa leaves at 5:30 p.m.

VALLE DE ÁNGELES

Valle de Ángeles, 23 km east of Tegucigalpa, leads a sort of double life. It's part playground for wealthy Tegucigalpa residents and tourists, and part still a rural Honduran mountain village. On weekends here you may feel a bit overwhelmed by the camera-toting, handicraft-buying crowd, but tough-looking cowboys still clomp around the cobblestone streets on horseback on their way into the surrounding pine forest.

As the name suggests, the town is set in a breathtaking high mountain valley at 1,310 meters, surrounded by mountains on three sides and dropping off into a valley on the fourth. Apart from enjoying the atmosphere and breathing the clean mountain air, many visitors come to Valle de Ángeles to shop for handicrafts in the dozen or so shops. The town is particularly known for wood carvings.

Practicalities

The only accommodations in town are at the **Posada del Ángel,** tel./fax 76-2233, offering 20 rooms around a large grassy courtyard. The rooms have hot water and cable TV, and rent for a very reasonable US$10 s or US$20 d. The hotel has its own restaurant, parking lot, and conference rooms. According to the owners, it will soon have a pool. It's best to reserve rooms ahead of time as they often fill up.

The most highly recommended restaurant in Valle de Ángeles is **La Canterita,** one block behind the church in a rustic but stylish converted house, tel. 76-2014. Dishes include stuffed jalapeños, lasagna *campesina* (made with tortillas), steak, jumbo shrimp, ceviche, and a daily special; US$6-9 per meal. Open daily for lunch and dinner, reservations recommended on weekends.

Restaurante Papagayo, one block below the square on the road leading out of town toward Tegucigalpa, tel. 76-2152, serves well-prepared midrange meals, including their famous *tortilla papagayo* stuffed with cheese, sausage, tomato, *chile,* onion, and beans. Other dishes on the menu include *pinchos,* chicken, and filet mignon; US$2-5 per plate. Open Tues.-Sunday.

Good low-priced eats can be found at **Casa Vieja** on the square, serving *pupusas, pinchos,* burgers, and other munchies inside or on the patio. Open Tues.-Sun. 11 a.m.-7 p.m.

Apart from the many shops lining the streets around Valle de Ángeles, handicrafts are also sold in the **Mercado Municipal de Artesanías,** in the market building where the Tegucigalpa buses turn around. Among the handicrafts sold in town are wood carvings, ceramics, pewter, tapestries, furniture, paintings, and much else.

Buses to Tegucigalpa leave daily until 5:30 p.m.

Three kilometers toward Tegucigalpa on the highway is **Parque Turístico,** where you'll find picnic tables amid the pine trees.

PARQUE NACIONAL LA TIGRA

The first protected area in Honduras, La Tigra was established as a reserve in 1952, and declared a national park in 1980. It covers 23,571 hectares across the top of the mountains above Tegucigalpa, of which 7,571 hectares form the core zone.

Because of the proximity to the La Rosario mines, the forests in La Tigra were heavily logged around the turn of the century, so only a few patches of truly virgin primary cloud forest remain. The mining company cut a dirt road across the mountain from La Rosario to Tegucigalpa, which exposed the heart of the forest for the exploitation of its precious woods for use in mines and surrounding villages. In spite of the depredations, La Tigra still offers a good opportunity to admire the flora and fauna of a high-altitude cloud forest, especially for those who don't have the time or desire to venture further afield to Celaque, Sierra de Agalta, La Muralla, or other, better-preserved forests.

La Tigra has a well-developed trail system, enabling casual hikers to enjoy a day or two wandering about the woods at their leisure, without fear of getting lost. Three main trails run between the western entrance of the park near Jutiapa and the eastern entrance at La Rosario; two of these are actual footpaths and the third is

the dirt road cut by the mining company, part of which is being allowed to deteriorate.

The two footpath trails unsurprisingly offer more opportunity to spot wildlife and enjoy the atmosphere of the forest. Though the dirt road does reach the highest accessible point in the park—Rancho Quemado at 2,185 meters—the views are limited by trees. The best spot to catch glimpses of the valleys below is from next to the Hondutel towers on a ridge above the road.

Other peaks in the park include Cerro La Estrella (2,245 meters), Cerro La Peña de Andino (2,290 meters), and Cerro El Volcán (2,270 meters). Some of the most pristine stretches of cloud forest remain in the region south of the trails, around Cerro El Volcán, but unfortunately the area is off limits to visitors.

Some Peace Corps workers have raved about the mountain-bike potential in the park, especially along the dirt road between Jutiapa and La Rosario, but mountain biking is currently prohibited by park management, who have inexplicably taken a somewhat adversarial attitude toward foreign visitors.

La Rosario

To get into the park from the east side, drive, hitch, or take a bus out to San Juancito from Valle de Ángeles. Buses to Cantarranas from Valle de Ángeles will drop you off at the *desvio* to San Juancito, from where you can walk 15 minutes into town. San Juancito holds several *pulperías* and restaurants, as well as a simple *hospedaje.*

From San Juancito, nestled into a small valley at the base of the mountain, a dirt road continues up the hill to La Rosario, the former mining complex. It's only a couple of kilometers up to the mines, but because of the steep grade it's a good hour-and-a-half walk, so hope one of the workers passes by in a truck to give you a lift.

La Rosario is an interesting collection of turn-of-the-century mining buildings clinging to the steep hillside, some in ruins and others in good condition. One of the buildings houses the visitor's center, where you can pay your entrance fee, get a trail map, look at the displays on local wildlife and geography, and chat with caretaker Don Magín, who is very knowledgable and speaks passable German and a few words of English.

LA ROSARIO MINING COMPANY

High up on a mountainside above the town of San Juancito, on the far side of La Tigra National Park from Tegucigalpa, lie the vestiges of what was for a time the richest mine in the western hemisphere—the New York and Honduras Rosario Mining Company, better known as **La Rosario.**

La Rosario was formed in 1880 by Julius J. Valentine and his four sons, Washington S., Ferdinand C., Louis F., and Lincoln, with the active encouragement of Honduran president Marco Aurelio Soto. A firm believer in the need to develop the Honduran economy with foreign capital, Soto offered the Valentines tax breaks and incentives so generous he kept the details of the contract secret for 17 years. By 1888 La Rosario was far and away the most powerful economic concern in the country, exporting US$700,000 in bullion annually. To ensure a continued free hand to operate as they pleased, mine owners led by Washington Valentine played an increasingly important role in national politics, going so far as to engineer the reelection of Pres. Luis Bográn in the 1888 presidential vote. The company was so closely identified with the U.S. presence in Honduras that for a short time the U.S. embassy was located in the mine complex at La Rosario.

The political machinations payed off handsomely, as the government invariably sided with the company in disputes with local villagers and small-scale Honduran miners over land, water, timber, and limestone. The government also repeatedly helped round up reluctant workers for the chronically understaffed mines.

Over the course of its 74 years of operation, La Rosario produced some US$100 million of gold, silver, copper, and zinc from slightly less than 6.5 million tons of ore. In the process the mine's U.S. owners and shareholders were made extremely wealthy, but the benefits were less evident in Honduras. In spite of the relatively high wages paid to miners, abysmal working conditions led to constant labor shortages as workers fled to their homes, many only to be rounded up by local militia and brought back to the mines. The owners' view of Honduran workers is evident in a letter written to shareholders by Washington Valentine in 1915: "the severe drought which occurred during the year past, while undoubtedly a great hardship upon the country as a whole, for the Company it had its great advantages. . . (it) induced many people to seek work in San Juancito thus there was an abundance and even a surplus of labor."

Also, the company almost entirely denuded the forests on the San Juancito side of the mountain in its insatiable thirst for timber, and eventually punched an adit through the far side of the mountain to access virgin stands of wood. Much of the original cloud forest at La Tigra was destroyed by the mines, and almost all of the flora seen along the trails in the park today is secondary growth.

By 1954 the richest veins of ore had been worked out, and when the miners struck to support the banana workers' strike on the north coast, it was enough to convince the New York owners to shut down most of their operations.

Just above the visitor's center, in the old mine hospital, is the park *hospedaje,* with clean, simple rooms. Bring a sleeping bag as no blankets are available and it's often chilly. No cooking facilities exist at present, but work is supposedly underway on a *comedor.*

Above La Rosario the dirt road continues across the top of the mountain to El Hatillo, on the far west side of the park. Several mines can be seen along this road, some blocked off and others still open. If you want to go exploring, take good care and be advised they are usually full of water and dripping wet. Between the Hondutel towers and La Rosario the road has been allowed to deteriorate.

Jutiapa

Less interesting than the mining complex at La Rosario, but considerably easier to get to from Tegucigalpa, is the western entrance to the park, via the village of Jutiapa. The visitor's center on this side is not as good as at La Rosario, and trail maps are often unavailable.

Buses leave Parque Herrera in Tegucigalpa daily to Limones, seven km from the visitor's center, at 6:30 a.m., 9:30 a.m., 12:30 p.m., and 5 p.m. From Limones it's about a two-hour walk uphill to the visitor's center. The 12:30 bus continues all the way to Jutiapa, only an hour's walk to the visitor's center. Sometimes it's possible to hitch from Limones, but as there's not much

*main office, La
Rosario mining
complex*

traffic, plan on having to walk. The Jutiapa bus descends at 5 a.m. and 2 p.m., while the Limones buses descend at 7:30 a.m., 10 a.m., and 5 p.m.

If you're driving, take the road to El Hatillo and continue to Ponce, where a dirt road turns to the right, signposted for the park.

Amatigra
For more information on the park, or if you want to make reservations for the La Rosario *hospedaje,* visit the office of Amatigra, Edificio Italia, Room 6, on Avenida República de Panamá a couple of blocks down from Avenida República de Chile, tel. 35-8494. Unfortunately the staff at Amatigra has gotten the idea they can charge foreign tourists as much as they like, so entrance prices have been recently jacked up to US$10, and an additional US$5 to camp in the park or sleep in the *hospedaje.* Camping in designated areas costs US$2 per person per night. According to Amatigra you're supposed to buy tickets in advance, but the *vigilantes* at the park are happy to take your money, and they look like they need the money more anyway.

OJOJONA

One of the loveliest of the many colonial villages near Tegucigalpa is Ojojona, 32 km from the capital at 1,390 meters, on the crest of the mountains sloping down toward the Pacific Coast. Thought to have been settled by the Spanish in 1579 on the site of a Lenca village, Ojojona, for much of the colonial era, played a larger and more important role than Tegucigalpa, because of the rich mines of El Aguacatal, Guasucarán, El Plomo, and Las Quemazones in the nearby hills.

Among the many colonial buildings in town are three churches, Iglesia San Juan Bautista (1824), Iglesia de Carmen (1819), and Iglesia del Calvario. In the Iglesia del Calvario, a few blocks from the square, hangs a colonial-era painting titled "Sangre de Cristo." Quite a vision of religious gore, it depicts a crucified Christ gushing blood onto sheep grazing below. The house with the wooden pillars on the square is the oldest building, built in 1723. For a time the house was owned by the family of Pablo Zelaya Sierra, and is now the local museum, although at last check it was closed for renovation.

Ojojona is known for the simple earthenware pottery made in surrounding villages and sold in several shops in town or, on weekends, at the outdoor market. A couple of kilometers from Ojojona is a viewpoint, **El Mirador,** from where you can enjoy views out toward the Pacific and into the interior of the country on a clear day.

Practicalities
The only hotel in town is **Posada Joxone** just off the square. The simple rooms around a garden courtyard go for US$2 pp, and the restaurant serves *carne asada, baleadas,* enchiladas, chicken, and other basic dishes at inexpensive prices.

A couple of other *comedores* serve up *plato típico.*

The last bus back to Tegucigalpa leaves at 5 p.m., charging US 25 cents for the 45-minute ride.

To get to Ojojona by car from Tegucigalpa, take the highway toward Choluteca until you reach a Dippsa gas station at a mountain crest, 24 km from the capital. From here a road turns right and leads eight km to Ojojona, passing through Santa Ana, where there is a colonial church with a lovely painted dome.

Guarisne and Guasucarán

The village of Guarisne, six km from Ojojona, is one of the region's most traditional Lenca communities, and is a center for ceramics. Near the town of Guasucarán is one of the country's best examples of a ruined colonial mining complex. To get there, drive the 16 km of rough dirt road and hire a guide for the several-hour hike. If you don't have your own wheels, take a once-daily bus from Ojojona, and either camp or hope you can find someone willing to put you up for a night.

EL SAUCE PETROGLYPHS

Of the several prehistoric petroglyph sites in the vicinity of Tegucigalpa, one of the most impressive and easiest to visit is near El Sauce, not far from Ojojona. The small village is a couple of kilometers east of the same gas station where the Ojojona road leaves the Choluteca highway, on the dirt road to San Buenaventura. The road heads straight across open fields, then winds down off the plateau to a valley below. At the bottom of the hill is El Sauce, and a 40 minute walk from there you'll find the petroglyphs. Once in the village, turn left off the main road and left again through the first gate. Continue to the small rancho at the end of this road, and ask someone to point the way to "La Cueva Pintada" (The Painted Cave), as the site is

known locally. The trail follows the edge of a small valley for about 15 minutes, reaching a point where another, smaller valley runs into it. At the junction is a small, usually deserted hut.

About another five minutes up the side valley, keep an eye on the rock overhangs—there's one on the right side (facing upriver) and three on the left. Each are filled with dozens of etched images and designs. Some modern grafitti has been added, but thankfully very little.

If you don't feel like spending too much time wandering around looking for the caves, ask one of the local kids to show you for a few lempira. Apart from the caves, the valley is a beautiful place for a walk in the countryside. In this same valley are the remnants of a small colonial-era mine works, including a mill and canal.

VALLE DE ZAMORANO

The highway from Tegucigalpa east to Danlí winds up into the mountains above the city, passing a dirt road turnoff to the left at the crest marked **La Montañanita,** which ends up in Santa Lucía.

On the far side of the mountains, the highway snakes down into the broad, fertile Valle de Zamorano, one of the richest agricultural regions in central Honduras. In the center of the valley, along the edge of the highway, is the **Escuela Agrícola Pan Americana,** set up in the 1040s by the United Fruit Company under the directorship of William Popenoe. The school trains farmers from across Central America. Students receive hands-on experience in the valley's fields.

A dirt road turning off the highway near the school leads to **San Antonio de Oriente,** a colonial village which was the subject of many well-known paintings by famed Honduran artist José Antonio Velásquez.

BOB RACE

LA MOSQUITIA
AND OLANCHO

The two largest departments in the country, Gracias a Dios and Olancho, combine to cover 36% of Honduras's territory, but have a population density of only about seven people per square kilometer, far lower than any other part of Honduras.

This is frontier country, populated by cowboys, loggers, and hunters—people accustomed to fending for themselves without anybody's help. It's not the sort of place you can expect to find a first-class hotel or haute cuisine, but if you're willing to rough it, wide open, unexplored expanses of tropical jungle, pine forest, savanna, raging rivers, and rugged mountains await.

LA MOSQUITIA

INTRODUCTION

If you came to Honduras in search of adventure and tired of traveling the same well-beaten gringo trail through Latin America, don't fail to leave a couple of weeks for La Mosquitia, otherwise known as the Mosquito Coast.

The Gracias a Dios department, which covers all of La Mosquitia, is the second largest in the country, but has a population of only 50,000. These inhabitants live in isolated villages and towns connected to each other mainly by boat, plane, or footpath. La Mosquitia has no road connection to the rest of the country, and four-wheeled transport is impossible, except on a couple of dirt roads near Puerto Lempira.

The La Mosquitia region boasts the highest percentage of indigenous groups in Honduras. Most of its inhabitants are either Miskito, Tawahka, Pech, or Garífuna. Indigenous is a relative term, though, since the ethnogeny of both the Miskito and Garífuna people is a fairly recent historical event—for more on this, see the special topics "The Voyage of the Garífuna" and "The Birth of a Race."

For anyone interested in ecotourism, La Mosquitia is hard to beat. Unbeknownst to most people, the largest remaining expanse of virgin tropical jungle in Central America is tucked in the middle of La Mosquitia—a massive swath of untracked forest stretching from the Caribbean coast south to the mountains of Olancho and south across the Nicaraguan border.

This Central American Amazon, like its South American counterpart, is being pressured on its edges by land-hungry peasants and cattle ranchers who are chopping and burning the forest at a vertiginous rate. In an effort to halt the tide of immigrants, or at least slow the destruction, in 1980 the Honduran government, in conjunction with UNESCO, created the **Río Plátano Biosphere Reserve,** protecting 800,000 hectares of primary jungle, plus a surrounding buffer zone. The **Tawahka Anthropological Reserve,** along the upper Río Patuca basin east and south of the Río Plátano Biosphere, connects to the Bosawas Reserve in Nicaragua, thus creating a huge corrider of protected forest.

Traveling In Mosquitia

La Mosquitia may be remote and undeveloped, but that doesn't mean it's cheap to travel there. Plane fares are reasonably priced, but boat trips can get expensive, especially if you hire a *viaje especial* (special trip), which is usually required for getting into the jungle. Cargo boats, which charge considerably less, occasionally travel between villages on rivers or along the coast.

With the growth of tourism in La Mosquitia, particularly to the Río Plátano Biosphere Reserve, locals now view visitors as potential income, and do not appreciate either backpackers trying to spend next to nothing or package tourists who blaze through with tour operators leaving nothing in the community. Justifiably, Mosquitia residents consider the land their own, and expect to see the benefits of foreign tourism directly in their pockets.

LA MOSQUITIA AND OLANCHO HIGHLIGHTS

- Boating up the Río Plátano, above Las Marías
- Hiking from Las Marías to the top of Pico Dama
- Seeing the dwarf forest on top of Sierra de Agalta
- Looking for quetzals in Parque Nacional La Muralla
- For the real adventurer, hiking and rafting from Dulce Nombre de Culmí through the Mosquitia jungle to the coast

---

THE LAND OF MOSQUITOES?

Yes, those nasty little bloodsuckers thrive all over La Mosquitia, but surprisingly that's not where the region got its name. The most common explanation holds the name derived from the word musket, or rifle, with which the Miskito were well supplied by the British. Supposedly the Spaniards took to calling the attacking Indians "mosqueteros" because of their weaponry, which none of the other Indian groups in Central America used. From this developed the name Mosquetos, which over the years became Miskito.

Another possible derivation is from Miskut, a tribal chief of the Táwira Sumu. Miskut's people lived near Cabo Gracias a Dios and are thought to have been the original Sumu group that evolved into the Miskito.

This does not mean locals are always out to gouge tourists or that they are unwilling to talk to them (far from it), but they have their own ideas about what should be charged for transport, guides, food, and lodging, and you are expected to pay it without complaint. For travelers on a budget, the best option is to visit La Mosquitia in a small group so you can split the costs of guides and boat transport. Often it's possible to hook up with other travelers in La Ceiba or the Bay Islands, and sometimes in Palacios.

Unless you're planning on flying everywhere in La Mosquitia (you won't see much of the jungle that way), don't go on a tight schedule. Any trip to the Río Plátano or Río Patuca jungles requires at least a week, or, more realistically, two. There is only one bank in all of La Mosquitia, and it won't change dollars, so be sure to bring plenty of lempira. Locals will usually accept or change dollars in a pinch, but always at bad rates.

Malaria is rampant in the coastal and savanna areas of La Mosquitia, but much less prevalent in the jungle. Though La Mosquitia did not get its name from those little bloodsucking bugs, known locally as *zancudos,* they are definitely well-known and prolific residents, particularly in the rainy season.

The Land

Much of La Mosquitia is a low-lying plain, by far the largest expanse of flat land in Honduras.

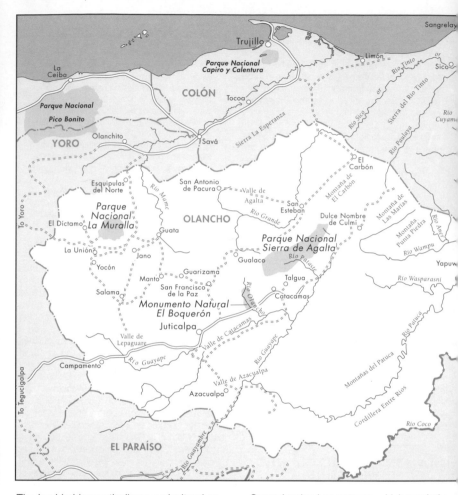

The land holds practically no agricultural potential, though, as the region is covered either by coastal mangrove swamp, tropical jungle, or marshy savanna dotted with Caribbean pine. Land-hungry migrants from Olancho and other parts of Honduras have been eagerly chopping down the jungle for farming and cattle ranching, but as they have slowly been realizing, the rich exuberance of the tropical rainforest has little to do with the underlying soil, which is nutrient-poor, thin, and easily eroded.

Several major river systems, which regularly flood, crisscross the Mosquitia plains including, from west to east, the Sico, Paulaya, Plátano, Sigre, Patuca, and Coco (or Segovia); this last forms the border with Nicaragua. The only mountains near the coast are the Montañas del Río Plátano, which run southwest into Olancho, connecting to the Sierra de Agalta. Farther east and south, forming part of the watershed of the Río Patuca, are the Sierra de Warunta and the Montañas de Colón. In general, the land slopes

LA MOSQUITIA AND OLANCHO

up gently from the coast to the mountains of Olancho, the source for the region's rivers.

La Mosquitia is the wettest part of the country, receiving 300-340 cm of rain on average annually. Rains regularly hit in May, June, and July, followed by a brief dry spell in August and September. Hurricane season is between October and December. February, March, and April are the most reliably dry months of the year, but wet weather can arrive at any time. Temperatures are invariably hot during the day,

often reaching 35° C, but it can be surprisingly cool at night. The coast is usually stroked with ocean breezes, which keeps the heat down.

History

In the pre-Columbian era, La Mosquitia was populated by the Pech, who lived across a wide area delimited by present-day Trujillo, the Olancho and Agalta Valleys, and the Río Patuca. In addition, several Sumu tribes inhabited the region east and south of the Río Patuca and across

THE BIRTH OF A RACE

Few ethnic groups in the world can trace their birth to historical events, and Honduras is home to two of them: the Garífuna (see special topic "The Voyage of the Garífuna"), and the Miskito. When Europeans first came to La Mosquitia, the region was inhabited by Pech Indians and several coastal and jungle subtribes of the Sumu. The Spaniards, intent on finding gold and quick riches, made few efforts to colonize La Mosquitia, and in the early 1600s the British began eyeing the region with interest.

In 1633 the first British settlement was established at Cabo Gracias a Dios. The colonists collected hardwood from the forests and traded peaceably with the Sumu, who were quickly smitten by British weaponry, manufactured goods, and rum. The coastal Sumu had always had a different physiognomy from their inland cousins, and in a few decades the differences became more dramatic. In part the Miskitos evolved from mixing with the English, but more so from several groups of slaves shipwrecked on the shores of eastern Honduras, the first in 1641. Unlike many other indigenous groups, the coastal Sumu tribes had an extremely open culture, which allowed them to mix freely with outsiders, a trait that sped up the process of racial evolution.

The first written mention of the Miskitos appeared in 1672, when the pirate John Exquemelin said they numbered about 1,600 people. In 1699 an anonymous English traveler wrote that "the Mosquetomen inhabit the sea-shore, pretty close to the sea-side, or on the sides of some lakes and lagunes hardby" between Cabo Camarón and Cabo Gracias a Dios.

It remains a mystery what process was underway in the latter part of the 17th century, which from the mixing of African, English, and Indian blood created a new race with a distinct language and culture, but by the turn of the century the Miskitos had been born. The English quickly saw the value of cultivating the Miskitos as allies against the Spanish, and in 1687 they invited the tribe's chief to Jamaica and crowned him Jeremy I, the first of the Miskito kings. In time the British also created governors, generals, and admirals at other Miskito settlements, who sometimes became more like independent warlords than servants of the king. The chiefs were never recognized as legitimate by their subjects until they had made a ritual trip to Jamaica, or later Belize, to receive the British blessing. Reportedly the crowning ceremonies were amusing spectacles of high-flowing speeches and much drunkenness.

The Miskitos needed little encouragement to fight the Spaniards. With a little training they became feared raiders with an insatiable thirst for attacking Spanish settlements. At first they joined pirate expeditions against Trujillo and Puerto Caballos, but soon took to launching their own attacks against San Pedro Sula, León and Granada in Nicaragua, Juticalpa in Olancho, and any other poorly defended Spanish settlement they ran across.

Miskito family on the Río Plátano

GUILLERMO COBOS

During the course of the 18th century the Miskitos gained complete ascendency over the Tawahka Sumu and the Pech, demanding tribute and often raiding the communities for slaves to sell to the English. Unable to compete with the fierce and well-armed Miskitos, the Pech and Tawahka abandoned their former territories. They fled into the jungle to escape attack, leaving the Miskitos the sole rulers of the shore.

With the Anglo-Hispanic Convention of 1786, the British agreed to evacuate the Mosquito Coast in return for Belize. The Miskitos however, were not ready to surrender to the Spanish. Some 1,300 immigrants from Spain arrived at Black River in 1788, but Miskitos attacked repeatedly and settlers were forced to flee to Trujillo, which became the eastern limit of Spanish control.

To this day, many Miskitos hold a special place in their hearts for the British, and fondly cherish the thought that they will return and kick out the *indios,* as they call the Spanish. Only a few Miskitos speak English, but many still have Anglo names. The Miskitos were left alone for the first half of this century, until the 1950s when the Honduran government began building schools in La Mosquitia to spread the use of Spanish. At about the same time Protestant missionaries, especially from the Moravian church, began evangelizing Miskitos.

Since that time, Spanish has slowly replaced English as the lingua franca of La Mosquitia, and the government has gradually begun to assert its authority in the region. But, as with the English and the African slaves who ended up on the Mosquitia shores, the Miskitos seem to be incorporating the Spanish immigrants rather than vice versa. Their open culture, unafraid of change, has proved to be the Miskito's strongest tool in facing the brave new world.

the Río Coco into Nicaragua. Little is known about the origin of these two groups or their society in pre-conquest times, other than that they are part of the Chibchan linguistic group and are thought to have migrated from the rainforests of Colombia to Central America. The ruins of what are believed to be Pech villages and ceremonial centers have been located along both the Caribbean coast and further inland as far as Olancho, but intensive archaeological work has yet to be undertaken.

Christopher Columbus was the first European to visit La Mosquitia. On his fourth voyage, after stopping at Guanaja and Trujillo Bay, Columbus sailed east along the coast until he came to the mouth of a major river, where he landed and spoke to the Indians living there through an interpreter he had brought from Guanaja. The river, which he named Río de la Posesión, could have been either the Aguán, Sico, or Patuca. Because some of the Indians apparently had rather large earlobes, Columbus named the region La Costa de las Orejas (The Coast of the Ears).

Following this landing, Columbus's fleet endured fierce weather for several weeks until the boats finally rounded Honduras's easternmost point and continued south along the coast of Nicaragua in calmer waters. In honor of the event, the point was named Cabo Gracias a Dios. After Columbus, in the 16th century the Spanish made a couple of abortive efforts to colonize La Mosquitia, but soon gave up and chased their dreams of gold and riches in the more hospitable climate of central Honduras. This left the coast open for the pirates who flocked over from Europe beginning in the late 16th century to prey on the Spanish treasure fleets in the Caribbean. The pirates used the Bay Islands and the protected, isolated lagoons of La Mosquitia as their bases.

When war broke out between England and Spain in 1625, English captains based in Bermuda began exploring the Honduran and Nicaraguan coast in earnest, eager to establish a foothold on the mainland. In 1633, the first English settlement was established at Gracias a Dios, from where the English began trading and interacting with the coastal Sumu.

By 1700, the English had cemented a firm alliance with the coastal tribes of the Tawahka—who had metamorphosed over the years into the Miskito—against their common enemy, the Spaniards. The Brits frequently launched raids from La Mosquitia against Trujillo and Puerto Caballos, and even struck inland to Olancho and southward to Nicaragua. The attacks had a devastating destabilizing effect on the Spanish colonies.

William Pitt settled Black River (now Palacios) in 1699, and shortly afterward migrants moved into Brewer's Lagoon (now Brus Lagunas). The Shoremen, as the new English settlers called themselves, were by this point more interested in logging, collecting dyewood, and smuggling than in raiding the Spaniards, but they had taught the Miskito too well, and couldn't always contain their allies. The constant harrassment eventually prompted the Spaniards into action, and by 1780 a major offensive had been launched against La Mosquitia and the Bay Islands. In March 1782, the Spaniards led a two-pronged attack against Black River and Brewer's Lagoon, one contingent coming by sea and the other, incredibly, marching overland through the jungle from Olancho. The two settlements were taken with little struggle, but most of the Shoremen and Miskitos escaped through the canals, evading capture and soon retaking the towns.

By this point, the shore colonies had become a serious headache for the British government, which was more worried about the situation in Europe than about a few loggers on the remote coast of Central America. In the Anglo-Spanish Convention, signed 14 July 1786, the British ceded all Central American settlements to the Spanish in exchange for Belize. By August of the following year all Shoremen had been evacuated to Belize, except for a few stragglers in the woods, and the Spanish took possession of Black River.

Colonial authorities soon discovered, however, that ownership is one thing and settlement quite another. Several boatloads of would-be migrants were shipped out to Mosquitia, but faced with the steaming jungle and hostile, violent Miskitos, most took the first opportunity to flee. Taking advantage of the general anarchy in Central America following independence from Spain in 1821, and in a bid to halt U.S. ascendency in the region, the British government again officially recognized the Miskito Kingdom, but the U.S. forced England to back down in 1860 through diplomatic pressure.

Although Honduras gained undisputed control over La Mosquitia in 1860, the region continued to be populated primarily by Miskitos, Tawahkas, Garífuna, Pech, and the occasional American or British logger until the 1950s, when the Honduran government began building schools in an effort to spread the use of Spanish.

The department of Gracias a Dios was created in 1957, and since that time the government has promoted migration into the region, with limited success.

In the 1980s, the Miskitos were again used as proxies in a foreign war, armed and encouraged by the U.S. CIA to fight the Sandinista government in Nicaragua. Honduras's Puerto Lempira was the main base for this front of the so-called Contra war. The violence led to major immigration from Nicaragua into Honduras, a trend which only recently began reversing.

Most residents of La Mosquitia survive on the fishing industry or as small-scale farmers. The fishing season is technically only between September and February, but as locals have little other means of income, many fish illicitly all year. Much of the lobster caught off the coast ends up on the tables of the Red Lobster restaurant chain in the United States.

In recent years, contraband cocaine has begun passing through La Mosquitia. Taking advantage of the huge stretches of unpatrolled coastline in this corner of Honduras, Colombian drug runners have started dropping off major shipments of coke on the beaches of La Mosquitia, where it's taken overland on its way north. Every once in a while a kilo or two will wash up on shore, and an entire village will be wired to the gills for a week or so.

PALACIOS

Situated on a spit of land at the mouth of the Río Sico, protected from the open ocean by a small lagoon, Palacios is a town of about 2,000, scattered across grassy pastures cut out of the jungle. Because planes fly daily between Palacios and La Ceiba, and because of the town's proximity to the Río Plátano, Palacios is a necessary stop-off point for visitors to the Biosphere Reserve. It's also a funky little town in its own right, worth visiting to experience the isolated life of La Mosquitia, and to check out nearby Garífuna and Miskito villages.

History

Black River, as the town was first called, was founded in 1699 by William Pitt, on the site of a Miskito village. A distant relative of the famed

British prime minister, Pitt was instrumental in maintaining the Shoremen's alliance with the Miskitos; in the process he became extremely wealthy. He had sugar plantations stretching up the Black River for 50 miles, 400 slaves, and a mansion built at the edge of the jungle.

Following the War of Jenkin's Ear between England and Spain in 1739, the British proclaimed sovereignty over Black River and sent military officers to build fortifications there and at Brewer's Lagoon. William Lawrie Pitt, grandson of the town's founder, officially relinquished control of Black River to the Spanish on 29 August 1787. The Spanish renamed the town Río Tinto, but the new name didn't protect it from repeated plunder by the Miskitos. The Spanish finally evacuated the town in September 1800.

The town, renamed Palacios, was not repopulated until the early part of this century, when the banana companies made an abortive attempt to start a plantation in the vicinity. The remains of their railroad can still be seen, mostly covered over by jungle. Palacios is still sometimes called La Criva, a corruption of Black River.

Three English cannons from the old fort and the graves of William Pitt and members of his family can still be seen in town; ask a local to point them out.

Practicalities

Options for eating and sleeping in Palacios are fairly limited. Don Felix Marmol runs a *pulpería* in a ramshackle, two-story wooden building, which is also the Isleña office and the town's informal gathering place. On the second floor of the building are a couple of fairly grim rooms going for US$2 a night. Next to the store is a newly built hotel, also owned by Felix, which he expects to run as a sportfishing lodge. Until that gets off the ground, he rents the rooms at fairly reasonable rates to travelers.

Between the store and the hotel is a small *comedor* with unexceptional meals for US$1. Check in with the cooks beforehand and ask what they have and when they're serving.

West of Felix's, facing the airstrip, is the two-story **Trek Hotel**, a sportfishing outfit run out of the United States. The hotel runs several boats with gear and guides for about US$1,400 for four days fishing, including airfare from San Pedro, lodging, and food. Fishing is mainly for snook, tarpon, kingfish, mackerel, and barracu-

CON MAN PAR EXCELLENCE

Near Black River was the site of the ill-fated Poyais Colony, one of the more impressive swindles in Central American history. Scotsman Gregor MacGregor, a former British soldier and a mercenary general in Bolivar's South American wars of independence, ended up on the Mosquitia Coast in 1820. He got along famously with Miskito King George Frederick. The king, who had a predisposition to like any Englishman, especially one with a large supply of rum, awarded MacGregor enormous land concessions around the mouth of the Black River.

MacGregor returned to England proclaiming himself the representative of the fictional nation of Poyais, currently looking for colonists. Calling himself His Highness Gregor I, Cazique of Poyais, MacGregor spent two years convincing politicians, financiers, and many others to back his project. In 1822 he published *Sketch of the Mosquito Shore, Including the Territory of Poyais, Chiefly Intended for the Use of Settlers,* enumerating the many wonders of the region, and notably failing to mention that the region was an undeveloped jungle.

MacGregor convinced hundreds to financially back the would-be colony, and over 200 suckers, including teachers, clerks, shopkeepers, and a banker, actually went to Honduras in late 1822. They arrived in the midst of severe rains to a patch of riverside jungle on the Black River, totally unprepared to deal with their surroundings. In their anger at being duped they alienated local Miskitos, who might have helped them, by refusing to swear allegiance to King George Frederick. The settlers were attacked by the Miskitos and decimated by disease; in the end, 50 bedraggled survivors were eventually picked up by a rescue ship from Belize.

Unperturbed by the fate of his "colony," MacGregor went on selling land to other Europeans for nine years before the situation got too hot, whence he bolted to Venezuela and lived a wealthy man until his death in 1845.

da, all on a catch-and-release basis. Contact Trek International Safaris, P.O. Box 19065, Jacksonville, FL 32245, tel. (800) 654-9915 or (904) 296-3236. The comfortable rooms, each with private bathroom and hot water, are sometimes available to walk-in travelers for US$10 a night, and, if business is slow, one-day fishing trips can be arranged for US$100 a day.

Far and away the finest food in Palacios, and probably all of Mosquitia, can be found at **The Restaurant on the Point,** run by an American couple. Hearty, home-style meatloaf, fish-fillet sandwiches, burgers, burritos, and (in season) lobster and conch are served up three meals every day for US$2-4. Portions are large. The patio restaurant is on the opposite side of the lagoon from Palacios, near the ocean. The only drawback to the restaurant is getting there— ask around for someone who can ferry you across the lagoon for hopefully not too much money. The owners plan to rent out a couple of simple rooms for US$3 a night, although the all-night generator might disturb your sleep a bit. Behind their house a trail leads to the beach.

The **Bahai Hospital** has a couple of western doctors on staff and is the best medical facility in western Mosquitia.

Getting There and Away

Isleña flies from Palacios to Trujillo (US$28) and La Ceiba (US$43) every day except Sunday, leaving at 11:45 a.m. Tickets can be arranged at Don Felix's store.

The legendary **Sami** flies a puddle jumper every day except Sunday from Belén (a 45-minute, US$5 boat ride from Palacios) to Brus Lagunas (US$13), Ahuas (US$16), and Puerto Lempira (US$25). He usually leaves in the morning—ask Don Felix to check times and seat availability in advance on the radio. Sometimes Sami flies through Palacios also.

Boat prices from Palacios to Belén, Cocobila, Raistá, Sangrelaya, Batalla, and elsewhere in the vicinity of Palacios are something of a racket. Expect to pay about US$5, sometimes more, to get across the lagoon to the villages on the peninsula. In fairness, gasoline in Mosquitia is extremely expensive as it all has to be brought in by boat. Local boatmen have agreed on prices, so generally haggling won't get you too far, although it's worth a try.

Boats from Palacios up to Las Marías on the Río Plátano, at last check, cost about US$100 roundtrip, including a couple of days at the village. For each extra day in Las Marías, expect to pay a bit more to the captain for the wait. In a *tuk-tuk,* or motorized canoe, the trip from Palacios takes 6-8 hours. Bring something soft to sit on (those wooden benches are a killer) and protection from the sun. A couple of outboard *lanchas* run the route in about half the time or less, but cost considerably more. Sometimes they operate out of Palacios, sometimes at Barra Plátano at the river mouth.

NEAR PALACIOS

Facing the Caribbean Sea on a narrow, sandy peninsula backed by the Río Sico and, farther east, the Laguna de Ibans, are a string of Garífuna and Miskito villages where most of the population in this part of La Mosquitia lives.

The Garífuna Villages

West of the mouth of the Río Sico lies the large Garífuna village of **Batalla.** Going west around Cabo Camarón from Batalla, walkable in a day on the beach, is **Sangrelaya,** another Garífuna village; trucks travel from here to Limón or Tocoa every day.

Several kilometers east of the mouth of the Río Sico is **Plaplaya,** the easternmost Garífuna settlement in Honduras. Plaplaya is home to the **Giant Leatherback Turtle Project,** run with the help of the Mopawi, a Mosquitia development agency, and a local Peace Corps volunteer. The project has set up a protected nesting area for the turtles, who grow up to 1,500 pounds and are the largest living turtle species. Basic rooms and meals can be found in Plaplaya by asking around.

The Miskito Villages

Approximately a two-hour walk east of Plaplaya is **Ibans,** and beyond, in quick succession, **Cocobila, Raistá, Belén,** and **Nuevo Jerusalem.** Walking between these Miskito settlements, it's difficult to tell where one stops and the next begins—they all blend together, houses and the occasional store and church scattered along grassy footpaths in the couple hundred meters of land between the ocean and Laguna de Ibans. The beach along this entire stretch is windswept and deserted.

Cold drinks and basic supplies are sold at *pulperías* in Ibans, Cocobila, and Belén, and you could probably find a room and a meal by asking around. Camping is allowed just about anywhere on the peninsula, but ask first.

The best setup for travelers is at the **Butterfly Farm (Finca Mariposa)** in Raistá, where you can rent a room for US$3 per person. The farm, started by a Peace Corps volunteer in 1995 and managed by locals, raises and exports butterfly larvae to U.S. research institutes. An interesting tour of the farm by manager Eddie Boddens costs US$2.50. Eddie's wife cooks up excellent meals for US$1.20 a meal— it's mainly rice, eggs, chicken, and beans, but somehow she has a knack for making it taste good. Occasionally you'll get a treat of *wabul,* a traditional Miskito drink made from bananas and coconut milk. The people at Raistá are very friendly, and the Finca is a peaceful place to hang out before or after a trip up the Río Plátano.

The office for Sami's five-seater airplane is in Belén, a five-minute walk east of Raistá. The Isleña office, where you can make reservations and buy tickets, is above a store in Cocobila. Boats back to Palacios usually cost US$5, although the Isleña boat is sometimes a bit cheaper. *Lanchas* and *tuk-tuks* up the Río Plátano can be negotiated in any of these villages, for the same prices as in Palacios. From the northeast corner of Laguna de Ibans, by Nuevo Jerusalem, locals have hacked out a canal to the Río Plátano, meaning boats no longer have to go out to the open ocean to get to the river. Don't go swimming in the canal as there are plenty of crocodiles lurking.

You could walk from Nuevo Jerusalem about three hours east along the beach to Barra Plátano, a village at the mouth of the Río Plátano. Boats up to Las Marías can be contracted in Barra Plátano. If your timing is exceptionally good, you might even find a boat already going and not have to pay for a *viaje especial* (special trip), but don't count on it. Rooms and food are available in Barra Plátano.

Cerro Baltimore

Named by a U.S. missionary some 50 years ago, Cerro Baltimore rises 1,083 meters from the south side of Laguna de Ibans. The jungle-clad peak is on the inside edge of the Biosphere Reserve, but in spite of its protected status cattle ranchers have begun invading and cutting down the forest on the southwest side. With a guide, you can climb Cerro Baltimore in three days, roundtrip. On the eastern flank of the mountain a trail cuts from the lagoon through the forest to Las Marías, on the Río Plátano—a three day walk. It can be difficult to find a boat ride back from Las Marías, unless you're willing to wait a few days. The boatmen are unhappy about this trail and have threatened to close it, since it takes potential business away from them. At last report it was still open. Sergio Boddens lives on the south side of the lagoon and will guide travelers. Contact him through his brother Eddie, the manager of the Butterfly Farm in Raistá.

RESERVA DE LA BIOSFERA DEL RÍO PLÁTANO

Created in 1980, the Río Plátano Reserve covers 800,000 hectares, expanded from 525,100 hectares in 1992. It encompasses a huge expanse of broadleaf tropical rainforest and patches of savanna grasslands across the Gracias a Dios, Olancho, and Colón departments. The reserve, a UN-ESCO World Heritage site, is bordered by the Río Paulaya on the northwest, the Caribbean Sea on the north, the Río Patuca to the east and south, and the Patuca and Agalta mountain ranges to the south and west. Other rivers within the reserve include the Río Sigre (Sikre) and the Río Twas, both of which empty into Laguna de Brus. Notable mountains include Cerro Baltimore (1,083 meters), Pico Dama (840 meters), Cerro Mirador (1,200 meters), Cerro Antilope (1,075 meters), and Montaña Punta Piedra (1,326 meters).

Most foreigners come to the Río Plátano to admire the plants and animals of the largest remaining virgin tropical forest in Central America, but there are also several pre-Columbian ruins both near Las Marías and in the southern section of the park in Olancho. Little is known about either the ruins or who built them. Persistent

THE RAINFOREST OF RÍO PLÁTANO

This jungle, the start of the high forest, was tall and orderly. Each tree had found room to grow separately. The trees were arranged in various ways, according to slenderness of leaf size, the big-leafed ones on the jungle floor, the towering trees with tiny leaves rising to great heights, and the ferns in between. I had always pictured jungle as suffocating spaghetti tangles, drooping and crisscrossed, a mass of hairy green rope and clutching stems. . . . This was more like a church, with pillars and fans and hanging flowers and only the slightest patches of white sky above the curved roof of branches.

Paul Theroux was a bit weak on geography in his popular novel, *The Mosquito Coast*—the Río Aguán, which his fictional American family followed up into the jungle, actually leads into one of the most heavily cultivated valleys in the country—but his description of primary rainforest certainly rings true. The Río Plátano rainforest is an example of one of the most complex and efficient ecosystems on the planet, a culmination of eons of evolution that is in danger of being destroyed completely within a couple of decades.

One of the great ironies of the process of deforestation is that land-hungry migrants see the lush forest and assume the soil underneath to be rich and productive, when in fact it's extremely thin and nutrient-poor. The evolutionary triumph of the rainforest is that almost all its nutrients are concentrated above ground—there's only a few centimeters of dirt in the forest. Under the dirt lies a mass of white threads, the rootlets of trees living in conjunction with a certain type of fungus, a sort of garbage collector of the forest that quickly decomposes any organic material and provides nutrients to the trees, which in turn supply the products of photosynthesis to the fungus. This is what plant biologists call a "mature system." As little as one-tenth of one percent of nutrients penetrate below the first five centimeters of the forest floor, meaning soil is one of the least important elements to the cycle.

The rainforest is composed of a dizzying variety of trees and plants, but they are extremely difficult to distinguish, as many have similar color bark and almost all have the same tear-drop shaped leaves. As one writer put it: "A naturalist in New England can easily learn all the species of native trees in the region in a single summer, but there are few people who, even after a lifetime of study, can confidently identify most of the trees in a patch of tropical American rainforest."

Trying to spot wildlife in the forest can also be frustrating. The Río Plátano jungle may support 80% of the mammal species in the country, but good luck finding all but a few of them. You won't have too much trouble running across the odd troop of noisy monkeys, but most other creatures have excellent camouflage and stay well hidden. Many are nocturnal. Rainforest birds in particular are difficult to find, as their nests are extremely well hidden to avoid predators.

rumor holds that a full-scale city called **Ciudad Blanca** lies in the middle of the jungle, waiting to be discovered.

Getting into the Reserve

The easiest access to the rainforest is up the Río Plátano from Palacios to the village of Las Marías, on the banks of the river 5-7 hours by boat from the coast. Between the coast and Las Marías it's mostly secondary forest and small riverside ranchos, but beyond the village the primary rainforest begins, continuing up to the mountains of Olancho.

Independent travelers can hire boats from Palacios or the nearby villages of Belén, Raistá, or Cocobila to Las Marías for about US$100 roundtrip, including a few days at Las Marías to explore the forest or take smaller boats upriver. It's worth finding a few travel companions to split the costs of the trip, as well as the guides at Las Marías. Finding a boat already headed upriver to hitch a ride on for not much money is difficult if not impossible. The best place to try is Barra Plátano, at the mouth of the river, which you can walk to in a few hours along the coast from Nuevo Jerusalem.

Trips up the Río Sigre with local guides are also available at Brus Lagunas. The Sigre features similar flora and fauna to the Río Plátano. The guide prices at Brus are higher than at Las Marías, but planes fly right into Brus from La Ceiba, eliminating the need to pay for an expensive boat ride to get to the start of the trip.

It's also possible to get into the rainforest from Dulce Nombre de Culmí, Olancho, on your own, hiring local guides as you go, but this is only for hardcore adventurers who can take care of themselves. The best option for those wanting to travel from Olancho to the coast, through the entire rainforest, is to contact **La Moskitia Eco Aventuras,** an outfit that offers combination hiking-and-rafting trips over the Olancho mountains and down the Río Plátano to the coast in 10-12 days, for between US$850 and US$1100 per person, depending on the size of the group. Shorter trips to the Río Plátano and rafting trips on the Río Patuca are also available. La Moskitia operates two offices, one in La Ceiba on Parque Bonilla, tel. 42-0104, and the other in Tegucigalpa, P.O. Box 3577, tel. 37-9398 or 21-0404, fax 21-0408.

Euro Honduras Tours runs well-recommended shorter tours of the Río Plátano and Río Sico regions, and can be reached in La Ceiba at tel. 43-3893 or tel./fax 43-0933. **Turtle Tours,** tel./fax 44-4431, based in Trujillo, also leads recommended trips to Mosquitia.

For unorthodox adventures in La Mosquitia with minimal amenities and flexible itineraries, consider taking a trip with **Derek Parent,** author of the only decent do-it-yourself adventuring book about La Mosquitia and something of a local legend. Derek charges US$35 per day, minimum two days and two participants; clients pay locals directly for food, accommodations, and guide services. He can be contacted in Canada at tel. (514) 698-2288 or e-mail: derekp@vir.com.

Las Marías

A mixed Miskito and Pech village of about 400 people, Las Marías is a collection of thatched huts spread over a large area on a rise above the Río Plátano. Located just downriver from the edge of the primary forest, Las Marías is an ideal base for hiking and river trips, and has become an unofficial headquarters for the Biosphere Reserve.

Las Marías appears to have a love-hate relationship with outsiders. The income from foreign visitors is much appreciated, but it has also created tensions and jealousies within the community, which is already divided along ethnic lines. Prices may seem somewhat outrageous for the goods and services offered, but keep in mind that money literally did not exist in Las Marías until just 10 years ago. Basic principles of supply and demand are simply not part of the way things work. Still, a trip to Las Marías and beyond remains quite reasonable, all things considered, especially when divided among a small group of travelers. Remember, it's not every day you get a guided trip into virgin rainforest.

Two *hospedajes* in town rent beds with mosquito nets for US$2.50 a night pp in comfortable, breezy buildings. Each hostel serve three very basic meals a day. The food is not well prepared and expensive at US$1.50 for mostly rice and beans, but there's not much choice. If you don't want to eat, let the cook know and expect black looks. The *hospedaje* further back from the river has somewhat better food. Camping is not appreciated by locals, unless you offer to pay to pitch a tent in someone's yard.

The local Peace Corps volunteer runs the **Mopawi office,** providing valuable information on the area and selling visitors maps and an assortment of local handicrafts. Mopawi is a local development agency that coordinates a variety of social and environmental projects in the region.

WHAT TO BRING ON A JUNGLE HIKE

light hiking boots
lightweight long-sleeve clothes, shorts for
    swimming
insect repellent and sunblock
hat
kerosene or gas stove
survival knife
compass
flashlights
waterproof matches and lighter
sheet or light sleeping bag
camera
malaria pills
water bottles
filter or purification tablets (preferably both)
binoculars for bird and animal watching
dry bags
accident insurance
tent or hammock with built-in mosquito net
first-aid kit with antiseptic, bandages,
    antibiotic, and snakebite kit

A BICULTURAL TOWN

Las Marías is one of the few settlements in La Mosquitia where two ethnic groups—Miskito and Pech—live side by side. The locals have a story about how the two groups met. Supposedly in the early part of the century, a group of Miskitos went upriver from the coast in search of cuyamel fish. Above the present site of Las Marías, at a place where there is a small beach on the banks of the river, the fishermen surprised a group of Pech bathing in the river. These Pech were, at that time, still very much jungle people, and the Miskitos didn't know what to make of them.

The Pech fled immediately, and the Miskitos returned to the coast to tell the tale to their compatriots. Eventually another group went upriver, this time with clothes, which they left on the beach. Hiding in the jungle nearby, the Miskitos watched the Pech return to the beach, find the clothes, and start putting them on all wrong—shorts over their head, shoes on their hands.

The Miskitos jumped out of their hiding spot and ran after the Pech, who fled into the jungle. One girl was too slow to escape, and the Miskitos captured her and brought her back to the coast, where they taught her Miskito and learned Pech. They returned upriver, and gradually the two groups began interacting and trading. Las Marías was founded about two generations ago, according to residents.

Whether the story is legend or fact, it says a lot about the two cultures. The coastal Miskitos have always been more worldly and domineering than the quieter, reserved Pech; these traits continue to the present day. The two still do not always get along with each other, and live in separate parts of the village—the Pech upstream and the Miskitos downstream.

For more information on Mopawi, see "Practicalities" under "Puerto Lempira," below.

The local water hole is a stream behind the medical center, away from the river. It's best to purify the water here, and many other places in Mosquitia. If you don't have purification tablets or a purifier, a couple of drops of bleach per quart will work. Don't drink the water from the river, as there are houses just upstream. Swimming in the river is considered safe; alligators are rare in the fast-moving water.

The small airstrip is used only by the Alas de Socorro mission plane, which comes for medical emergencies. If you really hate boats and have lots of money, Sami will fly a special charter to Las Marías.

Hiking and Boating from Las Marías

The Las Marías guides work on a strict rotation among all 80 households in the village, as it's the only way to keep everyone reasonably happy. Quality varies dramatically from one guide to the next—some are quite shy, and although possibly knowledgable don't know what gringos want to hear. For best results, keep asking questions. No English is spoken. Generally the older guides are better, but trying to request a specific guide has limited success. The rotation is managed by Martin Herrera, a young man who is not always too friendly but must be dealt with at least briefly to arrange the trip. At last report, guides cost US$6 per guide per day, extra on Sunday and holidays. For hiking trips with more than five people, two guides are required.

Trips upriver by *pipante,* narrow dugouts propelled by poles, cost a fair bit, as travelers must pay for three guides per *pipante* (two polers and one guide) plus US$4 per boat. Each *pipante* can only fit two visitors, so if you have a group of three, two boats and six guides are required.

It's hard to beat a boat ride through virgin jungle—birds and monkeys are easy to spot in the trees along the river's edge, and are not scared off by the noisy tromp of hikers. Further, a day's journey upstream from Las Marías are two sets of prehistoric rock carvings, **Walp'ulban'sirpi** and **Walp'ulban'tara.** The first, on a large rock in the river, resembles a person/serpent, while the second features several different figures and designs. Both can be visited in a two-day trip, with one night of camping.

Two to four days beyond the rock carvings lies the junction of the **Río Cuyamel,** where a hike begins to **Cerro Mirador,** at least a week roundtrip, but an excellent opportunity to fully appreciate both a river trip and multiday hike. Beyond Río Cuyamel are the wild headwaters of the **Río Plátano,** the very heart of the Biosphere Reserve and the most pristine jungle left in Central America. From Las Marías it takes a week to 10 days boating and hiking to reach the region. All times upriver change dramatically depending on how fast the river is running. A better option for those wanting to get into the headwaters area is to take a trip with Jorge Zalaverry of La Moskitia Eco Aventuras, from Dulce Nombre de Culmí across the mountains and down the Río Plátano.

Pico Dama, the jagged peak looming up out of the jungle not far from Las Marías, can be hiked in four to five days roundtrip, and offers great opportunities to see wildlife as well as stunning views over western La Mosquitia. For those wanting just a taste of jungle hiking, a viewpoint known as **Cerro Zapote** is a two- to three-hour walk from Las Marías, and offers vistas toward Cerro Baltimore and Laguna de Ibans. From Cerro Zapote you can see what a serpentine course the Río Plátano follows below Las Marías on the way to the coast.

Rio Sigre (Sikre)
Parallel to the Río Plátano to the east, running from the Olancho mountains into Brus Lagunas,

MAMMALS IN THE
RÍO PLÁTANO BIOSPHERE RESERVE

ENGLISH	SPANISH	MISKITO	PECH
opossum	tacuacín	Sikiski	maishí
three-toed sloth	perezoso de tres dedos	siwaiko	slwuá
two-toed sloth	perozoso de dos dedos	slwalko	siwuá
pygmy anteater	perico ligero	likor	kuráhuwuista
giant anteater	oso caballo	wingkutara	kurah ujáh
tanadua anteater	oso hormiguero	winkusirpi	kuráh
white-faced monkey	mono cara blanca	waklin	guayá
howler monkey	mono aullador (or olingo)	kong kong	huquí
spider monkey	mono araña (or mico)	urus	hurus
white-nosed coati	pizote	wistan	tuská
kinkajou	mico de noche	uyuk	wuachác
northern raccoon	mapachin (or oso lavador)	skusku	n/a
striped skunk	zorillo	piokrauat	wuahá
river otter	nutria (or perro de agua)	mamo	taoó
jaguarundi	jaguarundi	limi siksa	misto sonwá
ocelot	ocelot (or tigrillo)	krujuha	huç brú
mountain lion	león (or puma)	limi pauni	huc pawá
jaguar	tigre	limi bulni	huc cewáh
red brocket deer	tilopo	snapuka	ichaá pawua
white-tailed deer	venado cola blanca	sula waika pijini	ichaá kamazá
white-lipped peccary	jaguilla	wari	quitán
collared peccary	kekeo	buksa	wuareká
Baird's tapir	danto	tilba	chajú
squirrel	ardilla	buston	torenah
porcupine	eriso	haksuk	n/a
paca	tepiscuinte	ibijina	huaquí
agouti	guatuza	kiajki	barka
rabbit	conejo	bang bang	mi nih
nine-banded armadillo	cusuco	tayra	patuhá
naked-tailed armadillo	tumbo armadillo	takan-takan	yucrú
bat	murcielago	sankanki	tiquimi
vampire bat	murcielago vampire	sankanki tara	tiquimi

is the little-known Río Sigre, also called Río Sikre. The Río Sigre has the same flora and fauna as the Río Plátano, and can be visited with guides from Brus Lagunas. One- to four-day trips of hiking or boating cost between US$35 (with a group of five) and US$100 (with just one person) per day, all food and transport included. In Brus, contact Celio Colindres, who organizes the Comite Vigilante del Turismo Para Desarollo Nativo (Covitudena), Tourism Vigilance Committee For Native Development. Colindres can be contacted by calling 43-0400 in La Ceiba.

Río Sico and Río Paulaya

Until just a decade or so ago, the upper reaches of the Río Sico Valley (also called the Río Tinto or the Río Negro) and all of the Río Paulaya Valley were untouched jungle. Unfortunately, they've been invaded in recent years by a flood of land-hungry cattle ranchers from other parts of Honduras. In a move of questionable intelligence, the border of the Biosphere Reserve was set at the Río Paulaya itself, rather than the mountains on the western edge of the valley. So instead of encompassing the entire river valley, the reserve supposedly protects one side of the river but not the other. As no authorities patrol anywhere nearby, it's no surprise cattle ranchers have been hard at work hacking down the forest on both sides of the river. Although it hasn't completely disappeared yet, it seems the Río Paulaya jungle is unsalvageable.

Unless you enjoy the depressing sight of a disappearing forest, the only reason to head up the Paulaya Valley is to visit the **Piedra Floreada petroglyphs.** These impressive rock etchings, described by Alison McKittrick in an Instituto Hondureño de

Antropología e Historia (INAH) publication, are located on the Río Kiniskisné, a tributary of the Río Paulaya. Several figures and geometric shapes are carved into two large rocks, and the rocks are surrounded by unexcavated mounds that may cover a pre-conquest settlement. Local cattle ranchers know of the site and will guide visitors there from the town of Sico, which can be reached by boat from Palacios.

A trail follows the Río Paulaya upriver into a wild area of Olancho, near Dulce Nombre de Culmí, where there are other petroglyph sites similar to the Piedra Floreada. Formerly a central trade and communication route between coastal and inland Indian tribes, this path was also used extensively by smugglers and raiders from the English-controlled Mosquitia on their way to Olancho during colonial times.

BRUS LAGUNAS

Originally established as the English outpost named Brewer's Lagoon, Brus Lagunas is now a mainly Miskito settlement of about 5,000 on the southern edge of the lagoon of the same name. Apart from experiencing this quirky little town of wooden shacks spread over the savanna, which continues east from here across to Puerto Lempira, there's not a great deal to do. Brus's main attractions are sportfishing with an outfit on Cannon Island in the lagoon, and jungle trips up the nearby Río Sigre with local guides.

Considering the high population of alligators and crocodiles there, swimming in the lagoon is not recommended. Locals do it anyway, but everyone's got a story about someone losing an appendage, so it hardly seems worth the chance.

The one cannon on the grassy field in the middle of town originally came from Cannon Island, a fort used by Miskito Indians and British settlers in conflicts against the Spanish.

Practicalities

Official accommodations in town are limited to a few ultra-basic rooms run by the owner of the *pulpería* next to the docks; US$1.80. Cecelio Colindres, a half-French Honduran who has lived in Brus two decades, has helped organize a local jungle-guide

KAREN McKINLEY

plátano, rice, beans, shrimp, iguana, or whatever else the latest boat brought in. Beers are technically illegal in town, but are sold by, of all people, the family of the mayor. Ask around discretely.

The local Hondutel radiophone and telegram office is open Mon.-Fri. 8-11 a.m. and 2-4 p.m.

Brus has two airstrips. Sami and Alas use the one nearer to town by the water tank; Rollins uses the other, about a 40-minute walk further. Sami flies in daily except Sunday, and charges US$13 to Belén (near Palacios) or Ahuas, and US$20 to Puerto Lempira. Alas comes in irregularly, and generally charges US$10 to wherever the plane is going. For information on either, ask at the *pulpería* on the main street in the middle of town.

Rollins flies to and from La Ceiba on Wednesday and Saturday, charging US$40 one-way. The *pulpería* at the docks arranges Rollins flights. Usually a pickup drives out to each flight—ask when you get a ticket.

Lanchas from Brus across the lagoon and out to Barra Plátano cost about US$35 *viaje especial,* and it's rare to find a boat heading out there to hitch a ride on. It may be possible to find a boatman willing to navigate the canals and waterways across the savanna to the Río Patuca.

The **MV *Captain Rinel*** usually pulls into the lagoon once a week, and can take travelers eager for a tramp-freighter experience on the two-day run back to La Ceiba. Other boats occasionally come through on their way to Puerto Castilla, La Ceiba, or elsewhere.

Cannon Island

One of the finest sportfishing outfits in Honduras, Cannon Island offers weeklong fishing packages for US$3,000 per person. The price excludes airfare to San Pedro Sula, but includes lodging in one of three wooden cabins on the mosquito-free island, excellent homestyle cooking, and daily fishing trips aboard one of the lodge's six boats. The fishing excursions go to one of five rivers, the lagoon itself, or the open ocean in search of world-class snook, tarpon, snapper, barracuda, and the occasional shark, all catch-and-release. Guests are welcome to bring a favorite pole, but all equipment is provided. For information and reservations, contact Pan Angling at tel. (312) 263-0328, fax (503) 643-9224, or in La Ceiba at (504) 43-2487; e-mail: jdnovl@teleport.com.

DESTROYING A RAINFOREST~ HONDURAN STYLE

In spite of the growing national and international recognition of the Río Plátano Biosphere Reserve, campesinos, cattle ranchers, and mahogany loggers have been steadily hacking away at the edges of the reserve. The hardest-hit areas are along the Río Paulaya, in the southern mountains where roads cut into the forest from Olancho, and along the upper Río Patuca. In places depredations have hit not only the so-called "buffer zone," but up to 30 km inside the core zone of the reserve. One 1991 environmental study estimated that 60% of the forest in the buffer zone had been destroyed, and the process since then has if anything accelerated. In December 1995 the Reina administration, under pressure from cattle ranchers and *campesino* unions, declared the Paulaya valley a region for "agrarian reform," which migrants interpreted as a green light. The decree has since been rescinded, but the damage was done.

According to members of the Comite Vigilancia de Tierra (CVT), who have the thankless, often dangerous, and usually impossible task of patrolling the reserve, the first wave of invaders is usually poor peasants who work the land for a couple of years, get a title from the Agrarian Reform Institute, then turn around and sell it to large-scale cattle ranchers. These ranchers have amassed huge expanses of former jungle, if not legally than through threats and outright murder. The CVT, with only a few employees, no power to make arrests, and certainly no weapons with which to face the ranchers, stands little chance of stemming the tide, and the police and army don't appear interested in intervening. In fact, many hint that powerful members of the armed forces are involved in the whole shady business.

---

outfit and can also arrange rooms for visitors. Colindres, who speaks English, German, French, Spanish, and Miskito, has a beautiful pet ocelot at his house. For more information on tours from Brus, see Río Sigre under the Río Plátano Biosphere Reserve.

There are no restaurants in Brus, so ask around for someone who can cook you a meal. Expect

Although guests will encounter no problems, the American owner of Cannon Island is not well liked by the residents of Brus Lagunas, who resent that none of the money passing through the resort is ever seen in town.

RÍO PATUCA

Although the Río Coco, shared with Nicaragua, is longer, the Río Patuca is the longest river that runs completely inside Honduras. The Patuca's 500-km course winds from the mountains of the Olancho, El Paraíso, and Francisco Morazán departments into La Mosquitia. The middle reaches of the river are the homeland of the Tawahka Indians, the smallest indigenous group in Honduras.

Ahuas

The largest town on the Río Patuca, Ahuas has a population of about 1,800, almost all Miskito, spread out over the savanna and pine groves a couple of kilometers from the river. Missionaries have been hard at work at Ahuas, as evidenced by the several Protestant churches in town.

An exploratory oil well was sunk near Ahuas in the 1970s, and the remnants of the derrick are still nearby. The extremely anomalous big-rig truck in the middle of town was floated up the river by the oil crews, and left when the well was abandoned. A local recently got it cranked up again, but there's nowhere to drive it except out to the oil rig and back again.

One family in town offers rooms in a wooden shack for US$2.50 a night, not far from the airstrip, and another family near the "hotel" regularly cooks meals for visitors for US$1. A couple of *pulperías* in town sell basic supplies. The mission hospital near the airstrip usually has a western doctor in residence and offers good emergency care.

Ahuas is the base for Alas de Socorro, the mission-sponsored emergency plane service run by Geoff Goff. He is usually happy to take on passengers for US$10 a ride to wherever he's going, but his schedule is unpredictable. If his services aren't needed elsewhere, he will also charter special flights, but that can be expensive. Sami flies to Ahuas every day except Sunday at irregular hours. Reservations can be made at the hut next to the airstrip.

At Ahuas the Patuca is a wide and impressive river, bordered by a narrow strip of jungle. Boats frequently head downriver from here to Barra Patuca (3.5 hours, US$5) or upriver to Wampusirpi (7-8 hours, US$7). These narrow cargo/passenger boats are often quite packed and uncomfortable, so be prepared. *Viajes especiales* cost a great deal more.

Barra Patuca

At the mouth of the Río Patuca is the large Miskito town of Barra Patuca, with several stores and a couple of basic *hosepdajes*. Several families

downtown Ahuas

will gladly cook you a meal for a fee. Boats from Barra Patuca to Ahuas and Brus Lagunas are fairly frequent, but heading east to Puerto Lempira is difficult.

Upper Río Patuca

Seven to 10 hours upriver from Ahuas is **Wampusirpi,** a former Tawahka town that in recent years has been taken over by Miskitos, many having fled the violence of the Contra war in the 1980s. Wampusirpi is located where the Patuca emerges from the rainforest onto the pine savanna, which continues to the Caribbean coast. Basic lodging and meals can be arranged in town, although there are no hotels or restaurants per se.

Above Wampusirpi are the Miskito villages of, in order, Kurpa, Tukrun, Arenas Blancas, and Pimienta. Beyond Pimienta is Krausirpe—a Tawahka village that is the unofficial capital of the Tawahka. This is the proposed center of the Tawahka Anthropological Reserve, which if enacted will connect the Río Plátano Biosphere Reserve to the Bosawas reserve in Nicaragua. The Tawahka are strongly in favor of the reserve as a means to combat the constant incursions of Latino immigrants from Olancho along the Río Patuca.

With Tawahka guides, several hikes near Krausirpe are possible, including pre-conquest caves, petroglyphs, and jungle hikes in all directions. The Wankabila Trail cuts from Krausirpe over the mountains to the east and down into the Río Coco Valley and the town of Ahuasbila, where trucks can be found to Puerto Lempira.

Beyond Krausirpe is the village of Krautara, and continuing up the Patuca into Olancho are the Tawahka settlements of Yapuwás, Kamakasna, and Wasparasní.

PUERTO LEMPIRA

For most of its history an isolated little port in the farthest corner of La Mosquitia, Puerto Lempira experienced a boom in the 1980s, when it became the center of operations for the CIA-directed insurgency against the Sandanista government in Nicaragua. Little evidence remains of the past violence and intrigue. The town of about 5,000, on Laguna Caratasca, mainly survives

on fishing. It's also the capital of the Gracias a Dios department and the largest town in La Mosquitia. Mopawi, a Mosquitia development organization, is based here.

Puerto Lempira could be of interest to the inveterate adventurer who wants to check out this remote corner of the country, or a traveler intent on getting to Nicaragua the hard way, but has little to offer the casual traveler. Several nearby villages around the lagoon are worth a day's visit.

Practicalities

The two-story **Hotel Flores** in the center of town is the "best" lodging in Puerto Lempira; rooms have a/c, cable TV, and private bathroom. Unfortunately, the rooms are also boxlike, the power is constantly cutting out, and the a/c is not very effective. All in all, the hotel is overpriced at US$20 s, US$30 d. Next door is the **Anexo,** a better deal at US$5 s, US$7 d for a wooden room with fan.

On the opposite side of the street from the Flores, down a couple of blocks toward the airport, is **Hospedaje Modelo** with simple but clean wooden rooms with fans for US$4 d. The popular hotel is often full.

Hotelito Central on the second floor of a building on the main intersection in town has basic rooms for US$2 s or US$4 d with fan.

The Mopawi hostel has clean beds for US$3 per night, and is a good place to meet Peace Corps volunteers and other interesting folk. Aid workers have first chance, but the hostel is rarely full. Curfew at 10 p.m., which in Puerto Lempira is no major hardship.

A block from Hotel Flores is **Comedor Típicos,** which serves unoriginal but also clean and inexpensive meals of rice, beans, beef, and eggs. It's a favorite spot for locals to come drink a couple of beers.

The best food in town is at **Restaurant Caratasca** on the edge of the lagoon, an open-air cafe which doubles as a disco. The music is usually blaring even during the middle of the week, when no one's around. The food selection is limited but good, and costs US$3-5 per plate. The **pinchos,** a sort of shish kebab, are particularly tasty.

For entertainment, **Disco Wampus** on the docks can get hopping on weekends, and a couple of dive bars are nearby for the adventurous.

The one bank in town does not change foreign currency, but both the Isleña office at the airport and the Sosa office downtown change dollars at usurious rates if you're desperate. The migration office is a few blocks southwest of downtown.

The **Mopawi headquarters,** tel.98-7460, or in Tegucigalpa at tel. 37-7210, fax 37-2864, is on the edge of the lagoon, a few blocks south of the main dock. Formed in 1985 with the help of World Relief, the name derives from "Mosquitia Pawisa," which means Mosquitia Development in Miskito. The organization coordinates a variety of social and environmental projects in the region, and its workers are often excellent sources of information on La Mosquitia and its peoples. Mopawi operates a well-stocked store at its headquarters, selling all sorts of useful supplies and packaged food, as well as some T-shirts and maps.

Getting There and Away
The airstrip is a few blocks from downtown. Sosa flies to La Ceiba (US$45) on Tuesday, Thursday, and Saturday. Isleña flies there on Monday, Tuesday, Thursday, and Saturday. Sami also flies between Puerto Lempira and Ahuas, Brus Lagunas, and Belén (near Palacios) every day except Sunday.

The **MV *Captain Rinel*** pulls into the main dock usually once a week, and will gladly take on the random traveler wanting to spend a few days on the high seas on the way back to La Ceiba—cost negotiable.

Small *lanchas* are constantly zigging and zagging across the lagoon to various villages, and usually charge US$1 a ride if you're going their way.

Near Puerto Lempira
Of the many Miskito villages near Puerto Lempira, **Kaukira, Palkaka,** and **Mistruk** are reportedly worth visiting. **Laguna Caratasca** is well stocked with tarpon, snook, jack, grouper, and other fish; you'll need to bring your own tackle and hire a boat to take you out. The best season is between May and July.

A dirt road winds southwest from Puerto Lempira to the villages of **Mocorón, Rus Rus,** and **Ahuasbila,** the end of the road. Ahuasbila lies 265 km and 5-8 hours from Puerto Lempira, at the edge of the savanna where the jungle begins.

Between Mocorón and Rus Rus a road turns south to the Nicaraguan border at **Leimus,** where the dedicated adventure-traveler could try to cross into Nicaragua. An army post at Leimus will give you the once over, but there is no migration office, so get your passport stamped in Puerto Lempira. Usually one or two trucks a day go from Puerto Lempira to Leimus, leaving in the early morning for the three- to five-hour trip. At last check Evaristo López was running a truck to Leimus every day. Past Leimus, after crossing the Río Coco (also called Río Segovia), the road continues to Puerto Cabezas, Nicaragua.

OLANCHO

INTRODUCTION

The far-flung cattle-covered plains, rugged mountains, and thick pine forests of Olancho make up the "Wild East" of Honduras. Known affectionately by its residents as "La República Independiente de Olancho," the department has long maintained a Texas-style disdain for the central government; the people here hold the attitude that they can take care of their problems themselves, thank you very much.

This attitude arose during the colonial era, when pirates began raiding the north coast and cattle ranchers in the region found their outlet to the wider world cut off. The closest major marketplace was Guatemala City, at that time many long days away over rugged mountains, so *olanchanos* got used to doing without manufactured goods. Instead they developed self-sufficient haciendas where everything needed was made with the materials at hand.

Because of their minimal communication with the outside world, the people here commonly use certain old Spanish turns of phrase and odd words, many from Andalusia where a number of the Olancho colonists originated.

Another trait developed during the colonial era is the propensity of *olanchanos* to take justice into their own hands, seeking solutions to

vaqueros on the trail in Parque Nacional Sierra de Agalta

problems down the barrel of a gun, in a style not unlike the U.S. cowboys of a century ago. Residents nowadays claim their reputation for violence is much exaggerated, but it's still common to see tough-looking men walking around with guns stuck in their belts. One resident commented to a newspaper reporter, "The *olanchano* isn't violent, but you have to respect him."

Unless you're fool enough to insult some gun-slinging cowboy or make a pass at his girlfriend, visitors need not fear traveling in Olancho. Quite the opposite. *Olanchanos* tend to be courtly and hospitable with outsiders, proud to show off the land they love so much.

The Land

In a word: impressive. At 23,905 square km, Olancho is by far the largest of Honduras's 18 departments, covering 20% of the country's territory. Like much of Honduras, Olancho is criss-crossed by mountains—Sierra de Agalta, Sierra La Esperanza, Las Montañas del Patuca, La Cordillera Entre Ríos, and La Cordillera De Miscoso all cut through the department.

Unlike the rest of the country, however, these ranges are separated by broad valleys, once covered by pine forest and now pastureland for the department's cattle industry. Major valleys include the Catacamas or Olancho, Agalta, Lepaguare, Azacualpa, and Amacuapa. Altitudes range from 400 meters on valley floors to a high point of 2,354 meters in the Sierra de Agalta.

The mountains of Olancho give birth to several major river systems. The Río Guayape, famed for its gold, joins with the Río Guayambe to form the mighty Patuca, Honduras's longest river, running through the Olancho plains into the jungles of Mosquitia before reaching the coast after a journey of some 500 km. Parallel to the Patuca, forming the border with Nicaragua, is the even longer Río Coco (or Segovia). And in northwestern Olancho are the headwaters of the Paulaya and Sico Rivers.

Because of its size, describing Olancho's climate in general terms is not easy. Rainfall in the department ranges between 80 and 200 cm per year on average, depending on the region. The southern valleys tend to be driest, while the wettest areas are the mountain forests to the north. The dry season is usually February to April. Temperatures in Olancho also vary wildly, mostly depending on altitude, but it's usually comfortable—warm in the day and cool at night. Bring warm clothes if you plan to camp in the mountains.

History

Recent discoveries at the Cuevas de Talgua near Catacamas have led archaeologists to believe a sedentary village culture lived in the plains of Olancho 1,000 years before Christ. Little is known about the society, but evidence suggests it evolved on its own, rather than as an offshoot of the parallel cultures developing at that time in the Ulúa Valley.

Many different indigenous tribes inhabited Olancho when the Spanish arrived, including Pech, Lenca, Tawahka-Sumu, Tolupan, and perhaps descendants of Nahuatl immigrants, who later lost their original language and blended in with other groups. According to local legend, the Nahuatl arrived after a long journey from the north fleeing a great drought. The name Olancho is thought to be a derivation of a Nahuatl word meaning "land of tule trees," which are plentiful in Olancho's forests.

The Spanish era in Olancho began in 1524, when Gil González Dávila, coming from the north coast, and Hernando de Soto, marching overland from Nicaragua, met in the Valle de Catacamas and promptly started a fight over who had the rights to conquer Honduras. The internecine struggles continued for several years, and prevented the Spanish from conquering the rebellious Pech, Tolupan, and Sumu who lived in the region. Under the orders of Hernán Cortés, the first Spanish settlement in Olancho was founded in May of 1526 in the Valle de Agalta. Named Jeréz de la Frontera, the town was quickly sacked by Spaniards opposed to Cortés, who then founded another settlement, Villa Hermosa, somewhere in the vicinity of Juticalpa. Villa Hermosa was in turn leveled by a surprise attack by Indians the same year.

Having found gold in the rivers of Olancho, the Spaniards returned in force and stomped out the Indian revolt. By 1530 the town of San Jorge de Olancho had been established in the Valle de Olancho, and its inhabitants quickly forced black slaves and Indians to work the surrounding rivers for gold, especially the Río Guayape. Not long after, the towns of Juticalpa and Catacamas were established.

Either due to cruel treatment by the Spanish or a generally independent spirit, the indigenous peoples of the province were in constant rebellion for the first two centuries after the Spanish arrived. They regularly fled from the gold works, attacked villages, and massacred missionaries. The security of the region was further weakened as the English gained power on the north coast. Their allies, the Miskitos, regularly invaded Olancho by boat from the Patuca, Paulaya, or Sico rivers in search of gold or Indian slaves to sell to the English.

When the Spanish regained the north coast and expelled the British at the end of the 18th century, Olancho enjoyed a couple of decades of relative peace, but the advent of independence brought renewed violence. Always protective of their right to manage their own affairs, olanchanos resented efforts by the new Liberal government to assert control through taxation, and also disagreed with Liberal policies against the Church. In October 1828, beginning in the town of Gualaco, the tensions broke out into open rebellion against the central government.

In 1829, war raged throughout Olancho, except in Juticalpa, which remained loyal to the government. Because the olanchano fighters employed hit-and-run tactics rather than open battles, some historians consider the rebellion to be the first example of modern guerrilla warfare in the Americas.

General Francisco Morazán himself came to Olancho in late 1829 to lead the government troops, and managed to put an end to the rebellion with a feat of brave diplomacy. Between Juticalpa and San Francisco de la Paz, at that time a bastion of the rebels, is a stretch of windy road called "Las Vueltas de Ocote." Knowing the general was on his way, the rebels arrayed their forces at Las Vueltas, and waited in ambush. Morazán, aware the rebels were there, ordered his troops to halt just outside Las Vueltas, took off his sword, and walked into the hills alone and unarmed.

Stunned by this display of bravery, the rebels allowed Morazán into their camp. The general asked

COYOL WINE

A traditional Olancho drink, not seen as much these days as imported *aguardiente* and rum take over, coyol wine is a cross between hard cider and champagne. Local Indians once made the wine by climbing up a coyol palm, hollowing out a hole under the bud, and sucking the sap out with a reed. The sap, which is strongest in March and April, in the middle of the dry season, is then fermented for a few days or a week.

Nowadays, *olanchanos* can't be bothered climbing trees, so they generally just cut the whole thing down. A single tree can yield up to three gallons of wine. One Olancho historian, commenting on the early history of the wine, writes: "It is not known how the drink coming from the coyol palm was discovered, but the first who tried it can be called, with complete confidence, the first *olanchano*."

them to explain why they were rebelling. Over the course of the hot afternoon of 21 January 1830, he hammered out an agreement to end the rebellion, conceding to Olancho a certain degree of self-government. But many *olanchanos* continued to be unhappy with their new government, and for reasons still not entirely clear, a new, more widespread rebellion broke out in 1863. Conflicts this time had a markedly social character, pitting the lower class, small-scale mestizo ranchers and laborers against the wealthy criollo cattlemen.

The rebellion continued for two years, spreading into Yoro and threatening Trujillo, before it was put down with extreme brutality by President-General José María Medina, in a campaign known to this day in Olancho as "La Ahorcancina" ("The Hanging"). The heads of two rebel leaders, Bernabé Antuñez and Francisco Zavala, were stuck on pikes and left on a hillside overlooking Juticalpa for several years afterward, as a warning to any would-be rebels.

Whether from Medina's terror campaign or exhaustion after years of fratricidal war, Olancho settled into relative peace, resigned to remain technically one of the 18 departments in Honduras. The 1980's saw a renewed surge of violence in Olancho, but this time from the CIA-directed Contra war, part of which was based along the long, wild border between Olancho and Nicaragua.

Currently, Olancho concentrates on scraping out a living through cattle-raising, logging, and occasionally panning for gold. The odd North American miner still wanders into the wilder reaches of the department hoping for a rich strike. One of the poorer departments, Olancho is famous for exporting its poorer residents to other parts of the country in search of land or work. Olancho migrants are a big part of the spreading destruction of the Río Plátano and Río Patuca rainforests.

JUTICALPA AND VICINITY

The capital of Olancho, Juticalpa was founded as a small settlement, probably around 1530, on the site of a Tawahka Indian village near the then-capital of San Jorge de Olancho. Stone axes and arrowheads are still often found in town, particularly in the Belén neighborhood.

Situated at the southern end of the broad Valle de Catacamas 400 meters above sea level, Juticalpa's 87,600 residents make their living either working with the departmental government, cattle ranching, or as merchants for the surrounding area. Juticalpa is often a stop-off point when coming to Olancho from Tegucigalpa. It's a convenient town to take care of business and prepare for expeditions to Sierra de Agalta, La Muralla, La Mosquitia, or the nearby Monumento Natural El Boquerón.

Accommodations

The most expensive and, such as it is, the best hotel in town is **ApartHotel La Muralla,** tel./fax 85-1270, two blocks west of the square, charging

US$8 s or US$10 d for a modern room with fan, telephone, TV, and bathroom, a bit more for a/c.

On the same block is **Hotel Antuñez,** tel. 85-2250, a large building with an often sullen staff but a large selection of rooms at different prices, ranging from US$2.50 s for the most basic to US$4 for a decent upstairs single to US$7 with cable TV and a bathroom inside. The hotel runs a cafeteria and has free purified water.

Hotel El Paso, tel. 85-2311, on the road between the highway and the park, close to the bus station, has 30 rooms around an inside courtyard with parking available. The clean rooms go for US$4 s or US$7 d, with bath and fan. The friendly owners also run a *comedor.*

Dirt-cheap digs can be found at **Hospedaje America** a block southwest of the square; US$1.20 a bed.

Food and Entertainment

Far and away the best food in Juticalpa, universally recommended by locals, is **Restaurante La Fonda,** on the highway toward Tegucigalpa just past the gas station on the right-hand side, coming from town. The menu is nothing outrageous—steaks, chicken, *pinchos,* etc.—but the food is very well prepared and the portions are heaping. The hot beans, cream, and chips appetizer served in an ingenious ceramic mini-oven is excellent. Open daily 8 a.m.-9 p.m.; US$3-5 per plate. If you don't have your own wheels, take a taxi out from town and arrange to be picked up in an hour or so.

Restaurante Casa Blanca, in a bizarrely shaped little building a block southeast of the park, offers buffet-style meals Mon.-Sat. 7 a.m.-8 p.m. As with most eateries around here, emphasis is heavy on beef.

On the block behind the church is **Restaurante El Rancho,** serving *pinchos,* chicken, burgers, and sandwiches on benches and tables on a patio. Open daily 8 a.m.-10 p.m.

Tropical Juices on the park whips up excellent fruit shakes and juices Mon.-Sat. until 10 p.m.

A half a block off the park, next door to Banco Sogerin, is **Disco Nápoles,** the favorite spot for cowboys and their girls to kick up their heels on weekends.

Services

Hondutel, open daily 7 a.m.-9 p.m., and the post office are both a half block west of the park. Although Juticalpa has several banks, none change

---

**JUTICALPA
USEFUL TELEPHONE NUMBERS**

Police: 85-2028
Fire Department: 85-2910
Cruz Roja Ambulance: 85-2221

---

dollars, much less traveler's checks, on a regular basis. Bancahsa occasionally changes dollars. **La Confianza** store on the northwest corner of the park usually changes dollars, and sometimes so does **La Vivienda,** a half block away.

Getting There and Away

The **bus station** is near the highway at the entrance to town, one km from the park. **Aurora** and **Discovery,** tel. 85-2237 for both, run buses to Tegucigalpa 12 times daily (US$1.50, three hours), with three direct buses (US$2.50, two hours) at 6 a.m., 9 a.m., and 2 p.m. Frequent buses ply the highway between Juticalpa and Catacamas.

Two buses daily drive the seven-hour dirt road through Olancho to Tocoa for US$3.50, leaving at 3 a.m. and 5 a.m.

The 192-km, two-lane highway to Tegucigalpa from Juticalpa is in good shape and can be driven in two hours. Catacamas is 41 km from Juticalpa, while the turnoff to San Francisco de la Paz, which leads eventually to the north coast, is 10 km from Juticalpa on the Catacamas road.

Monumento Natural El Boquerón

Between Juticalpa and Catacamas is El Boquerón Natural Monument, a 4,000-hectare natural area covering two canyons and a mountain peak in the hills on the west side of the highway. Much of the surrounding area has been turned into pasture or farmland by local campesinos, but small patches of cloud forest and river-valley forest remain.

The main canyon, on the Río Olancho, has a very pleasant stretch of quiet forest with several swimming holes and plenty of opportunities for birdwatching. It can be visited easily in a day. To get to the canyon, get off the bus (or out of your car) from Juticalpa at the Río Olancho bridge between Km 194 and 195, and follow the dirt road along the edge of the river. Paths follow the river on both sides into the canyon, but the north side seems a bit easier to follow, at least for the first part of the hike.

Partway into the canyon, which is five km long, the path switches to the south side, and climbs up the hillside into pasture before reaching the village of **La Avispa**, about a three-hour hike from the highway at an easy pace. From La Avispa, you can hike back up over the top of **Cerro El Boquerón** (1,278 meters) and down the far side, looping back to the highway near the village of **Tempisque.** This would be a stiff and hot one-day hike, or a pleasant two-day walk, camping out around La Avispa.

In the Río Olancho canyon you'll also find the **Cueva de Tepescuintle,** with some impressive stalactites and stalagmites. In the 1940s an archaeologist found some evidence of pre-conquest habitation at the cave. Ask a local to show you the entrance for a few lempira, and bring a flashlight.

Not far from the highway near the Río Olancho is the site of **San Jorge de Olancho,** the region's early capital, which was wiped out by a natural disaster of mysterious character in 1611. William Wells, a North American traveler who passed through Olancho in the 1850s, reports the following local legend of the town's destruction in his book, *Explorations and Adventures in Honduras:*

The great wealth of Olancho in olden times had centered at the ancient town, which was once a sort of local emporium of fashion and luxury. The owners of cattle estates resided there, and collected immense treasure by mining operations on the Upper Guayape, and by purchasing gold of the Indians. The inhabitants, however, were niggardly; and, although they had such quantities of gold that the women wore nuggets of it in their hair, they withheld their hordes even from the Church, and were consequently stricken with Divine Wrath. In one of the churches a golden statue of the Virgin had been ordered by ecclesiastical authority, but the people were slow with the necessary contributions. The body of the statue was completed, but there being an indifferent supply of gold for the crown, the sacred brows were enriched with a "corona de

cuero" (a crown of hide). The padre of the church protested; but these infatuated wretches, unmindful of the wealth they were enjoying by the special favor of the Virgin, snapped their fingers in the face of this holy man! The infamous desecration of the Holy Mother was speedily avenged. While the population were collected in the church, the mountain broke forth with terrific violence, and in an hour the whole town was destroyed with showers of rocks, stones, and ashes. Many were killed, and the remainder fled affrightened out of the place. After the destruction, some few ventured back, but were seized with sudden sickness and died on the spot.

Locals claim the town was destroyed by a volcano, but since volcanic mountains do not exist in this part of Honduras, that seems unlikely. A massive landslide is a more likely explanation, especially considering the sheer cliff faces of El Boquerón, just behind the town's former location.

The survivors moved on to Olanchito in Yoro, bringing their patron saint, San Jorge, with them. Reportedly the remnants of a few buildings of the old town can still be seen—ask a local to point them out.

CATACAMAS AND VICINITY

A dusty town set against the base of the Sierra de Agalta, Catacamas is much like Juticalpa, only smaller, and is noteworthy mainly as a stopoff point for those on their way into the mountains. A few blocks toward the mountains from the main park (there are two in town) is a stairway leading up to **Cerrito de la Cruz,** a small hill with a cross on top affording good views over Catacamas and the valley.

Accommodations

Half a block south of the main park, around the corner from the bus station, is **Hotel La Colina,** tel. 95-4488, offering clean whitewashed rooms for US$7 d with hot water, fan, and TV. No singles.

Two doors down is the less expensive but still comfortable **Hotel Oriental,** charging US$1.80 for a basic cell, US$4 for a nicer double bed with bathroom, or US$6 with cable TV also. All rooms have fans.

Hotelito Central offers similar rooms at about the same price, two blocks northeast of the square.

The cheapest place in town is **Hospedaje El Hogar,** a block northeast of the square; US$1.20 pp.

Food and Entertainment

A funky little joint with wooden benches a block northeast of the park, **El Rinconcito Típico** has inexpensive burgers, chicken, steak, and *comida corriente*. The old Wurlitzer jukebox is well-stocked with great old and new ranchero tunes. Open daily for lunch and dinner.

Opposite Hospedaje El Hogar is **Restaurante Pollo Rico,** which offers a spacious patio dining area and the standard meals (good *pinchos*) for US$2-4; closed Tuesday.

The finest restaurant in town is the **Ace de Oro,** a half block off the main road, just past the center of town on the Dulce Nombre de Culmí side. Food is a bit expensive at US$5 for a full meal, but the chicken, steaks, fish, and (believe it or not) vegetarian dishes are excellent and filling. Credit cards accepted.

Buffet Ejecutivo between Hotels La Colina and Oriente has very good and inexpensive buffet meals daily 7 a.m.-8 p.m. It's a great spot for breakfast.

Tropical Juices next to the movie theater serves juices and fruit shakes Mon.-Sat. 10 a.m.-10 p.m.

The **Cine Maya** runs a daily double feature starting at 7:15 p.m.

Services

None of the banks in town change dollars or traveler's checks, but **Libreria Julio Verne** opposite Banco Atlántida will usually change cash.

Getting There and Away

The **Aurora/Discovery terminal,** tel. 95-4393, is on the south side of the park, and has nine regular buses to Tegucigalpa between 2:30 a.m. and 5 p.m. for US$2. Four direct buses leave daily at 3 a.m., 5:30 a.m., 11 a.m., and 2:30 p.m.

Local buses to Juticalpa leave from in front of the terminal all day until 6 p.m.

Buses to Dulce Nombre de Culmí depart from the market at 5 a.m., 6 a.m., and 1 p.m. for the 2.5-hour ride. The road is paved just seven km beyond Catacamas, and then turns into an all-weather dirt road.

Tegucigalpa is 232 km from Catacamas, and can be driven in 3-4 hours on the well-maintained paved highway. Juticalpa is 41 km from Catacamas.

Dulce Nombre de Culmí

A rough frontier town 59 km northeast of Catacamas, Dulce Nombre lies near the southern boundary of the Río Plátano Biosphere Reserve. It is the southern entry into La Mosquitia for those who want to cross from Olancho to the Caribbean coast via the Sico, Paulaya, Plátano, or Patuca rivers.

Formerly Dulce Nombre was a Pech village, but the influx of cattle ranchers and migrant campesinos has caused the Pech to retreat to outlying villages. A couple of Tawahka settlements are in the vicinity also. Facilities in Dulce Nombre are minimal. The only rooms in town are at **Hospedaje Kevin,** for US$2 a night, and there is a simple *comedor* nearby. A couple of *pulperías* sell basic supplies, but anyone planning a hike should bring everything needed.

North from Dulce Nombre de Culmí

A rough dirt road heads north from Dulce Nombre, leading to frontier villages and ranchos in the southernmost section of the Río Plátano Biosphere Reserve. Six km from town the road forks, the left branch to the village of **Las Marías** (not to be confused with the Las Marías on the Río Plátano near the Caribbean coast), from where you can make your way to the headwaters of the Río Plátano and Río Paulaya. The right branch continues to **La Llorana** and the source of the Río Wampu. On both of these routes are the unexcavated ruins of unknown pre-conquest civilizations, including **Las Crucitas, Marañones, Saguasón,** and others. Trucks from Dulce Nombre drive out these roads regularly—ask around in town. A truck/bus drives out to Las Marías every day.

Hiking from Dulce Nombre through the **Portillo de Will** and down the Río Paulaya valley to the town of Sico, above Palacios, is doable in 3-5 days along a well-beaten trail, much of it

THE CAVE OF GLOWING SKULLS

Four kilometers from Catacamas, near the village of Talgua, is the Cueva de Talgua, an extensive cavern long known about and explored by adventurous locals and the odd spelunker. In April 1994, four cavers clambering through the cave made an incredible discovery that has rewritten the history of pre-Columbian Honduras.

Hondurans Jorge Yáñez and Desiderio Reyes and Americans Tim Berg and Greg Cabe were about 2,000 feet inside the cave when they noticed an opening in a limestone wall 10 meters off the cave floor. Yáñez and Reyes scaled the wall, peered into the opening, and saw a scene out of a science-fiction movie: hundreds of skulls and bones apparently made of crystal, glowing in the light of their headlamps.

After reporting the discovery, the cave was examined by a team of archaeologists led by Dr. James Brady of George Washington University, who determined the bones had been placed on the ledge some 3,000 years ago by a hitherto unknown Mesoamerican civilization. Over the millennia since their burial, the bones were coated with calcite dripping from the cave roof, which preserved the remains and lent them their unearthly appearance.

In an apparent ritual burial, the bones of some 200 people had been carefully stripped of flesh, painted with a red ochre, and stacked in neat bundles along with pieces of ceramic and jade. As with many other Mesoamerican societies, caves were seen as entrances to the underworld, and the dead were evidently placed there to speed them on their journey to the next world. Further explorations revealed a second cave nearby, called the Cave of the Spiders, which held more bones and several pictographs on the cave walls. A third cave has since been found on a nearby mountainside.

Mounds above ground near the caves are believed to have been the villages of those buried in the caves. Little is known about these first *olanchanos,* other than they were relatively tall and healthy, and seemed to have traded with other societies in the region, judging from the pottery found. The earliest positive date of bones is from 1400 B.C.

As of 1996, entrance to the caves was supposedly restricted, though vandals had unfortunately managed to get in and disturb the cave. Most of the bones remain in place. The Honduran government plans to set up a visitor's center and museum at the site in the near future. A taxi out to the cave costs around US$5 each way. From the end of the road it's about a half-hour walk to the cave entrance.

BOB RACE

---

through pastures and patches of farmland hacked out of the jungle.

For more detailed information on trekking in this area without a tour group, get a copy of *La Mosquitia: A Guide to the Land of Savannas, Rain Forests and Turtle Hunters* by Derek Parent, 1995, available through the Adventure Travel Bookstore, e-mail: atbook@aol.com. Derek has wandered these mountains and rivers extensively, and has very detailed practical information in his book on traveling the region.

Jorge Zalaverry of La Moskitia Eco Aventuras runs ten- to twelve-day professional tours from Dulce Nombre through the mountains and down the Río Plátano. For more information, call 42-0104 or 21-0404, tel./fax 37-9398.

LA MURALLA

In far western Olancho, near the border with Yoro, is the broad mountain range of La Muralla ("The Wall"), containing probably the most extensive untouched swath of cloud forest in the country outside of Sierra de Agalta. La Muralla National Park is particularly famous for birdwatching. It's a very unlucky or impatient visitor who doesn't get a glimpse of the renowned quetzal while at the park.

La Unión

A small logging town about 200 km equally from Tegucigalpa and La Ceiba, set a couple of kilometers off the highway at an elevation of 800 meters, La Unión is the first stop for anyone going to visit La Muralla. **Hotel La Muralla** on the main street has bare rooms for US$1.70 s or US$3 d, and decent food is sold at **Merendero Mi Ranchito,** a concrete building with a thatched roof a couple of blocks toward the highway from the downtown park, as well as a couple of other *comedores.*

The **Cohdefor office** is helpful in arranging transport to La Muralla, and if a truck is going visitors are usually welcome to hop in. There's no gas station in town, but fuel is sold out of drums by various people—ask around.

Several buses pass daily on their way to Tegucigalpa, La Ceiba, or Trujillo. The first north coast bus passes at 9 a.m. and the last at 3 p.m., while the first Tegucigalpa bus passes at 7 a.m. and the last at 2 p.m.

The all-weather dirt-and-gravel road passing La Unión continues northward, reaching the Aguán Valley at El Mamé, between Olanchito and Savá, about two and a half hours from La Unión. To the south, it connects with the Tegucigalpa-Juticalpa highway at Valle de Lepaguare, just beyond Campamento. Tegucigalpa can be reached in about four hours from La Unión in a private vehicle.

Parque Nacional La Muralla

Covering 17,243 hectares between 900 and 2,064 meters, the park hosts forests ranging from pine on the lower fringes, to pine mixed with liquidambar (sweet gum) at the middle elevations, to broadleaf cloud forest on the peaks. Thirty seven mammal species not including bats have been spotted in the park, including jaguars, ocelots, white-faced and howler monkeys, and tapirs, as well as 150 bird species. Little biological investigation has taken place in the reserve, especially in the more remote reaches away from the visitor's center; it's likely other species will be identified.

La Muralla has a well-built visitor's center at 1,430 meters, offering three beds for visitors, displays on flora and fauna, and several detailed maps on the walls. Reservations for the beds (which are presently no cost) need to be made through the Tegucigalpa Cohdefor office;

call 22-1027. Otherwise it's no problem to pitch a tent on the lawn out front or sling a hammock. Bring warm clothes if you plan to sleep in a hammock, as it gets chilly at night. The trees in front of the visitor's center are great for birdwatching, especially in the early morning.

In the southwestern corner of the reserve a system of trails allows visitors to explore a section of the forest without a guide. The 3.7-km Pizote Trail makes a loop around a low peak, with several benches at strategic points to watch for birds. For the more ambitious, the 10-km Monte Escondido Trail descends into the Río Escondido Valley and up again into the center of the park. Getting to the lookout on Monte Escondido and back is a two-day trip.

Hikes deeper into the park, to the peaks of La Muralla (1,981 meters), Los Higuerales (1,985 meters), and Las Parras (2,064 meters), all require guides and several days in the woods. Cohdefor can arrange guides for about US$5 per day, and permission is required to camp in the park.

The visitor's center is 14 km from La Unión, reached by a rough dirt road connecting La Unión to the village of El Díctamo, further west. Those without a car can walk from town three hours uphill through pine forest and coffee plantations, or try to hitch, although traffic is not frequent. The best option is to catch a ride with one of the Cohdefor trucks, which usually go to the park every day during the week. The topographical map covering the park is 1:50,000 La Unión 2861 II.

VALLE DE AGALTA

Ten km from Juticalpa on the road to Catacamas, a dirt road turns north into the hills leading to the town of **San Francisco de la Paz** and then northeast to the Valle de Agalta, a broad, cattle-covered plain on the opposite side of the Sierra de Agalta from the Valle de Catacamas. Before reaching San Francisco de la Paz, the highway passes Las Vueltas de Ocote, marked by a bust of Francisco Morazán.

Gualaco

Settled in the early years of Olancho colonization, the logging and ranching town of Gualaco occupies the southwest end of the Valle de

HIKING IN SIERRA DE AGALTA

Although many visitors will want to hire a guide or go with a tour operator, it is possible to climb the highest peak in the Sierra without a guide, if you're confident of your orienteering skills. From Gualaco, drive north on the highway six km and look for a signpost on the east side of the road; the sign marks a faded dirt road heading into the pine forest, near the village of El Pacayal. This road continues about five km steadily uphill, the last two km progressively more steep and rough. Four wheel drive is recommended, and the road may be impassable by vehicle in the rainy season.

From the end of the road, a trail heads straight up the ridge, offering great views out over the Valle de Agalta. Keep an eye out for a flat spot on the hillside, about 45 minutes from the trailhead, where a trail splits off down to the right. Although the two trails join up farther ahead, the right hand trail is easier going.

From the junction, continue 2-3 hours along the hillside, across one stream, up over a ridge, and down to a river valley. The trail zigzags upstream along the river, crossing over it several times, so expect to get your feet wet. It's not always easy to stay on the trail, but just keep poking around and you'll find it. Along the edge of the river you'll find a simple thatched *champa,* which makes an excellent campsite for the first night out.

About 20 minutes from the campsite the trail arrives at **La Chorrera,** a lovely two-pronged waterfall pouring around a large boulder. Just below the falls, the trail crosses the river a last time, and heads straight up the mountainside. You'll know you're on the right track if you pass a section of roughly built steps just above the river.

From the river, it's about a four- to five-hour walk to the next campsite, high up on the side of the mountain. The trail upward is very faint in places, with many trees fallen across it requiring circumnavigation. If in doubt, keep looking around for machete marks, and backtrack until you're sure of the trail. There's only one path, and it stays on a compass bearing roughly between 160 and 200 degrees the whole way, following the ridge upward. Above the river the forest is pristine and full of wildlife. Troops of howler and spider monkeys are frequently seen, along with all manner of bird life.

After about four hours the trail levels off somewhat; at this point start looking for the second camp.

It's on the right side slightly below the trail, with a few flat spots to pitch tents and a couple of fire pits. A stream sometimes runs nearby, but it's best to bring up all the water needed from the river below.

Above the second camp the trail winds its tangled, steep way up the ridgeline to the peak in 1.5-2 hours. The vegetation here is so dense, most of the path seems to be more on root structures and branches than dirt. You'll also notice, about an hour above the camp, all the trees around are remarkably short—this is the famous dwarf forest of Agalta, consisting of stunted pines and oaks, gnarled and twisted by the wind and soaking wet from the near-permanent clouds. Everything is covered with lichens, moss, and ferns.

Apart from being an incredible sight on its own, the dwarf forest also allows visitors to admire truly stupendous views from La Picucha, across both the Catacamas and Agalta Valleys and over the mountains extending northward into the jungles of La Mosquitia. From La Picucha, a trail continues over to a nearby peak with a radio tower on it, where there is reportedly a route down to Catacamas.

Take particular care descending from La Picucha, especially between the second campsite and the river. It's much easier to get lost on the way down, as ridges branch off frequently. You'll see a couple of plastic tags, but not nearly enough. A wise hiker will bring a supply of colored string or plastic and tie off frequently when ascending, picking the tags up on the way down. From the highway to La Picucha it's a total elevation gain of 1,650 meters over a distance of roughly 10 kilometers.

SUGGESTED ITINERARY

Day One: Drive and hike from Gualaco to the river campsite.

Day Two: Hike up to the second campsite, taking time to look for animals.

Day Three: Wake up before dawn, climb the peak, descend to the river camp.

Day Four: Hike out to the highway and get back to Gualaco by midafternoon.

This could be shortened to three days by hiking all the way out to the highway on the same day as climbing the peak.

Agalta. Gualaco is the closest town to the La Picucha trail into the Sierra de Agalta.

The 17th century **Iglesia de San Jeronimo** on one end of the wide, treeless park features an elaborate facade with sculpted pillars. The two church towers were rebuilt in 1994 in an unfortunately less than subtle style, but the building is impressive nonetheless.

Hotel Camino Real on the road between the highway and the park has well-kept, simple concrete rooms around an interior parking lot for US$2 no bath, US$3 with.

On the park is **Hotelito Central** with similar prices.

Several *comedores* in town can serve up a meal. **Comedor Sharon** on the highway is particularly good and the owners are friendly and glad to talk to visitors.

The **Cohdefor office** is on the highway next to the gas station. Currently no maps are available, but you can look at the topo on the wall—which has the La Picucha trail marked in—and make a quick sketch to get an idea of distances, compass bearings, and elevations. The official in charge of the park or the local Peace Corps volunteer can supply good information, but the rest of the workers are mainly interested in logging and could care less about tourists.

About 10 minutes from Gualaco by car lies Aldea Jicalapa, and another half hour waking from there are the **Cavernas de Susmay,** three large dry caves and one with water in it.

Parque Nacional Sierra de Agalta

Over 60,000 hectares of mountain forest are protected in Sierra de Agalta, and in its core zone the park contains the most extensive cloud forest remaining in Honduras and Central America. Because of its remote location, Agalta's forest does not get as many visitors as La Tigra or Celaque, but those who have been there rate it as one of the country's most spectacular natural areas.

The range's isolation has also been its savior—loggers have not yet cut into the heart of the forest and with luck they never will. Around its perimeter, Sierra de Agalta is blanketed by dry pine forest, which is currently being logged. Above the pines, liquidambar (sweet gum) trees dominate, gradually giving way to the epiphyte- and vine-covered cloud forest, at elevations

between 1,700 and 2,000 meters. At the highest elevations grows a bizarre dwarf forest, created by high winds and heavy precipitation. Here stunted pine and oak trees between 1.5 and five meters high are cloaked in mosses and lichens.

The forests of Sierra de Agalta are considered a sort of transitional ecosystem, similar to the mountain forests of Costa Rica, while Celaque and other cloud forests in western Honduras are more like those of Guatemala and southern Mexico.

Over 200 species of birds have been identified in Sierra de Agalta, as well as a myriad of mammals rarely seen elsewhere in the country. Tapirs, sloths, ocelots, jaguars, and troops of howler, spider, and white-faced monkeys all reside in the park. Apart from its natural beauty and the rare flora and fauna it sustains, the Sierra de Agalta is a critical source of water for northeastern Honduras, forming the headwaters for the Patuca, Sico, and Paulaya rivers.

The easiest access to the Sierra is from Gualaco, in the Valle de Agalta, where a fairly well-developed trail reaches **La Picucha,** the highest point in the range at 2,354 meters. Lesser-known trails head into the mountains from Catacamas and from a dirt road cutting across the northeastern end of the mountains between Dulce Nombre de Culmí and San Esteban.

The topographical maps covering the park are 1:50,000 San Francisco de la Paz 2960 I, Catacamas 3060 IV, Dulce Nombre de Culmí 3061 II, and Valle de Agalta La Venta 3061 III.

San Esteban

At the northeastern end of the Valle de Agalta lies the cattle town of San Esteban, founded in 1805 and named in honor of Padre Esteban Verdelete, martyred by Pech Indians in the early 1600s. Because of its reputation for violence, most people do not spend much time in San Esteban. In addition, beyond the gas station and few *comedores* on the highway, there's little reason to stay here.

Los Encuentros

West of San Esteban is Los Encuentros, a ruin of unknown origin. To visit Los Encuentros, hitch a ride to the town of San Antonio de Pacura from San Esteban, and ask around for Chaveli-

THE HONDURAN HATFIELDS AND MᶜCOYS

For years San Esteban was known throughout the country as home to one of the longest-running and most violent family feuds in Central America. Bus drivers often blew right past town without stopping, and residents rarely ventured out on the streets at night for fear of being caught in the crossfire.

The Turcios and Nájeras families were once fast friends, but began feuding in 1987, some say from a dispute about land, others say because of a cock fight in the town square. Whatever the cause, the feud took some 30 lives over nine years. The families signed a public truce sponsored by the military on 2 June 1996. During the truce ceremony, the two families provided a tangible sign of the spread of arms in Olancho, a situation no doubt encouraged in part by disbanded Contra soldiers. Among the weapons relinquished at the ceremony were 13 AK-47s, a Mouser, and a 30-30 carbine. And you can bet each side kept a supply stashed away.

to, who will serve as a guide for the six-hour horseback ride to the site via the village of Naranjal. Several mounds and what appears to be a ball court—currently used as a soccer field by the local farmboys—are visible.

EL CARBÓN

Near the border of the Olancho and Colón departments, on the highway between San Esteban and the coast, is the village of Santa María del Carbón, usually just called El Carbón. It's one of the most traditional Pech communities left in Honduras. With the help of a highly motivated Peace Corps volunteer, the local Pech have begun organizing facilities for visitors, including accommodations and food in the traditional Pech style and guided trips into the surrounding mountains. The efforts are intended to promote tourism as a supplement to the meager local income and to encourage the preservation of Pech culture.

Efforts are underway, with the help of the Tourism and Environment Departments of the Honduran government, to declare a section of the nearby jungle a protected area. This would connect Sierra de Agalta to the Río Plátano Biosphere Reserve, thus establishing an unbroken wall of reserves on the southwestern border of La Mosquitia.

Practicalities

By the time of publication a thatched-hut *hospedaje* should have been built, but if not ask for the Peace Corps volunteer or Linton Escobar, the president of the local organization, to help find a room. These two are also the ones to speak to about arranging guided trips, and are eager to talk with visitors about Pech culture and customs.

Guides to La Cascada or the nearby mountains (see below) cost US$5 a day, or a bit more if you spend the night. Generally the guides are very friendly and happy to point out different plants, trees, birds, and animals along the way. One in particular, Natividad, is also a local *curandero* and knows more than most about the flora and fauna. He's also a useful guy to have around if you get bitten by a snake, as he knows an effective cure.

A variety of inexpensive and well-crafted *artesanías* are for sale in El Carbón, including excellent wooden chairs made with a pedal-lathe, woven baskets, bark hammocks, the traditional *tenpuca* drums made from a hollowed tree trunk and animal skin, and *camachas,* a sort of maraca.

El Carbón can be reached by any buses passing between Juticalpa and Tocoa or Trujillo, of which there are usually three or four a day in each direction, although this seems to change with regularity.

To get to El Carbón from the north coast, the best bet is to go to **Corocito,** a turnoff on the Tocoa-Trujillo road, by early morning and wait for the next bus heading to Olancho. The last passes around noon. Cotraipbal runs one bus from La Ceiba leaving at 6 a.m.

From Juticalpa, get a bus to Tocoa, Trujillo, or La Ceiba, or hitch from the turnoff on the Juticalpa-Catacamas road. If you're on a bus, be sure to let the driver know you want to get off at El Carbón.

The last bus in either direction usually passes El Carbón around 2 p.m.

KEVIN POSTMA

*Pech craftsman shows off his wares—
traditional Pech instruments*

La Cascada

Set in a jungle-clad valley a few hours hike (with a guide) from El Carbón is La Cascada, a gushing waterfall on the Río Ojo de Agua, which empties into the Río Sico. The hike from town leads through secondary forest, across some fields, and into a steep, narrow valley blanketed by virgin jungle.

About an hour of slippery, treacherous hiking from town brings you to **Lago de la Sirena,** a small lake at the base of the torrential falls, surrounded on three sides by lush hillsides. The lake is named for a spirit who allegedly protects the cuyamel fish. Those who catch cuyamel can expect an unpleasant visit from the Sirena in their dreams. For the full experience, take a swim out to a rock in the lake directly in front of the falls, and feel the power of the blast. It literally takes your breath away.

When on the trail, especially in the valley, let the guides go first as snakes are common. A towering *caoba* (mahogany) tree stands just above the trail, and the guides will lead you to it if you ask. The local guide group will soon be building an easier trail up the valley.

La Cascada can be visited in one day, but spending a night at the campsite at the mouth of the canyon is a pleasant experience, and gives you a chance to have a good talk with the guides. If your Spanish is not up to it, try convincing the local Peace Corps volunteer to come along and be your interpreter. Bring a tent if you want to camp.

Sierra del Carbón

The Sierra del Carbón, a northern extension of the Sierra de Agalta, runs from El Carbón into La Mosquitia, forming part of the headwaters of the Plátano, Sico, and Paulaya rivers. If a proposed natural reserve is created in these mountains, a huge corridor of protected forest will begin from here and stretch all the way into Nicaragua.

Guides from El Carbón can take visitors up any of the several peaks in the vicinity, including **Cerro El Diablo, Cerro Jesus Cristo,** and **Cerro Alpes.** From El Carbón the ecosystems change from pine forest, to dense, broadleaf jungle, to cloud forest in the higher reaches, and even patches of dwarf forest similar to that found on Sierra de Agalta mountaintops.

In the mountains, near the village of Agua Amarilla, a ruin of unknown origin covered with dense jungle was recently discovered. The ruin appears to have several acropolis-like structures. The Instituto Hondureño de Antropología e Historia is expected to survey it soon.

This is serious machete territory, dense forest with only occasionally-used footpaths running through it. Come prepared. The hard-core adventurer could hike across the mountains, with a guide, and end up in Dulce Nombre de Culmí in a few days.

BOB RACE

SOUTHERN HONDURAS

Though southern Honduras may not be a favorite tourist destination, tucked away in the mountains and coastal plains are a few hidden attractions worth visiting, especially for those passing through on their way to Nicaragua or El Salvador. Some of the best include the colonial mining towns of El Corpus and Yuscarán, the island-seaport of Amapala, and the cigar factories of Danlí.

THE PACIFIC COAST

Honduras's Pacific coast is a hot, dry plain facing the Gulf of Fonseca, which it shares with El Salvador and Nicaragua. Coastal beaches do exist, most notably at Cedeño, but unfortunately they can't compare with those in El Salvador. Most of the year the Pacific coast is scorchingly hot. The region's struggling economy, one of the poorest in the country, is dominated by shrimp farming and cattle ranching.

Three major rivers—the Choluteca, Goascorán, and Nacaome—trisect the narrow Choluteca Plain. The country's only volcanoes are found in this part of Honduras, as the volcanic chain of the Colinas de Juacarán beginning in El Salvador terminates in the gulf. Isla del Tigre is an example of one of these volcanoes, which are all extinct.

Much of the Pacific coastline is, or was, covered with mangrove swamps, but in recent years the growing shrimp-farming and cattle-ranching industries have severely threatened these fragile but important ecosystems. The **Bahía de Chismayo** not far from the El Salvador border is a protected area of mangroves in name, but shrimp farmers have been clamoring to be allowed there. One of the country's most forceful environmental groups, the Committee for the Preservation of the Fauna and Flora of the Gulf of Fonseca (CODEFFAGOLF), continues to work hard to stop the farmers' expansion.

The Choluteca Plain and surrounding hills have been heavily farmed for years, and the deforestation and massive use of pesticides and fertilizers have combined to wreak havoc on the land. Desertification is advancing relentlessly in the south, and many campesinos have been forced to migrate to other parts of the country because the land is no longer arable.

One unavoidable fact about the Choluteca Plain is the heat. For much of the year, especially outside of the May-October rainy season, it is unbearably hot, often reaching temperatures as high as 40° C. Rainfall on the Pacific coast is not as intensive as on the Caribbean side.

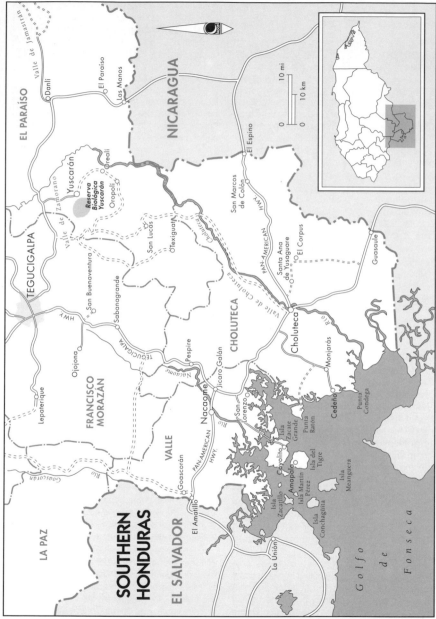

SOUTHERN HONDURAS

EL PARAÍSO

Valle de Jamastrán

Danlí

El Paraíso

Las Manos

NICARAGUA

Yuscarán

Reserva Biológica Yuscarán

Oropolí

Oreali

El Espino

San Marcos de Colón

TEGUCIGALPA

Valle de Zamorano

San Lucas

Texiguat

San Buenaventura

Sabanagrande

FRANCISCO MORAZÁN

Ojojona

Lepaterique

Santa Ana de Yusguare

El Corpus

PAN-AMERICAN

AMH

Guasaule

CHOLUTECA

Valle de Choluteca

TEGUCIGALPA HWY

Nacaome

Pespire

Jícaro Galán

Choluteca

Río

Monjarás

LA PAZ

VALLE

Goascorán

Río Goascorán

PAN-AMERICAN HWY.

El Amarillo

La Unión

EL SALVADOR

Nacaome

San Lorenzo

Coyolito

Isla Zacate Grande

Punta Ratón

Cedeño

Punta Condega

Amapala

Isla del Tigre

Isla Martín Pérez

Isla Zacatillo

Isla Conchagüita

Isla Meanguera

Golfo de Fonseca

0 10 mi

0 10 km

CHOLUTECA

Although it's the fifth-largest city in Honduras, with about 99,300 residents, Choluteca feels more like an overgrown village. The colonial downtown area, centered around the *parque central,* remains much as it was a few centuries ago, with narrow cobblestone streets, tiled-roofs, and one-level colonial buildings, most of which are in disrepair. The area around Choluteca was first explored by Andrés Niño in the 1522 expedition led by Gil González Dávila up the west coast of Central America from Panama. Originally called Xérex de la Frontera, the city of Choluteca was founded in 1541 by Capt. Cristóbal de la Cueva.

The name Choluteca, which is thought to mean "broad valley," derives from the pre-conquest inhabitants of the region, the Chorotega Indians. The Chorotega, related to the Toltec, were relatively recent arrivals themselves, having migrated from Chiapas, Mexico sometime before or around A.D. 1000.

During colonial times Choluteca grew quickly as a port and from the rich mines of El Corpus, in the hills above the Choluteca Plain. The town was originally settled on the west side of the Río Choluteca, but after being sacked and torched by pirates in the 17th century it was moved to its present location.

Anyone interested in the history and legends of Choluteca and the region, and who read Spanish, should look for two recently published books, *Por Cuentas Aquí En Choluteca* and *Por Cuentas Aquí En El Corpus.* Also, Padre Jesús who works in the *casa cural* across from the Catedral is very knowledgeable on local history.

In an effort to boost the town's tourism potential, officials have plans to restore many of the

---

SOUTHERN HONDURAS HIGHLIGHTS

- Visiting the colonial town of Yuscarán
- Touring a cigar factory in Danlí
- Admiring views over the Gulf of Fonseca from the volcanic peak of Isla del Tigre
- Spending a day in the mining village of El Corpus, in the hills above Choluteca

---

colonial buildings downtown and declare a several-block area a historic zone. The annual *Feria Patronal* of Choluteca, held 6-14 December, is reputed to be quite a bash, with lots of good food, music, dancing, and fireworks on the last night.

Orientation and Getting Around

Choluteca is essentially a one-story city extending along dusty streets from the downtown square. It's built along the east bank of the Río Choluteca, and the highway to Tegucigalpa leaves Choluteca on a suspension bridge crossing the river. In spite of its impressive-looking construction, the bridge is reportedly architecturally unsound and may need to be replaced soon.

The highway from Tegucigalpa continues east bypassing downtown on its way to San Marcos de Colón and the Nicaraguan border. Another highway turns off this road leading south to Guasaule, also on the Nicaraguan border. The city has two markets: the main, older one, Mercado San Antonio, is two blocks south of the square; the other, Mercado Nuevo, is six blocks farther south. Although Choluteca covers a lot of ground, most places of interest to travelers are within walking distance of the square in the northwest quadrant. One exception is the bus station, a dozen or so blocks southeast of the square. Taxis to the terminal and around town cost US 50 cents.

Sights

The **Catedral Inmaculada Concepción** on the square dates from at least 1643, the date on the baptismal font, but is thought to be older. The wood-paneled ceiling resembles the hull of a boat. In 1914 the facade was rebuilt to its present form.

Two blocks east of the cathedral is the older **Iglesia de La Merced,** also built at an unknown date, but thought to have been erected in the mid-16th century. It features interesting twisted columns on the outside. In colonial times the surrounding neighborhood housed the city's Indian and black population. The church is normally only open on Saturdays.

The colonial building on the southwest corner of the square is the former home of famed Cholutecan José Cecilio del Valle (1777-1834). The building now houses the local library, but the Instituto Hondureño de Antropología e Historia has plans to rebuild it and turn it into a

JOSÉ CECILIO DEL VALLE~"EL SABIO"

Known among Hondurans as "El Sabio," or "The Wise One," José Cecilio del Valle was born on 22 November 1777 to a wealthy landowning family. As a youth he was taken to Guatemala for his education, and at the age of 23 he graduated as a lawyer from the Universidad de San Carlos. At that time the first calls for independence from Spain

El Sabio

could be heard echoing through Central America, and del Valle quickly plunged into the nascent movement with a passion, editing the pro-independence newspaper *El Amigo de la Patria* and leading the Partido Evolucionista.

When independence was officially declared on 15 September 1821, del Valle was on the scene at the Palacio de Guatemala, and was one of the writers of the Act of Independence. He initially opposed the annexation of Central America by Mexico under Iturbide, but agreed to act as a deputy to the congress in Mexico. As a relentless defender of the rights of Central America, del Valle irritated Iturbide, who had him thrown in jail for six months. When the empire fell in 1824, del Valle regained his freedom and was elected deputy in the new congress of the Central American Union.

El Sabio was then appointed vice-president under Conservative Manuel Arce, but he refused to accept the office, campaining against the illegitimacy of Arce's regime. When Arce was overthrown in 1829, he competed against independence hero Francisco Morazán for the Central American presidency but lost. In the 1834 elections he was victorious, but died before he could take office.

Throughout his career del Valle was legendary for his intelligent and humanitarian proposals and his tireless efforts to unite the Americas. In 1822 he published a manifesto of sorts on his Pan-American beliefs, which ends with the words: "America from this moment will be my exclusive occupation—America by day when I write, by night when I think. The study most worthy of Americans is America."

museum. The statue in the middle of the square is of del Valle.

Accommodations

Of the less expensive hotels in town, **Hotel Santa Rosa,** tel. 82-0355, and **Hotel Bonsai,** tel. 82-2648, are both good values. The Santa Rosa, next to the old market, charges US$3 s or US$5 d for clean rooms—each with fan and private bathroom—around a small courtyard, while the Bonsai, half a block south of the square, charges US$2.80 for a room with fan and private bathroom, or US$6 for a newer room with a/c and TV.

One block south of the road leading out of town toward San Marcos de Colón is **Hotel Pacífico,** tel. 82-0838, and across the street from it is **Hotel Pacífico Anexo,** tel. 82-3249. Both charge US$3 s, US$6 d with private bathroom. The original Pacífico is a bit funkier than the Anexo.

For a bit more luxury at still reasonable prices, check out **Hotel Pierre,** tel. 82-0676, one long block south of the square on 6 Avenida. Its unremarkable but air-conditioned rooms with TV and private bathroom rent for US$10 s, US$13 d.

The motel-style **Hotel La Fuente,** tel. 82-0263, fax 82-0273, on the Panamericana, between the bridge and the Boulevard, has 40 clean, modern rooms—each with a/c, TV, and telephone—around a large pool for US$24 s, US$32 d. The hotel is convenient for those traveling through with a car.

By far the classiest and most expensive setup in town is **Hacienda Gualiqueme,** tel. 82-2750 or 82-2760, just across the bridge on the highway toward Tegucigalpa, on the right side. Rooms are spread across extensive grassy grounds, and each is tastefully furnished in dark tones, with tile floors, high ceilings, TV, a/c, and direct telephones. Amenities include a restaurant, pool, spa, and very helpful staff. Rooms cost US$48 s, US$54 d, or US$66 suite.

Food and Entertainment

Culinary selection in Choluteca is decidedly limited, but a couple of places in town serve up reasonably good meals.

Pizza King, a couple of doors down from the Hotel Pierre on 6 Avenida, tel. 82-0676, makes respectable, inexpensive pizza as well as burgers and sandwiches. Open daily 10 a.m.-10 p.m.

One of those classic general store-restaurants, where everyone stops in to catch up on the local gossip, **Comedor Central** on the square is a good place for snacks, breakfasts, light meals, and beers. Open Mon.-Sat. 6 a.m.-10 p.m. and on Sunday afternoon.

Cafe Frosty, two blocks south of the square on 3 Calle, serves cheap, unexceptional breakfasts, *comida corriente,* snacks, and ice cream.

One of the best restaurants in town is **El Conquistador** on the Panamerican, offering seating under a covered patio. The food can take a while, but it's worth the wait for the well-prepared seafood, steaks, beef stroganoff, soups, and sandwiches; US$3-6 per entree. Open daily 11 a.m. until all the customers are gone.

If you're up for a movie, head for one of the town's two theaters; **Cine Caribe** and **Cine Rex** are both near the market.

CHOLUTECA USEFUL TELEPHONE NUMBERS

Police: 82-0951, 82-0966, or dial 199
Hospital: 82-0231
Fire Department: 82-0503, or dial 198

Services

Banco Atlántida will exchange dollars but no traveler's checks, while Bancahsa will exchange both. Correos is on 2 Calle and 3 Avenida, and has Express Mail Service available. Next door is Hondutel, which receives faxes at tel. 82-0053.

Policlínica Ferguson, on 3 Calle and Avenida Central, tel. 82-0281 or 82-0300, can help with basic health problems.

Consulates

The **Consulado de El Salvador** is on the square; open Mon.-Fri. 8 a.m.-noon and 2-4 p.m., and other hours also if you ring the bell. The office issues tourist cards and visas the same day, normally costing US$10 for 90-day tourist cards and US$30 for visas. Fifteen-day transit visas are available free. Tourist cards and transit visas are both available at the border also.

The **Consulado de Nicaragua,** tel. 82-0127, is run out of the office of Dr. Orlando Sarria Alvarado, who issues Nicaraguan visas for US$25.

Getting There and Away

Royery runs buses to Tegucigalpa at 6 a.m., 7 a.m., and 1 p.m. daily from the main terminal; US$1.40. **Mi Esperanza,** tel. 82-0841, runs buses every hour between 4 a.m. and 6 p.m. from their own terminal a block and a half from the main terminal; also US $1.40.

Buses to Guasaule on the Nicaraguan border leave from the Mercado Nuevo daily every hour between 5 a.m. and 5 p.m. The buses invariably swing by the main terminal to pick up passengers before leaving town. It's an hour-and-a-half ride, and the bus drops passengers off right at the bridge over the border.

Buses leave the main terminal for San Marcos de Colón frequently between 4 a.m. and 6 p.m.; US 60 cents. From San Marcos you can continue on to the Nicaraguan border at El Espino. Buses also frequently leave the main terminal heading to El Amatillo at the Salvadoran border. All buses leaving from the terminal invariably take a spin through town to look for more passengers, so if you can't get to the terminal it's often possible to flag one down. Taxis to the terminal cost US 50 cents.

Buses to El Corpus leave regularly between 6:30 a.m. and 5 p.m. from the Mercado Nuevo.

The main highways leaving Choluteca toward Guasaule (47 km), San Marcos de Colón (56 km), El Amatillo (85 km), and Tegucigalpa (142 km) are all paved and in relatively good condition.

CEDEÑO

The Pacific coast town of Cedeño is a low-budget Honduran beach getaway, a fairly seedy collection of worn wooden buildings lining a reasonably decent stretch of sand. The few restaurant/discos in town are usually packed on the weekends and deserted during the week. In spite of being on the Bahía de Chismayo, waves can get fierce, depending on the tide and the season. Better, more isolated beaches than the one in town lie within walking distance a few minutes in either direction.

Practicalities
Of the couple of extremely minimal hotels in Cedeño, the best seems to be a concrete place with a yellow sign next to Restaurante Miramar, charging US$4 s or d with fan and private bathroom. The Hotel Las Vegas and Hotel Cedeño are grim.

Restaurante Miramar has about the best food in town, and turns into a hopping disco on weekends.

Four direct buses leave Cedeño daily for Tegucigalpa at 3:15 a.m., 6 a.m., 7:45 a.m., and 1 p.m., charging US$2. Buses frequently depart for Choluteca; US 50 cents. The last bus out of town leaves at 4:30 p.m.

The 34-km potholed road to the highway passes through sugar plantations and the dirt poor town of Mojarus. Along the way are turnoffs to Punta Ratón and Puesta del Sol, where reportedly good beaches can be found if you can get a ride out there.

AMAPALA

The only town on the volcanic island of Isla del Tigre, Amapala was once Honduras's primary Pacific port, but it has long been superseded by Puerto de Henecán near San Lorenzo. Amapala is now a decaying 19th-century relic, looking for a way to survive. The town boasts no obvious tourist attractions, apart from a couple of mediocre beaches nearby, though some travelers find the slightly surreal, lost-in-time feel of the place fascinating.

Isla del Tigre was first visited by Andrés Niño in 1522, but the Spanish didn't settle there initially. Pirates used the island as a hideout until 1770, when the governor of San Miguel, El Salvador ordered a town built. For a short time during the presidency of Marco Aurelio Soto, Amapala functioned as the capital of Honduras.

Although subject to the same heat as the Choluteca plain, the island is often graced by an ocean breeze, making the climate more hospitable. Isla del Tigre is six km in diameter, and the volcanic peak is 760 meters high. Until recently, a U.S. military contingent staffed a base at the peak, but it has been deserted.

Practicalities
Right at the end of the dock is the only actual "hotel" in Amapala, such as it is; the **Pensión Internacional** offers ultra-basic but spacious rooms upstairs above a family's house; US$1.70 pp. The balcony makes a good spot to hang out and contemplate the bay.

El Faro Victoria next to the dock has decent burgers, fish, chicken, and other snacks for US$2-4 per meal. The friendly owner, who speaks a bit of English picked up from the U.S. soldiers who used to be stationed on the island, also rents out rooms for US$6. Open for lunch and dinner Fri.-Sun., dinner only Mon.-Thursday.

None of the banks in town exchange foreign currency. It's often a good idea to bring a lot of change as breaking big bills on the island can sometimes be a problem.

Boats across to Coyolito should be only US 50 cents for the 10-minute trip, when going with other passengers, but the boatmen will invariably try to charge you more. From the dock in Coyolito, buses leave to San Lorenzo every 90 minutes between 5:30 a.m. and 3 p.m.; US 50 cents.

The 31-km paved but potholed road back to the main highway near San Lorenzo passes shrimp farms and mangrove swamps.

Around the Island
A dirt road of roughly 20 km rings Isla del Tigre. Many *campesino* families live along this road. From Amapala heading southwest, about 20 minutes from town by foot, just past the military installation, a dirt road turning inland leads in a stiff two-hour walk to the top of the volcano, the

site of a former U.S. DEA base, now deserted. The views, especially in the early morning when the sky is clear, are superb.

About 45 minutes from town via a short turnoff to the west lies **Playa Grande,** a swath of black sand facing El Salvador and lined with several fish restaurants. At the north end of the beach is La Cueva de la Sirena, an interesting red volcanic rock cave with two entrances, one on the ocean. Local legend has it Sir Francis Drake hid a stash of his ill-gotten booty here.

Another half hour up the main road is **Playa Negra,** where **Hotel Villa Playa Negra** sits on a hill above the beach. Once a more elaborate affair, the hotel suffered a fire recently and part of it burnt down. Several rooms are still available and rent for US$22 d with fan or US$40 with a/c. The restaurant has good food. For reservations call the hotel's office in Tegucigalpa at 37-8301 or 37-8822, fax 38-2457; the staff will pick you up at the dock in Amapala.

Continuing around from Playa Negra, there's not a lot to see along the road but a shrimp-packing plant and a few *campesino* settlements. Several decent beaches are reportedly accessible by trail from the road, including **Playa Brava,** which is said to have decent waves.

One bus circles the island each day, and there's some traffic in the morning—good for hitching rides—but in the afternoon it's usually deserted.

SAN LORENZO
AND THE TEGUCIGALPA HIGHWAY

San Lorenzo

A hot, unattractive town of 17,000 on the gulf, San Lorenzo's main reasons for existence are nearby Puerto de Henecán, the country's third-largest port after Puerto Cortés and Puerto Castilla, and the shrimp-packing plants in town.

Should you be unfortunate enough to have to stop in San Lorenzo for the night, the waterfront **Hotel Miramar,** tel. 81-2038, fax 81-2106, offers by far the best accommodations in town. It's often patronized by visiting businesspeople, and also has a restaurant. Air-conditioned rooms with two beds cost US$22.

One block toward the water from the square is the less expensive **Hotel Piasandu,** where rooms in a family's house rent for US$2.50 pp.

Several restaurants beyond Hotel Miramar serve up decent seafood, and there are a few basic *comedores* in the center of town.

Both Banco Atlántida and Banco de Occidente will change dollars.

Buses running between Choluteca and El Amatillo pull into the town market. If you're looking to catch a Tegucigalpa bus, it's best to go out to the highway and flag one down.

Many casual travelers may end up in San Lorenzo in order to get a bus to Coyolito, where boats cross the bay to Amapala. The buses leave the town market daily every 90 minutes between 8:30 a.m. and 4:30 p.m.; US 50 cents.

Jicaro Galán

Jicaro Galán is more just a few buildings at the junction of the Choluteca-Tegucigalpa highway and the Pan-American Highway than an actual town. On the Tegucigalpa side of the junction is **El Oasis Colonial,** tel. 81-4007 or 81-4009, fax 81-4006, with motel-style air-conditioned rooms around a pool for US$30 d. The hotel is popular with foreigners visiting the south on business. Jicaro Galán is 43 km from Choluteca and 99 km from Tegucigalpa.

Pespire

Set in a river valley just above the Choluteca plain, 82 km from Tegucigalpa, Pespire is a small, attractive colonial town with a lovely domed church and a historic two-story government building, both on the square.

Sabanagrande

Further up into the hills is Sabanagrande, 42 km from Tegucigalpa, a town of 4,000. The **Iglesia de Rosario** on the square has an elegant wooden roof and balcony. The best food in town is **Comedor Los Tucanes,** on the highway. Buses to Tegucigalpa cost US 50 cents.

EL CORPUS

A beautiful colonial mining town in the hills above Choluteca, El Corpus is without doubt one of the most attractive places to visit in southern Honduras. During the colonial era the town became the center of one of the richest mining regions in the country, and some mines in the surrounding hills still operate.

Apart from the cobblestone streets and colonial architecture in El Corpus itself, the surprisingly lush countryside all around makes the town seem like an oasis in the hot, dry south. Many paths lead up into the hills, including to a viewpoint where you can see out over the Gulf of Fonseca, into Nicaragua, and sometimes as far as El Salvador.

Practicalities

There are no official hotels currently in operation in El Corpus, but locals are usually willing to put people up for a small fee. The local Peace Corps volunteers are also usually happy to see visitors, and may let you stay in their house.

The **Bayside Cafe** (named after the Miami, Florida restaurant of the same name) has well-cooked *plato típico* and on occasion the owner will whip up something extravagant. Hours are variable; knock on the door and let the owner know when you want to eat.

Buses to Choluteca leave about every hour until midafternoon for the hour-long ride. To get to El Corpus by car, take the highway toward San Marcos de Colón from Choluteca, and keep an eye out for the turn-off to the right after Km 54.

SAN MARCOS DE COLÓN

San Marcos de Colón, a small town set at an elevation of 960 meters, is mainly visited by travelers on their way through to Nicaragua. Although the cool mountain air is a nice change from Choluteca, there's not much to do in town.

Practicalities

Hotelito Mi Esperanza, two blocks off the square, tel. 81-3062, has clean, tile-floor rooms for US$3 s or d for one bed with shared bathroom, US$4.50 with private bathroom, US$8 for two beds.

The best food in town is at **Restaurante Bonanza** half a block up the hill from the back of the church, with an extensive menu including spaghetti, shrimp, *pinchos,* nachos, and, believe it or not, gyros, for US$1.50-5 per meal.

DeliFruit Garomar one block off the square has *licuados,* juices, *baleadas, comida corriente,* and burgers at low prices.

The Hondutel and Correos offices are next to the market. Banco Atlántida and Bancahorro both change dollars but no traveler's checks or córdobas.

Getting There and Away

Direct buses to **Tegucigalpa** from San Marcos leave from the Mi Esperanza terminal next to the market five times daily between 6 a.m. and 4:45 p.m.; US$1.70. Buses to **Choluteca** leave frequently between 4:45 a.m. and 3:30 p.m.; US 60 cents.

Colectivo taxis to the border at El Espino, nine km away by paved road, cost US 50 cents, although they will often try to charge you more returning to town from the border.

DEPARTMENT OF EL PARAÍSO

The rolling hills and broad plains of the El Paraíso department in southeastern Honduras have long been favored by Hondurans for their rich agricultural potential and mineral wealth. The valleys of Jamastrán and Moroceli are dotted with farms and cattle ranches, and the surrounding hills are filled with coffee plantations.

Several major river systems are either born in or pass through El Paraíso, including the Río Choluteca, the Río Coco on the border with Nicaragua, and the Río Guayambre, one of the major tributaries of the Río Patuca flowing through Olancho and La Mosquitia to the Caribbean. The climate in El Paraíso is generally temperate and comfortable, with most villages and towns located between 800 and 1,000 meters.

DANLÍ

A sizable city of 116,000, Danlí lies in the midst of the Valle de Cuzcateca, which extends south to the town of El Paraíso, and not far from the rich Valle de Jamastrán. Apart from the cigar industry, the region's economy is derived mainly from cattle ranching and coffee production.

Keep those stogies rolling!

Sights

On the square, opposite **La Iglesia de la Inmaculada Concepción** is the **Museo del Cabildo,** housed in a decrepit two-story building built in 1857. It features an odd assortment of pre-Columbian and colonial-era trinkets and an old caretaker who will happily tell you about them if your Spanish is up to it.

Danlí has become the home of a burgeoning cigar industry. A dozen or so factories operate in the vicinity of the city, including Honduran Cuban Cigars, Cuban Honduran Tobacco, Placencia Tobacco, Central American Cigar, Tabacalera Occidental, and Puros Indios. **Honduran Cuban Cigars,** tel. 93-2089, fax 93-2294, an excellent hand-rolling factory on the road leading from town to El Paraíso, gives tours of their factory with advance notice.

The **Festival de Maíz,** held annually between 23 August and 1 September, is Danlí's major yearly party. Featured are music and dancing, and many different corn products for sale, including *chicha* (corn liquor), soups, *nacata-males, mantucas, atole* (a warm corn drink), and *totopostes.*

Accommodations

Two inexpensive hotels, both next to the gas stations at the entrance from El Paraíso, are **Hotel Apolo,** tel. 93-2177, US$3 s and US$5 d with private bathroom, and the more run-down **Hotel Danlí** across the street, US$2.50 s with private bathroom.

Hotel La Esperanza, tel. 93-2106, also near the gas stations, has nicer rooms around a one-story interior courtyard; US$9 s, US$11 d with private bathroom and fan, or a bit more with a/c and cable TV. Parking is available.

On the highway bypassing Danlí between Tegucigalpa and El Paraíso is **Gran Hotel Granada,** tel. 93-2499 or 93-2784, fax 93-2774, a one-story motel-style building favored by visiting businesspeople, with modern, comfortable rooms for US$20 pp with TV, hot water, and fans. The hotel has a cafeteria and restaurant.

Food

One block south of the square is **Restaurante El Español,** run by a Spaniard, with well-cooked standard meals including *churrasco, cerdo ahumado,* and chicken for US$3-5 per meal. Open daily 8 a.m.-10 p.m.

Pepylus, one block north of the church, tel. 93-2103, is probably the best restaurant in town, serving a wide range of meals including *cordon bleu,* shrimp, paella, fried snapper, steak, and American-style breakfasts for US$3-5 per meal. The dining room is in an indoor patio area.

Restaurante Kuan Ming, two blocks from the square on Calle Canal, tel. 93-2105, serves decent Cantonese food for US$2-4 per meal. Open daily 9 a.m.-10 p.m. On the main avenue between the square and the bus terminal is **Pollos La Cesta,** serving some of the tastier chicken in town for not much money. Open daily 8 a.m.-4 p.m. and 5-11 p.m.

DANLÍ TELEPHONE NUMBERS

Cruz Roja Ambulance: 93-2295
Fire Department: 93-2340, or dial 198
Police: 93-2224, 93-2253, or dial 199

CIGAR CAPITAL OF HONDURAS

Because of its reliable climate, with an average temperature of 75° F and an average 75% humidity, the region surrounding Danlí is considered a natural humidor perfect for cigar production. Taking advantage of these ideal conditions are eight cigar factories, and more may be coming to capitalize on the current boom in cigar smoking in the U.S. and Europe.

A few of the factories use mainly locally grown leaves to make a midrange, inexpensive cigar, while others blend leaves from Brazil, Panama, Costa Rica, the Dominican Republic, Nicaragua, and (believe it or not) Connecticut and Pennsylvania in the United States to create a hand-rolled, top-quality stogie, prized by connoisseurs and highly rated in *Cigar Aficionado* magazine. Wherever the leaves are from, when they first arrive at the factories, they need to be stacked in piles *(pilones),* sprayed with water, and left to sit for several months. Because of a chemical reaction in the leaves, the *pilones* literally cook themselves, reaching temperatures of 45° C. Each factory has its own master in charge of the *pilones,* who decides when the leaves have been properly cured and are ready to roll. This idiosyncratic process is probably the most crucial in establishing a certain cigar's flavor—two factories can buy the same leaves at the same time and because they cure them differently, produce completely different tasting cigars.

After leaving the *pilones,* the veins are removed from the leaves in a separate room, and the leaves are again sprayed and stacked. Rolling is accomplished in two stages: first the filler leaves, usually four of them, are rolled and cut to shape, and then put in a mold overnight. The next day the wrapper leaf—often an Ecuadoran Sumatra—is put on, and the cigar is moved into the humidor room for storage.

Because of the current rage of cigars in the United States and Europe, cigar factories are experiencing severe shortages in quality tobacco leaf, as the plant is notoriously tricky to grow properly. According to experts, to receive leaves for production now, a factory should have placed orders six years ago, thus none of the factories have enough tobacco to fill their bulging order sheets. Just about every cigar produced in Danlí has already been sold before even being rolled.

Almost all cigars rolled in Danlí are exported and are very difficult to come by in Honduras. One shop which does sell some Danlí cigars is Shakespeare and Co. Books in Tegucigalpa. Cigars rolled at the Flor de Copán factory in Santa Rosa de Copán, of a somewhat lower grade, are available all over. If you can arrange a tour with one of the local factories, you may be lucky enough to be allowed into the *bodega* to buy a box of your choice.

Licuados Gloria next to Hotel Apolo has *licuados,* juices, sweet breads, snacks, and inexpensive *comida corriente.*

Services
Bancahsa, Banco de Occidente, and Banco Atlántida all change dollars and sometimes traveler's checks. Hondutel and Correos are just off the park. The Correos offers Express Mail Service.

Getting There and Away
All buses leave Danlí from the central bus terminal near the exit of town toward Tegucigalpa. Discua, tel. 93-2217, and Emtra de Oriente run buses every hour or so to **Tegucigalpa,** charging US$1 for the two-hour ride.

Tegucigalpa is 93 km from Danlí by a well-maintained two-lane highway. Continuing past

Danlí toward Nicaragua, the road is in horrible shape to El Paraíso, and only marginally better to the border at Las Manos, 30 km from Danlí. Supposedly the funds have been allocated to repair the road, which is a good thing as currently it seems to have more potholes than pavement.

EL PARAÍSO AND THE NICARAGUAN BORDER

A midsize town 18 km from Danlí at one end of the Valle de Cuzcateca, El Paraíso doesn't offer much beyond its proximity to the Nicaraguan border at Las Manos, 12 km up the road.

Should you need to spend the night in town, **Hotel Isis,** on the square, tel. 93-4251, has clean rooms for US$4 s or US$6 d with private bathroom, less with a shared bathroom and more with a TV. The hotel also has a parking lot and a decent restaurant.

A gas station at the highway junction in town can give you a last fill-up if you're on your way to the border.

Minibuses to the border leave every hour or so from the terminal, charging US 25 cents. *Colectivo* taxis fitting four passengers will go for US$3 for the entire taxi.

Buses to Danlí leave frequently, charging US 30 cents for the bone-rattling ride. A few buses daily drive straight through from El Paraíso to Tegucigalpa for US$1.20.

Las Manos

The Nicaraguan-Honduran border at Las Manos is a collection of huts along the highway with a large gate across the middle, in the midst of green hills. The Honduran immigration office is open 8 a.m.-4 p.m., while the Nicaraguan office is open 8 a.m.-noon and 1 5 p.m.

Also at the border are a Hondutel office, *casa de cambio, comedor,* and *pulpería.* Buses continue into Nicaragua every hour or so from the border until midafternoon. The entire trip from Tegucigalpa to the border can be accomplished in three hours by bus, if you don't have to wait long at El Paraíso for a bus to Las Manos.

YUSCARÁN

One of the more charming colonial mining towns in Honduras, Yuscarán is a jumble of twisting cobblestone streets and plaster, tile roofed buildings perched on the edge of a mountain at an elevation of 850 meters. The town centers around an inviting square filled with trees and flowers. The climate is semitropical and the surrounding area is pleasingly lush.

Silver ore was discovered in the mountains above Yuscarán in the early 18th century, and shortly after that the town evolved in the haphazard manner that characterizes many mining towns. After hitting an early peak toward the end of the 18th century, the mines went into decline until the last decades of the 19th century, when there was a brief revival. Mining currently plays no role in the town's economy, but rumor has it foreign investors have been looking

at core samples with the idea of reopening some of the shafts.

Although only about 2,000 people live in Yuscarán itself, the town is the capital of the El Paraíso department. The best known *aguardiente* liquor in Honduras is produced here at the **El Buen Gusto** factory.

Sights

Apart from the simple **Iglesia Parroquial** on the square, built at an unknown date sometime in the mid-18th century, the only sight of note in town is **Casa Fortín,** a family house built in 1850. The two-story house, declared a national monument, serves as the town museum normally, but recently has not been in full operation. If it's closed, ask at nearby houses for the owners, who will let you in. Downstairs you'll find many mineral samples as well as mining and farming tools from the past century, while upstairs is a *sala ambiental,* or environmental room, featuring a display on the flora and fauna of the mountain above town.

After visiting Casa Fortín and the church, it's easy to spend an hour or two walking around the town admiring the rustic colonial architecture and cobbled streets.

Practicalities

The one hotel in town at the moment is **Hotel Carol,** at the entrance to town, tel. 81-7143, a good value at US$3 s with private bathroom for a clean room. Word around town is that a Dutchman is building a new hotel and restaurant in town which should be open by late 1997.

Two decent places to grab a meal in Yuscarán are **Típicos Monserrat** just off the square, and the less expensive **Restaurant Filomena de Cortés** (the name of the owner) in an unmarked building across from the Banco de Occidente.

Near Yuscarán

The mountains looming above town have recently been declared a biological reserve covering 2,240 hectares, accessed by a dirt road leading up to the Hondutel tower. Peaks inside the **Yuscarán Biological Reserve** include El Volcán (1,991 meters), El Fogón (1,825 meters), and Monserrat (1,783 meters). A display in the Casa Fortín shows the layout of roads and trails.

Although the forest is not in pristine condition, the views are wonderful and there are opportunities to birdwatch and explore some of the more than 100 mines in the mountains. Two mine shafts, **La Luz** and **Santa Gertrudis,** are reportedly being cleared out to serve as tourist attractions.

Two major sets of petroglyphs are not far from Yuscarán, one near the junction of the Río Oropolí and the Río Choluteca past the town of Oropolí, and the other near the village of Ore-

alí. Also off the dirt road leading to Oropolí is a hot spring near El Tamarindo. Two buses daily drive between Yuscarán and Oropolí.

Getting There and Away

Buses drive the 68 km to Tegucigalpa three times daily, leaving town at 7 a.m., noon, and 3 p.m. The 17 km spur to Yuscarán, paved in 1989, leaves the Danlí-Tegucigalpa highway between Km 47 and 48, at El Empalme.

BOB RACE

GLOSSARY

aguas calientes, aguas termales—hot or thermal waters, hot springs

alcalde—mayor

alfarda—an inclined plane of decorative stonework, an example of which can be seen at the Mayan ruins of El Puente

aguardiente—the favored Honduran poor-quality booze

artesanías—handicrafts

ayudante—helper, specifically a young man who helps the driver of a bus by seating passengers and collecting fares

baleada—a popular Honduran snack, made with a flour tortilla filled with beans, crumbly cheese, cream, and sometimes other ingredients, then grilled lightly

balneario—swimming spot

bando—a spicy fish stew popular on the north coast and the Bay Islands

bistec—beef steak

billiar—pool, billiards

bodega—storeroom

busito—literally, little bus, frequently used in rural areas

camacha—a traditional Pech instrument similar to a maraca

campesino—peasant, usually a small-scale farmer

canícula—a brief dry season in August during the middle of the rainy season

cantina—a low-priced bar, not always safe for women

caoba—mahogany, the most prized wood in Honduras

caracol—literally the shellfish conch, but also the nickname given to Bay Islanders by mainland residents

casa cural—the administration office of a church

caseta—toll building or place where admission is collected

cassava—a yucca dish made by the north coast Garífuna

cayuco—canoe

champa—a thatch-roofed hut with no walls

chichicaste—a stinging shrub found in Honduras

cipote—Honduran slang for a little kid

colones—Salvadoran currency

comida corriente—a set meal, usually the least expensive choice on a restaurant's menu

conejo—rabbit, often eaten in Honduras

criollo—a term used in colonial times to denote peoples of Spanish blood born in the Americas

cueva—cave

curandero—a healer using traditional indigenous spiritual techniques and herbal medications

desvio—turnoff, as from a highway onto another road. *Desvios* are frequently named in Honduras.

dugu—a Garífuna dance

encomienda—the colonial system of alloting Spaniards land and the right to tribute and labor from Indians living there

Fusep—the national police

guisado—stew

hacienda—a partially or fully self-sufficient ranch. The department of Olancho is known for its haciendas.

indio—the name given to Latinos by Miskito, Tawahka, and Pech Indians

jalón—word used to ask for a ride, as in hitchhiking

jejenes—sand flies

junco—a type of palm native to the Santa Bárbara region, used to make baskets, hats, and other crafts

lancha—launch, or a small, motor-powered boat

libra—pound, the unit of weight

licuado—a popular drink made by blending milk, sugar, and any of several fruits

Latino—people of mixed Spanish and indigenous blood, comprising most of the population of Honduras

machuca—a Garífuna stew made with fish, banana, and coconut milk

manzana—a unit of land measurement equal to 0.7 hectares; also, an apple

mestizo—a person of mixed indigenous and European blood, a term commonly used in the colonial era but less so now

milpas—a small patch of farmland on which peasants grow beans, corn, and other vegetables mainly for their own consumption rather than to sell

mondongo—tripe, or intestine, soup

nacatamale—a cornmeal food boiled in banana leaves and stuffed with spiced meat and vegetables

nance—a small fruit often sold on the street in bags as a snack

ocote—a type of pine tree common to the highlands of Honduras

olanchano—someone from the department of Olancho

pan de coco—coconut bread, a Garífuna specialty

panadería—bakery

papel de arroz—rice paper, or cigarette rolling paper

parque—park, usually the downtown square. Unlike many other Latin American countries, Hondurans do not use the word "plaza."

pastelito—a favorite Honduran snack consisting of a puff of dough filled with spiced beef and deep fried

patronatos—local organizations dedicated to preparing saint's-day festivals. In Tegucigalpa, these groups have evolved into grass-roots organizations pressuring the city government to improve neighborhood social services.

peatonal—pedestrian street

pinchos—a shish kebab-style meal with beef or chicken and vegetables served on a skewer

pipante—a dugout canoe propelled by poles, common in La Mosquitia

pisto—Honduran slang for cash or money

plato del día—"plate of the day," or an inexpensive set meal

plato típico—the Honduran national dish, which usually includes beef, fried plantain, rice, beans, a chunk of salty cheese, a dash of cream, and lots of tortillas

pulpería—a general store

punta—traditional Garífuna music, a modern version of which has become a popular Honduran dance music

pupusa—a thick tortilla filled with sausage and/or cheese, more common in El Salvador but also found in Honduras

quetzal—a legendarily beautiful bird living in the cloud forests

retablo—an altarpiece at a church; many are gilded and intricately carved

ron—rum

sacbé—an elevated Mayan roadway; one is visible at Copán

salón de billiar—pool hall

sampedrano—a resident of San Pedro Sula

sopa de caracol—conch soup, frequently made with coconut milk

tajadas—fried bananas or plantains, eaten like chips

tapado—a fish, yucca, and coconut dish made by the Garífuna

tenpuca—a traditional Pech drum

terminal de buses—bus terminal

timbre—a type of stamp sold at banks for different amounts, sometimes required to renew a tourist card

torta—a sandwich

tostones—slang term for Honduran 50-cent pieces

tramitador—someone who helps deal with official paperwork

tranquilo—relaxed, sometimes used to tell another person to relax

transito—the traffic police

tuk-tuk—a motorized canoe in La Mosquitia, so called for the noise it makes

tumulos—speed bumps

varas—a unit of land measurement equal to 838 square meters

viaje especial—a special trip, in a taxi or boat, which will cost more than a normal ride

vigilante—a guard

wabul—a traditional Miskito Indian drink made from bananas and coconut

zancudos—mosquitoes

zona viva—a district of a town or city known for its nightlife

SPANISH PHRASEBOOK

PRONUNCIATION GUIDE

Consonants

c   as **c** in **cat**, before **a**, **o**, or **u**; like **s** before **e** or **i**
d   as **d** in **dog**, except between vowels, then like **th** in **that**
g   before **e** or **i**, like the **ch** in Scottish **loch**; elsewhere like **g** in **get**
h   always silent
j   like the English **h** in **hotel**, but stronger
ll like the **y** in **yellow**
ñ   like the **ni** in **onion**
r   always pronounced as strong **r**
rr trilled **r**
v   similar to the **b** in **boy** (not as English **v**)
y   similar to English, but with a slight **j** sound. When y stands alone it is
    pronounced like the **e** in **me**.
z   like **s** in **same**
b, f, k, l, m, n, p, q, s, t, w, x as in English

Vowels

a   as in **father**, but shorter
e   as in **hen**
i   as in **machine**
o   as in **phone**
u   usually as in **rule**; when it follows a **q** the **u** is silent; when it follows an **h** or **g**
    its pronounced like **w**, except when it comes between **g** and **e** or **i**, when it's also
    silent

NUMBERS

0	*cero*	11	*once*	40	*cuarenta*
1 (masculine)	*uno*	12	*doce*	50	*cincuenta*
1 (feminine)	*una*	13	*trece*	60	*sesenta*
2	*dos*	14	*catorce*	70	*setenta*
3	*tres*	15	*quince*	80	*ochenta*
4	*cuatro*	16	*diez y seis*	90	*noventa*
5	*cinco*	17	*diez y siete*	100	*cien*
6	*seis*	18	*diez y ocho*	101	*ciento y uno*
7	*siete*	19	*diez y nueve*	200	*doscientos*
8	*ocho*	20	*veinte*	1,000	*mil*
9	*nueve*	21	*viente y uno*	10,000	*diez mil*
10	*diez*	30	*treinta*		

DAYS OF THE WEEK

Sunday — *domingo*
Monday — *lunes*
Tuesday — *martes*
Wednesday — *miércoles*

Thursday — *jueves*
Friday — *viernes*
Saturday — *sábado*

TIME

What time is it? — *¿Qué hora es?*
one o'clock — *la una*
two o'clock — *las dos*
at two o'clock — *a las dos*
ten past three — *las tres y diez*
six a.m. — *las seis a la mañana*
six p.m. — *las seis a la tarde*
today — *hoy*

tomorrow, morning
   — *mañana, la mañana*
yesterday — *ayer*
week — *semana*
month — *mes*
year — *año*
last night — *la noche pasada*
next day — *el próximo día*

USEFUL WORDS AND PHRASES

Hello. — *Hola.*
Good morning. — *Buenos días.*
Good afternoon. — *Buenas tardes.*
Good evening. — *Buenas noches.*
How are you? — *¿Cómo está?*
Fine. — *Muy bien.*
And you? — *¿Y usted?*
So-so. — *Así así.*
Thank you. — *Gracias.*
Thank you very much. — *Muchas gracias.*
You're very kind.
   — *Usted es muy amable.*
You're welcome; literally, "It's nothing."
   — *De nada.*
yes — *sí*
no — *no*
I don't know. — *Yo no sé.*
it's fine; okay — *está bien*
good; okay — *bueno*
please — *por favor*
Pleased to meet you. — *Mucho gusto.*
excuse me (physical) — *perdóneme*
excuse me (speech) — *discúlpeme*
I'm sorry. — *Lo siento.*
goodbye — *adiós*

see you later; literally, "until later"
   — *hasta luego*
more — *más*
less — *menos*
better — *mejor*
much — *mucho*
a little — *un poco*
large — *grande*
small — *pequeño*
quick — *rápido*
slowly — *despacio*
bad — *malo*
difficult — *difícil*
easy — *fácil*
He/She/It is gone; as in "She left," "He's
gone" — *Ya se fue.*
I don't speak Spanish well.
   — *No hablo bien español.*
I don't understand. — *No entiendo.*
How do you say . . . in Spanish?
   — *¿Cómo se dice . . . en español?*
Do you understand English?
   — *¿Entiende el inglés?*
Is English spoken here? (Does anyone
here speak English?)
   — *¿Se habla inglés aquí?*

TERMS OF ADDRESS

I — *yo*
you (formal) — *usted*
you (familiar) — *tú*
he/him — *él*
she/her — *ella*
we/us — *nosotros*
you (plural) — *vos*
they/them (all males or mixed gender)
— *ellos*
they/them (all females) — *ellas*

Mr., sir — *señor*
Mrs., madam — *señora*
Miss, young lady — *señorita*
wife — *esposa*
husband — *marido* or *esposo*
friend — *amigo* (male), *amiga* (female)
sweetheart — *novio* (male), *novia* (female)
son, daughter — *hijo, hija*
brother, sister — *hermano, hermana*
father, mother — *padre, madre*

GETTING AROUND

Where is . . . ? — *¿Dónde está . . . ?*
How far is it to . . .?
— *¿Qué tan lejos está a . . . ?*
from . . . to . . . — *de . . . a . . .*
highway — *la carretera*
road — *el camino*
street — *la calle*
block — *la cuadra*
kilometer — *kilómetro*

mile (commonly used near the
U.S. border) — *milla*
north — *el norte*
south — *el sur*
west — *el oeste*
east — *el este*
straight ahead — *al derecho* or *adelante*
to the right — *a la derecha*
to the left — *a la izquierda*

ACCOMMODATIONS

Can I (we) see a room?
— *¿Puedo (podemos) ver un cuarto?*
What is the rate? — *¿Cuál es el precio?*
a single room — *un cuarto sencillo*
a double room — *un cuarto doble*
key — *llave*
bathroom — *lavabo* or *baño*
hot water — *agua caliente*

cold water — *agua fría*
towel — *toalla*
soap — *jabón*
toilet paper — *papel higiénico*
air conditioning — *aire acondicionado*
fan — *abanico, ventilador*
blanket — *cubierta* or *manta*

PUBLIC TRANSPORT

bus stop — *la parada del autobús*
main bus terminal
— *terminal de buses*
railway station
— *la estación de ferrocarril*
airport — *el aeropuerto*
ferry terminal
— *la terminal del transbordador*

I want a ticket to . . .
— *Quiero un boleto a . . .*
I want to get off at . . .
— *Quiero bajar en . . .*
Here, please. — *Aquí, por favor.*
Where is this bus going?
— *¿Dónde va este autobús?*
roundtrip — *ida y vuelta*
What do I owe? — *¿Cuánto le debo?*

FOOD

menu — *lista, menú*
glass — *vaso*
fork — *tenedor*
knife — *cuchillo*
spoon — *cuchara, cucharita*
napkin   *servilleta*
soft drink — *refresco*
coffee, cream — *café, crema*
tea — *té*
sugar — *azúcar*
purified water — *agua purificado*
bottled carbonated water — *agua mineral*
bottled uncarbonated water — *agua sin gas*
beer — *cerveza*
wine — *vino*
milk — *leche*
juice — *jugo*
eggs — *huevos*
bread — *pan*

watermelon — *sandía*
banana — *plátano*
apple — *manzana*
orange — *naranja*
meat (without) — *carne (sin)*
beef — *carne de res*
chicken — *pollo*
fish — *pescado*
shellfish — *mariscos*
fried — *a la plancha*
roasted — *asado*
barbecue, barbecued — *al carbón*
breakfast — *desayuno*
lunch — *almuerzo*
dinner (often eaten in late afternoon)
    — *comida*
dinner, or a late night snack — *cena*
the check — *la cuenta*

MAKING PURCHASES

I need . . . — *Necesito . . .*
I want . . . — *Deseo . . .* or *Quiero . . .*
I would like . . . (more polite) — *Quisiera
    . . .*
How much does it cost? — *¿Cuánto cuesta?*
What's the exchange rate?
    — *¿Cuál es el tipo de cambio?*

Can I see . . . ? — *¿Puedo ver . . . ?*
this one — *ésta/ésto*
expensive — *caro*
cheap — *barato*
cheaper — *más barato*
too much — *demasiado*

HEALTH

Help me please. — *Ayúdeme por favor.*
I am ill. — *Estoy enfermo.*
pain — *dolor*
fever — *fiebre*
stomache ache — *dolor de estómago*
vomiting — *vomitar*

diarrhea — *diarrea*
drugstore — *farmacia*
medicine — *medicina*
pill, tablet — *pastilla*
birth control pills — *pastillas contraceptivos*
condoms — *contraceptivas*

BOOKLIST

HISTORY

General History and Information

Acker, Alison. *Honduras: The Making of a Banana Republic.* Boston: South End Press, 1988. Acker's account of Honduran history is somewhat cursory, but the slim volume makes good reading.

Alvarado, Elvia. *Don't Be Afraid, Gringo: A Honduran Woman Speaks from the Heart.* New York: Harper and Row, 1989.

Barry, Tom, and Kent Norsworthy. *Honduras: The Essential Guide to its Politics, Economy, Society and Environment.* Albuquerque: Resource Center Press, 1994. A responsible though relentlessly critical general overview of present-day Honduras.

Chapman, Anne MacKaye. *Masters of Animals: Oral Traditions of the Tolupan Indians, Honduras.* Philadelphia: Gordon & Breach Science Publications, 1992.

Davidson, William V. *Historical Geography of the Bay Islands, Honduras: Anglo-Hispanic Conflict in the Western Caribbean.* Birmingham: Southern University Press, 1979.

Gonzalez, Nancie L. *Sojourners of the Caribbean. Ethnogenesis and Ethnohistory of the Garifuna.* Urbana: University of Illinois Press, 1988.

Merrill, Tim L. *Honduras: A Country Study.* Washington, D.C.: U.S Government, 1995. Put out by the Department of the Army, this area handbook presents some rather obvious built-in biases—the historical account of the Contra affair, for example, is laughable—but it is nonetheless a good source of general information on Honduras.

Peckenham, Nancy, and Annie Street, eds. *Honduras: Portrait of a Captive Nation.* New York: Praeger, 1985. This collection of essays covering Honduran history from colonial times to the mid-1980s ranges from obscure to extremely enlightening.

Yuscarán, Guillermo. *Gringos In Honduras: The Good, the Bad, and the Ugly,* (1995) and *Velásquez: The Man and His Art.* (1994) Tegucigalpa: Nuevo Sol Publications. Otherwise known as William Lewis, Yuscarán has written several volumes of short stories about his adopted country (see below), as well as these two interesting short histories, one on Honduras's best-known painter.

Colonial Era

Chamberlain, R.S. *The Conquest and Colonization of Honduras, 1502-1550.* Washington: Carnegie Institute, 1957. In spite of its datedness, Chamberlain's book remains the only detailed, practically day-by-day account of Honduras's conquest.

Floyd, T.S. *The Anglo-Spanish Struggle for Mosquitia.*Albuquerque: University of New Mexico Press, 1967. The book focuses on a little-studied aspect of Central American colonial history: the centuries-long battle for the Caribbean coast between the English and the Spanish.

Newson, Linda. *The Cost of Conquest: Indian Decline under Spanish Rule in Honduras.* Boulder: Westview Press, 1986. Rather than trace the specific course of events in colonial Honduras, Newson relates the broad panorama of Honduras both before, during, and after colonization to assess its impact on the region's indigenous populations.

The Banana Companies

Amaya Amador, Ramón. *Prisión Verde.* Tegucigalpa: Editorial Baktun, 1983, third edition. Although technically a novel, Amaya's famed (in Latin America) work provides an excellent though chilling account of life in a banana plantation from the point of view of a Honduran worker.

Karnes, Thomas L. *Tropical Enterprise: The Rise of the Standard Fruit and Steamship Com-*

pany in Latin America. Baton Rouge: Louisiana State University Press, 1978.

Kepner, Charles David, Jr. and Jay Henry Soothill. *The Banana Empire: A Case Study of Economic Imperialism.* New York: Russell and Russell, 1935.

Langley, Lester and Thomas Schoonover. *The Banana Men: American Mercenaries and Entrepreneurs in Central America, 1880-1930.* Lexington: University of Kentucky Press, 1995. Although the first chapter is numbingly theoretical, the rest of the book is a fascinating account of the wild characters involved in creating and running the Central American banana empires. Special attention is payed to a man who deserves a full-length feature film to do his story justice, Lee Christmas.

McCann, Thomas. *An American Company: The Tragedy of United Fruit.* New York: Crown Publishers, 1976.

The Soccer War

Anderson, Thomas. *The War of the Dispossessed: Honduras and El Salvador, 1969.* Lincoln: University of Nebraska Press, 1981.

Durham, William H. *Scarcity and Survival in Central America: Ecological Origins of the Soccer War.* Stanford: Stanford University Press, 1070.

Honduras and the Central American Crisis

LaFeber, Walter. *Inevitable Revolutions.* New York: W.W. Norton, 1983. Not specifically about Honduras, LaFeber's classic work masterfully traces the development of U.S. foreign policy in the region and the coming of the revolutionary ferment of the 1970s and '80s.

Schulz, Donald E. and Deborah Sundloff Schulz. *The United States, Honduras, and the Crisis in Central America.* Boulder: Westview Press, 1994. Possibly the best book of Honduran history written in English, and maybe in Spanish too, the Schulzes minutely trace the course of Honduran history in the 1980s, with special emphasis on relations with the United States and the Contras. For anyone interested in understanding Honduras during that time, and today as well,

this extremely well-written, balanced, and occasionally very funny book is a must read.

LITERATURE AND TRAVELOGUES

19th-Century Travelers

For some reason, Honduras seemed to attract foreign travelers with literary proclivities during the past century. Of the four books listed below, Stephens's account is by far the most famous, as well as the most interesting and well-written.

Cecil, Charles. *Honduras: A Land of Great Depth.* New York: Rand McNally, 1890.

Soltera, María. *A Lady's Ride Across Honduras.* Gainesville: University of Florida Press, 1964.

Stephens, J.L. *Incidents of Travel in Central America, Chiapas, and Yucatan.* New York: Dover, 1969, two volumes. Originally published by Harper and Brothers, New York, 1841.

Wells, William. *Explorations and Adventures in Honduras.* New York: Harper, 1857.

Fiction

Henry, O. *Cabbages and Kings.* New York: Doubleday, Page and Co., 1904. O. Henry, the pen name for famed U.S. short story writter William Sydney Porter, spent some time in Puerto Cortés and Trujillo around the turn of the century, while on the run from the law. With the material gathered during his stay, he wrote this collection of stories.

Theroux, Paul. *The Mosquito Coast.* New York: Avon, 1982. This novel, along with the movie version starring Harrison Ford, has probably done more to put the Mosquitia region of northeastern Honduras on the map than anything else. Unfortunately, the site was apparently chosen by Theroux to represent the lowest state of humanity, and he shows little appreciation for anything Honduran.

Yuscarán, Guillermo. *Blue Pariah, Conociendo a la Gente Garífuna, Points of Light, Beyond Honduras, Northcoast Honduras, La Luz Hondureña.* Tegucigalpa: Nuevo Sol Publications. William Lewis, now know by his adopted name

Guillermo Yuscarán, lives in Honduras where he writes short stories, novels, and paints. A born storyteller, Yuscarán has published several fiction and nonfiction (see above) books on Honduras, which can be found in several bookstores and more expensive hotels in Tegucigalpa, San Pedro Sula, Copán, the Bay Islands, and the north coast beach towns.

RECREATION AND TRAVEL

Collins, Sharon. *Diving and Snorkeling Guide to Roatán and Honduras' Bay Islands.* Houston: Pisces Books, 1993. A slim volume, which is not bad but does not compare to *Diving the Bay Islands.*

Garoutte, Cindy. *Diving the Bay Islands.* New York: AquaQuest Publications, 1995. AquaQuest line: (800) 933-8989, (516) 759-0476. Locust Valley, NY. Garoutte's book is obviously the product of much time spent diving in the islands. Her book provides an excellent overview to diving on all the main islands, and is accompanied by some spectacular photos and useful dive-site locator maps.

Parent, Derek. *La Mosquitia: A Guide to the Land of Savannahs, Rain Forests and Turtle Hunters.* Intrepid Traveller Publications, 1995. If you really have the urge to go exploring on your own in La Mosquitia, be sure to get a copy of Parent's book, chock-full of first hand information on obscure treks—where to get guides, what to watch out for, and useful things to bring along.

Cruising Guide to the Honduras Bay Islands. Stamford: Wescott Cove Publishing Co. This guide is unfortunately currently out of print, although the publishers say another edition can be expected. If you call their office in Stamford, Connecticut, they will sell you a copy of their boating charts for the islands, which are excellent.

NATURAL HISTORY

Mader, Ron and Jim Gollin. *Honduras: Adventures in Nature.* Santa Fe: John Muir Publications, 1997. An overview of protected areas in Honduras, combining nuts and bolts travel practicalities with general environmental information.

Forests

Carr, Archie. *High Jungles and Low.* Gainesville: University of Florida Press, 1953. Well-known biologist Archie Carr spent several years in Honduras, most of it at the Escuela Agrícola Panamericana in the Valle de Zamorano. His account of this time combines plant and animal biology, particularly regarding the cloud forest and the tropical rainforest, with anecdotes and stories about local people. This well-written volume, obviously a labor of love, clearly shows the author's love for Honduras and its people. Carr also wrote "Animal Habitats In Honduras," one of the best English-language essays on the subject, which appeared in *The Bulletin of the American Museum of Natural History,* 1950, volume 96.

Forsyth, Adrian and Ken Miyata. *Tropical Nature: Life and Death in the Rain Forests of Central and South America.* New York: Charles Scribner's Sons, 1984. Not specifically about Honduras, this book is nonetheless a good overview of the workings of the rainforest ecosystem found in La Mosquitia.

Reef

Humann, Paul. *Reef Fish Identification, Reef Creature Identification,* and *Reef Coral Identification.* Jacksonville: New World Publishing, Inc. This three-volume set, published, respectively, in 1989, 1992, and 1993, is considered the best available on Caribbean reef life. The volumes can be ordered through the publisher by calling (904) 737-6558.

Birds

No bird guide exists just for Honduras, however two good regional guides cover most of the species found in the country.

Peterson, Roger Tory and Edward L. Chalif. *A Field Guide to Mexican Birds.* Boston: Houghton Mifflin, 1973.

Ridgely, Robert and John A. Gwynne, Jr. *A Guide to the Birds of Panama, with Costa Rica, Nicaragua, and Honduras.* Princeton: Princeton University Press, 1989.

INDEX

Italicized numbers indicate maps.

ABOUT THE AUTHOR

Chris Humphrey began traveling at the age of five, when he ventured across town to a friend's grandmother's house. He's been at it ever since. An inveterate explorer, Chris has a penchant for getting lost in rural regions and climbing to the top of whatever high point happens to be in the vicinity—be it mountains, trees, pyramids, or random tall buildings.

After a year-long stint working for two newspapers in Mexico City, Chris caught the journalism bug and now combines travel writing with freelance journalism on politics and culture from his base in the Condesa neighborhood of Mexico City. *Honduras Handbook* is his first travel guide.

When not staying up all night to meet deadlines, Chris likes to read whatever book comes his way, listen to music at full volume, try not to get hurt playing rugby, mountain biking, and climbing mountains, and do his utmost to keep his decrepit vehicles on the road.

MESA LANGE-SCOVEL

MOON TRAVEL HANDBOOKS
THE IDEAL TRAVELING COMPANIONS

Moon Travel Handbooks provide focused, comprehensive coverage of distinct destinations all over the world. Our goal is to give travelers all the background and practical information they'll need for an extraordinary travel experience. Every Handbook begins with an in-depth essay about the land, the people, their history, art, politics, and social concerns—an entire bookcase of cultural insight and introductory information in one portable volume. We also provide accurate, up-to-date coverage of all the practicalities: language, currency, transportation, accommodations, food, and entertainment. And Moon's maps are legendary, covering not only cities and highways, but parks and trails that are often difficult to find in other sources.

On the following pages is a complete list of Handbooks, covering North America and Hawaii, Mexico, Central America and the Caribbean, and Asia and the Pacific. To purchase Moon Travel Handbooks, please check your local bookstore or order by phone: (800) 345-5473 Monday-Friday 8 a.m.-5 p.m. PST. If you are calling from outside of the United States the number is (916) 345-5473.

"Amazingly detailed in a style easy to understand, the Handbooks offer a lot for a good price."
—**International Travel News**

"Moon [Handbooks] . . . bring a healthy respect to the places they investigate. Best of all, they provide a host of odd nuggets that give a place texture and prod the wary traveler from the beaten path. The finest are written with such care and insight they deserve listing as literature."
—**American Geographical Society**

"Outdoor enthusiasts gravitate to the well-written Moon Travel Handbooks. In addition to politically correct historic and cultural features, the series focuses on flora, fauna and outdoor recreation. Maps and meticulous directions also are a trademark of Moon guides."
—**Houston Chronicle**

"Moon Travel Handbooks offer in-depth historical essays and useful maps, enhanced by a sense of humor and a neat, compact format."   —**SWING**

"Perfect for the more adventurous, these are long on history, sightseeing and nitty-gritty information and very price-specific."   —**Columbus Dispatch**

"Moon guides manage to be comprehensive and countercultural at the same time . . . Handbooks are packed with maps, photographs, drawings, and sidebars that constitute a college-level introduction to each country's history, culture, people, and crafts."
—**National Geographic Traveler**

"An in-depth dunk into the land, the people and their history, arts, and politics."
—**Student Travels**

"Few travel guides do a better job helping travelers create their own itineraries than the Moon Travel Handbook series. The authors have a knack for homing in on the essentials."
—**Colorado Springs Gazette Telegraph**

NORTH AMERICA AND HAWAII

"These domestic guides convey the same sense of exoticism that their foreign counterparts do, making home-country travel seem like far-flung adventure."
—*Sierra Magazine*

Alaska-Yukon Handbook	**$17.95**
Deke Castleman and Don Pitcher	500 pages, 92 maps
Alberta and the Northwest Territories Handbook	**$17.95**
Andrew Hempstead and Nadina Purdon	497 pages, 72 maps,
Arizona Traveler's Handbook	**$17.95**
Bill Weir and Robert Blake	486 pages, 54 maps
Atlantic Canada Handbook	**$17.95**
Nan Drosdick and Mark Morris	436 pages, 61 maps
Big Island of Hawaii Handbook	**$13.95**
J.D. Bisignani	349 pages, 23 maps
British Columbia Handbook	**$15.95**
Jane King	375 pages, 69 maps
Colorado Handbook	**$18.95**
Stephen Metzger	447 pages, 59 maps
Georgia Handbook	**$17.95**
Kap Stann	360 pages, 50 maps
Hawaii Handbook	**$19.95**
J.D. Bisignani	1004 pages, 90 maps
Honolulu-Waikiki Handbook	**$14.95**
J.D. Bisignani	365 pages, 20 maps
Idaho Handbook	**$18.95**
Don Root	582 pages, 42 maps
Kauai Handbook	**$15.95**
J.D. Bisignani	330 pages, 23 maps
Maui Handbook	**$14.95**
J.D. Bisignani	393 pages, 35 maps
Montana Handbook	**$17.95**
Judy Jewell and W.C. McRae	454 pages, 52 maps
Nevada Handbook	**$16.95**
Deke Castleman	473 pages, 40 maps
New Mexico Handbook	**$15.95**
Stephen Metzger	337 pages, 47 maps
New York City Handbook	**$13.95**
Christiane Bird	272 pages, 19 maps
New York Handbook	**$19.95**
Christiane Bird	760 pages, 95 maps
Northern California Handbook	**$19.95**
Kim Weir	779 pages, 50 maps
Oregon Handbook	**$16.95**
Stuart Warren and Ted Long Ishikawa	520 pages, 33 maps

Road Trip USA	$22.50
Jamie Jensen	786 pages, 165 maps
Southern California Handbook	**$19.95**
Kim Weir	600 pages, 30 maps
Tennessee Handbook	**$17.95**
Jeff Bradley	490 pages, 44 maps
Texas Handbook	**$17.95**
Joe Cummings	598 pages, 70 maps
Utah Handbook	**$17.95**
Bill Weir and W.C. McRae	456 pages, 40 maps
Washington Handbook	**$19.95**
Don Pitcher	630 pages, 113 maps
Wisconsin Handbook	**$18.95**
Thomas Huhti	580 pages, 67 maps
Wyoming Handbook	**$17.95**
Don Pitcher	581 pages, 80 maps

ASIA AND THE PACIFIC

"Scores of maps, detailed practical info down to
business hours of small-town libraries. You can't beat
the Asian titles for sheer heft. (The) series is sort of
an American Lonely Planet, with better writing but
fewer titles. (The) individual voice of researchers
comes through."

—*Travel & Leisure*

Australia Handbook	**$21.95**
Marael Johnson, Andrew Hempstead,	
and Nadina Purdon	944 pages, 141 maps
Bali Handbook	**$19.95**
Bill Dalton	715 pages, 54 maps
Bangkok Handbook	**$13.95**
Michael Buckley	221 pages, 30 maps
Fiji Islands Handbook	**$13.95**
David Stanley	275 pages, 38 maps
Hong Kong Handbook	**$15.95**
Kerry Moran	347 pages, 49 maps
Indonesia Handbook	**$25.00**
Bill Dalton	1,351 pages, 249 maps
Japan Handbook	**$22.50**
J.D. Bisignani	952 pages, 213 maps
Micronesia Handbook	**$14.95**
Neil M. Levy	311 pages, 70 maps
Nepal Handbook	**$18.95**
Kerry Moran	466 pages, 51 maps

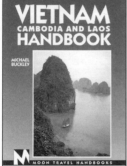

New Zealand Handbook	**$19.95**
Jane King	595 pages, 81 maps
Outback Australia Handbook	**$18.95**
Marael Johnson	424 pages, 57 maps
Pakistan Handbook	**$19.95**
Isobel Shaw	660 pages, 85 maps
Philippines Handbook	**$17.95**
Peter Harper and Laurie Fullerton	638 pages, 116 maps
Singapore Handbook	**$15.95**
Carl Parkes	300 pages, 28 maps
Southeast Asia Handbook	**$21.95**
Carl Parkes	1,103 pages, 196 maps
South Korea Handbook	**$19.95**
Robert Nilsen	824 pages, 141 maps
South Pacific Handbook	**$22.95**
David Stanley	913 pages, 147 maps
Tahiti-Polynesia Handbook	**$13.95**
David Stanley	243 pages, 35 maps
Thailand Handbook	**$19.95**
Carl Parkes	834 pages, 142 maps
Tibet Handbook	**$30.00**
Victor Chan	1103 pages, 216 maps
Vietnam, Cambodia & Laos Handbook	**$18.95**
Michael Buckley	691 pages, 112 maps

MEXICO, CENTRAL AMERICA, AND THE CARIBBEAN

"Travel guides published by Moon Publications are uniformly just as they are advertised: 'informative, entertaining, highly practical.' They satisfy all the needs of travelers on the road. At the same time they are colorful and educational enough to be enjoyed by those whose travel is confined to armchair-bound wishes and dreams." —*Worldviews*

Baja Handbook	**$15.95**
Joe Cummings	362 pages, 44 maps
Belize Handbook	**$15.95**
Chicki Mallan	363 pages, 45 maps
Cabo Handbook	**$14.95**
Joe Cummings	205 pages, 18 maps
Cancún Handbook	**$13.95**
Chicki Mallan	254 pages, 25 maps
Caribbean Handbook	**$16.95**
Karl Luntta	384 pages, 56 maps

Central Mexico Handbook	$15.95
Chicki Mallan	391 pages, 63 maps
Costa Rica Handbook	**$19.95**
Christopher P. Baker	750 pages, 74 maps
Cuba Handbook	**$19.95**
Christopher P. Baker	715 pages, 63 maps
Dominican Republic Handbook	**$15.95**
Gaylord Dold	350 pages, 24 maps
Honduras Handbook	**$15.95**
Chris Humphrey	350 pages, 40 maps
Jamaica Handbook	**$15.95**
Karl Luntta	312 pages, 17 maps
Mexico Handbook	**$21.95**
Joe Cummings and Chicki Mallan	1,457 pages, 232 maps
Northern Mexico Handbook	**$16.95**
Joe Cummings	500 pages, 68 maps
Pacific Mexico Handbook	**$17.95**
Bruce Whipperman	483 pages, 68 maps
Puerto Vallarta Handbook	**$14.95**
Bruce Whipperman	285 pages, 36 maps
Virgin Islands Handbook	**$13.95**
Karl Luntta	195 pages, 17 maps
Yucatan Peninsula Handbook	**$15.95**
Chicki Mallan	397 pages, 62 maps

OTHER GREAT TITLES FROM MOON

"For hardy wanderers, few guides come more highly
recommended than the Handbooks. They include
good maps, steer clear of fluff and flackery, and offer
plenty of money-saving tips. They also give you the
kind of information that visitors to strange lands—on
any budget—need to survive."

—*US News & World Report*

Moon Handbook	$10.00
Carl Koppeschaar	141 pages, 8 maps
Moscow-St. Petersburg Handbook	**$13.95**
Masha Nordbye	259 pages, 16 maps
The Practical Nomad	**$17.95**
Edward Hasbrouck	575 pages
Staying Healthy in Asia, Africa, and Latin America	**$11.95**
Dirk Schroeder	197 pages, 4 maps

WHERE TO BUY MOON TRAVEL HANDBOOKS

BOOKSTORES AND LIBRARIES: Moon Travel Handbooks are sold worldwide. Please contact our sales manager for a list of wholesalers and distributors in your area.

TRAVELERS: We would like to have Moon Travel Handbooks available throughout the world. Please ask your bookstore to write or call us for ordering information. If your bookstore will not order our guides for you, please contact us for a free catalog.

> **Moon Publications, Inc.**
> **P.O. Box 3040**
> **Chico, CA 95927-3040 U.S.A.**
> **tel.: (800) 345-5473, outside the U.S. (916) 345-5473**
> **fax: (916) 345-6751**
> **e-mail: travel@moon.com**

IMPORTANT ORDERING INFORMATION

PRICES: All prices are subject to change. We always ship the most current edition. We will let you know if there is a price increase on the book you order.

SHIPPING AND HANDLING OPTIONS: Domestic UPS or USPS first class (allow 10 working days for delivery): $3.50 for the first item, 50 cents for each additional item.

EXCEPTIONS: *Road Trip USA, Tibet Handbook, Mexico Handbook,* and *Indonesia Handbook* shipping $4.50; $1.00 for each additional *Road Trip USA, Tibet Handbook, Mexico Handbook,* and *Indonesia Handbook.*

Moonbelt shipping is $1.50 for one, 50 cents for each additional belt.

Add $2.00 for same-day handling.

UPS 2nd Day Air or Printed Airmail requires a special quote.

International Surface Bookrate 8-12 weeks delivery: $3.00 for the first item, $1.00 for each additional item. Note: Moon Publications cannot guarantee international surface bookrate shipping. Moon recommends sending international orders via air mail, which requires a special quote.

FOREIGN ORDERS: Orders that originate outside the U.S.A. must be paid for with an international money order, a check in U.S. currency drawn on a major U.S. bank based in the U.S.A., or Visa or MasterCard.

TELEPHONE ORDERS: We accept Visa or MasterCard payments. Minimum order is US$15. Call in your order: (800) 345-5473, 8 a.m.-5 p.m. Pacific standard time. Outside the U.S. the number is (916) 345-5473.

ORDER FORM

Prices are subject to change without notice. Be sure to call (800) 345-5473,
or (916) 345-5473 from outside the U.S. 8 a.m.–5 p.m. PST for current prices and editions,
or for the name of the bookstore nearest you that carries Moon Travel Handbooks.
(See important ordering information on preceding page.)

Name: _____ Date: _____

Street: _____

City: _____ Daytime Phone: _____

State or Country: _____ Zip Code: _____

QUANTITY	TITLE	PRICE

Taxable Total_____

Sales Tax (7.25%) for California Residents_____

Shipping & Handling_____

TOTAL_____

Ship: ☐ UPS (no P.O. Boxes) ☐ 1st class ☐ International surface mail

Ship to: ☐ address above ☐ other _____

_____

Make checks payable to: **MOON PUBLICATIONS, INC.**, P.O. Box 3040, Chico, CA 95927-3040 U.S.A.
We accept Visa and MasterCard. **To Order**: Call in your Visa or MasterCard number, or send a written order with your Visa or MasterCard number and expiration date clearly written.

Card Number: ☐ **Visa**   ☐ **MasterCard**

☐ ☐ ☐ ☐ ☐ ☐ ☐ ☐ ☐ ☐ ☐ ☐ ☐ ☐ ☐ ☐

Exact Name on Card: _____

Expiration date:_____

Signature: _____

MOONBELT

A new concept in moneybelts. Made of heavy-duty Cordura nylon, the Moonbelt offers maximum protection for your money and important papers. This pouch, designed for all-weather comfort, slips under your shirt or waistband, rendering it virtually undetectable and inaccessible to pickpockets. It features a one-inch high-test quick-release buckle so there's no more fumbling around for the strap or repeated adjustments. This handy plastic buckle opens and closes with a touch but won't come undone until you want it to. Moonbelts accommodate traveler's checks, passports, cash, photos, etc. Size 5 x 9 inches. Available in black only. **$8.95**

www.moon.com

MOON
PUBLICATIONS

Welcome to <u>Moon Travel Handbooks</u>, publishers of comprehensive travel guides to <u>North America</u>, <u>Mexico</u>, <u>Central America and the Caribbean</u>, <u>Asia</u>, and the <u>Pacific Islands</u>. We're always on the lookout for new ideas, so please feel free to e-mail any comments and suggestions about these exhibits to <u>travel@moon.com</u>.

If you like Moon Travel Handbooks, you'll enjoy our travel information center on the World Wide Web (WWW), loaded with interactive exhibits designed especially for the Internet.

Our featured exhibit contains the complete text of *Road Trip USA,* a travel guide to the "blue highways" that crisscross America between the interstates, published in paperback in 1996. The WWW version contains a large, scrollable point-and-click imagemap with links to hundreds of original entries; a sophisticated network of links to other major U.S. Internet sites; and a running commentary from our online readers contributing their own travel tips on small towns, roadside attractions, regional foods, and interesting places to stay.

Other attractions on Moon's web site include:

- Excerpted hypertext adaptations of Moon's bestselling *New Zealand Handbook, Costa Rica Handbook,* and *Big Island of Hawaii Handbook*

- The complete 75-page introduction to *Staying Healthy in Asia, Africa, and Latin America,* as well as the *Trans-Cultural Study Guide,* both coproduced with Volunteers in Asia

- The complete, annotated bibliographies from Moon's Handbooks to Japan, South Korea, Thailand, the Philippines, Indonesia, Australia, and New Zealand

- Current and back issues of Moon's free newsletter, *Travel Matters*

- Updates on the latest titles and editions to join the Moon Travel Handbook series

Come visit us at: **http://www.moon.com**

U.S.~METRIC CONVERSION

1 inch	=	2.54 centimeters (cm)
1 foot	=	.304 meters (m)
1 mile	=	1.6093 kilometers (km)
1 km	=	.6214 miles
1 fathom	=	1.8288 m
1 chain	=	20.1168 m
1 furlong	=	201.168 m
1 acre	=	.4047 hectares
1 sq km	=	100 hectares
1 sq mile	=	2.59 square km
1 ounce	=	28.35 grams
1 pound	=	.4536 kilograms
1 short ton	=	.90718 metric ton
1 short ton	=	2000 pounds
1 long ton	=	1.016 metric tons
1 long ton	=	2240 pounds
1 metric ton	=	1000 kilograms
1 quart	=	.94635 liters
1 US gallon	=	3.7854 liters
1 Imperial gallon	=	4.5459 liters
1 nautical mile	=	1.852 km

To compute celsius temperatures, subtract 32 from Fahrenheit and divide by 1.8. To go the other way, multiply celsius by 1.8 and add 32.

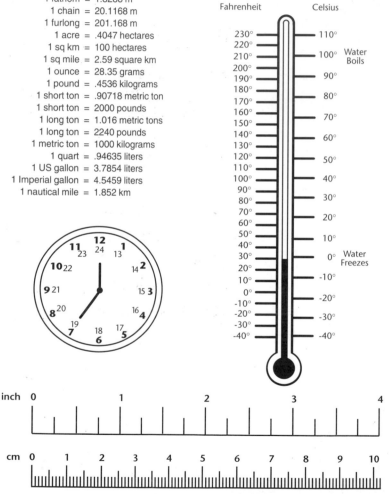